Pro .NET Benchmarking

The Art of Performance Measurement

Andrey Akinshin

Apress®

Pro .NET Benchmarking

Andrey Akinshin
Saint Petersburg, Russia

ISBN-13 (pbk): 978-1-4842-4940-6
https://doi.org/10.1007/978-1-4842-4941-3

ISBN-13 (electronic): 978-1-4842-4941-3

Managing Director, Apress Media LLC: Welmoed Spahr
Acquisitions Editor: Joan Murray
Development Editor: Laura Berendson
Coordinating Editor: Nancy Chen

Cover designed by eStudioCalamar

Cover image designed by Freepik (www.freepik.com)

Distributed to the book trade worldwide by Springer Science+Business Media New York, 233 Spring Street, 6th Floor, New York, NY 10013. Phone 1-800-SPRINGER, fax (201) 348-4505, e-mail orders-ny@springer-sbm.com, or visit www.springeronline.com. Apress Media, LLC is a California LLC and the sole member (owner) is Springer Science + Business Media Finance Inc (SSBM Finance Inc). SSBM Finance Inc is a **Delaware** corporation.

For information on translations, please e-mail rights@apress.com, or visit http://www.apress.com/rights-permissions.

Apress titles may be purchased in bulk for academic, corporate, or promotional use. eBook versions and licenses are also available for most titles. For more information, reference our Print and eBook Bulk Sales web page at http://www.apress.com/bulk-sales.

Any source code or other supplementary material referenced by the author in this book is available to readers on GitHub via the book's product page, located at www.apress.com/9781484249406. For more detailed information, please visit http://www.apress.com/source-code.

Printed on acid-free paper

Table of Contents

About the Author

 **Andrey Akinshin** is a senior developer at JetBrains, where he works on Rider (a cross-platform .NET IDE based on the IntelliJ platform and ReSharper). His favorite topics are performance and micro-optimizations, and he is the maintainer of BenchmarkDotNet (a powerful .NET library for benchmarking supported by the .NET Foundation). Andrey is a frequent speaker at various events for developers, and he is the program director of the DotNext conference. Andrey is also a PhD in computer science, a Microsoft .NET MVP, and a silver medalist of ACM ICPC. In his free time, he likes to study science (his primary research interests are mathematical biology and bifurcation theory). Previously, he worked as a postdoctoral research fellow in the Weizmann Institute of Science and as a research scientist in the Sobolev Institute of Mathematics SB RAS.

About the Technical Reviewers

John Garland is the Vice President of Learning Services at Wintellect and has been developing software professionally since the 1990s. His consulting clients range from small businesses to Fortune 500 companies. His work has been featured at Microsoft conference keynotes and sessions, and he has presented at conferences in North America, South America, and Europe. John lives in Cumming, GA, with his wife and daughter and is a graduate of the University of Florida with a Bachelor's Degree in Computer Engineering. He is the author of *Windows Store Apps Succinctly* and coauthor of *Programming the Windows Runtime by Example*. John is currently a Microsoft Azure Cloud Solution Architect, a member of the Microsoft Azure Insiders, a Microsoft Azure MVP, a Microsoft Certified Trainer, and a Microsoft Certified Azure Developer Associate.

Sasha Goldshtein is a Software Engineer at Google Research. He works on applying machine learning solutions to various Google products around conversation and dialogue, text classification, recommendation systems, and more. Before joining Google, Sasha spent more than ten years specializing in production debugging and performance optimization, taught courses around the world, and spoke at numerous international conferences. He is also the author of *Pro .NET Performance* (Apress, 2012).

Acknowledgments

I started to collect content for this book five years ago. The writing stage took about 2.5 years. I spent thousands of hours on it, but it would still have been impossible to finish all the chapters on my own. The book was created with the help of many talented developers.

First of all, I want to thank Ivan Pashchenko. He is the person who inspired me to share my knowledge and who reviewed not only this book but also dozens of my early blog posts. He supported me for many years, and he helped me to understand so many things that are essential for writing a good technical book. Thank you, Ivan!

Secondly, I want to thank all my unofficial reviewers: Irina Ananeva, Mikhail Filippov, Igor Lukanin, Adam Sitnik, Karlen Simonyan, Stephen Toub, Alina Smirnova, Federico Andres Lois, Konrad Kokosa, and Vance Morrison. They spent a lot of time reading raw drafts and found tons of mistakes and typos in the early stages of writing. Also, they gave a lot of good advice that helped me to make this book much better.

Thirdly, I want to thank the Apress team: John Garland and Sasha Goldshtein (official technical reviewers), Joan Murray (acquisitions editor), Laura Berendson (development editor), Nancy Chen (coordinating editor), Gwenan Spearing (original acquisitions editor), and all other team members who helped to publish this book. Sorry for all the failed deadlines and thanks for your patience. They make it possible to create a real book from my raw drafts and notes. They helped to structure the content, present my ideas in an understandable form, and fix my grammatical errors.

Next, I want to thank all BenchmarkDotNet contributors and users. It's so nice to see how this project not only helps developers to measure performance and analyze results, but also promotes good benchmarking practices and provokes in-depth discussions about benchmarking and performance. Especially, I want to thank Adam Sitnik for his tremendous contribution: the library wouldn't be so good without him.

Also, I want to thank everyone with whom I spoke about benchmarking and performance and everyone who writes and speaks about these topics. I learned a lot from private and public conversations, blog posts, GitHub discussions, Twitter threads, and StackOverflow questions (you will find a lot of links in the footnotes and in the reference list at the end of the book). Especially, I want to thank Matt Warren, Brendan

ACKNOWLEDGMENTS

Gregg, Daniel Lakens, Jon Skeet, Andy Ayers, Agner Fog, Raymond Chen, Bruce Dawson, Denis Bakhvalov, Aleksey Shipilev, Alexandre Mutel, Ben Adams, and hundreds of other developers who share their knowledge and contribute to open-source projects. This book contains a lot of great case studies that exist thanks to the people from the community who are passionate about performance.

Finally, I want to thank my family and all my friends and colleagues who believed in me, supported me, and kept asking "When will the book finally be published?"

Introduction

You should take the approach that you're wrong. Your goal is to be less wrong.

— Elon Musk

I wrote my first C# benchmark in 2004. This was a long time ago, so I don't remember exactly what I measured, but I guess that the source code looked like this:

```
var start = DateTime.Now;
// Some stuff
var finish = DateTime.Now;
Console.WriteLine(finish - start);
```

I remember my feelings about this code: I thought that now I know *everything* about time measurements.

After many years of performance engineering, I have learned a lot of new stuff. It turned out that time measurement is not a simple thing. There are too many factors that can affect our measurements. In this book, I want to take you on a fascinating journey into the wonderful world of benchmarking, where we learn how to conduct accurate performance measurements and avoid hundreds of possible mistakes.

In the modern world, it is very important to make your software fast. Good speed could be a reason why customers will use your product instead of a competitor's product. Poor speed could be a reason why users will stop using your product. But what does "fast" mean? When can we say that one program works "faster" than another? What should we do to be sure that our code will work "fast enough" everywhere?

If we want to make our application fast, the first thing we should learn is how to measure it. And one of the great ways to do it is benchmarking. According to the *New Oxford American Dictionary*, a benchmark is "a problem designed to evaluate the performance of a computer system." Here, you should ask further questions. What does "performance" mean? How can we "evaluate" it? Someone may say that these are very simple questions. However, they are so complicated that I decided to write an entire book about them.

About Content

This book contains nine chapters:

- Chapter 1 "Introducing Benchmarking"
  This chapter contains some basic information about benchmarking and other performance investigations, including benchmarking goals and requirements. We will also discuss performance spaces and why it's so important to analyze benchmark results.

- Chapter 2 "Common Benchmarking Pitfalls"
  This chapter contains 15 examples of common mistakes that developers usually make during benchmarking. Each example is pretty small (so, you can easily understand what's going on), but all of them demonstrate important problems and explain how to resolve them.

- Chapter 3 "How Environment Affects Performance"
  This chapter explains why the environment is so important and introduces a lot of terms that will be used in subsequent chapters. You will find 12 case studies that demonstrate how minor changes in the environment may significantly affect application performance.

- Chapter 4 "Statistics for Performance Engineers"
  This chapter contains the essential knowledge about statistics that you need during performance analysis. For each term, you will find practical recommendations that will help you use statistical metrics during your performance investigations. It also contains some statistical approaches that are really useful for benchmarking. At the end of this chapter, you will find different ways to lie with benchmarking: this knowledge will protect you from incorrect result interpretation.

- Chapter 5 "Performance Analysis and Performance Testing"
  This chapter covers topics that you need to know if you want to control the performance level in a large product automatically. You will learn different kinds of performance tests, performance anomalies that you can observe, and how to protect yourself from these anomalies. At the end of this chapter, you will find a description of performance-driven development (an approach for writing performance tests) and a general discussion about performance culture.

- Chapter 6 "Diagnostic Tools"
  This chapter contains a brief overview of different tools that can be useful during performance investigations.

- Chapter 7 "CPU-Bound Benchmarks"
  This chapter contains 24 case studies that show different pitfalls in CPU-bound benchmarks. We will discuss some runtime-specific features like register allocation, inlining, and intrinsics; and hardware-specific features like instruction-level parallelism, branch prediction, and arithmetics (including IEEE 754).

- Chapter 8 "Memory-Bound Benchmarks"
  This chapter contains 12 case studies that show different pitfalls in memory-bound benchmarks. We will discuss some runtime-specific features about garbage collection and its settings; and hardware-specific features like CPU cache and physical memory layout.

- Chapter 9 "Hardware and Software Timers"
  This chapter contains all you need to know about timers. We will discuss basic terminology, different kinds of hardware timers, corresponding timestamping APIs on different operating systems, and the most common pitfalls of using these APIs. This chapter also contains a lot of "extra" content that you don't actually need for benchmarking, but it may be interesting for people who want to learn more about timers.

The order of these chapters matters (e.g., Chapter 3 introduces a lot of terms used in later chapters), but I tried to make them as independent as possible. If you are interested in specific topics, you can read only the corresponding chapters: the essential part of the content should be understandable even if you skip the first chapters.

This book will provide a basic understanding of the core concepts and it will teach you how to use them for performance measurements. Technologies are changing—we get new versions of hardware, operating systems, and .NET runtime every year—but the basic concepts remain the same. If you learn them, you can easily adapt them to new technology stacks.

About examples

It's hard to learn benchmarking without examples. In this book, you will find a lot of them! Some of these examples are small synthetic programs that illustrate theoretical concepts. However, you will also find a lot of examples from real life.

Most of them are based on my own performance testing experience at JetBrains.[1] Thus, you will see some real-world problems (and possible solutions) that are related to JetBrains products like IntelliJ IDEA[2] (Java IDE), ReSharper[3] (Visual Studio plug-in), and Rider[4] (a cross-platform .NET IDE based on both IntelliJ IDEA and ReSharper). All products are very huge (Rider source code base contains about 20 million lines of code) and include a lot of performance-critical components. Many developers make hundreds of commits to these products every day, so keeping the performance level decent is not an easy task. I hope that you find these examples and techniques useful and find a way to use them in your own products.

Another source of experience for me is BenchmarkDotNet. I started it in 2013 as a small pet project. Today, it has become a highly adopted open-source library. During maintaining the project, I was involved in hundreds of pretty interesting discussions about performance. Some of the examples in this book may look too artificial, but almost all of them came from real life.

---

[1]https://www.jetbrains.com/
[2]https://www.jetbrains.com/idea/
[3]https://www.jetbrains.com/resharper/
[4]https://www.jetbrains.com/rider/

About expectations

We will talk a lot about performance, but we will not cover all kinds of performance topics. You **will not** learn the following things:

- How to write fast code

- How to optimize slow code

- How to profile applications

- How to find hotspots in applications

- And many other *performance*-related "how-tos"

There are many excellent books and papers on these topics; you can find some of them in the reference list at the end of the book. Note that **this book is focused only on benchmarking.** You will learn the following:

- How to design a good benchmark

- How to choose relevant metrics

- How to avoid common benchmarking pitfalls

- How to analyze benchmark results

- And many other *benchmarking*-related "how-tos"

Also, you should keep in mind that benchmarks don't fit all situations. You will not be a good performance engineer if your only skill is benchmarking. However, it's one of the most important skills. If you learn it, you will become a better software developer who is able to conduct very complex performance investigations.

CHAPTER 1

Introducing Benchmarking

It is easier to optimize correct code than to correct optimized code.

— Bill Harlan, 1997

In this chapter, we will discuss the concept of benchmarking, the difference between benchmarking and other kinds of performance investigations, what kind of problems can be solved with benchmarking, what a good benchmark should look like, how to design a benchmark, and how to analyze its results. In particular, the following topics will be covered:

- **Performance investigations**

    What does good performance investigation look like? Why is it important to define your goals and problems? What kind of metrics, tools, and approaches should you choose? What should you do with the performance metrics we get?

- **Benchmarking goals**

    When is benchmarking useful? How can it be used in performance analysis or marketing? How could we use it for improvement of our technical expertise or for fun?

- **Benchmarking requirements**

    What are the basic benchmarking requirements? Why is it important to write repeatable, noninvasive, verifiable, portable, and honest benchmarks with an acceptable level of precision?

© Andrey Akinshin 2019
A. Akinshin, *Pro .NET Benchmarking*, https://doi.org/10.1007/978-1-4842-4941-3_1

- **Performance spaces**

  Why should we work with multidimensional performance spaces
  (and what is it)? Why is it important to build a good performance
  model? How can input data and environment affect performance?

- **Analysis**

  Why is it important to analyze benchmark results? How are they
  interpreted? What is the bottleneck and why do we need to find it?
  Why should we know statistics for benchmarking?

In this chapter, we'll cover basic theoretical concepts using practical examples. If you
already know how to benchmark, feel free to skip this chapter and move on to Chapter 2.

Step 1 in learning how to do benchmarking or any other kind of performance
investigation is creating a good plan.

Planning a Performance Investigation

Do you want your code to work quickly? Of course you do. However, it's not always
easy to maintain excellent levels of performance. The application life cycle involves
complicated business processes that are not always focused on performance. When you
suddenly notice that a feature works too slowly, it is not always possible to dive in and
accelerate your code. It's not always obvious how to write code in the present for a fast
program in the future.

It's OK that you want to improve performance but have no idea what you should do.
Everything you need is just a good performance investigation away.

Any thorough investigation requires a good plan with several important steps:

1. Define problems and goals

2. Pick metrics

3. Select approaches and tools

4. Perform an experiment to get the results

5. Complete the analysis and draw conclusions

Of course, this plan is just an example. You may customize your own with 20 steps or skip some because they are obvious to you. The most important takeaway is that a complete performance investigation includes (explicitly or implicitly) all these steps at a minimum. Let's discuss each of them in detail.

Define Problems and Goals

This step seems obvious, but a lot of people skip it to immediately begin measuring or optimizing something. It's very important to ask yourself some important questions: What is wrong with the current level of performance? What do I want to achieve? And, how fast should my code work?

If you just start to randomly optimize your program, it will be just a waste of time. It's better to define the problems and goals first. I even recommend writing your problems and goals on a piece of paper, putting it next to your workplace, and keeping an eye on it during the performance investigation. This is a great visual reminder.

Here are some problem and goal statements for consideration:

- **Problem: We need a library that supports JSON serialization, but we don't know which one will be fast enough.**

  Goal: Compare two libraries (performance analysis).

  We found two good JSON libraries, both of which have all required features. It's important to choose the fastest library, but it's hard to compare them in the general case. So, we want to check which library is *faster on our typical use cases.*

- **Problem: Our customers use our competitor's software because they think it works faster.**

  Goal: Our customers should know that we are faster than the competition (marketing).

  In fact, the current level of performance is good enough, but we need to communicate to customers that we are faster.

- **Problem: We don't know which design pattern is most efficient in terms of performance.**

  Goal: Improve technical expertise of our developers (scientific interest).

  Developers do not always know how to write code effectively. Sometimes it makes sense to spend time on research and come up with good practices and design patterns which are optimal for performance-critical places.

- **Problem: Developers are tired of implementing boring business logic.**

  Goal: Change the working context and solve a few interesting problems (fun).

  Organize a performance competition to improve code base performance between developers. The team that achieves the best level of performance wins.

  Such challenges do not necessarily have to solve some of your business problems, but it can improve morale in your organization and increase developer productivity after the event.

As you can see, the problem definition can be an abstract sentence that describes a high-level goal. The next step is to make it more specific by adding the details. These details can be expressed with the help of *metrics*.

Pick Metrics

Let's say you are not happy with the performance of a piece of your code and you want to increase its speed twofold.[1] What increasing speed means to you may not be the same to another developer on the team. You can't work with abstracts. If you want clear problem statements and goals, you need concise well-defined metrics that correspond to the

---

[1]Of course, it's not a good problem definition. If you are going to make some optimizations, you need better reasons than just "unhappiness." Now we are talking about metrics, so let's say we have some well-defined performance requirements and our software doesn't satisfy our business goals (in this subsection, it doesn't matter what kind of goals we have).

goals. It's not always apparent which metric to enlist, so let's discuss some questions that will help you decide.

- **What do I want to improve?**

    Maybe you want to improve the *latency* of a single invocation (a time interval between start and finish) or you want to improve the *throughput* of this method (how many times we can call it per second). People often think that these are interrelated values and it doesn't matter which metric is chosen because all of them correlate to the application performance the same way. However, that's not always true. For example, changes in the source code can improve the latency and reduce the throughput. Examples of other metrics might be cache misses rate, CPU utilization, the size of the large object heap (LOH), cold start time, and many others. Don't worry if the terms are not familiar; we will cover them in future chapters.

- **Am I sure that I know exactly what I want to improve?**

    Usually, "No." You should be flexible and ready to change your goals after obtaining results. A performance investigation is an iterative process. On each iteration, you can choose new metrics. For example, you start with a simple operation latency. After the first iteration, you discover that the program spends too much time garbage collecting. Next, you start another metric: memory traffic (allocated bytes per second). After the second iteration, it turns out that you allocate a lot of int[] instances with a short lifetime. The next metric could be an amount of created int arrays. After some optimizations (e.g., you implement an array pool and reuse array instances between operations), you may want to measure the same metric again. Of course, you could use only the first metric (the operation latency). However, in this case, you look only at the consequences instead of the original problem. The overall performance is complicated and depends on many factors. It can be hard to track how changes in one place affect the duration of some method. Generally it is easier to track specific properties of the whole system.

- **What are the target conditions?**

    Let's say the chosen metric is the throughput: you want to handle 10000 operations per second. What kind of throughput is important for you? Do you want to improve the throughput under *average load* or under *peak load*? Is it a single- or multithreaded application? What level of concurrency is appropriate for your situation? How much RAM do you have on the target machine? Is it important to improve performance in all target environments or do you want to work under specific conditions?

    It's not always obvious how to choose the right target conditions and how these conditions affect the performance. Carefully think about relevant restrictions for your metrics. We will discuss different restrictions later in this book.

- **How should results be interpreted?**

    A good performance engineer always collects the same metric several times. On the one hand, it is good because *we can check* statistical properties of the metrics. On the other hand, it is bad because now *we have to check* these properties. How should we summarize them? Should we always choose mean? Or median? Maybe we want to be sure that 95% of our requests can be handled faster than N milliseconds; in this case, the 95th percentile is our friend. We will talk a lot about statistics and the importance of understanding that they are not just about result analysis but also about desired metrics. Always think about the summarizing strategy that will be relevant to the original problem.

To sum it up, we can work with different kinds of basic metrics (from latency and throughput to cache miss rate and CPU utilization) and different conditions (e.g., average load vs. under peak load), and summarize them in different ways (e.g., take mean, median, or 95th percentile). If you are unsure of which to use, just look at the piece of paper with your problem; the selected metrics should complement your goal and specify low-level details of the problem. You should have an understanding that if you improve selected metrics, it will solve your problem and make you, your boss, and the customers happy.

Once you are satisfied with the metrics, the next step is choosing how to collect them.

Select Approaches and Tools

In the modern world, there are many tools, approaches, and methods that provide performance metrics. Choose the performance analysis that is suitable for your situation and make sure that the tool you select has the required characteristics: precision of measurements, portability, the simplicity of use, and so on.

To decide, try to pick the best match to your problem and metrics, weighing some options to help you decide. So, let's talk about some of the most popular methods and corresponding tools.

- **Looking at your code**

  A senior developer with good experience can say a lot about performance even without measurements. Check the asymptotic complexity of an algorithm, think about how expensive the API is, or note an apparently ineffective piece of code. Of course, you can't know for sure without measurements, but often you can solve simple performance puzzles just by looking at your code with the help of thoughtful analysis. Be careful though, to keep in mind that *personal feelings and intuition can easily deceive you* and even the most experienced developers can get things wrong. Also keep in mind that technologies change, completely invalidating previous assumptions. For example, some method XYZ is superslow, and thus you avoid it for years. Then one day XYZ is fixed and superfast, but unless you're made aware of that somehow, you're going to continue avoiding it, and be less likely to discover the fix.

- **Profiling**

  What if you want to optimize your application? Where should you start? Some programmers start at the first place that looks "suboptimal": "I know how to optimize this piece of code, and I will do it right now!" Usually, such an approach does not work well. Optimization in a random method may not affect the performance of the whole application. If this method takes 0.01% of the total time, you probably will never observe any optimization effects. Or worse, you can do more harm than good. Trying to write "too smart" or fast code can increase code complexity, introduce new bugs, and just waste time.

To really make a difference, find a place where the application spends a significant part of its time. The best way to do it is profiling. Some people add measurements directly in the application and get some numbers, but that is not profiling. "Profiling" means that you should take a profiler, attach it to the application, take a snapshot, and look at the profile. There are many tools for profiling: we will discuss them in Chapter 6. The primary requirement here is that it must show the hot methods (methods that are called frequently) and bottlenecks of your application and should help you to locate where to start optimizing your code.

- **Monitoring**

  Sometimes, it is impossible to profile an application on your local computer; for example, when a performance phenomenon occurs only in the production environment or only rarely. In this case, monitoring can help you to find a method with performance problems. There are different approaches, but most commonly developers use built-in monitoring logic (e.g., they log important events with timestamps) or external tools (e.g., based on ETW [Event Tracing for Windows]). All of these approaches yield performance data to analyze. Once you have some performance troubles, you can take this data and try to find the source of this problem.

- **Performance tests**

  Imagine that you performed some amazing optimizations. Your application is superfast and you want to maintain that level of performance. But then somebody (probably you) accidentally makes some changes that spoil this beautiful situation. It's a common practice to write unit tests that ensure the business logic works fine after any changes in your code base. However, it is not enough to check only the business logic after your amazing optimizations. Sometimes it's a good idea to write special tests (so-called performance tests) which check that you have the same level of performance before and after changes. The performance tests can be executed on a build server, as part of a continuous integration (CI) pipeline.

It is not easy to write such tests, as it usually requires the same server environment (hardware + software) for all the benchmarking configurations. If the performance is very important for you, it makes sense to invest some time on the infrastructure setup and development of performance tests. We will discuss how to do it correctly in Chapter 5.

- **Benchmarking**

  Ask five different people what a benchmark is and you will get five different answers. For our purposes, it's a program that measures some performance properties of another program or piece of code. Consider a benchmark as a scientific experiment: it should provide some results that allow access to new information about our program, a .NET runtime, an operating system, modern hardware, and the world around us. Ideally, results of such an experiment should be repeatable and sharable with our colleagues, and they should also allow us to make a decision *based on the new information.*

Perform an Experiment to Get the Results

Now it's time for an experiment. At the end of the experiment (or a series of experiments), you will obtain results in the form of numbers, formulas, tables, plots, snapshots, and so on. A simple experiment may use one approach, while more complicated cases may call for more. Here is an example. You start with monitoring, which helps you find a slow user scenario. The profiling will help you to localize hot methods, and from there you compose several benchmarks to find the fastest way to implement the feature. Performance tests will help keep the performance on the same level in the future. As you can see, there is no silver bullet; all of the approaches have a purpose and use. The trick is to always keep the problems and metrics front in mind when you do this investigation.

Complete the Analysis and Draw Conclusions

Analysis is the most important part of any performance investigation. Once you get the numbers, you have to explain them, and be sure that your explanation is correct. A common mistake would be to say something like the following: "Profiler shows that method A is faster than method B. Let's use A everywhere instead of B!" Here is a better version of the conclusion: "Profiler shows that method A is faster than method B. We have an explanation for this fact: method A is optimized for the input data patterns that we used in the experiment. Thus, we understand why we got such results in the profiler sessions. However, we should continue the research and check other data patterns before we decide which method should be used in the production code. Probably, method A can be dramatically slower than method B in some corner cases."

A lot of performance phenomena are caused by mistakes in the measurement methodology. Always strive for a credible theory that explains each number from the obtained results. Without such theory, you can make a wrong decision and spoil the performance. A conclusion should be drawn only after careful analysis.

Benchmarking Goals

So now that we've covered the basic plan of a performance investigation, let's turn the focus to benchmarking and learn the important aspects of benchmarking step by step. Let's start from the beginning with benchmarking goals (and corresponding problems).

Do you remember the first thing to do at the beginning of any performance investigation? You should define a problem. Understand your goal and why it's important to solve this problem.

Benchmarking is not a universal approach that is useful in any performance investigation. Benchmarks will not optimize your code for you, nor do they solve all your performance problems. They just produce a set of numbers.

So before you begin, be sure that you need these numbers and understand why you need them. Lots and lots of people just start to benchmark something without an idea how to make conclusions based on the obtained data. Benchmarking is a very powerful approach, but only if you understand when and why you should apply it.

So moving on, let's learn about some of common benchmarking goals.

Performance Analysis

One of the most popular benchmarking goals is performance analysis. It is critical if you care about the speed of your software and can help you with the following problems and scenarios:

- **Comparing libraries/frameworks/algorithms**

    It's common to want to use existing solutions for your problem, selecting the fastest one (if it satisfies your basic requirements). Sometimes it makes sense to check carefully which one works the fastest and say something like "I did a few dry runs and it seems that the second library is the fastest one." However, it's never enough to make only a few measurements. If choosing the fastest solution is critical, then you must do the legwork and write benchmarks that fairly compare alternatives in various states and conditions and provide a complete performance picture. Good measurements always provide a strong argument to convince your colleagues, an added bonus!

- **Tuning parameters**

    Programs contain many hardcoded constants, including some that can affect your performance, such as the size of a cache or the degree of parallelism. It's hard to know in advance which values are best for your application, but benchmarking can fine-tune such parameters in order to achieve the best possible performance.

- **Checking capabilities**

    Imagine looking for a suitable server for your web application. You want it to be as cheap as possible, but it also should able to process N requests per second (RPS). It would be useful to have a program that can measure the maximum RPS of your application on different hardware.

- **Checking impact of a change**

    You implemented a great feature that should make users happy, but it's time-consuming, and you are worried about how it affects the overall performance of the application. In order to find out,

11

you will need to measure some performance metrics *before* and *after* the feature was included in the product.

- **Proof-of-concept**

    You have a brilliant idea to implement, but it requires a lot of changes, and you are unsure of how it will impact the level of performance. In this case, you can try to implement the idea in the "quick and dirty" style using measurements.

- **Regression analysis**

    You want to monitor how the performance of a feature is changing from change to change, so if you hear complaints like "It worked much faster in the previous release," you will be able to check if that's true or not. Regression analysis can be implemented via performance tests, but benchmarking is also an acceptable approach here.

Thus, performance analysis is a useful approach that allows solving a lot of different problems. However, it's not the only possible benchmarking goal.

Benchmarks as a Marketing Tool

Marketing, sales, and others really like to publish articles or blog posts that promote how fast a product is, and a good performance investigation report can do just that. While we programmers hyperfocus on source code and the technical aspects of the development process, we should be open to the idea that marketing is a legitimate and important goal. Writing performance reports based on benchmark results can be a useful activity in new product development. Unlike your benchmarking goals, when you write a performance report for others, you are summarizing all your performance experiments. You draw plots, make tables, and vet every aspect of your benchmark. You think about questions people might ask about your research, trying to answer them in advance, and you think about important facts to share. When we are talking about performance to marketing, there is no such thing as "too many measurements." A good performance report can make your marketing department look good, making everyone happy. It is also necessary to say a few words about *black marketing*, the situation when somebody presents benchmark results that are known (to the presenter) to be false. It's not ethical to do such things, but worth knowing about. There are several kinds of "black marketing" benchmarking:

- **Yellow headers**

  Taking some measurements and making unfounded claims, e.g. "our library is the fastest tool." A lot of people still believe that if something was posted on the Internet, it's obviously true, even without any actual measurements.

- **Unreproducible research**

  Adding some highly nonreproducible technical details with source code, tables, and plots. But no one can build the source, run your tools, or find the specified hardware because it's hard, and key implementation details are missing in the description.

- **Selected measurements**

  Picking and choosing measurements. For example, you can perform 1000 performance measurements for your software and the same for your competitor's software. But then you select the best results for your software and the worst for your competitors. Technically, you are presenting real results, which can be reproduced, but you are providing only a small subset of the true performance picture.

- **Specific environment**

  Finding a set of parameters that benefits you. For example, if you know that the competitor's software works fast only on computers with high amounts of RAM and an SSD, then you pick a machine with little RAM and an HDD. If you know that your software shows good results only on Linux (and poor results on Windows), then you choose the Linux environment. It's also usually possible to find a particular input data that will be profitable only for you. Such results will be correct, and it will be 100% reproducible, but it is biased.

- **Selected scenarios**

   Presenting only selected scenarios of benchmarking. You might do
   honest benchmarking comparing your solution to a competitor's
   in five different scenarios. Imagine that your solution is better only
   in one of these scenarios. In this case, you can present only this
   scenario and say that your solution is always faster.

   In summary, I think we all can agree that black marketing practices are unethical
and, worse, promote bad benchmarking practices. Meanwhile, "white" marketing
is a good tool to share your performance results. If you want to distinguish between
good and bad performance research, you need to understand it. We will discuss some
important techniques in Chapters 4 and 5.

Scientific Interest

Benchmarks can help you improve your developer skills and get in-depth knowledge
of software internals. It helps you to understand the layers of your program, including
central organization principles of modern runtimes, databases, I/O storages, CPUs,
and so on. When you read abstract theory about how hardware is organized, it's hard
to understand all the information and context. In this book, we will mainly discuss
academic benchmarks, small pieces of code which show something important. While
not useful on their own, if you want to benchmark big complex systems, first you must
learn how to benchmark at the granular level.

Benchmarking for Fun

Many of my friends like puzzle games with riddles to solve. My favorite puzzles are
benchmarks. If you do a lot of benchmarking, you will often meet measurement results
that you can't explain from the first attempt. You then have to locate the bottleneck
and benchmark again. On occasion, I have spent *months* trying to explain tricky code,
making it especially sweet when I find a solution.

   Perhaps you've heard of "performance golf."[2] You are given a simple problem that
is easily solved, but you have to implement the fastest and the most efficient solution.

---

[2]For example, see https://mattwarren.org/2016/05/16/adventures-in-benchmarking-
performance-golf/

If your solution is faster by a few nanoseconds than a friend's, you need benchmarking to show the difference. Note that it's important to know how to competently play with input data and environments (your solution could be the fastest only under specific conditions). Benchmarking for fun is a great way to unwind after a week of routine.

Now that you are familiar with the most common benchmarking goals, let's take a look at the benchmark requirements that will help us to achieve those goals.

Benchmark Requirements

Generally, any program that measures the duration of an operation can be a benchmark. However, a *good* benchmark should satisfy certain conditions. While there's no official list of benchmark requirements, the following is a list of useful *recommendations*.

Repeatability

Repeatability is probably the most important requirement. If you run a benchmark twice, you should get the same results. If you run a benchmark thrice, you should get the same results. If you run a benchmark 1000 times, you should get the same results. Of course, *it is impossible to get the exactly same result each time*, there is always a difference between measurements. But this difference should not be significant; all measurements should be close enough.

Note that the same code can work for various periods of time because of its nature (especially if it involves some I/O or network operations). A good benchmark is more than just a single experiment or a single number; it's a distribution of numbers. You can have a complicated measurement distribution with several local maximums as a benchmark output.

Even if the measured code is fixed and you cannot change it, you still have control over how to run it vis-à-vis multiple iterations, initializing the environment, or preparing specific input data. You can design a benchmark in multiple ways, but it must have repeatable output as a result.

Sometimes, it is impossible to attain repeatability, but that is the goal. In this book, we will delve into practices and approaches that will help you to stabilize your results. Even if your benchmark is consistently repeatable, it doesn't mean that everything is perfect. There are other requirements to be satisfied.

Verifiability and Portability

Good performance research does not happen in a vacuum. If you want to share your performance results with others, make sure that they will be able to run it in their own environment. Enlist your friends, colleagues, or people from the community to help you to improve your results; just be sure to prepare the corresponding source code and ensure that the benchmark is verifiable in another environment.

Non-Invading Principle

During benchmarking, you can often get the *observer effect*, that is, the mere act of observation can affect an outcome. Here are two popular examples from physics, from which the term came:

- **Electric circuit**

  When you want to measure voltage in an electric circuit, you connect a voltmeter to the circuit, but then you've made some changes in the circuit that can affect the original voltage. Usually, the voltage delta is less than the measurement error, so it's not a problem.

- **Mercury-in-glass thermometer**

  When you are using a classic mercury-in-glass thermometer, it absorbs some thermal energy. In a perfect scenario, the absorption, which affects the temperature of the body, would also be measured.

We have pretty similar examples in the world of performance measurements:

- **Looking for a hot method**

  You want to know why a program is slow or where to find a hotspot, but you don't have an access to a profiler or other measurement tools. So you decide to add logging and print to the current timestamp to a log file at the beginning and at the end of each suspicious method. Unfortunately, the cost of the I/O operation is high, and your small logging logic can easily cause a bottleneck. It's impossible to find the original hotspot now because you spent 90% of the time writing logs.

- **Using a profiler**

  Use of a profiler can impact a situation. When you work with
  another process, you make it slower. In some profiler modes, the
  impact can be small (e.g., in the sampling mode), but in others, it
  can be huge. For example, tracing can easily double the original
  time. We will discuss sampling, tracing, and other profiler modes
  in Chapter 6.

The takeaway here is that when you measure software performance, the observer
effect is usually present, so do keep it in mind.

Acceptable Level of Precision

Once I investigated a strange performance degradation. After some changes in Rider,
a test that covers the "Find Usages," the feature went from 10 seconds to 20. We did
not make any significant changes, so it looked like a simple bug. It was easy to find a
superslow method in my first profiling session. A piece of thoughtlessly copy-pasted
code was the culprit. The bug is fixed, right? But before pushing it to a remote repository,
I wanted to make sure that the feature works fast again. What measurement tool do
you think I used? I used a stopwatch! Not the `System.Diagnostics.Stopwatch` class,
but a simple stopwatch embedded in my old-school Casio 3298/F-105 wristwatch. This
tool has a really poor precision. It showed ~10 seconds, but it could be 9 or 11 seconds.
However, the accuracy of my stopwatch was enough to detect the difference between 10
and 20 seconds.

For every situation, there are tools that will solve problems, but none are good
enough for all kinds of situations. My watch solved the problem because the measured
operation took about 10 seconds and I did not care about a 1-second error. When
an operation takes 100 milliseconds, it would obviously be hard to measure it with
a physical stopwatch; we need a timestamping API. When an operation takes 100
microseconds, we need a high-resolution timestamping API. When an operation takes
100 nanoseconds, even high-resolution timestamping API is not enough; additional
actions (like repeating the operation several times) are needed to achieve a good
precision level.

Remember that operation duration is not a fixed number. If you measure an
operation 10 times, you will get 10 different numbers. In modern software/hardware,
noise sources can spoil the measurements, increase the variance, and ultimately affect
final accuracy.

Unfortunately, there is no such thing as the perfect accuracy: you will always have measurement errors. The important thing here is to know your precision level and to be able to verify that the level achieved is enough for solving your original problem.

Honesty

In a perfect world, every benchmark should be honest. I always encourage developers to present full actual data. In the benchmarking world, it is easy to fool yourself accidentally. If you get some strange numbers, there is no need to hide them. Share them and confess that you don't know why. We can't help each other improve our benchmarks if all our reports contain only "perfect" results.

Performance Spaces

When we talk about performance, we are not talking about a single number. A single measured time interval is usually not enough to draw a meaningful conclusion. In any performance investigation, we are working with a *multidimensional performance space*. It is important to remember that our subject of study is a space with any number of dimensions, dependent on many variables.

Basics

What do we mean by the "multidimensional performance space" term? Let's start with an example. We will write a web site for a bookshop. In particular, we are going to implement a page which shows all books in a category (e.g., all fantasy books). For simplification, we say that processing of a single book takes 10 milliseconds (10 ms) and all other things (like networking, working with a database, HTML rendering, etc.) are negligibly fast. How much time does it take to show this page? Obviously, it depends on the number of books in the category. We need 150 ms for 15 books and 420 ms for 42 books. In the general case, we need 10*N ms for N books This is a very simple *one-dimensional space* that can be expressed by a linear model. The only dimension here is the number of books N. In each point of this one-dimensional space, we have a performance number: how much time it takes to show the page. This space can be presented as a two-dimensional plot (see Figure 1-1).

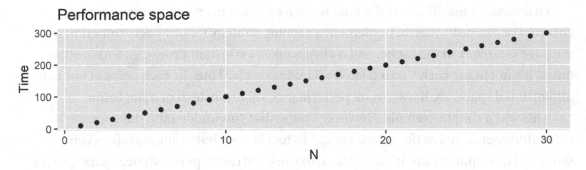

Figure 1-1. *Example 1 of a simple performance space*

Now let's say that processing a single book takes X milliseconds (instead of constant 10 ms). Thus, our space becomes two-dimensional. The dimensions are the number of books N and the book processing time X. The total time can be calculated with a simple formula: Time = N ∗ X (the plot is shown in Figure 1-2).

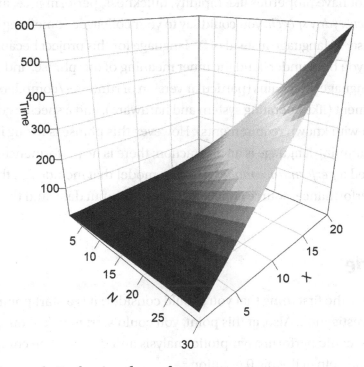

Figure 1-2. *Example 2 of a simple performance space*

Of course, in real life, the total time is not a constant even if all parameters are known. For example, we can implement a caching strategy for our page: sometimes, the page is already in the cache, and it always takes a constant time (e.g., 5 ms); other times, it's not in the cache, so it takes N ∗ X milliseconds. Thus, in each point of our two-dimensional space, we have several performance values instead of a single one.

This was a simple example. However, I hope that you understand the concept of "multidimensional performance space." In real life, we have hundreds (or even thousands) of dimensions. It's really hard to work with such performance spaces, so we need a *performance model* that describes the kind of factors we want to consider.

Performance Model

It's always hard to speak about "performance" and "speed" of programs, because different people understand these words in different ways. Sometimes, I see blog posts with titles like "Why C++ is faster than C#" or "Why C# is faster than C++." What do you think: which title is correct? The answer: both titles are wrong because a programming language does not have properties like rapidity, quickness, performance, and so on.

However, *in everyday speech*, you could say to your colleague something like "I think that we should use 'X' language instead of 'Y' language for this project because it will be faster." It's fine if you both understand the inner meaning of this phrase, and you are talking about specific language toolchains (particular version of runtimes/compilers/etc.), a specific environment (like operating system and hardware), and a specific goal (to develop a specific project with known requirements). However, this phrase is wrong in general because a programming language is an abstraction; there is no performance of language.

Thus, we need a *performance model*. This is a model that includes all the factors important for performance: source code, environment, input data, and the performance distribution.

Source Code

The source code is the first thing that you should consider; it is a start point of your performance investigation. Also, at this point, you could start to talk about performance. For example, you could perform asymptotic analysis and describe the complexity of your algorithm with the help of the big O notation.[3]

---

[3]We will discuss asymptotic analysis and the big O notation in Chapter 4.

Let's say that you have two algorithms with complexities O(N) and O(N^2). Sometimes, it will be enough to choose the first algorithm without additional performance measurements. However, you should keep in mind that the O(N) algorithm is not always faster than O(N^2): there are many cases when you have the opposite situations for small values of N. You should understand that this notation describes only the limiting behavior and usually works fine only for large values.

Sometimes it is hard to calculate the computational complexity of an algorithm (especially if it is not a traditional academic algorithm) even with the help of the amortized analysis (which we also will discuss later). For example, if an algorithm (which is written in C#) allocates many objects, there will be an implicit performance degradation because of the garbage collector (GC).

Also, the classic asymptotic analysis is an academic and fundamental activity; it does not respect features of modern hardware. For example, you could have CPU cache-friendly and –unfriendly algorithms with the same complexity but with entirely different performance characteristics.

All of the preceding doesn't mean that you should not try to analyze performance only based on source code. An experienced developer often can make many correct performance assumptions at a quick glance at the code. However, remember that source code is still an abstraction. Strictly speaking, we cannot discuss the speed of raw source code without knowledge of how we are going to run it. The next thing that we need is an environment.

Environment

Environment is the set of external conditions that affect the program execution.

Let's say we wrote some C# code. What's next? Further, we compile it with *a C# compiler* and run it on a *.NET runtime* that uses a *JIT compiler* to translate the Intermediate Language (IL) code to native instructions of a *processor architecture*.[4] It will be executed on a *hardware* with *some amount of RAM* and *some networking throughput*.

Did you notice how many unknown factors there are here? In real life, your program always runs in a particular environment. You can use the x86 platform, the x64 platform, or the ARM platform. You can use the LegacyJIT or the new modern RyuJIT. You can use different target .NET frameworks or Common Language Runtime (CLR) versions. You can run your benchmark with .NET Framework, .NET Core, or Mono.

---

[4]We will discuss all these terms in Chapter 3.

Don't extrapolate benchmark results of a single environment to the general case. For example, if you switch LegacyJIT to RyuJIT, it could significantly affect the results. LegacyJIT and RyuJIT use different logic for performing the most optimizations (it is hard to say that one is better than another; they are just different). If you developed a .NET application for Windows and .NET Framework and suddenly decided to make it cross-platform and run it on Linux with the help of Mono or .NET Core, many surprises are waiting for you!

Of course, it is impossible to check all the possible environments. Usually, you are working with a single environment which is the default for your computer. When users find a bug, you might hear, "it works on my machine." When users complain that software works slowly, you might hear "it works fast on my machine." Sometimes you check to see how it works on a few other environments (e.g., check x86 vs. x64 or check different operating systems). However, there are many, many configurations that will never be checked. Only a deep understanding of modern software and hardware internals can help you to guess how it will work in different production environments. We will discuss environments in detail in Chapter 3.

It's great if you are able to check how the program works in all the target environments. However, there is one more thing which affects performance: input data.

Input Data

Input data is the set of variables that is processed by the program. (it may be user input, the content of a text file, method arguments, and so on).

Let's say we wrote some C# code and chose our target environment. Can we talk about performance now or compare two different algorithms to check which one is faster? The answer is no because we can observe different algorithm speeds for various input data.

For example, we want to compare two regular expression engines. How can we do it? We might search something in a text with the help of a regular expression. However, which text and expression should we use? Moreover, how many text-expression pairs should we use? If we check only one pair and it shows that engine A is faster than engine B, it does not mean that it is true in the general case. If there are two implementations, it is a typical situation when one implementation works faster on one kind of input data, and another implementation is faster on another kind. It is nice to have a reference input set that allows comparing algorithms. However, it is difficult to create such a set: you should check different typical kinds of inputs and corner cases.

If you want to create a good reference set, you need to understand what's going on under the hood of your code. If you are working with a data structure, check different memory access patterns such as sequential reads/writes, random reads/writes, and some regular patterns. If you have a branch inside your algorithms (just an if operator), check different patterns for branch condition values: condition is always true, condition is random, condition values alternate, and so on (branch predictors on modern hardware do internal magic that could significantly affect your performance).

Distribution

Performance distribution is the set of all measured metrics during benchmarking.

Let's say we wrote some C# code, chose the target environment, and defined a reference input set. Could we now compare two algorithms and state, "The first algorithm is five times faster than the second one"? The answer is still no. If we run the same code in the same environment on the same data twice, we won't observe the same performance numbers. There is always a difference between measurements. Sometimes it is minor, and we overlook it. However, in real life, we cannot describe performance with a single number: it is always a distribution. In a simple case, the distribution looks like a normal one, and we can use only average values to compare our algorithms. However, you could also have many "features" that complicate the analysis. For example, the variance could be colossal, or your distribution could have several local maximums (a typical situation for big computer systems). It is really hard to compare algorithms in such cases and make useful conclusions.

For example, look at the six distributions in Figure 1-3. All of them have the same mean value: 100.

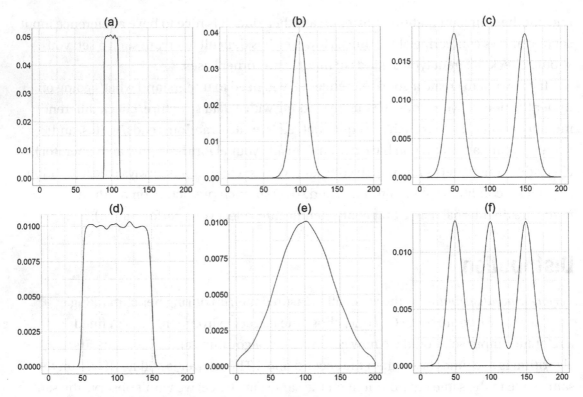

Figure 1-3. *Six different distributions with the same mean*

You may note that

- (a) and (d) are uniform distributions

- (b) and (e) are normal distributions

- (d) and (e) have much bigger variance than (a) and (b)

- (c) has two local maximums (50 and 150) and *doesn't contain* any values equal to 100

- (f) has three local maximums (50, 100, and 150) and *contains* many values equal to 100

It's very important to distinguish between different kinds of distributions because if you only look at the average value, you may not notice the difference between them.

When you are working with complex logic, it's typical to have several local maximums and big standard deviation. Fortunately, *in simple cases* you can *usually* ignore the distributions because the average of all measurements is enough for *basic* performance analysis. However, it does not hurt to occasionally check the statistical properties of your distributions.

Now that we have discussed the important parts of a performance model, it's time to put them together.

The Space

Finally, we can talk about *the performance space*, which helps combine source code, environment, and input data, and analyze how it affects the performance distribution. Mathematically speaking, we have a function from the Cartesian product of `<SourceCode>`, `<Environment>`, and `<InputData>` to `<Distribution>`:

$$\langle SourceCode\rangle \times \langle Environment\rangle \times \langle InputData\rangle \mapsto \langle Distribution\rangle.$$

It means that for each situation when we execute *the source code* in *an environment* on *the input data*, we get *a distribution* of measurements and a function (in a mathematical sense) with three arguments (`<SourceCode>`, `<Environment>`, `<InputData>`) that returns a single value (`<Distribution>`). We say that such a function defines a *performance space*. When we do a performance investigation, we try to understand the internal structure of a space based on a limited set of benchmarks. In this book, we will discuss which factors affect performance, how they do it, and what you need to keep in mind while benchmarking.

Even if you build such functions and they yield a huge number of performance measurements, you still have to analyze them. So, let's talk about the performance analysis.

Analysis

The analysis is the most important step in any performance investigation because experiment results without analysis is just a set of useless raw numbers. Let's talk about what to do to in order get the maximum profit from raw performance data.

The Bad, the Ugly and the Good

I sometimes refer to benchmarks as "bad" but honestly, they cannot be *good* or *bad* (but they can be *ugly*). However, since we use these words in everyday life and understand the implications, let's discuss them in those terms.

The Bad. *A bad benchmark* has unreliable, unclear results. If you write a program that prints some performance numbers, they always mean something, but perhaps not what you expect. A few examples:

- You want to measure the performance of your hard drive, but your benchmark measures performance of a file system.

- You want to measure how much time it takes to render a web page, but your benchmark measures performance of a database.

- You want to measure how fast a CPU can process arithmetical expressions, but your benchmark measures how effectively your compiler optimizes these expressions.

It is bad when benchmarks don't give you reliable information about the performance space. If you wrote "an awful benchmark," you're still able to analyze it the right way and explain why you have such numbers. If you wrote "the best benchmark in the world," you're still able to make a mistake in analysis. If you are using a super-reliable benchmarking framework, it does not mean that you will come up with the right conclusions. If you wrote a poor benchmark in ten lines based on a simple loop with the help of `DateTime.Now`, it does not mean that your results are wrong: if you understand extremely well what's going on under the hood of your program, you can get much useful information from the obtained data.

The Ugly. *An ugly benchmark* gives results that are hard to verify. It is not an indication of right or wrong, it just means that we may not be able to trust it. If you ignore important good practices of benchmarking, you can't be sure of getting correct results.

For example, imagine a poorly written piece of code. No one understands how it works, but it does, and it solves a problem. You can ruminate all day about terrible formatting, confusing variable names, and inconsistent style, but the program still works properly. The same holds true in the benchmark world: a really ugly benchmark can produce correct results if you can analyze it the right way. So while you can't tell someone that their results are wrong because his/her benchmark is awful, skips the warm-up stage, does an insufficient number of iterations, and so on, you can call out results as unreliable and request further analysis.

The Good. *A good benchmark* is a benchmark meets the following criteria:

- *The source code looks trustable.* It follows common benchmarking practices and avoids common pitfalls that can easily spoil results.

- *The results are correct.* It measures precisely what it is designed to measure.

- *Conclusions are presented.* It explains context for the results and provides new knowledge about the performance space (in lieu of raw performance numbers).

- *The results are explained and verified.* Supportive information about the results and why they can be trusted is offered.

Good performance investigation always includes analysis. Raw measurement numbers are not enough. The main result is a conclusion drawn based on analysis of the numbers.

On the Internet, you can find `Stopwatch`-based code snippets containing sample of output without comments. ("Look at this awesome benchmark" does not count.) If you have performance numbers, you have to interpret them and explain why you have these exact numbers. You should explain why we can extrapolate our conclusions and use it in other programs (remember how complicated the performance spaces could be).

Of course, that's not enough. A benchmark should always include the verification stage when trying to prove that results are correct.

Find Your Bottleneck

When you analyze benchmark results, always ask why a benchmark doesn't work faster. A benchmark usually has a limiting factor or a "bottleneck" that is important to identify for the following reasons:

- If you aren't aware of the bottleneck, it is challenging to explain the benchmark result.

- Only knowledge of the limiting factor allows verification of the set of metrics. Are you sure that your metrics fit your problem? This is a typical situation when a developer is trying to measure the total execution time, but it's better to measure specific things like a cache-miss count or memory traffic.

- Understanding the bottleneck will allow you to design a better benchmark and explore the performance space in the right direction.

- A lot of developers use benchmarking as a first stage trying to optimize something, but if you don't know the limiting factor, you won't know how to optimize.

The Pareto Principle (also called the 80/20 Rule) describes uneven distribution. For example, 20% of a given effort produces 80% of the results, 20% of the hazards causes 80% of the injuries, 20% of the bugs cause 80% of the crashes, and so on. We can apply the Pareto Principle to the bottlenecks (let's call it *The Bottlenecks Rule*[5]) and say that 20% of the code consumes 80% of the resource. If we go deeper and try to find the problem using this 20%, we can apply the Pareto Principle again and get the second-order Pareto Principle (or just Pareto^2). In this case, we are talking about 4% of the code (4% = 20% · 20%) and 64% of the resource (64% = 80% · 80%). In huge applications with a complex multilevel architecture, we can go even deeper and formulate the third-order Pareto Principle (or just Pareto^3). In this case, we get 0.8% of the code (0.8% = 20% · 20% · 20%) and 51.2% of the resource (51.2% = 80% · 80% · 80%). To summarize:

The Bottlenecks Rule:

- **Pareto^1: 20%** of the code consumes **80%** of the resource

- **Pareto^2: 4%** of the code consumes **64%** of the resource

- **Pareto^3: 0.8%** of the code consumes **51.2%** of the resource

Here we use "the resource" as an abstract term, but it's important to know what kind of resources limit performance and how they correspond to the different kinds of bottlenecks. In the book, we will learn that each kind has its own set of pitfalls and limiting factors to keep in mind (see Chapters 7 and 8). Understanding that allows you to focus on more important things for your particular situation.

Statistics

I wish that each benchmark could print the same number each time, but reality is that performance measurements have crazy and scary distributions. Of course, it depends on

---

[5]The Bottlenecks Rule was introduced by Federico Lois. You can watch his great talk about it and other performance topics on YouTube: www.youtube.com/watch?v=7GTpwgsmHgU

what kind of metric you choose, but you should be ready to get a distribution of a strange form (especially if you measure wall clock time). If you want to analyze benchmark results properly, you have to know basic concepts of statistics such as the difference between mean and median, along with the meaning of words like "outlier," "standard error," and "percentile." It's also good to know about the Central Limit Theorem and multimodal distributions. Big bonus points if you know how to do significance tests, feel comfortable when someone says "Null hypothesis," and can draw beautiful and incomprehensible statistical plots. Don't worry if you don't know all this stuff; we will discuss all of it in Chapter 4.

I hope now you understand why it's so important to spend some time on analysis. Now let's summarize what we have learned in this chapter.

Summary

In this chapter, you were briefly introduced to the main topics that are important for any developer who wants to write benchmarks, including the following:

- Good performance investigation and the steps it entails.

- Typical benchmarking goals and how can they help us make better software and improve our skills.

- Common benchmarking requirements and the difference between good and bad benchmarks.

- Performance spaces and why it's important to look at the source code, environments, and input data.

- Why the analysis is so important and how to make good conclusions.

In the subsequent chapters, we will dive into these topics in detail.

CHAPTER 2

Common Benchmarking Pitfalls

If you have spent less than a week studying a benchmark result, it is probably wrong.

— Brendan Gregg, author of *Systems Performance: Enterprise and the Cloud*, Prentice Hall, 2013

In this chapter, we will discuss the most common mistakes that people make when they try to measure performance. If you want to write benchmarks, you have to accept the fact that most of the time you will be wrong. Unfortunately, there is no universally reliable way to verify that you get the performance metrics you wanted to get. There are many pitfalls on different levels: C# compiler, .NET runtime, CPU, and so on. We will also learn some approaches and techniques to help you to write reliable and correct benchmarks.

Most pitfalls are especially painful for microbenchmarks with very short durations (such methods can take milliseconds, microseconds, or even nanoseconds). The pitfalls that we are going to discuss are relevant not only to microbenchmarks, but also to all other kinds of benchmarks. However, we will focus mainly on microbenchmarks for the following reasons:

1. The simplest microbenchmarks contain only a few lines of code. It usually takes less than one minute to understand what's going on in each example. However, simplicity is deceptive. You will see how hard it is to benchmark even very simple pieces of code.

2. Microbenchmarks are usually the first step in the world of benchmarking that developers usually take. If you want to write good real-world benchmarks, you should learn how to write

31

A. Akinshin, *Pro .NET Benchmarking*, https://doi.org/10.1007/978-1-4842-4941-3_2

microbenchmarks. The basic benchmarking routine is the same for both cases, and it is much easier to learn it on smaller examples.

In this chapter, we will look at some of the most common mistakes that people usually make during microbenchmarking. In each example, you will find "A bad benchmark" subsection. This will describe a benchmark that looks fine to some developers (especially to people who don't have any benchmarking experience) but produces wrong results. After that, "A better benchmark" will be presented. It's usually still not a perfect benchmark, and it still has some issues, but it shows the right way to improve your benchmarks. We can say that if "a bad benchmark" contains N mistakes, "a better benchmark" contains at most N-1 mistakes. I hope it will be a nice illustration of how to fix one of these mistakes.

One more thing: if you want to get not only knowledge but also some benchmarking skills, you should not mindlessly flip through examples. Try each example on your own computer. Play with it: check different environments or change something in the code. Look at the results and try to explain them yourself before you read the explanation in the book. You get benchmarking skills only if you get enough benchmarking experience.

General Pitfalls

We will start with the "General Pitfalls." All the examples will be presented in C#, but corresponding pitfalls are common not only for .NET, but for all languages and runtimes.

Inaccurate Timestamping

Before we start learning the pitfalls, let's talk about benchmarking basics. The first thing that you should learn here is timestamping.

How is the time of an operation measured? This question may seem obvious. We should take a timestamp before the operation (it's like asking the computer "What time is it now?"), execute the operation, and take another timestamp. Then, we subtract the first timestamp from the second one, and we get the elapsed time! The pseudocode may look like this (we use var here because the timestamp type depends on the used API):

```
var startTimestamp = GetTimestamp();
// Do something
var endTimestamp = GetTimestamp();
var totalTime = endTimestamp - startTimestamp;
```

But how exactly should we take these timestamps? The .NET Framework provides several APIs for timestamping. A lot of developers who are just starting to write benchmarks use `DateTime.Now`:

```
DateTime start = DateTime.Now;
// Do something
DateTime end = DateTime.Now;
TimeSpan elapsed = end - start;
```

And it works fine for *some* scenarios. However, `DateTime.Now` has many drawbacks:

- There are a lot of time-related surprises that can spoil your benchmark. For example, the current time can be suddenly changed because of daylight saving time. A possible solution is using `DateTime.UtcNow` instead of `DateTime.Now`. Also, `DateTime.UtcNow` has lower overhead because it doesn't have to do any calculations with time zones.

- The current time can be accidentally synchronized with the Internet. The synchronization happens pretty often and may easily introduce a few-second error.

- The accuracy of `DateTime.Now` and `DateTime.UtcNow` is poor. If your benchmark takes minutes or hours, it could be OK, but it's absolutely unacceptable if your method takes less than 1 millisecond.

There are many other time-related problems; we will discuss them in Chapter 9. Fortunately, we have another API called `System.Diagnostics.Stopwatch`. This class is designed to measure elapsed time with the best possible resolution. This is the best solution if we are talking about managed API in the .NET Framework. A usage example:

```
Stopwatch stopwatch = Stopwatch.StartNew();
// Do something
stopwatch.Stop();
TimeSpan elapsedTime = stopwatch.Elapsed;
```

Using the `StartNew()` and `Stop()` methods is the most convenient way to use `Stopwatch`. It's also good to know that there is no magic under the hood: these methods just call `Stopwatch.GetTimestamp()` twice and calculate the difference. `GetTimestamp()` returns the current number of `ticks` (tick is an abstract time unit used by Stopwatch and other timestamping APIs), which can be converted to real time with the help of the `Stopwatch.Frequency` field.[1] Usually, you don't need to use this, but the raw tick values can be useful when you do microbenchmarking (read more about it in Chapter 9). A usage example:

```
long startTicks = Stopwatch.GetTimestamp();
// Do something
long endTicks = Stopwatch.GetTimestamp();
double elapsedSeconds = (endTicks - startTicks)
    * 1.0 / Stopwatch.Frequency;
```

There are also some troubles with `Stopwatch` (especially on old hardware), but it's still the best available timestamping API. When you are writing a microbenchmark, it's nice to know how it works internally. You should be able to answer the following questions:

- What is the accuracy/precision/resolution of the chosen API?

- What are the possible values for the difference between two sequential timestamps? Could it be equal to zero? Could it be much bigger than the resolution? Could it be less than zero?

- What is the timestamping latency on your operating system? (How much time does it take to get a single timestamp?)

All of these topics and many implementation details are covered in Chapter 9. It's OK if you don't remember some tricky facts about `Stopwatch` internals, but you should be able to answer the preceding questions for your target environment.

OK, now it's time for examples!

---

[1]We should divide the tick delta by frequency to get the number of seconds. Both values are integer numbers, but the result should be a fractional number. So we have to convert the delta to double before performing the division operation. My favorite way to do this is multiplying the numerator by 1.0.

A bad benchmark

Let's say we want to measure how much it takes to sort a list with 10000 elements. Here is a *bad* DateTime-based benchmark:

```
var list = Enumerable.Range(0, 10000).ToList();
DateTime start = DateTime.Now;
list.Sort();
DateTime end = DateTime.Now;
TimeSpan elapsedTime = end - start;
Console.WriteLine(elapsedTime.TotalMilliseconds);
```

This is an awful benchmark: it has a lot of problems, and we just can't trust it. We will learn why it's so bad and how to fix all the problems later; now we are looking only at timestamping resolution.

Let's do some calculations. On Windows 10, the default frequency of DateTime updates is 64 Hertz. It means that we get a new value once per 15.625 milliseconds. Some applications (like a browser or a music player) can increase this frequency up to 2000 Hertz (0.5 milliseconds). Sorting 10000 elements is a pretty quick operation that typically works faster than 0.5 milliseconds on modern computers. So, if you use Windows and you close all nonsystem applications, the benchmark will print **0 milliseconds or ~15.625 milliseconds** (depends on how lucky you are). Obviously, such a benchmark is useless; we can't use these numbers for evaluating the performance of List.Sort().

A better benchmark

We can rewrite our example with the help of Stopwatch:

```
var list = Enumerable.Range(0, 10000).ToList();
var stopwatch = Stopwatch.StartNew();
list.Sort();
stopwatch.Stop();
TimeSpan elapsedTime = stopwatch.Elapsed;
Console.WriteLine(elapsedTime.TotalMilliseconds);
```

This is still a bad benchmark, and it's still unstable (if you run it several times, the difference between measurements will be huge), but for now we have a good timestamping resolution. The typical Stopwatch resolution on Windows is about

300–500ns. This code prints about **0.05–0.5 milliseconds** (depends on hardware and runtime), which is closer to the actual sorting time.

Advice: prefer Stopwatch over DateTime

In 99% of cases, Stopwatch should be your primary tool for timestamping. Of course, there are some corner cases, when you need something else (and we will talk about it later), but you don't need anything more in simple cases. This advice is simple and doesn't require additional lines of code. DateTime can be useful only if you *actually* need to know the current time (and you probably would want to do monitoring in this case instead of benchmarking). If you don't need the actual current time, use the right API: use Stopwatch.

Now we know how to write a simple benchmark with the help of Stopwatch. It's time to learn how to run it.

Executing a Benchmark in the Wrong Way

Now you know how to write a simple small benchmark. You also should know how to execute a benchmark. It may seem very obvious, but many developers suffer from incorrect benchmark results that were spoiled because the program was run the wrong way.

A bad benchmark

Open your favorite IDE, create a new project, and write the following simple program:

```
var stopwatch = Stopwatch.StartNew();
for (int i = 0; i < 100000000; i++)
{
}
stopwatch.Stop();
Console.WriteLine(stopwatch.ElapsedMilliseconds);
```

It doesn't measure anything useful, just a simple empty loop. The results have no practical importance; we will use it just for demonstration.

Let's run it. On my laptop, it prints values around **400** milliseconds (Windows, .NET Framework 4.6).[2] So, what's the main problem here? By default, each new project uses the Debug configuration. This is a configuration for debugging, but not for benchmarking. Many people forget to change it, measure the performance of the debug assemblies, and get wrong results.

A better benchmark

Let's switch to the Release mode and run this code again. On my laptop, it shows ~**40** milliseconds in Release. The difference is about 10 times!

Now it's your turn. Run this empty loop in both configurations on your machine and compare the results.

Advice: use Release without attached debugger in sterile environment

In fact, here I have a series of small tips. Let's discuss all the good practices that you should follow if you want to get reliable results.

- **Use Release instead of Debug**

    When you create a new project, you typically have two configurations: Debug and Release. The release mode means that you have `<Optimize>true</Optimize>` in your csproj file or use /optimize for `csc`.

    Sometimes (especially in the case of microbenchmarks), the debug version of the target method can run 100 times slower! Never use the Debug build for benchmarking. **Never**.

    Sometimes I see performance reports on the Internet that contain separated results for both modes. Don't do it! Debug results don't show anything useful. Roslyn compiler injects a lot of additional IL opcodes into the compiled assembly with only one goal: to simplify the debugging. Just-In-Time (JIT) optimizations are also

---

[2].NET Framework 4.6 honestly performs this loop, but be careful: in the future, some additional JIT optimizations could be implemented and this loop could be thrown away because it doesn't do anything useful (thus, the benchmark will print 0 milliseconds).

disabled in Debug. The performance of the debug build can be interesting for you only if you are developing some debugging tools. Otherwise, always use the Release mode.

- **Don't use attached debugger or profiler**

  Also, you never should use an attached debugger (e.g., embedded IDE debugger or external debugger like WinDbg or gdb) during the benchmarking. A debugger usually adds some performance overhead. It's not ten times overhead like the Debug build overhead, but it also can significantly spoil the results. By the way, if you use Visual Studio debugger (pressing F5), it disables JIT optimization by default even in the Release mode (you can turn off this feature, but it's enabled by default). The best way is to build a benchmark in the Release mode and run it in a terminal (e.g., cmd for Windows).

  If you use other kinds of attached applications (like performance or memory profilers), they also can easily spoil the performance picture. In the case of attached profiler, the overhead depends on the profiling kind (e.g., tracing adds bigger overhead than sampling), but it's always significant.

  Sometimes, you can use the internal diagnostic tools of the runtime. For example, if you run mono with the --profile=log:sample arguments, it produces a .mlpd file with information about the application performance profile. It can be useful for analysis of relative performance (hunting for hot methods), but the absolute performance will be affected by the mono profiler.

  It's OK to use the Debug build with an attached debugger or profiler only if you *debug* or *profile* the code. Don't use it for collecting final performance measurements, which should be analyzed.

- **Turn off other applications**

  Turn off all of the applications except the benchmark process and the standard OS processes. If you run a benchmark and work in an IDE at the same time, it can negatively affect the benchmark results. Someone may say that in real life our application works side by side with other applications, so we should measure performance in realistic conditions. Here is the problem with such conditions: their influence is unpredictable. If you want to work in realistic conditions, you should carefully check how these applications can affect your performance, which is not easy (we will discuss many useful tools in Chapter 6). And it's much better to check the performance in a sterile condition when you are not bothered by other applications.

When you design a benchmark, it's OK to perform dry runs directly from your favorite IDE. When you collect the final results, it's better to turn off the IDE and run it from the terminal.

Some benchmarks can take hours to finish. Waiting is boring, and so many developers like to do something else during the benchmarking: play some games, draw funny pictures in Photoshop, or develop another feature for a pet project. Of course, it's not a good idea. It can be OK if you clearly understand what kind of results you want to get and how they can be affected. For example, if you are checking a hypothesis that one method takes 1000 times more time than another method, it will be hard to spoil the conclusion by third-party applications. However, if you do microbenchmarking in order to check a 5%-difference hypothesis, it's unexpected to have heavy background processes: the experiment is not sterile anymore, and the results can't be trusted. Of course, you can be lucky and get correct results. But how can you be sure?

Be careful. Even if you shut down all the applications that can be terminated, an operating system still can run some CPU-consuming services. A typical example is Windows Defender, which can decide to do some heavy operations at any moment. In Figure 2-1, you can observe typical CPU noise on Windows.[3]

---

[3]It's a screenshot of ProcessHacker (a cool replacement for default Task Manager). The x axis denotes time, and the y axis denotes CPU usage. ProcessHacker uses two different colors for kernel CPU usage (red) and all CPU usage (green). Print readers: see the color copy of this figure in the download package for this book.

Usually, there are no heavy processes which could spoil a benchmark, but be prepared for the fact that some of the measurements could be much larger than others because of the CPU noise.

In order to avoid such situations, you should run a benchmark many times and aggregate the results. The CPU noise is random, so it typically spoils only some measurements, but not all of them. Also, you can verify that the environment is sterile with additional tools that monitor resource usage. In some cases, such tools also can affect the results, so you still have to perform sterile benchmark runs and use runs with monitoring for additional checks.

- **Use high-performance power mode**

  If you use a laptop for benchmarking, keep it plugged in and use the maximum performance mode. Let's play again with our empty loop benchmark. Plug out your laptop, choose the "Power saver" mode, and wait until 10% of battery energy remains. Run the benchmark. Then plug in the laptop, choose the "High performance" mode, and run the benchmark again. Compare the results. On my laptop, I have a performance improvement from ~**140** milliseconds to ~**40** milliseconds. We have a similar situation not only for microbenchmarks but also for any other applications. Try to play with your favorite programs and check how much it takes to finish different long-running operations. I hope that you will not run benchmarks on an unplugged laptop after this experiment.

Unfortunately, if you run a benchmark correctly, it doesn't mean that you always get "good" results. Let's continue to look at different microbenchmark pitfalls.

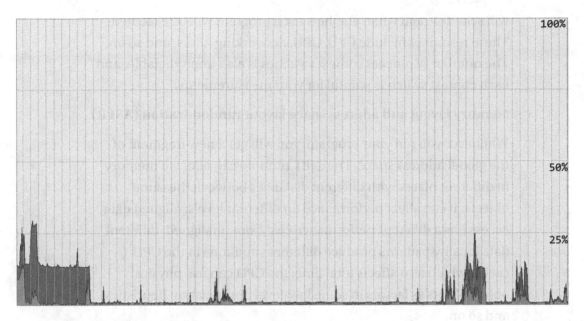

Figure 2-1. *Typical CPU noise on Windows*

Natural Noise

Even if you create a supersterile environment and run your benchmark according to the rules, natural noise still will be presented. If you run a benchmark twice, you will almost never get two identical results. Why? Well, there are a lot of noise sources:

- **There are always other processes which compete for computer resources**

  Even if you turn off all user processes, there are still a lot of OS processes (each of them has its own priority) that can't be turned off. And you always share resources with them. Since you can't predict what's happening in other processes, you also can't predict how it affects your benchmark.

- **Resource scheduling is nondeterministic**

  The operating system always controls the execution of your program. Since we always work in a multiprocessing and multithreading environment, it's also impossible to say how OS

41

will schedule and when and how each program will be executed. These resources include CPU, GPU, networking, disks, and so on. The number of process context switches is also unpredictable, and each context switch is painful for your measurements.

- **Memory layout and address space layout randomization (ASLR)**

  Whenever you run your program, you will get a new fragment of the global address space. The .NET runtime can allocate memory in different places with different distances between the same objects. It can affect performance on different levels: aligned data access has a different performance cost from unaligned; different data locality patterns produce different situations in the CPU cache, which also affects total time; the CPU can use physical object offsets as factors in some low-level optimization heuristics; and so on.

  Another interesting security feature of modern OS is ASLR; It protects you from malicious programs that try to exploit buffer overflows. It's a good feature, but it also adds some unpredictable numbers to the total wall clock time.[4]

- **CPU frequency scaling and boosting**

  A modern CPU can change the internal frequency dynamically, depending on the current workload. Unfortunately, it's another nondeterministic process; you can't predict when and how the frequency will be changed.

- **External environment matters**

  I'm not talking about the version of .NET Framework or your OS. I'm talking about real external environmental factors like temperature. Once, I had cooler problems on my laptop. The cooler was almost broken, and the CPU temperature was high all the time. When I was in my room, the laptop made loud noises

---

[4]You can find an example in the following article: de Oliveira, Augusto Born, Jean-Christophe Petkovich, and Sebastian Fischmeister. *How much does memory layout impact performance? A wide study*. Intl. Workshop Reproducible Research Methodologies, 2014.

and turned down after 10 minutes because the CPU temperature was too high. Fortunately, it was winter, so I opened a window, sat on the windowsill, and worked in a jacket, hat, and gloves. Should I tell you about performance? Well, it was superslow. And the most important thing: slowness was unpredictable. It was impossible to run any benchmarks because the variance was too high as well.

Of course, this was an extreme situation; you typically don't have such awful conditions. Here is another example which you can meet in real life: running benchmarks in the cloud. It's a perfectly valid case if you care about performance in the real environment. The data center environment of your cloud provider is important. There are so many external factors: environmental temperature, mechanical vibrations, and so on. We will discuss these factors in detail in Chapter 3.

Thus, it's OK to have a difference between similar measurements, but you always have to keep in mind how big the errors are. In this section, we will look at an example when natural noise matters.

A bad benchmark

Let's say we want to check if a number is prime. We are going to implement several ways to do it and compare performance. For now, we have only one `IsPrime` implementation, and we want to have the benchmarking infrastructure right now. So, we compare the performance of two identical calls (just to check that the benchmarking stuff works correctly):

```
// It's not the fastest algorithm,
// but we will optimize it later.
static bool IsPrime(int n)
{
  for (int i = 2; i <= n - 1; i++)
    if (n % i == 0)
      return false;
  return true;
}
```

```
static void Main()
{
  var stopwatch1 = Stopwatch.StartNew();
  IsPrime(2147483647);
  stopwatch1.Stop();

  var stopwatch2 = Stopwatch.StartNew();
  IsPrime(2147483647);
  stopwatch2.Stop();

  Console.WriteLine(stopwatch1.ElapsedMilliseconds + " vs. " +
                    stopwatch2.ElapsedMilliseconds);
  if (stopwatch1.ElapsedMilliseconds < stopwatch2.ElapsedMilliseconds)
    Console.WriteLine("The first method is faster");
  else
    Console.WriteLine("The second method is faster");
}
```

Try this snippet on your own computer and run it several times.

I already checked how it works on my laptop:

```
5609 vs. 5667
The first method is faster
```

And run it once again:

```
5573 vs. 5490
The second method is faster
```

Thus, we have two performance results for the same program with different conclusions. Our main mistake: we forget about the errors! If there is a difference between two measurements, it doesn't mean that one method works faster than another. We should check if the difference is bigger than the natural errors. Unfortunately, it's hard to evaluate the size of such errors. It's also hard to minimize these errors (you will find a lot of useful examples in this book). Usually, it's about 5–20% for a naive benchmark, but sometimes it can be 200–500%! So, be careful when you compare the performance of two methods!

Now it's time to improve the IsPrime benchmark.

A better benchmark

Thus, we want the following things:

1. Results should be stable; we should get the same conclusion each time.

2. If the methods take approximately the same time, we should get a corresponding message.

How can it be implemented? We can introduce a "maximum acceptable error" (let's say 20%[5] of the average of two measurements) and use it during comparison:

```
var error = ((stopwatch1.ElapsedMilliseconds +
            stopwatch2.ElapsedMilliseconds) / 2) * 0.20;
if (Math.Abs(stopwatch1.ElapsedMilliseconds -
            stopwatch2.ElapsedMilliseconds) < error)
  Console.WriteLine("There is no significant difference between methods");
else if (stopwatch1.ElapsedMilliseconds < stopwatch2.ElapsedMilliseconds)
  Console.WriteLine("The first method is faster");
else
  Console.WriteLine("The second method is faster");
```

Fix it in your snippet and try it. Here is my result:

```
542 vs. 523
There is no significant difference between methods
```

Hooray, we got the correct result!

Once again, however: this is not a perfect solution. You can't detect 5–10% performance deviation with such code: if one method actually works 7% longer than another, you don't notice it. But it can be OK if the performance difference is about two to three times (and it's obvious which method is faster). Be careful: it's *not always* OK; the natural performance noise can be really huge sometimes.

---

[5]20% is an example; this number depends on your benchmarking goals and business requirements. Also, it's a good idea to measure each case many times and check the difference between the minimal and maximal elapsed time: it provides the first approximation of the natural noise order. Thus, you get some initial rough value, which can be used as a maximum acceptable error. In the next chapters, we will discuss the standard deviation of the performance distributions and we will learn how to use this value for comparing different methods.

Advice: always analyze random errors

We can't prevent natural noise and random errors, so the best thing that we can do is the correct analysis. Perform many iterations of your benchmark, look at the variance, and keep in mind the order of these random errors. If you get two different performance numbers for two different methods (in our cruel world, you always get different numbers), compare the difference with the order of natural noise for each method before making any conclusions as to which method is faster (do we have significant difference between methods or not). We will discuss statistical methods for distribution comparison in Chapter 4.

In the next section, we will discuss other "surprises" we can observe in a distribution of measurements.

Tricky Distributions

In the previous sections, we discussed how to achieve the stable benchmark result. Unfortunately, you can't always describe a code performance with a single number.

A bad benchmark

Consider the following I/O benchmark:

```
byte[] data = new byte[64 * 1024 * 1024];
var stopwatch = Stopwatch.StartNew();
var fileName = Path.GetTempFileName();
File.WriteAllBytes(fileName, data);
File.Delete(fileName);
stopwatch.Stop();
Console.WriteLine(stopwatch.ElapsedMilliseconds);
```

Here we do a simple thing: create a new temp file, write 64MB data, and delete the file. What is the problem with this benchmark? We do only one iteration here! Are we sure that all I/O operations are equal?

A better benchmark

Now let's do several iterations and make some basic statistics:

```
int N = 1000;
byte[] data = new byte[64 * 1024 * 1024];
var measurements = new long[N];
for (int i = 0; i < N; i++)
{
  var stopwatch = Stopwatch.StartNew();
  var fileName = Path.GetTempFileName();
  File.WriteAllBytes(fileName, data);
  File.Delete(fileName);
  stopwatch.Stop();
  measurements[i] = stopwatch.ElapsedMilliseconds;
  Console.WriteLine(measurements[i]);
}
Console.WriteLine("Minimum = " + measurements.Min());
Console.WriteLine("Maximum = " + measurements.Max());
Console.WriteLine("Average = " + measurements.Average());
```

On my SSD (SanDisk SD8SNAT128G1002) + Windows (10.0.17134.285), I have the following values:

334,304,266,333,**2488**,575,371,**1336**,269,488,377,472,374,266,**15827**,...

And here is the program output:

```
Minimum = 265
Maximum = 19029
Average = 531.176
```

You can see that most values are about 250–500, but we also have some outliers (from 600 to 19000). If we increase the number of iterations, we will see that it was not a few accidental big values: we can consistently observe extremely high values from time to time (see Figure 2-2).

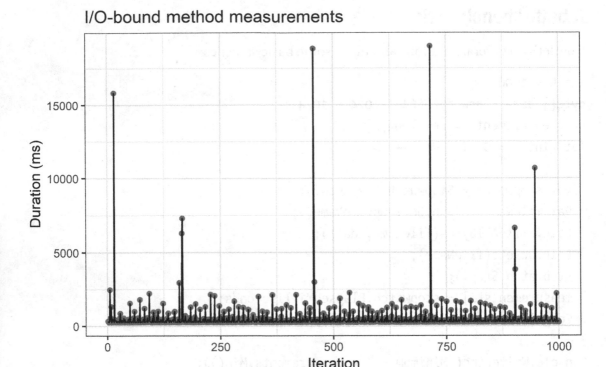

Figure 2-2. *I/O-bound method measurements*

Benchmarking of I/O operations is very hard, and it's a normal situation when it's impossible to describe the performance by one average number.

Advice: always look at your distribution

Fortunately, in many simple cases, we can just take the average value and work with it. But how can we be sure? But if we want to be sure that everything is OK, we always should check the distribution first. In Chapter 4, we will discuss in detail how to correctly analyze distributions.

In the next section, we will talk about the difference between the first measurement and the subsequent measurements (and why we can observe such effects).

Measuring Cold Start Instead of Warmed Steady State

If you execute some code for the first time (after the application was started), it is called **the cold start**. It includes a large amount of third-party logic (basically on the runtime and CPU levels): jitting of target methods, loading of assemblies, CPU cache warm-up, and so on. It also can include some user logic: initialization of business objects, running constructors of static classes, filling user caches, and so on. All of that can increase the work time and spoil the benchmark results.

Measuring the cold start is a rare task: developers typically do it only in situations when they are optimizing the startup time. In all other cases, it's a huge mistake if you include the initialization overhead in the final results. Thus, you should perform a **warm-up**: run the benchmark method several times in the idle mode (without measurements). "Warming up" means that we are waiting for a moment when all initialization and transitional processes are finished, and we will be in a **steady state**. "Steady state" means that all benchmark iterations do the exact same amount of work and there are no side effects. In other words, we should strive to a situation when we have the same state of the program before and after each iteration.

You should decide for yourself which state you want to measure: cold or warmed. For example, if you are working on the startup time of an application, you are interested only in the first benchmark iteration (subsequent iterations will be warmed). So, if you want to make several measurements of the cold start, you should restart the whole application each time.

However, most benchmarks work with the warmed program. Typically, you should warm up the program and only then perform target runs and measure its time.

How can we check that we are in the steady state? A short answer: we can't. Huge applications from real life with smart caching strategies and tricky multithreading scheduling can request tens or hundreds of warm-up iterations. Fortunately, for simple benchmarks, it's *usually* enough to do four or five iterations (run ten iterations to be sure). If each iteration works faster than the previous one, you probably are still not warmed (typically, you should observe some fluctuation around a single value at the steady state).

Now let's make sure that it's important to distinguish between cold and warmed states.

A bad benchmark

Consider the following benchmark:

```
int[] x = new int[100000000];
var stopwatch = Stopwatch.StartNew();
for (int i = 0; i < x.Length; i++)
  x[i]++;
stopwatch.Stop();
Console.WriteLine(stopwatch.ElapsedMilliseconds);
```

Here we have an `int` array with 100000000 elements, and we increment each element. What's wrong with this benchmark? We make a lot of memory reads/writes in the loop. Modern CPUs have a complicated hierarchical structure with a multilevel cache. When we run this code for the first time, this cache is unwarmed. Access to the main memory is too expensive, and this code will take a lot of time. Thus, the result will describe the cold state. Probably, that's not what we want.

A better benchmark

Let's do five iterations and measure the time for each of them:

```
int[] x = new int[100000000];
for (int iter = 0; iter < 5; iter++)
{
  var stopwatch = Stopwatch.StartNew();
  for (int i = 0; i < x.Length; i++)
    x[i]++;
  stopwatch.Stop();
  Console.WriteLine(stopwatch.ElapsedMilliseconds);
}
```

The typical output on my laptop (check how it works on your computer):

```
180
80
67
71
68
```

As you can see, the first iteration took about 180 milliseconds. That's our cold start time. After a few iterations, we can observe that measures are fluctuating around 70 milliseconds. Here we already achieved the steady state; that's our warmed time. The cold start benchmarking is too tricky, so such measurements should be handled in a special way. When we are talking about benchmarking in general, usually we assume a warmed state.

Here is an exercise for you: take some code from your work or pet project, and run it several times at the beginning of the Main method (with Stopwatch-based measurements). Compare the first measurement and subsequent measurements.

Make conclusions about how many iterations do you need before you get a steady state.

Advice: use different approaches for cold and warm states

Before actual benchmarking, you always should decide: do you want to measure the cold start or the warmed steady state? If you are interested in the cold start, you typically should restart the whole program (or restart a computer in some cases) before each iteration. Otherwise, you should make some warm-up iterations and get to the steady state before you start to collect target performance numbers.

In the next section, we discuss how many iterations we should do.

Insufficient Number of Invocations

When you make some micro-optimizations, it can be useful to measure a time of really small methods that take nanoseconds. If you are working with a hot method and you invoke it a million times per second, even a 10–20% performance boost can be important. However, it's hard to measure such methods.

Let's say we have a method that takes about 100 nanoseconds and we are trying to measure it with the help of Stopwatch:

```
var stopwatch = Stopwatch.StartNew();
Foo(); // 100ns
stopwatch.Stop();
// Print ElapsedTime
```

As we already know, the typical Stopwatch resolution on Windows is about 300–500ns. That's not enough to measure such a small method: the result most likely will be zero or the Stopwatch resolution. Even if a method takes microseconds, we still have natural noise, which spoils the repeatability of the benchmark. This problem can be solved if we invoke the method many times between measurements and divide the result into the number of invocations. Let's see how it works in an example.

A bad benchmark

We want to know how many divisors are there for the number 100000 (spoiler: 36). Let's solve this simple problem, measure it, and repeat the benchmark ten times (as usual, try this code on your computer):

```
const int N = 100000;
for (int iter = 0; iter < 10; iter++)
{
  var stopwatch = Stopwatch.StartNew();
  int counter = 0;
  for (int i = 1; i <= N; i++)
    if (N % i == 0)
      counter++;
  stopwatch.Stop();
  var elapsedMs = stopwatch.Elapsed.TotalMilliseconds;
  Console.WriteLine(elapsedMs + " ms");
}
```

Here is a typical output:

```
0.410468973641887 ms
0.475654133074913 ms
0.531752876344543 ms
0.308148026410656 ms
0.364641831252615 ms
0.460246731754378 ms
0.346864060498149 ms
0.308148026410656 ms
0.371752939554394 ms
0.274567792763341 ms
```

As you can see, the variance is huge: we have values from 0.27 to 0.53 milliseconds. The whole benchmark takes a small amount of time, so the random noise significantly affects measurements, and we get a new random error each time. It's hard to work with such measurements. If we make some optimizations and run the benchmark again, we can miss the difference, because the original measurement values may differ twofold.

A better benchmark

Let's repeat the measured code block 3000 times! Of course, we should divide the elapsed time by 3000 to get the actual time.

```
const int N = 100000;
const int Invocations = 3000;
for (int iter = 0; iter < 10; iter++)
{
  var stopwatch = Stopwatch.StartNew();
  for (int rep = 0; rep < Invocations; rep++)
  {
    int counter = 0;
    for (int i = 1; i <= N; i++)
      if (N % i == 0)
        counter++;
  }
  stopwatch.Stop();
  var elapsedMs = stopwatch.Elapsed.TotalMilliseconds
                  / Invocations;
  Console.WriteLine(elapsedMs + " ms");
}
```

The output:

```
0.356982772550016 ms
0.358534890455352 ms
0.358426564572221 ms
0.356142476585688 ms
0.358213231323168 ms
0.356969735518129 ms
0.356878397282608 ms
0.357596382184145 ms
0.358787255787751 ms
0.359197546588624 ms
```

Now it looks much more stable! Our result is about 0.356–0.359 milliseconds!

Advice: do many invocations

Well, sometimes it's hard to decide how many invocations you need. You should make at least enough invocations for preventing problems that you aware of. A general recommendation: when you are doing microbenchmarking, repeat the measurable code for at least 1 second. If you are in a hurry, 100ms *can be acceptable* in most cases. When you are working with a 10ms-loop, it's already easy to make mistakes because the benchmark precision is low, and the measurement variance is huge.

Now we know that an additional loop can help us to stabilize the results. However, such changes in the source code can bring additional problems. In the next section, we will discuss these problems and how to fix them.

Infrastructure Overhead

As you can see, a benchmark is more than just a code that you want to measure. A benchmark includes *an infrastructure*: additional code that helps you to measure time correctly and get reliable results. However, this infrastructure has overhead: any changes in a program can affect the measurements. Let's look at another example which illustrates the overhead.

A bad benchmark

We want to measure the conversion of 0.0 from double to int via Convert.ToInt32. We also know that such a microbenchmark should be wrapped into a loop (because the conversion duration is less than the Stopwatch resolution). Let's measure it:

```
var stopwatch = Stopwatch.StartNew();
for (int i = 0; i < 100000001; i++)
  Convert.ToInt32(0.0);
stopwatch.Stop();
Console.WriteLine(stopwatch.ElapsedMilliseconds);
```

Here you have the *observer effect* (we discussed it in Chapter 1): the loop is required for such micro-operations, but it also adds some performance costs. We don't measure only our target operation; we measure it together with the loop. There are many complicated cases when a loop can produce an additional unexpected performance effect (read more in Chapter 7). In simple cases, you always should keep in mind that the benchmark infrastructure (basically, it's all the code you wrote for performing measurements) always adds some overhead (and probably other performance effects).

A better benchmark

One of the possible solutions for "normalizing" results is just to measure benchmarking infrastructure (the loop in our case) for empty code (so called "overhead" or "idle" iterations), and subtract "empty" measurements from the "target" measurements. We can write something like this:

```
var stopwatchOverhead = Stopwatch.StartNew();
for (int i = 0; i < 100000001; i++)
{
}
stopwatchOverhead.Stop();
var stopwatchTarget = Stopwatch.StartNew();
for (int i = 0; i < 100000001; i++)
  Convert.ToInt32(0.0);
stopwatchTarget.Stop();q
var resultOverhead =
  stopwatchTarget.ElapsedMilliseconds -
  stopwatchOverhead.ElapsedMilliseconds
Console.WriteLine(resultOverhead);
```

You can find an example of results for RyuJIT-x64 on .NET Framework 4.6 in Table 2-1.

Table 2-1. *An Empty Loop vs.*
a Loop with ToInt32() Call

Method	Time
Overhead	~34ms
Target	~295ms
Result	~261ms

As you can see, the overhead takes more than 10% of the target measurements. Of course, it's a naive implementation; correct overhead evaluating may require more efforts in complicated benchmarks.

Advice: always calculate your infrastructure overhead

Remember that you always have the observer effect. Any additional time measurements always affect the performance of your code. In some cases, this overhead can be negligible, and in others, it can be significant. Anyway, it's a good thing to evaluate and get the knowledge of the part of the total measured time that you spend during basic benchmarking stuff.

Now we know how to get honest and repeatable results without included overhead. In the next section, we will talk about another important problem that can make distributions difficult to analyze.

Unequal Iterations

The lives of performance engineers would have been easier if each method had a fixed performance. Unfortunately, method performance might depend not only on the environment but also on the current program state. When you repeat a method a lot of times, be sure that each method invocation has the same performance cost and doesn't have side effects. Otherwise, you can't average it.

A bad benchmark

Let's say we want to measure the performance of List.Add. Write the following benchmark:

```
void Measure(int n)
{
  var list = new List<int>();
  var stopwatch = Stopwatch.StartNew();
  for (int i = 0; i < n; i++)
    list.Add(0);
  stopwatch.Stop();
  Console.Write("Capacity: " + list.Capacity + ", Time = ");
  Console.WriteLine("{0:0.00} ns",
    stopwatch.ElapsedMilliseconds * 1000000.0 / n);
}
```

It adds an element to a `list` n times and prints the total time and the result `list` capacity. Usually, when we do a lot of iterations, it does not matter exactly how many iterations we do; this number should just be sufficiently large. So, let's run this method for n = 16777216 and n = 16777217:

```
Measure(16777216);
Measure(16777217);
```

You can see an example of possible results in Table 2-2.

Table 2-2. *Performance of List.Add*

n	Capacity	Average Time
16777216	16777216	~6.62ns
16777217	33554432	~8.87ns

How is this possible? Why do we have a significant difference between measurements? The answer is simple: the Add method has two different run cases. In the first one, `list.Capacity > list.Count`, addition of a new element is cheap (because we have already the reserved memory for it). In the second case, `list.Capacity == list.Count`, we have to resize the internal array, which takes a lot of time.

16777216 is not a random number; it's 2^{24}. We can observe such effect for each power of two. You can see a plot with a series of Measure outputs for different N in Figure 2-3.

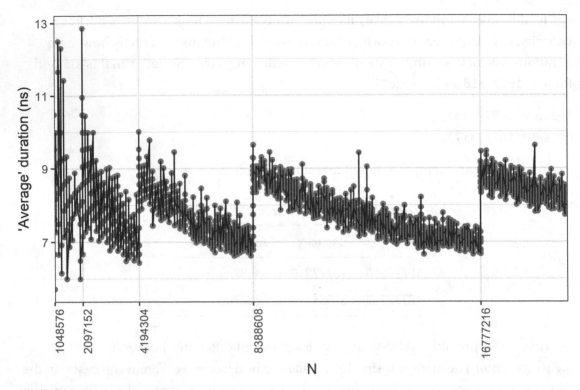

Figure 2-3. *"Average" duration of List.Add depending on the number of iterations*

Here are some of the List<T> implementation details with comments:

```
public void Add(T item)
{
  if (size == items.Length)
    EnsureCapacity(size + 1); // Here the list can be resized
  items[size++] = item;
  version++;
}

private void EnsureCapacity(int min)
{
  if (items.Length < min)
  {
    int newCapacity = items.Length == 0
      ? defaultCapacity : items.Length * 2;
```

```
    if ((uint)newCapacity > Array.MaxArrayLength)
      newCapacity = Array.MaxArrayLength;
    if (newCapacity < min)
      newCapacity = min;
    Capacity = newCapacity; // Calling the setter of the 'Capacity'
    property
  }
}

public int Capacity
{
  get { return items.Length; }
  set
  {
    if (value != items.Length)
    {
      if (value > 0)
      {
        // Setting new capacity has a side effect:
        //   it can create a new internal array
        T[] newItems = new T[value];
        if (size > 0)
          // Copying items to the new array
          Array.Copy(items, 0, newItems, 0, size);
        items = newItems;
      }
      else
      {
        items = emptyArray;
      }
    }
  }
}
```

Thus, the performance of the Add method depends on the current list Count and Capacity. It's wrong to calculate the average time of different Add calls (we may have many cheap calls and several expensive calls).

A better benchmark

There are several possible strategies that can solve this problem. For example:

- Measure pair Add/Remove together. In this case, each iteration doesn't change the list state and it doesn't have a side effect. It makes sense when you start and finish with an empty list: such a benchmark allows an evaluation of the performance cost of each element that should be added/removed.

- Allocate a list with huge capacity at the beginning of a benchmark (new List<int>(MaxCapacity)). Make sure that the program does not exceed this capacity. In this case, all the Add calls will be cheap.

Advice: measure methods that have a steady state

In the general case, the most important question is not "*How* to measure it?" but "*Why* do we want to measure it?" The best strategy always depends on what we want to achieve.

A recommendation: you should check that your average results don't depend on the number of iterations. If you run a benchmark with N iterations, also try 2*N, 5*N, 12.3456*N iterations. Make sure that each experiment has the same distribution and that there is no significant difference between them.

Now we know some of the commonest general pitfalls that are valid for many different languages and runtimes. It's time to learn some pitfalls that are specific for .NET.

.NET-Specific Pitfalls

.NET is a great platform. Each .NET runtime has many awesome optimizations that make your applications fast. When you want to write a superfast program, these optimizations are your best friends. When you want to design a benchmark, they are your worst enemies. A .NET runtime doesn't know that you want to measure performance; it tries to execute a program as fast as possible.

In the next sections, we will learn different runtime optimizations that can spoil our measurements. Let's start with a problem that affects loops in the benchmarks.

Loop Unrolling

We already know that fast methods should be wrapped in a loop for benchmarking. Do you know what happens with such loops on the assembly level?

Consider the following simple loop:

```
for (int i = 0; i < 10000; i++)
  Foo();
```

If we build it in Release and look at the assembly code for LegacyJIT-x86,[6] we will get something like this:

```
LOOP:
call  dword ptr ds:[5B0884h] ; Foo();
inc   esi                    ; i++
cmp   esi,2710h              ; if (i < 10000)
jl    LOOP                   ; Go to LOOP
```

This listing looks pretty obvious. Now let's look at the assembly code for LegacyJIT-x64:

```
LOOP:
call  00007FFC39DB0FA8      ; Foo();
call  00007FFC39DB0FA8      ; Foo();
call  00007FFC39DB0FA8      ; Foo();
call  00007FFC39DB0FA8      ; Foo();
add   ebx,4                 ; i += 4
cmp   ebx,2710h             ; if (i < 10000)
jl    00007FFC39DB4787      ; Go to LOOP
```

---

[6]Don't worry if you don't know anything about LegacyJIT-x86 and LegacyJIT-x64. We will discuss different JIT compilers later in the next chapter. Right now, you should know that we are talking about .NET Framework on Windows and comparing x86 and x64 versions of the same program. On modern versions of .NET Framework, you *usually* work with RyuJIT for x64, but LegacyJIT is still pretty popular.

What happened here? Our loop was unrolled! LegacyJIT-x64 performed **loop unrolling** and transformed the code to the following:

```
for (int i = 0; i < 10000; i += 4)
{
  Foo();
  Foo();
  Foo();
  Foo();
}
```

You can read more about different tricky JIT optimizations in Chapter 7. Right now, you should just know that you can't control which loops will be unrolled. In .NET Framework 4.6, LegacyJIT-x86 and RyuJIT-x64 can't do it. Only LegacyJIT-x64 knows how to do unrolling. It can unroll a loop only if the number of iterations is a constant (it is known in advance) and if it is divisible by 2, 3, or 4 (LegacyJIT-x64 tries to select the maximum divisor). However, it's not the best idea to use specific knowledge about JIT compiler optimization: it can be changed at any moment. The best possible solution is to keep the number of iterations at an auxiliary field so the JIT compiler will not be able to apply the optimization.

Do we really need to worry about this? Let's check it!

A bad benchmark

For example, we want to know how much time it takes to execute an empty loop with 1000000001 and 1000000002 iterations. This is another absolutely useless experiment, but it's a minimal reproduction case for the discussed problem. (For some reason, a lot of developers like to benchmark empty loops.)

```
var stopwatch1 = Stopwatch.StartNew();
for (int i = 0; i < 1000000001; i++)
{
}
stopwatch1.Stop();

var stopwatch2 = Stopwatch.StartNew();
for (int i = 0; i < 1000000002; i++)
{
```

```
}
stopwatch2.Stop();

Console.WriteLine(stopwatch1.ElapsedMilliseconds + " vs. " +
                  stopwatch2.ElapsedMilliseconds);
```

You can find an example of approximated results for LegacyJIT-x86 and LegacyJIT-x64 in Table 2-3.

Table 2-3. *Results for Empty Loops with Constants*

Iterations	LegacyJIT-x86	LegacyJIT-x64
1000000001	~360ms	~360ms
1000000002	~360ms	**~120ms**

How is it possible? The most interesting part: why do 1000000002 iterations work three times faster than 1000000001 iterations on LegacyJIT-x64? It's all about unrolling! 1000000001 is not divisible by or 2, 3, 4. So, LegacyJIT-x64 can't do unrolling here. But it's possible to unroll the second loop with 1000000002 iterations because this number is divisible by 3! It's also divisible by 2; the JIT compiler chooses the maximum divisor for the loop unrolling. Here are assembly listings for both loops:

```
; 1000000001 iterations
LOOP:
inc   eax            ; i++
cmp   eax,3B9ACA01h  ; if (i < 1000000001)
jl    LOOP           ; Go to LOOP

; 1000000002 iterations
LOOP:
add   eax,3          ; i += 3
cmp   eax,3B9ACA02h  ; if (i < 1000000002)
jl    LOOP           ; Go to LOOP
```

In the second case, we can see the add eax,3 instruction, which increments the counter by 3: we can see the loop unrolling in action! Now it's pretty obvious why the second loop works three times faster.

A better benchmark

We can be smarter than JIT and keep the number of iterations in fields. Be careful: it should be exactly the fields, not the constants!

```
private int N1 = 1000000001, N2 = 1000000002;

public void Measure()
{
  var stopwatch1 = Stopwatch.StartNew();
  for (int i = 0; i < N1; i++)
  {
  }
  stopwatch1.Stop();

  var stopwatch2 = Stopwatch.StartNew();
  for (int i = 0; i < N2; i++)
  {
  }
  stopwatch2.Stop();
}
```

So, the JIT compiler can't apply unrolling because he doesn't know a number of iterations. Furthermore, these values can be changed by someone in another thread, and it's too risky to do such optimization. Now we have the same results for all the configurations (see Table 2-4).

Table 2-4. *Results for Empty Loops with Variables*

Iterations	LegacyJIT-x86	LegacyJIT-x64
1000000001	~360ms	~360ms
1000000002	~360ms	~360ms

Yeah, the LegacyJIT-x64/1000000002 configuration is not so fast as in the first case. But now it's *a fair comparison*: we are not trying to get the maximum performance here, we are trying to compare the performance of two pieces of code.

Advice: use variables instead of constants in loops

You want to compare two different implementations of an algorithm: the loop is just a way to get meaningful results for pretty quick operations; it's not a real part of measured logic. Of course, we don't want to get different impacts from the loops on total performance. Thus, it's better to make N1 and N2 **variables instead of constants**. If you continue to read this chapter carefully, you may notice that we still use constants in loops. We do it *only for simplification* and use constants that are not divisible by 2 or 3. (LegacyJIT-x64, you can't unroll it!) All of these examples are not real benchmarks; they are just illustrations of benchmarking pitfalls. So, it's OK to use constants for such demonstrations, but please don't do it in real benchmarks.

Now we know how to how to prevent loop unrolling, but that's not the only runtime optimization. In the next section, we will learn how to prevent elimination of the loop body.

Dead Code Elimination

Modern compilers are very smart. In most cases, they are even smarter than developers who try to benchmark something. A typical benchmark contains some "fake" operations that are not actually used, because we don't care about the results, we care only about the duration of these operations. If the measured code doesn't produce any observable effects, the compiler can throw this code away. This optimization is called **dead code elimination** (DCE). Let's look at an example which shows this optimization in action.

A bad benchmark

Let's calculate square roots of all numbers from 0 to 100000000:

```
double x = 0;
for (int i = 0; i < 100000001; i++)
  Math.Sqrt(x);
```

Now let's measure the duration of this code. We know that the loop can add some overhead, so let's measure it as well and subtract overhead from the target measurements:

```
double x = 0;

var stopwatch = Stopwatch.StartNew();
for (int i = 0; i < 100000001; i++)
    Math.Sqrt(x);
stopwatch.Stop();

var stopwatch2 = Stopwatch.StartNew();
for (int i = 0; i < 100000001; i++);
stopwatch2.Stop();

var target = stopwatch.ElapsedMilliseconds;
var overhead = stopwatch2.ElapsedMilliseconds;
var result = target - overhead;
Console.WriteLine("Target   = " + target   + "ms");
Console.WriteLine("Overhead = " + overhead + "ms");
Console.WriteLine("Result   = " + result   + "ms");
```

The output example (Windows, .NET Framework, RyuJIT-x64, Release mode):

```
Target   = 37ms
Overhead = 37ms
Result   = 0ms
```

Hooray, it seems that Math.Sqrt works instantly! We can execute Math.Sqrt as many times as we want without any performance cost! Let's run it again:

```
Target   = 36ms
Overhead = 37ms
Result   = -1ms
```

Hooray, it seems that additional calls of Math.Sqrt can improve our performance! Although... Does it look believable? Not for a good performance engineer. Let's look at the assembly code for our target loop:

```
; for (int i = 0; i < 100000001; i++)
;   Math.Sqrt(x);
```

```
LOOP:
inc    eax        ; i++
cmp    eax,2710h  ; if (i < 10000)
jl     LOOP       ; Go to LOOP
```

Aha! JIT compiler has applied magic optimizations here! You may notice that we don't use the result of Math.Sqrt in any way. This code can be safely removed and this optimization spoils our benchmark. In both cases, we measure an empty loop. Because of the natural noise, we have variance in measurements, so it's a normal situation when we get a negative result (it just means that one measurement is bigger than another).

We still want to measure the performance cost of Math.Sqrt. How can we improve our benchmark?

A better benchmark

A typical workaround is to use the result somehow (let's rewrite the first part of the bad benchmark):

```
double x = 0, y = 0;

var stopwatch = Stopwatch.StartNew();
for (int i = 0; i < 100000001; i++)
  y += Math.Sqrt(x);
stopwatch.Stop();
Console.WriteLine(y);
```

Now the Math.Sqrt calls can't be removed because we need the result for printing the sum of square roots. Of course, we also add little overhead for the y += operation, which is a part of benchmarking infrastructure cost. Let's check how it works:

```
Target   = 327ms
Overhead = 37ms
Result   = 290ms
```

Now the Result is a positive number (290ms), which makes more sense.

Advice: always use results of your calculations

The modern compilers are smart, but we should be smarter! Our benchmarks shouldn't contain the code, which can be thrown away. The only way to do it is to use all results somehow. Roslyn and JIT compiler shouldn't know that we don't actually need this result. The simplest way here is to accumulate all calculated values and save it to a field. If you use a local variable, you should use it somehow after the measurements (`Console.WriteLine` is OK if you don't care about extra lines in the program output).

Be careful: any code which prevents DCE is also a part of your benchmark infrastructure; it increases the total time. You should be sure that this overhead is small and doesn't affect measurements significantly. Imagine that you get a `string` as a result. How can we use it? For example, we can add it to a global string accumulator like this:

```
string StringOperation() { /* ... */ }

// The benchmark
var stopwatch = Stopwatch.StartNew();
string acc = "";
for (int i = 0; i < N; i++)
  acc += StringOperation();
stopwatch.Stop();
```

Is it a good way to keep benchmark results? No, because the overhead of string concatenation is huge. Moreover, the overhead depends on the number of iterations: each iteration takes more time than the previous one because the length of the string `acc` grows. We need allocate more memory and copy more characters. How can we improve this benchmark? For example, we can accumulate string lengths:

```
string StringOperation() { /* ... */ }

// The benchmark
var stopwatch = Stopwatch.StartNew();
int acc = 0;
for (int i = 0; i < N; i++)
  acc += StringOperation().Length;
stopwatch.Stop();
```

This is much better because integer addition and getting the string lengths usually work much faster than any string operations. In most cases, we will not observe any significant performance overhead for this trick, but it perfectly solves the "DCE preventing" task: the compiler can't throw away `StringOperation()` calls because we use the result!

The DCE is not the only optimization that can eliminate some logic from our code. In the next section, we will talk about another cool optimization that also can reduce a program.

Constant Folding

Let's say we want to benchmark the following multiplication operation:

```
int Mul() => 2 * 3;
```

Does it look like a good method for multiplication benchmarking? Let's compile it (with optimizations) and look at the IL code:

```
ldc.i4.6
ret
```

`ldc.i4.6` means "Push 6 onto the stack as int32." `ret` means "Return from method, possibly with a value." (We take the value from the stack.)

Here you can see the multiplication result (6), which is hardcoded inside the program. The C# compiler is smart enough to precalculate such expressions at the compile time. The name of this optimization is **constant folding**. This optimization works for all kinds of constants including strings (e.g., `"a"` + `"b"` will be compiled to `"ab"`). It is great for performance, but not so great for benchmarking. We should be sure that it's impossible for the compiler to do any calculations in advance (if we want to measure these calculations). For example, we can keep our arguments in separate fields:

```
private int a = 2, b = 3;
```

```
public int Mul() => a * b;
```

Now, we can observe an honest `mul` opcode on the IL level:

```
ldarg.0
ldfld     a
ldarg.0
```

```
ldfld     b
mul
ret
```

ldarg.0 means "Load argument 0 onto the stack." The argument 0 here is this. ldfld <field>, which means "Push the value of field of object (or value type) onto the stack." mul means "Multiply values." Thus, in this code, we load this.a onto the stack, then load this.b onto the stack, then take the last two values from the stack, multiply them, push the result onto the stack, and return it.

The constant folding may look like a simple and predictable optimization, but this is not always true. Let's consider another interesting example.

A bad benchmark

Here is another question for you: which method is faster on RyuJIT-x64 (.NET Framework 4.6 without updates)?

```
public double Sqrt13()
{
  return
    Math.Sqrt(1) + Math.Sqrt(2) + Math.Sqrt(3) +
    Math.Sqrt(4) + Math.Sqrt(5) + Math.Sqrt(6) +
    Math.Sqrt(7) + Math.Sqrt(8) + Math.Sqrt(9) +
    Math.Sqrt(10) + Math.Sqrt(11) + Math.Sqrt(12) +
    Math.Sqrt(13);
}
public double Sqrt14()
{
  return
    Math.Sqrt(1) + Math.Sqrt(2) + Math.Sqrt(3) +
    Math.Sqrt(4) + Math.Sqrt(5) + Math.Sqrt(6) +
    Math.Sqrt(7) + Math.Sqrt(8) + Math.Sqrt(9) +
    Math.Sqrt(10) + Math.Sqrt(11) + Math.Sqrt(12) +
    Math.Sqrt(13) + Math.Sqrt(14);
}
```

If we carefully benchmark each method, we will get a result like in Table 2-5.

Table 2-5. *Results for Sqrt13 and Sqrt14 on RyuJIT-x64*

Method	Time
Sqrt13	~91 ns
Sqrt14	0 ns

It looks very strange. We added an additional square root operation, and it improved the performance of our code. Not just improved, it made it instant! How is this possible? It's time to look at the assembly code for each method:

```
; Sqrt13
vsqrtsd    xmm0,xmm0,mmword ptr [7FF94F9E4D28h]
vsqrtsd    xmm1,xmm0,mmword ptr [7FF94F9E4D30h]
vaddsd     xmm0,xmm0,xmm1
vsqrtsd    xmm1,xmm0,mmword ptr [7FF94F9E4D38h]
vaddsd     xmm0,xmm0,xmm1
vsqrtsd    xmm1,xmm0,mmword ptr [7FF94F9E4D40h]
vaddsd     xmm0,xmm0,xmm1
vsqrtsd    xmm1,xmm0,mmword ptr [7FF94F9E4D48h]
vaddsd     xmm0,xmm0,xmm1
vsqrtsd    xmm1,xmm0,mmword ptr [7FF94F9E4D50h]
vaddsd     xmm0,xmm0,xmm1
vsqrtsd    xmm1,xmm0,mmword ptr [7FF94F9E4D58h]
vaddsd     xmm0,xmm0,xmm1
vsqrtsd    xmm1,xmm0,mmword ptr [7FF94F9E4D60h]
vaddsd     xmm0,xmm0,xmm1
vsqrtsd    xmm1,xmm0,mmword ptr [7FF94F9E4D68h]
vaddsd     xmm0,xmm0,xmm1
vsqrtsd    xmm1,xmm0,mmword ptr [7FF94F9E4D70h]
vaddsd     xmm0,xmm0,xmm1
vsqrtsd    xmm1,xmm0,mmword ptr [7FF94F9E4D78h]
vaddsd     xmm0,xmm0,xmm1
vsqrtsd    xmm1,xmm0,mmword ptr [7FF94F9E4D80h]
vaddsd     xmm0,xmm0,xmm1
```

```
vsqrtsd      xmm1,xmm0,mmword ptr [7FF94F9E4D88h]
vaddsd       xmm0,xmm0,xmm1
ret

; Sqrt14
vmovsd       xmm0,qword ptr [7FF94F9C4C80h]
ret
```

vsqrtsd computes the square root of a floating-point value, vaddsd adds one floating-point value to another, and vmovsd moves a floating-point value. Thus, Sqrt13 calculates the whole sum each time, while Sqrt14 just returns a constant.

Aha! It seems that RyuJIT-x64 applied the constant folding optimization for Sqrt14. But why doesn't this work for Sqrt13?

Well, it's really hard to be a JIT compiler. You know a lot of awesome optimizations, and you don't have a huge amount of time to apply them (no one wants to have performance problems because of the JIT compilation). So, we need a trade-off between the time of JIT compilation and the number of applied optimizations. RyuJIT-x64 has a set of heuristics that help to make such decisions. In particular, if we are working with a small method, we can skip some optimizations because it probably should be fast enough. If a method is a big one, we can spend more time in the JIT compilation stage to improve performance. In our example, adding the Math.Sqrt(14) is a moment when we reach a heuristic threshold: from this point, RyuJIT applies additional optimization.

You should know that such things are possible, but it's not a good idea to use such knowledge in production code. If you want to improve the performance of an application by adding an additional Math.Sqrt here and there, please don't. The JIT implementation details can be changed at any moment. For example, the preceding issue was reported[7] and resolved,[8] so it can't be reproduced on .NET Framework 4.7+ (both Sqrt13 and Sqrt14 will take 0 nanoseconds because of the constant folding).

Let's fix the benchmark.

---

[7]https://github.com/dotnet/coreclr/issues/978
[8]https://github.com/dotnet/coreclr/issues/987

A better benchmark

The best way to avoid the constant folding is simple: don't use constants. For example, we can rewrite our code by introducing additional variables that keep our values:

```
public double x1 = 1, x2 = 2, x3 = 3, x4 = 4, x5 = 5, x6 = 6,
               x7 = 7, x8 = 8, x9 = 9, x10 = 10, x11 = 11,
               x12 = 12, x13 = 13, x14 = 14;
public double Sqrt14()
{
  return
    Math.Sqrt(x1) + Math.Sqrt(x2) + Math.Sqrt(x3) +
    Math.Sqrt(x4) + Math.Sqrt(x5) + Math.Sqrt(x6) +
    Math.Sqrt(x7) + Math.Sqrt(x8) + Math.Sqrt(x9) +
    Math.Sqrt(x10) + Math.Sqrt(x11) + Math.Sqrt(x12) +
    Math.Sqrt(x13) + Math.Sqrt(x14);
}
```

RyuJIT can't apply the constant folding here because there are no constants in the method.

Advice: don't use constants in your benchmarks

It's simple: if you don't have constants, the constant folding can't be applied. If you have any parameters that you want to pass to the target methods, introduce fields for these parameters. Such approach also provokes good benchmark design. It's typical to get different performance metrics from different input data. If you use parameters instead of hardcoded values, it will be easier to check different input values in the future.

.NET has many ways to eliminate different parts of your code. In the next section, we will discuss another one.

Bound Check Elimination

.NET is a great platform, and it allows you to write safe code. For example, if you try to get an element of array A with a nonexistent index (e.g. A[-1]), the runtime throws IndexOutOfRangeException. On the one hand, it is a good thing: the runtime protects us from writing incorrect code, as it's impossible to take a value from someone else's memory. On the other hand, it adds additional performance overhead.

73

Fortunately, the JIT compiler is smart enough to eliminate bound check sometimes. The name of this optimization is **bound check elimination** (BCE). The keyword here is *sometimes*; we can't control when the BCE is performed. Such optimizations are good for performance, but they are not so good for people who write benchmarks.

A bad benchmark

Let's say we have a big array with a constant length and we want to increment each element of this array. How should we design the benchmark loop? We can set the upper loop limit as a constant or as an array length. We get the same number of iterations in each case, and there is no difference in result. But is there a difference in performance?

```
const int N = 1000001;
int[] a = new int[N];

var stopwatch1 = Stopwatch.StartNew();
for (int iteration = 0; iteration < 101; iteration++)
  for (int i = 0; i < N; i++)
    a[i]++;
stopwatch1.Stop();

var stopwatch2 = Stopwatch.StartNew();
for (int iteration = 0; iteration < 101; iteration++)
  for (int i = 0; i < a.Length; i++)
    a[i]++;
stopwatch2.Stop();

Console.WriteLine(stopwatch1.ElapsedMilliseconds + " vs. " +
                  stopwatch2.ElapsedMilliseconds);
```

You can find an example of results (Windows, .NET Framework 4.6, RyuJIT-x64) in Table 2-6.

Table 2-6. *Performance of Array Modification Loop with Different Upper Bound Styles*

Experiment	Loop upper bound	Duration
1	N	~175ms
2	a.Length	~65ms

The reason of the performance difference is the BCE. The JIT compiler can skip bound checks when the upper limit is a.Length, but it can't do it when the upper limit is constant. It's not recommended to actively exploit such JIT compiler "features" during benchmarking: they depend on the runtime and its version. But we should know about it and design benchmarks in such a way that our results are not spoiled by different JIT decisions about the BCE.

A better benchmark

The main rule against BCE: use a consistent loop style for all your benchmarks. If you use a constant in one loop, use it everywhere (results for the same environment are in Table 2-7).

```
const int N = 1000001;
int[] a = new int[N];

var stopwatch1 = Stopwatch.StartNew();
for (int iteration = 0; iteration < 101; iteration++)
for (int i = 0; i < N; i++)
  a[i]++;
stopwatch1.Stop();

var stopwatch2 = Stopwatch.StartNew();
for (int iteration = 0; iteration < 101; iteration++)
for (int i = 0; i < N; i++)
  a[i]++;
stopwatch2.Stop();

Console.WriteLine(stopwatch1.ElapsedMilliseconds + " vs. " +
              stopwatch2.ElapsedMilliseconds);
```

Table 2-7. *Performance of Array Modification Loop with the Same Upper Bound Styles*

Experiment	Loop upper bound	Time
1	N	~175ms
2	N	~175ms

Now the results look much better.

Advice: use consistent loop style

If you want to use benchmark result for optimizing your software, use the same loop style as your production code. Of course, the preceding benchmark is a toy; real benchmarks are more complicated and can involve a lot of calls to the array indexer. You always have to keep in mind that the bound check has an additional performance cost, but sometimes the JIT compiler can eliminate it.

In the next section, we will learn how .NET can eliminate method calls.

Inlining

If you want to make your code readable, supportable, and beautiful, you probably don't like huge methods. Books about good code teach us that methods should be small; each method should solve its own small problem. If you have a 100-line method, it's usually possible to introduce additional small methods that are responsible for small subtasks. Someone may say: "Introducing additional methods adds a performance overhead because of additional calls." A general recommendation: *usually* you shouldn't care about it. The JIT compiler is the one who should care. Just write nice readable code and let the JIT compiler do all the dirty work. Besides, the call absence is not always good for performance. Sometimes, when you simplify a huge method by introducing additional calls, the JIT compiler will be able to optimize this simplified method well, which noticeably improves the performance (calls overhead will be negligibly small compared to these improvements).

However, this is only a general recommendation. The JIT compiler is *not always* as smart as we would like. Also, it's possible to disable inlining for a method, but it's impossible to make sure that a method will be inlined.

Consider the following method:

```
void Run1()
{
    for (int i = 0; i < N; i++)
    {
        // huge complicated logic
    }
}
```

If we do a lot of iterations of some huge complex logic, it makes sense to introduce a method for it. And we will keep the loop (and other benchmarking stuff) in the main method.

```
void Logic() =>// huge complicated logic
void Run2()
{
    for (int i = 0; i < N; i++)
        Logic();
}
```

The code looks perfect: each layer of abstraction has its own method. Steve McConnell[9] would be proud of us! However, such refactoring could affect performance. It's especially important in case of microbenchmarking.

A bad benchmark

In the next example, we will have two methods A and B. Both of them have a single double argument x. The A method just calculates $x * x$. The B method also calculates $x * x$, but it throws ArgumentOutOfRangeException for negative arguments.

```
double A(double x)
{
    return x * x;
}
```

```
double B(double x)
```

---

[9]Author of *Code Complete* (Microsoft Press, 2016).

```
{
  if (x < 0)
    throw new ArgumentOutOfRangeException("x");
  return x * x;
}

public void Measurements()
{
  double sum = 0;

  var stopwatchA = Stopwatch.StartNew();
  for (int i = 0; i < 1000000001; i++)
    sum += A(i);
  stopwatchA.Stop();

  var stopwatchB = Stopwatch.StartNew();
  for (int i = 0; i < 1000000001; i++)
    sum += B(i);
  stopwatchB.Stop();

  Console.WriteLine(
      stopwatchA.ElapsedMilliseconds + " vs. " +
      stopwatchB.ElapsedMilliseconds);
}
```

Check how it works on your computer. My results (Windows, .NET Framework 4.6, RyuJIT-x64) are in Table 2-8.

Table 2-8. *Performance of Different Strategies for Handling Invalid Values*

Method	Time
A	~2125ns
B	~2466ns

Why does the B method work so slowly? It contains only one additional check, but the difference in measurements between A and B looks too huge. The reason is simple: the A method was inlined because it's small and simple. The JIT compiler decided to not inline B because it's not so small.[10] Thus, we measure inlined A (*without* call overhead) and noninlined B (*with* call overhead), which is not fair. We need justice!

A better benchmark

The best available solution is to disable inlining with the help of the [MethodImpl] attribute:

```
[MethodImpl(MethodImplOptions.NoInlining)]
double A(double x)
{
  return x * x;
}

[MethodImpl(MethodImplOptions.NoInlining)]
double B(double x)
{
  if (x < 0)
    throw new ArgumentOutOfRangeException("x");
  return x * x;
}
```

New results:

Method	Time
A	~2125ms
B	~2466ms

Now we have the performance of method body + call overhead in both cases. We still observe the difference in measurements (because B has additional logic), but it's not so dramatic.

---

[10]Remember that we are talking about .NET Framework 4.6 only. You will observe another result with future versions of .NET Framework or .NET Core.

Advice: control inlining of the benchmarked methods

You should be sure that all benchmarked methods have the same inlining strategy. Since it's impossible to always force inlining (`MethodImplOptions.AggressiveInlining` is just a recommendation; the JIT compiler can ignore it), it's better to always disable inlining. `[MethodImpl(MethodImplOptions.NoInlining)]` is one of the simplest ways to do it (the JIT compiler can't ignore it).

If you don't want to write `MethodImplOptions.NoInlining` all the time and looking for a general approach, the delegates are your friends. Currently, JIT compilers can't inline them,[11] so you can wrap all benchmarked methods in delegates and pass them to your generic measurement logic.

JIT compilation has many smart optimizations, but it can apply them in different ways. We will discuss inlining in details in Chapter 7.

In the next section, we will discuss a situation when the final assembly code depends on additional conditions.

Conditional Jitting

Usually you will get identical assembly codes for the same method, regardless of how and when we call it. However, an executed code can sometimes affect how other methods will be jitted. Because of that, it may be dangerous to run several benchmarks in one program. The easiest way to explain this is with another example.

A bad benchmark

Consider the following code:

```
static string Measure1()
{
  double sum = 1, inc = 1;
  var stopwatch = Stopwatch.StartNew();
  for (int i = 0; i < 1000000001; i++)
    sum = sum + inc;
```

---

[11]It's true for .NET Framework 4.7.1, .NET Core 2.0, Mono 5.6. Who knows how smart .NET will be in the future…

```
    return $"Result = {sum}, Time = {stopwatch.ElapsedMilliseconds}";
}
static string Measure2()
{
    double sum = 1, inc = 1;
    var stopwatch = Stopwatch.StartNew();
    for (int i = 0; i < 1000000001; i++)
        sum = sum + inc;
    return $"Result = {sum}, Time = {stopwatch.ElapsedMilliseconds}";
}
static void Main()
{
    Console.WriteLine(Measure1());
    Console.WriteLine(Measure2());
}
```

Here we have two identical methods that measure the summation of double
variables. Each method returns the final value of sum and the elapsed time. The source
code looks clumsy, but it's a good small repro of one interesting effect. Let's run this
program on LegacyJIT-x86 (Windows, .NET Framework 4.6):

```
Result = 1000000002, Time = 3362
Result = 1000000002, Time = 1119
```

You probably expected to have the same result for both methods (because they are
identical). However, there is a threefold difference between measurements. Why? Let's
look at the assembly code of the *loop bodies* for each method:

```
; Measure1
fld1
fadd        qword ptr [ebp-14h]
fstp        qword ptr [ebp-14h]

; Measure2
fld1
faddp       st(1),st
```

It turned out that the first method keeps the sum value on the stack, and the second method keeps it in an FPU register. It's very important in such a short loop, so we have a significant performance difference. But why do we have different assembly codes for these methods?

The JIT compiler has a lot of different heuristics based on different factors. One such factor in LegacyJIT-x86 is the number of call sites. When we run the first method, the static constructor of the Stopwatch class wasn't executed. So, the JIT compiler has to add a few additional assembly instructions that check whether we need to call this static constructor or not. This call will be performed only once, but these assembly instructions will be inside the method forever. When we run the second method, the Stopwatch static constructor has already been executed. So, we don't need an additional check, and we can skip the described assembly instructions.

This check doesn't have any performance impact. But it increases the number of call sites. The floating-point registration logic for the LegacyJIT-x86 uses the number of call sites as a factor for choosing whether or not to register floating-point locals. Thus, we have different assembly listings and different performance.

There are two important lessons here:

- Execution of one benchmark can affect the performance of other benchmarks. So, it's recommended not to run several measurements in the same program because we can get different results depending on the benchmark order.

- If you remove the Stopwatch logic from methods, both of them will work fast. Thus, we made the first method slow by adding measurements logic. This is another example of the *observer effect*: when we add some measurement logic, we start to measure modified code instead of the original. Additional Stopwatch calls can spoil some optimizations in very short methods.

A better benchmark

It's better to run each benchmark in its own program. Just don't mix them and you will avoid some of these problems.

Another approach is to move the Stopwatch logic out from the method body:

```
[MethodImpl(MethodImplOptions.NoInlining)]
publicstatic double Measure1()
```

```
{
  double sum = 1, inc = 1;
  for (int i = 0; i < 1000000001; i++)
    sum = sum + inc;
  return sum;
}
[MethodImpl(MethodImplOptions.NoInlining)]
publicstatic double Measure2()
{
  double sum = 1, inc = 1;
  for (int i = 0; i < 1000000001; i++)
    sum = sum + inc;
  return sum;
}
public static void Main()
{
  var stopwatch1 = Stopwatch.StartNew();
  Measure1();
  stopwatch1.Stop();
  var stopwatch2 = Stopwatch.StartNew();
  Measure2();
  stopwatch2.Stop();
  Console.WriteLine(stopwatch1.ElapsedMilliseconds + " vs. " +
                    stopwatch2.ElapsedMilliseconds);
}
```

The result:

```
1119 vs. 1117
```

The second approach works for *this particular case,* but it's not a good solution in general. You can't control conditional jitting and you never know when it will spoil the measurements.

Advice: use own process for each benchmarked method

If you create an own process for each method, they can't affect each other. Yes, it's hard to do it manually each time, but it's a good practice which can prevent many problems. If you don't want to think about low-level JIT "features," it's always better to run each benchmark in isolation. Are you still not convinced of this? Then check out the next section, where we look at another benchmark isolation example.

Interface Method Dispatching

Conditional jitting is not the only reason why it's a good idea to isolate each benchmark in a separate process. In most cases, once the JIT compiler generates assembly code for a method, it will not be changed. However, there are exceptions.[12]

One such exception is **interface method dispatching**. When you call an interface method, the runtime should check the actual object type and find the corresponding method table. For this purpose, it generates a stub method which is called when you are trying to execute an interface method. This stub method depends on your current profile and can be regenerated. In other words, the performance cost of the interface method call can be implicitly changed by these calls. The important fact here is that one benchmark could affect the results of another benchmark.

Let's look at an example.

A bad benchmark

Let's say we have a simple interface, IIncrementer, which knows how to increment an int value. And we have two identical implementations of this interface. We also have a benchmark method, Measure, which takes an instance of the interface and run the Inc method in a loop:

```
interface IIncrementer
{
  int Inc(int x);
}
```

---

[12]For example, in .NET Core 2.x, the tiered jitting is introduced. If this feature is enabled, JIT can quickly generate a simple native code for the first invocation of a method. If this implementation is slow and the method is hot (you call it too many times), JIT can update the native code by a smarter and faster implementation.

```
class Incrementer1 : IIncrementer
{
  public int Inc(int x) => x + 1;
}
class Incrementer2 : IIncrementer
{
  public int Inc(int x) => x + 1;
}
static void Measure(IIncrementer incrementer)
{
  for (int i = 0; i < 100000001; i++)
    incrementer.Inc(0);
}

static void Main()
{
  var stopwatch1 = Stopwatch.StartNew();
  Measure(new Incrementer1());
  stopwatch1.Stop();

  var stopwatch2 = Stopwatch.StartNew();
  Measure(new Incrementer2());
  stopwatch2.Stop();

  Console.WriteLine(stopwatch1.ElapsedMilliseconds + " vs. " +
                    stopwatch2.ElapsedMilliseconds);
}
```

In the Main method, we measure the loop performance for the first interface implementation, and then for the second one. Someone who doesn't know about interface method dispatching can expect to get the same result. But we know how the runtime works, so unequal measurements will not be a surprise for us. The following are typical results on Windows, .NET Framework 4.6, and LegacyJIT-x64:

```
241 vs. 328
```

As you can see, the second case is much slower than the first one. In the first case, there is a single implementation of IIncrementer in the memory. So, the JIT compiler can generate a fast and simple stub that "knows" that there is only one possible method table for this call. In the second case, there are two implementations of IIncrementer, and the JIT compiler has to regenerate our stub. Now it's not so fast because it has to choose between two method tables. Of course, this is a simplification; the full algorithm is much more complicated, but I hope that you get the idea.

A better benchmark

Thus, the best choice for benchmarking is to run each target method in its own process. Mixing benchmarks in one program can lead to spoiled results.

Here our first program:

```
// Program1.cs
static void Main()
{
  var stopwatch1 = Stopwatch.StartNew();
  Measure(new Incrementer1());
  stopwatch1.Stop();

  Console.WriteLine(stopwatch1.ElapsedMilliseconds);
}
```

Here is our second program:

```
// Program2.cs
static void Main()
{
  var stopwatch2 = Stopwatch.StartNew();
  Measure(new Incrementer2());
  stopwatch2.Stop();

  Console.WriteLine(stopwatch2.ElapsedMilliseconds);
}
```

Now we can get the equal results:

```
// Program1
243
// Program2
242
```

It looks much better.

Advice: use a unique process for each benchmarked method

Isolating is always a good thing for benchmarks. Someone can say that we have to measure real performance in a real environment, so such isolation is wrong because we miss important runtime "features." And this makes sense, but now we are talking about how to design good benchmarks. Good benchmarks should provide repeatable, stable results regardless of the order. If you want to take effects like method interface dispatching into account, you have to design a proper set of benchmarks.

It is worth mentioning that such problems are not frequent. Usually, you will not suffer from conditional jitting or method interface dispatching. But you can't know about it in advance. It's also possible to have the order problem because of high-level logic like caching (the first benchmark initializes a cache and the second one works on a warmed cache). So it's a good idea, in general, to isolate each benchmark in a separate program.

This is the last benchmarking pitfall to be discussed in this chapter (but it's far from the last in this book). Let's summarize what we have learned.

Summary

In this chapter, we discussed some common pitfalls typical for people who have just started to write benchmarks. Some of them are general and can be applied to different languages and runtimes:

- **Inaccurate timestamping**

  DateTime-based benchmarks have many problems like pure resolution, so it's better to use Stopwatch for time measurements. We will discuss all .NET timestamping APIs and their characteristics in Chapter 9.

- **Executing a benchmark in the wrong way**

  Benchmarks should always be executed with enabled optimization (Release mode) without an attached debugger in a sterile environment.

- **Natural noise**

  Each benchmark iteration has random errors because of the natural noise.

- **Tricky distributions**

  Performance distributions often have a tricky form: they may have huge variance or include extremely high values. Such distribution should be carefully analyzed; we will discuss how to do this in Chapter 4.

- **Measuring cold start instead of warmed steady state**

  The first benchmark iterations are "cold" and can take much more time than subsequent "warm" iterations.

- **Insufficient number of invocations**

  In the case of microbenchmarks, the measured code should be repeated many times. Otherwise, errors will be huge because timestamping is limited on the hardware level and can't correctly measure high-speed operations.

- **Infrastructure overhead**

  Each benchmark includes an "infrastructure" part that helps you to get reliable and repeatable results. This infrastructure can affect results and spoil the measurements. Thus, the overhead should be calculated and removed from the final results.

- **Unequal iterations**

  If you repeat a code several times, you should be sure that all repetitions take the same amount of time.

We also have other kinds of pitfalls because of optimizations in .NET runtimes:

- **Loop unrolling**

  If you use a constant as the upper loop limit, the loop can be unrolled by different factors depending on the dividers of this constant.

- **Dead code elimination (DCE)**

  If you don't use the results of your code, the code can be completely removed.

- **Constant folding**

    If you use constants in expressions, these expressions can be precalculated at the compilation stage.

- **Bound check elimination (BCE)**

    If you manipulate array elements, the runtime can check the array bounds or skip these checks.

- **Inlining**

    Sometimes, the runtime can inline method calls, which can be pretty important for microbenchmarks. We will discuss inlining and similar optimizations in Chapter 7.

- **Conditional jitting**

    The final assembly code for a method can depend on the previous methods that were executed. So, it's a good idea to isolate benchmarks and run each benchmark in its own process.

- **Interface method dispatching**

    If you call an interface method, the performance of this call depends on loaded interface implementation. That's another reason why the benchmark isolation is a good idea.

I hope that now you understand why benchmarking can be difficult. Benchmarking (and especially microbenchmarking) requires in-depth knowledge of the target .NET runtime, modern operation systems, and modern hardware.

Of course, you shouldn't create own benchmarking infrastructure and solve all these problems each time you want to measure something. In Chapter 6, we will discuss *BenchmarkDotNet*, a library that can protect you from most pitfalls and help you to conduct a qualitative performance investigation.

However, BenchmarkDotNet is not a silver bullet: you still have to know how to design a benchmark correctly and what kind of runtime optimizations can spoil your results. It's not easy because you don't know in advance which optimizations will be applied to your program. It depends on your runtime (e.g., .NET Framework, .NET Core, or Mono), a specific version of C# compiler, a particular version of JIT compiler (e.g., `LegacyJIT-x86` or `RyuJIT-x64`), and so on. In the next chapter, we will talk about different environments and how application performance depends on it.

CHAPTER 3

How Environment Affects Performance

The environment is everything that isn't me.

— Albert Einstein

In Chapter 1, we discussed performance spaces. The main components of a performance space are source code, environment, and input data. The source code is a mathematical abstraction; it doesn't have the "performance" characteristic. If you want to talk about how fast your program is, you should put it in a real environment. In each environment, the source code will have a long journey before we can discuss performance (see Figure 3-1).

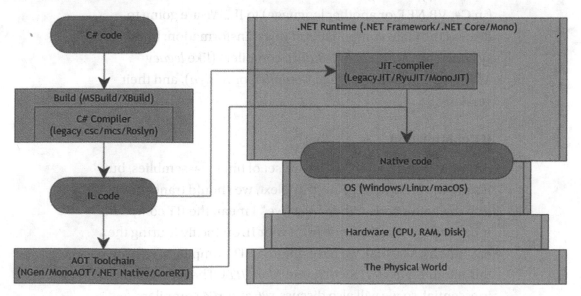

Figure 3-1. *Source code journey*

© Andrey Akinshin 2019

A. Akinshin, *Pro .NET Benchmarking*, https://doi.org/10.1007/978-1-4842-4941-3_3

In this chapter, we will discuss different factors affecting performance during this journey:

- **Runtime**

  Runtime is probably one of the most important parts of your environment. Today, .NET is more than just Windows-only .NET Framework; there are three different popular runtimes, and you should understand the differences between them. For example, you can get utterly different performance pictures if you run the same program on .NET Core and Mono. Another important thing is the version of your runtime. Even a small minor update can change the performance. We will discuss a brief history of each runtime, check out the most important versions, and learn some interesting "features." In the scope of this book, we will discuss the three most popular runtimes: **.NET Framework**, **.NET Core**, and **Mono**.

- **Compilation**

  It's a long way from the source code to executable binary files. It usually includes several stages:

  - **IL generation**

    The first typical stage is the transformation of our source code (in C#, VB.NET, or another language) to IL. We are going to discuss the main components of this transformation: build systems (like *MSBuild* or *XBuild*), compilers (like *legacy Microsoft C# compiler*, *Mono Compiler*, or *Roslyn*), and their versions.

  - **JIT compilation**

    After the IL generation, we have a set of binary assemblies, but it's not the final point of our trip. Next, we should transform it into the native code. When I say "we," I mean the JIT compiler. It produces the native code from your IL on the fly (during the execution). As usual, we have different JIT compilers (we will talk about *LegacyJIT*, *RyuJIT*, and *MonoJIT*). The target platform is essential, so we will also discuss *x86* and *x64* compilers.

– **Ahead-Of-Time (AOT) compilation**

JIT compilation is not the only way to get the native code: we can compile IL AOT (before the execution). The AOT compilation is also a very important scenario that changes the performance space. And of course, we have different AOT compilers (e.g., *NGen* [*Native Image Generator*], *Mono AOT*, *.NET Native*, and *CoreRT*). A good benchmark report usually includes what kind of compilation you use (JIT or AOT), the compiler type, its version, the target platform, and its parameters.

• **External environment**

The last section is about the environment of the runtime: there are many factors beyond the .NET ecosystem that also affect performance.

– **Operating systems**

The classic .NET Framework is Windows only, but we live in times of cross-platform .NET applications. You can run your C# programs on Windows, Linux, and macOS (and also on Sun Solaris, FreeBSD, or tvOS if you want). Each operating system has a lot of unique performance "features." We will recall a brief OS history, discuss each OS and its versions, and compare the performance of the same programs on different operating systems.

– **Hardware**

There are too many hardware configurations. We will talk about CPU, RAM, disks, networks, and other hardware components. The most important thing is that it's too hard to compare performance on different machines. There are a lot of low-level details that can affect the program. In this section, we will just briefly look at a variety of hardware and discuss the most important configuration parameters.

– **The physical world**

The hardware always exists in real physical conditions. The performance can be affected by many physical factors like temperature, vibrations, humidity, and others.

This chapter has three purposes:

1. **Introduce important codenames, titles, captions, and so on.**

   In this chapter, you will learn some new terms (e.g., *Rotor*, *CoreFx*, *mcs*, *SGen*, *Roslyn*, *RyuJIT*, *Darwin*, or *Sandy Bridge*), so if you skip this chapter and jump to a more interesting one, you can always come back to this one for a description of different environments, for short explanations of "what's what," and to understand why we should care about it.

2. **Provide ways to get information about the current environment.**

   If you write your own tools to analyze performance, it's pretty important to add logic for collecting information about the current environment. It's not obvious how to get the exact version of installed .NET Framework or .NET Core or determine the JIT engine (e.g., LegacyJIT or RyuJIT). In this chapter, you will learn how to collect detailed information about the environment of a .NET program.

3. **Explain why it's so important to care about your environment.**

   We will learn how minor differences between environments can significantly affect your results.

Each section in this chapter has the same structure. We start with an overview: history, versions, technology codenames, and so on. After that, you can read four different stories about how each technology can affect your benchmarks. These case studies are not random stories; each of them is presented for a reason. Each case contains a "Conclusions" part at the end that highlights things that you should learn from the corresponding story. Also, it contains an "Exercise" part. If you want, you can skip the exercises because some of them require special setup (e.g., hardware or operating systems) and a huge amount of time. However, if you decide to solve these problems, you will get skills that can be useful in real performance investigations. Some stories are based on my own developer experience, some of them are based on other people's research, and others are just pretty interesting code snippets.

Of course, in the scope of this book, we will not discuss *all possible environments*. We will not cover in detail Windows Servers, ARM processors, Mono LLVM (low-level virtual machine), GPU, and so on. We will briefly talk about many versions of each environment component, but we will not learn each version separately. It's just not necessary. You will never learn all versions of all technologies: there are too many of them, and we get a lot of new stuff every day. But it's important to have a general perspective (what kinds of environments do we have) and understand which components of the environment can affect performance (and how they can do it). In this case, you will be able to check all the important things during benchmarking.

Let's start with the most important part: .NET runtimes. Of course, you can work with only one runtime and know it very well, but you can't discuss ".NET performance" in general until you understand what's going on with other runtimes.

Runtime

Today, there are three popular .NET runtimes: .NET Framework, .NET Core, and Mono. Technically, all of them are more than just runtimes because they also include class libraries. However, people often call them runtimes because there is no better term ("framework" will be more correct, but it can be easily confused with .NET Framework). Thus, when you see the "runtime" term, it usually means "runtime and corresponding class libraries."

To be honest, .NET Framework, .NET Core, and Mono are not the only available .NET runtimes. There were many attempts to create other alternative .NET runtimes like *Silverlight, Moonlight, .NET Micro Framework*, and others. There are also many approaches to run C# code in a browser: *Blazor* (an experimental .NET web framework using C#/Razor and HTML that runs in the browser via WebAssembly), *Script#*, *Bridge. NET*, and so on. All of them are valid environments for .NET applications, but they are not as popular as .NET Framework, .NET Core, and Mono, so we are not going to discuss them in this book. You can find a nice overview of different .NET runtimes in [Warren 2018a].

All three runtimes that we are going to discuss are mature and widely adopted. In this section, we will briefly talk about each of them: we will discuss different topics like the history, available versions (and how to get these versions), and performance changes. In the end, you will find several case studies that demonstrate why it's so important to know the exact version of your runtime.

.NET Framework

.NET Framework is the first implementation of .NET created by Microsoft. To avoid misunderstanding between .NET Framework as a runtime and the ecosystem behind .NET, let's agree that .NET Framework as a runtime consists of two main parts: CLR (or Desktop CLR) and Framework Class Library (FCL). To clearly distinguish .NET Framework from other .NET implementations, people often use other titles like *Full .NET Framework* (or *.NET Full Framework*), *Microsoft .NET Framework*, or *Desktop .NET Framework*. In this book, when we say ".NET Framework," we mean the classic Windows-only .NET Framework by Microsoft.

Let's start from the beginning and remember the history of .NET Framework. It was created by Microsoft; the first version was released in 2002 (but the development was started in the late 1990s). In Table 3-1, you can see the list of .NET Framework versions.[1]

Table 3-1. *.NET Framework Release History*

Framework version	CLR version	Release date	Support ended
1.0	1.0	2002-02-13	2009-07-14
1.1	1.1	2003-04-24	2015-06-14
2.0	2.0	2004-11-07	2011-07-12
3.0	2.0	2006-11-06	2011-07-12
3.5	2.0	2007-11-19	2028-10-10
4.0	4.0	2010-04-12	2016-01-12
4.5	4.0	2012-08-15	2016-01-12

(continued)

---

[1] .NET Framework 4.8 was announced in [Lander 2018b], but it wasn't released at the moment of book writing. You can find the actual list of all versions here: https://docs.microsoft.com/en-us/dotnet/framework/migration-guide/versions-and-dependencies

Table 3-1. (*continued*)

Framework version	CLR version	Release date	Support ended
4.5.1	4.0	2013-10-17	2016-01-12
4.5.2	4.0	2014-05-05	Not announced
4.6	4.0	2015-07-20	Not announced
4.6.1	4.0	2015-11-30	Not announced
4.6.2	4.0	2016-08-02	Not announced
4.7	4.0	2017-04-05	Not announced
4.7.1	4.0	2017-10-17	Not announced
4.7.2	4.0	2018-04-30	Not announced
4.8	4.0	2019-04-18	Not announced

Some important facts that are good to know:

- Versions 1.0-3.0 of .NET Framework are obsolete and not supported by Microsoft anymore.

- Some legacy projects still use .NET Framework 3.5 because it's tough to upgrade the runtime. There are many significant changes between CLR 2 (used by .NET Framework 3.5) and CLR 4 (used by .NET Framework 4.0+).

- All .NET Framework 4.x versions are in-place updates for old 4.x versions (it includes CLR and FCL), and they use the same installation folder: C:\Windows\.NET Framework\V4.0.30319. Thus, if you install .NET Framework 4.5 and 4.7, all applications will use 4.7. You can't use two different 4.x versions of the .NET Framework on the machine at the same time. The CLR version for all 4.x versions is the same (CLR 4), but this doesn't mean that the same CLR implementation is used for execution: it gets updates with each .NET Framework update.

An example

You work on a Windows machine with .NET Framework 4.6.1 installed and develop a .NET Framework 4.0 application. If you execute it on this machine, 4.6.1 will be used. If you execute it on the computer of a friend who installed .NET Framework 4.7, 4.7 will be used. In this case, "4.0" in the properties of your project means that you can't use API from .NET Framework 4.5+ and that you can run this application on a machine with installed .NET Framework 4.0+. But it doesn't require a specific version of .NET Framework to be used for execution.

There are many essential changes between versions of the .NET Framework; you can get different performance metric values for the same code on different .NET Framework versions. Thus, it's important to know how to determine versions of the installed .NET Framework. You can do it via special keys in Windows Registry. For example, for .NET Framework 4.5+, you should look at the value of HKLM\SOFTWARE\Microsoft\ NET Framework Setup\NDP\v4\Full\Release. This is an internal number that can be mapped to the .NET Framework versions. The same version of the .NET Framework can have different internals numbers (depends on the Windows version and installed updates). You can find the minimum values of the Release value in Table 3-2.[2]

Table 3-2. *.NET Framework Registry Release Values*

Framework version	Minimum release value
4.5	378389
4.5.1	378675
4.5.2	379893
4.6	393295
4.6.1	394254
4.6.2	394802
4.7	460798
4.7.1	461308
4.7.2	461808

[2]The full actual manual can be found here: https://docs.microsoft.com/en-us/dotnet/ framework/migration-guide/how-to-determine-which-versions-are-installed

It's important to say a few words about the .NET Framework source code. The old versions of .NET Framework are known as closed source. However, we have access to the source code of some of these versions. *Shared Source Common Language Infrastructure* (*SSCLI*, codename "*Rotor*") is Microsoft's shared source implementation of the main parts of .NET Framework. The first version was released in 2002, and the second version (and the last one) of SSCLI was released in 2006[3]; it contains the essential parts of .NET Framework 2.0. You can find a good overview of the source code in [SSCLI Internals]. Unfortunately, there are no updates of SSCLI for .NET Framework 3.0, 3.5, 4.0, or 4.5. Later, Microsoft opened the source code of .NET Framework 4.5.1+ in a read-only mode. You can find it on the Microsoft Reference Source website.[4]

Today, .NET Framework is still a Windows-only runtime, which is a severe limitation for many developers. Fortunately, Microsoft has decided to create a free open source, cross-platform version: .NET Core.

.NET Core

.NET Core is an alternative implementation of .NET Framework. Originally, .NET Core was started as a fork of a .NET Framework subset, but it has become a mature full-featured independent platform.

.NET Core has been a free and open source project from the beginning (it uses the MIT License). The .NET Core Runtime is called *CoreCLR*[5] (instead of CLR in .NET Framework); it contains GC, JIT compiler, System.Private.CoreLib (a replacement for mscorlib), and some basic runtime-specific classes. The set of .NET Core foundation libraries is called *CoreFX*[6] (instead of FCL in .NET Framework); it contains all basic classes like collections, I/O, globalization, and so on. Another important project in the

---

[3]Unfortunately, official Microsoft links to the SSCLI download page are outdated and don't work anymore. Fortunately, the Internet remembers everything: you can find the source code here: `https://github.com/AndreyAkinshin/shared-source-cli-2.0`

[4]You can browse the source of the latest version of .NET Framework here: `https://referencesource.microsoft.com`. Old versions are available as .zip files in the Download section. The source code is also available on GitHub: `https://github.com/Microsoft/referencesource`.

[5]`https://github.com/dotnet/coreclr`

[6]`https://github.com/dotnet/corefx`

.NET Core ecosystem is *.NET Core SDK*,[7] which includes .NET Core, project templates, .NET Core command-line interface (CLI),[8] MSBuild, NuGet tools, and other components that help to develop .NET Core applications.

.NET Core is a cross-platform runtime (.NET Framework works only on Windows). Thus, there are a lot of .NET Framework components that can't be included in .NET Core because of the deep integration with Windows. However, some of them can be executed with .NET Core on Windows with the help of the *Windows Compatibility Pack* (see [Landwerth 2017b]). Since .NET Core 3.0, it has even been possible to develop Windows-only WPF and WinForms applications on .NET Core (see [Lander 2018a]).

Internally, the core part of the code base is the same for both .NET Core and .NET Framework. However, there are a lot of differences. Platforms have different release cycles: it can be hard to distinguish between versions of .NET Framework that contain particular changes from .NET Core. .NET Core includes a lot of cross-platform logic that is required for Linux and macOS. Meanwhile, .NET Framework has many backward compatibility hacks for Windows. There are a lot of commonalities between these runtimes, but we will talk about them independently.

Let's recall the brief history of .NET Core. .NET Core 1.0 was released on 27 June 2016. Since then, many versions have been released; you can see some of them in Table 3-3.[9]

Table 3-3.   *.NET Core Release History*

Runtime	SDK version	Release date
1.0.0	1.0.0-preview2-003121	2016-06-27
1.0.1	1.0.0-preview2-003131	2016-09-13
1.0.2	1.0.0-preview2-003148	2016-10-17
1.1.0	1.0.0-preview2.1-003177	2016-11-16

(*continued*)

---

[7]https://github.com/dotnet/core-sdk

[8]https://github.com/dotnet/cli

[9]You can find full actual release history here: https://github.com/dotnet/core/blob/master/release-notes/releases.csv

Table 3-3. (*continued*)

Runtime	SDK version	Release date
1.0.3	1.0.0-preview2-003156	2016-12-13
1.1.1	1.0.1	2017-03-07
1.0.4	1.0.1	2017-03-07
1.1.2	1.0.4	2017-05-09
1.0.5	1.0.4	2017-05-09
2.0.0	2.0.0	2017-08-14
1.0.7	1.1.4	2017-09-21
1.1.4	1.1.4	2017-09-21
1.0.8	1.1.5	2017-11-14
1.1.5	1.1.5	2017-11-14
2.0.3	2.0.3	2017-11-14
2.0.3	2.1.2	2017-12-04
2.0.5	2.1.4	2017-12-04
1.0.10	1.1.8	2018-03-13
1.1.7	1.1.8	2018-03-13
2.0.6	2.1.101	2018-03-13
1.0.11	1.1.9	2018-04-17
1.1.8	1.1.9	2018-04-17
2.0.7	2.1.105	2018-04-17
2.0.7	2.1.200	2018-05-08
2.0.7	2.1.201	2018-05-21
2.1.0	2.1.300	2018-05-30
2.1.1	2.1.301	2018-06-19
1.0.12	1.1.10	2018-07-10
1.1.9	1.1.10	2018-07-10
2.0.9	2.1.202	2018-07-10

(*continued*)

Table 3-3. (*continued*)

Runtime	SDK version	Release date
2.1.2	2.1.302	2018-07-10
2.1.2	2.1.400	2018-08-14
2.1.3	2.1.401	2018-08-14
2.1.4	2.1.402	2018-09-11
2.1.5	2.1.403	2018-10-02
1.0.13	1.1.11	2018-10-09
1.1.10	1.1.11	2018-10-09
2.1.6	2.1.500	2018-11-13
2.2.0	2.2.100	2018-12-04

There are some important facts that we should learn from this table:

- The first stable version of the runtime was released with *a preview version of the SDK*. If you try to play with early versions of SDK, you will have to work with .xproj+project.json files instead of the usual .csproj files. Many developers were unhappy about these changes, so it was decided to drop project.json-based projects and resurrect the *.csproj files to keep the backward compatibility with the old versions of MSBuild. However, if you want to check something on the old versions of the runtime, you don't need the old versions of SDK: newer SDK builds support old versions of the runtime.

- The same version of the runtime can be used with different SDK versions.

With .NET Core SDK and MSBuild 15+, Microsoft introduced an "improved" version of the .csproj format. It looks like this:

```
<Project Sdk="Microsoft.NET.Sdk">
  <PropertyGroup>
    <TargetFrameworks>net46;netcoreapp2.1</TargetFrameworks>
  </PropertyGroup>
</Project>
```

We will call it *SDK-style projects*. If a project uses the "original" format (with a huge number of lines in a .csproj file), we will call it just *classic projects*. SDK-style projects were introduced with .NET Core SDK, but that doesn't mean that you can use it only with .NET Core. In the preceding example, a project targets .NET Framework 4.6 (net46) and .NET Core 2.1 (netcoreapp2.1). If you develop a library that should be compatible with any target framework,[10] you can list all of them in each project, but it's not very convenient. This problem was solved with the help of *.NET Standard*. Here is the official definition of .NET Standard from Microsoft documentation[11]:

> The .NET Standard is a formal specification of .NET APIs that
> are intended to be available on all .NET implementations. The
> motivation behind the .NET Standard is establishing greater
> uniformity in the .NET ecosystem. ECMA 335 continues to
> establish uniformity for .NET implementation behavior, but there
> is no similar spec for the .NET Base Class Libraries (BCL) for .NET
> library implementations.

In Table 3-4, you can see mapping between .NET Standard and different .NET platforms.[12]

---

[10]There are a lot of them. You can find the full list here: https://docs.microsoft.com/en-us/dotnet/standard/frameworks

[11]https://docs.microsoft.com/en-us/dotnet/standard/net-standard

[12]It's not a full table. You can find the actual full version of this table here: https://docs.microsoft.com/en-us/dotnet/standard/net-standard. Moreover, actual mapping also depends on the version of .NET Core SDK. For example, .NET Standard 1.5 corresponds to .NET Framework 4.6.2 if you use .NET Core SDK 1.x and .NET Framework 4.6.1 if you use .NET Core SDK 2.x. If you are not sure that you correctly understand the concept of .NET Standard, it's recommended to watch [Landwerth 2017a].

Table 3-4. *.NET Standard Compatibility Matrix*

.NET Standard	1.0	1.1	1.2	1.3	1.4	1.5	1.6	2.0
.NET Core	1.0	1.0	1.0	1.0	1.0	1.0	1.0	2.0
.NET Framework	4.5	4.5	4.5.1	4.6	4.6.1	4.6.1	4.6.1	4.6.1
Mono	4.6	4.6	4.6	4.6	4.6	4.6	4.6	5.4
Xamarin.iOS	10.0	10.0	10.0	10.0	10.0	10.0	10.0	10.14
Xamarin.Mac	3.0	3.0	3.0	3.0	3.0	3.0	3.0	3.8
Xamarin.Android	7.0	7.0	7.0	7.0	7.0	7.0	7.0	8.0

Let's say that we have a library targeting .NET Standard 2.0. This means that we can use it with .NET Core 2.0, .NET Framework 4.6.1, or Mono 5.4. Here is the main thing that you should understand in the context of benchmarking: *.NET Standard is not a runtime; it's a set of APIs.* You can't *run* an application or unit tests[13] on .NET Standard. Thus, we can't discuss the performance of .NET Standard 2.0, but we can discuss the performance of .NET Core 2.0, .NET Framework 4.6.1, and Mono 5.4. And it doesn't make any sense to say something like ".NET Standard 1.3 works faster than .NET Standard 1.2."

It's very important to know the runtime version when we discuss performance. Let's learn how to detect the current version of .NET Core. Unfortunately, there is no public API which allows getting the current version of .NET Core at runtime. However, if we really want to know this version, we can use the following hack. The typical location of the runtime libraries in .NET Core SDK looks like this: dotnet/shared/Microsoft. NETCore.App/2.1.0/. As we can see, the full path includes the runtime version. Thus, we can take the location of an assembly that contains one of the base types (e.g., GCSettings), and find a part of the path with the exact version:

```
public static string GetNetCoreVersion()
{
  var assembly = typeof(System.Runtime.GCSettings).GetTypeInfo().Assembly;
  var assemblyPath = assembly.CodeBase.Split(new[] { '/', '\\' },
                    StringSplitOptions.RemoveEmptyEntries);
  int netCoreAppIndex = Array.IndexOf(assemblyPath, "Microsoft.NETCore.App");
```

---

[13]https://xunit.github.io/docs/why-no-netstandard

```
if (netCoreAppIndex > 0 && netCoreAppIndex < assemblyPath.Length - 2)
    return assemblyPath[netCoreAppIndex + 1];
return null;
}
```

It works for regular .NET Core installation, but it doesn't work for special environments like Docker containers.[14] In the case of Docker, you can get the runtime version from environment variables like DOTNET_VERSION and ASPNETCORE_VERSION (see [Hanselman 2018] for details).

For diagnostics, it can be also good to know the exact internal version of CoreCLR and CoreFX:

```
var coreclrAssemblyInfo = FileVersionInfo.GetVersionInfo(
    typeof(object).GetTypeInfo().Assembly.Location).FileVersion;
var corefxAssemblyInfo = FileVersionInfo.GetVersionInfo(
    typeof(Regex).GetTypeInfo().Assembly.Location).FileVersion;
```

Here is an example of possible values:

```
.NET Core 3.0.0-preview-27122-01
CoreCLR 4.6.27121.03
CoreFX 4.7.18.57103
```

As you can see, they do not match each other. The internal versions of CoreCLR and CoreFX are especially important when you are working on changes in .NET Core itself.

Each version of .NET Core has tons of performance improvements (see [Toub 2017], [Toub 2018]). If you care about the speed of your application, it's recommended to use the latest available version. However, the set of old .NET Core versions is an excellent guinea pig for benchmarking exercises.

The last thing that you should know is *.NET Core Configuration Knobs*.[15] Knobs are configuration parameters that help you to tune the runtime. You can enable a knob with the help of COMPlus_* environment variables. For example, if you want to enable

---

[14]https://github.com/dotnet/BenchmarkDotNet/issues/788

[15]You can find the full list of all knobs in .NET Core 2.2.0 on GitHub: https://github.com/
dotnet/coreclr/blob/v2.2.0/Documentation/project-docs/clr-configuration-knobs.md

`JitAggressiveInlining` (we will discuss JIT later in this chapter), you should set `COMPlus_JitAggressiveInlining=1`.

.NET Core was born in 2016, but it wasn't the first cross-platform .NET implementation. Developers were able to use .NET on Linux and macOS for years with the help of another .NET runtime: Mono.

Mono

Microsoft announced .NET Framework in 2000. It looked like a great runtime, but it was Windows only. Miguel de Icaza from Ximian decided to create his own open source version of .NET that works on Linux. It was a pretty successful attempt. After three years of development, Mono 1.0 was born. The first versions had many problems, bugs, and performance issues. However, the runtime evolved rapidly, and Mono became a good Linux/macOS alternative for .NET developers. Ximian was acquired by Novell in 2003. In 2011, Miguel de Icaza and Nat Friedman founded Xamarin, the new company that continued to develop Mono. In 2016, Xamarin was acquired by Microsoft. Since then, Mono has been a part of .NET Foundation.[16] While .NET Core is a good option for cross-platform applications in terms of reliability and performance, Mono is still widely used (mainly for mobile applications[17] and Unity applications[18]).

After the first Mono release in 2004, dozens of major and minor Mono versions were released. Each version has a huge list of changes; you can find all the details in the official release notes.[19] I want to highlight only some specific performance-related changes:

- **Mono 1.0** (2004-01-30): The first official Mono release.

- **Mono 1.2** (2006-11-02): Many common optimizations (inlining, DCE, constant folding, and so on), AOT compilation, Boehm GC.

- **Mono 2.0** (2008-10-01): Improved performance of operations on decimals and locking, reduced memory usage for generics.

---

[16]https://dotnetfoundation.org/
[17]https://visualstudio.microsoft.com/xamarin/
[18]https://unity3d.com/
[19]www.mono-project.com/docs/about-mono/releases/

- **Mono 2.2** (2009-01-09): New code generation engine with advanced optimizations, improved AOT, improved regex interpreter.

- **Mono 2.4** (2009-03-13): SIMD (Single Instruction Multiple Data) support, optimized XPath and resource loading.

- **Mono 2.6** (2009-12-14): LLVM support.

- **Mono 2.8** (2010-10-05): New GC engine support: SGen (the difference between Boehm and SGen is shown in Figure 3-2[20]; the lower straight line corresponds to SGen, the upper curved line corresponds to Boehm).

- **Mono 2.10** (2011-02-15): Significant SGen improvements like concurrent mark and sweeping.

- **Mono 3.0** (2012-10-19) A new task management system in SGen, low-level intrinstics for `ThreadLocal<T>`, `List<T>` optimizations.

- **Mono 3.2** (2013-07-24): LLVM 3.2 with better optimizations, SGen become the default GC, important AOT and LINQ optimizations, faster large object cloning and boxing, optimized `Marhshal.Read` and `Marshal.Write`.

- **Mono 3.4** (2014-03-31): Miscellaneous minor performance improvements.

- **Mono 3.6** (2014-08-12): New GC modes, improved lock performance, optimized EqualityComparer.

- **Mono 3.8** (2014-09-04) JIT improvements like better handling long remainders by the power of two, faster code for delegates that are only invoked once

- **Mono 3.10** (2014-10-04): Remove unnecessary locking from core metadata parsing functions, avoid cache thrashing of locals array when looping over enumerator.

---

[20]The picture was taken from the official release notes: `www.mono-project.com/docs/about-mono/releases/2.8.0/`

- **Mono 3.12** (2015-01-13): Major performance and memory consumption improvements on SGen, pushless code generations for x86.

- **Mono 4.0** (2015-04-29): Adoption of Microsoft's open source code (significant perf changes in many BCL classes like `System.Decimal`), floating-point optimizations, SGen tuning, many improvements in different places like `Interlocked`, `Thread.MemoryBarrier`, `Enum.HasFlag`, and so on.

- **Mono 4.2** (2015-08-25): More adoption of Microsoft's open source code (and more perf changes in BCL), updated delegate internals.

- **Mono 4.4** (2016-06-08) Unmanaged thin locks (10x perf improvements for locking in some cases), cooperative GC Mode.

- **Mono 4.6** (2016-09-13): Improved GC on Android, miscellaneous performance improvements.

- **Mono 4.8** (2017-02-22): Initial concurrent SGen support, further MS Reference Source Adoption.

- **Mono 5.0** (2017-05-10): Shipping Roslyn C# compiler (performance surprise for everyone who used old `mcs`), SIMD acceleration support enabling concurrent SGen GC by default, CoreFx + Reference Source Adoption, lazy array interfaces, reduced runtime memory usage, SIMD register scanning.

- **Mono 5.2** (2017-08-14): Experimental default interface methods support, optimized array stores, class initialization improvements, reduced minor collection pause times.

- **Mono 5.4** (2017-10-05): Concurrent method compilation, array element store optimization, load scalability improvements, `ValueType` write barrier optimization, Intrisificy `Marshal.PtrToStruct` for blitable types.

- **Mono 5.8** (2018-02-01): Modes for the SGen GC (balanced, throughput, pause).

- **Mono 5.10** (2018-02-26): ARM memory barriers, AOT size reduction via code deduplication.

- **Mono 5.12** (2018-05-08): jemalloc support.

- **Mono 5.14** (2018-08-07): better generic sharing, memory optimization for handles, LLVM inlining improvements, GC handling of very large objects.

- **Mono 5.16** (2018-1008): hybrid GC suspend, improved 32-bit floating-point math, intrinsics for Span<T> and ReadOnlySpan<T>.

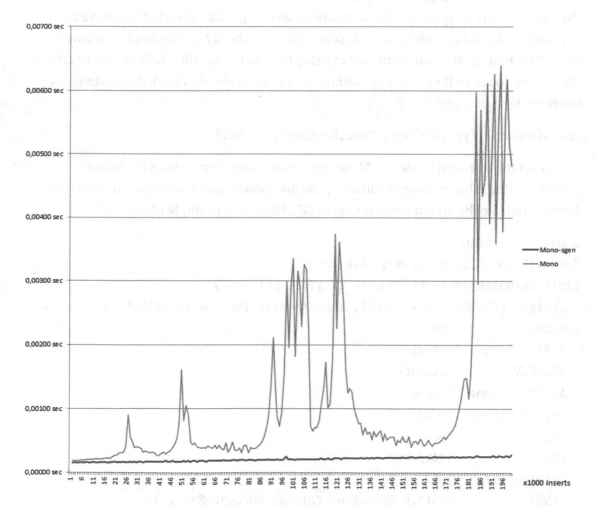

Figure 3-2. *Difference between Boehm and SGen in Mono 2.8*

As you can see from the changelog, each major release has important performance improvements. When you benchmark your code, it's very important to specify which version of Mono you are using. The changes affect the main Mono component: the JIT compiler, the implementation of base classes, and the GC. Speaking of GC, the runtime has two of them: *Boehm* and *SGen*. Boehm is a legacy one, SGen has been the default GC since Mono 3.2. It provides better performance and has many nice features. SGen has many possibilities for tuning, which will be covered in Chapter 8.

Mono is a cross-platform runtime. In this book, we usually discuss Windows, Linux, and macOS, but you can also use Mono 5.12+ on iOS, tvOS, watchOS, Sun Solaris, different flavors of BSD, Sony PlayStation 4, XboxOne, and so on.[21]

From the beginning, Mono was designed as an alternative runtime for existing .NET Framework programs. It doesn't have its own target framework. If you have an application that targets `net47` and `netcoreapp2.0`, the `net47` profile can be executed on both .NET Framework and Mono; `netcoreapp2.0` can be executed only on .NET Core. If you want to check if the current runtime is Mono, you should check the existence of the `Mono.Runtime` type[22]:

```
bool isMono = Type.GetType("Mono.Runtime") != null;
```

To get the installed version of Mono, you should run `mono --version` in the command line. This command will also print additional useful information about your Mono build like the architecture or default GC. Here is an example of output:

```
$ mono --version
Mono JIT compiler version 5.16.0.220
(2018-06/bb3ae37d71a Fri Nov 16 17:12:11 EST 2018)
Copyright (C) 2002-2014 Novell, Inc, Xamarin Inc and Contributors.
www.mono-project.com
    TLS:           normal
    SIGSEGV:       altstack
    Notification:  kqueue
    Architecture:  amd64
    Disabled:      none
    Misc:          softdebug
    Interpreter:   yes
    LLVM:          yes(3.6.0svn-mono-release_60/0b3cb8ac12c)
    GC:            sgen (concurrent by default)
```

---

[21]You can find the full list of supported platforms and architectures in the official documentation: www.mono-project.com/docs/about-mono/supported-platforms/

[22]www.mono-project.com/docs/faq/technical/#how-can-i-detect-if-am-running-in-mono

There are two builds of Mono for Windows: x86 and x64 (we will discuss different processor architectures later in this chapter). On Linux and macOS, only the x64 version of Mono is available.

Now it's time for a few exciting performance stories about different versions of different .NET runtimes.

Case Study 1: StringBuilder and CLR Versions

In .NET, `string` is an immutable type. It means that each operation like "concatenation" or "replace" creates a new instance of `string`. If you are working with huge strings, such operations allocate a lot of memory and take a significant amount of time. Fortunately, we have the `StringBuilder`[23] class, which was introduced in .NET Framework 1.1. It represents a mutable string and allows performing effective string operations without unnecessary memory allocations.

It looks very simple, but the internal implementation of `StringBuilder` is not so simple. Moreover, different versions of .NET Framework use different underlying algorithms.

Let's say that we want to implement a logging method `Log(string s)` that should collect all strings and join them into one huge string. Here is a naive implementation based on usual strings:

```
private string buffer = "";

public void Log(string s)
{
  buffer += s;
}
```

This is not an effective implementation because each call of `Log` will *create a new instance* of string, copy the content of `buffer` to this instance, copy the content of `s` to this instance, and save the instance back to the `buffer` field. As a result, we have many

---

[23]https://docs.microsoft.com/en-us/dotnet/api/system.text.stringbuilder

allocations, and we should spend a lot of time copying the same data between strings. Let's rewrite it with the help of StringBuilder:

```
private StringBuilder buffer = new StringBuilder();

public void Log(string s)
{
  buffer.Append(s);
}
```

How effective is this code? It depends.

In **.NET Framework 1.1-3.5 (CLR2)**, the implementation was pretty simple.[24] StringBuilder has an internal string field that represents the current value. In this context, we consider it as a mutable string because we can modify it via unsafe code. The initial capacity (length of this internal field) of StringBuilder by default is 16. When we call the Append method, StringBuilder checks if the capacity is big enough to keep additional characters. If everything is OK, it just adds new characters. Otherwise, it creates a new string with doubled capacity,[25] copies the old content to the new instance, and then appends target characters.

In **.NET Framework 4.x (CLR4)**, Microsoft made a lot of significant changes.[26] The most important change is about the internal representation: it's not a single string instance anymore. Now it's a linked list of chunks that contain char arrays for parts of the represented string. It allows optimizing many operations. For example, Append doesn't allocate a huge string when we don't have enough space: we can create new chunks and keep the chunks that contain the beginning of the string! The new implementation of the Append method is much better in CLR4. However, we don't have performance improvements for all methods. For example, ToString() works slower because we have to construct the final string from chunks (in CLR2, we had a ready string in the internal field). The indexer also works slower because we have to find the target chunk in the

---

[24]You can find the full source code for .NET Framework 2.0 here: `https://github.com/AndreyAkinshin/shared-source-cli-2.0/blob/master/clr/src/bcl/system/text/stringbuilder.cs`

[25]`https://github.com/AndreyAkinshin/shared-source-cli-2.0/blob/master/clr/src/bcl/system/text/stringbuilder.cs#L604`

[26]You can find the full source code for the latest version of .NET Framework here: `https://referencesource.microsoft.com/#mscorlib/system/text/stringbuilder.cs`

linked list (in CLR2, we could instantly get the target character because we had only one instance of a string). However, it's probably a good trade-off because a making a vast number of the Append calls is the most popular use case of StringBuilder. You can find more information about differences in StringBuilder implementations between CLR2 and CLR4 in [Guev 2017].

This is not the only change in StringBuilder that affects its performance; there are many other exciting stories. A few examples (we are not going to discuss all StringBuilder-related issues in this book, so it's recommended to read these GitHub discussions yourself):

- corefx#4632[27]: "StringBuilder creates unnecessary strings with Append methods"

- corefx#29921[28]: "ValueStringBuilder is slower at appending short strings than StringBuilder"

- corefx#25804[29]: "Iterating over a string builder by index becomes ~exponentially slow for large builders"

- coreclr#17530[30]: "Adding GetChunks which allow efficient scanning of a StringBuilder"

- msbuild#1593[31]: "Performance issue in ReusableStringBuilder.cs with large string and many appends"

Conclusions:

- **.NET Framework version matters.**

  Most modern .NET Framework applications are based on .NET Framework 4.x+ (CLR4). However, there are still many huge legacy projects that use .NET Framework 3.5 (CLR2). There are so many differences between 3.5 and 4.0. If you work with a legacy .NET

[27]https://github.com/dotnet/corefx/issues/4632
[28]https://github.com/dotnet/corefx/issues/29921
[29]https://github.com/dotnet/corefx/issues/25804
[30]https://github.com/dotnet/coreclr/pull/17530
[31]https://github.com/Microsoft/msbuild/issues/1593

Framework 3.5 project, you can't use measurements on .NET Framework 4.0 to make any conclusions about the performance of your application.

- **Major runtime updates can contain significant changes in basic algorithms.**

    Performance updates are not only about some advanced API or corner cases. Sometimes, you can get significant changes even for basic classes like `StringBuilder`.

- **Some updates change trade-offs.**

    When you read about performance changes in a changelog, it doesn't mean that you get better performance in the new runtime version for all possible use cases. Some updates can just change trade-offs: it can improve the performance of the most popular use cases and slow down some less popular scenarios. If you have some tricky logic, you can get a performance regression after an update.

AN EXERCISE

Write two programs that use `StringBuilder.Insert` and `StringBuilder.Remove`. One program should be much faster on .NET Framework 3.5 than on .NET Framework 4.0+. Another program should be much faster on .NET Framework 4.0+ than on .NET Framework 3.5. It's one of my favorite kinds of exercises because of the many developers who like to confidently say something like ".NET Framework 4.0+ is always faster than .NET Framework 3.5." This exercise should help you to understand that in-depth knowledge of runtime internals often allows writing a benchmark that demonstrates that one runtime is "faster" than another (no matter which runtime should be "faster").

Case Study 2: Dictionary and Randomized String Hashing

In old versions of .NET Framework, the `String` class had a well-known hash function that is the same between different application domains. It allowed performing a hash table attack on classes like `Dictionary` and `HashSet`: we can find a vast number of strings with equal hash codes in advance and put them in a dictionary. As a result, the algorithmic complexity of dictionary lookup will be O(N) instead of O(1).

In .NET Framework 4.5, it was decided to introduce randomized string hashing to prevent such attacks. Because of the backward compatibility,[32] a new hashing algorithm can't be enabled by default; it can break old code that is exploiting knowledge about legacy algorithms. However, if we are already under attack, we don't care about backward compatibility anymore and switch the hashing algorithm from legacy to randomized. Here is a fragment[33] of Dictionary source code (the Insert method, .NET Framework 4.7.2):

```
#if FEATURE_RANDOMIZED_STRING_HASHING

#if FEATURE_CORECLR
 // In case we hit the collision threshold
 // we'll need to switch to the comparer, which is
 // using randomized string hashing
 // in this case will be EqualityComparer<string>.Default.
 // Note, randomized string hashing is turned on
 // by default on coreclr so EqualityComparer<string>.Default will
 // be using randomized string hashing

 if (collisionCount > HashHelpers.HashCollisionThreshold &&
     comparer == NonRandomizedStringEqualityComparer.Default)
 {
    comparer = (IEqualityComparer<TKey>) EqualityComparer<string>.Default;
    Resize(entries.Length, true);
 }
#else
 if (collisionCount > HashHelpers.HashCollisionThreshold &&
    HashHelpers.IsWellKnownEqualityComparer(comparer))
 {
   comparer = (IEqualityComparer<TKey>)
   HashHelpers.GetRandomizedEqualityComparer(comparer);
```

---

[32]https://github.com/dotnet/corefx/issues/1534#issuecomment-143086216

[33]https://referencesource.microsoft.com/#mscorlib/system/collections/generic/dictionary.cs

```
   Resize(entries.Length, true);
 }
#endif// FEATURE_CORECLR

#endif
```

As you can see, if `collisionCount` is bigger than `HashHelpers.`
`HashCollisionThreshold` (it equals 100 in .NET Framework 4.7.2) and the legacy
`IEqualityComparer` is used, we change the `comparer`.

You can control this behavior via the `UseRandomizedStringHashAlgorithm`[34]
property in `app.config`. An example:

```
<?xml version ="1.0"?>
<configuration>
  <runtime>
   <UseRandomizedStringHashAlgorithm enabled="1" />
  </runtime>
</configuration>
```

In .NET Core, there are no problems with backward compatibility, so the randomized
string hashing is enabled by default. You can find more details about it in [Lock 2018].

Conclusions:

- **Performance of a method can be changed in the middle of a
  program.**

  In Chapter 2, we discussed that warm-up is important for
  benchmarking: the first call of a method can take much more time
  than subsequent calls. However, this is not the only case when
  a method performance can be changed. .NET Framework has a
  set of heuristics that can switch the internal implementation in
  special situations. If we want to design a good benchmark, we
  should be aware of such switches and cover different API use
  cases.

---

[34]https://docs.microsoft.com/en-us/dotnet/framework/configure-apps/file-schema/
runtime/userandomizedstringhashalgorithm-element

- **Internal algorithms can be tuned by app.config settings.**

  We already know that different .NET Framework versions could have performance differences because of changes in the implementation. However, we can manually switch some algorithms by values in `app.config` or via environment variables.

- **.NET Framework and .NET Core can have different algorithms for the same API.**

  .NET Framework and .NET Core share the main part of their code bases. Typically, we will get the same performance levels for the same base classes (it's not always easy to match .NET Framework and .NET Core versions, but you can check the source code for each version of each runtime). However, the behavior of some classes can be different even for the same versions: .NET Framework contains a lot of backward compatibility hacks that were removed in .NET Core.

AN EXERCISE

Try to implement a hash function attack on `HashSet` or `Dictionary` with disabled `FEATURE_RANDOMIZED_STRING_HASHING` (you should find over 100 different strings with the same hash codes). Write a benchmark that demonstrates performance difference between legacy and modern hashing behavior. This exercise should help you to learn how to exploit internal implementation details, find "corner cases," and demonstrate pure performance for common APIs, which usually work fast.

Case Study 3: IList.Count and Unexpected Performance Degradation

This story is about the development of JetBrains Rider. When Rider 2017.1 was released, it used Mono 4.9. Then, we started to upgrade it to Mono 5.2. Unfortunately, after the upgrade, some of the performance tests were red. Primarily, we had problems with the Solution-Wide Error Analysis (SWEA). On Mono 4.9, one of the tests took around **3 minutes** (we are trying to find all errors and warnings in huge solutions; it takes some time). After the upgrade, this test failed with **5 minutes** timeout. It was tough to investigate this issue because Mono 4.9/5.2 had poor abilities for profiling (advanced profiling was introduced only in Mono 5.6). If we run this test under profiling (`mono --profile`) with enough sampling frequency, it took about **30 minutes** and the snapshot is about **50 GB** (which is almost impossible to open). After a few weeks of unsuccessful profiling attempts, we decided to find other tests with the same problem and small total execution times. However, it turned out that the duration of almost all our tests were the same in both versions of Mono. So, we sorted all our tests by the performance difference between 4.9 and 5.2. In the top, we observed two kinds of tests: SWEA and code completion! A completion test looks like this: we open a file, move the caret to a specific place, press Ctrl+Space, wait for a completion list, press Enter, complete the statement. One such test took **4** seconds on Mono 4.9 and **18** seconds on Mono 5.2! The difference is huge, but it's pretty small in terms of profiling: it's much easier to make a performance snapshot for an 18-second session than for a 5-minute session. Of course, we didn't find the problem on the first attempt. Mono sampling showed an approximate place with the performance degradation. Next, we started to add Stopwatches here and there (it's 4->18 perf degradation; it should be easy to find it, right?) After another few days of investigating, we finally found the line that was responsible for the degradation. It contained just a `Count` call for an `IList<>` object. At first, I didn't believe that I found it correctly, so I created a minimal reproduction case and wrote a microbenchmark with the help of BenchmarkDotNet:

```
private readonly IList<object> array = new string[0];

[Benchmark]
public int CountProblem() => array.Count;
```

Here are the results on Linux:

```
BenchmarkDotNet=v0.10.9, OS=ubuntu 16.04
Processor=Intel Core i7-7700K CPU 4.20GHz (Kaby Lake), ProcessorCount=8
  Mono49     : Mono 4.9.0 (mono-49/f58eb9e642b Tue), 64bit
  Mono52     : Mono 5.2.0 (mono-52/da80840ea55 Tue), 64bit
```

Runtime	Mean	Error	StdDev
Mono49	5.038 ns	0.2869 ns	0.8459 ns
Mono52	1,471.963 ns	19.8555 ns	58.5445 ns

And here are the results on macOS:

```
BenchmarkDotNet=v0.10.9, OS=Mac OS X 10.12
Processor=Intel Core i7-4870HQ CPU 2.50GHz (Haswell), ProcessorCount=8
  Mono49      : Mono 4.9.0 (mono-49/f58eb9e642b Tue), 64bit
  Mono52      : Mono 5.2.0 (mono-52/da80840ea55 Tue), 64bit

Runtime |         Mean |      Error |      StdDev |
-------- |-------------:|-----------:|------------:|
  Mono49 |     5.548 ns |  0.0631 ns |    0.1859 ns |
  Mono52 | 2,443.500 ns | 44.6687 ns | 131.7068 ns |
```

As you can see, the Count invocation takes about **5** nanoseconds on Linux/macOS+Mono 4.9, about **1500** nanoseconds on Linux+Mono 5.2, and about **2500** nanoseconds on macOS+Mono 5.2. It significantly affects Rider in some different places like completion and SWEA. It's probably not a good idea to cast string[] to IList<object>, but we had such a "pattern" deep inside of different Rider subsystems and it's not easy to detect and refactor all of them.

OK, why do we have such a degradation here? If you read about Mono performance changes carefully, you probably noticed a remark about "Lazy array interfaces" in Mono 5.0. Here's a fragment from the official release notes[35]:

> **Lazy array interfaces** One curious aspect of C# is that arrays implement invariant interfaces as if they were covariant. This happens for IList<T>, ICollection<T> and IEnumerable<T> which means, for example, that string[] implements both IList<string> and IList<object>.
>
> Mono traditionally implemented this by creating the runtime-side metadata for all of those interfaces and that came with an extraordinary memory cost of creating a lot of interfaces that never ended up being referenced by C# code.
>
> With Mono 5.0 we now treat those interfaces as magic/special and use a different casting code-path. This allows them to be lazily

---

[35]www.mono-project.com/docs/about-mono/releases/5.0.0/#lazy-array-interfaces

implemented in arrays, which can save a lot of memory in LINQ-heavy workloads. As part of this work we refactored the casting code in the JIT to be simpler and more maintainable.

Unfortunately, there was a bug in the interface method dispatch implementation. We are in touch with developers from Mono, so this bug was quickly fixed[36] (Thank you guys!). We have patched Mono 5.2 with this fix and released Rider 2017.2 without any performance degradation (and some improvements).

Conclusions:

- **Runtime updates can unpredictably affect any parts of your code.**

  It's a good practice to read changelogs when you upgrade a runtime or third-party libraries. It can help you to find some serious problems in advance. However, you never know how these changes will affect your application. Don't trust your intuition and carefully measure performance before the update.

- **The implementation of simple API can be performance-critical for special cases.**

  Before this story, I didn't believe that would be possible to get serious performance problems because of the `IList<>.Count` implementation. When looking at such calls, you would usually think that you shouldn't care about its performance because it should always work superfast. However, even the simplest API calls could have a significant performance impact, especially if you call it too often, if you meet some corner cases, or if there are some bugs inside.

AN EXERCISE

Try to reproduce this issue locally. If you want to investigate performance changes at runtime, you should learn how to install (or build from source) different versions of runtime (e.g., Mono) and run a benchmark on each of them.

---

[36]https://github.com/mono/mono/pull/5486

Case Study 4: Build Time and GetLastWriteTime Resolution

The next story is also about Rider update. In Rider 2018.2, we decided to update Mono from 5.10 to 5.12. After the previous case study, we already know that it's a good practice to read changelogs carefully. Here is a short note from the Mono 5.12 release notes[37]:

> Added support for nanosecond resolution in file information on platforms where the information is available. This means the return value of APIs like `FileInfo.GetLastWriteTime ()` is now more precise.

Let's look at this change[38] in detail. Here are the values of `File.GetLastWriteTime(filename).Ticks` for the same file on Mono 5.10 and Mono 5.12 (1 tick = 100 nanoseconds):

```
          InternalTicks
Mono 5.10: 636616298110000000
Mono 5.12: 636616298114479590
```

As you can see, the old versions of Mono have information only about seconds (`10000000 ticks` is exactly `1 second`). In the new versions of Mono, we have information about milliseconds and microseconds. This is definitely a good improvement, but it's also a breaking change. However, it sounds like a small harmless change that wouldn't affect performance. In fact, it can. As usual, we decided to check that there are no performance regressions in the new version of Mono. And we found a lot of tests with increased duration. How is it possible? Let's figure it out!

Rider has a neat feature called the solution builder. As you can guess, it builds your solutions. Obviously, if a solution has already been built before, and a user asks to build it again, we shouldn't rebuild projects without any changes. The solution builder has a set of smart heuristics that help to detect such projects. One of the basic heuristics uses the last modification file time to find files without changes.

---

[37]www.mono-project.com/docs/about-mono/releases/5.12.0/
[38]https://github.com/mono/mono/pull/6307

The solution builder contains two parts. The first part is placed inside Rider host process, which uses the bundled version of Mono (this version is fixed for each Rider release). Here we save information about the last modification timestamps in a cache. The second part is placed inside an MSBuild[39] task, which uses the installed version of Mono (this version depends on the user environment). Here we check for the last actual modification timestamps. Next, we compare two timestamps (cached and actual) and decide whether to build a project or not.

Imagine a situation when Rider uses Mono 5.12 and a user has installed Mono 5.10. It means that the cached timestamp values have the milliseconds/microseconds data and the actual values don't have it. In the preceding example, these values are equal to 636616298114479590 and 636616298110000000. Thus, the probability that these two values are equal is very low. As a result, the solution builder rebuilds all the projects all the time; the feature is broken. Of course, we covered the solution builder by many tests, but these tests were executed only on Windows (for some historical reasons), where we use .NET Framework. On Linux/macOS, we didn't have such tests in Rider 2018.1, so the build was green. However, we discovered serious performance degradations for some tests because Rider executed extra builds. The bug was quickly found and fixed.

There was not a long performance investigation here, but this story still can teach us.

Conclusion:

- **Minor harmless changes can significantly affect performance.**

  This case study once again reminds us that it's very hard to predict how changes can affect the performance of a huge application. Don't forget to measure things and don't trust your intuition.

AN EXERCISE

As usual, try to reproduce the described change in Mono locally: download Mono 5.10 and 5.12, and then call `File.GetLastWriteTime(filename).Ticks` on a random file. Try to call it on .NET Framework and .NET Core.

---

[39]We will discuss it in the "Compilation" section.

Summing Up

In this section, we discuss the three most popular .NET runtimes: .NET Framework, .NET Core, and Mono. .NET Framework is a proprietary Windows-only runtime, while .NET Core and Mono are free and cross-platform runtimes. Now we know a short history of these runtimes and how to get the exact version of each of them.

Whichever runtime you use, don't forget that even minor changes in runtime updates can unpredictably affect performance in the most unexpected places. Don't forget to always measure all the performance-critical application use cases.

If you got some interesting benchmarking results on a single runtime, don't extrapolate your results on .NET in general. Remember that there are many .NET runtimes: each of them has its own implementation.

In the next section, we are going to talk about the transformation of the original source to native code.

Compilation

If you want to execute your C#[40] program, you should compile it first. After the compilation, we get a binary file that is based on the IL. When this file is executed by the runtime, we have another stage of compilation: runtime transforms it into native code. This process is known as JIT compilation. There are also a lot of tools that can do this transformation in advance (before the start of the application). This is known as AOT compilation. To avoid misunderstanding, we will call the first compilation stage IL generation.

In this section, we will discuss different topics about these three kinds of compilations:

- What kind of compiler we have and the differences between them.

- How to get the exact version of each compiler.

- How we can affect the compilation process.

Let's start with the first compilation stage: IL generation.

---

[40]Many languages can be used with the .NET platform. In addition to C#, we also have two pretty popular languages (Visual Basic .NET, F#), and many less popular languages like Managed C++ or Q#. Here and in the following, we will discuss C#, but almost all the facts are also valid for other .NET languages.

IL Generation

In this subsection, we will discuss tools that help us to *compile* and *build* the source code.

Compiling

If we want to compile a C# program, we need a *C# compiler*, which translates your C# code into IL.[41] Let's discuss the most popular compilers:

- **Legacy C#/VB compilers**

  In the epoch of C# 1..C# 5, we had C# and VB compilers as a part of .NET Framework. They were written in C++.

- **Roslyn**

  Roslyn is the modern open source[42] C# and Visual Basic compiler. It was pretty hard to maintain the legacy C#/VB compilers and introduce new features. So Microsoft decided to rewrite it in C#. Thus, Roslyn was born. The first Community Technology Preview (CTP) was presented in October 2011 and distributed as a part of Visual Studio 2010 SP1 (see [Osenkov 2011]). The first version of the compiler was released in July 2015 (see [Lander 2015]) with .NET Framework 4.6 and Visual Studio 2015. This version included the C# 6 and VB 14 support. All the subsequent releases of C# and VB are also based on Roslyn. The last version of C# supported by the legacy compiler is C# 5. Roslyn is distributed independently from .NET Framework; you can download a specific version of Roslyn via the Microsoft.Net.Compilers[43] NuGet package. You can find the full story of Roslyn in [Torgersen 2018].

---

[41]IL is also known as CIL (Common Intermediate Language) or MSIL (Microsoft Intermediate Language).

[42]https://github.com/dotnet/roslyn

[43]www.nuget.org/packages/Microsoft.Net.Compilers/

- **Mono C# Compiler**

  Historically, Mono had its own compiler: Mono C# Compiler.[44] It
  was developed as a cross-platform open source replacement of
  the Microsoft C# compiler. Initially, there were several different
  versions of the compiler (gmcs, smcs, dmcs).[45] Starting with Mono
  2.11, there is a universal compiler version: mcs. Starting with Mono
  5.0, the default compiler was changed from mcs to Roslyn, which
  is now shipped with Mono. However, mcs is still continuing to get
  updates in new versions of Mono.

If you have installed .NET Framework 4.x, you can find the legacy C# compiler in
C:\Windows\Microsoft.NET\Framework\v4.0.30319\Csc.exe. If you run it, you will see
a prompt message like this:

```
Microsoft (R) Visual C# Compiler version 4.7.3056.0 for C# 5
Copyright (C) Microsoft Corporation. All rights reserved.

This compiler is provided as part of the Microsoft (R) .NET Framework,
but only supports language versions up to C# 5,
which is no longer the latest version.
For compilers that support newer versions of the C# programming language,
see http://go.microsoft.com/fwlink/?LinkID=533240
```

The Roslyn compiler is not a part of the .NET Framework, so you should install it
separately. One of the typical installation paths on Windows looks like this: C:\Program
Files (x86)\Microsoft Visual Studio\2017\Community\MSBuild\15.0\Bin\Roslyn\
csc.exe (this path is valid for Visual Studio Community 2019). If you launch it, the
prompt message will look like this:

```
Microsoft (R) Visual C# Compiler version 2.9.0.63208 (958f2354)
Copyright (C) Microsoft Corporation. All rights reserved.
```

Note that the title of both compilers is the same (Visual C# Compiler), but Roslyn
has the lower version (2.9 instead of 4.7). This doesn't mean that it's an older version of

---

[44]It was renamed "Mono Turbo C# Compiler" in Mono 5.8: https://github.com/mono/mono/comm
   it/7d68dc8e71623ba76b16c5c5aa597a2fc7783f16

[45]https://stackoverflow.com/q/3882590

the C# compiler. When Roslyn was created, Microsoft started the versioning from 1.0. You can quickly detect the legacy compiler by the `"for C# 5"` suffix.

Building

If you have a huge solution with tons of files, it's pretty hard to manually specify all arguments that should be passed to the compiler. Fortunately, we can use a *build system* that orchestrates the compilation process: it controls not only how we compile separate files with source code, but how to build an entire solution with many projects and what kind of additional steps we need. There are several tools that can build .NET projects and solutions:

- **MSBuild**

    MSBuild is the most popular build tool in the .NET ecosystem. Initially, it was also a Windows-only closed source project distributed as a part of .NET Framework. Today, MSBuild is an open source and cross-platform project.[46] There are many ways to install it. For example, you can get it with Visual Studio, Build Tools for Visual Studio[47] or build it from sources. The latest versions of MSBuild ship Roslyn for compiling C# and VB files.

- **.NET Core CLI**

    CLI (command-line tool) allows performing all basic development operations: building, testing, deployment, and so on.[48] Internally, it has its own version of MSBuild.

- **XBuild**

    XBuild is a classic build tool for Mono. In the old days, it was the only way to build projects on Linux and macOS. Since Mono 5.0, XBuild has been deprecated because Mono ships MSBuild as the default build system.

---

[46]https://github.com/Microsoft/msbuild
[47]https://visualstudio.microsoft.com/downloads/#build-tools-for-visual-studio-2017
[48]You can download it here: www.microsoft.com/net/download

- **Other build systems**

  Many developers don't like pure MSBuild and try to use different build systems on top of it. Basically, they provide you a DSL (domain-specific language), which simplifies configuring your build process. Popular build systems include *Fake*, *Cake*, and *Nuke*.[49]

Today, the most popular toolset is MSBuild+Roslyn. However, some projects still may use the legacy C# compiler or XBuild. We discuss these technologies because they provide many good examples that demonstrate how changes in a compiler can affect the performance of your applications.

When MSBuild and the C# compiler were a part of .NET Framework, there were only a few widely used versions of the compiler. With the new Visual Studio 2017 Release Rhythm,[50] we get compiler updates all the time.

Build configurations

When you create a new solution in Visual Studio, you get two default build configuration: Debug and Release. If we open a `csproj` file for a classic application, we will find lines like this (some lines were removed for simplification):

```
<PropertyGroup Condition="'$(Configuration)|$(Platform)'=='Debug|AnyCPU'">
  <DebugSymbols>true</DebugSymbols>
  <DebugType>full</DebugType>
  <Optimize>false</Optimize>
  <OutputPath>bin\Debug\</OutputPath>
</PropertyGroup>
<PropertyGroup Condition="'$(Configuration)|$(Platform)'=='Release|AnyCPU'">
  <DebugType>pdbonly</DebugType>
  <Optimize>true</Optimize>
  <OutputPath>bin\Release\</OutputPath>
</PropertyGroup>
```

---

[49]https://fake.build/, https://cakebuild.net/, https://nuke.build/
[50]www.visualstudio.com/en-us/productinfo/vs2017-release-rhythm

The most important element for us is `<Optimize>`; this value is passed to the compiler and controls the optimization mode. By default, optimizations are disabled, but we can explicitly call compiler with enabled optimizations with the help of / optimize flag:

```
csc /optimize Program.cs
```

In a `csproj` file, we can define our own build configuration with custom rules for `<Optimize>`. We can even enable optimizations in Debug and disable it in Release. However, it's not a typical configuration. In this book, we will use the most common notation: Release means `<Optimize>true</Optimize>` and Debug means `<Optimize>false</Optimize>`. You can control the target configuration for MSBuild with the help of /p:Configuration:

```
msbuild /p:Configuration=Release Project.csproj
```

If you are using .NET Core SDK, you need `--configuration` or just `-c`:

```
dotnet build -c Release Project.csproj
```

Be careful: Debug (build configuration with *disabled* optimizations) is always the default option. It's great for debugging, but not so great for benchmarking.

Language version vs. compiler version

Sometimes, developers confuse C# version and C# compiler version. *C# version* is a specification. *C# compiler version* is a version of a program that translates C# source code to IL. Let's see what the difference is with the help of the legacy C# compiler. Consider the following program:

```
var numbers = new int[] { 1, 2, 3 };
var actions = new List<Action>();
foreach (var number in numbers)
    actions.Add(() => Console.WriteLine(number));
foreach (var action in actions)
    action();
```

There are two possible outcomes: 3 3 3 and 1 2 3. Old versions of the C# compiler created a single field for number, which was reused in all lambda expressions. After the end of the loop, the value of number is 3. Since all lambda expressions reference the same field, all of them will print 3 (you can find an explanation with more details in [Lippert 2009]). It was pretty confusing behavior for many developers, so the compiler team decided to make a breaking change in the compiler. Now, the compiler introduces a separate field per each loop iteration. Thus, we get 1 2 3 as the output because each lambda expression has its own field.

The breaking change was made in the compiler, not in the language version. Let's look at some possible compiling configurations in Table 3-5.

Table 3-5. *Closures on Different Versions of the Legacy C# Compiler*

Compiler version	Command line	Output
3.5.30729.7903 (C#3)	v3.5/csc.exe	3 3 3
4.0.30319.1 (C#4)	v4.0.30319/csc.exe	3 3 3
4.0.30319.33440 (C#5)	v4.0.30319/csc.exe	1 2 3
4.0.30319.33440 (C#5)	v4.0.30319/csc.exe /langversion:4	1 2 3

Let's discuss these in detail.

- **3.5.30729.7903** This is a *compiler version* that supports C# 3.

- **4.0.30319.1** This is a *compiler version* that supports C# 4.

- **4.0.30319.33440** This is a *compiler version* that supports C# 5.

- **4.0.30319.33440 with langversion:4** This is a *compiler version* that supports C# 5 and targets C# 4. We can specify the target language version for a C# compiler via the /langversion argument. Thus, we can run C# compiler 4.0.30319.33440 against C# 4 instead of C# 5. Basically, this means that we will not use C#5 language features like asynchronous methods. And it *doesn't mean* that we get the same IL code as in the "C# 4 compiler" (4.0.30319.1). As you can see, with /langversion:4, we still have 1 2 3 in output. The breaking change is still here.

The C# compiler produces IL code instead of native code. In the next section, we will discuss the next compilation stage: the JIT compilation. Sometimes, we will denote the compiler from this subsection as IL generator, "regular" compiler, or C# compiler to avoid confusion with the JIT compiler. To be short, we will also call it Roslyn because it's the most popular .NET compiler, but most of the conclusions can also be applied to the legacy C# compiler or other IL generators (for example, F# has its own compiler; this language is not supported by Roslyn).

Just-In-Time (JIT) Compilation

JIT compilation is a great technology that transforms IL code to native code (we will also call it *assembly* code or just *ASM* code). Here are some of the main advantages of the JIT compilation:

- IL code is hardware independent, so we can reuse the same binary file on different platforms.

- The JIT compiler compiles only methods that you really need.

- The generated code can be optimized for current usage profile.

- Some methods can be regenerated in order to achieve better performance.

In this section, we will discuss different JIT compilers in the .NET ecosystem.

The first versions of .NET Framework have two JIT compilers: *JIT32* and *JIT64* (for 32-bit and 64-bin versions of the runtime). Both compilers have independent code bases and different sets of optimizations. After years of development, it became very difficult to maintain and improve them, so it was decided to write a next-generation JIT compiler called *RyuJIT*.[51] Initially, JIT32 and JIT64 didn't have codenames (because .NET had only one JIT compiler for each platform). To avoid misunderstandings, we will use the terms *LegacyJIT-x86* and *LegacyJIT-x64* in this book.

The .NET team started to design RyuJIT in 2009, the development process was started in 2011, the first preview version was announced in September 2013 (see [RyuJIT 2013]), and it was finally released in 2015 (x64 only): RyuJIT became the default x64-JIT since .NET Framework 4.6. Thus, if you have a .NET 4.0 64-bit application, it will be automatically use RyuJIT after .NET Framework 4.6+ installation.

Early versions of RyuJIT had a lot of problems (especially on the CTP stage). Some of them are performance-related (RyuJIT produced slow code in comparison with LegacyJIT). Some of them are critical bugs that were the cause of huge problems in

---

[51]Here you can find a short story about origin of this name: `https://github.com/dotnet/coreclr/blob/master/Documentation/botr/ryujit-tutorial.md#why-ryujit`

some production systems.[52] However, now RyuJIT is a pretty stable, reliable, and fast JIT compiler. The development way was thorny, but eventually, we got a cool new JIT. Another interesting fact: the original source code of RyuJIT-x64 was based on LegacyJIT-x86, so you can find a lot of similar optimizations between these two JIT compilers.

If you want to switch back to LegacyJIT-x64 in .NET Framework, there are several ways. You can set `<useLegacyJit enabled="1" />` in the `configuration/runtime` section of your `app.config`, define the `COMPLUS_useLegacyJit=1` environment variable, or add a 32-bit DWORD Value `useLegacyJit=1` in the `HKEY_LOCAL_MACHINE\ SOFTWARE\Microsoft\.NETFramework` and `HKEY_CURRENT_USER\SOFTWARE\Microsoft\. NETFramework` Windows Registry subkeys. You can find the full actual instructions about disabling RyuJIT in [MSDOCS RyuJIT].

Let's start to understand what kind of JIT compiler (LegacyJIT or RyuJIT) is used for an x64-program. I want to tell you about one of my favorite hacks, which I used for years. Consider the following method:

```
int bar;

bool Foo(int step = 1)
{
  var value = 0;
  for (int i = 0; i < step; i++)
  {
    bar = i + 10;
    for (int j = 0; j < 2 * step; j += step)
      value = j + 10;
  }
  return value == 20 + step;
}
```

If you call this method on LegacyJIT-x64 with *enabled optimization*, Foo will return true: `value` will be equal to 21 instead of 11. You can find a detailed description of this bug with corresponding assembly listings in [Akinshin 2015]. A bug report was reported

---

[52]There is a famous post by Nick Craver from StackOverflow: [Craver 2015]. It's an intriguing story about bug advisory problems on StackOverflow production servers after upgrading .NET up to 4.6. It worth reading it and checking out all the links.

on Microsoft Connect,[53] but it was closed with status "Closed as Won't Fix. Due to several factors, the product team decided to focus its efforts on other items." Thus, if you run this code as an x64 application on .NET Framework and Foo returns true, LegacyJIT-x64 is used. Otherwise, the runtime uses RyuJIT-x64.

Another approach is based on the list of jit modules that is loaded into the current process. You can print this list as follows:

```
var modules = Process.GetCurrentProcess().Modules
  .OfType<ProcessModule>()
  .Where(module => module.ModuleName.Contains("jit"));
foreach (var module in modules)
  Console.WriteLine(
    Path.GetFileNameWithoutExtension(module.FileName) + " " +
    module.FileVersionInfo.ProductVersion);
```

In CLR2, you will see mscorjit. It always means LegacyJIT because it's the only JIT available in CLR2. In CLR4, RyuJIT-x64 has only one module: clrjit (formerly known as protojit). LegacyJIT-x64 has two modules: clrjit and compatjit. Thus, if you see compatjit in your module list, it means that LegacyJIT is used. RyuJIT-x86 is not available for .NET Framework; LegacyJIT-x86 is the only option for x86 programs.

Now let's talk about JIT compilers in .NET Core. .NET Core 1.x uses RyuJIT-x64 for x64 and LegacyJIT-x86 for x86 (the x86 version is available only for Windows). In .NET Core 2.0, LegacyJIT-x86 was replaced by RyuJIT-x86.[54] Eventually, all LegacyJIT-x86-related code was removed from the .NET Core source code.[55] .NET Framework and .NET Core share the same RyuJIT-x64 code base.[56]

In Mono, there is no well-known name for the JIT compiler, so we will call it *MonoJIT*. It's a part of the Mono runtime, so MonoJIT has improvements in each Mono update. In addition to the default JIT compiler, we also have a *Mono LLVM* option for JIT

---

[53]This page is not available anymore because the service has been retired.

[54]https://github.com/dotnet/announcements/issues/10

[55]https://github.com/dotnet/coreclr/pull/18064

[56]You can find some interesting technical details in this GitHub issue: https://github.com/dotnet/coreclr/issues/14250

compilation, which uses LLVM[57] for generating assembly code (available since Mono 2.6). You can control it via the `--nollvm` or `--llvm` arguments.

In Table 3-6, you can see a compatibility matrix between different JIT compilers and .NET runtimes.

Table 3-6. *Compatibility of JIT Compilers*

JIT	.NET Framework	.NET Core	Mono
LegacyJIT-x86	1.0+	1.x	—
LegacyJIT-x64	2.0+	—	—
RyuJIT-x86	—	2.0+	—
RyuJIT-x64	4.6+	1.0+	—
MonoJIT	—	—	1.0+
MonoLLVM	—	—	2.6+

In the next subsection, we will discuss another approach for generating native code.

Ahead-Of-Time (AOT) Compilation

JIT compiler generates the native code for a method when you want to call this method. This is the default strategy for most of the .NET applications, but it's not the only one. You can also compile your code AOT, generate native code for all methods, and produce binaries that don't need JIT compiler. AOT compilation has some advantages and disadvantages compared to JIT compilation: in some cases, it can provide significant performance improvements, but it can also do more harm than good.

Advantages (compared to JIT):

- **Better startup time**

    JIT compiler can take a lot of time during initial assembly loading and slow down the startup time. In the case of an AOT compiler, we don't have such problems.

---

[57]LLVM is a popular cross-platform solution for generating native code on different platforms based on own intermediate representation. You can find more information on the official site: `https://llvm.org/`

- **Lower memory usage**

  If several applications use the same assembly, the native image of the assembly can be shared between them. Thus, the total amount of used memory can be reduced.

- **Better optimizations**

  JIT compiler should work fast, and it doesn't have enough time for all "smart" optimizations. AOT compiler is not limited by compilation time, so it has an opportunity to "think well" about the best way to optimize your code.

Disadvantages (compared to JIT):

- **Optimizations are not always better**

  AOT compilation doesn't guarantee that all optimizations will be better. JIT compiler has knowledge about the current runtime session, so it can produce better assembly code. Also, it can generate better memory layout for generated code (e.g., if you have a call chain of methods, JIT compiler can put them near to each other).

- **API limitations**

  It's not always possible to use all .NET APIs with an AOT toolchain because you can't always compile everything AOT. For example, you can have problems with dynamic assembly loading, dynamic code execution, reflection, generic classes and interfaces, and other "advanced" APIs.

- **JIT/AOT binding overhead**

  If you have an interaction between AOT and JIT compiled methods, it can have noticeable performance overhead because of the expensive method address bindings.

- **Build process complication**

  AOT build usually takes much more time and you have to generate separate native binaries for all target platforms.

- **Huge size of binary files**

  JIT compiler can produce native code only for a method that you actually call. AOT compiler has to generate native code for all classes and methods because you don't know in advance which method will be called. JIT compiler can eliminate some branches based on the runtime information like values of static read-only values (e.g., IsSupported). AOT compiler has to generate code for all branches because it doesn't have values that will be computed in runtime.

Thus, the AOT compiler can be not a good option for all kinds of applications, but it can be pretty useful in some cases. Several engines provide AOT features for .NET:

- **NGen**

  NGen[58] is the classic and most famous AOT tool for .NET Framework. It can create native images (.ni.dll or .ni.exe) of the managed assemblies and install them into the native image cache. One of the interesting NGen features is MPGO[59] (Managed Profile Guided Optimization): it allows tracing your code during runtime, building "profile" data, and using it for better native code generation. MPGO works great when real-world usage scenarios are similar to these profiles.

- **CrossGen**

  CrossGen[60] is analogue of NGen (which is .NET Framework-specific) for .NET Core. It also generates native images for

---

[58]https://docs.microsoft.com/en-us/dotnet/framework/tools/
ngen-exe-native-image-generator

[59]https://docs.microsoft.com/en-us/dotnet/framework/tools/
mpgo-exe-managed-profile-guided-optimization-tool

[60]https://github.com/dotnet/coreclr/blob/v2.2.0/Documentation/building/crossgen.md

managed assemblies, but it's cross-platform: you can use it on Windows, Linux, or macOS. MPGO is also available for .NET Core (see [Le Roy 2017]).

- **Mono AOT**

  Mono also provides a tool for AOT compilation[61] that can be used by the `--aot` runtime arguments. It generates native images (with the extension `.so` on Linux; `.dylib` on macOS) that will be automatically used when the assembly is executed. Mono AOT has a huge number of options. For example, with `--aot=full`, you can enable the full AOT. This mode is designed for platforms that don't allow dynamic code generation: all of the target methods should be compiled AOT. Next, you can run the application with `mono --full-aot` (it's not an equivalent of `mono --aot=full`, it's another command!), which means that the JIT engine (and all the dynamic features) will be disabled. You can also use AOT on Xamarin.Android and Xamarin.iOS.[62]

- **.NET Native**

  If we are talking about UWP (Universal Windows Platform) applications, there is another interesting technology called .NET Native.[63] Many UWP applications are designed for mobile devices and have high requirements for startup time, execution time, memory usage, and power consumption. .NET Native uses C++ compiler on the back end; it is optimized for static precompilation and links the required parts of the .NET Framework directly in the app. When a user downloads an app, the precompiled native image is used. Thus, the startup time is much faster, and we don't have to spend the energy of a mobile device on the JIT compilation.

---

[61]www.mono-project.com/docs/advanced/runtime/docs/aot/

[62]https://xamarinhelp.com/xamarin-android-aot-works/, https://docs.microsoft.com/en-us/xamarin/ios/internals/architecture#aot

[63]https://docs.microsoft.com/en-us/dotnet/framework/net-native/

- **CoreRT**

  CoreRT[64] is a .NET Core runtime optimized for AOT compilation.
  It's cross-platform, which means that you can create native
  applications for Windows, Linux, and macOS. You can learn a lot
  about CoreRT internals in [Warren 2018b].

- **RuntimeHelpers**

  Unlike the preceding AOT approaches, `RuntimeHelpers` is a
  managed static class with handy methods that you can use
  for AOT compilation during runtime. Imagine that you have a
  method requiring "heavy" JIT compilation, but you don't want to
  wait on the first method call and you can't warm it up by calling
  it in advance because each invocation produces side effects. In
  this case, you can get the method handle via reflection and ask
  JIT compiler to generate native code in advance with the help of
  `RuntimeHelpers.PrepareMethod`.

Now let's discuss a few case studies about different kinds of compilation.

Case Study 1: Switch and C# Compiler Versions

`switch` is one of the basic C# keywords. Do you know how it works internally? Actually, it
depends on the version of your C# compiler. Consider the following code with `switch`:

```csharp
string Capitalize(string x)
{
  switch (x)
  {
    case "a":
      return "A";
    case "b":
      return "B";
    case "c":
      return "C";
```

---

[64]https://github.com/dotnet/corert

```
      case "d":
        return "D";
      case "e":
        return "E";
      case "f":
        return "F";
      case "g":
        return "G";
    }
    return "";
}
```

The legacy C# compiler 4.0.30319.33440 generates the following code:

```
; Phase 0: Dictionary<string, string>
IL_000d: volatile.
IL_000f: ldsfld class  Dictionary<string, int32>
IL_0014: brtrue.s IL_0077
IL_0016: ldc.i4.7
IL_0017: newobj instance void class Dictionary<string, int32>::.ctor
IL_001c: dup
IL_001d: ldstr "a"
IL_0022: ldc.i4.0
IL_0023: call instance void class Dictionary<string, int32>::Add
IL_0028: dup
IL_0029: ldstr "b"
IL_002e: ldc.i4.1
IL_0023: call instance void class Dictionary<string, int32>::Add
IL_0034: dup
IL_0035: ldstr "c"
; ...
; Phase 1:
IL_0088: ldloc.1
IL_0089: switch (
  IL_00ac, IL_00b2, IL_00b8,
  IL_00be, IL_00c4, IL_00ca, IL_00d0)
```

```
IL_00aa: br.s IL_00d6
; Phase 2: cases
IL_00ac: ldstr "A"
IL_00b1: ret
IL_00b2: ldstr "B"
IL_00b7: ret
IL_00b8: ldstr "C"
IL_00bd: ret
IL_00be: ldstr "D"
IL_00c3: ret
IL_00c4: ldstr "E"
IL_00c9: ret
IL_00ca: ldstr "F"
IL_00cf: ret
IL_00d0: ldstr "G"
IL_00d5: ret
IL_00d6: ldstr ""
IL_00db: ret
```

It allocates an internal static instance of `Dictionary<string, int>` and puts all values in this dictionary. This code is executed only once on the first call of the method.

Roslyn generates a smarter version for `switch` from the first version:

```
// Phase 1: ComputeStringHash
uint num = ComputeStringHash(x);
// Phase 2: Binary search
if (num <= 3792446982u) {
  if (num != 3758891744u) {
    if (num != 3775669363u) {
      if (num == 3792446982u) {
        if (x == "g") { return "G"; }
      }
    }
    else if (x == "d") { return "D"; }
  }
  else if (x == "e") { return "E"; }
}
```

```
else if (num <= 3826002220u) {
  if (num != 3809224601u) {
    if (num == 3826002220u) {
      if (x == "a") { return "A"; }
    }
  }
  else if (x == "f") { return "F"; }
}
else if (num != 3859557458u) {
  if (num == 3876335077u) {
    if (x == "b") { return "B"; }
  }
}
else if (x == "c") { return "C"; }
return "";
```

As you can see, there is not an additional dictionary anymore. We calculate a hash code for the given string and do a binary search. We need a runtime-independent value, so we use additional method instead of `string.GetHashCode`:

```
internal static uint ComputeStringHash(string s)
{
  uint num = default(uint);
  if (s != null)
  {
    num = 2166136261u;
    for (int i = 0; i < s.Length; i++)
      num = (s[i] ^ num) * 16777619;
  }
  return num;
}
```

Since all switch keys should be constants and known on the compilation stage, we can precalculate hash codes for all of them in advance. Next, we can sort the hash codes and implement a simple binary search by known values. It's pretty effective in terms of performance and memory.

Conclusion:

- **Performance can depend on the version of C# compiler.**

  The main part of the optimizations is the responsibility of JIT and AOT compilers. C# compiler just produces IL code from your source code. In most cases, it doesn't apply smart optimizations. However, some "advanced" language construction like `switch` can be translated to IL in different ways. When we discuss a new version of a compiler, we usually discuss new language features, but we also should be aware of changes in the existing features.

AN EXERCISE

Write a program with a huge switch statement. Try to write a benchmark that shows the performance difference between the legacy C# compiler and Roslyn.

Case Study 2: Params and Memory Allocations

C# has a lot of syntax sugar that allows writing laconic and understandable code. However, developers don't always think about the performance cost of this sugar. There is the `params` keyword, which helps us to create methods with a variable number of arguments:

```
void Foo(params int[] x)
{
// ...
}
```

It is a good approach in some cases. However, it may hide implicit object allocations from the developers. For example, what happens if you call such a method without arguments:

```
Foo();
```

The correct answer: it depends. If the project targets .NET Framework 4.5, Roslyn produces the following code:

```
IL_0000: ldc.i4.0
IL_0001: newarr      System.Int32
IL_0006: call        Foo(int32[])
IL_000b: ret
```

As you can see, a new empty array was created. It means that the runtime allocates a new object per method invocation without arguments.

In .NET Framework 4.6, Microsoft introduced a new API, `Array.Empty<T>`[65]: it returns an empty array instance. An implementation is pretty simple:

```
public class Array
{
  private static class EmptyArray<T>
  {
    internal static readonly T[] Value = new T[0];
  }
  public static T[] Empty<T>()
  {
    return EmptyArray<T>.Value;
  }
}
```

For each type T, we get at most one array instance which will be reused. Roslyn knows about this API. If a project targets .NET Framework 4.6+, Roslyn will generate an optimized version of the IL code:

```
IL_0000: call        !!0[] System.Array::Empty<int32>()
IL_0005: call        void ConsoleApp7.Program::Foo(int32[])
IL_000a: ret
```

In this case, the static `Array.Empty<T>` instance is used. This means that you shouldn't worry about unwanted memory allocation.

---

[65]https://docs.microsoft.com/en-gb/dotnet/api/system.array.empty

Conclusion:

- **Generated IL code can depend on project properties.**

  The compiler version is not the only factor that can affect
  generated code. The same version of the compiler can produce
  different IL code for the same language construction based on the
  target .NET Framework version and available API.

AN EXERCISE

Take a look at what IL code the legacy C# compiler generates for the preceding example on
.NET Framework 4.5 and 4.6.[66]

Case Study 3: Swap and Unobvious IL

Consider a simple method that takes two integer values, swaps them, and divides the
swapped variables (it doesn't look like a useful method, but it's a small example with
pretty exciting properties). There are many ways to implement this logic, and here is one
of the most obvious solutions:

```
public int SwapAndDiv1(int a, int b)
{
  var temp = a;
  a = b;
  b = temp;
  return a / b;
}
```

Here we swap the variables with the help of an additional variable, `temp`. It works, but
it looks too wordy: we need three lines of code and an additional variable. Fortunately,
C# 7.0 introduces the tuple syntax, which allows rewriting this method as follows:

```
public int SwapAndDiv2(int a, int b)
{
  (a, b) = (b, a);
  return a / b;
}
```

---

[66]We will discuss how to get the generated IL code in Chapter 6.

Now we can swap the values by one line of code without additional variables. This code is easier to read, and it looks more expressive. Now it's time for a puzzle: which method will get a more optimized IL representation? Someone can propose the following hypothesis: "The second method can swap variables without additional variables, so it should have a better IL representation." It may sound logical, but this hypothesis is based on what we have on the C# level. Let's check the hypothesis, compile the code with Roslyn 2.6.0.62309 (d3f6b8e7), and look at the IL listing. Here is the first method:

```
.method public hidebysig
    instance int32 SwapAndDiv1 (
        int32 a,
        int32 b
    ) cil managed
{
  ; Header Size: 1 byte
  ; Code Size: 10 (0xA) bytes
  .maxstack 8

  ; Swap
  IL_0000: ldarg.1   ; Loads 'a' onto the stack
  IL_0001: ldarg.2   ; Loads 'b' onto the stack
  IL_0002: starg.s a ; Pops the stack top value ('b') in the 'a' argument
  slot
  IL_0004: starg.s b ; Pops the stack top value ('a') in the 'b' argument
  slot

  ; Division
  IL_0006: ldarg.1
  IL_0007: ldarg.2
  IL_0008: div
  IL_0009: ret
}
```

As you can see, we have an additional variable on the C# level, but we don't have it on the IL level: Roslyn loads both variables onto the stack and stores them back in the reverse order. Here is the IL listing for the second method:

```
.method public hidebysig
    instance int32 SwapAndDiv2 (
        int32 a,
        int32 b
    ) cil managed
{
    ; Header Size: 12 bytes
    ; Code Size: 12 (0xC) bytes
    ; LocalVarSig Token: 0x11000002 RID: 2
    .maxstack 2
    .locals init (
        [0] int32 ; an additional variable 'temp'
    )

    IL_0000: ldarg.2    ; Loads 'b' onto the stack
    IL_0001: ldarg.1    ; Loads 'a' onto the stack
    IL_0002: stloc.0    ; Pops the stack top value ('a') in the local
                          variable 'temp'
    IL_0003: starg.s a ; Pops the stack top value ('b') in the 'a' argument
                          slot
    IL_0005: ldloc.0    ; Loads the local variable 'temp' onto the stack
    IL_0006: starg.s b ; Pops the stack top value ('temp') in the 'b'
                          argument slot

    ; Division
    IL_0008: ldarg.1
    IL_0009: ldarg.2
    IL_000A: div
    IL_000B: ret
}
```

Here you see a reversed situation: we don't have an additional variable on the C# level, but we have one on the IL level. This doesn't mean that we will get better performance in the first case, but it makes the situation easier for the next stages of the code source journey.

Conclusion:

- **Don't trust your intuition about compiler output.**

  Many developers try to guess the generated IL code, the native code, and the application performance based on what we have in the C# source code. Even if you have rich experience, your intuition is not your best friend here. You shouldn't make any conclusions based on your guesses; always check the generated code and carefully measure performance.

AN EXERCISE

What do you think: do we get any performance difference between `SwapAndDiv1` and `SwapAndDiv2`? Try to write a small benchmark and measure both methods. Check out the generated assembly code with different JIT compilers and compare it for both cases.[67] You can also implement your own methods that use different ways to swap two variables.

Case Study 4: Huge Methods and Jitting

A friend of mine told me a story about his project. He had some serious performance problems (current performance level did not satisfy business requirements). He tried many different approaches without luck. Eventually, he decided to try code generation. The idea was simple: native IL provides many constructions which are not available in pure C#. My friend tried to rewrite the hotspot in IL. He also decided to reduce the number of calls and inline everything into one huge method. After the first benchmark, it turned out that the generated method takes significantly more time than the original C# method. After quick research, the problem was found: the runtime spends 95% of the time during the JIT phase! The method was so big that it requires several seconds for generating native code. However, the second call of this method was superfast.

We will not reproduce this situation with all details, but we will write a small example that demonstrates this effect. Let's say we want to calculate the value of the following expression:

$$0 - 1 + 2 - 3 + 4 - 5 + \cdots - 999999 + 1000000$$

---

[67]We will discuss how to get the generated native code in Chapter 6.

Of course, we can do it via a simple for loop:

```
var result = 0;
for (var i = 1; i <= 1000000; i++)
  result += (i % 2 == 0 ? 1 : -1) * i;
```

Instead, we will try to generate this expression in IL without any loops:

```
// Regular code generation routine
var assemblyName = new AssemblyName {Name = "MyAssembly"};
var assembly = AppDomain.CurrentDomain
  .DefineDynamicAssembly(assemblyName, AssemblyBuilderAccess.RunAndSave);
var module = assembly.DefineDynamicModule("Module");
var typeBuilder = module.DefineType("Type", TypeAttributes.Public);
var methodBuilder = typeBuilder.DefineMethod(
  "Calc", MethodAttributes.Public | MethodAttributes.Static,
  typeof(int), new Type[0]);

// Generate the target method
var generator = methodBuilder.GetILGenerator();
generator.Emit(OpCodes.Ldc_I4, 0); // Put 0 on stack
for (var i = 1; i <= 1000000; i++)
{
  generator.Emit(OpCodes.Ldc_I4, i); // Put i on stack
  generator.Emit(i % 2 == 0 // Apply '+' or '-' on two top stack values
    ? OpCodes.Add : OpCodes.Sub);
}
generator.Emit(OpCodes.Ret); // Return the top value from stack

// Build the target type
var type = typeBuilder.CreateType();
// Lambda which call this method via reflection
Func<int> calc = () => (int) type.InvokeMember("Calc",
  BindingFlags.InvokeMethod | BindingFlags.Public |
  BindingFlags.Static, null, null, null);
```

```csharp
// Measure duration of the 1st and 2nd calls
var stopwatch1 = Stopwatch.StartNew();
calc(); // 1st call (cold start)
stopwatch1.Stop();
var stopwatch2 = Stopwatch.StartNew();
var result = calc(); // 2nd call (warmed state)
stopwatch2.Stop();

// Print results
Console.WriteLine($"Result    : {result}");
Console.WriteLine($"1st call : {stopwatch1.ElapsedMilliseconds} ms");
Console.WriteLine($"2nd call : {stopwatch2.ElapsedMilliseconds} ms");
```

Here is an example of possible results:

```
Result    : 500000
1st call : 612 ms
2nd call : 0 ms
```

If you try to run it on your machine, you can get other absolute numbers for the first call, but the conclusion will be the same: the first call takes a huge amount of time.

Conclusions:

- **Jitting of a single method can take a lot of time.**

  The JIT compiler can significantly slow down not only the startup time, but also the first call of a single method. Such a problem can be easily found if you profile the application.

- **Some optimization changes the trade-off between cold and warm start.**

  When you have two approaches, it's not always possible to say which one is faster. Like in the "The Tortoise and The Hare" story, some solutions can be slow on start and still come out ahead.

AN EXERCISE

Replace 1000000 in the code snippet with code generation with parameter n. Take measurements for different values of n and draw a plot that demonstrates the duration of the first call for each n. Try several JIT compilers (LegacyJIT, RyuJIT, MonoJIT) and compare plots. Find the value of n when each JIT starts to take more than 100ms on jitting. Try to write your own algorithms on pure IL and repeat the measurements. The exercise should give you the basic feeling of how expensive JIT compiler can be depending on the method body.

This was the last case study in this section. Let's summarize what have we learned.

Summing Up

In this section, we discussed different kinds of compilation:

- **IL Generation**

  When we create a new program on our favorite .NET-compatible language (e.g., C#, VB.NET, F#, Managed C++, or Q#), a compiler transforms it to IL. A build system orchestrates the compilation process and helps us to build projects and solutions. The most popular toolset is MSBuild+Roslyn, but there are other technologies like XBuild and the legacy C# compiler that are still used in the industry. By default, our programs will be compiled in the Debug mode (with disabled optimizations), which is great for debugging but not a good option for benchmarking. If we want to benchmark anything, we should switch to the Release mode (with enabled optimizations).

- **JIT Compilation**

  The IL code can be transformed to native code by the JIT compiler. It's happening in runtime on demand: runtime generates native code on the first method call. .NET Framework has three available JIT compilers: LegacyJIT-x86 (the only option for x86), RyuJIT-x64 (the default option since .NET Framework 4.6), and LegacyJIT-x64 (the default option before .NET Framework 4.6; can be manually enabled in the latest versions). .NET Core 2.0+ uses RyuJIT for both x86 and x64 architectures. Mono uses its own independent JIT compiler (MonoJIT), which can be switched to the LLVM back end (MonoLLVM).

- **AOT Compilation**

  The native code can be generated in advance with additional tools like NGen, CrossGen, Mono AOT, .NET Native, CoreRT, or RuntimeHelpers.PrepareMethod. Such an approach can reduce the application startup time and provide better optimizations, but it has some limitations (e.g., dynamic code execution, reflection, generics, and so on).

Now we know the most popular compiling and build tools in the .NET ecosystem. It's time to the discuss external environments that surround our runtimes.

External Environment

The environment of a program is a runtime. However, a runtime also has an environment. We use runtime on a specific *operating system* that is running on some *hardware* that exists in *the physical world*. In this section, we will discuss all these "external environments": why they matter and how they can affect performance.

Operating System

In the modern world, .NET is cross-platform. From the user's point of view, it's good because now you can run a .NET application on different operating systems. From the performance engineer's point of view, it's bad because now you should worry about performance on each operating system as well.

The duration of the same method call may vary depending on the operating system. Let's consider an example. In Figure 3-3, you can see a plot that demonstrates the duration of a single integration test in Rider 2018.2. The test shows completely different results on different OS. In June, we can observe around *9–16* seconds on Windows, around *58–77* seconds on Linux, and around *87–120* seconds on macOS. It doesn't mean that Windows is always fast and macOS is always slow: we also have tests where macOS is the champion and Windows is the slowest operating system, and in other tests, all three operating systems show the same result. If you look closely at the chart and compare May and August, you can notice a significant performance degradation on Linux and macOS (on Windows, the duration of the test has not changed). It seems that we had some destructive changes that randomly slowed down the cleanup on Linux and macOS.

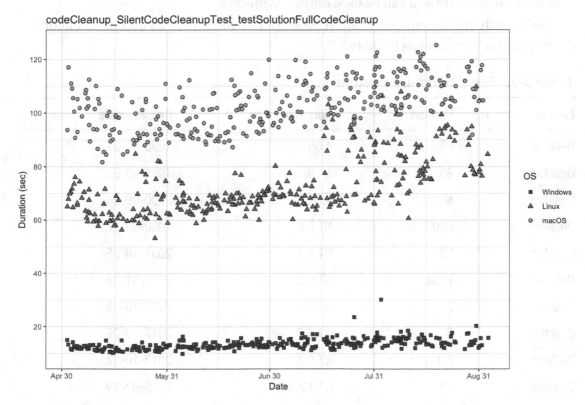

Figure 3-3. *Duration of a cleanup test in Rider 2018.2 on different OS*

In this subsection, we briefly recall the history of Windows, Linux, and macOS, look at the important operating system versions, and learn how to get these versions from the command line and managed code.

Windows is the only operating system that supports all three .NET runtimes because .NET Framework works only on Windows. On Unix-like operating systems (Linux and macOS), we can use only .NET Core and Mono. There are some other operating systems which can also be used for running .NET programs. For example, you can build .NET Core on FreeBSD as well. Mono supports different mobile OS (like Android, iOS, tvOS, and watchOS) and game consoles (like PlayStation 3, Xbox 360, and Wii). However, these operating systems are out of this book's scope, so we are going to discuss only Windows, Linux, and macOS.

Let's talk about each operating system in detail.

Windows

Windows is the homeland for .NET because .NET Framework was designed for this OS. Internally, many of the .NET Framework subsystems (like WPF) are tightly integrated with the Windows API and can be used only on Windows.

Let's briefly recall some important versions of Windows. You can find some major desktop and server editions in Table 3-7.

Table 3-7. *Some Windows Versions*

Edition	Version	Kernel version	Release date
Desktop	95	4.00	1995-08-24
Desktop	98	4.10	1998-06-25
Desktop	ME	4.90	2000-09-14
Desktop	2000	NT 5.0	2000-02-17
Desktop	XP	NT 5.1	2001-10-25
Desktop	Vista	NT 6.0	2007-01-30
Desktop	7	NT 6.1	2009-10-22
Desktop	8	NT 6.2	2012-10-26
Desktop	8.1	NT 6.3	2013-10-17
Desktop	10	NT 10.0	2015-07-29
Server	2000	NT 5.0	2000-02-17
Server	2003	NT 5.2	2003-04-24
Server	2003 R2	NT 5.2	2005-12-06
Server	2008	NT 6.0	2008-02-27
Server	2008 R2	NT 6.1	2009-10-22
Server	2012	NT 6.2	2012-09-04
Server	2012 R2	NT 6.3	2013-10-18
Server	2016	NT 10.0	2016-10-12
Server	2019	NT 10.0	2018-10-02

In the scope of the book, we will discuss mainly Windows 10 (desktop) because it's the most recent version of Windows and the end of mainstream support for Windows 8.1 was on January 9, 2018. .NET Framework 3.5+ supports Windows XP+[68] (and Windows Server 2003+), so sometimes we will discuss Windows XP, Vista, 7, 8, and 8.1 as well. Other Windows versions (like 1.01 or NT 3.1) are out of the scope of this book.

Since Windows 10 is the most interesting OS for us, it good to know the major updates for it; you can find them in Table 3-8.

Table 3-8. *Major Windows 10 Builds*

Version	Build	Marketing name	Codename	Release date
1507	10240	RTM	Threshold 1	2015-07-29
1511	10586	November Update	Threshold 2	2015-11-10
1607	14393	Anniversary Update	Redstone 1	2016-08-02
1703	15063	Creators Update	Redstone 2	2017-04-05
1709	16299	Fall Creators Update	Redstone 3	2017-10-17
1803	17134	April 2018 Update	Redstone 4	2018-04-30
1809	17763	October 2018 Update	Redstone 5	2018-11-13

It's also good to know how to check the exact version of it. In particular, we are interested in the full four-number versions like `10.0.15063.674`. On Windows, there are several ways to get the current operating system versions. For example, in Figure 3-4, you can see screenshots of the following programs:

---

[68] .NET Framework 1.0, 1.1., and 2.0 can be used on Windows 98/ME/2000.

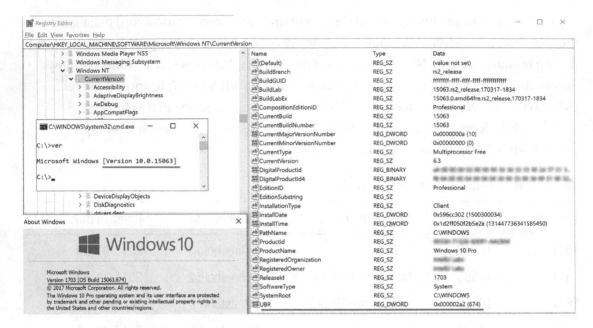

Figure 3-4. *Screenshots of different programs with Windows version*

- ver in the command line, which returns Microsoft Windows [Version 10.0.15063]. Now we know the main part of the version (build 15063 corresponds to 1703 "Creators Update"), but we don't know the revision version. ver prints the revisions only since 10.0.16299+.

- regedit (Registry Editor) with opened HKEY_LOCAL_MACHINE\ SOFTWARE\Microsoft\Windows NT\CurrentVersion\UBR. As you can see, the UBR (Update Build Revision) value is 674, which means that the full Windows version is 10.0.15063.674.

- winver, which provides a more user-friendly way to get the complete Windows version.

Linux

.NET Framework doesn't work on Linux, but we can use Mono and .NET Core for our .NET applications. There is a huge number of Linux distributions,[69] and of course, we can't discuss them all in this book. The main idea of checking different versions of Linux is to show how it can affect your performance. You should understand that it's not

---

[69]You can find the list of the most popular Linux distributions here: www.distrowatch.com

enough to say that you are working on Linux; it's also worth mentioning the title of the Linux distribution and its full version.

The main operating systems that are officially supported in the latest versions of Mono are Ubuntu, Debian, Raspbian, and CentOS. However, you can also use it on other distributions like openSUSE, Fedora, Linux Mint, and so on.

.NET Core supports several Linux distributions[70]: Red Hat Enterprise Linux, CentOS, Oracle Linux, Fedora, Debian, Ubuntu, Linux Mint, openSUSE, SUSE Enterprise Linux (SLES), and Alpine Linux.

In the scope of this book, we usually discuss only popular Debian-based distributions (e.g., Ubuntu), but the main parts of the explanations are applicable for other Linux distributions as well.

One of the best ways to check the distribution version in the command line is `lsb_release -a`.

Typical output for Ubuntu:

```
Distributor ID:  Ubuntu
Description:     Ubuntu 16.04.3 LTS
Release:         16.04
Codename:        xenial
```

macOS

macOS is another operating system developed by Apple. In Table 3-9, you can see the list of major versions with their codenames and kernel versions (the macOS kernel is known as Darwin). Previously, macOS was known as "Mac OS X" (10.0–10.7) and "OS X" (10.8–10.11), but it was renamed to macOS in 10.12 to be consistent with other operating systems by Apple like iOS, watchOS, and tvOS.

---

[70]Different versions of .NET Core support different distributions.

Table 3-9. *List of Major Mac OS X / OS X / macOS Versions*

Title	Version	Codename	Darwin	Release date
Mac OS X	10.0	Cheetah	1.3.1	2001-03-24
Mac OS X	10.1	Puma	1.4.1	2001-09-25
Mac OS X	10.2	Jaguar	6	2002-08-24
Mac OS X	10.3	Panther	7	2003-10-24
Mac OS X	10.4	Tiger	8	2005-04-29
Mac OS X	10.5	Leopard	9	2007-10-26
Mac OS X	10.6	Snow Leopard	10	2009-08-28
Mac OS X	10.7	Lion	11	2011-07-20
OS X	10.8	Mountain Lion	12	2012-07-25
OS X	10.9	Mavericks	13	2013-22-10
OS X	10.10	Yosemite	14	2014-10-16
OS X	10.11	El Capitan	15	2015-09-30
macOS	10.12	Sierra	16	2016-09-20
macOS	10.13	High Sierra	17	2017-09-25
macOS	10.14	Mojave	18	2018-09-24

There are several ways to check your Mac version from the command line. The first one is to run `sw_vers`, which will give you output like this:

```
ProductName:     Mac OS X
ProductVersion:  10.14.2
BuildVersion:    18C54
```

If you need only the version number, you can run `sw_vers -productVersion` (it returns `10.14.2` in this case). If you need extended information (including the kernel version), run `system_profiler SPSoftwareDataType`. here are some typical lines in the output:

```
System Version:  macOS 10.14.2 (18C54)
Kernel Version:  Darwin 18.2.0
```

Now let's check which values we get from C# code on Mono and CoreCLR:

```
Environment.OSVersion = "Unix 18.2.0.0"
```

macOS is based on Unix, so macOS and Linux have much in common. Unfortunately, it's not possible to distinguish Linux and macOS via `Environment.OSVersion` because it returns "Unix" for modern versions of both operating systems. If you want to check what kind of OS you have without additional dependencies, you can do the following hack based on uname from `libc`:

```
[DllImport("libc", SetLastError = true)]
private static extern int uname(IntPtr buf);

private static string GetSysnameFromUname()
{
  var buf = IntPtr.Zero;
  try
  {
    buf = Marshal.AllocHGlobal(8192);
    // This is a hacktastic way of getting sysname from uname ()
    int rc = uname(buf);
    if (rc != 0)
    {
      throw new Exception("uname from libc returned " + rc);
    }

    string os = Marshal.PtrToStringAnsi(buf);
    return os;
  }
  finally
  {
    if (buf != IntPtr.Zero)
      Marshal.FreeHGlobal(buf);
  }
}
```

The `GetSysnameFromUname()` returns "Linux" for Linux and "Darwin" for macOS.

There is another way to get full info about the current OS version: you can install the `Microsoft.DotNet.PlatformAbstractions` NuGet packages (which require .NET Framework 4.5.1+ or .NET Standard 1.3+) and use the `RuntimeEnvironment` class from the `Microsoft.DotNet.PlatformAbstractions` namespace. Here is an example of the `RuntimeEnvironment` properties on macOS:

```
RuntimeEnvironment.OperatingSystem          = "Mac OS X"
RuntimeEnvironment.OperatingSystemPlatform  = "Darwin"
RuntimeEnvironment.OperatingSystemVersion   = "10.14"
```

If you target .NET Core, you can also use `System.Runtime.InteropServices.RuntimeInformation`.[71] `RuntimeInformation.OSDescription` will return a string like this:

```
Darwin 18.2.0 Darwin Kernel Version 18.2.0: Mon Nov 12 20:24:46 PST 2018;
root:xnu-4903.231.4~2/RELEASE_X86_64
```

This API is also available for .NET Framework 4.7.1+, but it returns "Unix 18.2.0.0" on Mono.

Mono 5.18+ supports OS X 10.9 and later.[72] .NET Core 1.0 supports macOS 10.11, 10.12; .NET Core 2.0 supports macOS 10.12+. In this book, we will discuss macOS 10.12+.

In the next subsection, we will talk about the hardware environment for the operating system.

Hardware

In the modern world, there are an enormous number of different devices. If you open technical specification for your computer or mobile phone, you will find many characteristics that are important for performance. It's pretty hard to compare different

---

[71]https://docs.microsoft.com/en-us/dotnet/api/system.runtime.interopservices.
runtimeinformation

[72]Previously, Mono supported Mac OS X 10.7+, but the requirement was updated because of the limitations in the TLS stack. See https://github.com/mono/mono/issues/9581

hardware; it's not always possible to say which device is faster because different devices can be optimized for specific use cases and be better only in specific situations.[73]

In this subsection, we are going to briefly discuss the main hardware components: CPU, RAM, disks, network hardware, and others.

The CPU is the heart of any computer. It's an electronic circuitry which performs all the basic operations like arithmetic, logical, and I/O (input/output). There many different companies that produce CPU chips: the most famous and popular are *Intel*, *AMD*, and *VIA Technologies*. Each CPU has an architecture that defines an instruction set. One of the most popular architectures is x86, with a 32-bit instruction set developed by Intel. There is a 64-bit version of this architecture called x64 (also known as x86_64, AMD64, or Intel 64). Initially, Intel tried to create another 64-bit architecture called Itanium, but it wasn't popular because it didn't support existing x86-based programs. Meanwhile, AMD developed its own instruction set, AMD64, which was backward compatible with x86. It became very popular, so Intel also decided to adopt it. While x86 and x64 are very popular on server and desktop machines, there is another architecture called ARM, which is widely used on mobile and embedded devices because it was designed for low power consumption. There are 32-bit and 64-bit versions of ARM: ARM32 and ARM64 .NET Core 2.1+ supports ARM32,[74] so you can run it even on Raspberry Pi.[75] Meanwhile, Mono supports many other architectures like MIPS, PowerPC, SPARC (32 bits), s390x (64 bits), and others.[76] There are a huge number of different processor architectures by different manufacturers, but in the scope of this book, we will be focused on x86 and x64.

If you create a classic .NET application from a template, you can find the following line in the corresponding csproj file:

```
<PlatformTarget>AnyCPU</PlatformTarget>
```

This means that your application can target any platform, no special requirements are specified. If you want to run the application only on a specific platform, you can change this value (e.g., you can specify x86 or x64).

---

[73]If you really want to compare two hardware configurations, you can use www.userbenchmark. com to get the basic device characteristics. It doesn't mean that you will know which hardware is better "in general," but you will get some expectation about it.

[74]https://github.com/dotnet/announcements/issues/29

[75]https://github.com/dotnet/core/blob/v2.1.3/samples/RaspberryPiInstructions.md

[76]www.mono-project.com/docs/about-mono/supported-platforms/

There is another interesting option that can you meet in csproj files:

```
<Prefer32bit>false</Prefer32bit>
```

The default value of `Prefer32bit` is `true`. This means that if you create a new classic .NET Framework project on Windows-x64 (which supports both x86 and x64 programs), it will be executed using x86 instruction set. If you want to run it on x64, you should set `PlatformTarget=x64` or `Prefer32bit=false`. The "AnyCPU with Prefer32bit" mode has a special feature: it will correctly work on ARM-based Windows while an x86 program will fail on ARM (you can find more details in [Goldshtein 2012]). If you compile C# files directly via a compiler, you can specify the platform via the `/platform:` argument (possible values: x86, x64, `Itanium`, `arm`, `anycpu32bitpreferred`, `anycpu`).

We are not going to discuss all kinds of CPU, but it's still pretty important to show how performance depends on CPU internals. In the scope of this book, we will focus on Intel Core iX processors. This lineup includes Core i3, Core i5, Core i7, and Core i9 (i5 is superior to i3, i7 is superior to i5, i9 is superior to i7). Each model has several different generations of microarchitectures (Micro-arch); you can find some of them in Table 3-10. Usually, you can guess the microarchitecture by a processor number. The full specification can be found on Intel's official website.[77]

Table 3-10. *List of Recent Intel Core iX Processors*

Gen	Process	Micro-arch	Codename	Release date
1	45nm	Nehalem	Nehalem	2008-11-17
1	32nm	Nehalem	Westmere	2010-01-04
2	32nm	Sandy Bridge	Sandy Bridge	2011-01-09
3	22nm	Sandy Bridge	Ivy Bridge	2012-04-29
4	22nm	Haswell	Haswell	2013-06-02
5	14nm	Haswell	Broadwell	2014-09-05
6	14nm	Skylake	Skylake	2015-08-05
7	14nm	Skylake	Kaby Lake	2017-01-03
8	14nm	Skylake	Coffee Lake	2017-10-05

---

[77]www.intel.com/content/www/us/en/processors/processor-numbers.html

A CPU can have several *physical cores*; each core can process instruction independently. A technology called *Hyperthreading* allows emulating two *logical cores* on a single physical core. One of the basic CPU characteristics is *CPU frequency* (or *CPU clock rate*). It defines the number of clock cycles per second. Each assembly instruction takes one or several CPU cycles. If you open the technical specifications of your CPU, you can find a single value that describes the primary CPU frequency. However, it's not a constant: the frequency can be dynamically or permanently changed with the help of *overclocking, underclocking, CPU throttling*, or other techniques. CPU has many other characteristics which are important for performance: a number of *CPU cache levels* and their size, supported sets of instructions (like *SSE* or *AVX*), advanced supported technologies (like *Power reduction technology*), and so on.

CPU is not the only hardware component "responsible" for performance. There are many others:

- **RAM**

  Each program operates with RAM all the time. In terms of performance, the kind of RAM we have (e.g., *DDR2*, *DDR3*, *DDR3L*, *DDR4*), its latency, frequency, and the total memory size (bad things may happen if you don't have enough memory) are all important.

- **Disks**

  Programs also require different memory storage devices to save data permanently. Again, we have so many options to save our data: *HDD*, *SSD*, *SSHD*, *RAID*, different kinds of storage virtualization, and so on.

- **Network hardware**

  Modern applications actively interact with the Internet or the local network. Network bandwidth also becomes a bottleneck for the application performance. If you want to send data from one computer to another, the "data transportation process" may involve a huge number of different network devices with different types of commutation.

- **Other hardware components**

  Depending on the application use cases, other hardware components also may be pretty important. If the application mines cryptocurrency, the *GPU model* can be pretty important. Advanced rendering 3D engines are also sensitive to the GPU's capabilities, but its performance can also depend on the *screen resolution*. Other components like the battery and cooler are also important.

During my performance investigations at JetBrains, I have six different physical computers on my desks: three equivalent Mac mini with installed macOS, Windows, and Linux; a MacBook Pro, a Linux desktop, and a Windows laptop. The three equivalent Mac mini allow comparing performance on different operating systems without concerns about different hardware. I also have three different monitors: two with 4K resolution and one without the 4K support. Such a setup is not a luxury; it's my primary tool which significantly simplifies my performance investigations. Of course, we also have a huge pool of remote machines, but these can't be used for all of our tasks because our main products like Rider and IntelliJ IDEA are desktop applications. It's pretty important to check performance under conditions that are similar to the user environment. Some of the tricky problems are HiDPI-specific, so a physical monitor is required; many UI benchmarks can't be executed correctly via a remote session.

Everything depends on your use cases. However, there are some "main" components that can be bottlenecks for most applications: *CPU*, *memory*, *disks*, *network*. We will discuss CPU and memory in detail in Chapters 7 and 8. And now we have the last part of the environment to discuss: the physical world.

The Physical World

The hardware always exists in some real physical conditions. These conditions can also affect the performance of your applications. In this section, we are going to briefly discuss some of the physical factors that have an influence on performance: temperature, vibrations, physical location, and humidity.

Temperature

Temperature is one of the most important physical characteristics in terms of performance and reliability. Companies that have their own data centers spend a huge amount of money and effort on thermal control. Handling cooling issues is a serious challenge, there are many technologies and approaches that try to solve them. For example, Microsoft even decided to create data centers under the sea (see [Roach 2018]).

Cooling is important not only for data centers but also for desktop computers and laptops. There are several ways to save your CPU from overheating. One of the most obvious approaches is to use an external cooler. It's not always enough, so we have another option to reduce the temperature. Most modern processors have a cool feature called CPU throttling. It allows dynamically changing the CPU frequency depending on external factors. Thus, if heavy calculations cause too-high temperatures that can't be handled by a cooler, we can slow down the CPU and reduce the amount of generated heat. This is also called thermal throttling.

There are many interesting stories about performance problems and CPU throttling, but I'm going to tell you my favorite one. In July 2018, Apple started to sell a new generation of MacBook Pro, which included a model with six-core Intel Core i9 processors. It was supposed to be a high-performance device, but there was a bug in the thermal management system: when you started to do a lot of CPU-bound calculations, the temperature rose and the thermal throttling significantly slowed down the CPU clock rate. As a result, it worked slower than the cheaper MacBook of the same generation with the less advanced Core i7 processor. Some users complained (see [Lee 2018]) that it could outperform i7 only if you put the MacBook in a freezer. The bug was fixed by a software update in the macOS High Sierra 10.13.6 Supplemental Update.

Thermal throttling is not a rare event; I observe it all the time on different laptops. In general, it's a good technology because it protects your computers from damage. However, it's a serious problem for benchmarking: a sudden throttling can completely distort your performance measurements.

Vibrations

While temperature is important for CPU-bound programs, vibrations can affect disk-bound operations if you are using an HDD. It has mechanical parts, so any vibrations may affect its performance or reliability.

There is a famous video by Brendan Gregg called "Shouting in the Datacenter" (see [Gregg 2008]). In this video, Brendan screams at hard disk drives and shows real-time latency charts with peaks at the moments of screaming. This experiment demonstrates that even "scream" vibrations can significantly increase the latency of I/O operations.

There are some other interesting effects based on the sensitivity of HDD to vibrations. For example, in the kscope[78] project, Alfredo Ortega demonstrates how HDD can be used as a microphone: he measures the latency of disk operations and calculates the HDD frequency. He also uses this technique for another program called hdd-killer: if we play a sound with the current HDD frequency, it will resonate with the hardware and can seriously damage the hardware (in addition to causing changes in performance).

In [Shahrad 2017], scientists from Princeton University present an another attack based on acoustic resonance. They show how an attacker can disable a closed-circuit television (CCTV) system by targeting its digital video recorder (DVR) device. The same attack can also target a personal computer, causing a failure of an operating system.

Another interesting HDD "feature" is the active hard-drive protection. When the internal accelerometer detects excess acceleration or vibration, the hard drive unloads its heads to prevent damage. Thus, if you accidentally drop your laptop with an HDD during disk-bound benchmarking, you may observe performance regression at this moment.

As you can see, vibration is a serious issue for HDD performance. During benchmarking, you can get performance perturbations because of vibration, which can be incorrectly interpreted if you don't know about such phenomena. If you are using an SSD, you can ignore vibration because such disks have no moving parts. However, hard disk drives are still widely used, so it's good to know about possible performance problems.

Physical location

In the modern world, many people actively use different mobile applications on phones and tablets. The network becomes the bottleneck for most of such applications: performance depends on the signal strength. You have probably experienced a poor signal in the country or on a picnic in the woods: a browser and all the applications work superslow. Typical operations that are usually performed instantly may take many seconds or even minutes. Unfortunately, developers often forget about this during the development of their own mobile applications and run target benchmarks only with a good signal. This is probably not the best strategy if you want to make all of your users happy.

---

[78]https://github.com/ortegaalfredo/kscope/

Thus, developers who care about performance in all possible locations try to handle cases with poor signal. Some of the approaches look pretty interesting. For example, in [Colwell 2018], Brien Colwell speaks about a "distributed node device lab." Basically, it's a box with many Android and iOS devices. Such boxes were deployed in different cities to different locations: secure office buildings, base station, retail stores, data centers, moving cars/buses, and so on. With this approach, his team was able to detect places with poor signal, collect relevant metrics, make a recording of tests with performance problems, debug these tests, and fix them.

Some companies are trying to emulate poor connection in the office.[79] For example, in Facebook, there is a practice called "2G Tuesdays" (see [McCormick 2015]): they simulate a superslow Internet connection for an hour. It helps developers to get the same experience that other people with 2G Internet have. With this simple exercise, they can find features that are not optimized for a slow connection.

Humidity

Physical location is not the only factor that affects the signal strength. In [Luomala 2015], researchers from the University of Jyvaskyla investigated how temperature and humidity affect radio signal strength in outdoor wireless sensor networks. They conducted many experiments during different seasons (winter/summer) and times of day (day/night) in different weather conditions. They showed the relationship between the weather and radio signal strength. We already discussed that temperature may affect performance, but we talked about the hardware temperature and CPU-bound operations. According to the research, the outdoor temperature (and humidity) may affect network-bound operations. Thus, we can get different performance metrics in the same location depending on the weather.

The physical conditions are very important for any hardware. External factors like temperature, vibrations, physical location, humidity, and others have an influence on the application performance.[80] Hardware does not exist in a vacuum; don't forget about the physical world. If you know which external factors are important for a specific

---

[79]There are a lot of different ways to emulate low network connectivity. Here is a pretty interesting way to do it: https://stackoverflow.com/a/8630401

[80]External conditions can have pretty strange effects on hardware. Here is an interesting Twitter thread where John Hyphen explains why he was late: https://twitter.com/JohnHyphen/status/971405857446645761. His clock shows incorrect time because of the unbalanced frequency in the electricity grid.

benchmark (CPU-bound, disk-bound, and network-bound benchmarks are sensitive to different factors), you can predict possible problems that can spoil the measurements, and then you can stabilize the result by controlling external conditions.

Now let's discuss a few interesting stories about external environmental factors that can significantly affect performance.

Case Study 1: Windows Updates and Changes in .NET Framework

Developers usually care about the runtime versions and don't care about the OS version. However, the OS version can also be pretty important. For example, minor Windows updates can change the installed versions of the .NET Framework.

There was a bug known as coreclr#11574[81] in RyuJIT optimizations that affected .NET Framework 4.7. Consider the following code from the issue:

```
using System;

class Program
{
  static byte[] s_arr2;
  static byte[] s_arr3;

  static void Init()
  {
    s_arr2 = new byte[] { 0x11, 0x12, 0x13 };
    s_arr3 = new byte[] { 0x21, 0x22, 0x33 };
  }

  static void Main(string[] args)
  {
    Init();

    byte[] arr1 = new byte[] { 2 };
    byte[] arr2 = s_arr2;
    byte[] arr3 = s_arr3;
```

---

[81]https://github.com/dotnet/coreclr/issues/11574

```
    int len = arr1.Length + arr2.Length + arr3.Length;
    int cur = 0;
    Console.WriteLine("1: cur = {0}", cur);
    cur += arr1.Length;
    Console.WriteLine("2: cur += {0}, now {1}", arr1.Length, cur);
    cur += arr2.Length;
    Console.WriteLine("3: cur += {0}, now {1}", arr2.Length, cur);
    cur += arr3.Length;
    Console.WriteLine("4: cur += {0}, now {1}", arr3.Length, cur);
    Console.WriteLine("5: len is {0}", len);
  }
}
```

Because of the bug, this code snippet printed the following output:

```
1: cur = 0
2: cur += 1, now 1
3: cur += 3, now 6
4: cur += 3, now 7
5: len is 7
```

In the 3: cur += 3, now 6 line, we can see that the cur value is miscalculated: we got 6 instead of 4. The bug was fixed in .NET Framework September 2017 Security and Quality Rollup.

Let's say you have Windows 10 1703 installed (10.0.15063). The bug fix for this version was included in KB4038788[82] (a part of the .NET Framework September 2017 Security and Quality Rollup[83]), which corresponds to Windows 10.0.15063.608 (September 12, 2017). If you have an earlier version of 1703 (10.0.15063.x where x is 0, 13, 138, 250, 296, 297, 332, 413, 414, 447, 483, 502, or 540), you have this bug. If you have the update (10.0.15063.x where x is 608 or higher), you don't have the bug. .NET Framework versions are the same, and the main parts of Windows version (major.minor.build) are the same, but the logic of RyuJIT optimizations depends on the Windows revision number.

---

[82]https://support.microsoft.com/en-us/help/4038788/windows-10-update-kb4038788
[83]https://blogs.msdn.microsoft.com/dotnet/2017/09/12/
  net-framework-september-2017-security-and-quality-rollup/

If you share some performance results for .NET Framework, it's recommended to share also the full version of your Windows (include the revision number).

Conclusion:

- **Windows revision number matters.**

  The full versions of the installed .NET Framework may be not enough to fully describe the behavior of your applications. Windows updates can contain some important fixes for existing versions of the runtime.

AN EXERCISE

Check out other .NET Framework Security and Quality Rollups (you can find it in the Microsoft .NET Blog[84]) and try to find other JIT-specific changes.

Case Study 2: Meltdown, Spectre, and Critical Patches

Meltdown and Spectre are probably the biggest known CPU security vulnerabilities of the 21st century. They were disclosed on January 3, 2018, and it was huge news. Long story short: these vulnerabilities allow you to read data from OS kernels or other processes without permissions. It affects almost all modern CPUs (Intel, AMD, ARM) manufactured since 1995 (with some limitations). We will skip detailed descriptions of these vulnerabilities (because it's out of the scope of this book), but you can read more in [Meltdown] and [Spectre].[85]

This sounds impressive, but these vulnerabilities are security issues. Why should we care about performance here? Some of the most important security holes were fixed by OS patches (without hardware updates). These patches for most popular operating systems were published almost immediately. The only drawback was performance reduction of up to 30% (for some use cases). You can easily google many other reports about performance problems that occurred as a result of the vulnerability fixes. One of my favorite blog posts is [Gregg 2018] by Brendan Gregg.

---

[84]https://blogs.msdn.microsoft.com/dotnet/
[85]If you like stories about interesting vulnerabilities, it's also recommended to read [Foreshadow].

An important fact: we are talking about minor OS updates. Well, these performance updates contain huge changes and huge performance impacts, even though they are minor.

Conclusions:

- **The operating system versions matter.**

  Not only the major part, even the build and revision number matter a lot. And it's not only about .NET Framework; it's about the overall OS performance for all kinds of software.

- **Security fixes can slow down your applications.**

  If an update changelog doesn't include information about performance changes, it doesn't mean that you will not get a performance drop. It's a common situation when security patches fix vulnerabilities by sacrificing performance.

AN EXERCISE

Take hardware that is affected by Meltdown and do your own performance research. You should write some benchmarks and show the performance problems that were introduced by the security fixes. You may use old and new versions of your favorite OS or find a way to disable the Meltdown patches. It's not a quick and easy exercise, but it will help you to learn some important skills.

Case Study 3: MSBuild and Windows Defender

This is another story about Rider. Once, we bought new physical machines for our performance agent pool. We deployed Windows, Linux, and macOS images on them and started to run a specific part of our test suite several times per day. We checked the current level of performance; everything was fine. After a few days, we noticed a serious performance degradation for some tests on Windows. We tried to revert the latest commits, but it didn't help: these tests still took a tremendous amount of time. After an investigation, it turned out that the culprit was Windows Defender![86] The biggest part

---

[86]www.microsoft.com/en-us/windows/windows-defender/

of the degraded test involved a solution build, which produced many I/O operations. Windows Defender[87] can slow down such operations, especially if a process creates many exe and dll files. Unfortunately, it's not so trivial to disable Windows Defender: if you just turn it off in the settings, it will be enabled again after reboot. This is what happened on the day of degradation. There is a way to disable it permanently, but this approach wasn't applied to our updated Windows images because of a mistake. In Figure 3-5, you can see the performance plot for one of such tests: we had about **28** seconds with enabled Windows Defender and **4** seconds after this environment fix.

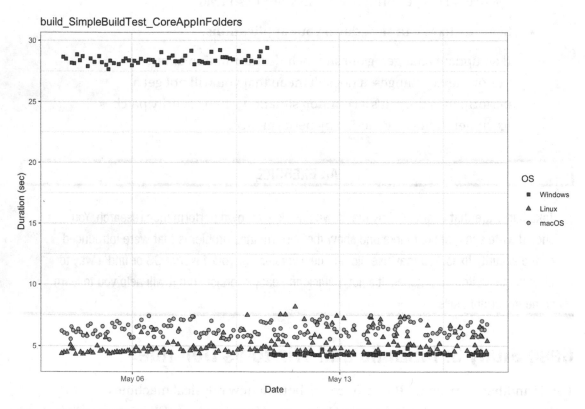

Figure 3-5. *Performance plot of Rider SimpleBuildTest*

There are a lot of OS processes that can slow down your benchmarks. For example, after another update of our macOS agents, we got a 300% performance degradation. After a short investigation, it turned out that the only problem was about the screen saver

---

[87]You can find it in the process explorer by looking for msmpeng.exe process.

process, which was accidentally enabled during the update. This is a common problem for macOS VMs; you can find more details in [Albrechtslund 2013].

Conclusion:

- **Some OS features can significantly slow down your program.**

  As you can see, Windows Defender has a significant impact on some workloads with a huge number of I/O operations. If you want to get better performance with local projects, it makes sense to add your work directory to the list of Windows Defender exclusions. During benchmarking, you can monitor the process explorer and check for any processes which do CPU, disk, or network operations. This sanity check will help you to verify that performance measurements are not spoiled by other processes.

AN EXERCISE

If you are working on Windows, check if Windows Defender is enabled and does it have your work directory in the exclusions list. Try to rebuild your project with enabled and disabled Windows Defender. If you are lucky enough and the build process of the project is simple, you will not observe any different for these configurations. In another case, you may also discover some interesting performance impacts.

Case Study 4: Pause Latency and Intel Skylake

Now let's talk about different CPU models. People often don't expect serious performance changes during an upgrade on the next CPU microarchitecture. If you ask your colleagues "What is the difference between fifth and sixth Intel Core iX generations?", you probably get an answer like "The sixth generation is better, it should work faster," but most developers can't explain why it works "faster" and what "better" means. In fact, next-generation CPUs are not always faster; some workloads can be even slower. Let's look at an example.

In the x86 instruction set, there is the `pause` instruction. It's used by `Thread.`
`SpinWait`[88] for spin-wait loops. This method may help to improve performance in
multithreaded applications because threads can acquire locks without expensive context
switching. In [Intel OptManual], section 8.4.7, we can find interesting information about
the `pause` latency:

> The latency of PAUSE instruction in prior generation
> microarchitecture is about **10 cycles**, whereas on Skylake
> microarchitecture it has been extended to as many as **140 cycles**.
>
> ...
>
> As the PAUSE latency has been increased significantly, workloads
> that are sensitive to PAUSE latency will suffer some performance
> loss.

140 CPU cycles may sound like a small value. For example, on a CPU with a 2.0GHz
frequency, it takes about $140 \cdot 1$ sec $/(2 \cdot 10^9)$ or 70 nanoseconds. Should we really worry
about it? With the original idea, the increased `pause` latency should have a positive
performance impact on highly threaded applications. However, everything depends on
the implementation. It turned out that this change affected many .NET applications. For
example, Alois Kraus reported about a 50% performance drop in some cases in [Kraus
2018]. The described situation is pretty typical for heavily multithreaded applications.
Imagine many threads that try to acquire a lock on the same object. To avoid heavy
context switches, each thread tries to do spin wait first. In .NET Core 2.0/.NET
Framework 4.7.2, the locking implementation contained many iterations with `Thread.`
`SpinWait(PlatformHelper.ProcessorCount * (4 << i))` calls, where `i` is the index of
an iteration. Such calls became pretty expensive with the 140 as the `pause` latency on the
big values of `i`: each thread continues to be alive, spending more and more CPU time on
each iteration. The corresponding .NET Core issue was reported in coreclr#13388.[89]
It was actively discussed on GitHub; you can find many interesting details there. The issue
was fixed in coreclr#13556[90] by replacing these expensive calls with `Thread.SpinWait`
`(4 << i)`: this small edit solved the original problem. The fix is available in .NET Core

---

[88]https://docs.microsoft.com/en-us/dotnet/standard/threading/spinwait
[89]https://github.com/dotnet/coreclr/issues/13388
[90]https://github.com/dotnet/coreclr/pull/13556

2.1.0 and .NET Framework 4.8 Preview.[91] Later, the implementation was significantly improved (see coreclr#13670[92] and coreclr#29989[93]).

Conclusions:

- **Processor model matters.**

  Typically, people don't care about the CPU model generations (especially when the frequency is the same). However, on some workloads, different CPU models can show a significant performance difference.

- **Some instructions can have performance regression in new versions of processors.**

  Most developers expect small performance improvements with hardware updates and don't expect any serious regression. But this is not always the case; performance is often about trade-offs. Engineers from Intel have decided to change the `pause` latency to optimize some workloads by sacrificing performance of other workloads.

AN EXERCISE

Read the GitHub discussion about this problem and [Kraus 2018]. Write your own multithreaded benchmark that shows the difference between .NET Core 2.0.0 and 2.1.0 (you will need a proper CPU).

Summing Up

When people say "program environment," they often mean a specific version of a particular runtime. However, any runtime has its own external environment: it's running on an operating system (like Windows, Linux, or macOS). An OS also has an external environment,

---

[91]https://github.com/Microsoft/dotnet-framework-early-access/blob/master/release-notes/NET48/dotnet-48-changes.md

[92]https://github.com/dotnet/coreclr/pull/13670

[93]https://github.com/dotnet/corefx/pull/29989

namely, hardware, which includes CPU (with a specific architecture like x86 or x64), RAM, disks, network hardware, and other components. And the hardware also has its own external environment: the physical world with variable temperature, vibrations, and humidity.

Benchmarking requires an understanding of these environmental factors and how they can affect performance. In this section, we briefly discussed each of them and introduced some terms and technologies. We will use them in subsequent chapters to illustrate some theoretical concepts. You won't be able to know each aspect of each environment component (and we are not going to discuss even a fraction of them). It's enough to understand which factors may be important for specific performance measurements. This knowledge will help you to design benchmark experiments and make correct conclusions.

Summary

The only thing that you should learn from this chapter is simple: **environment matters**. You can't discuss the performance of abstract source code in general case.

In this chapter, we covered the following environment-specific topics:

- **Runtime**

    - **.NET Framework**

        The original version of .NET platform by Microsoft. Initially, it was closed source. The source code of some core runtimes parts was open for reading (*Rotor*). Currently, the source code for the basic class library for .NET Framework 4.5.1+ is also available. Works only on Windows.

    - **.NET Core**

        An alternative implementation of .NET Framework by Microsoft. It's a cross-platform and open source project (available on GitHub).

    - **Mono**

        Another alternative implementation of the .NET platform. The first versions were maintained by Xamarin, but now the project belongs to .NET Foundation. It's a cross-platform and open source project (available on GitHub).

- **Compilation**

  - **IL generation**

    C# compiler translates your C# code into IL. There were two
    generations of C# compilers by Microsoft: *the legacy compiler*
    (C# 1 .. C# 5) and *Roslyn* (since C# 6). Mono had its own
    implementation of C# compiler (*msc*) but it was replaced
    by Roslyn in Mono 5.0.0. Another important component of
    the .NET infrastructure is a build system. The most popular
    build system, which was a part of .NET Framework from the
    beginning, is *MSBuild*. Mono had its own build system (*XBuild*)
    but it was replaced by MSBuild in Mono 5.0.0. There are some
    build toolchains on top of MSBuild like *.NET Core SDK* (the
    primary way to build and run SDK-style projects), *Cake, Fake,
    Nuke,* and so on.

  - **JIT compilation**

    JIT compiler translates your IL code into native code during
    runtime. The original JIT in .NET Framework is *LegacyJIT*.
    Since .NET Framework 4.6, it has been replaced by *RyuJIT* for
    x64 (you can still switch to LegacyJIT if you want). .NET Core
    has used RyuJIT from the beginning. Mono has its own JIT
    implementation (*MonoJIT*).

  - **AOT compilation**

    Besides JIT compilation, we have different AOT toolchains.
    AOT means that we create native code in advance (before
    the program execution is started). There are several ways to
    perform AOT, like *NGen, Crossgen, Mono AOT, .NET Native,* or
    CoreRT.

- **External environment**

  - **Operating system**

    There are many different operating systems. In this book, we
    will usually discuss Windows, Linux, and macOS.

175

- **Hardware**

  The most important hardware components are *CPU*, *RAM*, *disks*, and *network hardware*. In this book, Chapters 7 and 8 demonstrate how hardware capabilities affect performance.

- **The physical world**

  Many physical characteristics and external conditions like temperature, vibrations, and humidity are also important in terms of performance.

The environment is one of the key components of your performance space. Even minor changes in the environment could significantly affect benchmarks. If you want to share some performance results, it's a good practice to share as much information about your environment as possible.

Of course, you don't need all this information in all kinds of benchmarks. It's also good to think about possible bottlenecks and what component of the environment is important for your case. For example, in a CPU-bound benchmark, the most important environment factor is the processor model. In a disk-bound benchmark, it's worth it to check the disk model. If you are not sure which environment properties you need, it's better to write down more details than fewer details. Any of these answers could be very helpful for people who work with your benchmarks. Always think about your environment and don't forget to share it with performance results.

References

[Akinshin 2015] Akinshin, Andrey. 2015. "A Bug Story About JIT-X64." February 27. `https://aakinshin.net/blog/post/subexpression-elimination-bug-in-jit-x64/`.

[Albrechtslund 2013] Albrechtslund, Mads Fog. 2013. "Save CPU Time, Disable Screen Saver on Mac OS X VMs." `https://hazenet.dk/2013/06/01/save-cpu-time-disable-screen-saver-on-mac-os-x-vms/`.

[Colwell 2018] "Mobile Performance Testing in Real User Conditions." 2018. Presented at the Performance @Scale 2018, March 13. `https://atscaleconference.com/videos/mobile-performance-testing-in-real-user-conditions/`.

[Craver 2015] Craver, Nick. 2015. "Why You Should Wait on Upgrading to .Net 4.6." July 27. `https://nickcraver.com/blog/2015/07/27/why-you-should-wait-on-dotnet-46/`.

[Foreshadow] Weisse, Ofir, Jo Van Bulck, Marina Minkin, Daniel Genkin, Baris Kasikci, Frank Piessens, Mark Silberstein, Raoul Strackx, Thomas F. Wenisch, and Yuval Yarom. 2018. "Foreshadow-Ng: Breaking the Virtual Memory Abstraction with Transient Out-of-Order Execution." Technical report. https://foreshadowattack.eu/foreshadow-NG.pdf.

[Goldshtein 2012] Goldshtein, Sasha. 2012. "What AnyCPU Really Means as of .NET 4.5 and Visual Studio 11." April 4. http://blogs.microsoft.co.il/sasha/2012/04/04/what-anycpu-really-means-as-of-net-45-and-visual-studio-11/.

[Gregg 2008] "Shouting in the Datacenter." 2008. December 31. www.youtube.com/watch?v=tDacjrSCeq4.

[Gregg 2018] Gregg, Brendan. 2018. "KPTI/KAISER Meltdown Initial Performance Regressions." February 9. www.brendangregg.com/blog/2018-02-09/kpti-kaiser-meltdown-performance.html.

[Guev 2017] Guev, Timur. 2017. "StringBuilder: The Past and the Future." February 13. http://codingsight.com/stringbuilder-the-past-and-the-future/.

[Hanselman 2018] Hanselman, Scott. 2018. "Detecting That a .NET Core App Is Running in a Docker Container and SkippableFacts in XUnit." June 29. www.hanselman.com/blog/DetectingThatANETCoreAppIsRunningInADockerContainerAndSkippableFactsInXUnit.aspx.

[Intel OptManual] *Intel® 64 and IA-32 Architectures Optimization Reference Manual* (248966-033). 2016. www.intel.com/content/dam/www/public/us/en/documents/manuals/64-ia-32-architectures-optimization-manual.pdf.

[Kraus 2018] Kraus, Alois. 2018. "Why Skylake CPUs Are Sometimes 50% Slower – How Intel Has Broken Existing Code." June 16. https://aloiskraus.wordpress.com/2018/06/16/why-skylakex-cpus-are-sometimes-50-slower-how-intel-has-broken-existing-code/.

[Lander 2015] Lander, Rich. 2015. "Announcing .NET Framework 4.6." *Microsoft .NET Blog.* July 20. https://blogs.msdn.microsoft.com/dotnet/2015/07/20/announcing-net-framework-4-6/.

[Lander 2018a] Lander, Rich. 2018. "Announcing .NET Core 3 Preview 1 and Open Sourcing Windows Desktop Frameworks." *Microsoft .NET Blog.* December 4. https://blogs.msdn.microsoft.com/dotnet/2018/12/04/announcing-net-core-3-preview-1-and-open-sourcing-windows-desktop-frameworks/.

[Lander 2018b] Lander, Rich. 2018. "NET Core 3 and Support for Windows Desktop Applications." *Microsoft .NET Blog*. May 7. https://blogs.msdn.microsoft.com/dotnet/2018/05/07/net-core-3-and-support-for-windows-desktop-applications/.

[Landwerth 2017a] Landwerth, Immo. 2017. "Explaining .NET Standard Versioning in Front of My Fire Place." October 6. www.youtube.com/watch?v=vMRSlQ5modg.

[Landwerth 2017b] Landwerth, Immo. 2017. "Announcing the Windows Compatibility Pack for .NET Core." *Microsoft .NET Blog*. November 16. https://blogs.msdn.microsoft.com/dotnet/2017/11/16/announcing-the-windows-compatibility-pack-for-net-core/.

[Lee 2018] Lee, Dave. 2018. "MacBook Pro 15 (2018) - Beware the Core I9." July 17. www.youtube.com/watch?v=Dx8J125s4cg.

[Le Roy 2017] Le Roy, Bertrand, and Daniel Podder. 2017. "Profile-Guided Optimization in .NET Core 2.0." July 20. https://blogs.msdn.microsoft.com/dotnet/2017/07/20/profile-guided-optimization-in-net-core-2-0/.

[Lippert 2009] Lippert, Eric. 2009. "Closing over the Loop Variable Considered Harmful." November 12. https://blogs.msdn.microsoft.com/ericlippert/2009/11/12/closing-over-the-loop-variable-considered-harmful/.

[Lock 2018] Lock, Andrew. 2018. "Why Is string.GetHashCode() Different Each Time I Run My Program in .NET Core?" https://andrewlock.net/why-is-string-gethashcode-different-each-time-i-run-my-program-in-net-core/.

[Luomala 2015] Luomala, Jari, and Ismo Hakala. 2015. "Effects of Temperature and Humidity on Radio Signal Strength in Outdoor Wireless Sensor Networks." In *Computer Science and Information Systems (Fedcsis), 2015 Federated Conference*, 1247–55. IEEE. doi:https://doi.org/10.15439/2015F241.

[McCormick 2015] McCormick, Rich. 2015. "Facebook's '2G Tuesdays' Simulate Super Slow Internet in the Developing World." *The Verge*. October 28. www.theverge.com/2015/10/28/9625062/facebook-2g-tuesdays-slow-internet-developing-world.

[Meltdown] Lipp, Moritz, Michael Schwarz, Daniel Gruss, Thomas Prescher, Werner Haas, Stefan Mangard, Paul Kocher, Daniel Genkin, Yuval Yarom, and Mike Hamburg. 2018. "Meltdown." *arXiv Preprint arXiv:1801.01207*, January. https://meltdownattack.com/meltdown.pdf.

[MSDOCS RyuJIT] ".NET Framework - Troubleshooting RyuJIT." n.d. *Microsoft Docs*. https://github.com/Microsoft/dotnet/blob/master/Documentation/testing-with-ryujit.md.

[Osenkov 2011] Osenkov, Kirill. 2011. "Introducing the Microsoft 'Roslyn' CTP." *The Visual Studio Blog.* October 19. https://blogs.msdn.microsoft.com/visualstudio/2011/10/19/introducing-the-microsoft-roslyn-ctp/.

[Roach 2018] Roach, John. 2018. "Under the Sea, Microsoft Tests a Datacenter That's Quick to Deploy, Could Provide Internet Connectivity for Years." Microsoft News. June 5. https://news.microsoft.com/features/under-the-sea-microsoft-tests-a-datacenter-thats-quick-to-deploy-could-provide-internet-connectivity-for-years/.

[RyuJIT 2013] "RyuJIT: The Next-Generation JIT Compiler for .NET." *Microsoft .NET Blog.* September 30. https://blogs.msdn.microsoft.com/dotnet/2013/09/30/ryujit-the-next-generation-jit-compiler-for-net/.

[Shahrad 2017] Shahrad, Mohammad, Arsalan Mosenia, Liwei Song, Mung Chiang, David Wentzlaff, and Prateek Mittal. 2017. "Acoustic Denial of Service Attacks on Hdds." *arXiv Preprint arXiv:1712.07816*, December. https://arxiv.org/abs/1712.07816v1.

[SSCLI Internals] Pobar, Joel, Ted Neward, D. Stutz, and G. Shilling. 2008. "Shared Source Cli 2.0 Internals."

[Spectre] Kocher, Paul, Daniel Genkin, Daniel Gruss, Werner Haas, Mike Hamburg, Moritz Lipp, Stefan Mangard, Thomas Prescher, Michael Schwarz, and Yuval Yarom. 2018. "Spectre Attacks: Exploiting Speculative Execution." *arXiv Preprint arXiv:1801.01203*, January. https://spectreattack.com/spectre.pdf.

[Torgersen 2018] Torgersen, Mads. 2018. "How Microsoft Rewrote Its C# Compiler in C# and Made It Open Source." September 26. https://medium.com/microsoft-open-source-stories/how-microsoft-rewrote-its-c-compiler-in-c-and-made-it-open-source-4ebed5646f98.

[Toub 2017] Toub, Stephen. 2017. "Performance Improvements in .NET Core." *Microsoft .NET Blog.* June 7. https://blogs.msdn.microsoft.com/dotnet/2017/06/07/performance-improvements-in-net-core/.

[Toub 2018] Toub, Stephen. 2018. "Performance Improvements in .NET Core 2.1." *Microsoft .NET Blog.* April 18. https://blogs.msdn.microsoft.com/dotnet/2018/04/18/performance-improvements-in-net-core-2-1/.

[Warren 2018a] Warren, Matt. 2018. "A History of .NET Runtimes." October 2. http://mattwarren.org/2018/10/02/A-History-of-.NET-Runtimes/.

[Warren 2018b] Warren, Matt. 2018. "CoreRT - A .NET Runtime for AOT." June 7. https://mattwarren.org/2018/06/07/CoreRT-.NET-Runtime-for-AOT/.

CHAPTER 4

Statistics for Performance Engineers

Without data you're just another person with an opinion.

— W. Edwards Deming, a data scientist

In this chapter, we are going to discuss statistics and how to apply it to benchmarking. You will learn many useful approaches and techniques to help you improve your benchmark design and analyze the results.

There are many excellent books about statistics. For me as an author, it would be easy to name a few books and say: "Read them if you want to analyze benchmark results." However, there are several problems with this idea. First of all, most developers don't want to read books about statistics. And this is understandable: such books typically contain a lot of information that is irrelevant for your current task. Thus, most developers just don't find them useful and interesting enough. Even if you read some good books about statistics, the human mind has a nasty "feature": it quickly forgets information that it's not using. If you had statistics lessons in the past and don't have statistics experience in the present, you probably can't reproduce all the important formulas and approaches.

Even if you perfectly remember everything, it's often unclear how to apply statistics in the real world for *performance distributions*. "Performance distribution" means that we got this distribution from real performance measurements. Such distributions have many properties that may be nontypical for other data sources. Unfortunately, many classic academic approaches just don't work when you try to apply them to performance distributions. In this chapter, you will find many practical recommendations about how to use different metrics in real life. Here you will not find any classic examples about balls in a box or presidential elections. We will focus only on how to *use statistics in*

A. Akinshin, *Pro .NET Benchmarking*, https://doi.org/10.1007/978-1-4842-4941-3_4

benchmarking. Some of these recommendations can't be applied for statistical research in general. Also, they can be invalid for some specific performance investigations. However, they contain empirical rules that work in *most cases* and help you make initial hypotheses about your data.

In this chapter, we are going to cover the following topics:

- **Descriptive statistics**

  A set of measurements forms a distribution, which can be described by special statistical metrics: minimum, maximum, median, mean, percentiles, quartiles, variance, standard error, and others. We will discuss how to calculate all these values and correctly interpret them. Sometimes it's hard to work with raw numbers, so we will learn several ways to visualize data.

- **Performance analysis**

  How can two distributions be compared? How can a relationship between a method's performance and its parameters be detected? How can the parameters that have the most impact on performance be found? We are going to answer all these questions and cover important concepts like the null and alternative hypotheses, Type I and Type II errors, and p-values. Statistics can be useful not only after a performance experiment, but also during this experiment. You can adaptively choose the best number of iterations and other experiment options instead of choosing magic numbers in advance.

- **How to lie with benchmarking**

  It's pretty easy to fool yourself or others with the help of statistics. For self-defense, you need to know the most popular ways to lie with benchmarking. We will learn many deceiving techniques based on small samples, percentages, ratios, plots, and data dredging.

We are not going to cover the internal implementations of the statistical algorithms. In practice, it's almost always better to take an existing implementation and consider such algorithms as black boxes. The most important skills are related to the correct interpretation of statistical metrics rather than how they are calculated (only the simplest formulas will be presented). Some of the statements about statistics are not mathematically strict: this is to simplify the explanations and skip many footnotes about corner cases that you shouldn't worry about. In benchmarking, you don't need an in-depth knowledge of statistics: it's enough to know the main concepts and how they should be used.

We assume that we already have well-designed benchmarks that were executed in the right environment without any mistakes. The output of these benchmarks is not a single number; it's a set of different numbers that form a distribution (even if we are executing benchmarking in the same environment). Let's start with the basics and learn how to describe typical performance distributions.

Descriptive Statistics

In this section, we are going to discuss essential statistical metrics and visualizations that help to explore a single distribution.

Let's say that we have a benchmark that produces a single performance metrics in the output (e.g., the operation duration). If we run this benchmark n times, we will get a new number for each iteration. We will denote them as $x_1, x_2, \ldots, x_n$. This set of measurements is known as a *sample* x, and n is the *sample size*. It would be simpler if all these numbers were equal. Unfortunately, that's not the case: these measurements form a distribution that should be analyzed. Let's learn some approaches to help aggregate and analyze such samples. We will discuss such topics as basic sample plots (timeline plot, rug plot, histograms, density plots, waterfall plots), sample size, minimum, maximum, range, mean, median, quantiles, quartiles, percentiles, five-number summary, interquartile range (IQR), outliers, box plots, frequency trails, modes, standard deviation, variance, normal distribution, skewness, kurtosis, standard error, confidence intervals, and the central limit theorem.

Basic Sample Plots

Analyzing tons of raw numbers is hard. You can simplify this analysis with the help of good visualizations. A picture is worth a thousand numbers: you can instantly understand distribution properties with a good chart, but it's not always possible if you just look at numbers. There are several ways to draw a distribution. Here are some of the most popular ways:

- **Timeline plot**

  You can see an example of a timeline plot in Figure 4-1 (the central part with dots). It's the most direct way to display the measurements. For each iteration i (x axis), we draw a point that corresponds to the duration x_i (y axis) of this iteration.

- **Rug plot**

  You can see an example of a rug plot in Figure 4-1 (the right part with horizontal dashes). It's a one-dimensional plot with all measurements. It contains all x_i values on a single axis. You can imagine it as a "compressed" version of the timeline plot where the information about the iteration indexes is omitted.

- **Histogram**

  You can see an example of a histogram in Figure 4-2 (A). A histogram shows the *shape* of your distribution. It's a bar chart where each bar (also known as *bin*) shows how many measurements we have in the corresponding interval. If one bar is twice as high as another bar, it contains twice as many values from the sample. Usually, all bins have the same width, but you can choose your own binning functions (e.g., logarithmic). If you want to use the fixed width size, there are many different approaches to choosing this size.[1]

- **Density plot**

  You can see an example of a density plot in Figure 4-2 (B). A density plot is a "smooth version" of a histogram. It shows the distribution shape with the help of a smooth curve instead of a set of bins. If you don't care about specific bin heights and just want to know what the distribution looks like, the density plot is preferred because it has less visual noise. A histogram and a

---

[1]For example, Scott's normal reference rule, Rice rule, Freedman–Diaconis' choice, Doane's formula, square-root choice, Sturges' formula, and others.

density plot can be combined into one picture as presented in Figure 4-2 (C).

- **Density waterfall plots**

  If you have many distributions for the same benchmark, it may be hard to analyze them one by one. A waterfall plot combines many images and displays them on the same picture one under the other. A plot overlapping helps to make it compact. You can see an example of a density waterfall plot in Figure 4-2 (D).

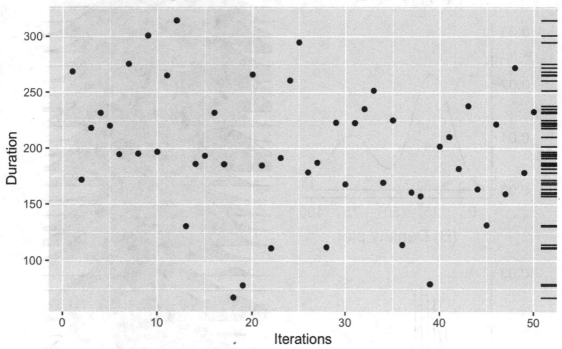

Figure 4-1. *Timeline and rug plots*

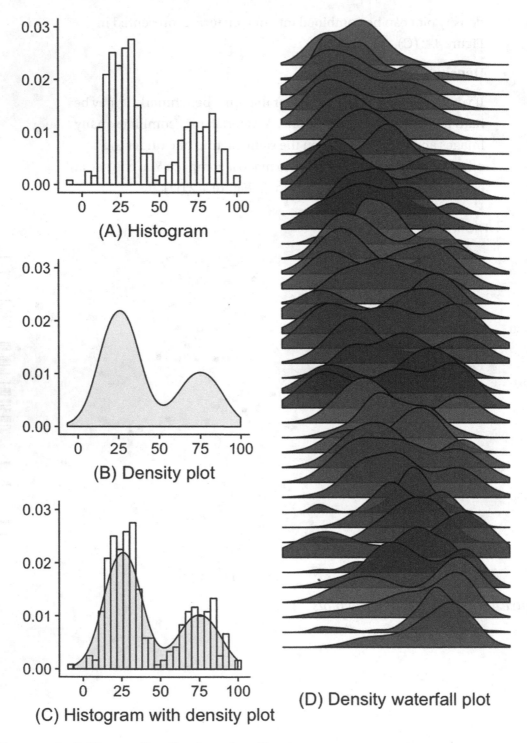

Figure 4-2. *Different distribution visualizations*

Plotting is an excellent way of representing data, but it has one serious disadvantage: it's hard to analyze plots automatically. You can instantly understand the distribution shape when you look at a single image, but if there are hundreds of distributions, you can't look at all of them at the same time. A waterfall plot may solve this problem for a single benchmark, but it's still an issue when you are working with many different methods and performance metrics. If you have a continuous benchmarking (you run a huge benchmark suite on a server each day), you probably don't want to examine all generated plots every day; you need only those plots with issues. So, it's important to have a way to detect "suspicious" distributions, which is hard if you only have a set of images: you need numeric metrics.

PRACTICAL RECOMMENDATIONS

It's always worth looking at a histogram or a density plot. However, a typical performance investigation includes dozens of experiments, and continuous plot monitoring may be time-consuming. It's recommended to look at the plots at the special moments of the investigation lifetime: e.g., after the first benchmark run (to get an idea about the distribution form), after the last benchmark run (to verify that your hypothesis is correct before making conclusions), and after a benchmark run with "suspicious" statistical metrics (to check the distribution for anomalies).

Sample Size

The **sample size** is the number n of measurements in a sample. The histograms and density plots show the distribution shape, but they don't contain information about the sample size. Thus, if you have three density plots for samples with n = 5, n = 100, and n = 10000, it's not always possible to say where the plot is for each sample. Meanwhile, the sample size is a very important characteristic: it's responsible for the accuracy. If you take many different samples with n = 5 for the same benchmark, you will get absolutely different density plots and values of the basic statistical metrics. If you take many samples with n = 10000, the results will be similar to each other. A big sample size helps to improve the result repeatability. However, extremely huge sample sizes are not optimal in terms of the total research duration: you may have to wait too much time for benchmark results. Thus, it makes sense to choose the minimal possible sample size that provides the required level of accuracy and repeatability.

PRACTICAL RECOMMENDATIONS

For the first benchmark run, it's recommended to take the sample size from 15 to 30. 15 is the value when the essential statistical characteristics (which we are going to discuss soon) usually start to show trustworthy values. 30 is the value when most statistical tests start to work and show believable results. Of course, 15 and 30 are just initial approximations: you can get good metrics estimation with 10 iterations or completely incorrect statistical test results with 40 iterations. If you make changes in the source code and rerun the benchmark trying to detect significant improvements like 5× speedup, you can try to do a few iterations (or even a single iteration). A single measurement doesn't provide any statistical metrics, but it helps to evaluate the magnitude of measurements roughly. Sometimes it's enough to say that a benchmark takes several milliseconds or several minutes. Benchmarks with complex distributions may require hundreds or even thousands of runs to get the correct metric values. It's recommended to make a lot of runs for final checks before making any conclusions.

Minimum, Maximum, and Range

The simplest distribution characteristics that we can calculate are the **minimum** and the **maximum** (or **min** and **max**). Together they form the **range**.

The minimum and the maximum values correspond to the best-case and worst-case performance or the fastest and the slowest measurements that we observe. The range provides us an idea what kind of values can we get for this benchmark.

PRACTICAL RECOMMENDATIONS

If you run a simple benchmark in a sterile environment, you may get a narrow range like (15.181ms, 15.226ms). If you don't care about better accuracy and you just want to compare two distributions, you may take any number from the interval (e.g., 15.2ms) and work with it: no other statistical characteristics are required. A benchmark with the (15.181ms, 15.226ms) range is most likely faster than a benchmark with the (629.4ms, 653.2ms) range. If the range is wide (there is a significant difference between the minimum and the maximum), you need more distribution metrics.

Mean

The **mean** or the **arithmetical average** is the most straightforward way to aggregate numbers: we should just sum up all numbers and divide the result by the number of elements. It's usually denoted as $\overline{x}$ or μ.

$$Mean: \overline{x} = \frac{x_1 + x_2 + \cdots + x_n}{n}$$

The mean is one of the most popular statistical metrics. Many developers use only the mean during performance investigations. What is the easiest way to compare the performance of the two methods? We can measure the duration of each method several times, calculate the mean for each method, and compare the means! In most simple cases it works fine. For example, the mean values of {99, 104, 105, 108, 114} and {503, 765, 653, 741, 593} are 106 and 651: the first method is obviously faster.

However, you never know in advance that it's OK. There are many problems with the mean. One of the most typical problems is a complex shape of distributions and extremely high values. For example, the mean of {95, 101, 304, 97, 295, 314} is 201 and the mean of {150, 125, 110, 5000, 115} is 1100, which may be pretty confusing because the mean values are far away from the measurements that we have in the distributions. Let's learn another metric that will help us to solve this problem.

PRACTICAL RECOMMENDATIONS

The mean value is a good starting point for distribution exploration. In simple cases (especially if the range is narrow), it may be enough just to check out the mean. However, it can be misleading in some cases: there are some distribution "features" that makes the mean value useless. In many simple cases when the difference between distributions is noticeable, the "relationship" between distributions and the mean values is the same. It creates a false sense of confidence that it's enough just to compare the mean values. However, you should never use only the mean value for analysis if you don't know the shape of the data.

Median

The **median** is another way to describe the "average" value of the sample. To find it, you have to sort all values and take the middle element. If the sample size is even, the median is the arithmetical average of two middle elements. For example, the median of

$\{1, 4, 7, 15, 20\}$ is 7 and the median of $\{1, 4, 7, 8, 15, 20\}$ is $(7 + 8)/2 = 7.5$. Thus, the median separates the lower half and the higher half of the measurement set.

The median solves the problem of extremely high and extremely low values that spoil the mean value. Imagine that a benchmark downloads a file from the Internet. All iterations finished fine except for one, which was terminated by timeout. Thus, we have the following sample: $x : \{150,125,110,5000,115\}$. The mean is 1100, but this number doesn't help to describe the data. The median is 125, which is much closer to actual "average" download time. By the way, some people use the "average" term to describe median or other "averaged" values like mean. To avoid misunderstanding, we will always use the terms "mean" and "median" instead of "average."

PRACTICAL RECOMMENDATIONS

Which metric should we use for describing the measurements set: the median or the mean? Fortunately, in most simple cases, these values are close to each other, and you can choose either of them. If there is a significant distance between them, additional analysis is required: you can't choose only one value, you need the median, the mean, and other metrics. Even if the values are close, we still don't know anything about the shape of the data and we still can't describe the distribution by a single number.

Quantiles, Quartiles, and Percentiles

The **q-quantiles** are cut points that divide the sample into q equal intervals.

We are already familiar with the **2-quantile**: it's the median that splits the sample into two parts. For example, the 2-quantile of $\{1, 2, 3, 4, 5, 6, 7, 8, 9\}$ is 5.

Another widely used kind of quantile is the **4-quantile** or **quartile**. The quartiles are three values Q_1, Q_2, Q_3 that split the sample into four equal parts. The second quartile Q_2 equals to the median. For example, the 4-quantiles of $\{1, 2, 3, 4, 5, 6, 7, 8, 9\}$ are 3, 5, and 7.

The range with the quartiles form the **five-number summary**: $\{Min, Q_1, Median, Q_3, Max\}$. These five values are commonly used as a short form of distribution representation: it doesn't describe the shape of the data, but it provides a general impression of the distribution. For example, the five-number summary of $\{1, 2, 3, 4, 5, 6, 7, 8, 9\}$ is $\{1, 3, 5, 7, 9\}$.

The difference between upper quartile Q_3 and lower quartile Q_1 is known as the Interquartile Range (IQR):

$$IQR = Q_3 - Q_1$$

The **percentiles** are 100-quantiles: the kth percentile p_k is the value that separates the lower k% of the measurement set from higher elements. The median and the quartiles can be expressed via percentiles:

$$p_{25} = Q_1, \quad p_{50} = Q_2 = \bar{x}, \quad p_{75} = Q_3$$

Sometimes the granularity of percentiles is not enough, and we need 1000-quantiles or **permilles**. The "permille" term is not usually used: people use percentiles instead. For example, the 99.9^{th} percentile corresponds to the 999th permille. We can continue to increase the granularity: the 99.95^{th} percentile is used for denoting the 9995th 10000-quantile.

The number of q-quantiles is $(q - 1)$. However, sometimes people introduce two additional fake quantiles: 0th and q^{th}, which are equal to the minimum and the maximum. Thus, the five-number summary can be expressed in percentiles like this: p_0, p_{25}, p_{50}, p_{75}, p_{100}. Technically, this is wrong (there are no 0th and 100th percentiles), but such notation is used in many articles and blog posts because it looks consistent.

Percentile values like p_{80}, p_{95}, p_{99}, and $p_{99.9}$ are often used during performance analysis of web applications. Many people think that values like p_{99} affect users very rarely and we shouldn't care about them. Now imagine a web page which makes 300 requests to additional resources like images, css, and javascript files. The probability that the latency of each request is less than the 99th percentile is $1 - 0.99^{300} \approx 0.95$. Thus, we have 95% probability that the total page loading time will be affected by the 99th percentile. If we consider the 99.9^{th} percentile, this value will be $1 - 0.99^{300} \approx 0.26$. The 26% probability is 3.7 times better than 95%, but it's still a huge number. Here is a simple exercise: open a popular web site like facebook.com or amazon.com, check out how many requests are processed, and calculate the probability of getting p_{90}, p_{95}, p_{99}, $p_{99.9}$, $p_{99.99}$ for one of the requests.

PRACTICAL RECOMMENDATIONS

The five-number summary (the range with the quartiles) is a common way to describe the distribution. If the range is wide and we are care about huge values, we may need a better granularity, which can be achieved with the help of percentiles. For example, this is a popular way of describing web request latencies.

Outliers

The **outliers** are very high or low values compared to other measurements. We will call them **upper and lower outliers** accordingly.

A typical performance distribution is presented in Figure 4-3. It shows the distribution of 1000 local runs of the Rider NuGetTest.uninstallOk (this test checks that we can correctly uninstall a NuGet package). This test includes some disk operations, so we are expecting to get some outliers. The mean value is 4.938 sec, but sometimes the test takes up to 26.930 sec. You can find many other real-life examples of outliers in [Gregg 2014b].

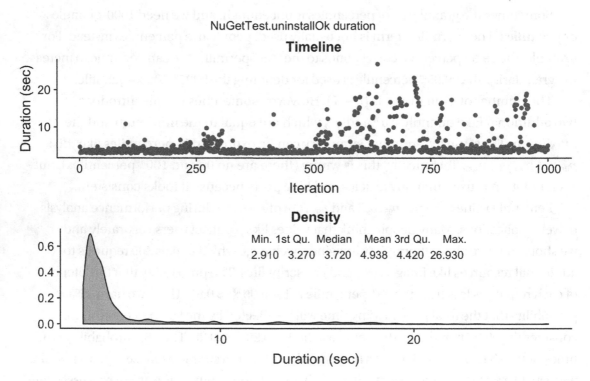

Figure 4-3. *Distribution with outliers*

There are many different ways to define which values are too high or low. One of the most popular approaches is the **Tukey's fences**[2]:

$$Lower\ Fence: Q_1 - 1.5 \cdot IQR; \quad Upper\ Fence: Q_3 + 1.5 \cdot IQR$$

---

[2]It's not the only outlier test; there are many other approaches: 6 sigma test, Chauvenet's criterion, Grubbs' test, Dixon's Q test, Peirce's criterion, and others.

All values that are smaller than the lower fence are the lower outliers. All values that are bigger than the upper fence are the upper outliers. In this formulas, 1.5 is the most popular factor for IQR, but you can use another value if you want to set another level of "sensitivity" to outliers.

It's important to understand why we have the outliers. There are two kinds of upper outliers:

- **Random noise (unwanted outliers)**

  In Chapter 2, we have already discussed that the performance measurements are noisy. We have many random errors because of different reasons: from other user and kernel processes that work in parallel with a benchmark to hardware timer quantizing errors (more about this in Chapter 9). We can't completely remove this noise, but we can clear the data and remove the unwanted outliers because they don't provide useful information and prevent us from getting accurate performance distribution.

- **True effects (wanted outliers)**

  In some benchmarks, there are outliers that we expect. Typically, you can observe extremely high values during I/O operations, network requests, database quires, and so on. Knowledge about such outliers is important because we will get them in production. It's a major part of real performance space that should be analyzed. We care about these outliers and we want to know the full list of them.

In most cases, the performance distributions have only upper outliers. However, the lower outliers also can be observed. Here are two examples:

- *Errors*

  Imagine that you are making a web request, but the network is accidentally not available. Such a request will be finished instantly; it produces an unusually low duration. These errors should also be handled and analyzed: it's a part of many performance and reliability analysis like the **Utilization Saturation and Errors (USE) Method** (see [Gregg 2017]). If you have a retry policy, such values can be transformed into regular

values or upper outliers, so we can miss important information if
we don't analyze errors separately.

- *Fast paths*

    Many software systems have different caching strategies. It's
    great for the application performance because we can process
    the repeated requests faster. But it's not so great if we want to
    benchmark the request processing time without caching. If it's
    impossible to disable caching or do cache invalidation[3] after each
    iteration, we should randomize our requests to avoid getting
    cached results. In this case, the lower outliers may notify us that
    we hit "fast paths" and skipped actual calculations.

PRACTICAL RECOMMENDATIONS

It's recommended to split your data into two groups: outliers and everything else. Next, you
can analyze the original sample with included outliers, the modified sample with excluded
outliers, and the full outlier list. For example, values like p_{95}, p_{99}, $p_{99.9}$ require a sample with
included outliers. When you use a sample with *excluded* outliers, many statistical distribution
characteristics like the mean value will become more stable and reliable metrics. Analysis of
wanted outliers (which can be explained by true effects) is very important; it's a part of the
performance space. You should make a decision about which piece of the data to use (with or
without outliers) based on the selected metrics and business goals.

Box Plots

The **box plot** (also known as the **whisker plot**) is a compact way to display the
minimum, Q_1, Q_2, Q_3, the maximum, the lower and upper fences, and the outliers at the
same time.

---

[3]http://thecodelesscode.com/case/220

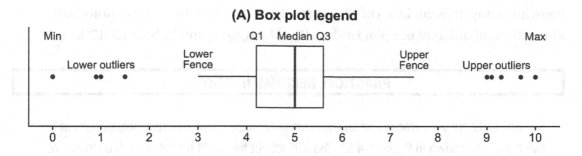

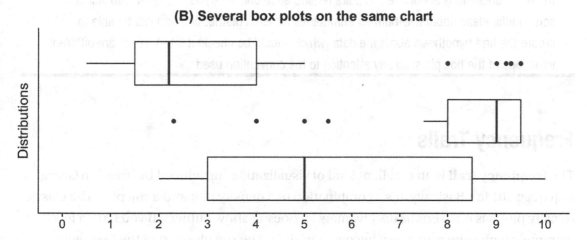

Figure 4-4. *Examples of box plots*

One of the most popular kinds of box plot is the **Tukey box plot**; you can see an example of it in Figure 4-4 (A). The box shows the positions of Q_1 and Q_3. The band inside the box shows the median. The box is extended by lines (also known as whiskers) that indicate the lower and upper fences. The outliers are presented as dots outside the whiskers.

The box plot has many variations. Usually, the box with the band always describes Q_1, Q_2, Q_3, but the rule for the whiskers can be different; it depends on the outlier detection algorithm used. The whiskers are often reduced to the nearest value from the sample (e.g., if we don't have a value that exactly equals $Q_1 - 1.5 \cdot IQR$, we finish to draw the lower whisker on the smallest value that is higher than the lower fence). That's why the whisker lengths in Figure 4-4 are not equal and the positions of the lower fence and the upper fence don't match the Tukey formula. If we don't have any values between Q3 and the lowest upper outlier, the upper whisker can be completely removed. Also, there are many different kinds of visual variations[4] (you can find explanations with illustrations of different box plot kinds in [Wickham 2011] and [Ribecca 2017]).

PRACTICAL RECOMMENDATIONS

The box plots are very efficient when you want to compare many different distributions at the same time, as shown in Figure 4-4 (B). You will not get the exact model of each distribution: the final conclusions about specific pairs require additional analysis. However, you will get some initial ideas about five-number summaries for each distribution and will be able to create the first hypothesis about the data (which should be checked later). There are different variations of the box plots, so pay attention to the convention used.

Frequency Trails

The **frequency trail** is an excellent kind of visualization introduced by Brendan Gregg in [Gregg 2014a]. Basically, it's a combination of a density plot and a rug plot. The classic density plot has one serious disadvantage: it doesn't show outliers. If you have a few extremely high values, they can become invisible. The rug plot part of the frequency trail plot solves this problem: it highlights the full list of outliers, which is very important for the distribution analysis. If we have many different distributions, it makes sense to combine several frequency trails into a waterfall plot by displaying them on the same image. You can see examples of frequency trail waterfall plots in Figure 4-5. The color palette can be arbitrary, but an inverted black-white palette is especially popular because it looks similar to the cover of the "Unknown Pleasures" album by Joy Division.

PRACTICAL RECOMMENDATIONS

The frequency trail is a good alternative to density plots when you want to look at the distribution shape and the list of outliers at the same time.

---

[4]For example, the classic box plot can be improved by additional information and transformed to the variable width box plot, the notched box plot, the vase plot, the bean plot, the bee swarm box plot, the highest density region box plot, the box-percentile plot, the letter-value box plot, or other kinds of box plot.

Figure 4-5. *Frequency trail waterfall plots*

Modes

Typically, density plots are not flat; they contain "low" and "high" areas. A local maximum of a density plot is known as **mode**; it's a point that contains a lot of measurements around it. On a histogram, such point will be presented by a bin that is higher than its neighbors.

If the density plot has a single local maximum, the distribution is called **unimodal**; you can see an example in Figure 4-6 (A). If the density plot has two local maximums, the distribution is called **bimodal**; an example is presented in Figure 4-6 (B). We say that the distribution is **multimodal** when the number of local maximums is more than one (the bimodal distribution is a special case of the multimodal distribution).

In real life, many performance distributions look like combinations of a multimodal distribution, random noise, and a set of outliers (you can see an example in Figure 4-6 (C)).

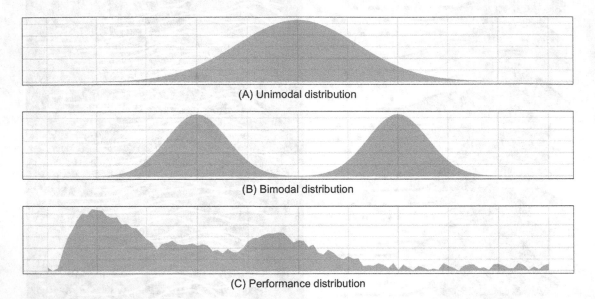

(A) Unimodal distribution

(B) Bimodal distribution

(C) Performance distribution

Figure 4-6. *Unimodal, bimodal, and performance distributions*

Thus, it's not always possible to say how many modes we have. However, it's usually possible to distinguish "simple" unimodal distributions and "complex" multimodal distributions. Let's discuss how to detect multimodal distributions. If you are not interested in a particular implementation, you can skip the rest of this subsection.

There are many different algorithms for multimodal distribution detection. Unfortunately, most classic academic algorithms don't work well on real data. The situation becomes worse when the sample size is small (less than 30–40 measurements). After many experiments, I finally found an approach that works acceptably. One approach that works really well with performance distributions is described in [Gregg 2015] by Brendan Gregg and based on the modal values (mvalues). If we have a histogram h with k bins $h_1, h_2, \ldots , h_k$ (the ith bin contains h_i measurements), the modal value h_m is defined as follows:

$$Modal\ Value\text{: } h_m = \frac{|h_2 - h_1| + |h_3 - h_2| + \cdots + |h_k - h_{k-1}|}{\mathrm{Max}(h_1, h_2, \ldots, h_k)}$$

In this formula, we summarize all elevations between neighboring bins and divide by the number of measurements in the highest bin. The minimal possible modal value is 2, which corresponds to the unimodal distribution. A modal value of a perfect bimodal distribution is 4.

The modal values and many other multimodality detection methods are very sensitive to given histograms. In Figure 4-7 (A), you can see a bimodal distribution with a histogram. If you look only at the histogram, you can easily say that the distribution is bimodal because the centers of the second and the fourth bins match the local maximums of the density plot. In Figure 4-7 (B), you can see the same distribution with another histogram. The bin size for both histograms are the same, but the first bin offsets are different. As a result, the second histogram looks unimodal: each bin contains the same number of values from the sample because of another histogram offset.

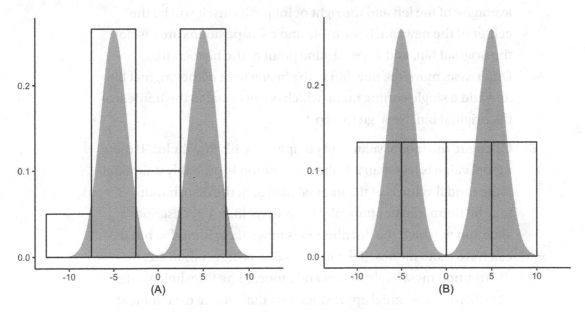

Figure 4-7. *Different histograms for bimodal distribution*

It's very important to build a good histogram. After a series of unsuccessful attempts, I finally came up with an algorithm for histogram building, which has been used in BenchmarkDotNet since v0.10.14.[5] It follows the following scheme (the particular implementation includes many additional corner case checks):

---

[5]See https://github.com/dotnet/BenchmarkDotNet/blob/v0.11.3/src/BenchmarkDotNet/
Mathematics/Histograms/AdaptiveHistogramBuilder.cs

1. Remove outliers based on the Tukey's fences.

2. Choose a value for the desired bin width w. It's recommended to use the Scott's normal reference rule and divide it by 2:

$$Desired\ Bin\ Width\ (modified\ Scott's\ rule): w = \frac{3.5s}{2\sqrt[3]{n}}.$$

3. Start with a histogram that contains a single bin with all values.

4. Find a bin that is bigger than w. If there are no such bins, the histogram is ready; go to step 6.

5. In the selected bin, find an interval of width w that contains the maximum number of measurements. Calculate the arithmetical average c of the left and the right point positions; it will be the center of the new bin. If the $c - w$ and $c + w$ positions are inside the original bin, add a new cutting point at the histogram. Otherwise, move the new bin to the inside area of the original bin and add a single cutting point, which is not equal to the borders of the original bin. Next, go to step 4.

6. Calculate the modal value and compare it with thresholds. If the modal value is less than 2.8, the distribution is probably unimodal. If the modal value is in the interval [2.8; 3.2], the distribution may be unimodal or bimodal. The interval [3.2; 4.2] describes a situation in which the distribution is most likely bimodal, but it can have more modes. If the modal value is bigger than 4.2, the distribution most likely has several modes. The threshold values (2.8, 3.2, 4.2) are initial approximations that can be used for first experiments. In case of modifications in the desired bin width formula, the threshold values should be adjusted.

The idea behind the algorithm is pretty simple. The modal values don't work correctly when we have a mode on the border between two bins like in Figure 4-7 (B). Thus, we are trying to find the "best" local maximum (step 4) and introduce a bin with the center equaling to the mode. Now, this mode is "protected" from being "split" and we are trying to find the next "best" local maximum.

It's not a classic kind of histogram and it doesn't have a special name. The approach doesn't have a formal proof, but it was tested on thousands of BenchmarkDotNet runs with different performance distributions. It turned out that it works really well on the real data, unlike some classic academic algorithms.

PRACTICAL RECOMMENDATIONS

One of the first things that you should check for in a distribution is multimodality. If a distribution is multimodal, many statistical metrics like the mean don't work as designed, and you can't use these values for meaningful conclusions. Meanwhile, you can still use the percentile analysis without any modifications.

The modal values provide a powerful approach for detecting multimodal distributions. It helps to identify "suspicious" distributions that probably can't be compared with "usual" metrics like the mean or the median.

Variance and Standard Deviation

The measurements vary from iteration to iteration. We can evaluate how huge the value spread is with the help of **variance**:

$$(Biased)\,Variance:\; s^2 = \frac{\left(x_1 - \bar{x}\right)^2 + \left(x_2 - \bar{x}\right)^2 + \cdots + \left(x_n - \bar{x}\right)^2}{n}$$

Here we just subtract the mean value $\bar{x}$ from each value x_i, summarize squares of $\left(x_i - \bar{x}\right)$, and divide the sum by the sample size n.

In practice, the **standard deviation** is usually used instead. It's just a square root from variance:

$$(Biased)\,Standard\,Deviation:\; s = \sqrt{\frac{\left(x_1 - \bar{x}\right)^2 + \left(x_2 - \bar{x}\right)^2 + \cdots + \left(x_n - \bar{x}\right)^2}{n}}$$

We denote the standard deviation as s, but you may also meet the σ symbol in many texts. Common short forms of the standard deviation in the source code are StdDev and SD.

You may notice the "(Biased)" prefix in the preceding formulas. These formulas would be correct if you collect *all* measurements. However, it's not possible to collect all of them because we can continue to take measurements without limitations. Thus, we have to evaluate the variance and the standard deviation with the help of a small sample. That's why we have a small error (bias). The error can be fixed with the help of Bessel's correction, which just replaces n in the divider by $n - 1$:

$$(Unbiased)\,Variance:\ s^2 = \frac{\left(x_1 - \overline{x}\right)^2 + \left(x_2 - \overline{x}\right)^2 + \cdots + \left(x_n - \overline{x}\right)^2}{n-1}$$

$$(Unbiased)\,Standard\ Deviation:\ s = \sqrt{\frac{\left(x_1 - \overline{x}\right)^2 + \left(x_2 - \overline{x}\right)^2 + \cdots + \left(x_n - \overline{x}\right)^2}{n-1}}$$

Bessel's correction is the source of confusion and misunderstanding. Which divider should we use: n or $n - 1$? In theory, $n - 1$ is better. From the practical point of view, it usually doesn't matter. When the number of observations n is low (less than five or ten), the errors are huge, and the evaluated values are rough approximations of the real variance and standard deviation. When the number of observations n is big enough (more than ten or fifteen), the difference between $1/n$ and $1/(n-1)$ becomes less than the accuracy that you care about. Bessel's correction exists for a reason, and it may be pretty important in some statistics applications. However, *usually* you do not have to worry about it during real performance investigations.

PRACTICAL RECOMMENDATIONS

The standard deviation can be used as a measure of "instability." It shows how big the difference between measurements can be. A low value shows that most of the measurements are close to the mean value, while a high value indicates that measurements can be far from the mean.

When you are comparing two distributions, a huge standard deviation may notify you that you can't compare the mean values. For example, if arithmetical averagesr of two distributions are 50 seconds and 52 seconds, but the standard deviation is about 15 seconds for each of them, you can't make any conclusions about which method is faster. In the next subsection, we will learn how to interpret the absolute value of the standard deviation.

Phrases like "the variance is big" are "the standard deviation is big" mean the same, but the first form is more popular because it's shorter. Meanwhile, the standard deviation is more often used in practice because it is expressed in the same units as the measurements and it's used in many useful formulas (some of them will be covered in the next subsections).

The mean and the standard deviation values are important metrics, but they still don't describe the distribution shape. In [Matejka 2017], you can find pictures of completely different distributions with the same values of $\bar{x}$ and s.

The standard deviation can be spoiled by outliers. If you calculate the standard deviation of a sample without outliers, you will get a more repeatable value, but you may lose some important information about the spread. Usually, it's a good practice to exclude outliers before the calculation but still look at them.

Normal Distribution

The normal distribution is one of the most famous and classic distributions that is important to know. You can see its bell-shaped density plot in Figure 4-8.

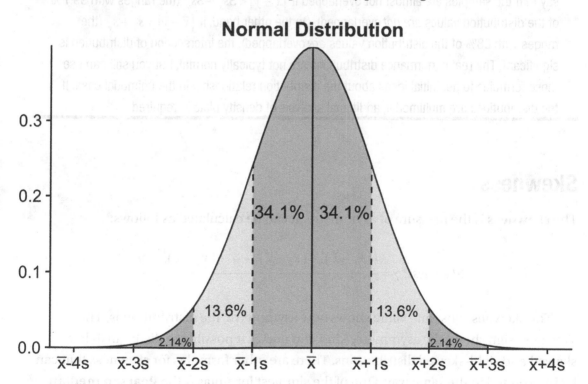

Figure 4-8. *Normal distribution*

The normal distribution has some important properties:

- The distribution is symmetric and unimodal.

- The mean equals to the median.

- The interval $[\bar{x}-1s; \bar{x}+1s]$ contains $\approx68\%$ of values.

- The interval $[\bar{x}-2s; \bar{x}+2s]$ contains $\approx95\%$ of values.

- The interval $[\bar{x}-3s; \bar{x}+3s]$ contains $\approx99.7\%$ of values.

The last property is known as the *three-sigma rules*. It states that almost all values ($\approx99.7\%$) in the normal distribution lie within three standard deviations of the mean.

PRACTICAL RECOMMENDATIONS

The normal distribution is a good mental model for the intuitive understanding of different metrics like the mean and the standard deviation in case of unimodal distributions. For example, if we have two samples x and y that are described by normal distributions, we can say that the samples are almost not overlapped if $|\bar{x}-\bar{y}| < 3s_x + 3s_y$ (the ranges with 99.7% of the distribution values *are not* overlapped). On the other hand, if $|\bar{x}-\bar{y}| > s_x + s_y$ (the ranges with 68% of the distribution values *are* overlapped), the intersection of distribution is significant. The real performance distributions are not typically normal, but you still can use these formulas to get initial ideas about the distribution relationship in the unimodal case. If the distributions are multimodal, additional analysis of density plots is required.

Skewness

The **skewness** is the measure of asymmetry. It can be calculated as follows:

$$Skewness:\ \gamma = \frac{\left((x_1 - \bar{x})^3 + (x_2 - \bar{x})^3 + \cdots + (x_n - \bar{x})^3 \right)/n}{s^3}$$

The skewness absolute value shows how asymmetric the distribution is. The skewness sign shows the asymmetry kind and makes it possible to distinguish left-skewed and right-skewed distributions. There are other formulas for skewness that can be interpreted in the same way. One of the simplest formulas is the **Pearson median skewness**:

$$Pearson\ Median\ Skewness:\ \gamma_{median} = \frac{3(\bar{x} - Q_2)}{s}$$

From this formula, it's obvious that the skewness sign can be easily evaluated by comparing the mean $\bar{x}$ and the median Q_2:

- If the mean is less than the median, the distribution is skewed left and Skewness < 0

- If the mean is equal to the median, the distribution is symmetrical and Skewness = 0

- If the mean is more than the median, the distribution is skewed right and Skewness > 0

You can see the corresponding density plots and box plots in Figure 4-9.

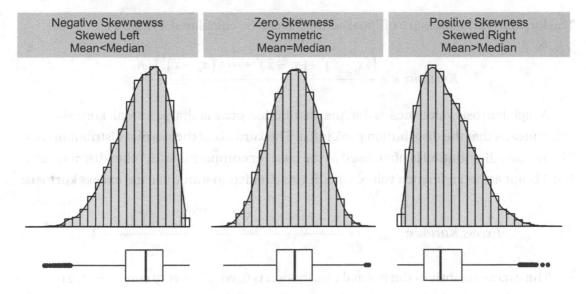

Figure 4-9. *Distribution with different skewness values*

The skewness of the normal distribution is zero because it's symmetrical. Note that Skewness = 0 doesn't always mean that the distribution is perfectly symmetrical. Most of the real performance distributions are right-skewed (the skewness is positive).

PRACTICAL RECOMMENDATIONS

The skewness provides the idea about the distribution symmetry without a direct look at the density plots. A combination of the negative skewness and huge standard deviation is unusual for performance distributions and may notify us that additional analysis is required. Outliers can distort the skewness values, so they should be excluded before the calculations. Skewness is unreliable on small sample sizes ($n < 15$) and multimodal distributions.

Kurtosis

The **kurtosis** is the measure of "peakedness." It can be calculated as follows:

$$Kurtosis: \kappa = \frac{\left(\left(x_1 - \overline{x}\right)^4 + \left(x_2 - \overline{x}\right)^4 + \cdots + \left(x_n - \overline{x}\right)^4\right)/n}{s^4}$$

A high kurtosis value means that the distribution peak is sharp. A small kurtosis value means that the distribution peak is flat. The kurtosis of the normal distribution is 3. The normal distribution is often used as the base for comparing with other distributions, but 3 is not a good reference value. Thus, it was decided to introduce the **excess kurtosis**:

$$Excess\ Kurtosis: \kappa_{excess} = \frac{\left(\left(x_1 - \overline{x}\right)^4 + \left(x_2 - \overline{x}\right)^4 + \cdots + \left(x_n - \overline{x}\right)^4\right)/n}{s^4} - 3$$

The excess kurtosis of the normal distribution is 0, which is very convenient. The difference between the kurtosis and the excess kurtosis is another popular topic for confusion. In many articles, books, blog posts, and programs, the excess kurtosis is denoted as just the kurtosis. Thus, if you see a phrase like "the kurtosis of the normal distribution," it's not possible to say the corresponding value in advance: it can be zero or three depending on the author's preferences.

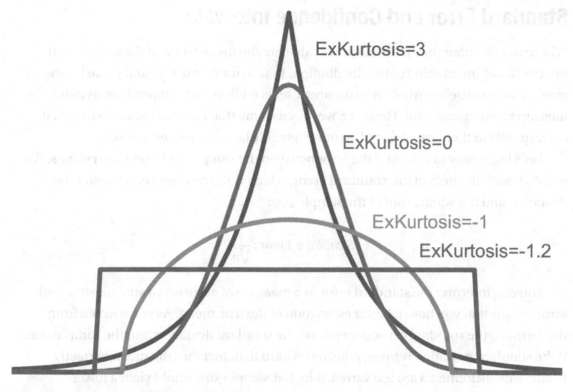

Figure 4-10. *Distribution with different excess kurtosis values*

Figure 4-10 should provide better "feeling" of the distribution form for different values of the excess kurtosis. The kurtosis describes the central peak of the distribution: a high kurtosis value corresponds to a sharper peak, and a low kurtosis value corresponds to a flat peak.

PRACTICAL RECOMMENDATIONS

The kurtosis is another number that helps us to imagine a distribution without charts. When you see the kurtosis value somewhere, check the local naming convention: it may be the excess kurtosis. Outliers can distort the kurtosis values, so they should be excluded before the calculations. Kurtosis is unreliable on small sample sizes ($n < 15$) and multimodal distributions.

Standard Error and Confidence Intervals

When we talk about the mean value, we calculate the mean value of the sample, but not the "true" mean value of the distribution. In fact, there is not a fixed value for the true mean because the whole measurement set is endless: we can produce as many measurements as we want. However, we may assume that the true mean exists and it corresponds to the mean value of an unimaginably large measurement set.

Let's learn how to calculate the error between the sample and true mean values. We will do it with the help of the **standard error**, which is the rate between the standard deviation and the square root of the sample size:

$$Standard\ Error : \frac{s}{\sqrt{n}}$$

You can interpret the standard error as a measure of accuracy: a smaller standard error means that you have a better estimation of the true mean. As you can see from the formula, the standard error depends on the standard deviation and the sample size. If the standard deviation is huge, it becomes hard to detect the true mean correctly because measurements are too varied. A higher sample size would yield a lower standard error. While the standard deviation shows the spread between different values in the distribution, the standard error shows the spread between mean values in different samples. Thus, it's also a measure of repeatability: if we run the whole experiment many times and get different distributions for the same benchmark, the difference between obtained values correlates with the standard error.

Now we can calculate the **margin of error**, which is the standard error multiplied by a critical value t^*:

$$Margin\ of\ Error : t^* \frac{s}{\sqrt{n}}$$

The critical value t^* is a "magic" constant that depends on the sample size and the **confidence level** (expressed in percentages). In Table 4-1, you can see the critical values for the most popular confidence intervals on different sample sizes.

Table 4-1. *Critical Values for Confidence Intervals*

n	80%	90%	95%	98%	99%	99.9%
2	3.078	6.314	12.706	31.821	63.657	636.619
3	1.886	2.920	4.303	6.965	9.925	31.599
4	1.638	2.353	3.182	4.541	5.841	12.924
5	1.533	2.132	2.776	3.747	4.604	8.610
6	1.476	2.015	2.571	3.365	4.032	6.869
7	1.440	1.943	2.447	3.143	3.707	5.959
8	1.415	1.895	2.365	2.998	3.499	5.408
9	1.397	1.860	2.306	2.896	3.355	5.041
10	1.383	1.833	2.262	2.821	3.250	4.781
11	1.372	1.812	2.228	2.764	3.169	4.587
12	1.363	1.796	2.201	2.718	3.106	4.437
13	1.356	1.782	2.179	2.681	3.055	4.318
14	1.350	1.771	2.160	2.650	3.012	4.221
15	1.345	1.761	2.145	2.624	2.977	4.140
16	1.341	1.753	2.131	2.602	2.947	4.073
17	1.337	1.746	2.120	2.583	2.921	4.015
18	1.333	1.740	2.110	2.567	2.898	3.965
19	1.330	1.734	2.101	2.552	2.878	3.922
20	1.328	1.729	2.093	2.539	2.861	3.883
100	1.290	1.660	1.984	2.365	2.626	3.392
1000	1.282	1.646	1.962	2.330	2.581	3.300
10000	1.282	1.645	1.960	2.327	2.576	3.292

The **confidence interval of the mean** is an interval around the mean with the margin of error as the radius. This means that the difference between any point from the interval and the mean is less than or equal to the margin of error:

$$Confidence\ Interval : \left[\bar{x} - t^* \frac{s}{\sqrt{n}}; \quad \bar{x} + t^* \frac{s}{\sqrt{n}} \right]$$

By definition, 99% of all confidence intervals with confidence level=99% include the true mean. The confidence intervals are often incorrectly interpreted, which leads to wrong conclusions. Here is the most common pitfall:

- Not true: "the true mean is most likely in the confidence interval, but if it's not in the interval, it *should be close to it*." In fact, the true mean can be far away from a confidence interval of a particular sample. The 99% confidence level says that such situations are unusual, but it doesn't say anything about the distance between the confidence interval and the true mean.

For performance distributions, the standard definition of the confidence interval doesn't work "as is." If a distribution is very skewed and has extremely high outliers, it's pretty hard to define the true mean. In practice, you can easily get a situation in which 80% of 99.9% confidence intervals don't have any common points. The situation can become better if we significantly increase the sample size, but it may be impractical: it significantly increases the whole experiment time without tangible benefits. It's much more efficient just to exclude the outliers from the sample and describe them independently. In simple cases, a 99.9% confidence level usually provides a pretty good accuracy that can be used for analysis.

The standard error helps you understand the influence of the sample size on the accuracy. Many people think that if we increase the sample size twice, the accuracy will also be increased twice, but this is a wrong assumption. Let's say that we change the sample size from 100 to 400. If the standard deviation is the same for both samples, the standard error will be changed from $s / \sqrt{100} = s / 10$ to $s / \sqrt{400} = s / 20$: Thus, increasing the sample size four times reduces the standard error twice. While all 100 iteration batches take the same amount of the experiment time, they contribute differently to the accuracy. The $100 \rightarrow 200$ sample size change reduces the error by $\approx 41\%$, but the $5100 \rightarrow 5200$ sample size change reduces the error only by $\approx 1\%$.

PRACTICAL RECOMMENDATIONS

The standard error is a measure of accuracy and repeatability for benchmark results. In the case of performance distributions, the confidence intervals don't work as designed, but it's still a good metric for the initial estimation between the sample and true mean values.

In practice, the 99.9% confidence level is recommended. For $n > 30$, you may use $t^* \approx 3.6$ as an approximation for the critical value.If you want to take another confidence interval, you can use choose a value from Table 4-1 (you can easily google an extended version of it). Usually, you shouldn't worry about the accurate value for t^* because it's enough to work with a rough approximation of the confidence interval. If you want to calculate the exact value, it's recommended to reuse an existing implementation (e.g., BenchmarkDotNet has API for it that is based on approximations from [ACM209] and [ACM395]).

The standard error also helps to choose the optimal sample size. When you change the sample size from n_1 to n_2, the standard error will be reduced by $\sqrt{n_2 / n_1}$. When n is small, each additional iteration noticeably improves the accuracy. At some point, it becomes meaningless to "pay" for the accuracy by our waiting time, because the accuracy impact of additional iterations is too small.

The Central Limit Theorem

The **central limit theorem** states that if we take many samples and calculate the mean for each sample, these mean values will form an approximately normal distribution. This theorem works only if the sample size in each case is big enough.

The most wonderful fact about the central limit theorem is that it works even on non-normal distributions. Your original data set can have many outliers and a complicated distribution shape, but the central limit theorem will work anyway.

People often make wrong conclusions based on the central limit theorem. Let's discuss a few common pitfalls:

- The central limit theorem doesn't work correctly when the sample sizes are small. For example, if you make a single measurement in each sample, the distribution based on the mean values will have the same shape with the original distribution.

- If we take a small number of samples ($n < 100$), we will not see a normal distribution on the density plot for mean values.

- If we do many iterations, the original distribution will not become normal, and we can't interpret the mean, the variance, the skewness, and the kurtosis as in the case of normal distribution.

- The range of the mean values across all samples is not always narrow; we still can have a huge difference between the mean values in different samples. The normal distribution based on the mean values has its own standard deviation, which depends on the sample size and can be expressed via the standard error.

You can find another beautiful explanation of the central limit theorem in [Minitab 2013].

PRACTICAL RECOMMENDATIONS

We know that a good benchmark should be repeatable, but it's not always easy to achieve repeatability if a distribution has a huge variance. The central limit theorem states that if we use a proper sample size, the mean values from different samples are distributed normally. Usually, we need at least 30 iterations in each sample. If we have huge outliers, the minimal sample size requirement should be increased.

Thus, you can evaluate the expected difference between the different experiments. Imagine that you want to compare performance between two methods, but the difference between the mean values of *these methods in a single experiment* is less than the difference between the mean values of *the same method in different experiments*. You can make the situation better by increasing the sample size in each experiment.

Summing Up

Descriptive statistics provides a rich set of metrics and approaches for distribution exploration:

- **Mean, standard deviation, skewness, and kurtosis**

  These values help you to get the first impression of the sample. The *mean* is the simplest way to aggregate your data. In many cases, it can be misleading, but usually, it's a good point to start. The *variance* (or the *standard deviation*, which is the square root of *variance*) shows the data spread. The *skewness* and the *kurtosis* are measures of the distribution asymmetry and peakedness. These values can be easily spoiled by *outliers* (extremely high or low values). One of the most popular ways to detect outliers is the *Tukey's fences*, but there are many alternative approaches (e.g., in [Gregg 2014b], the six-sigma test is described). The *normal distribution* is a good mental model for these values.

- **Quantiles**

  The quantiles divide the *range* (an interval between the *minimum* and the *maximum*) into equal parts. The most popular kinds of quantiles are the *median* (separate the data into two parts), the *quartiles* (separate the data into four parts), and the *percentiles* (separate the data into 100 parts). A distribution can be described by the *five-number summary*: Min, Q_1, Median, Q_3, Max or p_0, p_{25}, p_{50}, p_{75}, p_{100} (technically, the 0th and 100th percentiles do not exist, but people often use them for consistency instead of the minimum and the maximum values).

- **Accuracy**

  The *sample size* is critical for good accuracy; you can't make reliable conclusions about the distribution based on a few measurements. It's recommended to choose the initial sample size between 15 and 30, and make adjustments based on the results received. The *standard error* can be used as a measure of accuracy: it's directly proportional to the standard deviation (it's hard to achieve good accuracy with a huge spread) and inversely proportional to the sample size (the accuracy is better when we have many measurements). The *confidence interval of the mean* is a good estimation for the true mean. If it's too wide, the sample mean value can't be trusted.

- **Modes**

  In real life, many performance distributions are *multimodal*. This means that the distribution has several local maximums. In this case, typical metrics like the mean are not very useful.

It's very important to detect such distributions and handle them individually. One of the most powerful detection techniques is using modal values.

- **Visualization**

  Visualization is a powerful technique that helps you to understand the shape of your data instantly. The *timeline* plot is the most direct way to present the sample; it just shows the sample value for each iteration. The *rug plot* is a "compressed" version of the timeline plot: it's a one-dimensional plot with all measurements. The *histogram* is a bar chart that demonstrates the shape of data; it consists of bins that show the relative number of measurements in each small interval. The *density plot* is a "smooth version" of a histogram that shows the distribution shape with less visual noise. The *frequency trail* is a combination of a density plot and a rug plot; it's efficient when we want to highlight outliers on the density plot. The *waterfall plot* is a combination of many overlapped plots on the same image; it's efficient when we want to explore many density plots and frequency trails for the same benchmark. The *box plot* shows the minimum, Q_1, Q_2, Q_3, the maximum, the lower and upper fences, and the outliers at the same time; it's very efficient when we want to compare many distributions of different benchmarks at the same time. There are also many other different kinds of plots that also can be very useful.

PRACTICAL RECOMMENDATIONS

It's pretty time-consuming to check all possible statistical characteristics each time for each benchmark. Thus, it makes sense to check out only the most important metrics (which are chosen according to your gaols). First of all, it's recommended to check the distribution for multimodality and look at the outlier list. In the case of multimodal distributions, it makes sense to look at the density plot. If the distribution is unimodal, we can remove outliers and look at three values: the mean, the standard deviation, and the standard error. The mean provides the initial estimation of the "average" performance, the standard deviation helps to understand the "spread" of the values, and the standard error shows the "accuracy."

If we want to compare many distributions at the same time, we can check out the box plot or compare five-number summaries. The best way to explore the distribution is by looking at a histogram or a density plot. In the case of many outliers, it's better to look at a frequency trail plot. If we care about the worst cases and we have too many outliers or a huge variance, it makes sense to check out the percentiles (p_{95}, p_{99}, $p_{99.9}$). To make any conclusions based on the confidence interval, we need a proper sample size: it should be at least 30 (larger sample size is required if the distribution is very skewed or there are many outliers).

The statistical inference (the process of understanding distribution properties based on the descriptive statistics) is largely based on experience. After conducting a series of statistical research, you will understand how to select the most important metrics for your current investigation quickly. You can even build your own set of empirical rules that help you to interpret these metrics correctly and come up with relevant conclusions.

Working with a single distribution is an important skill for our next topic: the analysis.

Performance Analysis

We already know how to analyze a single distribution and calculate the basic statistical characteristics like the mean, the standard deviation, and the quartiles. It's time to learn how to use it for analysis of several distributions and optimization of the benchmarking process. In this section, we are going to discuss the following important topics:

- **Distribution comparison**

  We will learn how to compare two distributions with the help of different heuristics and statistical tests like Welch's t-test and the Mann–Whitney U test. We will cover many important concepts like the null and alternative hypotheses, Type I and Type II errors, and p-values.

- **Regression models**

  We will learn how to understand the relationship between the input data and the method performance. It requires knowledge of statistical approaches like polynomial regression models and curve fitting. We will also discuss how to analyze algorithmic

complexity and how to work with complex dependencies.
Performance depends not only on the input data but also on the
environment. We will learn basic ways to work with categorical
variables and to find the factors that affect performance.

- **Optional stopping**

    Statistics is a powerful tool when you want to analyze existing
    data. However, we can also use statistics during benchmarking.
    For example, instead of fixing the number of iterations in advance,
    we can stop the iteration process when the desired distribution
    characteristics are achieved.

- **Pilot experiments**

    Instead of guessing the perfect number of method invocations
    inside each iteration, we can perform a series of pilot iterations
    before actual measurements and find the best number of
    invocations.

The performance analysis is an essential skill for benchmarking. Without it, the
benchmark results are just numbers that can't be used for any conclusions. Moreover,
approaches like optional stopping and pilot experiments help to minimize the whole
experiment duration and get acceptable accuracy. Let's start with the most common
problem: comparing two distributions.

Distribution Comparison

Let's say you have two methods and you want to know which method is faster. During
benchmarking, we can collect performance samples x and y for both methods. After that,
we have to compare two sets of numbers. The distribution comparison is one of the basic
tasks in the performance analysis, but it's not an easy task. In Figure 4-11, you can see
density plots for three different methods. Can you tell which method is fastest?

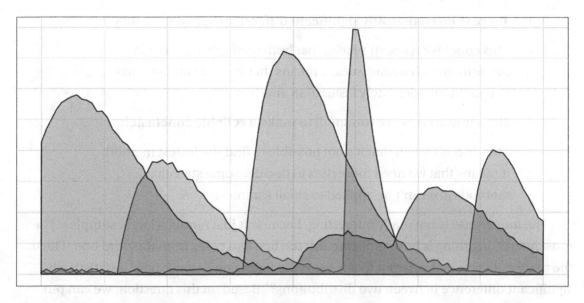

Figure 4-11. *Distributions that are difficult to compare*

Performance is often about trade-offs. Sometimes, one method can be faster than another one, but we can get an opposite situation in another sample. Multimodality and outliers are the most common problems that prevent us from comparing distributions. However, even if we have unimodal distributions without outliers, the comparison task can be difficult because of the huge variance and overlapped ranges. Let's learn how statistics can help us to solve these problems and automate distribution comparison.

When we compare two performance samples *x* and *y*, there are four possible outcomes:

1. **x is faster than y** .

   In fact, it doesn't mean the first method is always faster than the second one. But it means that we probably should prefer the first method if we want to have better performance.

2. **y is faster than x**.

   We have the same situation here: we can *pretend* that the second method is actually faster than the first one, and use this information for business decisions, but it doesn't mean that it's always true.

3. **There is no statistically significant difference between x and y**

   This conclusion doesn't mean that both methods have equal performance characteristics; it means that we just can't say that one method is definitely faster than another.

4. **The sample sizes are too small to make a reliable conclusion**.

   This doesn't mean that it's not possible to find the fastest method; it means that we need more data to decide. Some statistical methods just can't be applied to small samples.

The fourth case is not really interesting, because it just requires larger samples. The most interesting thing is how to distinguish the first two cases from the third one. Thus, the main question that we want to answer is the following: "Do we have a statistically significant difference between two distributions?" Based on this question, we can put forward two **hypotheses**:

- **Null hypothesis H_0**: there is no statistically significant difference

- **Alternative hypothesis H_1**: there is a statistically significant difference

For software developers, it's often hard to remember how to choose each hypothesis. Personally, I like to use other kinds of titles based on the searching results:

- **Negative hypothesis**: no, we didn't find a difference

- **Positive hypothesis**: hooray, we found a difference

Unfortunately, nobody uses them; almost all articles and blog posts contain the terms "null" and "alternative," so you should remember them. Here are a few mnemonics which can help you:

- **Letter rule**:

  Null hypothesis: there is **N**othing interesting

  Alternative hypothesis: there **A**ctually is something interesting

- **Do we have a statistically significant difference?**

  Null hypothesis: **N**o, we don't

  Alternative hypothesis: Ye**A**h, we do

Any conclusions that we make describe the collected data, but not our theory. It's impossible to prove that H_0 or H_1 for *distributions* is correct based on *samples* of measurements. However, we should make a business decision based on the collected samples (e.g., which algorithm should be used to get the best possible performance). Thus, we can *act* like H_0 or H_1 is true, but we should understand that some of our conclusions may be wrong.

The tests that we are going to cover allows rejecting the null hypothesis. Depending on the result (H_0 is rejected or H_0 is not rejected), there are two kinds of errors:

- **Type I error**: H_0 is true, but is rejected

- **Type II error**: H_0 is false, but is not rejected

Personally, I don't like the "Type I/Type II" notation; I prefer to use the terms "false positive" and "false negative":

- **Type I error = False positive**

   Our conclusion that we have a **positive** result is **false**

   We made an error when decided that the **positive** hypothesis is correct

   There is no difference, but we think that *there is* a difference

- **Type II error = False negative**

   Our conclusion that we have a **negative** result is **false**

   We made an error when decided that the **negative** hypothesis is correct

   There is a difference, but we think that *there is no* difference

Unfortunately, the "Type I/Type II" notation is used widely, so it's nice to remember which is which. Here are a few other mnemonics:

- **The number of vertical lines**[6]:

   Type I is a false **P**ositive; P has **one** vertical line

   Type II is a false **N**egative; N has **two** vertical lines

---

[6]https://stats.stackexchange.com/a/1620

- **The village boy and the wolf**[7]:

  The first error the villagers made (when they believed the boy) was a Type I error

  The second error the villagers made (when they didn't believe the boy) was a Type II error

- **The importance rule**:

  Type I: higher importance (we can *make* a wrong decision)

  Type II: lower importance (we can *miss an opportunity to make* a right decision)

You can see the classic form of all possible experimental outcomes in Table 4-2.

Table 4-2. *Error Types*

	H_0 is true	H_0 is false
H_0 is not rejected	No errors	Type II error
H_0 is rejected	Type I error	No errors

This representation may confuse some developers. Let's try to simplify this table. In statistics, we always work with H_0 because that's how mathematics works: we can only reject or not reject H_0, but we can't make conclusions about H_1. Thus, "H_0 is not rejected" is a common conclusion in statistics. It's strict, but it doesn't sound understandable for everyone. When we need to interpret the result, we mentally translate it into "we think that H_0 is true," which is a negative result; we don't have anything interesting. By analogy, we can translate "H_0 is rejected" to "we think that H_0 is false" or "we think that H_1 is true," which is a positive result; we found a difference between x and y. With this notation, Table 4-2 can be translated to Table 4-3.

---

[7]https://stats.stackexchange.com/a/17399

Table 4-3. *Error Types (Alternative Version)*

	Negative hypothesis is true	Positive hypothesis is true
We think that H-**Negative** is true	*True* **negative**	*False* **negative**
We think that H-**Positive** is true	*False* **positive**	*True* **positive**

It's not as strict as Table 4-2, but it looks more understandable and consistent. Now we are familiar with the basic "hypothesis and error" notation, it's time to make some conclusions!

In most simple cases (especially when one method is several times faster than another), the difference between the two distributions is obvious. However, if we want to automate distribution comparison, we need some formulas. Here are a few possible **heuristic tests** that we can apply to check that x is faster than y:

- **Range test:** $x_{max} < y_{min}$

   In many simple cases, the distribution tests are not overlapped at all. In such situations, we can just compare the maximum of the first distribution and the minimum of the second one. If the samples are large enough (it doesn't work well for $n \le 5$), it's most likely that the first method is faster then the second one.

- **Tukey test:** $Q_3(x) + 1.5 \cdot IQR_x < Q_1(y) - 1.5 \cdot IQR_y$

   The range test can be easily spoiled by outliers. If x contains a single extremely high value that is inside the y range, the ranges are overlapped. This problem can be resolved if we exclude the outliers. No need here to actually find all outliers; we can just compare the upper Tukey fence for the first distribution and the lower Tukey fence for the second one.

- **Three-sigma test:** $\bar{x} + 3s_x < \bar{y} - 3s_y$

   We know that 99.7% of values in the normal distribution are inside the $\pm3s$ interval around the mean. Thus, we can compare the upper interval bound for the first distribution and the lower bound for the second one. This test works great for distributions that are close to normal, but it doesn't work well for more complex distributions (e.g., multimodal).

These simple tests have a very small Type I (false positive) error rate: when we think that there is a statistically significant difference (H_0 is false, H_1 is true), we are most likely right. However, the Type II (false negative) error rate is huge: when the distribution ranges are overlapped, we most likely will fail to detect which method is faster even if there is a statistically significant difference. It's a typical situation when we work with small performance improvements (e.g., 1%–10%). Thus, we need an advanced statistical tool for such cases.

There are many different **statistical tests** that can help us in different kinds of situations. In benchmarking, there are two tests that provide the most reliable results:

- **Welch's t-test**

  This test helps us to compare mean values of x and y. In theory, this test can be applied to only normal distributions. In practice, it often gives reliable results for unimodal distributions when the sample sizes are large enough. Usually, you need at least 30–40 measurements in each sample to get reliable results.

- **Mann–Whitney U test**

  This test helps to check that a random measurement from one sample is larger than a random measurement from another sample. This test doesn't require normality, so it can be applied to all kinds of performance distributions. You can even use it with multimodal distributions of different shapes. It doesn't work at all for extremely small samples; you need at least five measurements in each sample.

Such tests don't give us a binary result; they provide a value between 0 and 1 called the **p-value**. You can interpret a statistical test like a function of two samples:

```
double StatisticalTest(double[] x, double[] y)
{
  // Some calculations
  return pValue;
}
```

For such tests, it's recommended to use a threshold for comparison: instead of checking that "the first method is faster than the second method," we will check that "the performance difference between the two methods is larger than a given value." The threshold can be relative (e.g., 1% of the baseline) or absolute (e.g., 15ms). The threshold approach allows reducing the Type I (false positive) error rate because it's more robust against the natural noise. Thus, we have to modify the signature of our method:

```
double StatisticalTest(double[] x, double[] y, double threshold = 0.0)
{
  // Some calculations
  return pValue;
}
```

These tests have different variations. When we check that the difference $x - y$ is not zero (or other fixed value), we are talking about a **two-sided test**. When we check that the difference $x - y$ is larger than a threshold, we are talking about a **one-sided test**. When we check that the absolute difference $|x - y|$ is larger than a threshold, we are talking about an **equivalence test**. If we already know how to perform a one-sided test, an equivalence test can be implemented based on the **two-one-sided tests (TOST)** approach: we can perform two one-sided tests and check that $x - y$ is larger than a threshold or $y - x$ is larger than a threshold.

The returned magic p-value number is a classic source of confusion and misunderstanding. The general rule that is used in a lot of research looks as follows: "If the p-value is less than 0.05, we can reject H_0." Here are a few facts to help you understand p-values better:

- **p-value<0.05 doesn't mean that H_1 is true.**

  It means that we observe "unusual" results. Even if we don't have a statistically significant difference, we still can observe small p-values; it's a normal situation.

- **p-value>0.05 doesn't mean that H_1 is true.**

  It means that we can't reject H_0 based on the given samples. If you have p-value=0.20, you can't make any conclusions about H_0 and H_1; you need more experiments for that.

- **0.05 is not a mandatory value.**

  It's just the historical p-value threshold, but you don't have to use this particular number. It's *not recommended* to increase it, but you may consider using smaller numbers. Typically, you can use 0.01 or even 0.001 in benchmarking.

- **p-values work correctly only in a series of experiments.**

  It's not enough to have a single experiment with p-value < 0.05 to reject H_0. You have to collect other samples, repeat the statistical test, and get many small p-values in a row to be sure the H_0 is false.

It's also important to understand the distribution of p-values. Imagine two normal distributions x and y where the true difference between means is $d = 7$ and the standard deviation for both distributions is $s = 10$. Let's consider different threshold values from 0 to 14 and repeat the following experiment 1000 times for each value: we will take samples from each distribution ($n = 20$) and check that the difference $x - y$ is *larger* than a threshold t with the help of *one-sided* Welch's t-test. Thus, the null hypothesis H_0 is $d \leq t$, and the alternative hypothesis H_1 is $d > t$. You can see histograms that present distributions of p-values for different thresholds in Figure 4-12.

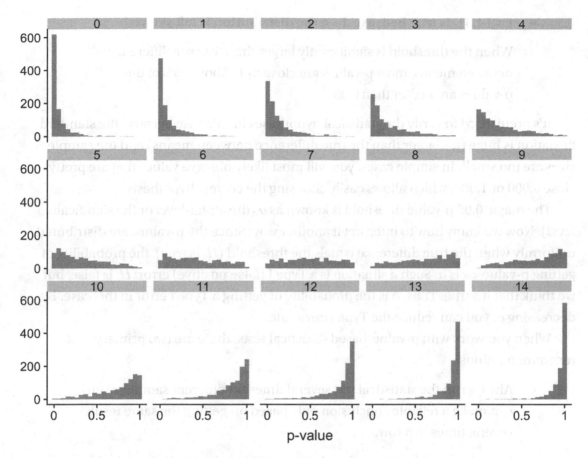

Figure 4-12. *p-value distributions for different thresholds*

Let's discuss some plots from this figure in detail:

- **t = 0, H₀ is false because d > 1, the distribution is right skewed.**

  When the threshold is significantly less than the true difference
  between means, most p-values are close to zero. However, there
  are still many p-values that are not small. Even when the threshold
  is zero, about 30% of the p-values are actually higher than 0.05.
  Thus, we can reject H_0 and say that the true difference between
  means is larger than zero only if we do several experiments.

- **t = 7, H₀ is true because d = t, the distribution is uniform.**

  When the threshold equals the true difference between means,
  the p-values are distributed uniformly. Thus, we can observe 0.05
  and 0.95 p-values with the same probability.

- **$t = 14$, H_0 is true because d $< t$, the distribution is left skewed.**

  When the threshold is significantly larger than the true difference between means, most p-values are close to 1. About 70% of the p-values are higher than 0.95.

It's pretty hard to verify the statistical hypotheses in this case because the standard deviation is huge (it's larger than the true difference between means) and the sample sizes are too small. In simple cases, you will most likely observe values that are pretty close 0.000 or 1.000, which allows easily choosing the correct hypothesis.

The magic 0.05 p-value threshold is known as α (the alpha-level or the significance level). Now we know how to interpret it another way. Since the p-values are distributed uniformly when the true difference equals the threshold (H_0 is true), the probability of getting p-value $<\alpha$ is α. Such a situation is a Type I (false positive) error: H_1 is false, but we think that it's true. Thus, α is the probability of getting a Type I error in this case. By decreasing α, you can reduce the Type I error rate.

When you work with p-value-based statistical tests, there are two primary recommendations:

- Always run the statistical test several times on different samples. You can make a reliable conclusion only based on getting the same results several times in a row.

- If you have too many p-values between 0.01 and 0.99, the sample size is probably not enough to make a statistically significant conclusion. Try to increase it.

- When you are sure that there is a tangible difference between x and y and want to prove it, you can use very small α like 0.001: it should be enough to detect a statistically significant difference with low Type I (false positive) error rate. When the difference between x and y is small (e.g., less than 1%) and the standard deviation is huge, it can be hard to prove that the difference is significant with a low α-level. However, if you did it, there is only a small chance that you did it wrong because α is responsible for the Type I (false positive) error rate. For example, in the Higgs boson experiment, $\alpha = 3 \cdot 10^{-7}$ was used, which means that the probability of getting incorrectly positive results is really small.

Now we know how to handle the fundamental task in the performance analysis: comparing two distributions. It's time to learn how to analyze several distributions.

Regression Models

Another important question in performance analysis is how the method performance depends on input parameters and environment. In statistics, there is an approach called **regression analysis**, which helps to answer this question.

In software development, the term "regression" has a negative meaning: it describes a situation when a feature worked fine before, but now it doesn't work (or it works incorrectly). "Performance regression" means that something worked fast before, but now it works slowly. In statistics, the term "regression" has another meaning. Originally, it was introduced by Francis Galton. One of his most famous researches describes a phenomenon when tall parents, on average, have children with a smaller height. The name of this effect is "regression toward the mean" (this concept is also well-covered in [Kahneman 2013]), which has a biological meaning. Later, the term "regression" was adopted by statisticians; it's used for describing a relationship between different variables (for example, the input data and the method performance).

In performance analysis, the regression models help to explore the performance space. With a regression model built on several samples, we can understand how the input data affects the performance and extrapolate this result for prediction of performance in real-life situations. One of the most popular usages of regression models in computer science is the **asymptotic analysis**. Consider the following three methods:

```
public int GetLength(int[] a)
{
  return a.Length;
}

public int ArraySum(int[] a)
{
  int n = a.Length;
  int sum = 0;
  for (int i = 0; i < n; i++)
    sum += a[i];
  return sum;
}
```

```
public void BubbleSort(int[] a)
{
  int n = a.Length;
  for (int i = 0; i < n; i++)
  for (int j = 0; j < n - i; j++)
    if (a[j] > a[j + 1])
    {
      var temp = a[j];
      a[j] = a[j + 1];
      a[j + 1] = temp;
    }
}
```

The first one returns the length of an array, the second calculates the sum of elements in an array, and the third sorts numbers in an array with the help of the bubble sort. In the asymptotic analysis, we can describe the performance of this method by the big O notation. We can say that the **algorithmic complexities** of these methods are as follows:

- GetLength: $O(1)$ (constant time complexity)

- ArraySum: $O(n)$ (linear time complexity)

- BubbleSort: $O(n^2)$ (quadratic time complexity)

Such dependencies can be visualized with the help of scatter plots. In the two-dimensional case, this plot has the performance metric on one axis and the target input variable on the other axis. In Figure 4-13, we can see the values of $O(1)$, $O(n)$, and $O(n^2)$ for different values of n.

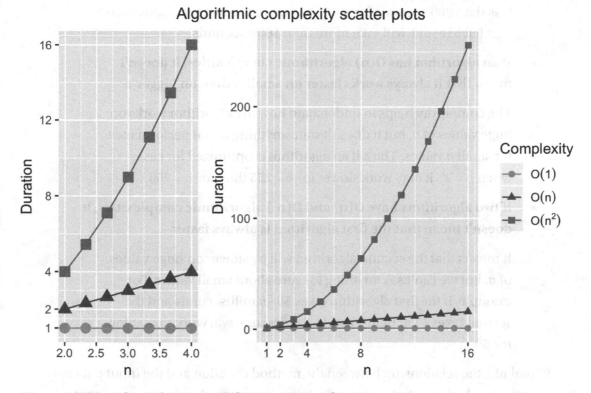

Figure 4-13. *Algorithmic complexity scatter plots*

The algorithmic complexity is often incorrectly interpreted, so let's discuss a few common pitfalls:

- **The algorithmic complexity is not the method duration**

    It just specifies the upper bound for the algorithm duration, which works even for huge n values. For example, $O(n^2)$ means that there is constant C such that the method duration is less than $C \cdot n^2$ for any n. In practice, it's useful to know how fast the duration will increase when n is increased. The constant C can have a pretty high value. For example, we can set =100 , which means that ArraySum will take less than $100n$ seconds. It may sound obvious that it takes less than 100 seconds for $n = 1$, but the most important fact here is that this condition will be valid for huge n values. The BubbleSort complexity is (n^2) , which means that $100n$ can't be used for the upper bound duration. Of course, BubbleSort takes less than 100 seconds for $n = 1$ and less than 200 seconds for $n = 2$, but there are huge n values such that BubbleSort will take more than $100n$ seconds.

- **If an algorithm has O(n) algorithmic complexities, it doesn't mean that it always works faster on small n than on bigger n**

   The complexity helps to understand how the algorithm works on huge values of n, but it doesn't state anything about performance for small n values. Thus, if an algorithm is optimized for cases when $n = 2^k$, it may work slower for $n = 255$ than for $n = 256$.

- **If two algorithms have O(n) and O(n²) algorithmic complexities, it doesn't mean that the first algorithm is always faster**

   It means that the second algorithm will be slower on huge values of n, but we can't say anything for sure about small values. For example, if the first algorithm takes $50 \cdot n$ milliseconds and the second takes $1 \cdot n^2$ milliseconds, the first one will work slower for $n < 50$.

In real life, the relationship between the method duration and the input data may be complicated. Let's say that we have the following expression for an array: `array.OrderBy(x => x).Take(1)`. What is the algorithmic complexity of this method? In .NET Core 2.1, the internal implementation uses the quickselect algorithm. It has the $O(n)$ best-case and average-case complexity. But the worst-case complexity is $O(n^2)$. This means that if the number in the array follows a special pattern (like `2 4 6 8 10 5 3 7 1 9`), the performance will be much worse than on the average case. In Table 4-4, you can see corresponding measurements for two cases: `Equal` (all numbers are zeros) and `QsWorst` (the worst case for the quickselect algorithm).

Table 4-4. *Quickselect Performance*

n	Case	Mean	StdDev
1000	Equal	42.16 μs	0.1068 μs
1000	QsWorst	8,853.04 μs	84.8771 μs
10000	Equal	415.93 μs	0.9477 μs
10000	QsWorst	876,433.01 μs	4,960.2892 μs

As you can see, when we increase n 10 times (1000 → 10000), the duration of `Equal` increases 10 times, but the duration of `QsWorst` increases 100 times, which can be explained by $O(n)$ and $O(n^2)$ complexity. The behavior was improved[8] and now it always has $O(n)$ complexity because it just calculates the minimum element (the fix is available in .NET Core 3.0). Thus, the actual performance depends not only on the number of elements in an array, but also on the array content and the runtime version.

However, in simple cases, it's often possible to build a regression model and explain how performance depends on the input data. A regression model provides more useful information about method performance than the algorithmic complexity does: instead of the determining the upper bound, it allows building a function that returns an estimation for method performance based on its parameters.

The simplest regression model is the **linear regression model**. It's useful when you are sure that you have a linear dependency between the parameters and the performance. Such a model is expressed by the following equation:

$$\textit{Linear regression}: \text{Duration} = \alpha_0 + \alpha_1 n$$

where α_0 and α_1 are some constants.

It can be a good prediction model when the dependency is really linear. However, sometimes it can be quadratic.[9] In this case, we can use the **quadratic regression model**:

$$\textit{Quadratic regression}: \text{Duration} = \alpha_0 + \alpha_1 n + \alpha_2 n^2$$

A cool fact about the linear regression model: it's a special case of the quadratic regression. This means that if we are not sure if the algorithm is linear or quadratic, we can build a quadratic model and check α_2. If this value is close to zero, the algorithm is most likely linear. If this value is far from zero, the algorithm is not linear, but we don't know its degree. Fortunately, we can build the **polynomial regression model**:

$$\textit{Polynomial regression}: \text{Duration} = \alpha_0 + \alpha_1 n + \alpha_2 n^2 + \alpha_3 n^3 + \alpha_4 n^4 + \cdots$$

---

[8]https://github.com/dotnet/corefx/pull/32389

[9]There is an interesting blog called "Accidentally Quadratic" with stories about situations when an algorithm has the quadratic complexity, but it wasn't obvious: https://accidentallyquadratic.tumblr.com/

If the coefficients α_3, α_4, ... are close to zero, the model is most likely quadratic. Such equations can be built with the help of **the method of least squares**.[10] The regression is not always polynomial; it can be expressed by any kind of function. The problem of finding this function is known as **curve fitting**.[11] You may come up with an idea of this curve from a scatter plot, make a hypothesis about the regression kind (e.g., $O(n \log n)$ or $O\left(\sqrt{n}\right)$), and build the corresponding model.

A common problem that often arises in regression analysis is **overfitting**. It relates to the situation when the built curve perfectly fits the data we have, but doesn't show the true dependency between the method performance and its parameters. The risk of overfitting is high when the sample size is small. For example, it's always possible to build a perfect linear model when you have only two points (you should just connect them by a line). If you have three points, it's always possible to build a perfect quadratic model even if the true model is logarithmic or cubic. In fact, any k points allow building a perfect polynomial model of degree $k - 1$. Thus, if we have 1000 points, we can build a polynomial model of degree 999, but it's unlikely a correct model. To avoid overfitting, you always have to check how the model works on data that is not used for the construction of the regression model. This approach is known as **cross-validation**.

Another important kind of performance analysis tries to answer how the performance depends on the environment. Here we usually work with **categorical variables**. You can interpret it as a value from an enum (a predefined set of non-numeric values). For example, you can consider a JIT kind (LegacyJIT or RyuJIT), a runtime (.NET Framework, .NET Core, or Mono), or an operating system (Windows, Linux, or macOS). In the simplest case, you already know the environment factor that you want to check. For example, in JetBrains Rider, a typical factor that is important for performance is the operating system. In Figure 4-14, you can see performance measurements for a test that expands an ASP.NET template and performs some operations on it.

---

[10]You can find an implementation of this method and other similar algorithms in the MathNet. Numerics NuGet package: see `https://numerics.mathdotnet.com/`

[11]You can find the most truthful explanation of how curve fitting works in real life here: `https://xkcd.com/2048/`

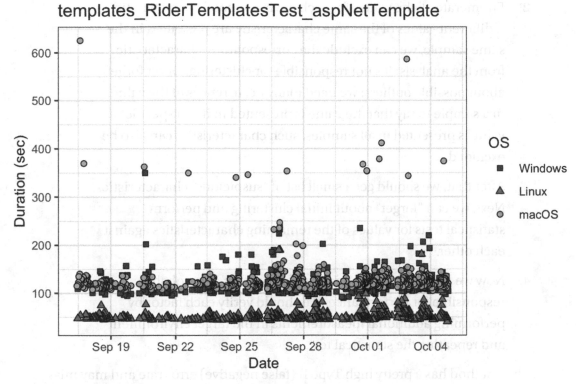

Figure 4-14. *Performance clustering by OS*

Different operating systems are denoted by different shapes and colors. As you can see, we obviously have **clustering** here: the test works much faster on Linux than on Windows or macOS. A good visualization may provide some initial hypothesis about factors affecting performance. Next, you can perform a statistical test against samples from a different OS. For example, we can apply one-sided Mann–Whitney U test, which checks that the difference between the macOS sample and the Linux sample is statistically significant with a 60-second threshold.

However, we don't always know which environment factors really affect performance. Imagine that we have hundreds of characteristics for each measurement, but we don't know which of them are important. In this case, we can do the following:

1. Find the cluster in one performance measurements. Since we have one-dimensional data, we don't need "advanced" cluster detection algorithms. It's recommended to use a simple method like **Jenks natural breaks optimization**. After that, you should get several samples with statistically significant differences between them.

2. Enumerate all the values for each environmental characteristic. If different values of the same characteristic are presented in the same sample, we can exclude the corresponding characteristic from the analysis: it's not responsible for clustering. Don't forget about possible outliers: we need many occurrences of the values in a sample to say that the value is presented in it. If a specific value is presented in all samples, such characteristics can also be excluded.

3. After that, we should get a small list of "suspicious" characteristics. Next, we can "forget" about initial clustering and perform statistical tests for values of the remaining characteristics against each other.

4. Now we have a list of "suspicious" factors that are probably responsible for performance. We should verify each factor by performing additional measurements in the target environment and repeating the statistical test.

Such a method has a pretty high Type II (false negative) error rate and may miss some cluster effects. However, it also has very small Type I (false positive) error rate, so we will not be disturbed by a false alarm. Meanwhile, if we have an obvious clustering, we will probably find it. You can come up with your own checks based on your business goals and the environment part of the performance space. You can even use some machine learning–based approaches, but simple checks and heuristics may be much more effective in real life. In huge software products, you typically don't need all existing clustering effects: you need only the most major effects, which are superobvious when you are looking at a scatter plot. Such effects can be easily detected with very simple checks that can be quickly implemented without complicated mathematics.

The use of regression models is a very powerful technique that helps you to understand your performance space better. It allows you to determine dependencies between the input data, the environment, and the performance. When you know how to use them, you can make a prediction about the duration of your methods under different conditions.

Optional Stopping

A typical benchmark includes many magic numbers, including the hardcoded number of iterations. The process of benchmarking has a unique "feature": we can do as many measurements as we want. On one hand, this is good because if we don't have enough performance data, we always can do additional iterations. On the other hand, it's bad because we can't collect *all* measurements. Here the problems begin. Since we have an endless set of measurements, how many iterations should we do? Is it enough to take ten measurements? Or do we need ten thousand of them? Usually developers set the number of iterations based on the amount of time that they are ready to wait. If an iteration takes 10 milliseconds, we can do hundreds of them. If an iteration takes 5 minutes, it can be the only iteration. Most developers don't want to wait too long, and the endless set transforms into a pretty small collection of numbers.

Usually, developers pick them at random: "Let's make 100 iterations; I guess that should be enough." This isn't the best strategy because most likely a random number is less than necessary (accuracy is poor) or more than necessary (we are waiting for results too long). There is a solution to this problem: we can choose the magic numbers *adaptively* during the run. In statistics, this approach is known as the **sequential analysis**.

Let's consider a part of a hypothetical performance investigation log:

- We are going to run the benchmark 5 times.

- It seems that 5 is not enough because the variance is too huge. Let's try to run the benchmark 100 times.

- Now the variance is OK, but it takes too long run the benchmark 100 times. Let's try 20 iterations.

- Now the variance is still OK, and all runs takes an acceptable amount of time.

This investigation has one major problem: the goals are poorly chosen. Here are the described goals:

- We want to run the benchmark 5 times.

- We want to run the benchmark 100 times.

- We want to run the benchmark 20 times.

However, it would be better to set the following goal:

- We want to get a low standard error (less than 2.5 seconds); the number of iterations should be as minimal as possible.

Thus, you will use magic numbers anyway. However, it's very important which numbers to choose. Instead of asking "How many iterations should I choose?", you should ask yourself "What kind of distribution characteristics I want?" The benchmark design should include the desired metric values of the future distributions. Once these conditions are achieved, we can stop the iteration process.

The optional stopping requires collecting **cumulative metrics**. These are intermediate statistical characteristics that are recalculated after each iteration. In Figure 4-15, you can see an example of a timeline plot that includes cumulative means and confidence intervals. Such plots can help you understand the relationship between the sample size and the final metrics. As you can see, if we stop the iteration process after a few iterations, the confidence interval will be huge; it can't be used for reliable conclusions. After the first 10 iterations, the confidence interval becomes smaller, but it's still pretty big (it equals to [36.53; 47.97] while the cumulative mean is 42.25). After 30 iterations, the confidence interval equals [35.98; 42.19] while the cumulative mean is 39.08.

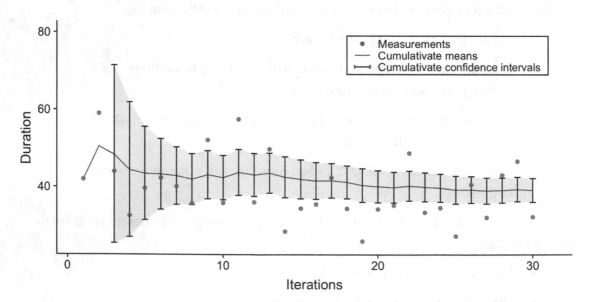

Figure 4-15. *Timeline plot with cumulative means and confidence intervals*

Once you have the cumulative metrics, you can formulate the **stopping criteria** based on that. Here are a few options:

- Stopping criteria for warm-up iterations may be based on fluctuations. We know that the first iteration can be heavy. Usually, the second iteration takes less time than the first one because it's performed in a warmed-up state. However, one iteration may be not enough for full warm-up. The third iteration may be faster than the second one because it's performed in a more warmed state. While each iteration takes less time than the previous one, the warm-up is in progress. Once fluctuations are started, we can assume that the warm-up is finished (it's not true in the general case). Thus, we can wait for fluctuations before we terminate the warm-up process.

- Stopping criteria for actual iterations (which we use in the final results) may be based on the standard error. For example, we can specify an absolute or relative threshold for the standard error and wait until we reach it. Since the standard error is $s/\sqrt{n}$, it decreases when we increase the sample size.[12] Thus, it's almost always possible to find the sample size with a standard error less than a given value.

- Stopping criteria for any kind of iteration may be a logical formula that includes several conditions. For example, it's recommended to set the upper limit for the number of iterations. If you didn't achieve your requirements after 100 iterations, it's most likely that a few dozen additional iterations will not help: it's better to stop the experiment and look at the distribution and statistical metrics. After that, you can understand that it's impossible to reach the desired distribution characteristics in a reasonable amount of time or that you need special stopping criteria for this particular benchmark.

You can use the preceding criteria or create your own based on the business goals. However, the metric that you use in the stopping criteria has an important requirement: the cumulative metrics should form a convergent series. For example, you shouldn't use

---

[12]We assume that the standard deviation is not changing significantly with additional iterations. The only exception from this rule supposes that new iterations take more time than the previous. In this case, the benchmark doesn't have a steady state, and it doesn't make sense to discuss its distribution.

the desired results of statistical tests: if you use stopping criteria based on p-values, it may significantly increase the Type I (false positive) error rate.

In Figure 4-16 (A), you can see cumulative p-value plot (based on the Welch's t-test) for 20 experiments when H_0 is true (we *don't have* a statistically significant difference). The picture resembles random noise because such p-values are uniformly distributed. In Figure 4-16 (B), you can see the same experiments, but the plot is scaled to the [0.00, 0.10] p-values range. Sometimes, a cumulative p-value function "dives" under the 0.5 threshold and "emerges" from under it. If the sample size is fixed from the beginning, we will get uniformly distributed p-values as a result. However, if we stop the iteration process once p-value <0.05 is observed, we will get too many small p-values, which leads to the false H_0 rejecting. In Figure 4-16 (C), a histogram of such p-values is presented. As you can see, the [0.00, 0.05] interval contains left-skewed distribution, which is untypical for p-values obtained from correct experiments. Knowledge of the expected p-value distribution helps to verify your own results and check someone else's research. You can find an example of such verification in [Lakens 2014a].

In Figure 4-16 (D,E,F), you can see the same experiment, but H_0 is false (we *have* a statistically significant difference). In this case, once a cumulative p-value function "dives" under the 0.5 threshold, it remains under it. This experiment has a pretty small difference between means, so sometimes we need many measurements to get a reliable result, but we eventually achieve p-value <0.05, which helps to reject H_0 correctly.

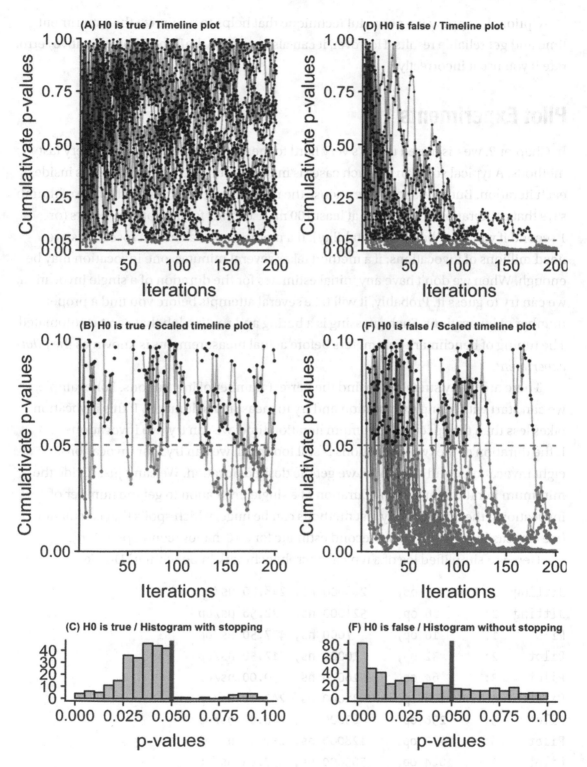

Figure 4-16. *Cumulative p-values*

Optional stopping is a powerful technique that helps to minimize the experiment time and get reliable results. However, it can also increase the Type I (false positive) error rate if you use it incorrectly.

Pilot Experiments

In Chapter 2, we discussed that it's very hard to measure the performance of very fast methods. A typical solution for such cases is making many method invocations inside each iteration. But how should we choose the number of invocations? The rule of thumb says that an iteration should take at least 100 milliseconds for acceptable results (or 1 second if you want better repeatability). If a method takes a few microseconds, we need millions of invocations; if a method takes several minutes, one invocation may be enough. When we don't have any initial estimates for the duration of a single invocation, we can try to guess it. Probably, it will take several attempts before you find a proper number of invocations. Such guessing is a boring and routine job that can be automated. The tuning of benchmark parameters before actual measurements is known as the *pilot experiment*.

There are many strategies to find the perfect number of invocations. For example, we can start with a single invocation and try to measure its duration. If this invocation takes less than the specified minimum iteration time, we can try two invocations. If the duration of the two invocations is still too small, we can try four invocations, eight invocations, and so on until we get the desired duration. We can't just divide the minimum iteration time by the duration of a single invocation to get the number of invocations: the error for very fast methods can be huge, which spoils that calculation (we can easily get a 1000-nanosecond estimate for a 10-nanosecond operation).

Here is a simplified log of a typical microbenchmark in BenchmarkDotNet:

```
Jitting  1:      1 op,    248000 ns, 248.00 µs/op
Jitting  2:     16 op,    521000 ns,  32.56 µs/op
Pilot    1:     16 op,      7000 ns, 437.50 ns/op
Pilot    2:     32 op,     10000 ns, 312.50 ns/op
Pilot    3:     64 op,     16000 ns, 250.00 ns/op
Pilot    4:    128 op,     31000 ns, 242.18 ns/op
Pilot    5:    256 op,     63000 ns, 246.09 ns/op
Pilot    6:    512 op,    128000 ns, 250.00 ns/op
Pilot    7:   1024 op,    305000 ns, 297.85 ns/op
```

```
Pilot    8:     2048 op,    500000 ns, 244.14 ns/op
Pilot    9:     4096 op,    998000 ns, 243.65 ns/op
Pilot   10:     8192 op,   2189000 ns, 267.21 ns/op
...
Pilot   18: 2097152 op, 523762000 ns, 249.74 ns/op
```

Let's discuss it in detail.

- *Jitting 1*: this is the first iteration of the jitting phase. During this iteration, the JIT compiler generates the native code for the method. BenchmarkDotNet runs a single invocation of the given method and measures its duration. In this example, 1 op means "1 operation," which equals to one invocation by default. As you can see, a single iteration takes 248,000 nanoseconds.

- *Jitting 2*: this is the second iteration of the jitting phase. We already know that the given method is pretty fast, so we are switching to another benchmark mode where we have 16 consecutive method invocations inside a loop body. This manual loop unrolling helps us to achieve better accuracy in nanobenchmarks. During this iteration, the JIT compiler generates the native code for the described loop. The 16 invocations of a method take 521000 nanoseconds, which means that a single invocation takes approximately 32.56 μs (microseconds).

- *Pilot 1*: Now it's time for the pilot stage. First of all, we try to repeat an iteration with 16 invocations. It takes 7000 nanoseconds instead of 521,000! The first jitting call had a huge overhead, but now we have a better estimation of the approximated average invocation time: 437.50 nanoseconds.

- *Pilot 2*: 7000 nanoseconds is not enough to get reliable results. Let's increase the number of invocations twice and measure the duration of 32 operations. It takes 10000 nanoseconds. It doesn't equal to 2∗7000 nanoseconds because the previous iteration was spoiled by natural noise. The increased number of invocations reduces the noise influence and allows getting a better approximation for the average invocation duration: 312.50 nanoseconds. Let's continue to increase the number of invocations until the total iteration time reaches an acceptable value.

- *Pilot 18*: After 18 pilot iterations, the iteration duration becomes 523,762,000 nanoseconds (0.52 seconds). Thus, the average invocation time is 249.74 nanoseconds. It is significantly better than our first approximation, which is 248,000 nanoseconds. It doesn't make sense to continue increasing the number of invocations because it doesn't improve the accuracy: we achieved a reliable and repeatable estimation for a single invocation duration. If we use a larger number of invocations, the total experiment time will be increased without any benefits in terms of accuracy. Thus, we can continue to do 2,097,152 invocations per iteration during warm-up and actual stage when we collect the measurements that form our final performance distribution.

Of course, you can use other strategies for the pilot experiment. For example, you can invoke the method in a `while` loop until the minimum iteration time is achieved. Don't use this approach for actual measurements: iteration with an unequal number of invocations also can spoil the results. Such a `while` loop also requires a separate warm-up stage: the first experiment can be spoiled by cold start effects like assembly loading or jitting.

The pilot experiment is a powerful technique that helps to find the best benchmark parameters and achieve a better trade-off between the accuracy and the total benchmarking time.

Summing Up

In this section, we covered two important approaches to analyzing a group of distributions:

- **Distribution comparison**

    When we want to compare two distributions, we work with two hypotheses: H_0 (*there is no* difference) and H_1 (*there is* a difference). The conclusions may include errors of two kinds: Type I (false positive: *there is no* difference, but *we think that there is* a difference) and Type II (false negative: *there is* a difference, but *we think that there is no* difference). In most simple cases, we can apply simple heuristics (range test, Tukey test, or three-sigma test) or honest statistical tests: Welch's t-test (works only for unimodal distributions that are close to normal), Mann–Whitney U test (works for any kind of distribution). Such tests provide a p-value that should be compared with α-level threshold (typical value is 0.05). If we get many small p-values (less than α) in a series of experiments, H_1 is most likely true (we have a difference between distributions). When H_0 is true, p-values are distributed uniformly, which means that α is the Type I (false positive) error rate.

- **Regression models**

  Regression models help to detect relationships between the input data, the environment, and the performance. Asymptotic analysis helps to express the algorithmic complexity by the big O notation (e.g., $O(n^2)$ or $O(n \log n)$). In many cases, we can use polynomial models (e.g., linear model or quadratic model), but other cases require advanced curve fitting. When we want to understand how the environment affects performance, we should work with categorical variables (e.g., OS: Windows/Linux/macOS). We can find the most important environment factors with the help of clustering and check that they really affect performance with the help of statistical tests.

Also, we discussed two approaches of adaptive benchmarking:

- **Optional stopping**

  Instead of guessing the perfect number of iterations, we can define a stopping criteria: the iteration process should perform until the desired distribution properties are achieved. You shouldn't use p-values for it because it can significantly increase the Type I (false positive) error rate.

- **Pilot experiments**

  Some experimental parameters (like the number of invocations inside each iteration) can be determined in advance. In the pilot experiment (which is performed before the actual experiment), we can run a series of iterations with different characteristics in order to determine the best benchmark parameters for our accuracy requirements.

Adaptive benchmarking helps you to design the benchmark correctly, achieve the desired accuracy, and minimize the total benchmark duration. These approaches have been successfully used in BenchmarkDotNet for years. Even with BenchmarkDotNet, you should still understand the concept of adaptive benchmarking; the library will not design a benchmark for you. BenchmarkDotNet provides some default values for the target distribution requirements, but it works fine only in simple cases. In complicated cases, you have to tune these numbers or even define your own statistics criteria.

However, knowledge of all analysis techniques doesn't protect you from mistakes and wrong conclusions. Let's learn how statistics may deceive you and force you into wrong business decisions.

How to Lie with Benchmarking

The title of this section is inspired by a great book by Darrell Huff, *How to Lie with Statistics* (see [Huff 1993]). This book contains many examples that demonstrate how easily people can be fooled with the help of special ways of presenting the data. When we are talking about benchmarking, this topic becomes pretty important because it's very easy to make incorrect conclusions based on benchmark results even if nobody tries to deceive you.

This section has two goals:

- **Self-defense from others**

    Many performance reports that you can find in articles, blog posts, StackOverflow answers, and GitHub discussions often contain misleading numbers and plots that may push you to a wrong decision. It's good to know how to detect different deceptive techniques.

- **Self-defense from yourself**

    Even when you are working with your own set of benchmarks, it's pretty easy to interpret results incorrectly and fool yourself. If you want to prevent such a situation, you should learn the most common mistakes that developers usually make.

If you think that the knowledge of statistics is sufficient protection, I highly recommended you to read [Kahneman 2013], which demonstrates how bad human intuition handles pretty simple statistics tasks. One of the main book ideas is the following: the human mind has two "systems": "System 1" (fast but not so smart) and "System 2" (slow but smart). The first ideas that we have about something are provided by "System 1": we get them instantly, but they are often wrong. If we carefully think about the subject, "System 2" will provide more accurate and correct answer, but it can take some time. Unfortunately, people don't always carefully think when they make decisions and use answers coming from System 1. This may lead to incorrect conclusions about the benchmark results.

In this section, we will try to activate our "System 2" and learn how to use it in benchmarking. We are going to cover the most common ways to lie with benchmarking and what you need to pay attention to in order to recognize a lie.

Lie with Small Samples

When you are analyzing raw data, intuition is your worst enemy. It tries to find patterns everywhere, and it finds it (even if there are no patterns). Here is an exercise: based on the following measurements, which method is faster?

```
A: 58 ms 62 ms 57 ms 60 ms 66 ms
B: 61 ms 67 ms 70 ms 77 ms 73 ms
```

If you think like most people, you say "A faster than B" because in each column, the "A" value is less than the "B" value.

I have to confess: I generated all ten numbers based on the same benchmark with the following source code:

```
static long Measure()
{
  var data = new byte[64 * 1024 * 1024];
  var stopwatch = Stopwatch.StartNew();
  var fileName = Path.GetTempFileName();
  File.WriteAllBytes(fileName, data);
  File.Delete(fileName);
```

```
  stopwatch.Stop();
  return stopwatch.ElapsedMilliseconds;
}
```

It's one of my favorite guinea pigs for such experiments: it creates a file with 64 MB of data and removes it. Now we can generate ten numbers as we get in the preceding:

```
Console.Write("A: ");
for (int i = 0; i < 5; i++)
  Console.Write(Measure() + " ms ");
Console.WriteLine();
Console.Write("B: ");
for (int i = 0; i < 5; i++)
  Console.Write(Measure() + " ms ");
```

It still may seem that the probability of getting such results is pretty low. Let's do some math. The chance that one measurement will be less than another is about 50% (the I/O operations don't produce stable performance values, so it's pretty unlikely to have equal measurements). The chance that each number from the "A" row will be less than the corresponding number from the "B" row is $(1/2)^5$ or 3.125%. That's not a small number. Let's say that 22 readers of this book decide to try this code snippet. The probability that no one gets such a strange result is $(1 - 0.03125)^{22}$ or 49.7%. This means that there is a 50.3% chance that at least one of them will get a result that looks like "A faster than B." It's pretty similar to the Birthday Paradox, which states that there is a 50% chance that in a room of 23 people, 2 of them will have the same birthday (read more about it in [Azad 2007]).

It's a common situation when a small sample contains insidious data anomalies that look like patterns. If you often do benchmarking, you will often get "extraordinary" results in small samples because of the random noise. You may be tempted to make conclusions based on that, which may lead to wrong business decisions. Knowledge of statistics will help you to protect yourself from such situations and correctly verify all your performance hypotheses.

When the sample size is small, most of the statistical metrics are unreliable because you can't calculate the correct values for the true distribution based on a few measurements. You can't understand if the distribution is multimodal or unimodal, you can miss possible outliers, you can't get a proper value of the standard deviation, and so on. A small sample size may be used for getting a first impression about the measurements, such as "the method takes several seconds" or "the method takes several microseconds." But it's not enough to make a meaningful conclusion about the distribution. For example, when the difference between the two methods is 10–20%, you can't detect it correctly if $n = 5$.

Lie with Percents

Let's say that you made a performance improvement: a method which took 200ms before now takes 100ms. How do you describe this change with percentages? It depends on your baseline. If the baseline is 200ms, we have $(200 - 100)/200 * 100\% = 50\%$ improvement. If the baseline is 100ms, we have $(200 - 100)/100 * 100\% = 100\%$ improvement. The ratio is the same, but the result is different: 50% vs. 100%.

Someone may say that it's cheating and the baseline should always be the original value (the "before" state). Here we have another hack: we can let readers choose the baseline themselves. Usually, people don't like to do complicated math in their minds, so they try to choose the simplest baseline for calculations. Let's say that you made a 2.5× performance improvement. Compare the following two sentences:

> A method which took **250** seconds before, now takes **100** seconds.

and

> A method which took **100** seconds before, now takes **40** seconds.

In both cases, we have a 2.5× speedup. However, many people mentally translate it to 150% in the first case and 60% in the second case. It's much easier to use 100 seconds as a baseline because it's the most natural divider when we are talking about percentages. Of course, if you spend several seconds thinking, you will understand that your first intuitive guess was wrong. Kahneman's System 1 and System 2 in action! Usually, people don't like to apply math everywhere: they just quickly scan a text. Thus, for many people, the $250 \rightarrow 100$ improvement makes more impression than the $100 \rightarrow 40$ improvement.

Operations with percentages are a frequent source of wrong conclusions. Let's say that our project had a good level of performance in May. The metric used is RPS. In June, we had a 40% degradation in terms of RPS. In July, we made some improvements and got a 50% speedup *compared to June*. Thus, we have the following picture:

```
May  : Baseline
June : -40%
July : +50%
```

The question: what can you say about performance changes between May and July? Probably, the first idea that appeared in your head was "Performance in July was better because the 50% speedup beat the 40% degradation." Now, let's do some calculations. If a method performed around 100 RPS in May, the 40% degradation means that we had $100 \cdot (1 - 0.40) = 60$ RPS in June. The 50% speedup means that we had $60 \cdot (1 + 0.50) = 90$ RPS in July:

```
May  : Baseline | 100 RPS
June : -40%      |  60 RPS
July : +50%      |  90 RPS
```

As you can see, we still have a degradation comparing to May.

Here is another performance quiz for you (try to answer as fast as you can). Let's say that we decided to optimize a method and we have two alternative improvements. After benchmarking, it turns out that the first optimization reduces the method duration by 98%, and the second one reduces it by 99%. By how much is the second implementation faster than the first one?

Typically, the first number that arises in mind is 1%, but the correct answer is "two times." Probably, you solved this quiz correctly because you were waiting for a trick. However, many people often incorrectly interpret such situations when they try to read benchmark results quickly and don't expect any tricks.

Many performance reports use such tricks to create a *feeling* that the situation is better or worse than in reality. While such reports do not contain deliberately false data, the described manipulations may force you to think out wrong conclusions.

Lie with Ratios

If you determined that one method is faster than another, the next logical question is "how many times faster?" The typical approach is to divide the mean value of the first method sample by the mean value of the second method sample. However, this doesn't work well in general, because it's another kind of situation where we can't describe the answer with a single number. The correct approach is to build the ratio distribution z:

$$z_1 = \frac{x_1}{y_1}, \quad z_2 = \frac{x_2}{y_2}, \quad \ldots, \quad z_n = \frac{x_n}{y_n}$$

This is a paired method, which means that you need samples of equal size. As a result, you have another distribution that has its own statistical metrics: mean, variance, and so on.

Consider the following two samples:

$$x = \{200,200,200,200,200\}, \quad y = \{100,100,100,100,10000\}$$

The x sample is superstable: all its elements equal to 200. The y sample also is pretty stable (almost all its elements equal to 100), but it has a single huge outlier. Now let's build the ratio distribution:

$$z = \{2,2,2,2,0.02\}$$

How much faster is x than y? Let's consider two ways to calculate it: the ratio of the means and the mean of the ratio:

$$\frac{\overline{x}}{\overline{y}} \approx 0.1, \quad \overline{z} \approx 1.6$$

The first answer says that x is 10 times *faster* than y, but the second answer says that x is 1.6 times *slower* than y. Which answer is better? In fact, both answers are bad because we can't describe the answer by a single number in this case. The best answer contains information about the ratio distribution. For example, we can present it as follows:

$$\min(z) = 0.02, \quad \max(z) = 2, \quad Q_2(z) = 2, \quad \overline{z} \approx 1.6, \quad s_z \approx 0.89, \quad n_z = 5$$

After a quick analysis, we can understand that in most cases y is faster than x, but sometimes x may be significantly faster. We also know that the ratio sample size is five, which is not enough for meaningful conclusions; you probably need more data.

In most real-life benchmarks, $\overline{x}/\overline{y}$ and $\overline{z}$ have close values and the z range is narrow, so people often use phrases like "10 times improvement." It's OK to say something like that if you have already checked the ratio distribution and know that the difference between z_{min} and z_{max} is small. It's not a good idea to provide too many metrics in each performance report: it's hard to read and understand such reports. You should highlight only the important metrics and provide a way to check out the full list of statistics characteristics. Unfortunately, developers quickly get used to narrow ranges and forget to check the ratio distribution before making their final conclusions.

We can also not provide the scaled result and suggest to a reader to evaluate it himself. Look at the following table and try to quickly compare the performance of methods A and B:

	Mean	Skewness	Kurtosis	StdDev
A	523ms	0.34	2.64	752ms
B	929ms	0.39	2.31	983ms

Probably, the first impression was something like "A works two times faster than B" because of the Mean column. The Skewness and Kurtosis columns don't provide useful information for this problem, but they "hide" the standard deviation column: a reader can stop to read the table because of the "boring" columns. Meanwhile, the standard deviation column contains very important information: it has very huge values. The sample sizes and the standard errors are not presented, so we don't have enough data for any meaningful conclusions about A and B. The difference between means (406 ms) can be easily explained by "bad" samples: it's very easy to get such a value when the variance is huge and the sample sizes are small. We can't say that A is faster than B without a proper statistical test or a density plot based on larger samples. However, many developers finish analyzing the results after the Mean column and reach unreliable conclusions.

Lie with Plots

Plotting is a great way to visualize your data and quickly understand the form of the distribution. However, it can also be a dangerous weapon that forces you to make wrong conclusions.

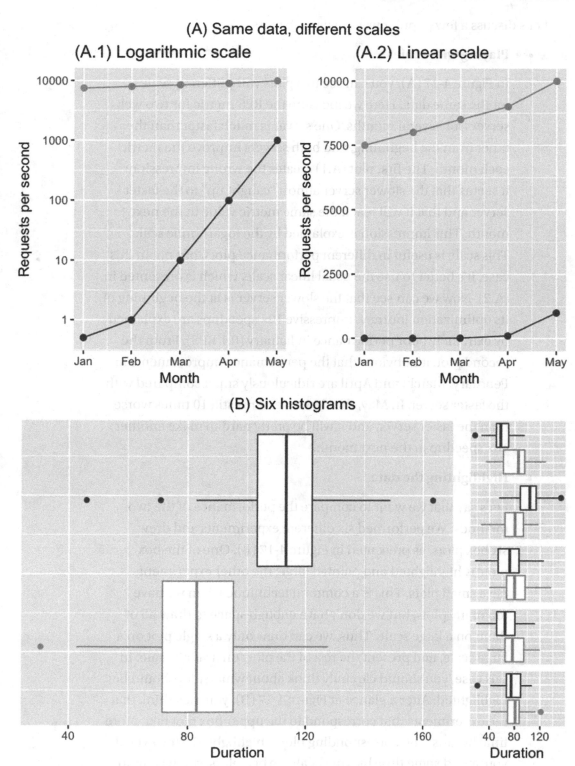

Figure 4-17. *Lie with plots*

Let's discuss a few popular ways to lie with plots:

- **Playing with scales**

  In Figure 4-17 (A), you can see two plots with different scales for the same data. Here we measure the RPS metric for two web servers for several months. One server is much faster than the other from the beginning, and both servers improve the metric each month. The first plot (A.1) creates the wrong impression: it seems that the slower server almost "caught up" to the faster server and that it will reach the same metric value in the next month. This impression is explained by the logarithmic scale. This scale is useful in different performance plots, but not in this case. It's better to use the usual linear scale, which is presented in (A.2). Now we can see that the slower server is at the beginning of its optimization journey. Impressive 10× speedups are explained by extremely poor performance in January (0.1 RPS). From the second plot, it's obvious that the performance improvements in February, March, and April are ridiculously small compared with the faster server. In May, the slower server is still 10 times worse than the faster server, and it will be pretty hard to make another 10× speedup in the next month.

- **Highlighting the data**

  Let's say that we want to compare the performance of the two methods. We performed six different experiments and drew six box plots, as presented in Figure 4-17 (B). One of the box plots is highlighted and painted large; the other experiments have small plots. This is a common technique when we have too many plots, but we don't have enough space to draw all of them on a large scale. Thus, we can draw only a single plot on a large scale, and present the rest of the plots on a small scale. In this case, you should carefully think about which plot should be highlighted. After a glance at Figure 4-17 (B), you may think that the experiments that correspond to the upper box plot take more time because the corresponding plot is highlighted. However, if you spend some time looking at all the box plots, you will figure out that it's impossible to say which method is faster: we have opposite results in different experiments.

- **Hiding the data**

  Sometimes, we have unwanted data that we don't want to highlight. In this case, we can choose a special visualization form. For example, if we have too many outliers that we don't want to present, we can choose a density plot over a frequency trail plot. A density plot is a popular kind of visualization, and it's OK to use it. However, we know about one of its features: it "hides" outliers. It's still an honest way to present the data, but it doesn't show *all the data*. If the distribution is multimodal, but we don't want to tell anyone about it, we can choose a box plot over a density plot. In this case, we also use a popular and honest kind of visualization, but we choose it because it hides information that we don't want to share with others. Each plot kind shows only specific properties of a distribution: there is no compact and accurate way to present all possible distribution characteristics (especially if we have many distributions). Thus, we will always hide some information. Usually, when we finish the analysis, we are trying to find a visualization approach that highlights the most interesting parts of the performance space. However, it's also possible to intentionally choose a plot that hides it.

There are many different ways to lie with plots (you can find other interesting examples of deceiving plots in [Wainer 1984]). A good visualization is a complicated task that usually takes much time and effort. It's a common situation when a researcher doesn't have enough time and just picks a random plot. Another typical situation: a researcher knows how to draw only one kind of plot and uses it everywhere instead of looking for the best visualization for each specific case. In such a situation, there is a high risk that a deceiving plot will be drawn unintentionally. When you read reports by other people, always pay attention to how the visualization is presented and why a specific plot kind is used.

Lie with Data Dredging

Imagine that we made some minor performance improvements and we really want to demonstrate a positive impact of it in real-world scenarios. We set up a benchmark, collect 100 pairs of samples, perform statistical tests, and calculate p-values. Unfortunately, only two of them have p-values <0.05, which is not enough to say that we have a statistically significant difference. We know that it's OK to have a few small p-values when H_0 is true because they are distributed uniformly. We didn't show all the experiment results to anyone yet, and we still want to prove that our performance improvements matter. How can we convince others of this? Maybe we can show only pairs of samples with p-values <0.05?...

The described technique is known as **p-hacking**. It's not a good practice, but unfortunately, it's highly abused in many types of scientific research. We already discussed another example of it in the "Optional Stopping" section: terminating of the iteration process after achieving small p-value is a reliable way to support H_1 and show that we really have a significant effect even when H_1 is false.

While many people use p-hacking *intentionally* (they know that H_1 is false, but want to show that it's true), the p-hacking effect can accidentally spoil your conclusions even if you don't want it to. *Unintentional* p-hacking happens when you have a strong temptation to accept H_1 based on a few small p-values without additional checks.[13]

Several different approaches can save you from unintentional p-hacking. One of my favorites is the **Holm–Bonferroni correction**. The idea is simple: when we get a set of p-values from different experiments, we should sort them in descending order, and rank the sorted array. After that, we should multiply each p-value by its rank. You can see an example of such correction in Table 4-5. The original p-value set has two values that are less than 0.05: 0.009 and 0.015. After correction, they become 0.063 and 0.090, which are larger than our 0.05 α-level. Some values may become more than 1.0, but you shouldn't worry about it while you are comparing it with α.

---

[13]In [Lakens 2014b], Daniel Lakens describes an interesting effect called "bi-polar p-value disorder."

Table 4-5. *Holm–Bonferroni Correction*

p-value	Rank	Corrected p-value
0.962	1	0.962
0.673	2	1.346
0.313	3	0.939
0.120	4	0.480
0.042	5	0.210
0.015	6	0.090
0.009	7	0.063

p-hacking is an example of **data dredging**. All such techniques are based on a simple idea. Let's say that we don't have a statistically significant effect, but we want to demonstrate that we have it. In this case, it's almost impossible to achieve the zero Type I (false positive) error rate. If we perform a huge number of statistical experiments, we will typically get a few "untypical" results. Including only such experiments in the final report makes it possible to convince other people of incorrect results.

Data dredging has many variations. Another popular example relates to the **multiple comparison problem** in clustering. There is a saying: *"He who seeks will always find."* This perfectly describes this approach. Imagine that we have a set of performance samples in different environments. Each environment is described by hundreds of characteristics, from the RyuJIT version to the SSD model. If we split the samples by each characteristic and perform statistical tests against different subsamples, we will probably get several characteristics with low p-values. This may lead to an incorrect conclusion that these characteristics affect performance. Fortunately, such a hypothesis can be easily checked: you should perform additional experiments in two environments (splitted by the selected characteristic) and repeat the statistical test on the new samples.

Data dredging is an unethical approach that helps lead to incorrect conclusions based on the real data. If you don't trust a researcher, you always try to repeat the described experiment and check whether it's possible to reproduce the results or not (a decent performance investigation should include enough information for reproduction). If you have the full raw data set, you can also analyze it yourself and check the distribution of p-values: you already know how it looks with and without the data dredging.

Summing Up

In this section, we discussed several techniques that allow lying with benchmarking:

- **Small samples**

  When the sample size is small, the chance to get "extraordinary" results is high. With small sizes, you can easily miss outliers or incorrectly calculate the standard deviation. Typically, statistical tests can't be applied to small samples.

- **Percentages**

  If we want to calculate performance difference in terms of percentages correctly, we need a proper baseline (typically, it's the "before" state). It's incorrect to sum or subtract percentages from different experiments: the results don't provide any meaningful numbers.

- **Ratios**

  The ratio of two distributions can't be described by a single number in general; we have to work with the distribution of ratios. In many simple cases, the ratio of mean values provides a "correct" answer, but it's untrustworthy without the distribution analysis: it can be easily spoiled by outliers or a huge standard deviation.

- **Plots**

  Plots may provide a wrong impression of the data. For example, you can use special scales to highlight or hide an important part of the performance space.

- **Data dredging**

  When the H_0 is true, the Type I (false positive) error rate is typically more than zero. If you perform enough experiments, you will find samples with low p-values that support H_1. Presenting only such experiments may convince other people of wrong results. This technique is known as p-hacking, but there are other approaches based on looking for something "unusual" in the performance space. For example, if you have hundreds of environmental characteristics for a small set of experiments, you will probably find a few that "supposedly" affect performance.

All of these described ways to lie don't contain knowingly false data: on the contrary, all of them are based on real measurements. There are two kinds of conclusions:

- **Direct way**

  Here the report contains wrong conclusions. For example, you can present incorrectly calculated metrics or try to prove H_1 based on p-hacked samples.

- **Indirect way**

  Here the report doesn't contain any conclusions, it just presents the data in a "special way." However, the presentation form forces intuition to work against the reader, which can lead to wrong conclusions. This approach is much more efficient because our own conclusions are usually more trustable than conclusions of other people.[14]

In this section, we didn't cover all possible ways to lie with benchmarking, so stay alert and always carefully analyze performance distributions before making conclusions. Don't trust your intuition and check everything twice.

Summary

In this chapter, we covered the following topics:

- **Descriptive statistics**

  We learned many metrics that can describe a single distribution: from the mean and the standard deviation to the skewness and the confidence interval. You don't need to remember how to calculate all these metrics, but you should remember how to interpret them. We also learned many useful visualization

---

[14]You can find more information about this effect in the following Wikipedia article: https://en.wikipedia.org/wiki/Confirmation_bias

techniques: from histograms and density plots to box plots and frequency trails. A good visualization significantly simplifies the investigation process.

- **Performance analysis**

  We learned several approaches for the performance analysis. Two distributions can be compared with the help of statistical tests, and the regression models can help you understand how the performance depends on the input data and the environment. Adaptive techniques like optional stopping and pilot experiments use statistics during benchmarking and help to optimize the measurements in terms of the whole experiment duration and the accuracy.

- **How to lie with benchmarking**

  We also learned many deceptive techniques that may force us to incorrect result interpretations. Since we know about them, we can recognize them in performance research and avoid popular mistakes in our own performance investigations.

This chapter is not a complete introduction to statistics. It's a practical guide with the most useful techniques for real-world performance distribution. However, we didn't discuss many statistical methods and approaches that also can be useful in different kinds of investigations. If you want to improve your knowledge of statistics, it's recommended to read other books like [Downey 2014], [Freedman 2007], [Wasserman 2010], and [Boslaugh 2012].

Note that this chapter is not a classic statistics theory; it's a guide for a practicing performance engineer that should help him or her to analyze performance measurements, correctly interpret the results, and optimize the benchmarking process. Thus, some topics are not fully covered, and not all of the statements are mathematically strict. However, this shouldn't be a problem in real performance investigation. It's much more important just to be familiar with the main concepts and know how to work with them.

References

[ACM209] Ibbetson, D. 1963. "Algorithm 209: Gauss." *Magazine Communications of the ACM* 6 (10). ACM: 616. https://dl.acm.org/citation.cfm?id=367664.

[ACM395] Hill, Geoffrey W. 1970. "Algorithm 395: Student's T-Distribution." *Magazine Communications of the ACM* 13 (10). ACM: 617–619. http://dl.acm.org/citation.cfm?id=355599.

[Azad 2007] Azad, Kalid. 2007. "Understanding the Birthday Paradox." April 26. https://betterexplained.com/articles/understanding-the-birthday-paradox/.

[Boslaugh 2012] Boslaugh, Sarah. 2012. *Statistics in a Nutshell: A Desktop Quick Reference.* 2nd ed. O'Reilly Media, Inc.

[Downey 2014] Downey, Allen B. 2014. *Think Stats: Exploratory Data Analysis.* 2nd ed. O'Reilly Media, Inc. http://greenteapress.com/thinkstats/.

[Freedman 2007] Freedman, David, Robert Pisani, and Roger Purves. 2007. *Statistics.* 4th ed. WW Norton & Company.

[Gregg 2014a] Gregg, Brendan. 2014. "Frequency Trails: Introduction." February 2. www.brendangregg.com/FrequencyTrails/intro.html.

[Gregg 2014b] Gregg, Brendan. 2014. "Frequency Trails: Detecting Outliers." February 2. www.brendangregg.com/FrequencyTrails/outliers.html.

[Gregg 2015] Gregg, Brendan. 2015. "Frequency Trails: Modes and Modality." June 17. www.brendangregg.com/FrequencyTrails/modes.html.

[Gregg 2017] Gregg, Brendan. 2017. "The USE Method." August 24. www.brendangregg.com/usemethod.html.

[Huff 1993] Huff, Darrell. 1993. *How to Lie with Statistics.* WW Norton & Company.

[Kahneman 2013] Kahneman, Daniel. 2013. *Thinking, Fast and Slow.* Farrar, Straus and Giroux.

[Lakens 2014a] Lakens, Daniel. 2014. "What P-Hacking Really Looks Like: A Comment on Masicampo & LaLande (2012)." September 30. http://daniellakens.blogspot.com/2014/09/what-p-hacking-really-looks-like.html.

[Lakens 2014b] Lakens, Daniel. 2014. "The Probability of P-Values as a Function of the Statistical Power of a Test." May 29. http://daniellakens.blogspot.com/2014/05/the-probability-of-p-values-as-function.html.

[Matejka 2017] Matejka, Justin, and George Fitzmaurice. 2017. "Same Stats, Different Graphs: Generating Datasets with Varied Appearance and Identical Statistics Through Simulated Annealing." In *CHI 2017 Conference Proceedings: ACM SIGCHI Conference on Human Factors in Computing Systems*, 1290–1294. ACM. www.autodeskresearch.com/publications/samestats.

[Minitab 2013] "Explaining the Central Limit Theorem with Bunnies & Dragons." 2013. The Minitab Blog. October 15. http://blog.minitab.com/blog/michelle-paret/explaining-the-central-limit-theorem-with-bunnies-and-dragons-v2.

[Ribecca 2017] Ribecca, Severino. 2017. "Further Exploration #4: Box Plot Variations." September 27. http://datavizcatalogue.com/blog/box-plot-variations/.

[Wainer 1984] Wainer, Howard. 1984. "How to Display Data Badly." *American Statistician* 38 (2): 137–147.

[Wasserman 2010] Wasserman, Larry. 2013. *All of Statistics: A Concise Course in Statistical Inference*. Springer Science & Business Media.

[Wickham 2011] Wickham, Hadley, and Lisa Stryjewski. 2011. "40 Years of Boxplots." *American Statistician*, July. http://vita.had.co.nz/papers/boxplots.pdf.

CHAPTER 5

Performance Analysis and Performance Testing

The first principle is that you must not fool yourself — and you are the easiest person to fool.

— Richard Feynman, 1974

In most cases, benchmarking is a kind of performance investigation. Benchmarks allow getting new knowledge about software and hardware. This knowledge can be used later for different kinds of performance optimization.

Once you get the desired level of performance, you usually want to keep this level. And you typically don't want to have situations when someone from your team accidentally spoils your performance improvements. How can we prevent such situations? Well, how do we usually prevent situations when someone spoils our code base? We write tests! If we don't want to have any performance regressions, we need *performance tests*! Such tests can be a part of your CI pipeline, so it will be impossible to make any unnoticed performance degradations![1]

So, it looks simple: we write performance tests and get profit! Sounds good, doesn't it? Unfortunately, it's harder than it sounds. In performance tests, it's not enough to just measure performance metrics of your code; you also have to know how to process these values. A benchmark without analysis is not a benchmark, it's just a program that prints some numbers. You always have to explain the benchmark results.

When you run a benchmark locally, you have all the relevant source code under your hands: you can read it, you can play with it. You can do additional actions depending on the current state of the investigation. You can look at the current data and make a

---

[1] In theory.

© Andrey Akinshin 2019
A. Akinshin, *Pro .NET Benchmarking*, https://doi.org/10.1007/978-1-4842-4941-3_5

decision about the next step. When a benchmark becomes a performance test, you should automate this process. This is much harder because the automation logic should handle future changes to the source code. You don't know the future, you don't know the performance metrics that you will get tomorrow, you can't look at the future distribution plots, and you can't make nonautomated decisions about future problems. Everything should be automated! And this is a huge challenge: you have to predict possible problems and write algorithms for analysis without knowledge of the data. You should design not only a set of benchmarks, but also a set of performance asserts and alarms that should notify you in case of any problems.

The title of this chapter is "Performance Analysis and Performance Testing" instead of just "Performance Testing." These topics are close to each other: performance testing requires a deep understanding of performance analysis approaches. Meanwhile, you can apply performance analysis techniques not only for performance testing but also for regular benchmarks (which don't include automatic asserts) and performance investigations. All problems and solutions will be discussed in the context of performance testing, but you should keep in mind that almost all of this can be used for benchmarking in general. We are going to cover the following topics:

- **Performance testing goals**

  What problems do we want to solve? What exactly do we want when we are talking about performance tests? We should clearly understand our goals before the start; we should understand what we want to achieve.

- **Kinds of benchmarks and performance tests**

  There are a lot of different kinds of performance tests. You should decide what your test should look like and what exactly it should measure. For example, it can be a stress test that checks what's going on with your web server under high load. Or it can be a user interface test that checks that UI controls are responsive and work without delays. Or it can be an asymptotic test that verifies that the algorithmic complexity of a method is $O(N)$. Or it can be a functional test that measures the latency of a single operation. Knowledge of these kinds allows you to choose how to write performance tests in each situation.

- **Performance anomalies**

  The duration of a test is not a single number; it's always a distribution. Sometimes, this distribution looks "strange." For example, it can be multimodal, or it can have an extremely huge variance. We say that distributions of "unusual shape" are *performance anomalies*. It's not always a problem, but hunting for performance anomalies can usually help you to find many problems that you can't find in another way.

- **Strategies of defense**

  When should we run our performance tests: before or after the merge into the main branch in a version control system? Should we run performance tests per each commit or it will be enough to run it once per day? How much time should we spend on performance testing and what kind of degradation could we detect in each case? Can we implement completely automatic CI logic? Or do we always have to do things manually? What can we do if a product with performance problems has already been released? There are different strategies of defense from performance degradations: each of them has advantages and disadvantages, and each of them helps you to solve a specific set of problems.

- **Performance space**

  For each test, you can collect many metrics. You can measure the total wall-clock time, and you can check out the hardware counters or the number of GC collections. You can collect these metrics only from a single branch or from several branches. There are a lot of ways to get performance numbers, and you should know about them because this knowledge will help you choose which of them will work best for you.

- **Performance asserts and alarms**

  Everything is simple with functional tests because they are usually deterministic. If you don't have tricky race conditions, a test always have the same result. It's clear when a test is green;

depending on your requirements, you can easily check it with a series of assertions.

In the case of performance tests, everything is more complicated. Remember that a test output is a series of numbers; you have new numbers per run even on the same machine. Moreover, in some cases, you have to compare data from different machines. The standard deviation can be huge, so it can be hard or even impossible to detect 5-10% degradation. It's very important to define your alarm criteria and answer a simple question: *"When is a test red?"*

- **Performance-driven development (PDD)**

  This approach is similar to test-driven development (TDD) with one exception: instead of the usual functional tests, we write performance tests. The idea is simple: you shouldn't start to optimize anything before you write corresponding performance tests that are red. Indeed, it sounds simple, but it's a very powerful technique; it will help you to save a lot of time and nerves.

- **Performance culture**

  Unfortunately, performance tests will not work well if members of the team don't care about performance. You need a special kind of culture in your team and your company. Not only is performance testing about technologies; it's also about attitude.

There is no universal approach that allows getting a performance testing system for free in any project. The best approach *for you* depends on *your* performance requirements and on CI/human resources. In this chapter, we will learn basic information about performance tests that will help you to understand which practices can be helpful for your projects and your team.

Many examples in this chapter are based on development stories about IntelliJ IDEA, ReSharper, and Rider. I will mention these projects without additional introductions.

Let's start with performance testing goals!

Performance Testing Goals

In the modern world, we often release new versions of our software. We are trying to fix old bugs and implement excellent new features. Sometimes, though, these new features do not work as well as expected. However, this is a normal situation: it's tough to write new code without introducing new problems. That's just how it works. Hopefully, your users understand this and will wait for a new version with fixes. However, in many cases, it's almost inexcusable when you're breaking old features or make them slow. As a performance engineer, the worst user feedback I ever get was like: "The new version of your software works so slowly that I have to roll back to the previous version" or even "I have to switch to the product of your competitors." *Sometimes we have performance degradations*—this is the problem that we are going to solve in this chapter. We have defined the problem, and now it's time to define the goals!

Goal 1: Prevent Performance Degradations

This is our primary goal: *prevent performance degradations*. Some developers may confuse this goal with "make software fast" or "make users happy with our performance." Be careful! When we say "prevent performance degradations," this is not about the overall level of performance or the happiness of our users. "Prevent performance degradations" means that each version of our software should work *as fast as or faster* than the previous one.

Remark 1. Programming is always about trade-offs; we can't constantly improve the performance of all features in our program. Sometimes we have to slow down one part because we want to speed up another part (e.g., we spend time on loading caches on startup, which allows fast request processing in the future). This trade-off can be a conscious decision, and it's completely OK. However, in most cases, developers slow down features accidentally. In large programs, it's tough to measure performance impact on the whole product even for small changes. Thus, our goal actually sounds like this: *prevent accidental performance degradations*.

Remark 2. In this book, there is no strict general definition of performance degradation. You should define this term for yourself because it depends on your business goals and requirements. If you are reading this chapter, you probably already have some performance problems, or you expect them in the future. Try to formalize the term "performance degradation" for your situation. Here are a few very simplified examples of how the definition may depend on the context:

- *Sometimes even 1% degradation can be a huge problem.*

  An example: Let's say we have a web server that processes requests. We host this server in the cloud, and we pay a cloud provider for the time resources at a fixed rate. In our spherical example in a vacuum, each request always takes 100 ms. 1% degradation means that we will get 101 ms per request after a deployment. If we have billions of such requests, the total processing time will increase noticeably.[2] The most important thing is that our bills will also increase by 1%.

- *Sometimes even 500% degradation can be not a problem.*

  An example: We have a server that displays statistics about user activities. Let's say that we don't need real-time statistics; it's enough to refresh it daily. So, we have a console utility that regenerates a statistic report and deploys it. With the help of cron,[3] we run it every day at 02:00 AM. The utility takes 1 minute, so the report is ready at 02:01 AM. A developer from your team decided to implement additional "heavy" calculations: now the report contains new useful information, but the total generation time is 6 minutes; the report is ready at 02:06 AM. Is this a problem? Probably not, because analytics will review the report only in the morning. If the utility takes 10 hours, it can be a problem, but nobody cares about five extra minutes in this case.

---

[2]Very small changes in the hot paths can significantly affect performance. A friend of mine has a nice example from a production system when a single .EndsWith('/') call caused a regression of 20% in RPS: the metric was changed from around 55000 to around 38000. The problem was solved with the help of a very simple optimization: the EndWith call was replaced by [variable. Length-1] == '/'.

[3]Cron is a time-based job scheduler in Unix-like computer operating systems.

- *Sometimes it's impossible to talk about degradations in terms of percentages.*

  An example: Because of a complicated multilevel hierarchical cache, 20% of requests take 100 ms, 35% of requests take 200 ms, and 45% of requests take 300 ms. After some changes, 20% of requests take 225 ms, 35% of requests take 180 ms, and 45% of requests take 260 ms. Is this a good change or a bad change? Do we have a performance regression in this case? (Try to calculate the average processing time for both cases.) Well, this is another trade-off problem: we can't answer this question without business requirements.

We will discuss different performance degradation criteria in the "Performance Asserts and Alarms" section.

Remark 3. In large software products, it's very hard to prevent *all* possible performance degradations. "Prevent all performance degradations" sounds like "prevent all bugs" or "prevent all security vulnerabilities." Theoretically, it's possible. In practice, it requires too many resources and too much effort. You can write thousands of performance tests, and you can buy hundreds of CI servers that run these tests all the time. And it will help you to catch *most problems* in advance, but probably not all of them. Also, some performance degradations may not affect the business goals, so doesn't always make sense to fix them. Thus, when we say "prevent all performance problems," we usually mean "prevent most of them that matter."

Goal 2: Detect Not-Prevented Degradations

Since it's almost impossible to prevent *all* performance degradations, we have a second goal: *detect not-prevented degradations.* In this case, we can fix them and recover the original performance. Such problems can be detected on the same day, in the same week, in the same month, and even one year later. We will discuss what kinds of problem we can detect in different moments in the "Strategies of Defense" section. The most important thing here is that we want to detect these problems before users/customers find them and start to complain about them.

Goal 3: Detect Other Kinds of Performance Anomalies

Degradation is not the only problem we can get. In this chapter, we will discuss so-called "performance anomalies," which include clustering, huge variance, and other kinds of "strange" performance distributions. Usually (but not always) such anomalies help to detect different kinds of problems in the business logic. If you implement a system for performance analysis, it makes sense to check the performance space for these anomalies as well. One cool thing about it: some anomalies can be detected in a single revision, so you don't have to analyze the whole performance history or compare commits.

Goal 4: Reduce Type I Error Rate

If you skipped the chapter about statistics (Chapter 4), I will explain this goal in simple terms. A Type I error (*false positive* result) means that there is no performance degradation, but performance tests detect "fake" problems. Consequences: developers spend some time on investigations in vain. This is not just a waste of our most precious resource (time of developers), it's also a substantial demotivating factor. Having a few Type I errors per month is OK. Moreover, you should expect to have such errors; it's too hard to implement an excellent performance testing system with zero Type I error rate. However, if you get several false positive results per day, developers will not care about it. And it sounds reasonable: what's the point to spend time on useless investigations each day? You can have "real" problems among the "fake" problems, but you will miss them: developers will ignore all alarms because they are likely false alarms. The whole idea is destroyed: performance tests do not benefit and instead distract your team members.

Thus, you should monitor Type I errors. If you have too many of them, it makes sense to reduce performance requirements and weaken the degradation criteria. It's better to miss a few real problems than to have a completely useless set of performance tests.

Goal 5: Reduce Type II Error Rate

Type II error (*false negative* result) means that there is performance degradation, but we failed to detect it. Consequences: serious performance problems can be delivered to users with the next update. In this case, we didn't solve our main problem; we didn't prevent degradation. Since it's impossible to prevent all performance degradation, we can try to keep the number of such situations low.

It sounds like a consequence of the first goal, but I decided to form it as a separate goal because the Type II error rate is also a metric that describes our performance testing system. It's not enough to just write a bunch of performance tests and let them live their lives. You should monitor how successful your performance framework is. For example, you can form a monthly report like: "In January, we detected 20 performance problems and fixed them before the release. Three problems were detected by performance tests after the release, and two problems were reported in February by dissatisfied users." Such reports allow the following:

- Evaluation of the effectiveness of performance tests

- Detection of weaknesses and pieces of code that should be covered by additional performance tests

- If you detected many problems in time, it will encourage the team to write new performance tests

- If you didn't have any significant issues (both detected and nondetected), you probably don't need performance tests for these projects, and it doesn't make sense to invest time into it in the future.

Goal 6: Automate Everything

It's not easy to formulate proper degradation criteria and get low Type I and Type II error rates. Sometimes you may be tempted to monitor performance manually instead of writing a reliable system for performance tests. For example, performance tests can produce thousands of numbers that are aggregated and displayed in a monitoring service. Next, you (or one of your colleagues) check performance reports every day, manually look for problems, and notify the rest of the team of the results. This is not a good approach because there are always many problems with the human factor: the person who is responsible for monitoring can be sick, on vacation, or busy. In this case, we will not get any alarms even if we have essential problems. In addition, he or she can miss some dangerous problems due to inattentiveness.

Unfortunately, it's hard to automate everything. In huge projects, it's almost impossible to implement a reliable and automated performance monitoring system with low Type I and Type II error rates. Sometimes you *have to* analyze some data manually. In this case, you can try to automate everything that can be automated. For example, let's say we have a huge integration test that typically takes 5 minutes. After some changes, it takes 6 minutes, so the main analyst gets a notification. Now he or she should investigate it. How can automation help? Here are a few ideas:

- **Automatic reports**

  You can generate a full report about the problem automatically. Such a report could include links to the commits (if you have a web service that allows browsing your code base), a list of authors of these changes, performance history of this test, links to other tests from the same test suite with new performance problems (they can be related), and so on. The main idea here is that the analyst shouldn't look for additional data; all necessary information should be collected automatically. You can even automatically create an issue in your issue tracker and easily track all performance problems.

- **Automatic bisecting**

  It's not always possible to run all performance tests for each commit. Imagine that one of your daily performance tests is red and there are N=127 commits in this day by ten different people. How do you find the commit that introduces the problem? It's a good idea to start to bisect these commits. Let's check the commit 64 (for simplification, assuming that we have a linear history without branches). If the test is red, it means that the problem was introduced before this commit, and we are going to check commit 32. If the test is green, it means that the problem was introduced after this commit, and we are going to check commit 96. If we continue this process, we can find the commit with problem after $log_2(N)$ iterations (in the perfect world without branches). Manual bisecting is a waste of developers' time. This process can also be automated: the report should include the specific commit and the author of this commit (this person should start to investigate the issue).

- **Automatic snapshots**

  One of the first steps in such investigations is profiling. Once we get a slow test, we can automatically take a performance snapshot before and after the change. In this case, the analyst can just download both snapshots and compare them. It can allow finding the problem even without the need to download the sources and build it locally: many stupid mistakes can be found only with the snapshots.

- **Automatic step-by-step analysis**

  If you have a 1-minute degradation in a huge integration test, you probably have a problem in a single subsystem instead of a project-wide problem. In this case, you can measure separate steps for both cases and compare them automatically. After that, a notification (or an issue) can contain additional information like "it seems that we have a problem with these two steps; the rest of the steps doesn't have noticeable degradation."

- **Automatic continuous profiling**

  If you have a pool of servers with services that sometimes suffer from accidental performance drops, you can try to profile them automatically. If the overhead of such profiling is too big, you can randomly profile only a part of the pool. For example, pick 10% of the servers and profile them for 30 seconds, then pick another 10%, and so on. You can play with the exact numbers and get a profile snapshot at the moment the problem reproduced (maybe it will not be on the first try). The randomized approach helps to reduce the profiling overhead on your production system.

Try to come up with your ways to automate routine. You should manually do only work that cannot be automated and requires creativity. If a series of performance investigations has common parts, you should try to automate these parts. It allows saving the time of developers and simplifying the investigation process for people who don't have distinctive performance skills.

Summing Up

Let's summarize. Our main problem: sometimes we have performance degradations. If we understand what "performance degradation" means well, we can try to prevent accidental performance degradations (Goal 1). Unfortunately, we can't prevent all of them, so we want to detect not-prevented degradations in time (Goal 2) and detect other kinds of performance problems (Goal 3). We also want to reduce Type I error (false positive: there are no degradations, but we detect "fake" problems) rate (Goal 4) and Type II error (false negative: nondetected degradations) rate (Goal 5). Everything that can be automated should be automated (Goal 6).

Now we know our problems and goals. It's time to learn what kinds of performance tests we can choose.

Kinds of Benchmarks and Performance Tests

There are many kinds of approaches that can be used as performance tests. In this section, we briefly discuss some of them:

- **Cold start tests**: situations when we care about startup time

- **Warmed-up tests**: situations when an application is already running

- **Asymptotic tests**: tests that try to determine the asymptotic complexity (e.g., $O(N)$ or $O(N^2)$)

- **Latency and throughput tests**: instead of asking "How much time does it take to process N requests?", we ask "How many requests can we process during a time interval?"

- **Unit and integration tests**: if you already have some usual tests (which are not designed to be performance tests), you can use the raw durations of these tests for performance analysis

- **Monitoring and telemetry**: looking at the production performance in real time

- **Tests with external dependencies**: tests that involve some part of the external world that we can't control

- **Other kinds of performance tests**: stress/load tests, user interface tests, fuzz tests, and so on

All of these kinds can be applied not only for performance testing but also for regular benchmarking. Let's start with the cold start tests.

Cold Start Tests

There are different kinds of cold start test depending on which part of your software environment is cold. Here is a list of some of the cold start levels:

- **Method cold start**

  When you run a method for the first time, a lot of time-consuming things may happen on different levels: from JIT compilation and assembly loading on the runtime level to some first-time calculations for static properties on the application logic level.

- **Feature cold start**

  Difference between cold and warm time for a method can be negligibly small. However, it can be noticeable when we are talking about thousands of methods and many assemblies. Because of that, a user can experience delays when he or she launches a feature for the first time (especially if this feature involves tons of methods that were not invoked before).

- **Application cold start**

  Startup time is important for many kinds of applications. And it's definitely crucial for desktop and mobile applications. The perfect situation is a situation when the user instantly gets a ready application after a double-click on a shortcut (or launching it any other way). Any delay can make him or her nervous. Imagine a situation when you should quickly make a few edits in a file. You open it in your favorite text editor and... . And you have to wait a few seconds until the text editor is initialized. If you edit files often and close the editor each time, these few seconds can be irritating.

For some people, startup time is critical; they might prefer a pure-featured text editor that starts instantly over a full-featured text editor that starts in a few seconds.

- **OS cold start**

  If your benchmark interacts with different OS resources, a physical restart can be required for a cold start test.

- **Fresh OS image**

  Sometimes it's not enough to reboot the operating system; we may need a fresh image of the system. The old test runs can make any changes on the disk that can be important for subsequent launches. For example, Rider uses a pool of TeamCity agents for running hundreds of build configurations with tests every day. TeamCity refreshes the agent images once per several days: then the fun begins. Sometimes, we have a significant performance difference between the last (warmed) test run on the old image and the first (cold) test run on the new image (without any changes in the source code base). We don't use a fresh OS installation each time, because such approach has a huge infrastructure overhead and the described problems are not frequent.

Let's try the following exercise. Take a machine with installed Windows and restart it. Open a video file with your favorite movie in your favorite video player, watch the movie, and close the player. Next, run the RAMMap[4] utility (a part of the Sysinternals suite). This utility allows performing advanced physical memory usage analysis and provides many low-level details. Check out the "Standby" category for "MappedFile" on the "Use Counts" tab (we will discuss all these categories in Chapter 8); the memory usage should be huge. Next, open the "File Summary" tab and sort all files by the "Standby" column. Now find the file with the movie on this tab. You should see a huge amount of "Standby" memory for it (you can see my RAMMap instance in Figure 5-1).

---

[4]https://docs.microsoft.com/en-us/sysinternals/downloads/rammap

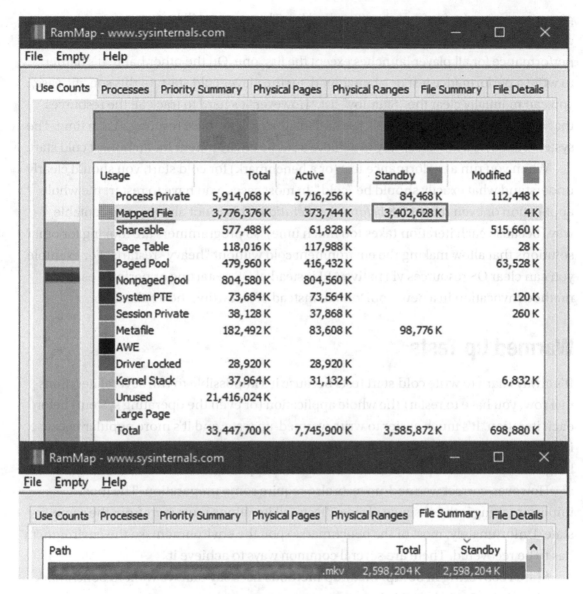

Figure 5-1. *RAMMap shows huge "Standby" memory use for closed file*

How is this possible? We closed the player; there are no more applications that use this file. Why do we see it in RAMMap? And what does "Standby" mean?

You can imagine the "Standby" category as a memory cache. After closing the player (which loaded the whole movie file into main memory), there is no need to clear the memory instantly. We can mark this memory as "free" (thus, you will not see it in the Task Manager as a part of "usual" memory) and clear it later when another application asks for additional memory allocation. However, if we decide to watch the movie again, the video player can *reuse* the file from the "Standby" list. The startup will be faster because we don't have to load the file into memory again. On the one hand, it's great: we have better performance for all player launches except the first one. On the other hand, it's harder to write a performance test or a benchmark for the player cold start. In this specific case, you can manually clear the "Standby" list.[5] However, it's hard to track all the resources that can be reused in the general case and manually clear these resources each time. The system reboot is a universal way to achieve a sterile environment for an honest cold start.

When you run a performance test (or a benchmark) for cold start, you should clearly understand what exactly should be "cold." In most cases, you have to restart the whole application or even reboot OS *before each iteration*. This is not always an acceptable way (because each iteration takes too much time), so programmers are looking for other solutions that allow making the environment cold without "heavy" restarts. For example, you can clear OS resources via native API instead of OS restarting or perform each method invocation in a new AppDomain instead of restarting the application.

Warmed Up Tests

It's always hard to write cold start tests because it's impossible to run several iterations in a row: you have to restart the whole application (or even the operating system) before each iteration. It's much easier to write warmed-up tests, and it's more popular because in many applications (especially for web services), you usually don't need to care how long startup takes; the performance of a warmed application is more interesting.

However, correct warmed-up tests also require some preparation. The most important thing is the absence of side effects: all iterations must start from the same state. Unfortunately, most of the benchmarks spoil the environment, so the environment has to be recovered. There are several common ways to achieve it.

State recovering in Setup/Cleanup methods Let's say that we want to benchmark the List<int>.Sort() method:

```
void ListSortBenchmark()
{
  list.Sort();
}
```

---

[5]In the RAMMap utility, open the "Empty" menu and click on "Empty Standby List." In this menu, you can clear other memory lists as well.

Regardless of the initial state, the list will be sorted after the first iteration. It's not interesting to perform benchmarking of sorting of a sorted list. Thus, we have to choose the "reference initial state" that should be recovered after each iteration. Let's say that the initial state is a reversed array. Here is an example of the setup method:

```
void IterationSetup()
{
  for (int i = 0; i < list.Count; i++)
    list[i] = list.Count - i;
}
```

It solves the "recovered state problem," but now we have another problem: the IterationSetup method should be invoked before each benchmark call; it can affect the measurements. Usually, we write code like this with IterationCount iterations:

```
var stopwatch = Stopwatch.StartNew();
for (int i = 0; i < IterationCount; i++)
{
  ListSortBenchmark();
}
stopwatch.Stop();
long sum = stopwatch.ElapsedMilliseconds;
long average = sum / IterationCount;
```

Now we have to call IterationSetup() before each iteration. We can write it as follows:

```
var stopwatch = Stopwatch.StartNew();
for (int i = 0; i < IterationCount; i++)
{
  IterationSetup();    // Setup inside measurements
  ListSortBenchmark();
}
stopwatch.Stop();
long sum = stopwatch.ElapsedMilliseconds;
long average = sum / IterationCount;
```

In this case, the duration of IterationSetup() will be included in ElapsedMilliseconds and increase the average time (the setup method can be heavy and take a lot of time). It's better to exclude IterationSetup() from the measurements:

```
long sum = 0;
for (int i = 0; i < IterationCount; i++)
{
  IterationSetup();    // Setup outside measurements
  var stopwatch = Stopwatch.StartNew();
  ListSortBenchmark();
  stopwatch.Stop();
  sum += stopwatch.ElapsedMilliseconds;
}
long average = sum / IterationCount;
```

Such approach can be fine for macrobenchmarks (if we sort tons of elements), but in the case of microbenchmarks (let's say list.Count < 100), we can get big errors because of these interrupts between stopwatch measurements. In Chapter 2, we discussed that we should use many iterations for microbenchmarks because the Stopwatch resolution is not enough to handle nanosecond operations: if we try to measure the duration of a single ListSortBenchmark call, the ElapsedMilliseconds will have an inaccurate value. In the preceding example, the loop multiplies the error instead of reducing it! Moreover, IterationSetup calls between measurements can produce additional side effects. For example, if this method allocates memory, it can cause a sudden garbage collection during the measurements.

In such cases, it can be useful to evaluate the overhead separately. For example, we can write something like this:

```
public void SetupRunCleanup()
{
  Setup();
  Run();
  Cleanup();
}
```

```
public void SetupCleanup()
{
  Setup();
  Cleanup();
}
```

Next, you can get `Duration(Run)` as `Duration(SetupRunCleanup)` - `Duration(SetupCleanup)`. This trick is not always successful (especially if `Setup` and `Cleanup` allocate many objects and have complex performance distributions), but it usually works for simple cases.

Another factor that can affect the benchmark is the CPU cache. The effect of this cache on the program is simple: the recently read data can be read much faster than data that hasn't been read by anyone for a long time. In `ListSortBenchmark`, we should choose the optimal strategy for the CPU cache state. When you sort the array for the first time, CPU loads the list content (or a part of the list in the case of a huge list) into the cache. Next iterations will be faster because we already have the elements (or some of the elements) in the cache. Here we should choose between a cold and a warm state for it. The decision depends on how you are going to use the `Sort` method in the real application. If you work with elements before sorting, you get a warm list: everything is OK with the benchmark because it also uses the warmed list. If you don't touch the elements before sorting, you get a cold list in real life. In this case, the benchmark requires cache invalidation in the setup method as well (we will discuss how to do it in Chapter 7).

Preparing many "initial" states in advance If we have enough memory and a small number of iterations, we can prepare several instances of the benchmark input in advance. Let's say that we are going to run `IterationCount` iterations (it's a constant) with lists of equal size `ListSize` (it's also a constant). In this case, we can create an array of lists and fill all the list instances with the same data:

```
private List<int>[] lists = new List<int>[IterationCount];

public void GlobalSetup()
{
  for (int i = 0; i < IterationCount; i++)
  {
    lists[i] = new List<int>(ListSize); // All lists have the same size
```

```
  // And the same "reversed" elements:
  for (int j = 0; j < ListSize; j++)
    lists[i].Add(ListSize - j);
  }
}
```

Next, we take a new list for each iteration:

```
public void ListSortBenchmark()
{
  var stopwatch = Stopwatch.StartNew();
  for (int i = 0; i < IterationCount; i++)
    lists[i].Sort(); // We use lists[i] instead of the same list instance
  stopwatch.Stop();
  long sum = stopwatch.ElapsedMilliseconds;
  long average = sum / IterationCount;
}
```

The approach also has its own problems. Given how those lists are created, there is a high tendency for those objects to live in approximate sequential memory; therefore all the CPU cache pollution is not enough to not skew the results. A better approach for that kind of test is to create all the lists and ensure that the amount of memory used by those is higher by at least 10× the maximum size of the CPU total cache available. Then we should create another list with a random uniform distribution of numbers and iterate over that list to get the indexes. As you are always running the same sequence, the memory effects would be reduced to the index list (therefore diminishing its impact on the benchmark results) and at the same time ensuring a uniform distribution cache pollution. We will discuss more details about this topic in Chapter 8.

State recovering inside a benchmark We already discussed a similar problem in Chapter 2 (the "Unequal Iterations" section) when we tried to benchmark the List. Add method. This method has a side effect: we have the different number of elements before and after the List.Add invocation. When the list capacity is not enough for an extra element, the next List.Add call will cause the internal array resizing, which takes too much time and spoils the results. If we want to write a repeatable benchmark, all side effects should be annihilated. One of the possible solutions is to benchmark the List. Add/List.Remove pair:

```
public void AddRemoveBenchmark()
{
  list.Add(0);
  list.RemoveAt(list.Count - 1);
}
```

Is this a good solution? The answer depends on what you actually want to achieve. Consider several possible goals:

- *We want to know the duration of list.Add.*

  Actually, we want to gain knowledge of the list.Add duration and use it for solving a real problem (e.g., writing a fast algorithm). The solution of the problem is our "true" goal, but not the knowledge itself. This is important because the correct way to benchmark list.Add *depends* on how you are going to use it.

- *We want to add many elements in a list and want to know how much time does it take.*

  In this case, we probably have to benchmark the addition of N elements instead of a single one. Remember that not all of the Add calls are equal: some of them can produce resizing of the internal array. You can play with the initial state, the initial capacity, the number of elements, and so on. If you want to know the duration of the adding of N elements, you should benchmark this. The performance cost of a single Add is useless for you because you can't multiply it by N (in the general case) to get the result.

- *We are going to make a few edits in the Add implementations and check for performance improvements/degradations.*

  Any performance changes in the Add method will also affect the performance of the Add/RemoveAt pair. It will be hard to say something about how much the edits affect the Add method (quantitative changes), but we can say is it better or worse (qualitative changes). Also, we still have to check cases with the resizing of the internal array carefully.

- *We are going to use a list as a stack (with Push/Pop operations) with the known maximum capacity and want to know the duration of the "average" operation.*

    In this case, the Add/RemoveAt benchmark is a great solution because there is no difference between Add and RemoveAt here: we have to measure these methods together.

As you can see, everything depends on the goal. There are many ways to use quick operations like list.Add, but the algorithm performance depends on how you use it. Typically, you can't get the "reference" operation duration, because this duration depends on the use case. Always ask yourself: why do you want to get knowledge about method performance? How are you going to use this method?[6] If you answer these questions first, it will help you to design a good benchmark and decide when you need a cold start test and when you need a warmed-up test (or a combination of the two).

Asymptotic Tests

Sometimes it's impossible to run all tests on huge data sets. But we can run them on several small data sets and extrapolate the results.

Let's consider an example. In IntelliJ IDEA, there are a lot of code inspections (as in any IDE). From the user's point of view, an inspection is a logic that shows a problem with your code (from compilation errors and potential memory leak to unused code and spelling problems). From the developer point of view, an inspection is an algorithm that should be applied to the source code. Different algorithms are independent and don't affect each other. When IntelliJ IDEA analyzes a file, it applies all inspections to each file. Since there are so many inspections, they should be efficient. Even a single nonoptimal inspection could be a reason for performance problems in the whole IDE.

Well, how should we choose which inspection is "nonoptimal"? There is a simple rule: a proper inspection should have an $O(N)$ complexity where N is the file length. If the inspection complexity is (N^2), we will get a performance problem with huge files.

Thus, our metric here is not time; it's the *computational complexity*. This approach has a couple of important **advantages**:

---

[6]If you have several possible use cases, you have to consider all of them.

- **Portability**

  Results almost always don't depend on hardware: we should get the same result on slow and fast computers.

- **Benchmarks take less time**

  The inspection performance impact can be noticeable only in huge files. There are hundreds of inspection; we have to wait too long until we benchmark each inspection on each huge file from the test data. The asymptotic approach allows getting reliable results in less time. We can apply an inspection to a few small files, measure the analysis durations, and calculate the asymptotic complexity. Thus, we can check that the the inspection works fast enough without using huge files.

It also has two important **disadvantages**:

- **Many iterations**

  We can't build a regression model with one or two iterations. We have to run many iterations if we want to build a reliable model that produces correct results.

- **Complicated implementation**

  It's not easy to build a good regression model. If you are lucky enough, your performance function is polynomial. If you are not lucky, the performance function can't be approximated by an analytic function. Even if the function type is known (and you have only to find the coefficient), it's not always easy to build such model with a small error.

Thus, asymptotic analysis is not a silver bullet for all kinds of benchmarks, but it can be extremely useful when we want to get measurements for huge input data and we don't want to wait too long.

Latency and Throughput Tests

There are many ways to benchmark the same code. The final conclusions depend on the question we want to answer and the metric that we use. Let's say that we process some requests. It doesn't matter what kind of requests we have and how we process them.

283

Consider a couple of questions (and corresponding metrics) that we can use in this situation.

- **(A)** "How much time (T) do we need to process N requests?"

  The metric here is the *latency* of processing of N requests (the time interval between the start and end of processing).

- **(B)** "How many requests (N) can we process in the fixed time interval T?"

  The metric here is the processing *throughput*. Such case is also called *capacity planning* or *scalability analysis*.

These metrics may sound too abstract. Let's look at a code sample that measures each metric. The full infrastructure for measurements can be huge; we will look only at small and simple benchmarks to illustrate the idea.

- **(A)** In the first case, N is fixed. Thus, we have to do N iterations and measure the time between start and finish:

```
// Latency
var stopwatch = Stopwatch.StartNew();
for (int i = 0; i < N; i++)
  ProcessRequest();
stopwatch.Stop();
var result = stopwatch.ElapsedMilliseconds;
```

- **(B)** In the second case, T is fixed. We don't know how many requests can we process, so we will process requests until the time is over. In real life, it's typically complicated multithreaded code, but we can write a very simple single-threaded benchmark:

```
// Throughput
var stopwatch = Stopwatch.StartNew();
int N = 0;
while (stopwatch.ElapsedMilliseconds < T) {
  N++;
  ProcessRequest();
}
var result = N;
```

If we have a linear dependency between N and T, there is no difference between these approaches. However, the difference can be huge if the dependency is nonlinear.

Let's say that we know the exact formula for $T(N)$:

$$T(N) = C \cdot \log_2(N),$$

where C is a constant. The initial value for C was 2, but after a refactoring, it has become 4. You can see the T values for both cases and different N (32,64,128,256,512,1024) in Table 5-1.

Table 5-1. $T = C \cdot \log_2(N)$ *Dependency for C=2 and C=4*

N	$\log_2(N)$	$T_{C=2}$	$T_{C=4}$
32	5	10	**20**
64	6	12	24
128	7	14	28
256	8	16	32
512	9	18	36
1024	10	**20**	40

Imagine that a manager asks you about the performance drop: "How much slower does it work now"? Further, imagine that he or she is not a very good manager and doesn't want to hear anything about nonlinear dependencies and logarithms[7]; you should provide a single number as an answer.

Let's calculate the answer for both cases.

- **(A)** Let's check how much time (T) it takes to process $N = 1024$ requests. When $C = 2$, $T = 20sec$. When $C = 4$, $T = 40sec$. The performance drop is $40sec/20sec$ or 2x.

---

[7]Of course, not all managers behave like this. Many of them are great people with strong professional skills who are deeply involved in the development process. Unfortunately, our hypothetical manager is not one of them.

- **(B)** Let's check how many requests (N) we can process in $T = 20$ seconds. When $C = 2$, $N = 1024$. When $C = 4$, $N = 32$. Performance drop is 1024/32 or 32x.

So, what's the answer? 2x or 32x? Well, there is not one single correct generic answer. If you want to describe a situation in a general case, you should provide the model ($T = C \cdot \log_2(N)$ in our case) as an answer. If you want to describe a specific case, you should clearly define the case.

Usually, the target metric depends on your business goals. If the business goal is "Process $N = 1024$ requests as fast as possible," you should use the "latency approach" **(A)**. If the business goal is "Process as many requests as possible in $T = 20sec$," you should use the "throughput approach" **(B)**. If you have other business goals, you should design a set of benchmarks or performance tests that correspond to your goals. "Correspond" means that you measure the target case *and* use the correct set of metrics.

If you look at Table 5-1, you may think that capacity planning (the "throughput approach") is similar to asymptotic analysis. This is not always true. Asymptotic analysis requires several measurements for building the performance model. Capacity planning can be implemented with a single measurement. However, you can use asymptotic analysis *for* capacity planning: the knowledge of T values for $N = 32, \ldots, 1024$ allows predicting T for huge N like 2048, 4096, 8192, and so on without actual measurements.

Unit and Integration Tests

Some people are afraid of performance testing because it looks too complicated: they should make a lot of preparation (especially for cold/warm/stress tests), choose correct performance metrics, probably do some tricky math (especially for asymptotic analysis), and so on. I have some good news: if you have "usual" integration tests, you can use them as performance tests! There are many kinds of test classifications. In this book, we will use the term "integration test" for all not-unit tests: functional tests, end-to-end tests, component tests, acceptance tests, API tests, and so on. The main property of such tests that is important for performance testing is duration: the integration tests usually work much longer than instant unit tests. In fact, you can use any of your tests (even "usual" unit tests), which takes a noticeable amount of time (let's say more than ten milliseconds). If a test takes several microseconds or nanoseconds, we can't use it "as is" because the natural errors are too big; we have to transform such tests into "true" benchmarks. If a test takes more than ten milliseconds (or even several seconds or minutes, it's much better), we can *try* to use it as a performance test without additional modifications.

It may sound strange because we don't control accuracy for such tests, we don't do many iterations, we don't calculate statistics, and we don't do anything that we usually do in benchmarking. These tests *were designed* to check the correctness of your program, not performance. It seems that raw duration of unit and integration tests can't be used in performance analysis.

To me, it sounds strange to have so many performance data and don't use it. Yes, errors are huge, accuracy is poor, results are unstable, everything is terrible. But this doesn't mean that we can't *try* to use it. In performance tests, every iteration is expensive because it consumes the CI resources and increases our waiting time. From the practical point of view, a good suite of performance tests is always a trade-off between accuracy and the total elapsed time. The unit and integration tests will be executed anyway because we have to check the correctness of the business logic. We will get the duration of these tests anyway without additional effort. It's also a performance data. Moreover, it's a performance data that we have *for free*. If it's possible to get some useful information from this data (somehow), we should definitely do it!

A few words about terminology for the rest of this section. We can't use the term "performance test" anymore because now we consider all tests as performance tests. In the context, we introduce a few additional terms (they're not official terms, but we will use them for a while):

- **Explicit performance tests**

    These tests were designed to evaluate performance. Explicit tests may require special hardware and tricky execution logic (with warm-up, many iterations, metrics calculation, and so on). The result of such test is a conclusion about performance (like "the test works two times slower than before" or "the variance is too huge").

- **Implicit performance tests**

    These tests are "usual" tests that are designed to check logic. Each run of such tests has a duration, its performance number, which we get as a side effect. The result of such a test is a conclusion about correctness (green status for correct logic and red status for incorrect logic). "Implicit performance tests" means that these tests are not designed as performance tests, but we still can use them as such.

- **"Mixed" performance tests**

   It may sound obvious, and we will not discuss such tests in detail, but I still have to highlight this idea: you can check logic and performance at the same time. For example, we can write a huge integration stress test that covers the most performance-critical pieces of our code. Such a test can check that everything works correctly even under load (some race conditions can appear in such situations) *and* that we don't have a performance regression in such a case.

Now we know that we can use both explicit performance tests (which are designed to measure performance) and implicit performance tests (which are designed for something else, but we can still use them as performance tests). However, there is a huge difference between them. Let's compare explicit and implicit performance tests by several factors:

- **Persistent CI agent**

   When we measure performance, it's a good idea to run performance tests on the same hardware each time. It's very hard (or sometimes impossible) to evaluate the performance impact of your changes when you compare the "before" performance data from one agent with the "after" data from another agent. It's always better to have persistent CI agent (or set of agents) for explicit performance tests. This is not mandatory, but it's highly recommended. In case of implicit performance tests, there is no such requirement[8]; they should work correctly on any agent.

---

[8]Of course, there are exceptions to anything. Implicit performance tests may require some special environment like a specific operating system, a specific amount of memory, a specific drive (HDD or SSD), or even a specific processor model. With such tests, we can check many statements like "The program shouldn't crash if we have only 2GB of RAM" or "If a processor doesn't support SSE 4.1, we should use an old slow algorithm instead of our default fast algorithm, which uses modern processor instructions."

- **Virtualization**

  Virtualization is a great invention that helps us to organize a flexible cloud infrastructure. However, a virtual environment is a poison for the accuracy of explicit performance tests. You never know who else is running benchmarks on the same hardware at the same time. Explicit performance tests usually require a dedicated real (not virtual) agent. Implicit performance tests should work correctly in any environment.[9]

- **Number of iterations**

  Most explicit performance tests require several iterations. Remember that performance of a method is not a single number; it's a distribution. We can't evaluate errors and build a confidence interval if we have only one iteration. And we can't compare two revisions if we don't know errors and variance. Of course, sometimes a test can be too expensive (it consumes too much time), so you can't afford to run it several times. Implicit performance tests typically need only one iteration.[10]

---

[9]This is not always true. An example: there are many paid desktop programs with a trial period. This means that you can use a program for free at the beginning (let's say for 30 days). After that, you need to pay if you want to continue. Of course, smart rogues found a workaround: they install the program on a virtual machine, use it for 30 days, and create a new virtual machine with a new trial period. Developers often try to protect their programs from such exploits. The obvious solution is to prohibit running the program on virtual machines. Thus, they should implement a method that checks if the environment is virtual, and they should write tests for this method. The only way to check this logic is to run these tests in different virtual environments or without it.

[10]This is also not true. A simple example: we have a race condition in a test which fails our test in 1% of the cases. If we run a test only once, it can pass; on the CI server, such a test will be flaky because it can switch its status from green to red without any changes or reasons. A simple solution: we can run such test (with potential race conditions) 100 times. If it's a flaky test, it should fail after 100 iterations with a good probability.

- **Writing easiness**

  It's easy to write implicit performance tests.[11] I mean that every
  method which somehow calls your code can be a test. Different
  teams have different standards of coding, but most of them agree
  that the source code should be covered by tests. Some good
  development practices require writing tests (e.g., before writing
  a bug fix, you should write a red test for this bug and make it
  green with your fix). Typically, you get tests as an "artifact" of the
  development process. You write tests because it will simplify your
  life in the future and make you more confident in the quality of
  your code. Most of the unit tests are deterministic: a test is red,
  or a test is green. Moreover, it's usually obvious when a test is
  green. If you are writing a method Mul(x,y) that should multiply
  two numbers, you know the expected output. Mul(2,3) should
  be 6. Not 5, not 7; there is only one correct answer: 6. When we
  are writing explicit performance tests and making performance
  asserts, it's always complicated. For example, yesterday Mul took
  18 nanoseconds; today it takes 19 nanoseconds. Is it a regression
  or not? How should we check it? How many iterations do we
  need? How should we evaluate errors? And the most important
  question: is the test red or green? If you have clear answers to
  all questions about performance asserts, ask your teammates
  about it. Are you sure that you have the same point of view? It's so
  hard to write performance tests because there are no strict rules
  here. You should come up with your own performance asserts
  that satisfy your performance goal. It's hard because there is no
  "absolute green status," and there is no single "correct" way to
  write "performance asserts." There are only trade-offs.

---

[11]I confess: There are many footnotes in this section in which I tried to deceive you. I just tried
to show that there are always exceptions. However, I'm not going to explain all exceptions for
each case, as there are too many of them. In this book, I'm trying to show only general ideas,
principles, and approaches. It's tough to write about performance testing because for each
example, there are so many counterexamples. For each situation in which a particular fact works
well, there are hundreds of situations in which this same fact won't work. If you see a sentence
and you don't agree with it, imagine that there is a footnote with additional explanations.

- **Time of execution**

  Speaking of trade-offs, the most interesting one is between accuracy and the execution time. Performance tests wouldn't be so fun if we had unlimited amount of time. I wish I could perform billions of iterations for each of my benchmark or performance tests. Unfortunately, the world is cruel, and we don't have such opportunities. There is the natural upper limit for the total execution time of a test suite. It can be 10 seconds, 10 minutes, 2 hours, or 5 days: it depends on your workflow. But you have this limit anyway; you can't spend months and years for a single suite run. It would be great if you could run all of your performance tests during a few hours. If the total time is limited and you have too many tests, you can afford the only small number of iterations. It can be 100 iterations, or 10 iterations, or even a single iteration. And sometimes you have to deal with this single iteration. Implicit performance tests should be as fast as possible, there is no reason (typically) to repeat the same thing over and over. In the case of the explicit performance tests, each additional iteration can increase the accuracy. Of course, there is a "desired" level of accuracy and a "recommended" number of iterations. Usually, it doesn't make sense to "pay" for additional iterations by execution time after that point.

- **Variance and errors**

  Since the explicit performance tests are designed to get reliable performance results, we do everything to stabilize them: use real dedicated hardware, make many iterations, and calculate statistics. In case of the implicit performance tests, we (typically) don't care about variance and errors: we can run it inside a virtual machine, we can choose a new CI agent each time, we can always do only one iteration, and so on. Variance and errors are typically huge.

Well, does it make any sense to analyze the performance of "usual" tests (a.k.a. implicit performance tests) if it's so unstable? A general answer: it depends. A more specific answer: you will never know if you don't try. In the "Performance Anomalies" section later in this chapter, we will discuss many approaches that can be easily applied to implicit performance tests. When you work with a huge code base, it's impossible to cover all methods by performance tests: you don't have enough time and resources. However, if someone made a simple mistake (most of the mistakes are simple) and get a huge performance regression (most of the regressions due to simple mistakes are huge), you can easily catch it with your "usual" unit and integration tests (if you use them as implicit performance tests).

Monitoring and Telemetry

In this subsection, we will talk about two additional and interesting techniques of performance analysis:

- **Monitoring**

    Monitoring is a typical solution for web servers: we can watch for life indicators of the server with the help of special tools like Zabbix[12] or Nagios.[13]

- **Telemetry**

    Telemetry is a widely used technology in software development[14] that allows collecting information on the usage of user applications. Such data is typically anonymous and doesn't include any sensitive information. However, it can include important information about the performance of different operations. While usual monitoring is a great approach for web services, telemetry is our main "monitoring" tool for desktop applications (however, it can also be useful for the client side of web services). There is an existed API for telemetry by Microsoft,[15] but we can implement our own set of tools.

    For example, Mozilla Firefox collects data[16] about memory usage and operation latencies.

---

[12]www.zabbix.com/

[13]www.nagios.org/

[14]In fact, telemetry has been used since the 19th century for many different applications including meteorology, oil and gas industry, motor racing, transportation, agriculture, and so on. Check out the Wikipedia page for interesting examples: https://en.wikipedia.org/wiki/Telemetry

[15]https://docs.microsoft.com/en-us/azure/application-insights/ app-insights-windows-desktop

[16]https://wiki.mozilla.org/Performance/Telemetry

Of course, telemetry can include only general usage data without any performance statistics. For example, .NET Core CLI Tools use[17] telemetry for collecting information about .NET Core SDK usage.[18] The collected telemetry datasets are open and available for everyone, but they don't include any information about performance.

Strictly speaking, monitoring and telemetry are not kinds of benchmarks or performance tests. If you look at the list of benchmarking requirements from Chapter 1, the first requirement (and one of the most important) is repeatability. Forget about it! Each second you have a new situation; the external world is constantly changing. It's hard to write performance asserts for such data, but there are a few useful approaches:

- **Common trends**

  It's hard to perform a precise analysis, but you can track common trends. For example, you can compare statistics (like average, p_{90}, p_{99}, and so on) of a web page load duration on the previous week (with the previous version of your web service) and the current week (with an updated web service version). If you see a statistically significant difference, it's a reason for a performance investigation.

- **Thresholds**

  If you have a low latency requirement for some operations, you can introduce thresholds and send telemetry data in cases of failure. Imagine that you develop a desktop application and you want to keep the startup time low. Let's say that 1 second on modern hardware (you can collect information about the hardware as well) is your upper limit. Of course, a user can have some heavy processes running at the same time, so let's say that the threshold is 2 seconds. If the startup time is more than 2 seconds, a telemetry alarm should be sent. Probably, you will get a few such alarms every day because you can't control the user

---

[17]https://docs.microsoft.com/en-us/dotnet/core/tools/telemetry

[18]This feature is enabled by default, but you can disable it with the `DOTNET_CLI_TELEMETRY_OPTOUT` environment variable.

environment. However, if you start getting dozens or hundreds of such alarms after the publishing of a new version, you have an issue for investigation.

- **Manual watching**

  It's hard to predict all the things that can go wrong. It's even harder to automate the analysis of performance plot and write a system that automatically notifies us about all suspicious things. We will talk about performance anomalies later in this chapter. Thus, it's a common practice when a special person (or a group of people) are looking for performance charts. Popular services require 24/7 monitoring: in case of any problems (not only performance problems but also availability and business logic issues), the reaction must be immediate. Unfortunately, it's almost impossible to automate this process. But you can use dashboards and alarm systems to make life easier.

Tests with External Dependencies

Sometimes, we have a performance-critical scenario that involves something from the external world. In this case, the final performance distribution is affected by it. Unfortunately, we can't control the external world. Let's consider a couple of examples:

- **External services**

  In Rider, we have some tests that cover NuGet features like install, uninstall, or restore. The logic of the test is simple: we just check that we can correctly perform these operations in small and huge solutions. Most of the tests are using our local NuGet repository, but some of them are using the nuget.org and myget.org servers. The primary goal of these tests is checking that the logic is correct, but we can also use it as performance tests. In Figure 5-2, you can see a typical performance plot for one of our NuGet tests. On March 22, 2018, nuget.org was down (see [Kofman 2018]). On April 16, 2018, api.nuget.org was blacklisted in Russia.[19] On

---

[19]https://github.com/NuGet/NuGetGallery/issues/5806

May 6, 2018, there were some serious problems with search API in the NuGet Gallery (see [Akinshin 2018]). We learn about these incidents immediately because we are watching the performance plots all the time. On the one hand, it's hard to use such tests for honest performance regression testing: we get false positive results (a performance test is red, but there are no changes in the code base). On the other hand, all these problems are relevant to the behavior that users have in the product. It's good to be notified about it as soon as possible.

- **External devices**

  Many years ago, I was involved in an interesting project. My colleagues and I worked on a program that communicates with OWEN TRM 138.[20] This is an industrial measurement device with eight channels that can measure different characteristics, such as temperature, amperage, and voltage. If you connect it to eight different points of a machine detail and measure the temperature at these points, the program can extrapolate the data and build a 2D map of the temperature surface. Everything should work in real time: if the user changes some connection points, the map should be recalculated instantly. The real-time visualization was an important feature, so we checked that the time intervals between changes in the experimental setup and a new visualization. Unfortunately, sometimes we experienced unpredictable delays: OWEN TRM 138 provided data a few seconds late. Thus, it was almost impossible to make reliable performance measurements (because the delays were *unpredictable*). Eventually, we stopped to measure the whole cycle and started to measure different stages: fetching data, extrapolating, building an image, and so on. It solved the problem because measurements of the device-independent stages were pretty stable.

---

[20]www.owen.ru/uploads/re_trm138.pdf (In Russian.)

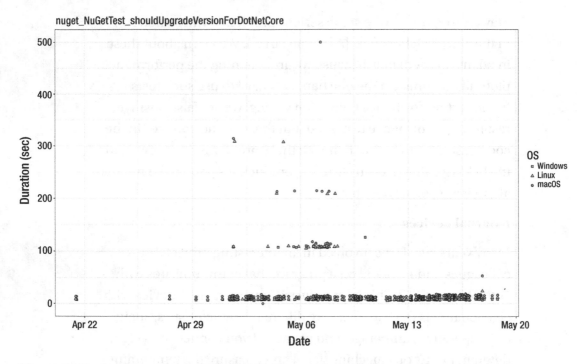

Figure 5-2. *Performance plot of a NuGet test in Rider*

The general advice: if you have some parts of the external world that affect your performance and you can't control it, try to isolate it. It's still nice to see the whole picture and get the performance distribution of the whole operations (monitoring/telemetry), but you can't build reliable performance tests on top of it. For such stages, you should measure test stages that you can control (without any interaction with the external world).

Other Kinds of Performance Tests

There is a huge number of different approaches that can be used for writing performance tests. This section is just an overview of possible techniques; we are not going to cover all of them. However, there are a few more performance test kinds that are worth mentioning: stress/load tests, user interface tests, and fuzz tests.

- **Stress/load tests**

  You should always know the limitations of your software product. Usually, it's a good idea to cover these limitations by performance tests. When we are talking about performance stress tests, we usually mean integration tests. Such testing is especially useful for web services that handle a huge number of users at the same time. A typical mistake for server application benchmarking is focusing only on a situation without load (we send a single request to the server and measure the response time). In real life, you have many users who send requests at the same time. The most interesting thing is that the way the server process these requests depends on the volume of these requests. Fortunately, there are existing solutions that can help to automate this process (e.g., Apache JMeter, Yandex. Tank, Pandora, LoadRunner, Gatling).

- **User interface tests**

  It's not always easy to implement a correct infrastructure for user interface tests, because you usually can't run it a "headless" mode; you need a "graphical environment" for such tests. For example, in the IntelliJ IDEA code base, there are some user interface tests that check whether the IDE interface is responsive. In the CI pipeline, these tests are running on dedicated agents that are connected to physical 4K monitors.

  There are also many libraries and frameworks that can help you to automate testing of the interface in your product (e.g., Selenium).

- **Fuzz tests**

  We already know that the performance space is complicated and a method duration can depend on many different factors. Let's say that there is an algorithm that processes a list of integers and makes some calculations. We implemented a faster version of this algorithm and now we want to verify that it really works faster. How should we compare them? Obviously, we can create a reference set of lists and benchmark both algorithms on each list from the set. Even if the new algorithm shows great results on all these pregenerated lists, we can't be sure that it will always be faster than the original algorithm. What if there is a corner case that spoils the performance of the new implementation? Unfortunately, we can't enumerate all possible lists of integers and check each of them. In such cases, we can try a technique called *fuzzing*. The idea is simple: we should generate random lists until we find input which causes problems.

A very simplified version may look as follows:

```
for (int i = 0; i < N; i++)
{
  var list = GenerateRandomList();
  var statistics = RunBenchmark(NewAlgorithm, list);
  if (HasPerformanceProblem(statistics))
    ReportAboutProblem(list);
}
```

Fuzzing is a powerful approach used in different areas of software engineering. It can be applied even for searching for bugs in RyuJIT (see [Warren 2018] for details). If we can discover bugs in a JIT compiler that were unnoticed by developers and passed all unit tests, we definitely can try it in benchmarking.

Here is another situation: a user complains about performance problems, you know that these problems most likely relate to specific parameter values, but you don't know the exact values that cause the problems, and it's not possible to get information about the user setup. If you are not able to try all possible setups, you can try to find it with the help of fuzzing.

Fuzzing can be also a part of your continuous integration pipeline: you can generate new input data each time and check for unusual performance phenomena.

However, fuzzing has one important drawback. It breaks one of the main benchmark requirements: the repeatability. The fuzz benchmarks are a special kind with only one goal: to catch undesirable results. However, you still should make each run of a fuzz benchmark repeatable by saving the input data or a random seed that is used for data generation.

Summing Up

There are many kinds of benchmarks and performance tests. In this section, we discussed only some of them. To be honest, all *kinds* of performance tests are not exactly *kinds*. They are like *concepts*, *ideas*, or *approaches* that you can mix in any combination. For example, you can use *asymptotic analysis* for *capacity planning* for a web server in the *warmed state* under *load*. Of course, you shouldn't implement all the discussed test categories in each product: you can select only a few of them or invent your own kinds of performance tests relevant to your problems. The main rule is simple: you should design such tests that correspond to the business goals and take a reasonable amount of time. If you write some benchmarks or performance tests, you should clearly understand what kind of problems are you going to solve. Typically, figuring out the problem takes more than half of the time that goes into finding the solution. Based on this understanding, you can choose the best techniques (or combinations of them) that fit your situation.

Performance Anomalies

In simple words, a performance anomaly is a situation when the performance space looks "strange." What does this mean? Well, you can choose your own definition. It's a situation when you look at a performance plot and say: "This plot seems unusual and suspicious; we might have a problem with it. We should investigate it and understand why we have such plot."

An anomaly is not a problem that should be fixed; it is a characteristic of the performance space that you should know. All anomalies can be divided into two groups: **temporal** and **spatial**. A temporal anomaly assumes that you have a history (a set of revisions or commits) that is analyzed. For example, you can find a problem that was introduced by recent changes in the source code. A spatial anomaly can be detected in a single revision. For example, it can be based on a difference between environments or a strange performance distribution of a single test.

In this section, we discuss some of the more common performance anomalies:

- **Degradation.** Something worked quickly before, and now it works slowly.

- **Acceleration.** Something worked slowly before, and now it works quickly.

- **Temporal clustering.** Something suddenly changed for several tests at the same time.

- **Spatial clustering.** Performance results depend on a parameter of the test environment.

- **Huge duration.** A test takes too much time.

- **Huge variance.** The difference between subsequential measurements without any changes is huge.

- **Huge outliers.** The distribution has too many extremely high values.

- **Multimodal distributions.** The distribution has several modes.

- **False anomalies.** A situation when the performance space looks "strange," but there's nothing to worry about here.

Each anomaly subsection has a small example with a table that illustrates the problem. After that, we discuss the anomaly in detail and why it's so important to detect it. Some of the subsections also contain a short classification of the anomaly kinds.

In the last two subsections, we will discuss problems that can be solved by hunting for these anomalies and recommendations about what can you do with performance anomalies.

Let's start from one of most famous anomalies: the performance degradation.

Degradation

Performance degradation is a situation when a test works slower than before. It's a **temporal** anomaly because you detect a degradation by comparing several revisions.

An example. You can see a performance test history of a single test in Table 5-2. Compare the performance history before and since May 20.

Table 5-2. *An Example of Degradation*

Day	May 17	May 18	May 19	May 20	May 21	May 22
Time	*504 ms*	*520 ms*	*513 ms*	**2437 ms**	**2542 ms**	**2496 ms**

Performance degradation is one of the most common anomalies. When people talk about performance testing, one of the typical goals is to prevent performance degradation. Sometimes it's the only goal (before people start to explore the performance state and discover exciting things).

There are two main kinds of performance degradations:

- **Cliff**

  A cliff degradation is a situation when you have a statistically significant performance drop after a commit. You can see an example of the cliff degradation in Figure 5-3.

- **Incline**

   An incline degradation is a situation when you have a series of
   small performance degradations. Each degradation can't be
   easily detected, but you can observe a performance drop when
   you look at the history for a period. For example, your current
   performance can be 2 times worse than a month ago, but you
   can't point to a commit that ruined everything because there are
   too many commits with a small performance impact. You can see
   an example of the incline degradation in Figure 5-4.

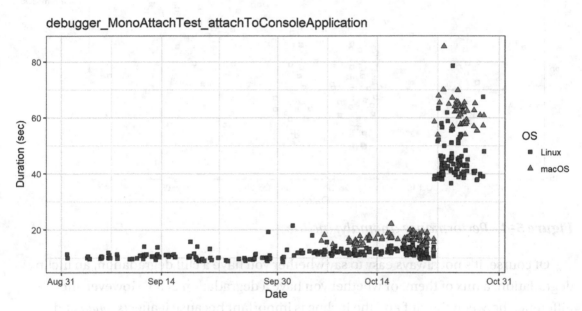

debugger_MonoAttachTest_attachToConsoleApplication

Figure 5-3. *Performance anomaly: cliff*

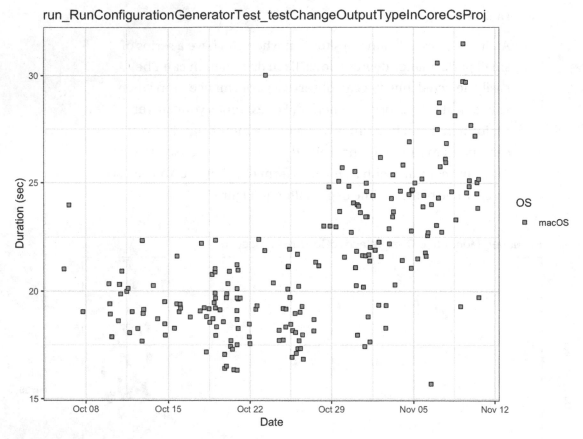

Figure 5-4. *Performance anomaly: incline*

Of course, it's not always easy to say whether you have a cliff degradation, an incline degradation, a mix of them, or whether you have a degradation at all. However, the difference between the cliff and the incline is important because it affects *when* and *how* you are going to detect a degradation: the cliff can be detected on a specific commit (even before a merge), and the incline can be detected during the retrospective analysis.

Acceleration

Performance acceleration is a situation when a test works faster than before. It's a **temporal** anomaly because you detect acceleration by comparing several revisions.

An example. You can see a performance test history of a single test in Table 5-3. Compare the performance history before and since April 08.

Table 5-3. *An Example of Acceleration*

Day	Apr 05	Apr 06	Apr 07	Apr 08	Apr 09	Apr 10
Time	954 ms	981 ms	941 ms	*1 ms*	*2 ms*	*1 ms*

It's very important to distinguish *expected* and *unexpected* accelerations:

- **Expected accelerations**

  An expected acceleration is a good anomaly. For example, you make an optimization, commit it, and see that many tests work much faster now. There's nothing to worry about! However, it still makes sense to track such anomalies because of the following reasons:

  – *Tracking optimization impact*

  Even if you are sure that the optimization works, it still makes sense to verify it. Of course, you should perform local checks first, but it's better to have several verification stages: it reduces the risk that a problem can go unnoticed. Also, you get a better overview of the features that were improved.

  – *Team morale*

  However, tracking such acceleration can be good for morale in your team. When you implement a feature, you instantly see the result of your work. When you fix performance problems all the time, it can be demoralizing due to lack of feedback.[21] People should see a positive impact of their work. A single performance plot with significant performance improvements can make a developer very happy.

- **Unexpected accelerations**

  An unexpected acceleration is always suspicious. You can meet a lot of developers who can say something like the following:

---

[21]If something works slowly, users often complain about it all the time. Typically, if something works fast enough, nobody tells you about it.

"I didn't change anything, but now the software works faster. Hooray!" Unfortunately, an unexpected speedup can often mean a bug. I had observed many situations when a developer *accidentally* turned off a feature and got a performance improvement. Such situations can pass all the tests, but you can't hide them from the performance plots! Investigations of unexpected accelerations don't help you with performance, but they can help you to find some bugs.

Temporal Clustering

Temporal clustering is a situation when several tests have significant performance changes at the same time. It's a **temporal** anomaly because you detect it by comparing several revisions.

An example. You can see a performance test history of three tests in Table 5-4. Compare October and November results for Test1 and Test2.

Table 5-4. *An Example of Temporal Clustering*

Day	Oct 29	Oct 30	Oct 31	Nov 01	Nov 02
Test1	*1.4 sec*	*1.3 sec*	*1.4 sec*	**2.9 sec**	**2.8 sec**
Test2	*4.3 sec*	*4.2 sec*	*4.4 sec*	**8.8 sec**	**8.7 sec**
Test3	5.3 sec	5.3 sec	5.4 sec	5.4 sec	5.3 sec

One of the performance testing goals is automation. A simple "you have a problem somewhere here" is a good thing, but it's not enough. You should provide all data that can help to investigate the problem quickly and easily.

One of the ways to do it is by tracking the grouped changes. If you get 100 tests with problems after a change, it doesn't mean that you should create 100 issues in your bug tracker and investigate them independently. It's most likely that you have a few problems (or only one problem) that affect many tests. Thus, you should find groups of the tests that likely suffer from the same problem.

Let's discuss a few possible group kinds.

- **Suite degradation**

  Most of the projects have a test hierarchy. You can have several projects in a solution, several test classes in a project, several test methods in a class, and several input parameter sets for a method. When you are looking for performance degradation or another performance anomaly, you should try to highlight test suites[22] that share the same problem.

  Let's look at an example in Table 5-5. Here we have two suites: A and B, three tests in each suite. We have some measurements before and after some changes. We have different measurement values for all tests, but some of them can be explained by natural noise. You can note that performance delta in the B suite is not significant: it's about 1% (typical fluctuations for usual unit tests). Meanwhile, we have a noticeable time increase for tests from the A suite: around 10-18%. The fact that we got a performance degradation for all tests of the suite at the same time is a reason to assume that we have the same problem with the whole suite.

Table 5-5. An Example of Suite Degradation

Suite	Test	Time (before)	Time (after)	Delta
A	A1	*731 ms*	**834 ms**	**103 ms**
A	A2	*527 ms*	**623 ms**	**96 ms**
A	A3	*812 ms*	**907 ms**	**95 ms**
B	B1	345 ms	349 ms	4 ms
B	B2	972 ms	966 ms	−6 ms
B	B3	654 ms	657 ms	3 ms

---

[22]Different developers use different definitions for the term "suite." In the context of a project or a team, you can have a clear definition. For example, you can say that a suite is a test class that is marked with the `TestFixture` attribute in a NUnit project. In this book, we use a higher level of abstraction and say that a suite is a group of tests that have the same place in the test hierarchy. For example, a suite can be a set of tests in a project or a single test with different sets of input parameters (test cases).

- **Paired degradation/acceleration**

  This is another kind of very common problem. In a suite, you often have an initialization logic. It can be an explicit setup or an implicit lazy initialization. In this case, you can have a test that works slowly not because of the test logic, but because it includes the initialization logic. Let's look at an example in Table 5-6. As you can see, before the change all test methods take about 100 ms except Foo which takes 543 ms. After the change, Foo takes 104 ms (acceleration), Bar takes 560 ms (degradation), and other tests don't have statistically significant changes. In such cases, we can assume that the order of tests was changed: Foo was the first test in the suite before the changes; after the changes, Bar is the first test. This is not always true, but it's a hypothesis which should be checked. Why should we care about it? The initialization logic should always move away from the tests to a separate method. It's not only a good practice, but it's also important from the performance point of view. A huge deviation from the setup can hide real performance problems in the tests. Let's do some calculations with rounded example values. If a test takes 100 ms and a setup takes 400 ms, they take 500 ms together. If we have a 30 ms degradation, this comprises 30% of the test time (a significant change) and only 6% of the total time, which can be ignored because of huge errors. If you have a setup logic inside one of the tests, it's not a bug, but it's a design flaw. Usually, it's a good idea to get rid of it (if possible).

Table 5-6. *An Example of Suite Degradation*

Test	Time (before)	Time (after)	Delta
Foo	**543 ms**	*104 ms*	**-439 ms**
Bar	*108 ms*	**560 ms**	**452 ms**
Baz	94 ms	101 ms	7 ms
Qux	103 ms	105 ms	2 ms
Quux	102 ms	99 ms	-3 ms
Quuz	98 ms	96 ms	-2 ms

- **Correlated changes in time series**

  If you can detect a correlation between two time series in your tests, it can be interesting to check that you always have this correlation. In Table 5-7, you can see an example of some latency and throughput measurements. The latency is just a raw duration, the throughput is a number of RPS. We run these tests on different agents with different hardware, so we can't apply "usual" degradation analysis here. However, we can notice a pattern: Throughput≈2 sec / Latency. For example, if Latency = 0.1 sec, we get Throughput = 2 sec / 0.1 sec = 20. This pattern can be explained by parallelization: we have two threads on each agent that process our requests. We can observe such patterns on all agents except Agent4. So, we can assume that something is wrong with parallelization here. Of course, we can detect this problem in other ways. However, the correlation analysis helped us to formulate a hypothesis for future investigation (something is wrong with the Latency/Throughput) and get additional important information (we have this problem only on Agent4). Such facts can save a lot of investigator time because you can collect all such suspicious patterns automatically. You can find another example of such analysis in [AnomalyIo 2017].

Table 5-7. *An Example of Correlated Changes in Time Series*

Day	Agent	Latency	Throughput
Jan 12	Agent1	100 ms	20.12 RPS
Jan 13	Agent1	105 ms	19.01 RPS
Jan 14	Agent2	210 ms	9.48 RPS
Jan 15	Agent2	220 ms	8.98 RPS
Jan 16	Agent3	154 ms	12.89 RPS
Jan 17	Agent3	162 ms	12.41 RPS
Jan 18	**Agent4**	**205 ms**	**4.95 RPS**
Jan 19	**Agent4**	**209 ms**	**5.02 RPS**

Spatial Clustering

Spatial clustering is a situation when the performance of some tests significantly depends on some test or environment parameters. It's a **spatial** anomaly because you detect it with a single revision.

An example. In Table 5-8, you can see average durations of three tests depend on an operating system. Compare durations of Test1 and Test2 for Windows vs. Linux/macOS.

Table 5-8. *An Example of Spatial Clustering*

	Test1	Test2	Test3
Windows	**5.2 sec**	**9.3 sec**	1.2 sec
Linux	*0.4 sec*	*0.6 sec*	1.4 sec
macOS	*0.4 sec*	*0.7 sec*	1.2 sec

Sometimes, it's obvious that test performance can depend on some properties of the environment. Sometimes, it's not obvious enough. Moreover, some external factors can unexpectedly affect the performance only of a specific set of tests. If you check your product on different machines with different environments, it's a good idea to check the difference between performance measurements for the same test in different environments.

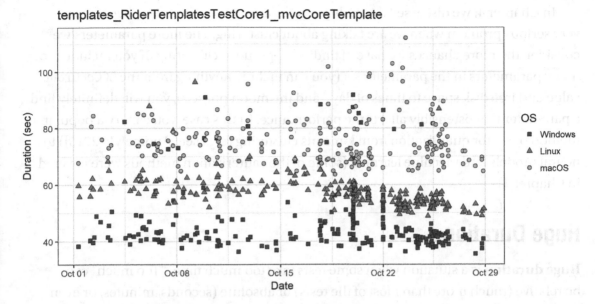

Figure 5-5. *Performance anomaly: spatial clustering*

Let's consider an example. The same version of ReSharper should work on different versions of Visual Studio (VS). For example, ReSharper 2017.3 should work on VS 2010, VS 2012, VS 2013, VS 2015, and VS 2017. The ReSharper team has a suite of integration tests that are executed on all versions of Visual Studio. It's not a rare situation when some changes spoil performance only on a specific version of Visual Studio. Moreover, if we work only with a single revision (without performance history), we can observe that some tests work fast on VS 2010, VS 2012, VS 2013, and VS 2015 and work slowly on VS 2017. It's a good practice to look for such situations and try to investigate them.

Another example is about Rider. Rider should work fast on all supported operating systems. It uses .NET Framework on Windows and Mono on Linux/macOS. Most of the tests have about the same duration on different operating systems, but some of them demonstrate huge differences. In Figure 5-5, you can see performance measurements for .NET Core ASP.NET MVC template (create a solution from the template, restore NuGet packages, build it, run the analysis, and so on). As you can see in the figure, these tests work faster on Windows than on Linux or macOS. Also, it has a huge variance, but we will discuss it in the next subsection.

The clustering anomaly can be applied to a single revision instead of a set of revisions. It doesn't show problems which were introduced by recent changes, but it can show problems that you have right now (and had for a long time).

In Chapter 4, we discussed the multiple comparisons problem. This becomes a very serious problem when we are talking about clustering. The more parameters we consider, the more chances we have of finding a "pseudo" clustering. If you include too many parameters in the parameter set (you can include anything from the GCCpuGroup value and free disk space to times of day[23] and the moon phase[24]), you will definitely find a parameter that ostensibly affects the performance. In this case, you can try a popular method of vector quantization from k-means clustering (e.g., see [AnomalyIo 2015]) to neural models and machine learning (some of the cauterization methods were covered in Chapter 4).

Huge Duration

Huge duration is a situation when some tests take too much time. "Too much" can be relative (much more than most of the tests) or absolute (seconds, minutes, or even hours). It's usually a **spatial** anomaly because you are looking for the slowest test per revision.

An example. In Table 5-9, you can see examples from the top five slowest tests. Compare the first test and the fifth test.

Table 5-9. *Examples of Huge Duration*

Place	Test	Time
1	Test472	**18.54 sec**
2	Test917	**16.83 sec**
3	Test124	5.62 sec
4	Test952	0.42 sec
5	Test293	0.19 sec

---

[23]Times of day can be an essential parameter if we monitor the performance of a popular web service.

[24]In programmers' folklore, the moon phase is the final reasonable explanation of an anomaly when all other plausible hypotheses are rejected.

First of all, try to answer the following questions:

- What is the maximum acceptable duration of a single test?

- What is the maximum acceptable duration of the whole test suite?

- Check out the durations of tests in your project. What is the typical duration of the whole test suite? Find the slowest test (or a group of the slowest tests). Is it possible to test the same thing in less time?

It's always great when you can run all of your tests quickly. When we are talking about usual unit tests, it's a typical situation when thousands of tests take a few seconds. However, the situation is worse with integration and performance tests. Sometimes, such tests can take minutes and even hours.

If you are going to speed up the test suite, it doesn't mean that you should implement some crazy optimizations. There are many examples of success stories when people significantly reduce the total test suite duration by a small change. In [Kondratyuk 2017], a developer changed `localhost` to `127.0.0.1` and got a 18x speedup of a test suite. In [Songkick 2012], the test suite time was reduced from 15 hours to 15 seconds by a series of different improvements. In [Bragg 2017], the test suite time was reduced from 24 hours to 20 seconds.

If the duration of the whole test suite is your pain point and affects the development process, here are a couple of classic techniques that can minimize it:

- **Run tests in parallel if possible**

   If you are care only about the total build time, you should try to run tests in parallel. Be careful: in this case, you will not get reliable performance results. Also, it's not always possible to run arbitrary tests in parallel because they can work with the same static class or share resources (e.g., files on a disk).

- **Replace integration tests by unit tests if possible**

   If you have a ready framework for integration tests, it's usually much simpler to write an integration test instead of a unit test. Unit tests require some effort: you have to isolate a part of the system correctly, mock other parts, generate synthetic data, and so on. You typically shouldn't do it in integration tests: the whole system with real data is ready for your checks. However, if you want to check only a single feature, a unit test is a recommended way. If you run the unit tests before the integration tests, the increased feature covering by additional unit tests can also improve the build time: in case of failed unit tests, you can skip the integration test phase.

Huge Variance

Huge variance is a situation when some tests have too much variance. "Too much" can be relative to other tests (much more than most of the tests), relative to the mean value (e.g., mean = 50 sec, variance = 40 sec), or absolute (seconds, minutes, or even hours). It can be a **temporal** anomaly (if you analyze a performance history) or a **spatial** anomaly (if you analyze several iterations for the same revision).

An example. In Table 5-10, you can see durations of several invocations for the same test and the same revision (no changes were made). Find the minimum and maximum values.

Table 5-10. *An Example of Huge Variance*

InvocationIndex	Time
1	2.34 sec
2	54.73 sec
3	5.15 sec
4	186.94 sec
5	25.70 sec
6	92.52 sec
7	144.41 sec

Another example from the IntelliJ IDEA test suite is presented in Figure 5-6. It's a stress test with a huge number of threads. It takes 100–1000 seconds on Linux/Windows and 1000–4000 seconds on macOS.

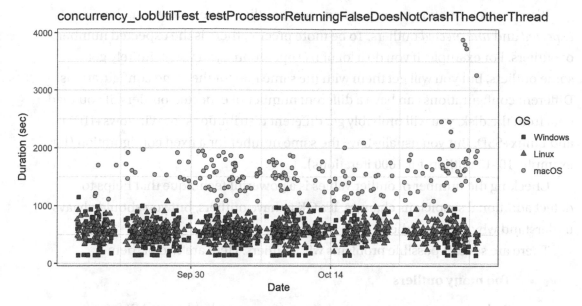

Figure 5-6. *Performance anomaly: variance*

Huge Outliers

Huge outliers is a situation when the outliers values are too big (much bigger than the mean value) or there are too many outlier values (e.g., significantly more than before). It can be a **temporal** anomaly (if you analyze a performance history) or a **spatial** anomaly (if you analyze several test iterations for the same revision).

An example. In Table 5-11, you can see durations of several invocations for the same test and the same revision (no changes were made). Find the outlier.

Table 5-11. *An Example of Huge Outliers*

InvocationIndex	Time
1	100 ms
2	105 ms
3	103 ms
4	**1048 ms**
5	102 ms
6	97 ms

It's a normal situation when you have some outlier values. However, there are *expected* and *unexpected* outliers. To be more precise, there is the expected number of outliers. For example, if you do a lot of I/O operations, you will definitely get some outliers, but you will get them with the same rate for the same configurations. Different configurations can have a different number of expected outliers. If you read data from the disk, you will probably get different distributions for Windows+HDD and Linux+SSD. But you usually have the same number for a fixed configuration (for example, 10–15 outliers for 1000 iterations).

Checking the number of outlier values is a powerful technique that helps to detect additional suspicious changes. It's OK to have outliers, but you should always understand why you have them.

There are several possible problems with outliers. Here are two of them:

- **Too many outliers**

  Sometimes you make some changes (for example, change API for reading data from the disk) and accidentally increase the number of outliers (e.g., 40–50 instead of 10–15). In this case, the standard deviation is also increased, so you have an additional way to detect the problem.

- **Extremely huge outliers**

  Outliers are always bigger than the mean value. It's usually OK if the difference between the maximum outlier and the mean value is huge (e.g., mean = 300 ms, max = 2600 ms). However, sometimes these values are extremely high (e.g., mean = 300 ms, max = 650000 ms). Such a situation can be a sign of a serious bug that can hurt your users.

Multimodal Distributions

Multimodal distribution is a situation when the distribution has several modes (we already covered this topic in Chapter 4). It can be a **temporal** anomaly (if you analyze a performance history) or a **spatial** anomaly (if you analyze several iterations for the same revision).

An example. In Table 5-12, you can see durations of several invocations of the same test. As you can see, the total time is around 100 ms or 500 ms.

Table 5-12. *An Example of Multimodal Distribution*

InvocationIndex	Time
1	*101 ms*
2	**502 ms**
3	**504 ms**
4	*105 ms*
5	*103 ms*
6	**510 ms**
7	*114 ms*

When you run some simple synthetic benchmarks, you usually don't observe such situations. However, it's a pretty common situation in real-life performance measurements. For example, in Figure 5-7, you can see measurements for the OutputLineSplitterTest_testFlushing from the IntelliJ IDEA test suite. This test takes about 0 sec or 10 sec. The test name (which contains testFlushing) helps us to assume that we do output flushing only in some cases, but not every time. This is not always a mistake; it can be a "by design" behavior. However, it's very important to detect such situations in advance because we can't use the average value (which is around 5 sec for testFlushing) in case of a multimodal distribution. We already discussed multimodal distribution and how to detect them in Chapter 4.

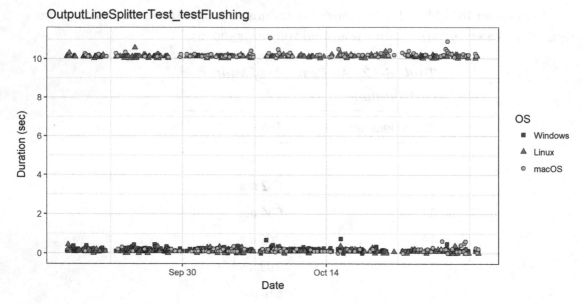

Figure 5-7. *Performance anomaly: bimodal distribution*

False Anomalies

False anomaly is a situation that looks like an anomaly but there are no problems behind it. A false anomaly can be temporal (if you analyze a performance history) or spatial (if you analyze only a single revision).

An example. Let's say that we have a test that takes 100 ms:

```
public void MyTest() // 100 ms
{
  DoIt();              // 100 ms
}
```

We decided to add some heavy asserts (200 ms), which check that everything is OK:

```
public void MyTest() // 300 ms
{
  DoIt();              // 100 ms
  HeavyAsserts();      // 200 ms
}
```

On the performance plot, we will see something that looks like a performance degradation (100 ms ->300 ms), but there is no performance problem here; it's an expected change of the test duration. If you have a recently introduced anomaly, it's a good practice to check the changes in the source code first. Found changes in a test body at the beginning of an investigation can save hours of useless work. You can also use a proactive approach and set an agreement in your team: each person who makes any performance-sensitive changes on purpose should mark them somehow. For example, a test can be marked with a special comment or an attribute. Or you can create common storage (a database, a web service, or even a plain text file) that contains all information about such changes. It doesn't matter which way you choose if all the team members know how to view the history of the intentional performance changes in each test.

If you have an anomaly, it doesn't always mean that you have a problem. It's a regular situation to have an anomaly because of some natural reason. If you hunt for anomalies all the time and investigate each of them, it's important to be aware of "false anomalies" that don't have any actual problems behind them.

Let's discuss some frequent reasons for such anomalies.

- **Changes in tests**

    This is one of the most common false anomalies. If you make any changes in a test (add or remove some logic), it's obvious that the test duration can be changed. Thus, if you have a performance anomaly like degradation in a test, the first thing that you should check is if there are any changes in the test. The second thing for checking is any changes that spoil the performance on purpose (e.g., you can sacrifice performance for the sake of correctness).

- **Changes in the test order**

    The test order can be changed at any moment; there can be several reasons for this, including test renaming. It can be painful if the first test of the suite includes a heavy initialization logic. Let's say we have five tests in a test fixture with the following order (revision A): Test01, Test02, Test03, Test04, Test05. Our test framework uses lexicographical order to execute tests. In revision B, we rename Test05 to Test00. You can see possible consequences of such renaming in Table 5-13. It's most likely that we have an example of the "Paired degradation/acceleration" anomaly: now we have a new slow test, Test00, instead of the old slow Test01. We have already discussed that it's a good idea to move the initialization logic to a separate setup method, but it's not always possible. If we know about such a "first test effect" and we can't do anything about it, we will still get a notification about an anomaly here.

Table 5-13. *Example of Changes in the Test Order*

Revision	Index	Name	Time
A	1	**Test01**	**100ms**
A	2	Test02	20ms
A	3	Test03	30ms
A	4	Test04	35ms
A	5	**Test05**	**25ms**
B	1	**Test00**	**105ms**
B	2	**Test01**	**20ms**
B	3	Test02	20ms
B	4	Test03	30ms
B	5	Test04	35ms

- **Changes in CI agent hardware**

  It's great if you can run performance tests on the same CI agent (a physical machine) all the time. However, the agent can break down, and it can be hard to find an identical replacement. Any changes in the environment can affect performance: from a minor change in the processor model number to the RAM memory size. It's always hard to compare measurements from different machines because the actual changes are unpredictable. If you want to perform nanobenchmarks, you typically need a set of identical physical CI agents.

- **Changes in CI agent software**

  You can get some trouble with the same agent without hardware replacement. It's a common practice when admins install operating system updates from time to time. They can be minor security updates or major OS updates (e.g., Ubuntu 16.04 → Ubuntu 18.04). Any environment change can affect performance. This leads to a situation when you see a suspicious degradation or acceleration on performance plots without any changes in the source code.

- **Changes in CI agent pool**

  Only the luckiest have an ability to run tests on a CI agent pool with dedicated identical machines. A much more frequent situation is a dynamic pool of CI agents: you can't predict which hardware/software environment will be used for the next test suite run. Something is constantly changing in such a pool: some machines are turned off, some machines are put into operation, some machines get updates, some machines are occupied by developers who do performance investigations, and so on. Such a situation means increased variance (because of the constant jumping between) and performance anomalies based on the changes in the pool. In Figure 5-8, you can see a performance anomaly for `MonoCecil` test in Rider for macOS agents around October 20. Nothing was changed in the source code; the degradation was caused by a planned update of all macOS agents. The updating process consumes CPU and disk resources and affects the performance of tests (it wasn't a special performance test; it was a regular test that runs on regular agents from the pool). As soon as the update finished, the performance returned to the "normal level" (if you can say "normal" for a test with such variance).

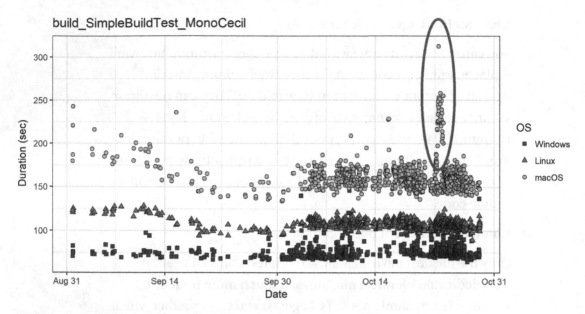

Figure 5-8. *False performance anomaly: agent problems*

- **Changes in the external world**

  If you have any external dependencies, they can be a persistent source of performance anomalies. Unfortunately, it's not always possible to get rid of these dependencies. Once a dependency becomes a part of your tested logic, you start to share the performance space with it. The classic example of such a dependency is an external web service. You can download something from the web or test an authentication method. For example, I had such a problem with NuGet Restore tests in Rider. These tests checked that we could restore packages correctly and fast. The first version of these tests used nuget.org as a source feed for all NuGet packages. Unfortunately, these tests were *very* unstable. Once a day, there was such a situation in which one of the tests was failing because of slow nuget.org responses. On the next iteration, we created a mirror of nuget.org and deployed it on our local server. We (almost) didn't have fails any more, but the variance was still huge for these tests. On the final iteration, we started to use a local package source (all the packages were downloaded on the disk before the test suite is started). We got (almost) stable tests with low variance. It should be noted that it's not an honest test refactoring. We sacrificed a part of the logic (downloading packages from a remote server) for the sake of the false anomaly rate.

- **Any other changes**

  Our world is constantly changing. Anything can happen at any minute. You should always be ready to meet false performance anomalies. A performance engineer who is responsible for the processing of the anomalies should know what kinds of false anomalies are frequent for the project infrastructure. Checking if an anomaly is false should be the first thing that you should do before a performance investigation. This simple check helps to save time and prevent a situation in which a false anomaly becomes a Type I (false positive) error.

Underlying Problems and Recommendations

Usually, performance anomalies notify us about different problems in a project. Here are some of them:

- **Performance degradation**

  It may sound obvious, but the biggest problem with this anomaly is the degradation of the performance. Usually, people start to do performance testing because they want to prevent degradations.

- **Hidden bugs**

  Missed asserts are bugs in tests, but you can have similar bugs in the production code. If a test has a huge variance, the first thing that you should ask is the following: "why do we have such variance here?" In most cases, you have a nondeterministic bug behind it. For example, it can be a race condition or a deadlock (with termination on timeout but without assert).

- **Slow build process**

  You have to wait too long before all tests are passed on a CI server. It's a typical requirement that all tests should pass before an installer will be available, or a web service will be deployed. When the whole test suite takes 30 minutes or even 1 hour to run, it's acceptable. However, if it takes many hours, it slows down your development process.

- **Slow development process**

  If a test is red and you are trying to fix it, you have to run the test locally again and again after each fix attempt. If a test takes 1 hour, you have only eight attempts with a standard 8-hour working day. Moreover, it doesn't make any sense to wait for the test result without any actions, so developers often switch to another problem. The developer context switch is always painful. Also, the huge test duration implies huge errors. When a test takes 1 hour, you are usually OK with an error of a few minutes. In such a situation, it's hard to set up strict performance asserts (we will talk about this later).

- **Unpredictably huge duration**

  We already talked about a huge test duration: this is not a good thing. When you have an *unpredictably huge* test duration, it's much worse. In such case, it's hard to work on the performance of such tests. If you have timeouts (which are popular solutions because tests may hang), the test can be flaky because the total duration can *sometimes* exceed the timeout.

- **It's hard to specify performance asserts**

  Let's look again at Figure 5-6. You can see a performance history plot of a concurrency test from the IntelliJ IDEA test suite. Some of the runs can take 100 seconds (especially on Windows), and others can take 4000 seconds (especially on macOS). We can observe both kinds of values on the same revision without any changes. Imagine that you introduce a performance degradation. How do you catch it? Even if you have a performance degradation of **1000 seconds**, you can miss it because the variance is too huge.

- **Missed asserts**

    Many times, I have seen tests with *green* performance history as
    follows: 12.6 sec, 15.4 sec, 300.0 sec, 14.3 sec, 300.0 sec,
    16.1 sec, ... A typical example: we send a request and wait for
    a response. The waiting timeout is 5 minutes, but there is no
    assert that we got the response. After 5 minutes, we just terminate
    waiting and finish the test with the green status. It may sound like
    a stupid bug, but there are a lot of such bugs in real life. Such tests
    can be easily detected if we look for the tests with extremely high
    outliers.

- **Surprising delays in production**

    Have you ever had a situation when you do an operation that is
    usually performed instantly, but it hangs an application for a few
    seconds? Such situations are always annoying users. There are
    many different reasons for such behavior. Usually, it's hard to fix
    them because you typically don't have a stable repro. However,
    some of them can also be a cause of outliers on your performance
    plot. If you systematically have outliers on a CI server, you can add
    some logs, find the problem, and fix it.

- **Hacks in test logic**

    Have you ever had flaky tests with race conditions? What is the
    best way to fix such tests? There is an incorrect but popular
    hotfix: putting Thread.Sleep here and there. Usually, it fixes the
    flakiness; the test is always green again. However, it fixes only
    symptoms of a problem, but not the problem. Once such fix is
    committed, it's hard to reproduce this problem again. And it's
    hard to find tests with such "smart fixes."[25] Fortunately, such hacks
    can be seen with the naked eye on the performance plots. Any
    Thread.Sleep calls or other hacks that prevent race conditions

---

[25]Of course, there are some ways. For example, I like to find all Thread.Sleep usages in our code
base. If I find such a call in our test base, I remove it and see what will happen. Usually, some
tests become red or flaky. After that, I'll try to fix bugs that were revealed.

or similar problems can't be hidden from a good performance engineer.

- **False anomalies**

    The main problem with a false anomaly is obvious: you spend time on investigations, but you do not get a useful result.

There are several general recommendations for handling performance anomalies:

- **Systematic monitoring**

    This is the most important recommendation: you should monitor performance anomalies all the time. Since, a real application can have hundreds of them, you can use the dashboard-oriented approach: for each anomaly, we can sort all tests by the corresponding metrics and look at the top. Look at the tests with the highest duration, the highest variance, the highest outliers, the highest modal values, and so on. Try to understand why you have these anomalies. Do you have any problems behind them? Could you fix these problems? You can look at such a dashboard one time at month, but it will be much better if you will do it every day: in this case you can track new anomalies as soon as they are introduced.

- **Serious anomalies should be investigated**

    If you systematically track anomalies, you can find a lot of serious problems in your code. Sometimes, you can find performance problems that are not covered by performance tests. Sometimes, you can find problems in business logic that are not covered by functional or unit tests. Sometimes, it turns out that there are not any problems: an anomaly can be a false anomaly or a natural anomaly (which is caused by "natural" factors you can't control like network performance). If you don't know why you have a particular anomaly, it's a good practice to investigate it. If you can't do it right now, you can create an issue in your bug tracker or add the anomaly to a "performance investigation list." If you ignore found anomalies, you can miss some serious problems, which will be discovered only in the production stage.

- **Beware of high false anomaly rates**

    If the Type I (false positive) error rate is huge, the anomaly tracking system becomes untrustable and valueless. It's better to miss a few real issues and increase the Type II (false negative) error rate than overload the team with false alarms, which can undo all your performance efforts. If you see a performance anomaly, the first thing that you should do is check for natural reasons. Typically, these checks don't take too much time, but they can protect you from useless investigations. Here are a few check examples:

    - **Check for changes in test**

        If somebody changed the source code of the test in a corresponding revision, check these changes.

    - **Check for changes in test order**

        Just compare test orders for the current revision and for the previous one.

    - **Check the CI agent history**

        Did you use the same agent for the current and previous results? Did you make any changes in the agent hardware/software?

    - **Check typical sources of false anomalies**

        If you are looking for performance anomalies all the time, you probably know the most common causes of false anomalies. Let's say you download content from an external server with 95% uptime. If the server is down, you are doing retries until the server is up again. Such behavior can be a frequent source of outliers without any changes. If you know that a group of tests suffer from such phenomena, the first thing that you should check is log messages about retries.

- **Beware of alert fatigue**

  It's great when you can track down all your performance
  problems. However, you should understand how many issues
  can be handled by your team. If there are too many performance
  anomalies in the queue, the investigation process becomes an
  endless and boring activity. You can't fix performance issues all
  the time: you also have to develop new features and fix bugs.

Summing Up

There are too many kinds of performance anomalies to fully discuss here. Most of them
can be easily detected with the help of very simple checks. You don't typically need
advanced techniques because the basic anomaly checkers catch most of the problems.
In Rider, we usually look only at the "Huge variance" and "Clustering" anomalies. The
first implementation of our "performance analyzer" took about 4 hours: it was a C#
program that downloads data from a TeamCity server with an R script, which aggregates
this data and draws a performance plot for the most suspicious tests. In those days,
I created a few dozen performance investigation issues for different people. Many of
them were real problems that were hidden among thousands of unit tests. And to this
day, we continue to find important problems every week. We also have many advanced
analyzers that look for tricky performance issues. However, basic "Huge variance" and
"Clustering" supply us with a huge list of problems to be investigated.

I believe that checking for performance anomalies is a healthy thing for any huge
project that requires performance tests. It helps to detect critical problems in time
before users start to suffer after the next software update. Each project is unique, with
its own set of performance anomalies. Everything depends on your domain area. You
can find many interesting examples of different projects on the Internet. I recommend
that you read about flow anomalies in distributed systems (see [Chua 2014]), anomalies
in correlated time series (see [AnomalyIo 2017]), and other methods of performance
anomaly analysis in different cases (see [Ibidunmoye 2016], [Dimopoulos 2017],
[Peiris 2014]).

There is no universal way to write analyzers that will work great for every project.
Knowledge of the main performance anomalies allows you to check the performance
history of your test suite and write analyzers that will work great for your program.

Strategies of Defense

There are several ways to prevent or detect performance degradation. In this section, we talk about some common ways to do this.

Here is a list of discussed approaches:

- **Precommit tests:** looking for performance problems before a merge into the master branch.

- **Daily tests:** looking for performance problems in the recent history.

- **Retrospective analysis:** looking for performance problems in the whole history.

- **Checkpoint testing:** looking for performance problems in special moments of the development life cycle.

- **Prerelease testing:** looking for performance problems just before a release.

- **Manual testing:** looking for performance problems manually.

- **Postrelease telemetry and monitoring:** looking for performance problems after a release.

I call these approaches "Strategies of defense against performance problems," but this not a well-known term, and other terms may also be used. For example, Joe Duffy calls them "test rings" in [Duffy 2016].

For each approach, we will cover the following characteristics:

- **Detection time:** when can a performance degradation be detected?

- **Analysis duration:** how much time does it take to detect a problem?

- **Degree of degradation:** what kind of degradation can be detected? Is it huge (50-100% or more), medium (5-10%), or small (less than 1%)?[26]

- **Process:** automatic, semiautomatic, or manual? What should the developers do in each case and how can it be automated?

---

[26]Of course, these are very rough estimates; they're just some examples. The exact estimation depends on your business requirements and the performance space. In some cases, 1% can be a huge degradation or 200% can be a small one.

Pre-Commit Tests

We use this approach at the JetBrains .NET team. The idea is simple: you can't commit directly to master.[27] Instead, you have to create a feature branch and run a build configuration that should merge it into master. This build configuration runs all the tests and merges it only if all the tests are green. Thus, it's impossible to get stable[28] red tests in the master. This mechanism can be used not only for a functional test but also for performance tests. There are many variations of this approach, but the idea is always the same: we check all the changes for any performance degradation automatically before we have these changes in the master branch.

- **Detection time:** *on time.*

  The best thing about this approach is simple: we detect all performance degradations in advance automatically. There is no need to solve any new performance problems because we don't have any of those (in theory, of course).

- **Analysis duration:** *short.*

  Since we won't wait too long before our changes will be merged, the precommit tests should work quickly. It's great if a typical precommit test suite run doesn't take more than a few hours.

- **Degree of degradation:** *huge.*

  Of course, there are some limitations. We don't have any possibility of doing a lot of iterations (because we have to run all the tests very quickly). Thus, we can catch only huge degradations (e.g., 50% or 100%); it's almost impossible to detect small degradations (e.g., 5% or 10%). If we try to do this, it will increase the total run duration or Type I (false positive) error rate.

---

[27]Here we mean the main branch; in your repository, it can have another name like "default," "trunk," "release," "dev," or something else.

[28]This doesn't solve all the problems. For example, we still can merge flaky tests (tests that are sometimes red).

- **Process:** *automatic.*

   I just want to repeat one of my favorite parts about this way:
   it's completely automatic, meaning that no human actions are
   required.

Daily Tests

Unfortunately, we can't always run all the tests per each commit or merge. The reason
is simple: some tests (especially integration tests or smart performance tests) take too
much time. The common solution for such case is daily tests. These are a special set of
tests that are checked one time per day.[29] Of course, you can choose any interval of time:
for example, you can run once-weekly or even once-monthly tests.

- **Detection time:** *1 day late.*

   With daily tests, we detect performance degradations when they
   are already in master.

- **Analysis duration:** *up to 1 day.*

   Daily tests don't have "a few hours run" limitation; we can use up
   to 24 hours. If that's not enough, we can try weekly tests and spend
   up to 7 days per a test suit.

- **Degree of degradation:** *medium.*

   Since we have a lot of time, we can do many iterations and detect
   medium performance degradation (like 5% or 10%).

- **Process:** *semiautomatic.*

   Daily tests should be a part of your CI pipeline; the build server
   should run them every day automatically. However, if some tests
   are red (we have a performance degradation), the incident should
   be investigated manually. Typically there are a few team members
   who monitor the status of daily tests all the time and notify a team
   in case of any trouble.

---

[29]Some teams call them nightly tests because they usually run them at night when there is some
free time on CI agents.

Retrospective Analysis

This is one of my favorite approaches. The idea: we take all historical data for all tests and analyze it.

- **Detection time:** *late*.

   Unfortunately, some degradations will be detected late (probably after a week or after a month). However, it's better to detect such cases after a month inside the team than to let customers detect them after a few months.

- **Analysis duration:** *it depends*.

   We don't have any duration limitations; we can spend as much time as we want. If we don't have enough historical data, we can even take specific commits, build them, and run some additional iterations. Everything is possible in the retrospective analysis!

- **Degree of degradation:** *small*.

   We can detect any kind of performance degradations (even less than 1%)! In fact, the main limitation here is how much we are ready to allocate in terms of resources.

- **Process:** *semiautomatic*.

   The same situation as in the case of daily tests: we can run retrospective analysis automatically, but all issues found should be investigated manually.

Checkpoints Testing

Sometimes you know that your changes are dangerous. For example, you do a big refactoring, you rewrite a performance-critical algorithm, or you upgrade your runtime version (e.g., Mono or .NET Core). If you are not sure that there are no performance degradations in your changes, you can run performance tests in the master branch and in your branch. After that, you can compare results. Thus, we have a checkpoint (a huge change that should be checked) and we want to reduce risks.

- **Detection time:** *on time.*

  This approach allows preventing performance degradations
  before they will be merged into master.

- **Analysis duration:** *it depends.*

  In fact, the merge deadline is our only limitation. We can do as
  many tests as we want before we are sure that it's safe to merge it.

- **Degree of degradation:** *small.*

  Since we have a lot of time, we also can do a ridiculous number of
  iterations, and find even very small degradations.

- **Process:** *almost completely manual.*

  It's the developer's responsibility to check dangerous changes;
  it's not possible to automate this. If you suspect that you can have
  some performance problems in your branch, you should run tests
  manually. If you find any problems, you should investigate them
  manually. There is no automation here (except for running tests
  and branch comparison).

Pre-Release Testing

There is a special kind of checkpoint: the release. Your customers will be unhappy if,
after the software update, they get performance problems. So, each release should be
carefully checked before it's published. For some projects, the full test suite can take
several days. In this case, you don't have an opportunity to run these tests every day or
for each dangerous branch. But you can run such suite once per release candidate to be
sure that you didn't skip any really serious problems.

- **Detection time:** *very late.*

  Usually, developers run prerelease performance tests before the
  release. And they hope that there are not any problems; it's an
  additional check just to be sure. However, if you discover a serious
  performance problem a few days before the release, it can be a
  huge problem (especially if you have strict deadlines).

- **Analysis duration:** *it depends.*

  Well, it's up to you: it depends on your release cycle. How much time do you typically have between the release candidate and the actual release? Some teams spend only a few days for the final stage of testing, while others spend months. You should find an acceptable trade-off between how fast you want to deliver your product and how critical performance degradation can be.

- **Degree of degradation:** *it depends.*

  It depends on the duration of analysis. The rule is simple: the more time you spend, the more minor degradations can be found.

- **Process:** *almost completely manual.*

  The same situation as in the usual checkpoint case. You should manually run tests before release, and you should manually check the report and investigate all the issues.

Manual Testing

Of course, your QA team can test the software manually. Usually, this is not the best way because it requires a lot of man-hours, but it can help to find some performance problems that you didn't cover in your tests. It's a good practice to write new performance tests as soon as you find a new performance problem manually.

- **Detection time:** *late.*

  This approach allows checking changes that are already merged. Typically, the manual testing is a part of your workflow: you can check your daily builds,[30] you can check some internal milestone builds, you can check "checkpoints," you can check preview versions, and you have to check the release candidate.

- **Analysis duration:** *it depends.*

  It always takes too much time. The exact number of spent hours depends on the target product quality and capabilities of the QA team.

---

[30]Or nightly builds; there is no difference between these terms.

- **Degree of degradation:** *huge.*

  Usually, manual testing allows detecting only huge performance degradations because it's hard to detect a small performance regression with the human eye.

- **Process:** *completely manual.*

  You start to test software manually, you test it manually, and you investigate it manually. There is no automation here.

Post-Release Telemetry and Monitoring

Many people think that their performance adventure ends after a release. In fact, it's just starting. It's impossible to fix all bugs or to resolve all performance issues in advance. Some of them can be detected immediately after the release. Other problems may show up after a prolonged period of time: you can't detect them with other strategies of defense, because they might take multiple releases to become statistically significant.

- **Detection time:** *too late for the current release, but not too late for the next one.*

  It's never too late to fix performance problems. It's bad if you missed some problems in the current release, but it's much worse if you do nothing about it. You will always get "it works too slowly" feedback from your users or customers. It's very important to collect all performance issues from each release. There are several ways to do it:

  - **Monitoring**

    In case of a web service, you can monitor performance metrics of your servers in real time. You can manually compare them with expected metrics or set up automatic alarms about performance problems.

  - **Telemetry**

    If you can't monitor your software (desktop programs, mobile applications, embedded systems, the client side of a web page, and so on), you can collect telemetry data and regularly process it.

333

- **Issue tracker**

  If you have an issue tracker, group all performance-related issues with the help of tags or issue fields.

- **New tests**

  It's almost impossible to cover all use cases by performance tests. Never stop writing tests! If you continue to write new tests, you probably will discover new problems.

- **Analysis duration, Degree of degradation, Process:** *it depends.*

  It's up to you how you collect, analyze, and process performance issues after a release.

Summing Up

You can see the overview of all strategies in Table 5-14 ("T&M" means "telemetry and monitoring"; "DoD" means "Degree of degradation").

Table 5-14. *Overview of Strategies of Defense*

Strategy	Detection time	Analysis duration	DoD	Process
Precommit tests	On time	Short	Huge	Automatic
Daily tests	1 day late	Up to 1 day	Medium	Semiautomatic
Retrospective analysis	Late	It depends	Small	Semiautomatic
Checkpoint testing	On time	It depends	Small	Almost completely Manual
Prerelease testing	Very late	It depends	It depends	Almost completely Manual
Manual testing	Late	It depends	Huge	Completely manual
Postrelease T&M	Too late	It depends	It depends	It depends

Each approach has its advantages and disadvantages. It's up to you how to test your software. If you care about performance a lot, it makes sense to use several approaches (or all of them) or their combination. Of course, we didn't cover all possible options for performance testing; we just discussed some main directions. You can come up with an approach that will be the best for your own situationr.

Performance Subpaces

In Chapter 1, we discussed performance spaces. It's time to learn about *performance subspaces*. They are covered by different factors that can affect performance. Knowledge about these factors can help you to complete your performance investigation. In this section, we will talk about the most important subspaces:

- **Metric subspace**: what do we measure: wall-clock time, asymptotic complexity, hardware counter values, or something else?

- **Iteration subspace**: how many iterations do we do?

- **Test subspace**: how many tests do we analyze in the same suite?

- **Environment subspace**: how many different environments do we use?

- **Parameter subspace**: what parameter values do we use?

- **History subspace**: are we working with a single branch or looking at the whole repository?

Let's discuss each subspace in detail.

Metric Subspace

When we analyze performance reports, we are always working with some metrics. Different metrics can provide different performance pictures. For example, two tests can have the same value in one metric and different values in another. Relevant metrics should be chosen based on your business goals. If you don't know which metrics are more important for you, you can try several options and check out which metrics are useful for your investigations. Here are a few possible metrics for you:

- **Wall-clock time**

  This is an honest test duration. It can be measured via Stopwatch or be fetched from a CI server.

- **Throughput**

  How many operations can we process per second?

- **Asymptotic complexity**

  What is the asymptotic complexity of your algorithm? $O(N)$? $O(N*log(N))$? $O(N^3)$?

- **Hardware counters**

  There are plenty of them. You can use "general" counters for all cases (e.g., "Retired Instructions") or "specific" counters for specific tests (e.g., "Branch mispredict rate" or "L2 Cache Misses"). We will talk about hardware counters in detail in Chapter 7.

- **I/O metrics**

  You can collect all the metrics provided by OS for network and disk operations. It often helps to locate a real bottleneck correctly.

- **GC.CollectionCount**

  This is one of my favorite metrics. One of the main problems with "time" and "counter" metrics is variance. You can't control OS and how it schedules the execution time for different processes. If you run a test ten times, you will probably get ten different results. With GC.CollectionCount, you should get a stable value. Let's consider an example:

```
var gcBefore = GC.CollectionCount(0);
var stopwatch = Stopwatch.StartNew();

// Dummy code with huge number of allocations
int count = 0;
for (int i = 0; i < 10000000; i++)
  count += new byte[1000].Length;
Console.WriteLine(count);

stopwatch.Stop();
var gcAfter = GC.CollectionCount(0);
Console.WriteLine($"Time: {stopwatch.ElapsedMilliseconds}ms");
Console.WriteLine($"GC0: {gcAfter - gcBefore}");
```

Run it several times and write down the values of Time and GC0. You can see an example of the result in Table 5-15. Despite the fact that the Time value varies, the

GC0 value (the number of collections in Generation 0) is the same for all runs. We will discuss GC metrics in detail in Chapter 8.

Table 5-15. *Wall-Clock Time and GC.CollectionCount Metrics*

Run	1	2	3	4	5
Time	6590ms	6509ms	6241ms	7312ms	6835ms
GC0	16263	16263	16263	16263	16263

Remark. Of course, GC.CollectionCount has limitations. If you are working with a nondeterministic multithreaded algorithm, you can get different values even for GC. CollectionCount. But this value will be still more "stable" than the pure wall-clock time. If an algorithm is allocation-free, this metric is useless because it's always zero.[31]

Iteration Subspace

When you run a test, you can always choose the number of iterations. Let's discuss cases when you do a single iteration or a set of iterations.

- **Single iteration**

  This is the most popular and simple case: we always do exactly one iteration of a test. On the one hand, it's great because it's a very simple situation: we have only one measurement per revision. Performance history looks simple as well; it's just a function from a commit to a single number (for each metric). On the other hand, we have limited data: we don't know any information about the performance distribution for the test. Imagine that you have the following measurements for two subsequential commits: 50 ms and 60 ms. Do we have a problem? You can't say anything about it because you don't know the distribution.

---

[31]Unless you want to keep it allocation-free, and therefore know that even 1 byte should be considered a regression.

- **Many iterations**

  If you do many iterations, you have much more data! On the one hand, that's great because you can run many cool analyses. On the other hand, now you kind of have to do these analyses. Additional iterations are not free: you pay for them with time and machine resources. If you decide to do many iterations, you should understand how you are going to use this data (it also helps you to choose the best number of iterations). For example, it allows comparing commits. If you have a (50ms) vs. (60ms) situation, you can't say for sure that there is a performance degradation here. If you have a (50ms;51ms;49ms;50ms;52ms) vs. (60ms;63ms;61ms;49ms; 61ms) situation, you can say that it's most likely a degradation. If you have a (50ms;65ms;56ms;61ms;58ms) vs. (60ms;48ms;64ms;53ms;5 0ms) situation, you can say that most likely nothing is changed.

Test Subspace

A single test is not always the only source of the metrics. You can take smaller or bigger units. For example, you can take a small test part or group several tests. Thus, we have the following option:

- **Whole test**

  This is probably the most common way. You write a test that measures only one target case. Such testing may require a preparation (e.g., you should set an initial state up and warm the target logic up), but one test measures only one thing.

- **Test stage**

  In some cases, an honest test separation can be expensive. Imagine that you have a huge desktop application and you want to measure the "shutdown" time: the interval between a moment when a user clicks the close button and the moment when the application process is finished. Such tests require a lot of preparatory work. For example, you can spend 5 minutes for initialization (emulation of active work in the application) and only 1.5 seconds on the shutdown logic. If we perform 12 iterations inside the test, the whole test will take more than 1 hour. A whole hour of testing for a single test that takes 1.5 seconds! That looks like a waste of our time and machine resources.

Unfortunately, we can't significantly improve the situation for the shutdown test. However, we can something else: we can use these 5 initialization minutes to our advantage! In fact, we have an integration test that takes a lot of time and performs a lot of different operations. Let's introduce "test stages" and measure each test separately. We can measure the application load time and duration of some typical operations in the same tests. On the one hand, this move looks dirty and breaks the rules of classic unit testing: instead of measuring each feature in a separate test, we measure all kinds of different stuff in the same test. On the other hand, we have no choice (don't hate the player; hate the game!). Tests should be fast. In the case of performance tests, it's impossible to run them really fast, but the whole performance testing suite should take a reasonable amount of time. Test stage is a powerful technique that can save you a lot of time.

- **Test suite**

  When we analyze many tests together, we can do a lot of additional analysis. It's very important to perform a correlation analysis. For example, if you have a performance degradation after some changes, it's useful to find the whole scope of tests that have this degradation.

Environment Subspace

A huge part of this book is about different environments. There are so many important details: hardware, operating systems, build toolchain, runtime, JIT, and so on. If you have a huge project with many tests and run them all the time, you probably have several CI agents. The same test can be executed on different build agents. Even if the configuration (hardware+software) is the same for all agents, you still can get different results between them. If you don't have a huge pool of agents, you can manually check test suites in different environments. You can't be sure how a particular change affects performance until you check it in many different environments. The environment subspace can be used during analysis of the following anomalies:

- **Spatial clustering**

  When you have metrics for the same test from several agent, you can try to find factors that affect performance. It can be the operating system, the processor model, or any other parameter of your environment.

- **Temporal anomalies**

  If you are investigating the performance history of a single test, it can be useful to compare durations of the test runs on different CI agents. If a performance degradation or another anomaly appeared at that moment when the CI agent was changed, the first thing that you should check is the difference between the CI agent environments.

Parameter Subspace

The same test can be executed on different sets of input parameters. You can get different durations depending on the parameters. Here are a few things that you can check:

- **Nontrivial dependencies**

  Let's say that we have a test that processes many requests. The requests can be processed in several threads. How does the performance depend on the degree of parallelization? You may get a 2x performance boost when a single-thread implementation is replaced by a two-thread solution. However, switching from four threads to eight may slow down the benchmark because of inefficient and heavy locking. You can find the best parallelization degree only if you check several possible values.

- **Asymptotic complexity**

  Let's say that we have a test that checks whether a given string of length M is contained in a text of length N. The time complexity depends on the underlying algorithm. For example, it can be

$O(N \cdot M)$ for a trivial implementation or $O(N + M)$ for a smarter algorithm. You can easily miss some important degradation if the test works only for short search patterns and doesn't check the larger cases. The knowledge of the complexity allows you to extrapolate results on huge inputs without actually having to test them.

- **Corner cases**

  Let's say that we have a test with the quicksort algorithm. In the best and average case, the complexity is $O(N \cdot \log N)$, but it becomes $O(N^2)$ in the worst case. The knowledge of the worst-case performance also may be very important (especially if we have a risk on a performance attack on the program). The worst possible performance is another valuable metric that we can collect during testing.

- **Duration range**

  Let's say that we have a test that parses text with a regular expression. In this case, the test duration may vary in a huge range depending on the expression complexity and the text. It's not enough to just check a few input cases to get reliable performance metrics. Good performance coverage for such a test requires hundreds of inputs that correspond to different real-life situations and corner cases. Speaking of corner cases: there are regular expression denial of service (ReDoS) attacks that can significantly slow down your code. One of the most famous .NET Framework 4.5 ReDoS exploits against MVC web applications is described in [Malerisch 2015]: the `EmailAddressAttribute`, `PhoneAttribute`, `UrlAttribute` classes contained regular expressions that can be forced to calculate an exponential number of states on special inputs. The vulnerability was fixed in Microsoft Security Bulletin MS15-101.[32] As you can see, the subspaces can be analyzed together: here we have an interesting performance issue that involves the environment and performance subspaces.

---

[32]https://docs.microsoft.com/en-us/security-updates/SecurityBulletins/2015/ms15-101

The parameter subspace analysis is very complex because you usually can't check all possible inputs. However, you still should try to cover different cases for the same method. The benchmark metrics for a single test of input parameters can't be extrapolated to the method performance in general.

History Subspace

When we are talking about performance testing, one of the most important subspaces is the history subspace. The source code is changing all the time. Some popular repositories have dozens or even hundreds of commits (revisions) per day. In each situation, you are looking at a set of commits; applicable analysis depends on this set. Let's discuss the main types of such commit sets.

- **History moment (single revision)**

  If you only have a single revision, you can look for spatial anomalies: there are plenty of them. You can't find any performance degradations here, but you still can find a lot of problems that can be critical for your production environment.

- **Linear history (single branch)**

  If you have several revisions, you can look for spatial anomalies like degradation/acceleration. If you find a problem that is introduced in the latest release, you can bisect the history and find a commit with relevant changes.

- **Treelike history (selected branches or whole repository)**

  Sometimes, it makes sense to analyze several branches or even *the whole repository*. The number of performance measurements are always limited. If you are looking for anomalies like "Huge variance" or "Huge outliers," you can join performance history of the master branch and all feature branches. Analysis of this "mixed" history can produce a lot of false positive results, but it usually easily finds serious problems that are hard to detect based on a single branch because you don't have enough measurements.

Summing Up

The performance space contains many subspaces like the metric subspace, the iteration subspace, the test subspace, the environment subspace, the parameter subspace, the history subspace, and others. Each of these subspaces or their combination can have a significant impact on performance. The knowledge of the situation in a few points of the whole space doesn't allow extrapolating these results in general. Understanding the performance space helps you to perform high-quality performance investigation: you can discover more anomalies and find the factors that affect performance. Of course, it's not possible to carefully check the whole space: there are just too many possible combinations. The rich investigation experience will help you to guess factors that most likely affect the performance. You may also find interesting ideas in other people's stories: they increase your erudition and improve your performance intuition.

Performance Asserts and Alarms

One of the biggest challenges in performance testing is automated problem detection. When you do a regular local performance investigation, it's not always easy to say if you have a performance problem or not. The performance space can be really complicated, and it takes time to collect all relevant metrics and analyze them. In the world of performance testing, you have to automate this decision. There are two main kinds of such decisions, which can be expressed as *performance asserts* and *performance alarms*.

When a performance assert is triggered, we're sure that something is wrong with the performance. Asserts can be effectively applied to processes with 100% automation like the precommit testing. If a performance assert fails, it means that the corresponding test is red. Thus, it should have a low Type I (false positive) error rate. Unfortunately, it's almost impossible to get rid of errors completely, but the errors should be quite rare (otherwise, we get flaky tests).

When a performance alarm is triggered, we are not sure that something is wrong; the situation requires a manual investigation. Alarms can be effectively applied to situations when a performance plot looks "suspicious." Such alarms can be aggregated into a single dashboard, which is processed by developers on a regular basis. It's a typical situation when you have several false alarms per day because this doesn't interfere with the development process. Usually, it doesn't take a lot of time to check out such alarms and make a decision that we have nothing to worry about. Meanwhile, some

343

serious problems can be detected in time with this approach, which reduces Type II (false negative) errors. Alarms work well for anomalies like clustering or huge variance: in these cases, we can't afford to have a red test for all such anomalies. Moreover, if a test has a huge variance, it's hard to write a strict performance degradation assert with a small false positive rate. An alarm can solve this problem: you can get a few notifications per week for no good reason,[33] but you will also be notified when someone spoils the performance for real. The alarm approach is also useful for trade-off situations when we sacrifice performance in one place for some benefits in other areas. In such cases, developers definitely should be notified about it (in many cases, changes are made unintentionally), but the situation should be resolved manually.

Asserts and alarms usually have similar implementations (the only difference is how we report the results). In general, the logic looks very simple: we calculate some statistics (average test duration, variance, minimum/maximum time, P99, and so on) and compare it with a *threshold*. And this is the trickiest part: how should we choose the correct threshold value? In this section, we will discuss four different approaches (with an overview of the most important advantages and disadvantages):

- **Absolute threshold:** a hardcoded value in the source code (like 2 seconds or 5 minutes)

- **Relative threshold:** a hardcoded ratio to a reference value (like 2 times faster than another method)

- **Adaptive threshold:** comparing current performance with the history without hardcoded values (like it shouldn't be slower than yesterday)

- **Manual threshold:** a special developer who watches the performance plots all the time and who is looking for problems

Let's discuss each kind of threshold in detail.

---

[33]However, I think that we have a good reason for that: huge variance is almost always a bad thing. If you get false alarms about such tests all the time, you will be tempted to reduce the variance.

Absolute Threshold

Probably, this is the most popular kind of threshold because it has the simplest implementation. Typically, it looks as follows:

```
const int TimeoutMs = 2000; // 2 seconds

[Fact] // xUnit test
public void MyTest()
{
  var stopwatch = Stopwatch.StartNew();
  DoTest(); // Target logic
  stopwatch.Stop();
  Assert.True(stopwatch.ElapsedMilliseconds < TimeoutMs);
}
```

The implementation depends on the unit test framework:

- **NUnit, MSTest:** both frameworks provide [Timeout] attributes, which all allow you to set timeout in milliseconds.

- **xUnit:** As of xUnit 2.0 (and in subsequent versions like 2.1, 2.2, 2.3), the framework doesn't support timeouts[34] because it's pretty hard to achieve stable time measurements with parallelization enabled by default in xUnit 2.x. Thus, you have to implement the timeouts manually like in the preceding example. In this case, it's highly recommended to disable parallelization.

However, you can always set a timeout in the code with the help of stopwatch. Also, you have to implement it manually when you are looking for performance anomalies. For example, you can do 20 iterations, calculate the standard deviation, and compare it with the threshold.

- **Simple implementation**

  You can implement it with a few lines of code. In case of NUnit or MSTest, a single [Timeout] attribute is usually enough. In case of xUnit or a complicated check, you need two lines with Stopwatch (Start/Stop) and a single line with assert.

---

[34]https://xunit.github.io/releases/2.0

Although the implementation is quite simple, this approach has some important problems.

- **Portability**

    Not all computers are equally fast. A test can satisfy a 2000ms timeout on your machine in 100% runs, but it can fail on a slow machine of your colleague or in a virtual environment on a CI server.

- **Flakiness**

    When a timeout is close to actual test duration, the test can be red *sometimes* depending on the duration variance and other resource-consuming processes in OS, which can slow down this test.

- **Maintainability**

    When I see a test with a hardcoded absolute timeout, I always look at the test history. Typically, it looks like in Table 5-16. You can see that developers change the hardcoded value in the source code all the time. This is not a healthy thing. If such commits are a common practice in your team, it's always easier to increase the timeout of a red test instead of doing an investigation in case of real performance problems.

Table 5-16. *Example of Absolute Timeout History*

Revision	Timeout	Comment
N	5000	Increased timeout because test works too slow on my machine
N-1	3000	Test timeout adjustments
N-2	7000	Some new CI agents are too slow; increase timeouts
N-3	4562	Decrease timeouts to minimum possible values
N-4	5000	Test is flaky, it's red in 3% cases on CI; increase timeout
...	...	...

Meanwhile, absolute thresholds can be the last line of defense against test hanging. If a test typically takes a few seconds, you can safely set a rough timeout like 1 minute. In this case, if a test is red because of the timeout, it's definitely a good thing because it notifies us about serious problems like the following:

- Test is hanged because of a deadlock. The timeout helped us to save time on a CI agent.

- Test takes 1.5 minutes instead of a few seconds because of a bug. Hooray, performance asserts helped to find a performance degradation.

- The variance is huge, a test takes from 1 second to 5 minutes (probably because of the moon phase). Typically, this means a serious bug in the source code; such anomalies should be investigated.

If you want to use accurate absolute timeouts (like 5 seconds in our example), you probably should use alarms instead of asserts. For example, you can manually check all tests that have several alarms per week. This isn't a perfect solution, but the implementation is really simple (if you already have an "alarm infrastructure").

If you don't like the idea of absolute timeouts, there are other ways to implement performance tests. Let's talk about relative thresholds.

Relative Threshold

Relative thresholds try to solve the portability problem. The idea is simple: we write a reference (Baseline) method (or a set of reference methods) and evaluate its "average" performance. There are several kinds of relative thresholds:

- **Relative method performance**

  You can introduce a Baseline and measure the relative performance of all methods to the baseline. When you are marking changes in the source code, you can calculate relative performance against the baseline instead of analyzing the absolute numbers.

- **Relative machine or environment performance**

  The baseline approach can also be used for comparing performance between different machines.[35] The same trick can be used to compare performance between several runtimes on the same hardware. For example, Mono and .NET Core have different startup time overheads. In theory, the relative threshold is not a correct approach because the performance ratio between different methods can be different for each machine/environment. In practice, this approach usually works for most *simple cases*.

- **Handling portability issues**

  You should understand that this is not the perfect solution, but it usually works pretty well for simple cases.

- **Flakiness**

  The same as in the absolute threshold case: sometimes you will get false alarms.

- **Maintainability**

  Relative thresholds are still hardcoded; you should manually change it in case of important changes like changes in the test.

Adaptive Threshold

Probably, this is the most powerful and the most complicated kind of alarm. Here you don't have any hardcoded thresholds, you only have the performance history of the test. This history can include any metrics that you want to collect. At the moment of performance testing, you compare the current state with the whole history.

- **No hardcoded values**

  You shouldn't keep many magic numbers in the source code anymore. You even shouldn't think about how fast the code

---

[35]Such an approach is used for some performance tests in IntelliJ IDEA: `https://github.com/JetBrains/intellij-community/blob/181.5451/platform/testFramework/src/com/intellij/testFramework/CpuTimings.java`

should be. An algorithm will check automatically that you don't have any performance degradations or other anomalies.

- **Slow reaction to changes in the test**

    If you change the logic of the test (for example, add a few heavy asserts), you should retrain your algorithm and wait while the algorithm "learns" the new baseline. Meanwhile, you will get false alerts. Of course, you can introduce a way to mark a test as "changed" or clear the performance history, but it's usually not as simple as changing a hardcoded threshold.

- **Smart algorithm is required**

    You should manually implement an algorithm that compares the performance history and the current state. Unfortunately, no universal algorithm solves this problem in general or works for all projects. There are some ready solutions, but you should check which one works for you. Don't forget about possible pitfalls like the optional stopping problem (which we discussed in Chapter 4).

Manual Threshold

When we discussed the strategies of defense against performance anomalies, the last one was the manual testing. If we can't cover tests by performance asserts, we always can generate performance alarms. It's not easy to detect all "suspicious" tests because this requires a threshold. However, you can easily generate "worst of the worst" tests.

For example, let's imagine that we are looking for tests with huge variance but we can't say when the variance is huge. Let's calculate the variance for each test and sort the results. We can generate the "Top 10" tests with the biggest variances each day. Performance plots for these ten worst tests should be checked manually, and a developer should decide the following for each test: do we have a problem here or not? I call this the "dashboard-oriented approach."

Another example: we are looking for performance degradation but we can't say when we really have a degradation. Let's calculate the difference between average performances from this week and the previous week. Yes, I know that the average is an awful metric and the distribution can be too complicated. But if something really bad happens with the test, you typically will see it in the "worst of the worst" tests. We call it "manual threshold" because a developer should manually check a test in order to say "It doesn't look like a normal test to me."

This approach is not accurate, and it requires manual checking of these reports every day. However, it can help discover some performance anomalies that were not caught by performance asserts. Since we don't have real performance asserts here, the final Type I (false positive) error rate is zero. The Type II (false negative) error rate is reduced because you can find some missed problems. Of course, the reduction is not free; you pay for it with the working time of your team members.

It's not recommended to use only this approach for performance testing because it's time-consuming and you can't manually check out all your tests every day. But it can be a good addition to your automated performance testing infrastructure because it helps to find some tricky problems that can't be automated because corresponding checks usually have a huge false positive rate.

- **Handle even supertricky cases**

  You can detect very tricky problems that are almost impossible to cover by a smart algorithm. Typically, an experienced developer can instantly say if you have a performance problem or not with a quick glance at the performance plot.

- **Complete lack of automation**

  You should manually check most suspicious tests every day.

Summing Up

If you want to implement a reliable system that helps you to handle all kinds of performance problems, you need both performance asserts and alarms. Asserts helps you to automatically prevent degradations before the changes are merged with a high confidence. Alarms help you to monitor the whole test suite and notify you about problems that cannot be detected with a low false positive rate.

You can use different kinds of thresholds in both cases. Absolute thresholds are the simplest way to implement it, which is good for a start, but it's not a reliable way in the longer term: this approach has a lot of issues with portability, flakiness, and maintainability. Relative threshold is better: it solves some of the issues, but not all of them. Adaptive thresholds are great, but it's not easy to implement them, and you should carefully handle cases when you change the test performance on purpose. Manual threshold is also an effective technique that helps you to find problems not currently covered by automatic thresholds, but it requires a special performance engineer who systematically monitors performance charts.

There is no single universal approach that will be great for all kinds of projects. However, combinations of different approaches for performance asserts and alarms can protect you even from very tricky and nonobvious performance problems.

Performance-Driven Development (PDD)

You are probably familiar with TDD (Test-Driven Development). PDD (Performance-Driven Development) is a similar technique with one important difference: it uses performance tests instead of the usual functional and integration tests. Usually, it looks as follows:

- **Define a task and performance goals**

- **Write a performance test**

- **Change the code**

- **Check the new performance space**

In this section, we discuss this approach in detail: how it should be used and how useful it can be in daily performance routine. The PDD is not a solution for all kinds of situations, but this concept can be useful when you want to minimize the risk of introducing performance issues.

Define a Task and Performance Goals

As we already know, any performance-related work should start with defining goals. PDD is a technique that is suitable only for a specific set of goals. You should use it only if it fits your current task. There are three primary kinds of tasks/goals that can be solved via PDD. Each kind (I will provide codenames for future reference) should be started with a performance test.

- **Codename: "Optimizations"**

  Task: Optimize ineffective code

  Goal: We should achieve "better" performance

351

It's not a good idea to blindly optimize different parts of your code. A performance test can help you to verify that you actually optimized something and evaluate the performance boost.

- **Codename: "Feature"**

  Task: Implement a new feature

  Goal: The feature should be fast

  When a feature is already implemented, there is always a temptation to say something like "It *seems* that it works fast enough." A proper performance test helps to set your business requirements in advance. This case is pretty similar to a situation in classic TDD.

- **Codename: "Refactoring"**

  Task: Refactoring in performance-sensitive code

  Goal: We should keep the same level of performance (or make it better)

  It's pretty hard to say that you didn't introduce any performance degradations if you don't have a baseline. A baseline helps you to verify that everything is OK.

In each case, the task should correspond to your business goals. "Better performance," "fast feature," and "same level of performance" are abstract, ineffective terms. The PDD forces you to formalize the goal and specify the required metric values.

Write a Performance Test

This is the most important part of PDD. You shouldn't do anything before you get a reliable performance test (or a test suite). "Optimizations" and "Feature" should be started with a red test; "Refactoring" should be started with a green test that can be easily transformed to a red one.

If you can't write a performance test, something is going wrong. Usually, it means that you have problems with performance goals. For example, you want to optimize a method because it "looks ineffective." In this case, you should prove that it's ineffective by a red performance test. Your performance requirements should be strictly defined.

If you can't write a *red* test that corresponds to performance requirements, you probably don't need optimizations because you can't demonstrate that the method is ineffective.

Keep in mind that the test should be green at the end. If you made your optimizations, but the test is still red, you may be tempted to change performance asserts. Be careful: it's a slippery slope! Indeed, sometimes you collect new information, and you have to change something in the test. In this case, you also have to check that the test is still red before the optimizations. PDD assumes that an optimization is always a transition from a red performance test to a green one. There are many cases when you can't achieve such transition. And it's the coolest "feature" of PDD: it protects you from premature or wrong optimizations!

Now it's time to discuss five typical steps of writing such tests.

- **Step 1: Write target method**

  Just write a method that covers the target case. Imagine that you are writing a functional test that covers your code. As in the case of ordinary tests, you should try to isolate logic and measure only logic that matters to you. In the "Optimizations" case, you should cover only logic that you are going to optimize and nothing else. In the "Feature" case, you should cover the feature (and only the feature) in advance (as you usually do in typical TDD). In the "Refactoring" case, you should cover only the performance-critical part of the architecture that you are going to refactor. It's always better to have several performance tests. If you came up only with a single one, try to parametrize it. If you read a file, try files with different sizes. If you process a dataset, try different datasets.

- **Step 2: Collect metrics**

  As a minimum, you have to measure raw test duration. However, it's better to collect some additional metrics like hardware counters, GC collections, and so on. Do many iterations, accumulate them, and calculate statistics numbers. Run tests not only on your developer machine but also on machines of your colleagues and on a server.

- **Step 3: Look at the performance space**

  It's not enough to just collect raw metrics; you should carefully look at them. Check out how the distribution looks. Does it have one mode or several modes? What about the variance? How does the performance depend on the test parameters? Is the dependency linear or not? What's the maximum parameter value that produces a reasonable duration for the performance test? If you practice PDD on a regular basis, you will come up with your own checklist soon. Looking at the performance space doesn't require too much time (especially if it's not your first time), but it can save a lot of time later. Knowledge about some "features" of the test performance space will help you to find tricky places in your source code that you should be aware of.

- **Step 4: Write performance asserts**

  Now it's time to transform your business goals into performance asserts. Remember that the test should be red for "Optimizations" cases. Many developers skip this step. You may be tempted to say: "OK, I know how much time it takes now. I can optimize my code and check how much it takes after that. Next, I will write performance asserts." This is a bad practice: it can destroy your business goal. If you want to optimize a method twice, write a corresponding assert. If you discover new things during optimizations (like "Hey, I can optimize it ten times!" or "It's just impossible to optimize more than 50%"), you always can change the assert later. But you still have to express your original intention in the form of performance asserts. I have seen many times when developers say something like "After these crazy hacks I get 5% speedup, now I'm going to commit it" (whereas 5% speedup doesn't have business value and crazy hacks mutilate the code and move it to the "impossible to maintain" state). Original performance asserts don't protect you from all such cases, but they will make you think twice before committing code that doesn't solve the original problem.

- **Step 5: Play with the test status**

  Next, you should check that you wrote good performance asserts. In the "Optimizations" case, try to transform the red test to a green one by commenting the "heaviest" part of your code. In the "Refactoring" case, try to add a few `Thread.Sleep` calls here and there and make sure that the test is red now. In the "Feature" case, check empty and `Thread.Sleep` implementations. You should be sure that you wrote performance asserts correctly (at the end, tests should be green in case of success or red in case of failure).

Once you have a good performance test with correct performance asserts and you learned what the performance space looks like, it will be time to write some real code!

Change the Code

Now it's time to remember your original goals and optimize the product, implement new features, or perform refactoring. You can be completely focused on your task without fearing to introduce a performance problem.

The classic TDD approach assumes that you should write a code that makes your test red. It can be useful for PDD as well. For example, if you are developing a feature, you can write a naive implementation first. Such implementation should work correctly, but it can be slow. You should get a situation with green functional/integration/unit tests and red performance tests. After that, you can start to optimize the code until you reach your original performance goals. It should be very easy to verify it with one click because you have the performance tests.

Check the New Performance Space

Remember that it's not always possible to cover all possible problems by automatic performance asserts. So, it's nice to check the part of the performance space that can be affected by your changes.

Here is another example from my personal experience. Rider on Unix uses Mono as a runtime for the ReSharper process. Each version of Rider is based on a fixed bundled version of the Mono runtime. Sometimes, we have to upgrade Mono to the next stable release. We never know how this upgrade can affect the Rider performance. We have a lot of tests, but it's almost impossible to cover all cases in a huge product that can be affected by changes in the runtime. So, we create two revisions with the same Rider code base and different versions of Mono. After that, we do several dozen runs of the whole test suite on the same hardware and different operating systems (Windows, Linux, macOS). Next, we build dashboards for different metrics that have the biggest differences between revisions. Next, I start to manually check the top tests in these dashboards and look at their performance plots. My favorite metric is variance: we have found plenty of problems by looking at tests that have huge differences between variance for old and new versions of Mono. Unfortunately, it's almost impossible to automate this process because the high Type I (false positive) error rate. However, sometimes, in perhaps 1 test out of 100, we find very serious problems that actually affect the product.

Summing Up

PDD is a powerful technique that provides a reliable way to do performance-sensitive tasks. It allows you to control performance of your code during development and prevent many bugs and degradations in advance. Also, it forces you to formalize your performance goals and write many performance tests.

However, this approach also has one important disadvantage: it creates an immense amount of work, most of which is likely extraneous for most projects and most types of code. While TDD can be used on daily basis, it's not recommended to use PDD all the time. You should be sure that the benefits from PDD (decreased risk of introduced performance problems) are worth the time and resources that you spend on writing performance tests in advance.

Performance Culture

Performance testing is a discipline that consists of two components. The first one is the technical part, which we discussed in previous sections. It answers the question of how the performance testing should be implemented. The second one is *performance culture* (this term was taken from an awesome blog post by Joe Duffy, see [Duffy 2016]). It answers the question of how to make performance testing work. You can implement an awesome performance testing toolkit with excellent anomaly detection algorithms and smart performance alarms/asserts. However, it will not work if there is not much performance culture in your team. *Performance testing is not only about technologies;*

it's also about attitude. In this section, we will discuss some core principles of the
performance culture:

- **Shared performance goals:** all team members should have the same
  performance goals.

- **Reliable performance testing infrastructure:** infrastructure should
  work great, and developers should trust it.

- **Performance cleanness:** you shouldn't be tolerant to performance
  problems and your list of unexamined performance anomalies
  should be empty.

- **Personal responsibility:** each developer is responsible for the
  performance of his or her code.

As usual, let's start with the performance goals.

Shared Performance Goals

All team members should share common performance goals. They should clearly
understand it. It doesn't matter what kind of goals do you have.

It's OK if you don't care about performance at all if all team members don't care
about performance. It can be applied not only to performance but to every business goal.
It's hard to work with the same team on the same product with people who don't share
goals with you. Such situations produce many communication problems and spoil the
business process.

If a decent performance level is your business goal, it should be obvious for all
developers in the team. Remember that when we say "good performance," this isn't
the best wording. The target performance level should be formalized and expressed
with some metric. In this book, there are many chapters that explain again and again
why it's so important to formalize your goals. There is a reason for that. There are many
situations when a performance engineer speaks with another team member and says
something like "We have a performance degradation after your recent changes: could
you please fix it?" If he or she gets an answer like "I'm too busy, I am not going to fix it, it
works fast enough," we can't say whether it make sense to fix the problem or not because
we don't know the performance goals of this team. Moreover, there are no unified
business goals in the team that are clear for everyone.

If such a situation exists, you have to formalize goals. For example, you can say that a web server should process at least 1000 RPS. Or you can say that any operation on the UI thread shouldn't take more than 200 ms.

It's worth noting that some teams can live without strict formalized performance goals. I have seen many cases in which a team has an empirical understanding of the goals. If you can work without conflict over performance and still achieve your goals, that's great; keep up the good work![36]

It doesn't matter what kind of goals you have and how you express them, as long as all team members agree with them.

In [Duffy 2016] (see the "Management: More Carrots, Fewer Sticks" section therein), Joe Duffy said: "In every team with a poor performance culture, it's management's fault. Period. End of conversation." That's a controversial statement, but it seems to be true for most teams. Originally, performance culture was an approach to help you achieve performance goals. However, if you really care about performance, the performance culture should become one of the goals for management. It's not something that you can get for free: a performance culture requires hard work and many conversations with your team members. All of them should have common values and views, and management should make some investment in it. Here is another quote from the post: "Magical things happen when the whole team is obsessed about performance."

Reliable Performance Testing Infrastructure

If developers don't trust performance tests, these tests are useless. Here are the three most important requirements:

- **All tests should be green**

  If you constantly have some red or flaky tests, nobody will care about "one more test" with some performance problems.

---

[36]Here is a quote from Federico Andres Lois about his development experience in RavenDB: "RavenDB team behaves like that. Our goal is to be the fastest database out there, everybody understands that even if there is no formal goal. So everybody does their part, and when in doubt they ask the resident performance expert on their timezone of convenience. Having said that, almost never would performance improvements trump a new feature or correctness. We flag that feature, and then an expert would look into how to make it blazing fast as soon as it is stabilized."

- **Type I (false positive) error rate should be low**

  If you get false alarms about performance problems all the time, you will probably start to ignore them because you will spend your time on the investigation without any benefits from it.

- **It should be easy to write a performance test**

  Writing performance tests is usually an optional task. If such tests require complicated routine work, developers will be tempted to skip it.

If you want to force developers to use a tool (e.g., a performance testing infrastructure), it should be reliable and easy to use. The developers should trust the tool and enjoy using it. Otherwise, it will not work.

Performance Cleanness

There is a well-known criminological theory called "the Broken Windows theory" (see [Wilson 1982]). Here is the key rule from the original article:

If a window in a building is broken and is left unrepaired, all the rest of the windows will soon be broken.

This rule can also be applied to software development. If you have many performance problems here and there, or if you have a lot of tests with suspicious anomalies without an assignee, you will get new performance problems all the time.

Once you get performance cleanness, there are two important rules to save it:

- **Zero tolerance for performance problems**

  If you have a new performance problem, it should be investigated on the spot. Try to forget about backlog lists and thoughts like "I'm too busy right now, will take a look at the next week." It will be much harder to investigate the issue a week later: other problems can be introduced and "the rest of the windows will soon be broken." Of course, it's ideal when you instantly fix any performance problems. In many cases, though, this can be impossible because you have many other higher-priority issues that can't be postponed. But, in terms of zero tolerance for performance problems, it doesn't matter that you can't always achieve this ideal situation.[37]

- **Regular checking of the performance anomaly list**

  I should say it again: it's pretty hard to catch all problems automatically. New problems that are not covered by performance tests with strict asserts can be introduced at any moment. Thus, it's a very good practice to have some performance alarms and dashboards and to check them regularly.

Of course, these rules are valid only for projects with corresponding business goals. The performance cleanness can significantly simplify keeping a decent level of performance. Once you achieve the cleanness, it's much easier to support it than trying to find the most important issues in the midst of "performance chaos."

Personal Responsibility

Performance cleanness is the responsibility of each developer. In many teams, there are a few developers who know a lot about performance and everyone thinks that they should handle all the performance problems. Why?

Let's say you are going to commit a new feature. If you want to have clean code in your repository, you are responsible for your code. Imagine that there is a developer who is responsible for the clean code: you commit dirty code, and this developer will clean this code for you: make basic formatting, choose proper names for variables, and so on. But this sounds ridiculous, right? No developer will fix your code style for you.

Why is it a common practice to have a performance geek who should solve all the performance problems? It's good to have someone who knows a lot about performance and optimization and can help you with a tricky situation. But he or she shouldn't do all tasks.

---

[37]Here is another quote from Federico Andres Lois about RavenDB: "RavenDB took an entirely different path back in 3.0 time frame. They hired a dedicated guy (they assigned me exclusively) to investigate any potential venue to improve performance.... And while we did a lot of good stuff, most of the work was actually uncovering the architectural deficiency issues that we would need to fix for 4.0. The team started to pick up the theme of the usual optimizations and apply the cookie cutter techniques rapidly, but because with Oren we did a general theme to post on the internal and external channels, we got 3× here, 2× there, 30% there, etc. There was no week without one of two of those, for like a year. So the culture shifted pretty fast."

You should care about the performance of your code. You should care about performance cleanness. *It's your personal responsibility.*

Summing Up

If I had to choose between a team of developers who have strong performance skills and a team of developers who have strong performance culture, I would choose the second team. If developers have the performance culture, they can read books and blog posts about performance, optimizations, and runtime internals, they can learn how to use tools for profiling and benchmarking, and they can adopt some good practices and techniques. Without the performance culture, their performance skills will probably not help to develop a product with a small number of performance problems.

The *shared performance goals* help you to communicate with each other. A *reliable performance testing infrastructure* helps you to easily solve routine technical tasks. The *performance cleanness* helps you maintain the product without any "broken windows." *Personal responsibility* helps to make the code of each developer better and faster. All these things together help you to get the *performance culture* in your team and develop awesome, fast, and reliable software.

Summary

Performance analysis is an essential skill for every performance engineer. It helps to do in-depth performance investigations and implement a reliable infrastructure for performance testing. In this chapter, we discussed the most critical topics for performance analysis:

- **Performance testing goals**

  The basic goals are to prevent performance degradations, detect not-prevented degradations, detect other kinds of performance problems, reduce Type I (false positive) and Type II (false negative) error rates, and automate everything. You can also have your own goals, but you still have to remember these primary goals, which are relevant for most projects.

- **Kinds of benchmarks and performance tests**

  There are many of them like cold start tests, warmed-up tests, asymptotic tests, latency and throughput tests, user interface tests, unit and integration tests, monitoring and telemetry, tests with external dependencies, stress/load tests, user interface tests, fuzzing tests, and so on. A good performance test suite usually includes a combination of these kinds.

- **Performance anomalies**

  Degradation is not the only performance problem that you can have. There are many other anomalies like acceleration; temporal and spatial clustering; huge duration, variance, outliers; and multimodal distributions. If you want to get rid of all performance problems, you should systematically check out your test suite. Probably, you will get many false anomalies, but it's still worth it to monitor your anomalies.

- **Strategies of defense**

  There are many strategies of defense against performance problems. Here are some of them: precommit tests, daily tests, retrospective analysis, checkpoint testing, prerelease testing, manual testing, postrelease telemetry and monitoring. As usual, it makes sense to use a combination of some or all of these approaches.

- **Performance space**

  In most performance investigations, we work with a multidimensional performance space that contains many subspaces like metric subspace, iteration subspace, test subspace, CI agent subspace, environment subspace, and history subspace. Understanding these subspaces allows collecting more data for the investigation and finding the factors that actually affect performance.

- **Performance asserts and alarms**

  Performance asserts are automatic checks used in performance tests with a low false positive rate. Performance alarms are notifications about performance problems that can't be used directly as an assert because of a high false positive rate. Both asserts and alarms can use different kinds of thresholds: absolute, relative, adaptive, and manual.

- **PDD**

    This technique is similar to classic TDD with performance tests instead of the usual unit/functional/integration tests. It helps you to optimize the product, implement new features, or perform refactoring with confidence that you will not spoil the performance (or that you will make it even better).

- **Performance culture**

    Performance testing is not only about technologies, it's also about attitude. The key components of the performance culture are shared performance goals, good management, reliable performance testing infrastructure, performance cleanness, and personal responsibility. The performance culture is required if you want to make performance testing work.

Of course, it's not possible to cover all aspects of performance testing in a single chapter. However, we discussed some of the most important techniques and ideas that will help you to improve your investigator skills and start to cover your product with performance tests.

References

[Akinshin 2018] Akinshin, Andrey. 2018. "A Story About Slow NuGet Package Browsing." May 8. https://aakinshin.net/blog/post/nuget-package-browsing/.

[AnomalyIo 2015] "Anomaly Detection Using K-Means Clustering." 2015. Anomaly.io. June 30. https://anomaly.io/anomaly-detection-clustering/.

[AnomalyIo 2017] "Detect Anomalies in Correlated Time Series." 2017. Anomaly.io. January 25. https://anomaly.io/detect-anomalies-in-correlated-time-series/.

[Bragg 2017] Bragg, Gareth. 2017. "How We Took Test Cycle Time from 24 Hours to 20 Minutes." October 12. https://medium.com/ingeniouslysimple/how-we-took-test-cycle-time-from-24-hours-to-20-minutes-e847677d471b.

[Chua 2014] Chong, Freddy, Tat Chua, Ee-Peng Lim, and Bernardo A. Huberman. 2014. "Detecting Flow Anomalies in Distributed Systems." In *Data Mining (ICDM), 2014 Ieee International Conference*, 100–109. IEEE. https://arxiv.org/abs/1407.6064.

[Dimopoulos 2017] Dimopoulos, Giorgos, Pere Barlet-Ros, Constantine Dovrolis, and Ilias Leontiadis. 2017. "Detecting Network Performance Anomalies with Contextual Anomaly Detection." In *Measurement and Networking (M&N), 2017 IEEE International Workshop*, 1-6. IEEE. doi:https://doi.org/10.1109/IWMN.2017.8078404.

[Duffy 2016] Duffy, Joe. 2016. "Performance Culture." April 10. http://joeduffyblog.com/2016/04/10/performance-culture/.

[Ibidunmoye 2016] Ibidunmoye, Olumuyiwa, Thijs Metsch, and Erik Elmroth. 2016. "Real-Time Detection of Performance Anomalies for Cloud Services." In *Quality of Service (IWQoS), 2016 IEEE/ACM 24th International Symposium*, 1–2. IEEE. doi: https://doi.org/10.1109/IWQoS.2016.7590412.

[Kofman 2018] Kofman, Svetlana. 2018. "Incident Report - NuGet.org Downtime on March 22, 2018." March 22. https://blog.nuget.org/20180322/Incident-Report-NuGet-org-downtime-March-22.html.

[Kondratyuk 2017] Kondratyuk, Dan. 2017. "How Changing 'Localhost' to '127.0.0.1' Sped Up My Test Suite by 18x." June 9. https://hackernoon.com/how-changing-localhost-to-127-0-0-1-sped-up-my-test-suite-by-1-800-8143ce770736.

[Malerisch 2015] "Microsoft .NET MVC ReDoS (Denial of Service) Vulnerability - CVE-2015-2526 (MS15-101)." 2015. Malerisch.net. September 10. http://blog.malerisch.net/2015/09/net-mvc-redos-denial-of-service-vulnerability-cve-2015-2526.html.

[Peiris 2014] Peiris, Manjula, James H. Hill, Jorgen Thelin, Sergey Bykov, Gabriel Kliot, and Christian Konig. 2014. "PAD: Performance Anomaly Detection in Multi-Server Distributed Systems." In *Cloud Computing (Cloud), 2014 IEEE 7th International Conference*, 769–776. IEEE. doi: https://doi.org/10.1109/CLOUD.2014.107.

[Songkick 2012] "From 15 Hours to 15 Seconds: Reducing a Crushing Build Time." 2012. Songkick. July 16. https://devblog.songkick.com/from-15-hours-to-15-seconds-reducing-a-crushing-build-time-4efac722fd33.

[Warren 2018] Warren, Matt. 2018. "Fuzzing the .NET JIT Compiler." October 28. http://mattwarren.org/2018/08/28/Fuzzing-the-.NET-JIT-Compiler/.

[Wilson 1982] Wilson, James Q., and George L. Kelling. 1982. "The Police and Neighborhood Safety: Broken Windows." *Atlantic Monthly* 127 (2): 29–38.

CHAPTER 6

Diagnostic Tools

If all you have is a hammer, everything looks like a nail.

— Abraham Maslow

Benchmarking is only one of the performance investigation steps. In this chapter, you will find a brief overview of the some important diagnostic tools that can be useful for the whole investigation. We will learn the following kinds of tools:

- **Benchmarking harness**

  This tool automatically benchmarks the specified method and displays corresponding metrics. It tells you how much time it takes to perform this method, but it doesn't always tell you why you have such values.

- **Performance profiler**

  This tool measures performance metrics for each called method inside an application. It tells you where the performance bottleneck of the application is and allows exploring performance profiles with detailed information about consumed CPU resources for each method.

- **Memory profiler**

  This tool measures memory traffic for an application. It tells you how many objects were allocated and allows exploring memory snapshots with detailed information about the graph of alive and dead objects of each class.

© Andrey Akinshin 2019

A. Akinshin, *Pro .NET Benchmarking*, https://doi.org/10.1007/978-1-4842-4941-3_6

- **C#/VB decompiler**

  This tool takes a .NET assembly and shows C#/VB code (even if you don't have original source code).

- **IL decompiler**

  This tool takes a .NET assembly and shows IL code for requested classes and methods.

- **ASM Decompiler**

  This tool takes a .NET assembly or an existing .NET process and shows the native code for requested classes and methods.

- **Debuggers**

  This tool allows debugging .NET assemblies. The debugger is especially useful when it can also show C#/IL/ASM disassembly listings and debug external code (with or without symbols).

- **System monitoring tool**

  This tool monitors all processes in the operating system and shows performance, memory, and other metrics for the system in general and for individual processes and their threads.

The tools will be presented in the following groups:

- **BenchmarkDotNet**

  We will discuss the only one benchmarking harness: BenchmarkDotNet. This is the most adopted library, used in many popular open source and closed source projects.

- **Visual Studio Tools**

  Visual Studio is an IDE, but it has some important embedded tools that are useful for performance investigations. We will discuss the embedded memory/performance profiler and debugging tools.

- **JetBrains Tools**

  JetBrains has many different tools that provide advanced support for performance/memory profiling and decompilation. We will discuss dotPeek, dotTrace, dotMemory, ReSharper, and Rider.

- **Windows Sysinternals**

  This is a suite of independent tools for Windows that can simplify different steps of performance investigations and collect system metrics. We will discuss RAMMap, VMMap, and ProcessMonitor.

- **Other Useful Tools**

  There are many other tools in the .NET ecosystem that can also be useful in different scenarios. We will discuss ildasm, monodis, ILSpy, dnSpy, WinDbg, PerfView, Mono Console Tools, perfcollect, Process Hacker, and Intel VTune Amplifier.

The topic of diagnostic tools is huge, and it's not possible to cover all of them in detail in this chapter. The aim of this chapter is to provide an overview of some available tools. However, you will not find step-by-step tutorials that teach you how to use them: you will have to study them yourself. You are free to choose any tools you like: you can look for them on the Internet or build your own software. In this chapter, we are going to briefly discuss some features of *some* tools that can be used during performance investigations.

For each tool, you will find some useful information: the URL of the official website, links to useful resources, the license, and the supported operating systems. The "free/commercial" label means that the general license is commercial, but there are some free options (e.g., for open source projects, for students and teachers, for small teams, and so on). You can find the full information about the discounted and complimentary licenses on the official websites.

BenchmarkDotNet

BenchmarkDotNet is a powerful .NET library for benchmarking with tons of features that help to design benchmarks, execute them, and analyze performance results. I'm proud to say that I'm the project lead of this library. I started BenchmarkDotNet in 2013 as a small pet project. Today, it's a highly adopted open source project supported by the .NET Foundation. BenchmarkDotNet is used for performance experiments in the most popular .NET projects including .NET Core. Here is a usage example:

```
using System;
using System.Security.Cryptography;
using BenchmarkDotNet.Attributes;
using BenchmarkDotNet.Running;
```

```
namespace MyBenchmarks
{
  [ClrJob(baseline: true), CoreJob, MonoJob, CoreRtJob]
  public class Md5VsSha256
  {
    private SHA256 sha256 = SHA256.Create();
    private MD5 md5 = MD5.Create();
    private byte[] data;

    [Params(1000, 10000)]
    public int N;

    [GlobalSetup]
    public void Setup()
    {
      data = new byte[N];
      new Random(42).NextBytes(data);
    }

    [Benchmark]
    public byte[] Sha256() => sha256.ComputeHash(data);

    [Benchmark]
    public byte[] Md5() => md5.ComputeHash(data);
  }

  public class Program
  {
    public static void Main(string[] args)
    {
      var summary = BenchmarkRunner.Run<Md5VsSha256>();
    }
  }
}
```

This program will generate an output like this:

```
BenchmarkDotNet=v0.11.0, OS=Windows 10.0.16299.309 (1709/Redstone3)
Intel Xeon CPU E5-1650 v4 3.60GHz, 1 CPU, 12 logical and 6 physical cores
```

```
Frequency=3507504 Hz, Resolution=285.1030 ns, Timer=TSC
.NET Core SDK=2.1.300-preview1-008174
  [Host]      : .NET Core 2.1.0-preview1-26216-03
                (CoreCLR 4.6.26216.04, CoreFX 4.6.26216.02), 64bit RyuJIT
  Job-HKEEXO : .NET Framework 4.7.1
                (CLR 4.0.30319.42000), 64bit RyuJIT-v4.7.2633.0
  Core        : .NET Core 2.1.0-preview1-26216-03
                (CoreCLR 4.6.26216.04, CoreFX 4.6.26216.02), 64bit RyuJIT
  CoreRT      : .NET CoreRT 1.0.26414.01, 64bit AOT
  Mono        : Mono 5.10.0 (Visual Studio), 64bit
```

Method	Runtime	N	Mean	Error	StdDev	Ratio
Sha256	Clr	1000	8.009 us	0.0370 us	0.0346 us	1.00
Sha256	Core	1000	4.447 us	0.0117 us	0.0110 us	0.56
Sha256	CoreRT	1000	4.321 us	0.0139 us	0.0130 us	0.54
Sha256	Mono	1000	14.924 us	0.0574 us	0.0479 us	1.86
Md5	Clr	1000	3.051 us	0.0604 us	0.0742 us	1.00
Md5	Core	1000	2.004 us	0.0058 us	0.0054 us	0.66
Md5	CoreRT	1000	1.892 us	0.0087 us	0.0077 us	0.62
Md5	Mono	1000	3.878 us	0.0181 us	0.0170 us	1.27
Sha256	Clr	10000	75.780 us	1.0445 us	0.9771 us	1.00
Sha256	Core	10000	41.134 us	0.2185 us	0.1937 us	0.54
Sha256	CoreRT	10000	40.895 us	0.0804 us	0.0628 us	0.54
Sha256	Mono	10000	141.377 us	0.5598 us	0.5236 us	1.87
Md5	Clr	10000	18.575 us	0.0727 us	0.0644 us	1.00
Md5	Core	10000	17.562 us	0.0436 us	0.0408 us	0.95
Md5	CoreRT	10000	17.447 us	0.0293 us	0.0244 us	0.94
Md5	Mono	10000	34.500 us	0.1553 us	0.1452 us	1.86

You can find the full documentation for the latest version of BenchmarkDotNet on GitHub, so I'm not going to describe how to use all the features. Instead, I want to talk about the philosophy of tools for benchmarking. I think that a good benchmarking library should satisfy the following requirements:

- **It should do all routine tasks for you**

  A typical benchmark includes a lot of boilerplate code. Users
  shouldn't write it each time when they want to measure
  performance. A benchmarking tool should automatically run
  several iterations, and each iteration should include several
  method invocations. It should run several warm-up iterations
  and remove them from the report. It should isolate benchmarks
  from each other and run each benchmark in a separate process.
  If you want to check several different environments, it should
  automatically perform benchmarks in each environment and
  aggregate the results. It should automatically evaluate its own
  overhead and subtract it from the measured values. All the
  dirty work should be done by the benchmarking library. During
  benchmarking, users should be able to focus on the measured
  logic instead of the benchmarking infrastructure.

- **It should protect you from known pitfalls**

  It shouldn't allow you to run benchmarks in the DEBUG mode
  (without optimizations). It should control inlining and make sure
  that all benchmarks use the same inlining policy. It should use the
  best available timestamping API. The best benchmarking practices
  (like warm-up and isolation) should be enabled by default.

- **It should choose the best benchmarking mode for you**

  Approaches of adaptive benchmarking should be implemented.
  Instead of asking the user about the number of iterations, it
  can use optional stopping. Instead of asking the user about the
  number of method invocations inside each iteration, it should
  find the best value during the pilot experiment. By default, users
  shouldn't worry about infrastructure parameters: the library has
  to find the best possible values by default.

- **It should be highly configurable**

  Each benchmark experiment is unique, with its own
  requirements. Users should be able to disable all the smart
  features. For example, if they want to measure the cold start,

it should pe possible to disable warm-up. If they know that
benchmarks don't affect each other, they may want to disable the
process isolation to speed up the whole experiment. It's nice when
somebody else chooses the number of iterations for you, but it
should also be possible to set it manually.

- **It should have a user-friendly API**

  This requirement is valid for any library. The API should be
  understandable and well documented. It should support different
  approaches: some users like to configure benchmarks in the
  command line, some users like to use attributes, some users like
  to use fluent API. The library should provide different ways to
  configure the benchmarking process.

- **It should know statistics for you**

  The library should be able to calculate all the basic statistics
  characteristics like the mean and the median, the standard
  deviation and the confidence interval, the quartiles and the
  percentiles, and the skewness and the kurtosis. It should know
  how to detect outliers, how to perform statistical tests like Welch's
  t-test or the Mann–Whitney U test, and how to check distributions
  for multimodality.

- **It should help you to analyze results**

  If the library can calculate all possible statistical metrics, it doesn't
  mean that it should print all of them each time. The library should
  highlight all the essential features of the calculated distribution.
  We know that we can get a huge difference between the mean
  and the median, but these values are often close to each other.
  If the library will print both values each time, users will learn to
  ignore one of them. It's better to show only the mean by default
  and present the median only when it's important. We know that
  it's important to distinguish between unimodal and multimodal
  distributions. However, most simple performance distributions
  are unimodal. It doesn't make sense to print "Everything is OK,
  the distribution is unimodal" each time. It's better to print a
  warning in case the distribution is multimodal. It should tell you

if the distribution is spoiled by outliers. The basic report should contain only important data in the most compact form. It's great if it can calculate the mean value with the highest possible precision, but does it really make sense to print 6.38319573993657 ms? The most users care only about the most significant digits, so it will be enough to print just 6.383. The library can perform the Mann–Whitney U test and print the p-value, but it will be better to print a conclusion based on it (many users don't remember how to correctly interpret p-values). The library should tell you when the results are unreliable because of the initial settings (e.g., small sample size or insufficient iteration time). The final summary table should be as small as possible but contain the most important numbers and facts. Users should be able to read it and quickly understand what's going on with the data.

- **It should collect information about environment**

  A good performance report should include the most important information about the environment like OS version, processor model, used runtime, JIT compiler kind, and so on.

- **It should provide basic diagnostics data**

  A benchmarking library is not a profiler or a decompiler, but it can perform some basic diagnostics logic and provide the minimal diagnostics data. For example, it can measure the amount of allocated memory, evaluate values of hardware counters, print IL and native listings for the main methods, generate a trace file based on ETW events, check runtime optimizations like inlining or tail call optimizations, and so on. It should help users to understand why they have such a performance report and what kinds of additional tools they need.

- **It should generate many reports and draw plots**

  The information about performed measurements should be available in different formats like CSV, JSON, XML, HTML, Markdown, AsciiDoc, and others. Developers often share their performance results, so the library should support different dialects of Markdown that can be posted to GitHub,

StackOverflow, JIRA, or other services. The distribution should be shown with the help of different plots like histograms, timeline plots, density plots, bar plots, box plots, frequency trails, and so on. The library should know how to generate any kinds of report that can be useful during performance analysis.

BenchmarkDotNet has become popular because it tries to follow all these requirements. Of course, the library is not perfect; it has some bugs and missed features. However, BenchmarkDotNet gets better with each version thanks to community contributions.

You should understand that any benchmarking library (including BenchmarkDotNet) is not a silver bullet. It will not write a benchmark for you. It will not analyze benchmarking reports for you. It just *helps* to design and execute benchmarks. Thus, you still have to know the benchmarking methodology, and you still have to know about possible pitfalls. You still should know about JIT optimizations like DCE, BCE, and constant folding. You still should know about natural noise and possible huge variance; you should check the distribution manually, and you should know how to analyze it.

There is no magic library that solves all these problems for you: they are still your responsibility. BenchmarkDotNet just allows you to skip the boilerplate part of a benchmark and focus on the target code. It's especially useful for beginners who don't know about the discussed problems (or for people who just don't want to think about all of that right then). The library does not guarantee that all your benchmarks are correct. But at least you do not have to worry about common stupid benchmark bugs. It's a handy tool for bootstrapping benchmarks, so we will discuss it several times in this book.

URL: `https://github.com/dotnet/benchmarkdotnet`

Open source (MIT); free; cross-platform.

Resources: `https://benchmarkdotnet.org/`, [Sitnik 2017a], [Sitnik 2017b], [Sitnik 2018].

Visual Studio Tools

Visual Studio is the most popular IDE for .NET development. We are not going to discuss Visual Studio as an IDE; we will talk only about a few features that can be useful during performance investigations.

URL: `https://visualstudio.microsoft.com/vs/`

Closed source; free/commercial; Windows-only.

Embedded Profilers

Visual Studio has many different profiling modes:

- CPU usage

- Memory usage

- Resource consumption for XAML

- Network usage for UWP Apps

- GPU usage for Direct3D

- Energy usage for UWP Apps

A screenshot is presented in Figure 6-1.

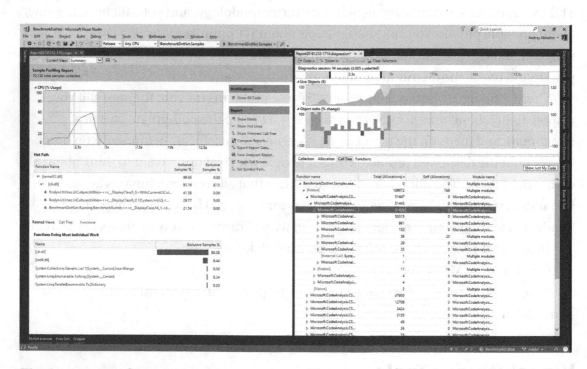

Figure 6-1. *Performance and memory profilers in Visual StudioURL: https://docs.microsoft.com/en-us/visualstudio/profiling*

Disassembly View

Visual Studio has several tool windows for low-level debugging:

- **Disassembly**: a disassembly listing of a method.

- **Registers**: plain text information about all available register values. It supports different groups of registers: CPU, CPU Segments, Floating Point, MMX, 3DNow!, SSE, AVX, AVX-512, MPX, Neon, Neon Float, Neon Double, and CPU flags.

- **Memory**: several tool windows that show a dump of a specified segment of memory. It can interpret memory as 1/2/4/8-byte integers or 32/64-bit floating-point numbers and display them in different formats (hexadecimal, signed numbers, unsigned numbers).

All the tool windows can be found during debugging in the Debug→Windows menu.

By default, the debugger in Visual Studio suppresses some JIT optimizations to provide better debugging experience. Unfortunately, it spoils the native code even in the Release mode. If you want to get the real native code, you should disable the "Suppress JIT optimization on module load" check box in the settings.[1]

A screenshot is presented in Figure 6-2.

---

[1]You can find more information about it in the documentation: https://docs.microsoft.com/en-us/visualstudio/debugger/jit-optimization-and-debugging

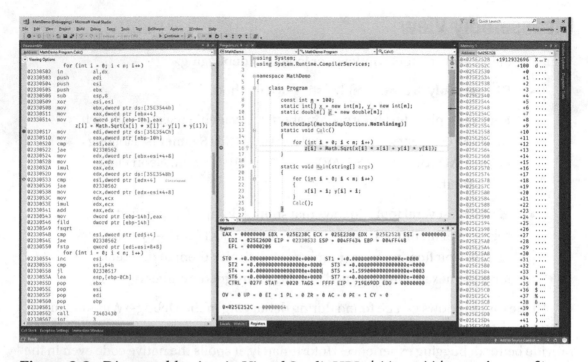

Figure 6-2. *Disassembly view in Visual StudioURL:* `https://docs.microsoft.`
`com/en-us/visualstudio/debugger/how-to-use-the-disassembly-window`

JetBrains Tools

JetBrains has a suite of tools for .NET development. In this section, we are going to
discuss some profiling, decompiling, and debugging features.

dotPeek

dotPeek is a free .NET decompiler and assembly browser. Here are some of the useful
features:

- Decompilation to C# and IL

- Export decompiled code to Visual Studio projects and generation of
  pdb files

- Find usages of any symbol

- Quick navigation to a type, symbol, or anything else

A screenshot is presented in Figure 6-3.

Figure 6-3. *dotPeek URL:* $www.jetbrains.com/decompiler/$ *Closed source; free; Windows-only*

dotTrace and dotMemory

dotTrace and dotMemory are .NET performance and memory profilers. Here are some of the useful features of both products:

- **Support for various .NET applications**

    It supports different kinds of .NET Framework applications (including desktop apps, IIS, IIS Express, Windows services, UWP, and so on) and .NET Core applications.

- **Rich visualizations**

    Both profilers have a lot of visualization views, which allows you to investigate different kinds of issues. For example, dotMemory has the timeline view with real-time data collection, sunburst diagram, call tree chart, and many tree views that help to examine relations between objects in a snapshot.

- **Comparing snapshots**

  When you want to evaluate the impact of a particular change, you can capture performance or memory snapshots before and after the change and compare them. It's useful when you want to verify that the change fixes a performance problem (or that the change doesn't introduce performance degradations).

- **Many execution options**

  You can use dotTrace as a stand-alone desktop application, via command line, or via profiling API. You can attach to local or remote applications (remote profiling is especially useful when you have a problem in a web application on a server).

Here are some special features of dotTrace:

- **Different profiling modes**

  dotTrace supports the following types of profiling:

  - **Sampling**. The idea of this approach is simple: the profiler at the call stacks for all threads from time to time. With this information, it can find methods that take too much time (because they will often appear in captured call stacks). This approach has the lowest possible overhead, but it's not accurate: it can miss some fast methods and it can't calculate the number of calls for each method. It's useful when you want to find a performance bottleneck without significant profiler overhead.

  - **Tracing**. In the tracing mode, the profiler gets special entry and exit events for each method with the help of code instrumentation. As a result, it may add some overhead to each call; the measured time can be distorted. It's useful when you want to know the exact number of calls for each method.

  - **Line-by-line**. This approach is similar to tracing, but it works with state-ments instead of methods. It has bigger overhead than tracing. It's useful when you are looking for the slowest statement in a huge method.

  - **Timeline**. In the timeline mode, the profiler collects temporal information about call stacks, thread state data, memory allocation, garbage collections, and I/O operations. The results are presented with the help of the Timeline

Viewer, which displays recorded events on a timeline diagram. It's useful when the chronological order of events does matter; it allows detecting UI freezes, excessive GC and I/O operations, and lock contention.

- **Support for advanced cases**

    dotTrace has a lot of additional features like profiling async calls, analyzing slow HTTP requests, SQL queries, and file system operations.

Here are some special features of dotMemory:

- **Powerful automatic inspections**

    dotMemory automatically detects common memory issues in your snapshots like string duplicates, sparse arrays, leaking event handlers or WPF bindings, and others.

- **Support for raw memory dumps**

    You can work with raw Windows memory dumps as regular snapshots, explore them via standard view panes, and apply inspections.

dotTrace 2018.3 and dotMemory 2018.3 are Windows-only applications, but future versions should support .NET Core and Mono profiling on Linux and macOS. Screenshots of dotTrace and dotMemory are presented in Figure 6-4 and Figure 6-5.

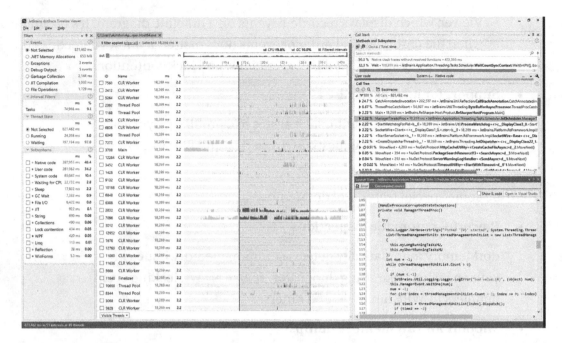

Figure 6-4. *dotTrace*

Figure 6-5. *dotMemoryURL: www.jetbrains.com/profiler/, www.jetbrains. com/dotmemory/Closed source; free/commercial; Windows-only*

ReSharper

ReSharper is a Visual Studio extension for .NET developers. It has many useful features, but I want to highlight only one: IL Viewer. It allows viewing IL code for the current file in a separate tool window. Thus, you can check out the generated IL listing without switching from Visual Studio to another program. ReSharper and dotPeek use the same decompilation engine.

A screenshot is presented in Figure 6-6.

Figure 6-6. *ReSharper IL ViewerURL: www.jetbrains.com/resharper/Closed source; free/commercial; Windows-only.Resources: [Balliauw 2017a], www. jetbrains.com/help/resharper/Viewing_Intermediate_Language.html*

Rider

Rider is a fast and powerful cross-platform .NET IDE. We are not going to discuss Rider as an IDE. Instead, we will talk only about the following features:

- **Embedded decompiler**

  With the help of the dotPeek engine, Rider is able to show decompiled C# code for any third-party classes even without symbols.

- **External code debug**

  Even if you are working with a simple console application, you can attach to any .NET application and debug the decompiled code of any class without original source code or symbols. You can even set breakpoints in the decompiled sources and analyze the execution of third-party assemblies. While most of the classic .NET tools are Windows-only, Rider supports external debug for Mono and .NET Core on Linux and macOS.

- **Embedded profiler**

  Rider contains an embedded dotTrace engine, which allows profiling your application from the IDE.

  URL: `www.jetbrains.com/rider/`

  Closed source; free/commercial; cross-platform.

  Resources: [Balliauw 2017b], `www.jetbrains.com/help/rider/Debugging_External_Code.html`

Windows Sysinternals

Windows Sysinternals is a set of advanced system utilities for Windows. This suite includes many different tools that form the following groups:

- **File and Disk Utilities:** tools that can obtain detailed information about disks (e.g., resource permissions, disk usage, disk mapping, information about encrypted files) and disk manipulation tools (e.g., scheduling file operations for the next reboot, defragmentation, working with symbolic links).

- **Networking Utilities:** tools that can work with Active Directory, named pipes, sockets, and remote computers. It also includes PsPing, which allows performing basic network latency and bandwidth measurements.

- **Process Utilities:** tools that can monitor and control processes, their threads, and handles.

- **Security Utilities:** tools that can operate with users, their sessions and permissions.

- **System Information:** tools that can collect different information about the operating system, processes, memory, devices, and hardware.

- **Miscellaneous:** other tools that help to work with registry, encodings, screens, and desktops.

In this section, we are going to discuss a few tools that can be especially useful during performance investigations: RAMMap, VMMap, and Process Monitor.

URL: `https://docs.microsoft.com/en-us/sysinternals/`

Closed source; free; Windows-only.

RAMMap

RAMMap shows a detailed low-level view of all kinds of memory in the operating system. It allows exploring different kinds of memory (Active, Standby, Modified, and so on) for different usage types (Process Private, Mapped Files, Sharable, and so on). You can analyze the memory of each process, physical memory pages, and ranges.

You can find more information about different kinds of memory in Windows in [Russinovich 2017] and [Russinovich 2019].

A screenshot is presented in Figure 6-7.

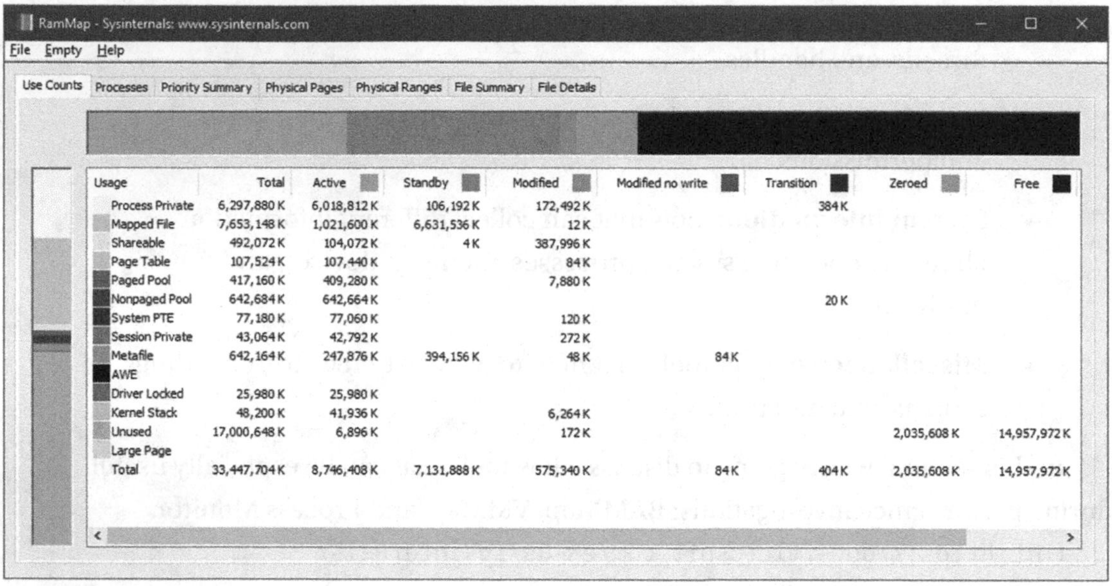

Usage	Total	Active	Standby	Modified	Modified no write	Transition	Zeroed	Free
Process Private	6,297,880 K	6,018,812 K	106,192 K	172,492 K		384 K		
Mapped File	7,653,148 K	1,021,600 K	6,631,536 K	12 K				
Shareable	492,072 K	104,072 K	4 K	387,996 K				
Page Table	107,524 K	107,440 K		84 K				
Paged Pool	417,160 K	409,280 K		7,880 K				
Nonpaged Pool	642,684 K	642,664 K				20 K		
System PTE	77,180 K	77,060 K		120 K				
Session Private	43,064 K	42,792 K		272 K				
Metafile	642,164 K	247,876 K	394,156 K	48 K	84 K			
AWE								
Driver Locked	25,980 K	25,980 K						
Kernel Stack	48,200 K	41,936 K		6,264 K				
Unused	17,000,648 K	6,896 K		172 K			2,035,608 K	14,957,972 K
Large Page								
Total	33,447,704 K	8,746,408 K	7,131,888 K	575,340 K	84 K	404 K	2,035,608 K	14,957,972 K

Figure 6-7. *RAMMapURL:* $https://docs.microsoft.com/en-us/sysinternals/downloads/rammap$

VMMap

VMMap shows a detailed low-level view of memory for a process. While RAMMap helps to explore memory in the whole operating system, VMMap is always working with a single process. It provides advanced data for all memory segments that are used by this process.

A screenshot is presented in Figure 6-8.

VMMap - Sysinternals: www.sysinternals.com

File Edit View Tools Options Help

Process: JetBrains.ReSharper.Host64.exe
PID: 2388

Committed: 1,183,888 K

Private Bytes: 723,636 K

Working Set: 794,604 K

Type	Size	Committed	Private	Total WS	Private WS	Shareable WS	Shared WS	Locked WS	Blocks	Largest
Total	6,116,352 K	1,183,888 K	723,636 K	794,604 K	657,188 K	137,416 K	31,536 K		5447	
Image	443,780 K	440,852 K	34,176 K	138,376 K	3,708 K	134,668 K	30,612 K		2280	25,952 K
Mapped File	49,152 K	49,152 K		1,668 K		1,668 K	72 K		18	25,308 K
Shareable	26,856 K	4,096 K		1,064 K		1,064 K	836 K		29	20,484 K
Heap	151,300 K	129,776 K	129,712 K	98,224 K	98,220 K	4 K	4 K		406	16,192 K
Managed Heap	1,063,040 K	506,116 K	506,116 K	506,108 K	506,108 K				2344	393,216 K
Stack	66,560 K	4,440 K	4,440 K	2,676 K	2,676 K				202	1,024 K
Private Data	4,302,756 K	49,456 K	49,192 K	46,488 K	46,476 K	12 K	12 K		168	4,194,432 K
Page Table										
Unusable	12,908 K									60 K
Free	137,432,837,056 K								109	137,387,537,472 K

Address	Type	Size	Committed	Private	Total WS	Private ...	Sharea...	Share...	Lock...	Blocks	Protection	Details
0000000000010000	Heap (Shareable)	64 K	64 K		4 K		4 K	4 K		1	Read/Write	Heap ID: 2 [COMPATABILITY]
0000000000020000	Shareable	32 K	16 K		12 K		12 K	12 K		2	Read	
0000000000030000	Shareable	100 K	100 K		100 K		100 K	100 K		1	Read	
0000000000050000	Thread Stack	1,024 K	120 K	120 K	100 K	100 K				3	Read/Write/Guard	Thread ID: 14228
0000000000150000	Shareable	16 K	16 K		12 K		12 K	12 K		1	Read	
0000000000160000	Shareable	12 K	12 K		12 K		12 K			1	Read	
0000000000170000	Private Data	4 K	4 K	4 K	4 K	4 K				1	Read/Write	
0000000000180000	Heap (Private Data)	200 K	116 K	116 K	116 K	116 K				2	Read/Write	Heap ID: 1 [LOW FRAGMENTATION]
00000000001C0000	Heap (Private Data)	200 K	8 K	8 K	8 K	8 K				2	Read/Write	Heap ID: 3 [LOW FRAGMENTATION]
0000000000200000	Private Data	2,048 K	540 K	540 K	540 K	540 K				43	Read/Write	Thread Environment Block ID: 14228
0000000000400000	Heap (Private Data)	200 K	4 K	4 K	4 K	4 K				2	Read/Write	Heap ID: 5 [LOW FRAGMENTATION]
0000000000440000	Shareable	4 K	4 K		4 K		4 K			1	Read/Write	

Timeline...   Heap Allocations...   Call Tree...   Trace...

Figure 6-8. *VMMapURL:* `https://docs.microsoft.com/en-us/sysinternals/downloads/vmmap`

Process Monitor

Process Monitor is an advanced monitoring tool for Windows that shows real-time file system, Registry, and process/thread activity. It allows viewing all kinds of low-level OS events (e.g., CreateFile/OpenFile/CloseFile, LoadImage, RegQueryKey/RegCloseKey, ThreadCreate/ThreadExit, and so on). It's also possible to get all available metadata for each event, including full thread stack traces with integrated symbol support for each operation. Since Windows has a huge number of such events, Process Monitor allows setting different kinds of complicated filters, which helps you to catch only the events that you want to see.

A screenshot is presented in Figure 6-9.

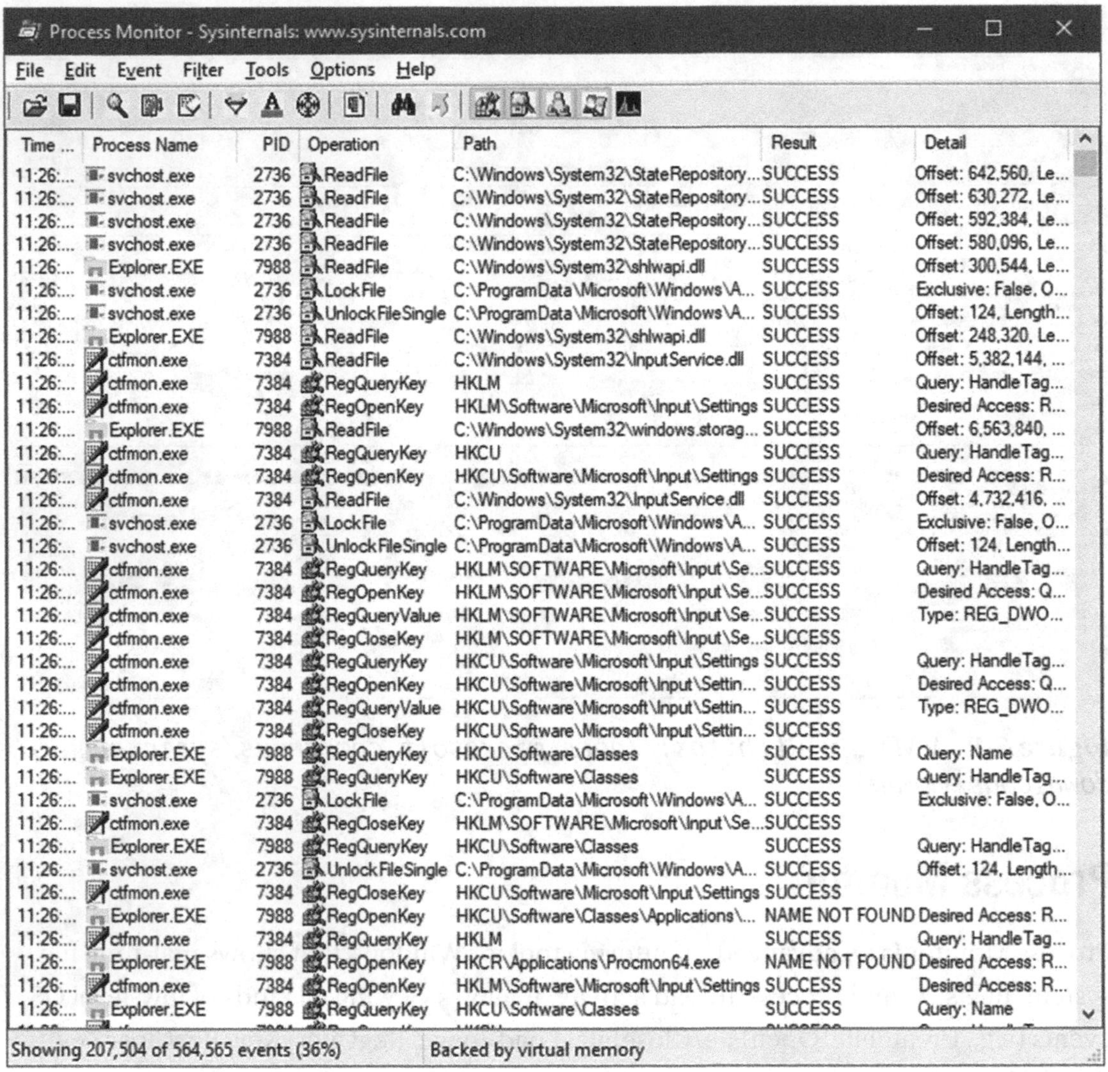

Figure 6-9. *Process MonitorURL:* $https://docs.microsoft.com/en-us/$ $sysinternals/downloads/procmon$

Other Useful Tools

In this section, we are going to discuss other useful tools from different vendors which can also simplify performance investigations.

ildasm and ilasm

ildasm allows getting IL disassembly for a .NET assembly and dumping it into a text file. It's a companion tool to the ilasm, which builds a .NET assembly from the IL sources. Thus, you can decompile an assembly to IL with ildasm, make a few changes, and create a modified assembly with ilasm. Both tools are installed with Visual Studio and available from the Developer command prompt. Typical installation paths of these tools look like `c:\Program Files (x86)\Microsoft SDKs\Windows\v10.0A\bin\NETFX 4.7.1 Tools\ildasm.exe` and `c:\Windows\Microsoft.NET\Framework\v4.0.30319\ilasm.exe`.

Let's say that we have a `Program.cs` file with the following content:

```
using System;
namespace ConsoleApp
{
  class Program
  {
    static void Main(string[] args)
    {
      Console.WriteLine("Hello World!");
    }
  }
}
```

Let's compile it with the help of Roslyn:

```
csc Program.cs
```

Now we have the `Program.exe` assembly, which can be decompiled to IL:

```
ildasm.exe Program.exe /out:Program.il
```

This command creates `Program.il` with the full IL metadata of our assembly. In the middle of this file, we can find the following lines:

```
.class private auto ansi beforefieldinit ConsoleApp.Program
       extends [mscorlib]System.Object
{
```

```
.method private hidebysig static void  Main(string[] args) cil managed
{
  .entrypoint
  // Code size       13 (0xd)
  .maxstack  8
  IL_0000:  nop
  IL_0001:  ldstr      "Hello World!"
  IL_0006:  call       void [mscorlib]System.Console::WriteLine(string)
  IL_000b:  nop
  IL_000c:  ret
} // end of method Program::Main

.method public hidebysig specialname rtspecialname
        instance void  .ctor() cil managed
{
  // Code size       8 (0x8)
  .maxstack  8
  IL_0000:  ldarg.0
  IL_0001:  call       instance void [mscorlib]System.Object::.ctor()
  IL_0006:  nop
  IL_0007:  ret
} // end of method Program::.ctor

} // end of class ConsoleApp.Program
```

Let's open this file in a text editor and change IL_0001: ldstr "Hello World!" to
IL_0001: ldstr "Modified" and compile it back to the executable file:

```
ilasm.exe Program.il
```

Now, if we execute Program.exe, we will get "Modified" instead of "Hello World!".

This approach is especially powerful when you want to make a few changes in the
assembly without rebuilding the project in the command line.

URL: https://docs.microsoft.com/en-us/dotnet/framework/tools/ildasm-exe-
il-disassembler

Closed source; free; Windows-only

monodis

monodis is a Mono version of ildasm. It makes the preceding example with modification of IL code cross-platform. monodis prints the IL listing to the output, so we can rewrite `ildasm.exe Program.exe /out:Program.il` like this:

```
monodis Program.exe ❯ Program.il
```

ilasm also exists in Mono (the title is the same).

URL: `www.mono-project.com/docs/tools+libraries/tools/monodis/` Open source; free; cross-platform

ILSpy

ILSpy is a .NET assembly browser and decompiler. It's a pretty simple decompiler, without many UI features. However, it allows using its decompilation engine via the `ICSharpCode.Decompiler` NuGet package. Thus, you can easily embed this decompiler into your own tools.

Originally, ILSpy was a Windows-only application, but now we have a cross-platform version based on Avalonia.[2]

A screenshot is presented in Figure 6-10.

---

[2]`https://github.com/AvaloniaUI/Avalonia`

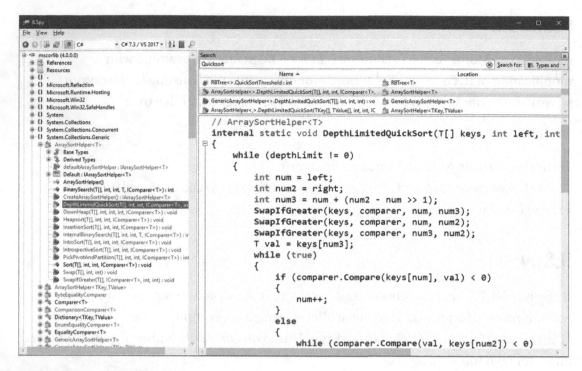

Figure 6-10. *ILSpyURL: https://github.com/icsharpcode/ILSpy, https://github.com/icsharpcode/AvaloniaILSpy Open source (MIT); free; cross-platform*

dnSpy

dnSpy is a debugger and .NET assembly editor. Here are some of its useful features:

- Decompilation to C#, VB, and IL

- Edit assemblies in C#/VB/IL and edit metadata

- Debug .NET Framework, .NET Core, and Unity assemblies without source code

- Powerful IL code hex editor

The decompilation engine is based on ILSpy and the compilation engine is based on Roslyn.

The most powerful feature of dnSpy is assembly editing: you can easily change any IL instruction in a third-party assembly even without its source code. It significantly simplifies experiments when you are trying to find a performance problem in one of your project dependencies. Even when you are working with your own assembly, dnSpy allows making minor code fixes without time-consuming solution recompilation.

A screenshot is presented in Figure 6-11.

Figure 6-11. *dnSpyURL:* `https://github.com/0xd4d/dnSpy` *Open source (GPLv3); free; Windows-only.*

WinDbg

WinDbg is the most powerful low-level debugger for Windows. It allows profiling native and .NET Windows applications. A rich set of commands helps to get any kind of information needed during debugging. The `.loadby sos clr` command loads a special WinDbg extension called SOS (Son of Strike): it provides many additional commands for .NET applications. With WinDbg, you can examine all runtime objects, threads, call stacks, locks, and heaps; you can also explore managed and unmanaged memory, registers, and disassembly listings.

The classic version of WinDbg has a poor user interface, and it's not easy to use it. Fortunately, there is a modern version of WinDbg with reworked UI, which is available via the Microsoft Store (see [Luhrs 2017]).

A screenshot of this modern version is presented in Figure 6-12.

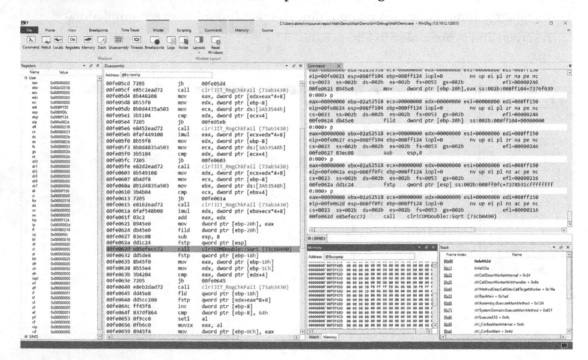

Figure 6-12.   *WinDbgURL:* `https://docs.microsoft.com/en-us/windows-hardware/drivers/debugger/debugger-download-tools` *Closed source; free; Windows-only.Resources:[Goldshtein 2016b],* `https://docs.microsoft.com/en-us/windows-hardware/drivers/debugger/debugging-using-windbg,` `http://windbg.info/doc/1-common-cmds.html,` `https://theartofdev.com/windbg-cheat-sheet/`

Asm-Dude

Asm-Dude is an extension for Visual Studio 2015+ that improves the disassembly support. Here are some of the useful features:

- **Enhanced disassembly tool window**

    The extension applies syntax highlighting in the disassembly tool window and provides QuickInfo tooltips with detailed information about each assembly instruction and its performance characteristics.

- **ASM language support**

    You can also get syntax highlighting, QuickInfo tooltips, code completion, code folding, signature help, and label analysis in the editor. It's significantly simplifying the editing of assembly programs.

    URL: `https://github.com/HJLebbink/asm-dude`

    Open source (MIT), Free, Windows-only.

Mono Console Tools

Mono has several embedded tools that can be useful during investigations.

For example, Mono allows viewing the generated native code for any method. Let's say we have the following program:

```
using System;
namespace MyApp
{
  class Program
  {
    static void Main()
    {
      int x = 3, y = 4;
      double z = Math.Sqrt(x * x + y * y);
      Console.WriteLine(z);
    }
  }
}
```

We can ask mono to compile this method without actual execution with the help of the following command on Linux/macOS:

```
$ MONO_VERBOSE_METHOD=MyApp.Program:Main mono
         --compile MyApp.Program:Main Program.exe
```

Here is the Windows version:

```
> SET MONO_VERBOSE_METHOD=MyApp.Program:Main
> mono --compile MyApp.Program:Main Program.exe
```

At the end of the command output, we will find an assembly listing like this:

```
0000000000000000    subq        0x8, %rsp
0000000000000004    movl        0x19, %eax
0000000000000009    cvtsi2sdl   eax, %xmm0
000000000000000d    movsd       xmm0, -0x8(%rsp)
0000000000000013    fldl        0x8(%rsp)
0000000000000017    fsqrt
0000000000000019    fstpl       -0x8(%rsp)
000000000000001d    movsd       -0x8(%rsp), %xmm0
0000000000000023    nop
0000000000000026    movabsq     $0x106f05fc8, %r11
0000000000000030    callq       *%r11
0000000000000033    addq        $0x8, %rsp
0000000000000037    retq
```

Also, mono allows running your program with the Mono log profiler:

```
$ mono --profile=log Program.exe
```

As a result, you will get the output.mlpd file, which can be opened via the mprof-report or Xamarin Profiler.[3] The mono profiler has a lot of different options, which you can learn about in the official documentation.

URL: https://github.com/mono/mono/

Open source (MIT/BSD), free, cross-platform

Resources: www.mono-project.com/docs/, www.mono-project.com/docs/debug+profile/profile/profiler/

PerfView

PerfView is a free performance analysis tool. It can collect ETW events and explore collected data. ETW is a built-in Windows mechanism (with special support for .NET applications) with extremely low overhead, which makes PerfView very useful for production system monitoring.

A screenshot is presented in Figure 6-13.

---

[3] https://docs.microsoft.com/en-us/xamarin/tools/profiler

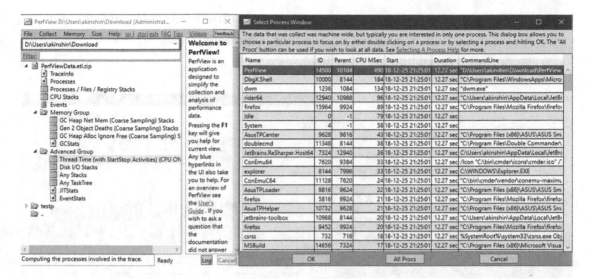

Figure 6-13. *PerfViewURL:* `http://aka.ms/perfview` *Open source (MIT); free; Windows-only.Resources: [Goldshtein 2016a]*

perfcollect

perfcollect is a bash script that automates performance measurements for .NET Core applications on Linux. The collected traces can be viewed using PerfView on Windows.

URL: `http://aka.ms/perfcollect`

Open source (MIT), free, Linux-only

Resources: [Kokosa 2017], [Goldshtein 2017], `https://github.com/dotnet/coreclr/blob/master/Documentation/project-docs/linux-performance-tracing.md`

Process Hacker

Process Hacker is a free, powerful, multipurpose tool that helps you monitor system resources, debug software, and detect malware. It's an "advanced" version of the default Windows task manager. There is also a similar tool from the Sysinternals suite called Process Explorer.[4]

Process Hacker has a detailed view for each process with general statistics (CPU, Memory, I/O usage), performance charts, dozens of .NET performance metrics (like GC heap sizes, the number of jitted methods, the number of thrown exceptions, and so on),

---

[4]`https://docs.microsoft.com/en-us/sysinternals/downloads/process-explorer`

loaded .NET assemblies, information about threads (with stack traces), environment variables, tokens, modules, handles, and memory segments.

A screenshot is presented in Figure 6-14.

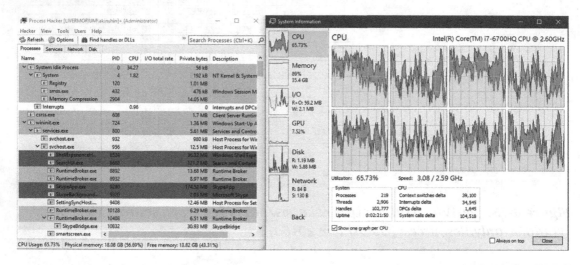

Figure 6-14.   Process HackerURL: https://github.com/processhacker/ processhacker Open source (GPLv3); free; Windows-only

Intel VTune Amplifier

Intel VTune Amplifier is an advanced general-purpose profiler. It knows about hundreds of hardware counters that are supported by Intel CPUs. In especially complicated performance investigations, it's almost impossible to make any conclusions without these counters.

VTune has a lot of different profiling modes for different use cases from four groups: "Hotspots," "Microarchitecture," "Parallelism," and "Platform Analysis." Each mode is highly configurable: the many different settings allow customizing your profile session and getting only metrics that you really need. One of my favorite modes is "Microarchitecture Exploration": it allows getting a lot of different hardware counters that are not available in other profilers.

It has advanced support for different languages like C, C++, C#, Fortran, Java, Python, Go, and Assembly. VTune 2019+ has advanced support for .NET Core applications.

A screenshot is presented in Figure 6-15.

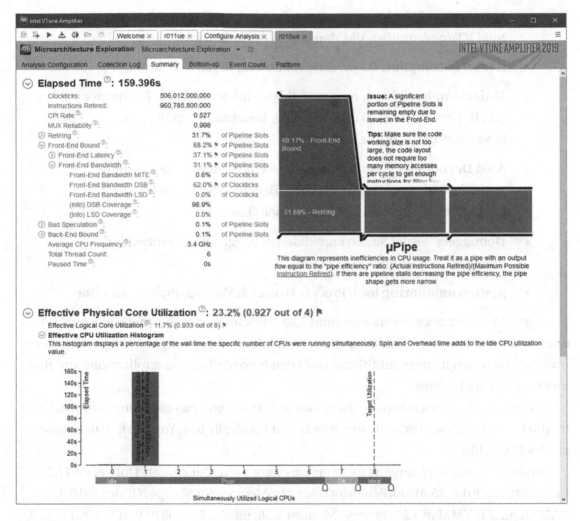

Figure 6-15. *Intel VTune AmplifierURL:* $https://software.intel.com/en-us/$
vtune Closed source; commercial; cross-platform.Resources: [Lander 2018]

Summary

In this chapter, we briefly discussed different diagnostic tools that can be useful during
performance investigations:

- **Benchmarking harness**: BenchmarkDotNet

- **Performance profiler**: Visual Studio embedded profiler, Rider
  embedded profiler, dotTrace, Intel VTune Amplifier, Mono Console
  Tools, perfcollect with PerfView

- **Memory profiler**: Visual Studio embedded profiler, dotMemory, Intel VTune Amplifier, VMMap, Mono Console Tools

- **C#/VB decompiler**: ILSpy, dnSpy, dotPeek, Rider, ReSharper

- **IL decompiler**: ildasm, monodis, ILSpy, dnSpy, dotPeek, ReSharper (via IL Viewer), Intel VTune Amplifier, BenchmarkDotNet (via `DisassemblyDiagnoser`)

- **ASM Decompiler**: Visual Studio disassembly view (which is more powerful with Asm-Dude), WinDbg, BenchmarkDotNet (via `DisassemblyDiagnoser`), Mono Console Tools

- **Debuggers**: Visual Studio embedded debugger, Rider embedded debugger, WinDbg

- **System monitoring tool**: Process Hacker, RAMMap, Process Monitor

A good benchmark answers questions like "How long does this method take?", but it doesn't answer questions like "Why does this method take so long?". A full performance investigation often involves additional tools that help to diagnose applications and make meaningful conclusions.

Of course, this not a complete list of available tools; you can easily find more of them on the Internet. I described only those tools that I typically use. You are free to choose any tools you like.

In this chapter, the following tool versions were used: BenchmarkDotNet v0.11.3 Visual Studio 2017 (15.9), dotPeek/dotTrace/dotMemory/ReSharper/Rider 2018.3, RAMMap 1.51, VMMap 3.25, Process Monitor 3.50, ildasm 4.0.30319.0, ILSpy 4.0 Beta 2, dnSPy 5.0.10, WinDbg Preview 1.0.1812.12001, PerfVew 2.0.26, Asm-Dude 1.9.5.3, Mono 5.16, ProcessHacker 3.0.1563, Intel VTune Amplifier 2019 Update 2. Updated versions of these tools can include changes in the feature set and license policy.

References

[Balliauw 2017a] Balliauw, Maarten. 2017. "Exploring Intermediate Language (IL) with ReSharper and dotPeek." January 19. https://blog.jetbrains.com/dotnet/2017/01/19/exploring-intermediate-language-il-with-resharper-and-dotpeek/.

[Balliauw 2017b] Balliauw, Maarten. 2017. "Debugging Third-Party Code with Rider." December 20. https://blog.jetbrains.com/dotnet/2017/12/20/debugging-third-party-code-rider/.

[Goldshtein 2016a] Goldshtein, Sasha. 2016. "PerfView: Measure and Improve Your App's Performance for Free." Presented at DotNext Piter 2016, June 3. www.youtube.com/watch?v=eX644hod65s.

[Goldshtein 2016b] Goldshtein, Sasha. 2016. "WinDbg Superpowers for .NET Developers." Presented at DotNext Moscow 2016, December 9. www.youtube.com/watch?v=8t1aTbnZ2CE.

[Goldshtein 2017] Goldshtein, Sasha. 2017. "Profiling a .NET Core Application on Linux." February 27. http://blogs.microsoft.co.il/sasha/2017/02/27/profiling-a-net-core-application-on-linux/.

[Kokosa 2017] Kokosa, Konrad. 2017. "Analyzing Runtime CoreCLR Events from Linux – Trace Compass." August 7. http://tooslowexception.com/analyzing-runtime-coreclr-events-from-linux-trace-compass/.

[Lander 2018] Lander, Rich. 2018. ".NET Core Source Code Analysis with Intel® VTune™ Amplifier." *Microsoft .NET Blog*. October 23. https://blogs.msdn.microsoft.com/dotnet/2018/10/23/net-core-source-code-analysis-with-intel-vtune-amplifier/.

[Luhrs 2017] Luhrs, Andy. 2017. "New WinDbg Available in Preview!" August 28. https://blogs.msdn.microsoft.com/windbg/2017/08/28/new-windbg-available-in-preview/.

[Russinovich 2017] Yosifovich, Pavel, Mark E. Russinovich, David A. Solomon, and Alex Ionescu. 2017. *Windows Internals, Part 1*. 7th ed. Microsoft Press.

[Russinovich 2019] Russinovich, Mark E., David A. Solomon, Alex Ionescu, and Andrea Allievi. 2019. *Windows Internals, Part 2*. 7th ed. Microsoft Press.

[Sitnik 2017a] Sitnik, Adam. 2017. "Collecting Hardware Performance Counters with BenchmarkDotNet." April 4. https://adamsitnik.com/Hardware-Counters-Diagnoser/.

[Sitnik 2017b] Sitnik, Adam. 2017. "Disassembling .NET Code with BenchmarkDotNet." August 16. https://adamsitnik.com/Disassembly-Diagnoser/.

[Sitnik 2018] Sitnik, Adam. 2018. "Profiling .NET Code with BenchmarkDotNet." September 28. https://adamsitnik.com/ETW-Profiler/.

CHAPTER 7

CPU-Bound Benchmarks

Knock, knock.

Branch prediction.

Who's there?

— A classic programming joke

One of the most common bottlenecks in many benchmarks is CPU. Proper design and analysis of CPU-bound benchmarks require knowledge of different runtime and hardware "features" that can affect performance. Each .NET runtime has a lot of different optimizations that can improve (or spoil) performance of your code. Each CPU microarchitecture has a lot of low-level mechanisms that also affect measurements. If you are not aware of these optimizations and mechanisms, it's hard to design some benchmarks and interpret the measured metrics correctly. In this chapter, we are going to cover the following topics:

- **Registers and Stack**

  We will discuss when a JIT compiler keeps the intermediate values in registers and when it uses the stack for it.

- **Inlining**

  We will discuss when a JIT compiler can inline your methods and why it's important.

- **Instruction-Level Parallelism (ILP)**

  We will discuss one of the most important hardware features, ILP, which allows processing multiple instructions at the same time inside a single thread.

© Andrey Akinshin 2019
A. Akinshin, *Pro .NET Benchmarking*, https://doi.org/10.1007/978-1-4842-4941-3_7

- **Branch Prediction**

  We will discuss the ability of modern CPUs to predict which branches will be taken in your programs. Correct predictions help to improve conditions for the ILP. It's important in the context of benchmarking because the input data can significantly affect the method performance based on the correct prediction rate.

- **Arithmetic**

  We will discuss what kind of problems we can get with benchmarks that use arithmetic operations. We will talk about hardware (floating-point numbers and IEEE 754) and runtime (different environments and JIT optimizations) features.

- **Intrinsics**

  We will discuss cases when a JIT compiler can generate a "smart" native implementation for specific methods and statements.

The full explanation of each topic is pretty huge because it includes a lot of low-level details about runtime and hardware internals. However, you don't actually have to know all the internals during benchmarking. In this chapter, we are going to cover only high-level concepts that are good to know. In each section, you will find four case studies that demonstrate how these concepts can affect even small and simple benchmarks. Each case study contains four sections:

- **Source code**

  A small set of benchmarks that demonstrate an interesting performance effect. You can find the source code of all examples in the attachment to this book.

- **Results**

  Benchmark results in a *specific* environment. If you can't reproduce the result on your own machine, check out the versions of your OS, .NET Core, .NET Core SDK, runtime, JIT compiler, and the CPU model. The performance always depends on your environment: anything can spoil the described performance phenomena or introduce another one.

- **Explanation**

  A short description of the observed results. We will often look at the generated IL and native code in order to understand what's going on in the corresponding example.

- **Discussion**

  General recommendations about the discussed effects, additional interesting information, links to GitHub issues, and other references for further reading. Many case studies are based on some great StackOverflow questions and answers: you will find the corresponding links at the end of the subsection.

You will learn the commonest mistakes which developers usually make because they are not aware of some benchmarking pitfall. This knowledge will help you to design better CPU-bound benchmarks and correctly interpret their results.

Registers and Stack

When we have a local variable, the JIT compiler can put it into registers or on the stack. Operations with registers are usually much faster than operations with stack values. Thus, the JIT compiler decision can have a significant impact on performance. It's impossible to keep all local variables in registers because the number of registers is limited: the JIT compiler should use it wisely. Different CPU instruction sets have different numbers of registers.

Case Study 1: Struct Promotion

In most cases, when we use a struct value in local variables, the JIT compiler keeps its fields on the stack. In some special cases, the fields can be saved into registers. Such an approach is known as *struct promotion* or *scalar replacement*. It's implemented in RyuJIT, but you can't manually enable or disable this feature for a particular method. Let's learn an example that demonstrates some limitations of struct promotion.

Source code

Consider the following BenchmarkDotNet-based benchmark:

```
public struct Struct3
{
  public byte X0, X1, X2;
}

public struct Struct8
{
  public byte X0, X1, X2, X3, X4, X5, X6, X7;
}

public class Benchmarks
{
  public const int Size = 256;

  private int[] sum = new int[Size];
  private Struct3[] struct3 = new Struct3[Size];
  private Struct8[] struct8 = new Struct8[Size];

  [Benchmark(OperationsPerInvoke = Size, Baseline = true)]
  public void Run3()
  {
    for (var i = 0; i < sum.Length; i++)
    {
      Struct3 s = struct3[i];
      sum[i] = s.X0 + s.X1;
    }
  }

  [Benchmark(OperationsPerInvoke = Size)]
  public void Run8()
  {
    for (var i = 0; i < sum.Length; i++)
    {
```

```
    Struct8 s = struct8[i];
    sum[i] = s.X0 + s.X1;
  }
 }
}
```

Here we have two structs: Struct3 with three byte fields and Struct8 with eight byte fields. We also have two benchmarks: Run3 and Run8. In each benchmark, we calculate the sum of the first two struct fields in a loop. The only difference between Run3 and Run8 is the used struct.

Results

Here is an example of results (Windows 10.0.17763.195, Intel Core i7-6700HQ CPU 2.60GHz, .NET Core 2.1.5, RyuJIT-x64):

```
Method |    Mean |    StdDev | Ratio |
--------- |----------:|------------:|-------:|
   Run3 | 1.100 ns | 0.0091 ns |  1.00 |
   Run8 | 1.579 ns | 0.0115 ns |  1.44 |
```

As you can see, Run8 works much slower. Run8 uses Struct8, which is similar to Struct3 but contains five additional fields. These fields are not actually used in the benchmark, but we still have a ~30–50% performance drop.

Explanation

Let's look at the native code of the Run3 loop body:

```
; Run3
lea    r8,[r8+r10+10h]              ; r8 = &struct3[i]
movzx  r10d,byte ptr [r8]           ; r10d = X0
movzx  r11d,byte ptr [r8+1]         ; r11d = X1
movzx  r8d,byte ptr [r8+2]          ; r8d  = X2
mov    r8,rdx                       ; r8 = &sum
cmp    eax,dword ptr [r8+8]         ; if (i > sum.Length)
jae    00007ffe`e62a2b74            ;    throw
add    r10d,r11d                    ; r10d += r11d
mov    dword ptr [r8+r9*4+10h],r10d ; sum[i] = r10d
```

As you can see, we find the location of struct3[i] and load the three corresponding fields X0, X1, and X2 into registers r10d, r11d, and r8d. This is the struct promotion in action! We don't actually need X2, but JIT loads all the fields by default. Next, we add r11d to r10d and save the result to sum[i].

Now, let's look at the native code of the Run8 loop body:

```
; Run8
mov     rdx,qword ptr [rdx+r8*8+10h] ; rdx = struct8[i]
mov     qword ptr [rsp+20h],rdx      ; [rsp+20h] = struct8[i]
mov     rdx,qword ptr [rcx+8]        ; rdx = &sum
mov     r9,rdx                       ; r9 = &sum
cmp     eax,dword ptr [r9+8]         ; if (i > sum.Length)
jae     00007ffe`e6272b7a            ;    throw
movzx   r10d,byte ptr [rsp+20h]      ; r10d = X0
movzx   r11d,byte ptr [rsp+21h]      ; r11d = X1
add     r10d,r11d                    ; r10d += r11d
mov     dword ptr [r9+r8*4+10h],r10d ; sum[i] = r10d
```

Here we load struct8[i] onto the stack first. After that, we load the first two fields of struct8[i] from the stack to registers r10d and r11d. Next, we add r11d to r10d and save the result to sum[i].

As you can see, RyuJIT was able to apply struct promotion in Run3, but not in Run8. This result can be explained by a limitation of RyuJIT in .NET Core 2.1.5: it can't promote structs that have more than four fields.

Discussion

In .NET Core 1.x/2.x, the implementation of scalar replacement has many different limitations. For example, the promoted struct has to follow some rules[1]:

- It must have only primitive fields.

- It must not be an argument or a return value that is passed in registers.

- It can't be larger than 32 bytes.

- It can't have more than 4 fields.

---

[1]https://github.com/dotnet/coreclr/issues/6733#issuecomment-240623400

In general, it's not recommended to rely on these particular heuristics during optimization because they might be changed in future versions of RyuJIT. Also, these rules are not valid for other JIT compilers like LegacyJIT-x64 or MonoJIT. However, if you really want to optimize some hot methods and the .NET Core version is fixed, you can use this knowledge, but it makes sense to check such optimizations after each .NET Core update (you can automate it with the help of performance tests).

We discussed this case study because the knowledge of the struct promotion concept helps to interpret some benchmark results correctly. If you are designing a small benchmark based on a real application, it's not recommended to modify the used structs even if some of its fields are not actually used in the benchmark. Any modifications in the struct layout may introduce unpredictable performance changes.

This particular benchmark also has some interesting memory-alignment performance issues. We will continue to discuss this in Chapter 8.

See also:

- coreclr#6839 "Promote (scalar replace) structs with more than 4 fields"[2]

- coreclr#6733 "Scalar replacement of aggregates"[3]

- CoreCLR design docs: "First Class Structs"[4]

This case study is based on StackOverflow question 38949304.[5]

Case Study 2: Local Variables

"Introduce a local variable" is a popular refactoring that can improve the readability of your code. This code modification doesn't change the logic, so developers don't expect situations when this refactoring will have an impact on the application performance. However, *any changes* in the source code may lead to performance changes.

---

[2]https://github.com/dotnet/coreclr/issues/6839
[3]https://github.com/dotnet/coreclr/issues/6733
[4]https://github.com/dotnet/coreclr/blob/v2.2.0/Documentation/design-docs/first-class-structs.md
[5]https://stackoverflow.com/q/38949304

Source code

Consider the following BenchmarkDotNet-based benchmarks:

```
public struct Struct
{
  public Struct(uint? someValue)
  {
    SomeValue = someValue;
  }

  public uint? SomeValue { get; }
}

public class Benchmarks
{
  [Benchmark(Baseline = true)]
  public uint? Foo()
  {
    return new Struct(100).SomeValue;
  }

  [Benchmark]
  public uint? Bar()
  {
    Struct s = new Struct(100);
    return s.SomeValue;
  }
}
```

Here we have two benchmarks: Foo and Bar. Both methods do the same thing: they create an instance of Struct (which is a value type wrapper for the uint? type) and return the only field of it. However, Bar differs from Foo: it saves the struct instance to a local variable instead of using it in the return expression. The performed logic is identical for both cases, but we have minor changes on the C# level. Typically, we don't expect any performance changes during simple code refactoring like this.

Results

Here is an example of results (Windows 10.0.17763.195, Intel Core i7-6700HQ CPU 2.60GHz, .NET Core SDK 2.1.403, .NET Core 2.1.5, RyuJIT-x64):

```
Method |    Mean |   StdDev | Ratio |
------- |---------:|----------:|------:|
   Foo | 6.597 ns | 0.0433 ns |  1.00 |
   Bar | 4.975 ns | 0.0439 ns |  0.75 |
```

As you can see, Bar works ~20–30% faster than Foo. How is that possible?

Explanation

Let's look at the generated IL code (Roslyn 2.9.0.63127):

```
// Foo()
.maxstack 1
.locals init (
  [0] valuetype Struct V_0
)
IL_00: ldc.i4.s   100
IL_02: newobj     System.Void System.Nullable`1::.ctor(!0)
IL_07: newobj     System.Void Struct::.ctor(System.Nullable`1)
IL_0c: stloc.0    // V_0
IL_0d: ldloca.s   V_0
IL_0f: call       System.Nullable`1 Struct::get_SomeValue()
IL_14: ret

// Bar()
.maxstack 2
.locals /*11000001*/ init (
  [0] valuetype Struct s
)
IL_00: ldloca.s   s
IL_02: ldc.i4.s   100
IL_04: newobj     System.Void System.Nullable`1::.ctor(!0)
IL_09: call       System.Void Struct::.ctor(System.Nullable`1)
```

```
IL_0e: ldloca.s    s
IL_10: call        System.Nullable`1 Struct::get_SomeValue()
IL_15: ret
```

As you can see, there are some minor differences between these methods. Foo creates Struct via newobj, loads the result to a local variable, and loads the address of this variable. Meanwhile, Bar creates Struct via call (which saves the result to a local variable) and instantly loads the address of this variable. Both implementations are equivalent, but they use different IL instructions.

Now let's look at the generated native code for Foo():

```
; Foo()
sub  rsp,18h
xor  eax,eax;                ; Initialize Struct
mov  qword ptr [rsp+10h],rax ; Store Struct into stack

mov  eax,64h                 ; eax = 100
mov  edx,1                   ; edx = 1

xor  ecx,ecx;                ; Initialize SomeValue
mov  qword ptr [rsp+8],rcx   ; Store SomeValue into stack
lea  rcx,[rsp+8]             ; rcx = pointer to SomeValue
mov  byte ptr [rcx],dl       ; SomeValue.HasValue = 1
mov  dword ptr [rcx+4],eax   ; SomeValue.Value = 100

mov  rax,qword ptr [rsp+8]   ; rax = pointer to SomeValue
mov  qword ptr [rsp+10h],rax ; Store SomeValue to a different location on
                               stack
mov  rax,qword ptr [rsp+10h] ; rax = pointer to SomeValue

add  rsp,18h
ret
```

As you can see, the stloc.0/ldloca.s pair forces RyuJIT to generate some redundant mov instructions. And here is the native code for Bar:

```
; Bar()
push  rax
xor   eax,eax               ; Initialize Struct
mov   qword ptr [rsp],rax   ; Store Struct into stack
```

```
mov    eax,64h                      ; eax = 100
mov    edx,1                        ; edx = 1

lea    rcx,[rsp]                    ; rcx = pointer to SomeValue
mov    byte ptr [rcx],dl            ; SomeValue.HasValue = 1
mov    dword ptr [rcx+4],eax        ; SomeValue.Value = 100
mov    rax,qword ptr [rsp]          ; rax = pointer to SomeValue

add    rsp,8
ret
```

It looks more efficient because it doesn't have redundant instructions.

Discussion

Any code refactorings that don't change logic can change the generated IL code. Any changes in the IL code can unpredictably affect the efficiency of the generated code. When developers design benchmarks based on real-life scenarios, they often do some small refactorings to improve the readability of the benchmark. Unfortunately, these refactorings can introduce additional performance effects and spoil (or improve) the performance. When you are refactoring an existing benchmark, it's recommended to verify that your code changes don't have an impact on the results.

In such cases, the performance depends on the compiler version. The preceding example is valid for Roslyn 2.9.0.63127 (which is bundled in .NET Core SDK 2.1.403), but the behavior can be changed in future versions (see roslyn#30284[6] for details).

It's a pretty common situation when minor changes in source code lead to interesting performance effects. For example, in StackOverflow question 53452713,[7] you can find a simple Java benchmark that becomes faster after replacing 2 * i * i by 2 * (i * i).

This case study is based on StackOverflow question 52565479.[8]

---

[6]https://github.com/dotnet/roslyn/issues/30284
[7]https://stackoverflow.com/q/53452713
[8]https://stackoverflow.com/q/52565479

Case Study 3: Try-Catch

A proper exception handling is important if you want to develop stable .NET applications. A lot of developers put try-catch blocks here and there "just in case." They don't expect performance penalty because exceptions are considered as rare events. It may seem that if the source code doesn't throw any exceptions, the try-catch overhead shouldn't be noticeable. Unfortunately, this is not always true because the JIT compiler can modify the generated native code when a try-catch block is added.

Source code

Consider the following BenchmarkDotNet-based benchmarks:

```
public class Benchmarks
{
  private const int N = 93;

  [Benchmark(Baseline = true)]
  public long Fibonacci1()
  {
    long a = 0, b = 0, c = 1;
    for (int i = 1; i < N; i++)
    {
      a = b;
      b = c;
      c = a + b;
    }
    return c;
  }

  [Benchmark]
  public long Fibonacci2()
  {
    long a = 0, b = 0, c = 1;
    try
    {
```

```
    for (int i = 1; i < N; i++)
    {
      a = b;
      b = c;
      c = a + b;
    }
  }
  catch {}
  return c;
  }
}
```

Here we have two methods, Fibonacci1 and Fibonacci2, which calculate the 93rd Fibonacci number.[9] However, Fibonacci2 wraps the main loop in try-catch. This code doesn't throw any exceptions, so we probably shouldn't expect any performance overhead because of it, right?

Results

Here is an example of results (Windows 10.0.17763.195, Intel Core i7-6700HQ CPU 2.60GHz, .NET Core 2.1.5, RyuJIT-x64):

```
    Method |       Mean |    StdDev | Ratio |
----------- |----------:|----------:|------:|
 Fibonacci1 |   41.07 ns | 0.1446 ns |  1.00 |
 Fibonacci2 |  102.93 ns | 0.3394 ns |  2.50 |
```

In this environment, Fibonacci2 works 2.5 slower than Fibonacci1.

Explanation

Let's look at the generated native code for Fibonacci1:

```
; Fibonacci1
xor   eax,eax       ; a = 0
mov   edx,1         ; c = 1
```

---

[9]It equals to 12,200,160,415,121,876,738. It's the largest Fibonacci number that can be represented using long.

```
mov   ecx,1            ; i = 1
LOOP:
mov   r8,rdx           ; b = c
lea   rdx,[rax+r8]     ; c = a + b
inc   ecx             ; i++
cmp   ecx,5Dh          ; if (i < 93)
mov   rax,r8           ;    a = b
jl    LOOP             ;    goto LOOP
mov   rax,rdx          ; result = c

ret                    ; return result
```

This implementation is pretty simple. The a, b, and c variables are represented using registers rax, r8, and rdx.

Now let's look at the generated native code for Fibonacci2:

```
; Fibonacci2
sub   esp,10h                      ; Reserve space
lea   rbp,[rsp+10h]                ;    on stack
mov   qword ptr [rbp-10h],rsp      ;

xor   eax,eax                      ; a = 0
mov   qword ptr [rbp-8],1          ; c = 1
mov   edx,1                        ; i = 1
LOOP:
mov   rcx,qword ptr [rbp-8]        ; b = c
add   rax,rcx                      ; a += b
mov   qword ptr [rbp-8],rax        ; c = a
inc   edx                          ; i++
cmp   edx,5Dh                      ; if (i < 93)
mov   rax,rcx                      ;    a = b
jl    LOOP                         ;    goto LOOP
mov   rax,qword ptr [rbp-8]        ; result = c

lea   rsp,[rbp]                    ; Recover stack pointer
pop   rbp                          ;
ret                               ; return result
```

The a and b variables are still using registers rax and rcx. However, the c variable is placed on the stack (qword ptr [rbp-8]) instead of registers. Fibonacci2 works much slower than Fibonacci1 because the read/write operations with stack values take much more time than operations with registers.

The only difference between Fibonacci1 and Fibonacci2 is a try-catch in Fibonacci2. We don't have any native instructions for exception handling because Fibonacci2 doesn't throw any exceptions. However, the existence of the try-catch block forced RyuJIT to put the c variable on the stack, which spoiled the method performance.

Discussion

This case study is based on StackOverflow question 8928403.[10] In this question, the author asks why a method with try-catch works *faster* than a method without exception handling. But we have the opposite result with RyuJIT! Performance always depends on the environment. The question was asked in 2012; the original measurements used .NET Framework 2.0 with LegacyJIT-x86 and old versions of the C# compiler. Here is a quote from the Jon Skeet's answer[11]:

> Possibly the try/catch block forces more registers to be saved
> and restored, so the JIT uses those for the loop as well... which
> happens to improve the performance overall. It's not clear
> whether it's a reasonable decision for the JIT to not use as many
> registers in the "normal" code.

The underlying problem is the same (the JIT compiler uses registers in one case and the stack in another case), but the result is the opposite. That's why it's not a good idea to use such knowledge during performance optimizations: different JIT compilers use different algorithms that can be changed at any moment. However, this knowledge is extremely useful during performance investigations when you are trying to explain some interesting performance effects.

---

[10]https://stackoverflow.com/q/8928403
[11]https://stackoverflow.com/a/8928476

Case Study 4: Number of Calls

The number of calls in a method is an important factor for some JIT compiler heuristics. The overhead of these calls can be small, but it can force the JIT compiler to change the generated native code for other statements in the same method.

Source code

Consider the following BenchmarkDotNet-based benchmarks:

```
public class X {}

[LegacyJitX86Job]
public class Benchmarks
{
  private const int N = 100001;

  [Benchmark(Baseline = true)]
  public double Foo()
  {
    double a = 1, b = 1;
    for (int i = 0; i < N; i++)
      a = a + b;
    return a;
  }

  [Benchmark]
  public double Bar()
  {
    double a = 1, b = 1;
    new X(); new X(); new X();
    for (int i = 0; i < N; i++)
      a = a + b;
    return a;
  }
}
```

Here we have two methods: Foo and Bar. Both methods add one double variable to another one in a loop. However, the Bar method has three additional constructor calls.

Results

Here is an example of results (Windows 10.0.17763.195, Intel Core i7-6700HQ CPU 2.60GHz, .NET Framework 4.7.2, LegacyJIT-x86 v4.7.3260.0):

```
Method |     Mean |     StdDev | Ratio |
------- |---------:|-----------:|------:|
   Foo | 103.5 us | 0.4686 us |  1.00 |
   Bar | 309.7 us | 1.4324 us |  2.99 |
```

The Bar method works three times slower than the Foo method. The only difference that we have is three additional constructor calls in Bar. These calls should be executed almost instantly and they shouldn't introduce a noticeable overhead. So, why do we have these results?

Explanation

Let's look at the generated native code for Foo (only the main part is shown):

```
; Foo()
xor    eax,eax      ; i = 0

LOOP:
fld1                ; load 1 into st(0)
faddp  st(1),st     ; st(1) += st(0)
inc    eax          ; i++
cmp    eax,186A1h    ; if (i < 100001)
jl     LOOP         ;   goto LOOP
```

Here we load 1 in the st(0) and add it to st(1). st(0) and st(1) are x87 FPU data registers (see [FPUx87] for details). Now let's look at the generated native code for Bar:

```
; Bar()
mov    ecx,569952Ch
call   017130c8       ; new X();
mov    ecx,569952Ch
call   017130c8       ; new X();
mov    ecx,569952Ch
call   017130c8       ; new X();
xor    eax,eax        ; i = 0
```

```
LOOP:
fld1                        ; load 1 into st(0)
fadd    qword ptr [esp] ; st(0) += [esp]
fstp    qword ptr [esp] ; [esp] = st(0)
inc     eax             ; i++
cmp     eax,186A1h      ; if (i < 100001)
jl      LOOP            ;   goto LOOP
```

Here we keep the result on the stack (qword ptr [esp]) and perform read/write stack operations on each loop iteration. At the beginning of the method, we can see three calls of the X constructor. These calls don't have a noticeable overhead. However, LegacyJIT-x86 decided to use the stack for the calculations instead of registers because it uses the number of calls for this decision.

Discussion

The described performance phenomena in the preceding example is valid only for LegacyJIT-x86; you will not observe a performance drop for *this case study* with other JIT compilers. However, the number of calls in a method still can be used by any JIT compiler as a factor for different optimizations. In general, you shouldn't try to optimize methods by reducing the number of additional calls: this factor is important only in some specific cases. When you get a situation when adding/removing an additional call leads to unexpected performance changes (larger than the expected call duration), you should check how these calls affect the generated native code of the whole method.

A similar example was already discussed in Chapter 2 ("Conditional Jitting" section). This case study is based on StackOverflow question 32114308.[12]

Summing Up

When we have local variables, the JIT compiler can store it into registers or on the stack. When these local variables are primitive types or structs, this decision may have a significant impact on performance. In this section, we covered several factors that are important for this decision:

---

[12]https://stackoverflow.com/q/32114308

- The number of fields in a struct definition.

- Explicitly introducing a local variable from an expression.

- Existence of a try-catch block that wraps the measured logic.

- The number of calls in a method.

When you design a small benchmark based on a real application, you can easily introduce some conditions that are important for JIT heuristics. It's good to have a minimal benchmark that demonstrates an important performance effect. However, any changes in the source code may lead to additional unexpected performance changes. Be careful when you are prettifying your benchmarks! If you want to compare two small benchmarks or if you want to apply benchmark results for optimization of a real application, it's a good practice to check how the JIT compiler handles the local variables.

Of course, some benchmarks can be huge and involve hundreds of additional methods. It's almost impossible to check the native code for each invoked method in each performance investigation. Fortunately, **you shouldn't worry about the "stack vs. registers" problem in most cases**: this problem actually affects performance in real-life benchmarks only infrequently. Meanwhile, when you hit this problem and get results you can't explain, you have one more thing to check.

Inlining

The topic of inlining has already been discussed in this book several times. When the JIT compiler *inlines* a method, it means that a call of this method is replaced by its body. It's not easy to decide when we should use inlining because this optimization has some advantages and disadvantages.

Advantages:

- **Eliminated call overhead**

    When we call a method, we always have some overhead. For example, we perform a couple of additional instructions (`call`, `ret`). Sometimes, we have to save some register values before the call and restore them after the call. Inlining eliminates this overhead. It can be important for hot methods that should be superfast.

- **Opportunity for other optimizations**

  Once a method is inlined, other optimizations like constant folding or code elimination are possible.

- **Better register allocation**

  In some cases, when a method is inlined, the JIT compiler can use the registers better because it shouldn't pass arguments to the called method.

Disadvantages:

- **Increasing code size**

  On the CPU level, we have an *instruction cache*, which helps to load the executed code faster. Duplication of the inlined method native code across its usages may hurt the instruction cache performance. This effect is almost invisible on small programs, but it can affect applications with a huge source code base.

- **Preventing further inlining**

  Imagine three methods A, B, C where A calls B and B calls C. If the JIT compiler inlines B into A, A may become too complicated, which will prevent further inlining C into A. Meanwhile, the C→B inlining can be more profitable than B→A inlining.

- **Worse register allocation**

  You may think about a method as a scope for the JIT compiler where it tries to use registers as best as possible. Since the number of registers is limited, an inlined method may lead to worse conditions for register usage. In the previous section, we already discussed many cases when we have a performance drop because some variables are placed on the stack instead of registers.

Thus, inlining can be a good optimization or a bad optimization. Usually, the JIT compiler tries to make a decision that is best for performance. However, these decisions are not always obvious, and they may lead to unexpected performance phenomena. Let's look at some case studies that help us to recognize situations when the knowledge about inlining is important for performance investigations.

Case Study 1: Call Overhead

When we have a hot method, we want to make it as fast as possible. Typically, a call of a simple method takes a few nanoseconds. If a method also takes a few nanoseconds, the call overhead may increase its duration twice. This overhead can be eliminated with the help of inlining. Unfortunately, it's not always possible to inline a method. Let's look at an example that shows what kind of performance drop we could get when it's impossible to inline a hot method.

Source code

Consider the following BenchmarkDotNet-based benchmarks:

```
public class Benchmarks
{
  private const int N = 1000;
  private int[] x = new int[N];
  private int[] y = new int[N];
  private int[] z = new int[N];

  [Benchmark(Baseline = true)]
  public void Foo()
  {
    for (int i = 0; i < z.Length; i++)
      z[i] = Sum(x[i], y[i]);
  }

  [Benchmark]
  public void Bar()
  {
    for (int i = 0; i < z.Length; i++)
      z[i] = VirtualSum(x[i], y[i]);
  }

  public int Sum(int a, int b) => a + b;

  public virtual int VirtualSum(int a, int b) => a + b;
}
```

Here we have three int arrays of the same length: x, y, and z. In the declared benchmarks Foo and Bar, we perform z[i] = x[i] + y[i] for all array elements. Instead of the direct calculations, the sum operation is extracted to a separate method. Foo uses Sum (a nonvirtual method), and Bar uses VirtualSum (a virtual method).

Results

Here is an example of results (macOS 10.14.2, Intel Core i7-4870HQ CPU 2.50GHz, .NET Core 2.1.3, RyuJIT-x64):

```
Method |    Mean |   StdDev | Ratio |
------ |--------:|---------:|------:|
   Foo | 1.121 us | 0.0148 us |  1.00 |
   Bar | 2.311 us | 0.0196 us |  2.06 |
```

As you can see, Bar works two times slower than Foo.

Explanation

VirtualSum can't be inlined because it's marked as a virtual method. According to the set of RyuJIT heuristics in .NET Core 2.1.3, virtual methods can't be inlined here. Sum can be inlined because there are no factors that prevent inlining. Foo works two times faster than Bar because it used the inlined version of the sum operation and it doesn't have the Sum call overhead.

Discussion

Here are some conditions that *typically* prevent inlining:

- **MethodImplOptions.NoInlining**

  We can annotate a method with [MethodImpl(MethodImplOptions.NoInlining)], which notifies the JIT compiler that this method shouldn't be inlined. In this case, inlining can't be applied even if a method is empty.

- **Big methods**

  When a method is "big" (it contains too many IL instructions), it will not be inlined by default. There are no strict criteria for when a method is "big." Different JIT compilers have different rules for that. In some cases, we can ask the JIT compiler to inline a "big" method with the help of [MethodImpl(MethodImplOptions. AggressiveInlining)], but it still can decide to not inline it.

- **Exception handling**

  If a method contains a try/catch block, it can't be inlined because such optimization will spoil the call stack during exception handling.

- **Virtual methods (in most cases)**

  The JIT compiler can't inline virtual methods (in most cases) because they can be overridden in a derived class. However, there are some special cases when it's possible to inline both virtual and interface calls. Also, this behavior can be changed in the future (see coreclr#9908[13] for details).

- **Recursive methods**

  Recursive methods can't be inlined because it's impossible to completely inline the whole recursive chain. However, it's potentially possible to inline the "first recursive step."

The JIT compilers in .NET have a lot of different heuristics that are responsible for the inlining policy. You can find some information about these heuristics in [Notario 2004], [Morrison 2008], and [Ayers 2016]. Inlining is a complicated topic because it's hard to predict how a particular rule affects the performance of a real application in general (e.g., see [Amit 2018]).

Typically, you may rely on some specific rules that definitely prevent inlining and be sure that a recursive method or a method with the [MethodImpl(MethodImplOptions. NoInlining)] attribute can't be inlined. However, you can't be sure that a particular method will always be inlined: different JIT compilers (or different versions of the same JIT compiler) can have different inlining policies. To make the final decision, the JIT compiler does a series of "observations" about each method.[14] Next, it combines these

---

[13]https://github.com/dotnet/coreclr/issues/9908

[14]You can find some of these observations for RyuJIT here: https://github.com/dotnet/coreclr/blob/v2.2.0/src/jit/inline.def

observations with the help of very tricky rules. Here is my favorite method in the RyuJIT implementation[15]:

```
// EstimateCodeSize: produce (various) code size estimates based on
// observations.
//
// The "Baseline" code size model used by the legacy policy is
// effectively
//
//   0.100 * m_CalleeNativeSizeEstimate +
//  -0.100 * m_CallsiteNativeSizeEstimate
//
// On the inlines in CoreCLR's mscorlib, release windows x64, this
// yields scores of R=0.42, MSE=228, and MAE=7.25.
//
// This estimate can be improved slightly by refitting, resulting in
//
//  -1.451 +
//   0.095 * m_CalleeNativeSizeEstimate +
//  -0.104 * m_CallsiteNativeSizeEstimate
//
// With R=0.44, MSE=220, and MAE=6.93.

void DiscretionaryPolicy::EstimateCodeSize()
{
// Ensure we have this available.
  m_CalleeNativeSizeEstimate = DetermineNativeSizeEstimate();

// Size estimate based on GLMNET model.
// R=0.55, MSE=177, MAE=6.59
//
// Suspect it doesn't handle factors properly...
// clang-format off
  double sizeEstimate =
```

---

[15].NET Core 2.2.0 version is presented. You can find the full source code here: https://github.com/dotnet/coreclr/blob/v2.2.0/src/jit/inlinepolicy.cpp

```
   -13.532 +
     0.359 * (int) m_CallsiteFrequency +
    -0.015 * m_ArgCount +
    -1.553 * m_ArgSize[5] +
     2.326 * m_LocalCount +
     0.287 * m_ReturnSize +
     0.561 * m_IntConstantCount +
     1.932 * m_FloatConstantCount +
    -0.822 * m_SimpleMathCount +
    -7.591 * m_IntArrayLoadCount +
     4.784 * m_RefArrayLoadCount +
    12.778 * m_StructArrayLoadCount +
     1.452 * m_FieldLoadCount +
     8.811 * m_StaticFieldLoadCount +
     2.752 * m_StaticFieldStoreCount +
    -6.566 * m_ThrowCount +
     6.021 * m_CallCount +
    -0.238 * m_IsInstanceCtor +
    -5.357 * m_IsFromPromotableValueClass +
    -7.901 * (m_ConstantArgFeedsConstantTest > 0 ? 1 : 0) +
     0.065 * m_CalleeNativeSizeEstimate;
// clang-format on

// Scaled up and reported as an integer value.
  m_ModelCodeSizeEstimate = (int)(SIZE_SCALE * sizeEstimate);
}
```

As you can see, this method contains a lot of "magic" numbers that are involved in the decision process. If you have a huge experience of reading generated native code for C# methods, you can guess which method will be inlined in some cases for a particular version of the JIT compiler. However, the inlining policy is evolving all the time, which means that these assumptions can obsolete in future versions of the JIT compiler.

Case Study 2: Register Allocation

In the previous section, we covered many cases in which we have a performance drop because the JIT compiler decides to use the stack instead of the register for some variables. Let's discuss one more case that involves inlining.

Source code

Consider the following BenchmarkDotNet-based benchmarks:

```
public class Benchmarks
{
  private const int n = 100;
  private bool flag = false;

  [Benchmark(Baseline = true)]
  public int Foo()
  {
    int sum = 0;
    for (int i = 0; i < n; i++)
    for (int j = 0; j < n; j++)
    {
      if (flag)
        sum += InlinedLoop();
      sum += i * 3 + i * 4;
    }
    return sum;
  }

  [Benchmark]
  public int Bar()
  {
    int sum = 0;
    for (int i = 0; i < n; i++)
    for (int j = 0; j < n; j++)
    {
      if (flag)
        sum += NotInlinedLoop();
```

```
      sum += i * 3 + i * 4;
    }
    return sum;
}

[MethodImpl(MethodImplOptions.AggressiveInlining)]
public int InlinedLoop()
{
    int sum = 0;
    for (int i = 0; i < 10; i++)
        sum += (i + 1) * (i + 2);
    return sum;
}

[MethodImpl(MethodImplOptions.NoInlining)]
public int NotInlinedLoop()
{
    int sum = 0;
    for (int i = 0; i < 10; i++)
        sum += (i + 1) * (i + 2);
    return sum;
}
}
```

Here we have two benchmarks, Foo and Bar, which perform some calculations in a loop. They don't calculate anything useful, but they will help us to show an interesting performance effect.

Both Foo and Bar have a call to another method with additional calculations. Foo calls InlinedLoop, which is marked with AggressiveInlining; Bar calls NotInlinedLoop, which is marked with NoInlining. The logic of InlinedLoop is identical to that of NotInlinedLoop; the only difference between them is the inlining policy.

The InlinedLoop and NotInlinedLoop calls are conditional: they will be performed only if flag == true. In our benchmarks, flag is always false, which means that we are not going to actually perform these calls. Since we don't actually call these methods, we may think that we shouldn't get any performance effects because of these calls. This is a valid assumption for some JIT compilers, but it's not always true.

Results

Here is an example of results (Windows 10.0.17763.195, Intel Core i7-6700HQ CPU 2.60GHz, .NET Framework 4.7.2, LegacyJIT-x86):

```
Method |      Mean |    StdDev | Ratio |
------- |----------:|----------:|------:|
   Foo | 23.403 us | 0.2643 us |  1.00 |
   Bar |  8.495 us | 0.0560 us |  0.36 |
```

As you can see, Foo (with an AggressiveInlining call) works three times slower than Bar (with a NoInlining call).

Explanation

Let's look at the generated native code for Foo (only the main part is presented):

```
; Foo
xor   ebx,ebx                  ; sum = 0
xor   ecx,ecx                  ; i = 0

LOOP1:
xor   edx,edx                  ; edx = 0
mov   dword ptr [ebp-10h],edx ; j = 0
mov   eax,dword ptr [ebp-18h] ; eax = &this
movzx eax,byte ptr [eax+4]     ; eax = flag
mov   dword ptr [ebp-14h],eax ; [ebp-14h] = flag

LOOP2:
cmp   dword ptr [ebp-14h],0    ; if (flag == false)
je    AFTER_CALL               ;   goto AFTER_CALL

xor   edi,edi                  ; <InlinedLoop Body>
xor   esi,esi                  ; <InlinedLoop Body>
lea   eax,[esi+1]              ; <InlinedLoop Body>
lea   edx,[esi+2]              ; <InlinedLoop Body>
imul  eax,edx                  ; <InlinedLoop Body>
add   edi,eax                  ; <InlinedLoop Body>
inc   esi                      ; <InlinedLoop Body>
```

```
cmp    esi,0Ah                     ; <InlinedLoop Body>
jl     014304A9                    ; <InlinedLoop Body>
add    ebx,edi                     ; sum += InlinedLoop();

AFTER_CALL:
lea    eax,[ecx+ecx*2]             ; eax = i * 3
add    eax,ebx                     ; eax += sum
lea    ebx,[eax+ecx*4]             ; sum = eax + i * 4

inc    dword ptr [ebp-10h]         ; j++
cmp    dword ptr [ebp-10h],64h     ; if (j < 100)
jl     LOOP2                       ;    goto LOOP2
inc    ecx                         ; i++
cmp    ecx,64h                     ; if (i < 100)
jl     LOOP1                       ;    goto LOOP1
```

As you can see, InlinedLoop was actually inlined (we asked the JIT compiler to do it via AggressiveInlining). The generated code for InlinedLoop is pretty efficient: it performs all the calculations using registers only. Unfortunately, this inlined snippet affected the rest of the method: the JIT compiler decided to keep the j loop counter on the stack (dword ptr [ebp-10h]).

Now let's look at the generated native code for Bar (only the main part is presented):

```
; Bar
xor    esi,esi                     ; sum = 0
xor    edi,edi                     ; i = 0

LOOP1:
xor    ebx,ebx                     ; j = 0

LOOP2:
mov    eax,dword ptr [ebp-10h]     ; eax = &this
cmp    byte ptr [eax+4],0          ; if (flag == false)
je     0143051A                    ;    goto AFTER_CALL

mov    ecx,dword ptr [ebp-10h]     ; ecx = &this
call   dword ptr ds:[1214D5Ch]     ; call NotInlinedLoop
add    esi,eax                     ; sum += NotInlinedLoop();
```

```
AFTER_CALL:
lea    eax,[edi+edi*2]          ; eax = i * 3
add    eax,esi                  ; eax += sum
lea    esi,[eax+edi*4]          ; sum = eax + i * 4

inc    ebx                      ; j++
cmp    ebx,64h                  ; if (j < 100)
jl     01430506                 ;    goto LOOP2
inc    edi                      ; i++
cmp    edi,64h                  ; if (i < 100)
jl     014304FE                 ;    goto LOOP1
```

It looks pretty similar to Foo, with two important differences. The first one: we have a direct call to NotInlinedLoop instead of the inlined body. The second one: both loop counters i and j are using registers edi and ebx. That's why it works faster than Foo: operations with registers are usually more efficient.

Discussion

If you remove the [MethodImpl(MethodImplOptions.AggressiveInlining)] attribute from the InlinedLoop method, it will not be inlined, and we will get the same duration for both methods. By default, LegacyJIT-x86 makes the right decision.

The preceding example looks too artificial because it doesn't calculate anything useful. We discussed it because it allows showing disadvantages of inlining with a small number of lines. In real life, such a situation can arise in pretty complicated pieces of code that are hard to analyze. In most simple examples, inlining usually improves performance (or just doesn't make it worse). It may create a false sense of confidence that inlining is always a good optimization.

Applying of AggressiveInlining for hot methods can improve performance, but you should be sure that it's a good idea (such a decision requires careful measurements). Mindless usage of AggressiveInlining on all methods can lead to serious performance problems that are really hard to find.

Case Study 3: Cooperative Optimizations

Inlining can be profitable for performance not only because of the call overhead elimination, but also because it can create opportunities for other optimizations.

Source code

Consider the following BenchmarkDotNet-based benchmarks:

```
public class Benchmarks
{
  private double x1, x2;

  [Benchmark(Baseline = true)]
  public double Foo()
  {
    return Calc(true);
  }

  public double Calc(bool dry)
  {
    double res = 0;
    double sqrt1 = Math.Sqrt(x1);
    double sqrt2 = Math.Sqrt(x2);
    if (!dry)
    {
      res += sqrt1;
      res += sqrt2;
    }

    return res;
  }

  [Benchmark]
  public double Bar()

  {
    return CalcAggressive(true);
  }

  [MethodImpl(MethodImplOptions.AggressiveInlining)]
  public double CalcAggressive(bool dry)
  {
    double res = 0;
    double sqrt1 = Math.Sqrt(x1);
```

431

```
    double sqrt2 = Math.Sqrt(x2);
    if (!dry)
    {
      res += sqrt1;
      res += sqrt2;
    }
    return res;
  }
}
```

Here we have the Calc method with a bool argument dry. When dry is true, this method returns zero. When dry is false, it returns the sum of square roots of the x1 and x2 fields. We also have the CalcAggressive method with the same implementation, but it's marked with [MethodImpl(MethodImplOptions.AggressiveInlining)]. Two benchmarks are presented: Foo, which calls Calc(true), and Bar, which calls CalcAggressive(true).

Results

Here is an example of results (Windows 10.0.17763.195, Intel Core i7-6700HQ CPU 2.60GHz, .NET Framework 4.7.2, LegacyJIT-x86):

```
Method |      Mean |    StdDev |
------- |----------:|----------:|
   Foo | 1.5214 ns | 0.0972 ns |
   Bar | 0.0000 ns | 0.0127 ns |
```

As we can see, Foo takes ~1.5 nanoseconds and Bar works almost instantly. How is that possible?

Explanation

Let's look at the native generated code for Foo:

```
; Foo
push   ebp
mov    ebp,esp
mov    edx,1
call   dword ptr ds:[0F94D50h]    ; call Calc
```

```
popebp
ret

; Calc
fldz                          ; load 0 into stack (res)
fld    qword ptr [ecx+4]      ; load x1 into registers
fsqrt                         ; sqrt(x1)
fld    qword ptr [ecx+0Ch]    ; load x2 into registers
fsqrt                         ; sqrt(x2)
and    edx,0FFh               ; if (!dry)
je     012C04BA               ;   goto SUM
fstp   st(0)                  ; discard sqrt2
fstp   st(0)                  ; discard sqrt1
jmp    FINISH                 ; goto FINISH
SUM:
fxch   st(1)                  ; swap FPU registers
faddp  st(2),st               ; res += sqrt1
faddp  st(1),st               ; res += sqrt2
FINISH:
ret                           ; return result
```

In the Foo method, we call Calc, which always calculates values of sqrt(x1) and sqrt(x2). Only after that does it check the dry value: if it's true, the calculated values are discarded.[16] In our benchmark, dry is always true, but the JIT compiler doesn't know about that. It will be better to move square root calculations inside the if (!dry) { } scope, but LegacyJIT-x86 is not smart enough: the generated code is pretty straightforward, and it exactly matches the original C# program.

Now let's look at the native generated code for Bar:

```
; Bar
push   ebp
mov    ebp,esp
cmp    byte ptr [ecx+4],al
fldz                          ; load 0 into stack (res)
```

---

[16]If you are not fully understand how FPU data registers (st(0), st(1), st(2)) work, it's
    recommended to read [FPUx87].

```
pop     ebp
ret
```

Because of the [MethodImpl(MethodImplOptions.AggressiveInlining)] attribute, LegacyJIT-x86 was able to inline CalcAggressive. After inlining, if (!dry) becomes if (false) (because dry is true), and the JIT compiler was able to completely eliminate this scope with res += sqrt1 and res += sqrt2 statements. After that, the sqrt1 and sqrt2 become unused variables and LegacyJIT-x86 decided to eliminate square root calculations as well. The final versions of the generated code (after all the optimizations) just return zero without any additional calculation.

In the BenchmarkDotNet output, we can also find the following warning for Bar: "The method duration is indistinguishable from the empty method duration." According to the BenchmarkDoNet approach, the duration of an empty method with matching signature (like double Empty() { return 0; }) is considered zero. The Bar method contains instructions that take some time, but these instructions are considered as the call overhead, which is automatically subtracted from the actual measurements. That's why we have 0 ns in the summary table.

Discussion

Cooperative optimizations are very powerful and they can significantly improve the performance of your applications. Unfortunately, it's not always easy to control them. In the preceding example, AggressiveInlining helped to get performance benefits from inlining and code elimination, which were working together on LegacyJIT-x86. However, you can't always predict how your current JIT compiler will process all usages of the inlined method. You can optimize your code with the help of AggressiveInlining in *some specific cases*, but you should be sure that it doesn't spoil your performance in other cases (like in the previous case study).

In the context of benchmarking, you should understand that cooperative optimizations are very fragile: any changes in the source code can enable or disable inlining policy for your methods and affect conditions for further optimizations.

Case Study 4: The "starg" IL Instruction

We already know that inlining has some limitations. For example, virtual or recursive methods can't be inlined. However, some of the inlining limitations are not so obvious (and, as usual, they can depend on the JIT compiler version).

Source code

Consider the following BenchmarkDotNet-based benchmarks:

```
public class Benchmarks
{
  [Benchmark]
  public int Calc()
  {
    return WithoutStarg(0x11) + WithStarg(0x12);
  }

  private static int WithoutStarg(int value)
  {
    return value;
  }

  private static int WithStarg(int value)
  {
    if (value < 0)
      value = -value;
    return value;
  }
}
```

In the Calc benchmark, we calculate the sum of two methods: WithoutStarg(0x11) and WithStarg(0x12). The WithoutStarg method just returns its argument. The WithStarg method also returns its argument, but it performs one additional check first: if the value is less than zero, it assigns -value back to this argument.

Results

Here is an example of results (Windows 10.0.17763.195, Intel Core i7-6700HQ CPU 2.60GHz, .NET Framework 4.7.2, LegacyJIT v4.7.3260.0):

Job	Mean	StdDev
LegacyJIT-x64	0.0000 ns	0.0000 ns
LegacyJIT-x86	1.7637 ns	0.0180 ns

435

As you can see, `Calc` works instantly on LegacyJIT-x64, but it takes a few nanoseconds on LegacyJIT-x86.

Explanation

We can find a hint which will help us to understand these results in the source code of the `Decimal` constructor from an integer value[17]:

```
public Decimal(int value) {
// JIT today can't inline methods that contains "starg" opcode.
// For more details, see DevDiv Bugs 81184: x86 JIT CQ:
// Removing the inline striction of "starg".
  int value_copy = value;
  if (value_copy >= 0) {
    flags = 0;
  }
  else {
    flags = SignMask;
    value_copy = -value_copy;
  }
  lo = value_copy;
  mid = 0;
  hi = 0;
}
```

Here we can see an interesting comment: it says that LegacyJIT-x86 can't inline methods that contain the `starg` opcode. It stores the value on top of the evaluation stack in the argument slot at a specified index.[18] The `Decimal` constructor is a small hot method in some programs, so it would be nice to inline it where it's possible. In order to avoid LegacyJIT-x86 inlining limitations, we don't have a `value = -value` assignment in this constructor. Instead, we have the `value_copy = -value_copy` assignment, which is performed on the `value` copy. This simple trick allows you to avoid the `starg` opcode on the IL level and to unblock inlining on LegacyJIT-x86.

---

[17]https://github.com/dotnet/coreclr/blob/v2.1.5/src/mscorlib/src/System/Decimal.cs#L157

[18]You can find more information in the official documentation: https://docs.microsoft.com/en-us/dotnet/api/system.reflection.emit.opcodes.starg

Now let's look at the IL code of the WithStarg method:

```
IL_0000: ldarg.0      // 'value'
IL_0001: ldc.i4.0
IL_0002: bge.s        IL_0008

IL_0004: ldarg.0      // 'value'
IL_0005: neg
IL_0006: starg.s      'value'

IL_0008: ldarg.0      // 'value'
IL_0009: ret
```

Here we have starg.s, which should block inlining of this method on LegacyJIT-x86. Let's check this hypothesis and look at the native code for this method:

```
; Calc/LegacyJIT-x86
push  ebp
mov   ebp,esp
mov   ecx,12h                      ; ecx = 12h
call  dword ptr ds:[11B4D74h]      ; call WithStarg
add   eax,11h                      ; eax += 11h
pop   ebp
ret                                ; return eax

; WithStarg/LegacyJIT-x86
mov   eax,ecx                      ; eax = 12h
test  eax,eax                      ; if (eax >= 0)
jge   FINISH                       ;    goto FINISH
neg   eax                          ; eax = -eax
FINISH:
ret                                ; return eax
```

As we can see, we pass 12h to the WithStarg method, get the returned value, add 11h to it, and return the sum. The WithoutStarg method was successfully inlined, so we don't see the corresponding call. The WithStarg method wasn't inlined and we can see its call overhead in the summary table (~1.8 ns).

Now let's look at the native code of this method on LegacyJIT-x64:

```
; Calc/LegacyJIT-x64
mov     eax, 12h
add     eax, 11h
ret
```

Both methods were inlined; `Calc` works almost instantly (we get the "method duration is indistinguishable from the empty method duration" message in the BenchmarkDotNet output).

Discussion

Sometimes, the JIT compiler has nonobvious conditions that prevent inlining. Different JIT compilers have their own sets of inlining heuristics, which can be changed after runtime update. When a JIT compiler fails to inline a method, we have a corresponding ETW event that contains the fail reason. You can get this information with the help of the BenchmarkDotNet [`InliningDiagnoser`] attribute: it will notify you about all failed inlining optimizations. For the preceding example, we will get the following message: "Fail Reason: Inlinee writes to an argument."

You can find more information about the discussed LegacyJIT-x86 limitation in [Akinshin 2015].

This case study is based on StackOverflow question 26369163.[19]

Summing Up

Inlining is a powerful optimization. Here are some facts about it that are good to know:

- Inlining is critical for hot methods that take a few nanoseconds. When such a method is inlined, the method call overhead is eliminated. This optimization may increase the throughput of such a method noticeably.

- You can disable inlining of a specific method with the help of the [`MethodImpl(MethodImplOptions.NoInlining)`] attribute. There

---

[19]https://stackoverflow.com/q/26369163

are some other implicit factors that automatically disable inlining (exception handling, recursion, virtual modifier, and others).

- You can't force the JIT compiler to always inline a method, but you can use the [MethodImpl(MethodImplOptions. AggressiveInlining)] attribute to ask the JIT compiler to inline some methods (if possible) that are not inlined by default. For example, the JIT compiler doesn't inline "huge" methods that contain "too many" IL opcodes (the "too many" threshold value depends on the specific JIT compiler implementation). In some cases, these "huge" methods can be inlined if AggressiveInlining is enabled.

- It's not recommended to mindlessly apply AggressiveInlining to all methods. In general, the JIT compilers knows better when the inlining will be profitable. In some cases, we can get performance benefits with AggressiveInlining, but it may lead to performance degradations in other cases.

- Inlining is more than just a call overhead elimination. It's especially profitable with other JIT compiler optimizations like constant folding or DCE. It also affects the register allocation: after inlining, the JIT compiler may get better or worse conditions for efficient register usage.

Knowledge about inlining is also important when you are writing handwritten benchmarks (which don't use BenchmarkDotNet or other benchmarking frameworks). Consider the following code:

```
void Main()
{
  // Start timer1
  for (int i = 0; i < n; i++)
    Foo();
  // Stop timer1

  // Start timer2
  for (int i = 0; i < n; i++)
    Bar();
  // Stop timer2
}
```

```
void Foo() { /* Benchmark body */ }
void Bar() { /* Benchmark body */ }
```

Here we want to compare the performance of Foo and Bar. Imagine that Foo was inlined in the Main method and Bar wasn't. Even if Foo is actually slower than Bar, we can get the opposite result because of inlining. This particular case can be fixed with the help of MethodImplOptions.NoInlining:

```
[MethodImpl(MethodImplOptions.NoInlining)]
void Foo() { /* Benchmark body */ }
[MethodImpl(MethodImplOptions.NoInlining)]
void Bar() { /* Benchmark body */ }
```

Now both methods will *not be* inlined, which means that competition conditions are "fairer." However, you can't always control attributes for all methods (especially if you want to benchmark methods from third-party assemblies). In this case, you can benchmark a delegate that contains a reference to the benchmarked method.[20]

However, this doesn't resolve all the issues. Imagine that a method is inlined in a real application, but it's not inlined in the corresponding benchmark because you did some minor code changes that hit the JIT compiler inlining limitations. In this case, the benchmark results are not relevant to the situation that we get in real life. If you are using BenchmarkDotNet, you can get information about failed inlining with the help of the [InliningDiagnoser] attribute. You can also manually get this information via corresponding ETW events.

Instruction-Level Parallelism

ILP is a powerful CPU technique that helps to improve the performance of your applications significantly. In this chapter, we will *not going* to discuss all the details of CPU internals: you don't need this information for benchmarking. In practice, it's enough just to know the general concepts. This knowledge will help you to design proper benchmarks and interpret the results correctly. If you want to know more about this topic, it's recommended to read [Hennessy 2011]. In this book, we are just going to

---

[20].NET Framework 4.7.2, .NET Core 2.2, and Mono 5.18 can't inline delegates.

discuss a series of case studies that demonstrate the performance effects of ILP on very simple benchmarks.

Let's discuss the main concept of the ILP. On the CPU level, we have different execution units that are responsible for the processing of different instructions. While one execution unit performs the current instruction, other units are usually idle. Since this is not an efficient way to utilize your CPU, modern hardware allows execution of several instructions in parallel. Here we are not talking about multithreading: the parallelization is performed for a single thread on a single CPU core.

One of the key ILP mechanism is the *out-of-order execution*: the CPU can "look forward" at the "future" instructions and process them in advance (at the same time as the current instruction).

Another important ILP mechanism is *instruction pipelining*. When CPU is executing an instruction, it's performing several execution "stages" (e.g., instruction fetching, instruction decoding, execution, writing results, and so on). When the first stages of the current instruction are already performed, we can start to perform these stages for the next instruction (we shouldn't wait until the current instruction is completely finished).

If you open [Agner Instructions] (a list of CPU instruction performance characteristics for different CPUs), you will see that typically we have two different metrics: *latency* and *reciprocal throughput* expressed in CPU cycles. Some examples of these values for Intel Skylake are presented in Table 7-1.

Table 7-1. *Latencies and Reciprocal Throughputs of some Skylake Instructions*

Instruction	Operands	Latency	Reciprocal throughput
MOV	r8/r16,r8/r16	1	0.25
MOVQ	x,x	1	0.33
POP	r	2	0.5
PUSH	r	3	1
VMASKMOVPS	m128,x,x	13	1
DPPS	x,x,i	13	1.5
DIV	r8	23	6
FBLD	m80	46	22
FRSTOR	m	175	175

For example, the latency of MOVQ x,x is one. It means that the duration of a single instruction (from start to end) takes one CPU cycle. The reciprocal throughput of this instruction is 0.33. This means that if we have a series of 3000 such instructions, they can be performed with 1000 CPU cycles (0.33 CPU cycles on average). However, it doesn't mean that we are able to perform a single instruction using 0.33 CPU cycles: it's impossible to execute any instruction faster than a single CPU cycle.

ILP allows getting better performance, but it makes it harder to measure individual instructions because any instruction has several performance metrics. Everything depends on *how we use* these instructions in our source code. In practice, the actual "average" instruction duration is between the latency and the reciprocal throughput. In some cases, it's even impossible to measure the latency correctly because it's impossible to write such a program that performs a series of the same instructions without ILP effects.

In this section, we are going to discuss four case studies that demonstrate how ILP may affect benchmark results.

Case Study 1: Parallel Execution

ILP is a common problem during benchmarking that may lead to incorrect result interpretation. Let's discuss a very simple example where this problem occurs.

Source code

Consider the following BenchmarkDotNet-based benchmarks:

```
public class Benchmarks
{
  private const int n = 10001;
  private int x = 3;

  [Benchmark(Baseline = true)]
  public int Div1()
  {
    int a = 1;
    for (int i = 0; i < n; i++)
    {
      a /= x;
    }
```

```
  return a;
}

[Benchmark]
public int Div2()
{
  int a = 1, b = 2;
  for (int i = 0; i < n; i++)
  {
    a /= x;
    b /= x;
  }
  return a + b;
}

[Benchmark]
public int Div3()
{
  int a = 1, b = 2, c = 3;
  for (int i = 0; i < n; i++)
  {
    a /= x;
    b /= x;
    c /= x;
  }
  return a + b + c;
}

[Benchmark]
public int Div4()
{
  int a = 1, b = 2, c = 3, d = 4;
  for (int i = 0; i < n; i++)
  {
    a /= x;
    b /= x;
    c /= x;
```

```
    d /= x;
  }
  return a + b + c + d;
}

[Benchmark]
public int Div5()
{
  int a = 1, b = 2, c = 3, d = 4, e = 5;
  for (int i = 0; i < n; i++)
  {
    a /= x;
    b /= x;
    c /= x;
    d /= x;
    e /= x;
  }
  return a + b + c + d + e;
}
}
```

Here we have five benchmarks. In each of them, we perform integer division operations in a loop. In Div1, all the divisions are performed with a single variable a. In Div2, the loop body contains two division operations with two independent variables a and b. In Div3, Div4, and Div5, we have three, four, and five operations on different variables.

Results

Here is an example of results (Windows 10.0.17763.195, Intel Core i7-6700HQ CPU 2.60GHz, .NET Framework 4.7.2, LegacyJIT-x64 v4.7.3260.0):

```
Method |    Mean   |   StdDev  | Ratio |
------- |---------:|----------:|------:|
  Div1 |   75.5 us | 0.2012 us |  1.00 |
  Div2 |   75.5 us | 0.2196 us |  1.00 |
  Div3 |   80.6 us | 0.3359 us |  1.07 |
  Div4 |  100.0 us | 0.3588 us |  1.33 |
  Div5 |  126.1 us | 0.4532 us |  1.67 |
```

As you can see, Div1 and Div2 have very similar durations. It may look strange because Div2 has two division operations instead of a single division in Div1. Div3 takes a little bit more time than Div2 (5 microseconds). Div4 takes 20 microseconds longer than Div3. Div5 takes 26 microseconds longer than Div5.

Explanation

Let's use Intel VTune Amplifier to get more metrics for our benchmarks. We write the Main method of the program in the following way:

```
var b = new Benchmarks();
b.Div1();
b.Div2();
b.Div3();
b.Div4();
b.Div5();
```

Also, we increase n to 100,000,000 (which will help to get meaningful results). Next, we profile this new program in the "Microarchitecture Exploration" mode. The results are presented in Figure 7-1.

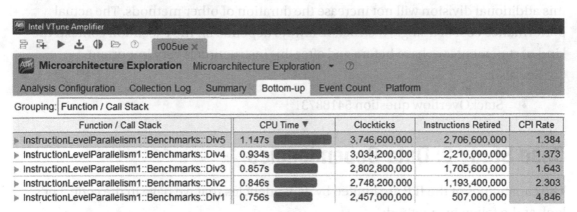

Figure 7-1. *VTune report for the "Parallel Execution" case study*

In this report, we can see three essential columns:

- Clockticks: how many CPU clock ticks were performed

- Instruction Retired: how many instructions were executed

- CPI Rate (cycles per instruction rate): how many CPU clock ticks were performed per instruction *on average*

445

The most interesting methods in the summary table are `Div1` and `Div2`, which have very similar durations. We have this situation because the CPU was able to perform `a /= x` and `b /=x` in parallel. Let's look at the VTune report again. The numbers of clock ticks for `Div1` and `Div2` are close to each other (they are not equal because the VTune profile session of a console application is not so accurate as BenchmarkDotNet execution toolchain). Meanwhile, the `CPI Rate` of `Div2` is two times lower than the `CPI Rate` of `Div1`. This means that we were able to execute two times more instructions at the same time.

`Div3` takes a little bit longer than `Div2` because we are too close to the parallelism capacity. When we continue to add additional division operations in `Div4` and `Div5`, the total duration noticeably increases because we reach the ILP capacity: we can't perform additional divisions in parallel with existing operations. The `CPI Rates` for `Div4` and `Div5` are almost the same, which proves that we hit the parallelism limitations.

Discussion

ILP helps to execute code faster, but it makes it harder to write proper benchmarks. Also, we can't extrapolate our conclusions to other benchmarks because of ILP. When we add an additional division operation in `Div1`, it doesn't increase the method duration. This doesn't mean that this operation is performed instantly. We can't expect that this additional division will not increase the duration of other methods. The actual performance cost of a single instruction always depends on the execution context: the kind of statements we have before and after this instruction is very important.

See also:

- StackOverflow question 54188731[21]

Case Study 2: Data Dependencies

The capabilities of the ILP are limited by dependencies that we have in the code. Let's look at the following method:

```
int Calc(int a, int b, int c)
{
  int d = a + b;
```

---

[21]https://stackoverflow.com/q/54188731

```
    int e = d * c;
    return e;
}
```

Here we can't execute both arithmetic operations (a + b and d * c) in parallel because the second operation depends on the result of the first operation. It's a pretty simple example of a *data dependency*. Let's look at an example that shows how such dependencies can affect benchmark results.

Source code

Consider the following BenchmarkDotNet-based benchmarks:

```
public class Benchmarks
{
    private int n = 1000001;
    private double x0, x1, x2, x3, x4, x5, x6, x7;

    [Benchmark(Baseline = true)]
    public void WithoutDependencies()
    {
        for (int i = 0; i < n; i++)
        {
            x0++; x1++; x2++; x3++;
            x4++; x5++; x6++; x7++;
        }
    }

    [Benchmark]
    public void WithDependencies()
    {
        for (int i = 0; i < n; i++)
        {
            x0++; x0++; x0++; x0++;
            x0++; x0++; x0++; x0++;
        }
    }
}
```

Here we have two methods: `WithoutDependencies` and `WithDependencies`. In both cases, we are performing eight `double` increments in a loop. In the first case (`WithoutDependencies`), we are incrementing eight *different variables*. In the second case (`WithDependencies`), we are incrementing *the same variable* eight times.

Results

Here is an example of results (macOS 10.14.2, Intel Core i7-4870HQ CPU 2.50GHz, .NET Core 2.1.3):

Method	Mean	StdDev	Ratio
WithoutDependencies	3.503 ms	0.0327 ms	1.00
WithDependencies	10.560 ms	0.1149 ms	3.02

As you can see, `WithoutDependencies` works three times faster than `WithDependencies`.

Explanation

The `WithoutDependencies` method works much faster because we don't have any dependencies between the increment statements and the ILP can improve the loop performance. In the `WithDependencies` method, there is a dependency between the subsequent increments: we should finish the previous statement before we start the next one. Thus, we can't improve the performance with the help of the ILP.

Discussion

You may ask: "How do we have to evaluate the *actual* duration of the `double` increment?" The right answer: there is no such thing as the *actual* duration of `double` increment. You may ask: "Which benchmark is the *correct* one?" The right answer: both benchmarks are *correct*, but they are measuring different things. The application performance depends on how we use these increments in the source code. Any data dependencies may limit the ILP and reduce the performance.

In the instruction tables (like [Agner Instructions]), we can find the latency and reciprocal throughput of some instructions, but these values will not help us to guess the performance metrics of a method without actual measurements (however, they can help us to make a hypothesis that explains these measurements). These values correspond to

the "corner cases," which are not useful in performance investigations without the full
source code.

Case Study 3: Dependency Graph

In the previous case study, it was obvious where we have data dependencies between
instructions. However, these dependencies are not always obvious at first sight. The
full data dependency graph may be pretty complicated, which makes it harder to guess
where the ILP can optimize our code.

Source code

Consider the following BenchmarkDotNet-based benchmarks:

```
public class Benchmarks
{
  private double[] a = new double[100];

  [Benchmark]
  public double Loop()
  {
    double sum = 0;
    for (int i = 0; i < a.Length; i++)
      sum += a[i];
    return sum;
  }

  [Benchmark]
  public double UnrolledLoop()
  {
    double sum = 0;
    for (int i = 0; i < a.Length; i += 4)
      sum += a[i] + a[i + 1] + a[i + 2] + a[i + 3];
    return sum;
  }
}
```

449

Here we have two benchmarks: Loop and UnrolledLoop. Both of them calculate the sum of elements in a double array. However, in the UnrolledLoop method we have the manual unrolling: instead of a single addition per loop iteration, we add four elements to sum each time. For simplification, we use a constant that is divided by four as the array length.

Results

Here is an example of results (macOS 10.14.2, .NET Core 2.1.3, Intel Core i7-4870HQ CPU 2.50GHz):

```
      Method |     Mean |    StdDev |
------------- |---------:|----------:|
        Loop | 82.04 ns | 1.3756 ns |
UnrolledLoop | 51.69 ns | 0.6441 ns |
```

As you can see, UnrolledLoop works ~30–40% faster.

Explanation

The addition of double values is not an associative operation. It means that (a + b) + c is not always equal to a + (b + c) (we will discuss this fact in detail in the "Arithmetic" section). Thus, the CPU is not allowed to reorder subsequent additions. It creates implicit dependencies between operations. You can see the dependency graphs in Figure 7-2 (the Loop graph is shown on the top half; the UnrolledLoop graph is shown on the bottom half).

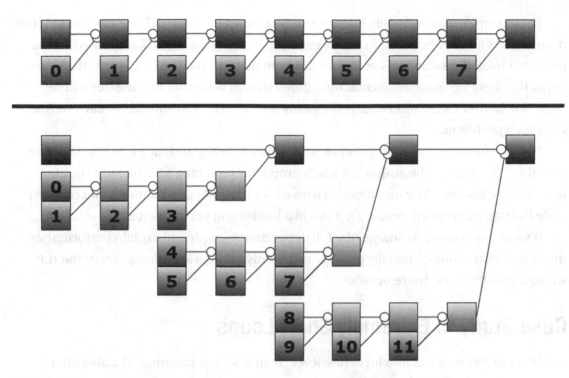

this figure will be printed in b/w

Figure 7-2. *visualization for the "Dependency Graph" case study*

In the Loop method, we have subsequent dependencies between all operations. On the first iteration, we should perform sum += a[0]. *Only after that,* we can perform sum += a[1]. This operation requires the value of sum after the first iteration: these additions can't be executed in parallel. *Only after the second operation,* we can perform the third one. There is no place for the ILP here: all the statements should be executed one after another.

The situation in the UnrolledLoop method is much better: the expressions a[0] + a[1] + a[2] + a[3] and a[4] + a[5] + a[6] + a[7] are independent: there are no dependencies between them. Thus, we can calculate the values of the a[i] + a[i + 1] + a[i + 2] + a[i + 3] expression from different iterations in parallel. Of course, we can't execute *all of them* in parallel because of the ILP limitations. However, the situation is still better than in the Loop case. That's why we have ~30–40% performance boost.

Discussion

In the discussed case studies, the dependencies between statements were pretty simple. In real applications, the dependency graph may be pretty complicated, which complicates the analysis. In some cases, we don't have dependencies on the C# level, but they exist on the native code level.

For example, in coreclr#993,[22] a performance problem in RyuJIT was discovered (this problem has already been fixed). In the example in this issue, RyuJIT generated native code that used the same register for two different operations. The CPU was not able to apply ILP there because the second operations should wait until this register will be "free" for further calculations. Such situations are rare, but you should be ready to work with such problems.

You can find another example of an unobvious data dependency in StackOverflow question 25078285.[23] The author got a 50% drop after replacing a 32-bit loop counter with a 64-bit counter. The investigation uses a C++ example and contains a lot of native code listings, but it worth reading it if you like interesting performance case studies.

It's not always easy to analyze the full dependency graph and explain performance measurements,[24] but it's usually possible using only general knowledge about the ILP without low-level hardware details.

Case Study 4: Extremely Short Loops

Modern hardware contains a lot of low-level "features" that can unpredictably affect your benchmarks. Let's discuss one more interesting example.

Source code

Consider the following program:

```
public class Program
{
  private static int n = 10000000;
  private static int rep = 100;

  static void Main()
  {
    MeasureAll();
    MeasureAll();
  }
}
```

---

[22]https://github.com/dotnet/coreclr/issues/993

[23]https://stackoverflow.com/q/25078285

[24]There are some tools that can do it for you. Here is a good example: https://godbolt.org/z/ba0ZWy.

```csharp
public static void MeasureAll()
{
  Measure("Loop 00", () => Loop00());
  Measure("Loop 01", () => Loop01());
  Measure("Loop 02", () => Loop02());
  Measure("Loop 03", () => Loop03());
  Measure("Loop 04", () => Loop04());
  Measure("Loop 05", () => Loop05());
  Measure("Loop 06", () => Loop06());
  Measure("Loop 07", () => Loop07());
}

public static void Measure(string title, Action action)
{
  var stopwatch = Stopwatch.StartNew();
  for (int i = 0; i < rep; i++)
    action();
  stopwatch.Stop();
  Console.WriteLine(title + ": " + stopwatch.ElapsedMilliseconds);
}

public static void Loop00()
{
  for (int i = 0; i < n; i++) { }
}

public static void Loop01()
{
  for (int i = 0; i < n; i++) { }
}

public static void Loop02()
{
  for (int i = 0; i < n; i++) { }
}
```

453

```
public static void Loop03()
{
  for (int i = 0; i < n; i++) { }
}

public static void Loop04()
{
  for (int i = 0; i < n; i++) { }
}

public static void Loop05()
{
  for (int i = 0; i < n; i++) { }
}

public static void Loop06()
{
  for (int i = 0; i < n; i++) { }
}

public static void Loop07()
{
  for (int i = 0; i < n; i++) { }
}
}
```

Here we have eight empty loops, which are measured with the help of a Stopwatch instance. We purposefully aren't using BenchmarkDotNet here, in order to completely eliminate the possibility of hitting unknown BenchmarkDotNet bugs. The performance effect that we are going to discuss is so noticeable that we can neglect good benchmarking practices like warm-up and distribution analysis.

Results

Here is an example of results (Windows 10.0.17763.195, Intel Core i7-6700HQ CPU 2.60GHz, .NET Framework 4.7.2, RyuJIT-x64):

```
Loop 00: 727
Loop 01: 352
```

```
Loop 02: 371
Loop 03: 369
Loop 04: 752
Loop 05: 352
Loop 06: 348
Loop 07: 349
Loop 00: 692
Loop 01: 344
Loop 02: 351
Loop 03: 349
Loop 04: 702
Loop 05: 345
Loop 06: 347
Loop 07: 351
```

As you can see, Loop00 and Loop04 work two times slower than other loops.

Explanation

I don't have a proper explanation for these results. Unfortunately, Intel keeps many low-level hardware features secret and doesn't include them in the official manuals. Anyway, this effect is pretty stable (I reproduced it on 30+ different computers), so it should be discussed. Here I want to share some of my investigation notes.

Observation 1.

This effect is valid only for RyuJIT-x64; it's not reproduced on LegacyJIT-x86, LegacyJIT-x64, or MonoJIT. RyuJIT generates the following code for the empty loop:

```
LOOP:
inc eax
cmp eax,edx
jl LOOP
```

I also have a reproduction case on pure assembly that proves that it's a CPU microarchitecture phenomenon (it's not affected by the .NET runtime). Also, it works the same way on Windows, Linux, and macOS (it's not affected by the operating system).

Observation 2.

This effect is valid only for Intel Haswell and subsequent Intel Core processor families like Broadwell, Skylake, and Kaby Lake. It's not reproduced on older processors like Sandy Bridge and Ivy Bridge.

Observation 3.

In the preceding example, we have "slow" and "fast" loops. The exact indexes of the slow loops depend on the memory layout of the generated native code. *Any changes* in the source code can change the layout and corresponding results. To be more specific, a loop is slow when the cmp/jl pair is placed on the border of two 64-byte segments like this:

```
00007FFEB1AF377C  inc  eax
00007FFEB1AF377E  cmp  eax,edx
00007FFEB1AF3780  jl   00007FFEB1AF377C
```

I checked a lot of different hypothesis including features of the instruction cache, MacroFusion,[25] and branch prediction,[26] but all of them were rejected.

Observation 4.

The CPI Rate for the fast loop is 0.333, which means that CPU executes all three instructions at one cycle. The CPI Rate for the slow loop is 0.666. That's why it works two times slower than the fast loops.

If you have any plausible explanations of this performance effect, please let me know.

Discussion

Despite the fact that I have no explanation for this effect, the effect does exist. It can easily spoil your nanobenchmarks if you don't know about it, because the actual performance depends not only on your source code, but also on the memory layout of the generated native code. Let's say we want to compare the performance of the two

---

[25]This kind of optimization can "join" the cmp and jl instruction into a single "macro instruction" that can be performed in one CPU cycle. We have the following sentence in the [Intel Manual] (section 2.3.2.1): "Macro fusion does not happen if the first instruction ends on byte 63 of a cache line, and the second instruction is a conditional branch that starts at byte 0 of the next cache line." It looks similar to our situation, but it's not the actual problem.

[26]We will discuss this in the next section.

methods, Foo and Bar, which take a few nanoseconds. In order to get reliable results, we wrap them in loops as follows:

```
for (int i = 0; i < n; i++)
  Foo();

for (int j = 0; j < n; j++)
  Bar();
```

If one loop will hit the border of the 64-byte segment, and another loop will not, the measurement will be spoiled by different ILP strategies. There is an approach to resolve this problem called loop unrolling. For example, we can rewrite the loop for the Foo method like this:

```
for (int i = 0; i < n / 16; i++)
{
  Foo(); Foo(); Foo(); Foo();
  Foo(); Foo(); Foo(); Foo();
  Foo(); Foo(); Foo(); Foo();
  Foo(); Foo(); Foo(); Foo();
}
```

In this case, we resolve the preceding ILP problem and reduce the loop overhead. This trick is used in BenchmarkDotNet by default, which allows getting reliable results even for nanobenchmarks. You can control the number of calls in the loop body with the help of UnrollFactor property (check out the official documentation for details); the default value is 16. If you are using your own short loops inside your benchmarks, BenchmarkDotNet will not protect you from this problem or other problems that are specific for short loops (e.g., see StackOverflow question 53695961[27]). When you have a high-speed operation inside a loop (which takes several nanoseconds), it's always recommended to unroll it manually.

Summing Up

The ILP is a common source of mistakes in benchmark result interpretation. The ability to execute several instructions of the same thread in parallel on the same CPU core is "hidden" from developers on the hardware level: you can't control it, and it's pretty hard to analyze how it affects your code.

---

[27]https://stackoverflow.com/q/53695961

In this section, we discussed four kinds of possible problems:

- We can observe no performance changes after adding a statement in the source code because it can be executed in parallel with existing instructions.

- The source code may contain dependencies between statements, which prevents ILP. Thus, you can have two benchmarks that perform the same number of native instructions but have different durations because of these dependencies.

- The data dependency graph may be pretty complicated because some of the dependencies can be implicit.

- The performance of a short loop can depend on the memory layout of the native code (which you can't control). Fortunately, it doesn't affect unrolled versions of this loops.[28]

You should understand that there are no incorrect benchmarks[29]; there are only incorrect interpretations of the benchmark results. Each benchmark is a program that prints some numbers. The task of a performance engineer is to combine these numbers with knowledge about the environment (hardware, operating system, runtime, and so on) and make correct conclusions about the measured code.

Branch Prediction

Branch prediction is another CPU technique that helps to increase possibilities for the ILP. We already know that the out-of-order execution helps to look at the further instructions and execute them ahead of time if it's possible. It works pretty well when we have a linear program without any branches. But what if we have a program like this:

---

[28]Here is a more correct version of this statement: "I had never observed situations when ILP affected huge loops *noticeably* in *simple* benchmarks." I'm sure that it's possible to find a specific case when it's important. However, you probably shouldn't worry about it because it's hard to hit such cases in real life. Meanwhile, the described problem with small loops actually affects many simple nanobenchmarks.

[29]Usually we say that a benchmark is incorrect when it doesn't measure the metrics that it has to measure.

```
if (flag)
  Foo();
else
  Bar();
```

It's impossible to actually perform Foo or Bar before we get the value of flag. Since a typical program contains a lot of if conditions, ternary operators, switch statements, and loops, it becomes pretty hard to get proper benefits from the out-of-order execution. The situation becomes much better with the help of the branch predictor. This is a part of the CPU that tries to guess which branch will be taken based on the previously evaluated condition values. Internally, this is a very complicated piece of hardware. We are not going to cover its internals because you don't need low-level knowledge of branch prediction algorithms in most cases. In practice, it's enough just to understand the basic concept. In this section, we will look at four case studies that show how the input data may affect the performance of the same program. This will help you to design better benchmarks based on the branches that you have in your code.

Case Study 1: Sorted and Unsorted Data

When we want to measure the duration of a method, we typically focus on the source code and the environment. However, there is one more performance space component that we usually forget: the input data. Let's look an example that shows how it can affect the performance metrics.

Source code

Consider the following BenchmarkDotNet-based benchmark:

```
public class Benchmarks
{
  private const int n = 100000;
  private byte[] sorted = new byte[n];
  private byte[] unsorted = new byte[n];

  [GlobalSetup]
  public void Setup()
  {
```

```
  var random = new Random(42);
  for (int i = 0; i < n; i++)
    sorted[i] = unsorted[i] = (byte) random.Next(256);
  Array.Sort(sorted);
}

[Benchmark(Baseline = true)]
public int SortedBranch()
{
  int counter = 0;
  for (int i = 0; i < sorted.Length; i++)
    if (sorted[i] >= 128)
      counter++;
  return counter;
}

[Benchmark]
public int UnsortedBranch()
{
  int counter = 0;
  for (int i = 0; i < unsorted.Length; i++)
    if (unsorted[i] >= 128)
      counter++;
  return counter;
}

[Benchmark]
public int SortedBranchless()
{
  int counter = 0;
  for (int i = 0; i < sorted.Length; i++)
    counter += sorted[i] >> 7;
  return counter;
}

[Benchmark]
public int UnsortedBranchless()
```

```
  {
    int counter = 0;
    for (int i = 0; i < unsorted.Length; i++)
      counter += unsorted[i] >> 7;
    return counter;
  }
}
```

Here we have two byte arrays: sorted and unsorted. Both arrays contain the same set of random elements in a different order: the sorted array contains sorted elements, and the unsorted array contains randomly shuffled elements. In the SortedBranch and UnsortedBranch benchmarks, we enumerate the corresponding arrays and calculate the number of elements that are greater than or equal to 128 with the help of a simple if statement like if (sorted[i] >= 128) counter++. In the SortedBranchless and UnsortedBranchless benchmarks, we perform the same logic, but instead of the if statement, we increment the counter by an expression like sorted[i] >> 7. When an array element is greater than or equal to 128, this expression will be equal to 1, which means that counter will be incremented by 1. When an array element is less than 128, this expression will be equal to 0, which means that counter will not be changed. As you can see, these algorithms are equivalent, but the last two benchmarks are branchless (the loop bodies don't contain any branches).

Results

Here is an example of results (macOS 10.14.2, Intel Core i7-4870HQ CPU 2.50GHz, .NET Core 2.1.3):

```
            Method |       Mean |    StdDev | Ratio |
------------------- |----------:|----------:|------:|
      SortedBranch |  65.75 us | 0.6622 us |  1.00 |
    UnsortedBranch | 424.04 us | 4.9999 us |  6.45 |
   SortedBranchless |  65.82 us | 0.4978 us |  1.00 |
 UnsortedBranchless |  65.03 us | 0.8578 us |  1.00 |
```

As you can see, SortedBranch works six to seven times faster than UnsortedBranch. Meanwhile, SortedBranchless and UnsortedBranchless have approximately the same duration.

Explanation

Let's imagine that the branch predictor is a small creature who is living inside the CPU. In our example, this creature will have a short memory: it will remember only the last value of the condition that it's trying to predict. It will always assume that the condition will have the same value we observed last time. Let's say it has to predict values of the a[i] >= 128 expression for the following small array: a = {0, 32, 64, 96, 128, 160, 192, 224}. In this case, this creature will perform the following chain of reasoning:

- a[0] >= 128 (it's **false** because a[0] == 0)

  *"I don't have a previous value of this condition. Probably, it's **false**."*

  The prediction is **correct**.

- a[1] >= 128 (it's **false** because a[1] == 32)

  *"Last time this expression was false. Probably, it's **false** again."*

  The prediction is **correct**.

- a[2] >= 128 (it's **false** because a[2] == 64)

  *"Last time this expression was false. Probably, it's **false** again."*

  The prediction is **correct**.

- a[3] >= 128 (it's **false** because a[3] == 96)

  *"Last time this expression was false. Probably, it's **false** again."*

  The prediction is **correct**.

- a[4] >= 128 (it's **true** because a[4] == 128)

  *"Last time this expression was false. Probably, it's **false** again."*

  The prediction is **incorrect**.

- a[5] >= 128 (it's **true** because a[5] == 160)

  *"Last time this expression was true. Probably, it's **true** again."*

  The prediction is **correct**.

- a[6] >= 128 (it's **true** because a[6] == 192)

*"Last time this expression was true. Probably, it's **true** again."*

The prediction is **correct**.

- a[7] >= 128 (it's **true** because a[7] == 224)

*"Last time this expression was true. Probably, it's **true** again."*

The prediction is **correct**.

Here we get seven of eight correct predictions. This is a pretty good result! Now let's do the same for another array which contains the same elements in another order: a = {224, 0, 192, 32, 160, 64, 128, 96}.

- a[0] >= 128 (it's **true** because a[0] == 224)

*"I don't have a previous value of this condition. Probably, it's **false**."*

The prediction is **incorrect**.

- a[1] >= 128 (it's **false** because a[1] == 0)

*"Last time this expression was true. Probably, it's **true** again."*

The prediction is **incorrect**.

- a[2] >= 128 (it's **true** because a[2] == 192)

*"Last time this expression was false. Probably, it's **false** again."*

The prediction is **incorrect**.

- a[3] >= 128 (it's **false** because a[3] == 32)

*"Last time this expression was true. Probably, it's **true** again."*

The prediction is **incorrect**.

- a[4] >= 128 (it's **true** because a[4] == 160)

*"Last time this expression was false. Probably, it's **false** again."*

The prediction is **incorrect**.

- a[5] >= 128 (it's **false** because a[5] == 64)

*"Last time this expression was true. Probably, it's **true** again."*

The prediction is **incorrect**.

- a[6] >= 128 (it's **true** because a[6] == 128)

  *"Last time this expression was false. Probably, it's **false** again."*

  The prediction is **incorrect**.

- a[7] >= 128 (it's **false** because a[7] == 96)

  *"Last time this expression was true. Probably, it's **true** again."*

  The prediction is **incorrect**.

In this case, all eight predictions are incorrect.

Of course, the real branch predictors are much smarter than our imaginary creature and they have much more memory for the condition value history. However, the general idea is the same: they try to predict future values based on existing observations. When these values follow a specific pattern (e.g., all of the values are equal), it's much easier to predict future values than when the values are completely random.

When the prediction is correct, we can evaluate the corresponding *correct* branch out of order and get noticeable performance benefits.

When the prediction is incorrect, we evaluate the corresponding *incorrect* branch out of order. When we get the actual value of the condition, we have to revert the evaluation results and evaluate another branch. Such a situation is known as *branch mispredict* and it has a huge performance penalty because we have to spend time on reverting existing results and evaluating another branch without out-of-order benefits.

That's why UnsortedBranch works so much slower than SortedBranch: when we are working with the unsorted array, we have a huge branch mispredict rate. We don't see a difference between the SortedBranchless and UnsortedBranchless benchmarks because both methods don't contain conditions which involve the array elements. They work as fast as SortedBranch because they don't have a performance penalty because of the branch mispredict.

Discussion

Branch prediction is another technique that's good for performance, but not so good for benchmarking. When you have branches in the source code, it's impossible to determine its "actual" duration in a specific environment in general because this duration depends on the input data. Proper benchmark design, in this case, requires checking different input patterns that can give you different measurements.

This case study is based on StackOverflow question 11227809.[30] In the most popular answer to this question, you can find another interesting branch prediction interpretation based on trains and railroad junctions.

Case Study 2: Number of Conditions

Let's say that we have a simple if/else block:

```
if (/* Expression */)
{
  /* Statement1 */
}
else
{
  /* Statement2 */
}
```

When we are working with C# source code, we often consider such expression as an atomic unit. On the C# level, we have exactly two possibilities: the expression is true (Statement1 should be executed) or the expression is false (Statement2 should be executed). This is a good mental model when we are thinking about the program logic. However, when we are thinking about performance and branch prediction, we can have more possibilities here in the case of a composite expression.

Source code

Consider the following BenchmarkDotNet-based benchmarks:

```
public class Benchmarks
{
  private const int n = 100000;
  private int[] a = new int[n];
  private int[] b = new int[n];
  private int[] c = new int[n];
```

---

[30]https://stackoverflow.com/q/11227809

```csharp
[Params(false, true)]
public bool RandomData;

[GlobalSetup]
public void Setup()
{
  if (RandomData)
  {
    var random = new Random(42);
    for (int i = 0; i < n; i++)
    {
      a[i] = random.Next(2);
      b[i] = random.Next(2);
      c[i] = random.Next(2);
    }
  }
}

[Benchmark(Baseline = true)]
public int OneCondition()
{
  int counter = 0;
  for (int i = 0; i < a.Length; i++)
    if (a[i] * b[i] * c[i] != 0)
      counter++;
  return counter;
}

[Benchmark]
public int TwoConditions()
{
  int counter = 0;
  for (int i = 0; i < a.Length; i++)
    if (a[i] * b[i] != 0 && c[i] != 0)
      counter++;
  return counter;
}
```

```
[Benchmark]
public int ThreeConditions()
{
  int counter = 0;
  for (int i = 0; i < a.Length; i++)
    if (a[i] != 0 && b[i] != 0 && c[i] != 0)
      counter++;
  return counter;
}
}
```

Here we have three int arrays, a, b, and c, and three benchmarks, OneCondition, TwoConditions, and ThreeConditions. All the benchmarks calculate the number of cases when a[i] != 0 && b[i] != 0 && c[i] != 0. In the ThreeConditions method, we just use this expression without any modifications. In the TwoConditions method, we replaced "a[i] != 0 && b[i] != 0" with "a[i] * b[i] != 0" (we assume that the element values are small enough and the multiplication can be evaluated without overflow). In the OneCondition method, we replaced the whole expression with "a[i] * b[i] * c[i] != 0".

Also, we have the RandomData parameter. When RandomData is true, we fill all arrays by random numbers from 0 to 1. When RandomData is false, we don't fill arrays, which means that all elements are zeros.

Results

Here is an example of results (macOS 10.14.2, Intel Core i7-4870HQ CPU 2.50GHz, .NET Core 2.1.3, RyuJIT-x64):

Method	RandomData	Mean	StdDev	Ratio
OneCondition	False	130.15 us	1.9242 us	1.00
TwoConditions	False	89.68 us	1.5718 us	0.69
ThreeConditions	False	58.51 us	0.4505 us	0.45
OneCondition	True	227.79 us	1.7919 us	1.00
TwoConditions	True	419.46 us	2.9244 us	1.84
ThreeConditions	True	717.50 us	6.7728 us	3.15

As you can see, when `RandomData` is false, `OneCondition` is the slowest benchmark, and `ThreeConditions` is the fastest one. When `RandomData` is true, we have the opposite situation: `OneCondition` is the fastest benchmark, and `ThreeConditions` is the slowest one.

Explanation

When `RandomData` is false, `OneCondition` is the slowest benchmark because it performs more operations than other benchmarks. The integer multiplication is a "heavy" operation; it takes much more time than a comparison of an integer number with zero or the && operation. `OneCondition` has two multiplications and one comparison; `TwoConditions` has one multiplication, two comparisons, and one && operation; `ThreeConditions` has three comparisons and two && operations. The methods with more multiplication operations take more time.

When `RandomData` is true, the branch prediction is starting to affect performance because we have a high branch mispredict rate. Instead of working with the whole expression, the branch prediction is trying to predict individual comparisons separately.

Now let's look at the `ThreeConditions` native code:

```
; ThreeConditions/RyuJIT-x64
sub     rsp,28h                         ; Move stack pointer
xor     eax,eax                         ; counter = 0
xor     edx,edx                         ; i = 0
mov     r8,qword ptr [rcx+8]            ; r8 = &a
cmp     dword ptr [r8+8],0              ; if (a.Length <= 0)
jle     FINISH                          ;   goto FINISH
START:
mov     r9,r8                           ; r9 = &a
cmp     edx,dword ptr [r9+8]            ; if (i >= a.Length)
jae     OUT_OF_RANGE                    ;   goto OUT_OF_RANGE
movsxd  r10,edx                         ; r10 = i
cmp     dword ptr [r9+r10*4+10h],0 ; if (a[i] == 0)
je      CONTINUE                        ;   goto CONTINUE
mov     r9,qword ptr [rcx+10h]          ; r9 = &b
cmp     edx,dword ptr [r9+8]            ; if (i >= b.Length)
jae     OUT_OF_RANGE                    ;   goto OUT_OF_RANGE
cmp     dword ptr [r9+r10*4+10h],0 ; if (b[i] == 0)
```

```
je      CONTINUE                    ;    goto CONTINUE
mov     r9,qword ptr [rcx+18h]      ; r9 = &c
cmp     edx,dword ptr [r9+8]        ; if (i >= c.Length)
jae     OUT_OF_RANGE                ;    goto OUT_OF_RANGE
cmp     dword ptr [r9+r10*4+10h],0  ; if (c[i] == 0)
je      CONTINUE                    ;    goto CONTINUE
inc     eax                         ; counter++
CONTINUE:
inc     edx                         ; i++
cmp     dword ptr [r8+8],edx        ; if (i < a.Length)
jg      START                       ;    goto START
FINISH:
add     rsp,28h                     ; Restore stack pointer
ret                                 ; return counter
OUT_OF_RANGE:
call    IndexOutOfRangeException    ; throw IndexOutOfRangeException
int     3                           ;
```

As you can see, inside the a[i] != 0 && b[i] != 0 && c[i] != 0 expression, we have six jump instructions! Three of them are range checks, which are always false in the preceding example. The other three jumps correspond to the a[i] != 0, b[i] != 0, and c[i] != 0 checks. First of all, the branch predictor should predict the value of a[i] != 0. If it is false, the whole expression is false. If it is true, the branch predictor should predict the value of b[i] != 0. If it is false, the whole expression is false. If it is true, the branch predictor should predict the value of c[i] != 0. Since all of the arrays contain random data, we will suffer from branch mispredict three times.

The mispredict penalty in this case is much bigger than the duration of a multiplication operation. That's why ThreeConditions is the slowest method. TwoConditions works faster because it suffers from mispredict two times. In the case of the OneCondition method, there is at most one branch mispredict per iteration.

Discussion

One of the most popular benchmarking goals is to determine which method is faster. Even if we know the exact environment, performance may still depend on the input data. As you can see, the OneCondition method can be the fastest one or the slowest one depending on the content of the arrays.

This case study is based on StackOverflow question 35531369.[31]

Case Study 3: Minimum

In this case study, we will try to measure the performance of two simple methods that calculate a minimum of two numbers. We will benchmark the two following implementations:

```
int MinTernary(int x, int y)
{
  return x < y ? x : y;
}

int MinBitHacks(int x, int y)
{
  return x & ((x - y) >> 31) | y & (~(x - y) >> 31);
}
```

The first implementation looks obvious, but it has one significant problem: it could suffer from branch mispredictions because of a condition in the expression. Fortunately, it is possible to rewrite it without a branch with the help of bit hacks.

Here we calculate (x-y); the sign of this expression depends on which number is less. Then, (x-y) >> 31 gives a bit mask that contains only zeros or ones. Next, we calculate an inverted mask: ~(x - y) >> 31. Now we and our operands and the corresponding bit masks (the minimum number get the 11...11 mask). That's all: the or operator returns the correct result. Here is an example for x=8 and y=3 (assuming 8-bit numbers):

```
Expression      | Binary   | Decimal
     x          | 00001000 | 8
       y        | 00000011 | 3
     x-y        | 00000101 | 5
    (x-y)>>31   | 00000000 | 0
   ~(x-y)>>31   | 11111111 | -1
x&( (x-y)>>31)  | 00000000 | 0
y&(~(x-y)>>31)  | 00000011 | 3
Result          | 00000011 | 3
```

---

[31]https://stackoverflow.com/q/35531369

As you can see, there is no branch here: we compute the minimum using only bit operations.

Source code

Consider the following BenchmarkDotNet-based benchmarks:

```
public class Benchmarks
{
  const int N = 100001;

  private int[] a = new int[N];
  private int[] b = new int[N];
  private int[] c = new int[N];

  [Params(false, true)]
  public bool RandomData;

  [GlobalSetup]
  public void Setup()
  {
    if (RandomData)
    {
      var random = new Random(42);
      for (int i = 0; i < N; i++)
      {
        a[i] = random.Next();
        b[i] = random.Next();
      }
    }
  }

  [Benchmark]
  public void Ternary()
  {
    for (int i = 0; i < N; i++)
    {
      int x = a[i], y = b[i];
```

471

```
    c[i] = x < y ? x : y;
  }
}

[Benchmark]
public void BitHacks()
{
  for (int i = 0; i < N; i++)
  {
    int x = a[i], y = b[i];
    c[i] = x & ((x - y) >> 31) | y & (~(x - y) >> 31);
  }
}
}
```

Here we have two benchmarks, Ternary and BitHacks, which put the minimum value of a[i] and b[i] to c[i] in a loop. Each benchmark has its own way to calculate the minimum: Ternary uses the ternary operations (with a branch), and BitHacks uses bit hacks (without branches).

Also, we have the RandomData parameter. When RandomData is true, we fill the a and b arrays with random numbers. When RandomData is false, we don't fill arrays, which means that all elements are zeros.

Results

Here is an example of results (Windows 10.0.17763.195, Intel Core i7-6700HQ CPU 2.60GHz, .NET Framework 4.7.2 (JIT 4.7.3260.0); Mono x64 5.180.225):

Method	Job	RandomData	Mean	StdDev
Ternary	LegacyJitX64	False	136.0 us	1.9197 us
BitHacks	LegacyJitX64	False	170.3 us	1.1214 us
Ternary	LegacyJitX86	False	142.3 us	1.2358 us
BitHacks	LegacyJitX86	False	177.6 us	1.6017 us
Ternary	Mono	False	157.8 us	1.3883 us
BitHacks	Mono	False	231.0 us	4.5545 us
Ternary	RyuJitX64	False	126.0 us	1.4962 us

BitHacks	RyuJitX64	False	172.8 us	1.9703 us
Ternary	LegacyJitX64	True	498.2 us	4.3987 us
BitHacks	LegacyJitX64	True	171.4 us	0.9027 us
Ternary	LegacyJitX86	True	577.1 us	5.5484 us
BitHacks	LegacyJitX86	True	179.5 us	1.4957 us
Ternary	Mono	True	159.3 us	1.2456 us
BitHacks	Mono	True	229.0 us	2.0781 us
Ternary	RyuJitX64	True	504.3 us	5.2434 us
BitHacks	RyuJitX64	True	173.1 us	1.0211 us

And here are the mean values regrouped into a better summary table (without information about the standard deviation):

	RandomData=False		RandomData=True	
	Ternary	BitHacks	Ternary	BitHacks
LegacyJIT-x86	142.3 us	177.6 us	577.1 us	179.5 us
LegacyJIT-x64	136.0 us	170.3 us	498.2 us	171.4 us
RyuJIT-x64	126.0 us	172.8 us	504.3 us	173.1 us
Mono	157.8 us	231.0 us	159.3 us	229.0 us

When RandomData is false, the BitHacks method always works more slowly than Ternary. When RandomData is true, the BitHacks method works faster on LegacyJIT-x86, LegacyJIT-x64, RyuJIT-x64, but not on Mono.

Explanation

First of all, let's discuss the situation on .NET Framework (LegacyJIT-x86, LegacyJIT-x64, RyuJIT-x64). When RandomData is false, BitHacks works more slowly than Ternary because it contains more instructions. When RandomData is true, Ternary gets a performance penalty because of the branch mispredicts. The BitHacks method duration is not affected by the RandomData value because it doesn't contain conditional logic in the loop body.

473

The situation becomes much more interesting on Mono. We can make a few interesting observations about it:

- Ternary always works faster than BitHacks on Mono (even when RandomData is true).

- Mono version of the Ternary method works much faster than the same code on .NET Framework when RandomData is true.

- We get approximately the same duration for RandomData=False and RandomData=True on Mono for both benchmarks.

Let's look at the native code. For simplification, we will look at the generated code for MinTernary and MinBitHacks methods. Here is the corresponding listing for RyuJIT-x64:

```
; MinTernary/RyuJIT-x64
cmp  edx,r8d ; if (x < y)
jl   LESS    ;   goto LESS
mov  eax,r8d ; result = y
ret          ; return y
LESS:
mov  eax,edx ; result = x
ret          ; return x
```

This looks very straightforward: we just compare x and y and return the minimum value. Now let's look at the same method on Mono:

```
; MinTernary/Mono5.180.225-x64
sub     $0x18,%rsp      ; move stack pointer
mov     %rsi,(%rsp)     ; save rsi on stack
mov     %rdi,0x8(%rsp)  ; save rdi on stack

mov     %rdx,%rdi       ; rdi = x
mov     %r8,%rsi        ; rsi = y
cmp     %esi,%edi       ; compare x and y
mov     %rsi,%rax       ; rax = rsi (y)
cmovl   %rdi,%rax       ; rax = rdi (x) if (x < y)

mov     (%rsp),%rsi     ; restore rsi from stack
mov     0x8(%rsp),%rdi  ; restore rdi from stack
```

```
add     $0x18,%rsp      ; restore stack pointer
retq                    ; return rax
```

Here Mono uses the *Conditional move* (the cmovl instruction). The cmovl %rdi,%rax moves the value from %rdi to %rax only if the previous cmp instruction "decided" that x < y. The execution of the cmovl instruction is not affected by the branch predictor. The mono implementation of Ternary doesn't have branch mispredict performance penalty because there is no branch on the native code level (despite the fact that we have a condition in the source C# code).

Now we can explain our observation. The RandomData value doesn't have a performance impact on the Ternary and BitHacks methods on Mono because neither of them contain branches. The BitHacks method takes more time than the Ternary method because it contains more "heavy" instructions. The Ternary method works faster on Mono than on .NET Framework when RandomData is true because the Mono implementation doesn't actually have branches (.NET Framework implementation contains the jmp instruction) and it doesn't have the branch mispredict penalty.

Discussion

All of the main performance space components (source code, environment, input data) are important. In the preceding example, we can't say which method (Ternary or BitHacks) is faster: the performance depends on the environment and the input data at the same time. Even if you see an if statement in a C# program, it doesn't mean that you will get a real branch on the native code level: everything depends on the C# and JIT compilers.

Branchless versions of different algorithms may look interesting because they are not affected by branch mispredict. This makes it easier to analyze the performance of such methods (we shouldn't enumerate different input data sets).

There is a cool project called movfuscator[32] that can transform a program into a series of the mov instructions. Both programs (the original one and its movfuscated version) are equivalent. From the academic point of view, it's a very interesting project because it allows making branchless versions of any program. Unfortunately, the movfuscated programs are superslow, which makes them unusable.[33]

---

[32]https://github.com/xoreaxeaxeax/movfuscator

[33]You can try to play in the branchless DOOM; the source code can be found here: https://github.com/xoreaxeaxeax/movfuscator/tree/master/validation/doom. It takes approximately 7 hours to render a single frame.

See also:

- coreclr#21615[34]: "Branchless TextInfo.ToLowerAsciiInvariant / ToUpperAsciiInvariant"

This case study is based on [Akinshin 2016a].

Case Study 4: Patterns

In the first branch prediction case study ("Sorted and Unsorted Data"), we imagined that the branch predictor is a creature who remembers only the latest evaluated value of each condition. The real branch predictors are much smarter; they can perform correct predictions even if the data follows a specific pattern.

Source code

Consider the following BenchmarkDotNet-based benchmark:

```
public class Benchmarks
{
  private int[] a = new int[100001];

  [Params(
    "000000000000",
    "000000000001",
    "000001000001",
    "001001001001",
    "010101010101",
    "random"
    )]
  public string Pattern;

  [GlobalSetup]
  public void Setup()
  {
    var rnd = new Random(42);
```

```
  for (int i = 0; i < a.Length; i++)
    a[i] = Pattern == "random"
      ? rnd.Next(2)
      : Pattern[i % Pattern.Length] - '0';
}

[Benchmark(Baseline = true)]
public int Run()
{
  int counter = 0;
  for (int i = 0; i < a.Length; i++)
    if (a[i] == 0)
      counter++;
    else
      counter--;
  return counter;
}
}
```

Here we have an int array that is filled by zeros and ones according to the specified pattern. In the only benchmark, we compare each element of the array with zero: if it equals to zero, we increment counter; otherwise, we decrement counter. Thus, the numbers of instruction are the same for all kinds of patterns.

Results

Here is an example of results (macOS 10.14.2, Intel Core i7-4870HQ CPU 2.50GHz, .NET Core 2.1.3):

Pattern	Mean	StdDev	Ratio
000000000000	86.30 us	0.5490 us	1.00
000000000001	90.75 us	0.5556 us	1.05
000001000001	95.63 us	0.4887 us	1.11
001001001001	109.50 us	0.5972 us	1.27
010101010101	141.40 us	0.4198 us	1.64
random	434.80 us	3.5712 us	5.04

As you can see, the benchmark with the 000000000000 pattern is the fastest one, and the benchmark with the random pattern is the slowest one.

Explanation

The branch predictor provides the best performance when all of the condition values are the same. In this case, we don't have branch mispredict at all. When the pattern is random, we have the highest branch mispredict rate (and the worst performance) because it's pretty hard to predict random values. We also have some "intermediate" results between these two cases: the branch predictor is able to "recognize" some specific patterns. In the preceding example, the worst pattern is 010101010101 because the predicted value is changing on each iteration. However, the benchmark with this pattern still works three times faster than the random case.

Discussion

If you want to know more about branch prediction internals, it's recommended to read [Intel Manual], [Rohou 2015], [Edelkamp 2016], [Luu 2017], and [Mittal 2018]. The branch predictor is a very complicated part of CPU; different CPU models have different branch prediction algorithms. They may involve some unobvious factors; some parts of these algorithms can be kept secret. Here is a quote from [Agner Microarch]:

> 3.8 Branch prediction in Intel Haswell, Broadwell and Skylake
>
> The branch predictor appears to have been redesigned in the Haswell, but very little is known about its construction.
>
> The measured throughput for jumps and branches varies between one branch per clock cycle and one branch per two clock cycles for jumps and predicted taken branches. Predicted not taken branches have an even higher throughput of up to two branches per clock cycle.
>
> The high throughput for taken branches of one per clock was observed for up to 128 branches with no more than one branch per 16 bytes of code. If there is more than one branch per 16 bytes of code then the throughput is reduced to one jump per two clock cycles. If there are more than 128 branches in the critical part of the code, and if they are spaced by at least 16 bytes, then

apparently the first 128 branches have the high throughput and the remaining have the low throughput.

These observations may indicate that there are two branch prediction methods: a fast method tied to the μop cache and the instruction cache, and a slower method using a branch target buffer.

As you can see, it's pretty hard to learn all the details of branch predictor internals on all existing CPUs. However, you usually don't need this knowledge in practice: you can design great benchmarks and analyze the results correctly with the help of the core concept of branch prediction.

Summing Up

Branch prediction increases the power of the ILP capabilities near branches. Here are some conclusions based on the discussed case studies:

- Performance depends on the input data. Even if we perform the same number of instructions each time, a method duration may be different depending on the branch conditions.

- If we have a composite expression like "a && b && c" as a branch condition, we can consider it as an atomic unit in the C# code flow. On this level, we have only two options: the expression is true (and we take the branch) or the expression is false (and we don't take the branch). However, it's translated to three jump instructions on the native code level. This, the branch predictor has to perform three independent predictions. In the worst case, we can get three branch mispredictions for this expression.

- Even if you have an explicit branch on the C# level (e.g., an if statement or an expression with the ternary operator), some JIT compilers can be smart enough to replace it with a branchless native implementation. In this case, the code execution will not be affected by random data because the branch predictor has nothing to predict.

- Usually, the best case for a branch predictor is a situation when the branch condition has the same value all the time. The worst case is a situation when the branch condition values are random. However, there are a lot of "intermediate" cases: modern branch predictors are able to "recognize" some regular patterns and provide good performance. It will be still worse than the best case, but it can be much better than the worst case with random data.

When you are designing a benchmark with branches, you should carefully check different input data patterns. Of course, you shouldn't enumerate all kinds of patterns for each condition in each benchmark. Usually, it's enough to check the best case (all condition values are the same), the worst case (all condition values are random), and some real cases (with data from real-life scenarios). Typically, these cases provide enough measurements for conclusions.

Arithmetic

Arithmetic operations like addition and multiplication are very common in many kinds of programs. It's very easy to use them, but it's not so easy to benchmark them (especially when the calculations involve floating-point numbers).

Usually, we skip low-level explanations of different effects because you don't actually need them during benchmarking. In this section, we have to briefly discuss operations with floating-point types like `float`, `double`, and `decimal`: it will help to understand some performance results of benchmarks that involve arithmetic operations.

The `float` and `double` types follow the IEEE 754 standard, which states that a floating-point number is represented by a *sign S*, an *exponent E*, and a *mantissa M* which can be converted to the real value by the following rule:

$$V = \left(-1\right)^{s} \cdot \mathbf{1}.M \cdot 2^{E - E_{bias}}$$

After this formula, most developers stop reading texts about floating-point numbers because things become too complicated and confusing. Instead of the classic theory, we will use another approach, which was introduced in [Sanglard 2017] by Fabien Sanglard. According to the *Sanglard interpretation*, a floating-point number is represented by a *sign*, a *window* between two consecutive powers of two, and an *offset* within that window. All numbers can be splitted into nonoverlapped intervals (windows): [0.125; 0.25), [0.25; 0.5), [0.5; 1), [1; 2), [2; 4), and so on. Each window also can be split into nonoverlapped subintervals (buckets). If we want to convert a number to the IEEE 754 notation, we should find the window that contains this number. The index of the window is the exponent value. Next, we should find the bucket inside the window that contains the number. The bucket index (offset) is the mantissa value. If the number is negative, we should do the same for the absolute value of this number and put 1 in the sign bit.

Unfortunately, we can't represent every real number in computer memory: the range and the precision depends on the number of bits that we have. In Table 7-2, you can see the main characteristics of the 32-bit, 64-bit, and 80-bit floating-point numbers.

Table 7-2. *Characteristics of the Floating-Point Numbers*

	Sign	Exponent	Mantissa	Digits	Lower	Upper	E_{bias}
32bit	1	8	23	≈7.2	$1.2 \cdot 10^{-38}$	$3.4 \cdot 10^{+38}$	127
64bit	1	11	52	≈15.9	$2.3 \cdot 10^{-308}$	$1.7 \cdot 10^{+308}$	1023
80bit	1	15	64	≈19.2	$3.4 \cdot 10^{-4932}$	$1.1 \cdot 10^{+4932}$	16383

For example, a 32-bit number contains 1 bit for the sign, 8 bits for the exponent, and 23 bits for the mantissa. It's enough to represent numbers from $1.2 \cdot 10^{-38}$ to $3.4 \cdot 10^{+38}$, but we can keep approximately 7.2 digits for each number.

Let's do a simple exercise and calculate the real value of the following IEEE 754 32-bit number[35]:

```
Sign Exponent                Mantissa
 0 10011100 11011100110101100101001
```

- The sign *S* is zero, which means that the number is positive (1 denotes negative numbers).

- The exponent *E* is $10011100_2 10011100_2$ or 156_{10}. In order to find the window, we should subtract E_{bias} from it: this trick helps to encode very small and very huge numbers using a non-negative number as an exponent. For 32-bit numbers, $E_{bias} = 127$(see Table 7-2), $E - E_{bias} = 156 - 127 = 29$. Thus, our window is $[2^{29}; 2^{30}]$ or [536,870,912; 1,073,741,824].

---

[35]You can explore the details of this number here: `https://float.exposed/0x4e6e6b29`

- The mantissa M is $11011100110101100101001_2 1101110011010110$
  0101001_2 or $7{,}236{,}393_{10}$. Since we have 23 bits in the mantissa, the
  window should be divided into 2^{23} (8,388,608) buckets; the index of
  our bucket (the offset within the window) is 7,236,393.

Our window is [536,870,912; 1,073,741,824]. If we split into 2^{23} subintervals, we get 64
as the bucket size. Since we know the bucket index (the offset), we can easily calculate
the value:

$$V = 536\ 870\ 912 + 64 \cdot 7236393 = 1\ 000000064$$

The same value can be obtained with the classic formula. In this formula, we use $\mathbf{1}.M$
because the mantissa has the leading 1 by default; it helps to save one bit in memory.
The value of $1.M$ is $1.11011100110101100101001_2$ or $15'625'001_{10} \cdot 2^{-23}$. Thus, we get:

$$V = (-1)^0 \cdot \left(15\ 625\ 001 \cdot 2^{-23}\right) \cdot 2^{156-127} = 15\ 625\ 001 \cdot 2^6 = 1\ 000\ 000\ 064$$

In .NET, we have only two native types that follow the IEEE 754 representation: float
(32-bit) and double (64-bit). .NET doesn't have a type for 80-bit floating-point numbers,
but the runtime still can use such values for intermediate calculations. There is one
additional standard type that can handle real values: decimal (128-bit). However, this
is not a native type; it's a struct. It has a custom implementation, based on four int
fields,[36] which doesn't follow the IEEE 754 standard. It was designed for financial and
monetary calculations. In C#, you can specify the type that you want to use with the help
of special postfix: 1.0f is float, 1.0d is double, 1.0m is decimal.

Each floating-point type has its own set of "features." For example, if we convert
1,000,000,064 to float and print it in the 10-digit form (((float)1000000064).
ToString("G10")), we will get 1000000060 instead of 1000000064. Despite the fact that
1,000,000,064 is perfectly represented in IEEE 754, the runtime rounds it because the
float precision is not enough to handle 10-digit numbers. This number can be perfectly
represented in decimal. Another interesting fact: 1000000064.00m.ToString() will print
1000000064.00 because decimal keeps the knowledge about two zeros after the decimal
point. You can find more interesting facts about decimals in [Skeet 2008].[37]

---

[36]You can find its source code here: https://referencesource.microsoft.com/#mscorlib/
system/decimal.cs

[37]You can also find it here: http://csharpindepth.com/Articles/General/Decimal.aspx

On the hardware level, there are several sets of instructions that can operate with IEEE 754 numbers. The first x86-compatible instruction set that supports IEEE 754 is x87: it was introduced in the first math coprocessor by Intel: Intel 8087. Later, Intel designed other instruction sets like SSE and AVX, which also support IEEE 754 operations.

Different JIT compilers use different sets of instructions for `float` and `double` operations. For example, LegacyJIT-x86 knows how to work only with x87. LegacyJIT-x64 is better; it knows how to work with SSE (if it's available). RyuJIT is even better; it knows how to work with AVX (if it's available).

Most of the classic arithmetic rules don't work with floating-point numbers. Here is one of the most famous IEEE 754 equations[38]:

$$0.1d + 0.2d \neq 0.3d$$

We have such situations because `0.1d`, `0.2d`, and `0.3d` can't be perfectly presented in IEEE 754 notation:

```
0.1d ~ 0.1000000000000000055511151231257833
+0.2d ~ 0.2000000000000000011102230246251565
-------------------------------------------
         0.3000000000000000044408920985006262

  0.3d ~ 0.2999999999999999888977697537484355
```

Many arithmetic rules don't work with `float` and `double` in general: $(a + b) + c \neq a + (b + c)$, $(a \cdot b) \cdot c \neq a \cdot (b \cdot c)$, $(a + b) \cdot c \neq a \cdot c + b \cdot c$, $a^{x+y} \neq a^x \cdot a^y$, and so on. Such behavior is not surprising for people who know IEEE 754. However, there is an important fact about floating-point numbers in .NET that developers usually don't know: operations with `float` and `double` are nondeterministic. This means that the same program can produce different floating-point results under different conditions.

Here is my favorite example from [Skeet 2008][39]:

```
static float Sum(float a, float b) => a + b;
static float x;
static void Main()
{
```

---

[38]See also: https://0.30000000000000004.com/

[39]You can also find it here: http://csharpindepth.com/Articles/General/FloatingPoint.aspx

```
        x = Sum(0.1f, 0.2f);
float y = Sum(0.1f, 0.2f);
Console.WriteLine(x == y);
// y = y + 1;
// Console.WriteLine(y);
// GC.KeepAlive(y);
}
```

It seems that this program should always print True. However, LegacyJIT-x86 will prints True only in the DEBUG mode; in the RELEASE mode, we will get False. How is that possible? We can find a clue in the specifications:

> ECMA-335, I.12.1.3 "Handling of floating-point data types"
>
> The nominal type of the variable or expression is either *float32* or *float64*, but its value **can be represented internally with additional range and/or precision**.

In the RELEASE mode, LegacyJIT-x86 uses an 80-bit floating-point number for y. We don't have the 80-bit floating-point type in .NET, but the runtime can use it for intermediate calculations. If you uncomment one of the commented lines, it may force LegacyJIT-x86 to use float for y, which changes the program output.

If you want to understand all nuances of using floating-point types, it's recommended to read [Goldberg 1991].

Case Study 1: Denormalized Numbers

Let's continue to talk about IEEE754. In Table 7-3, you can see the lower window bound, the upper window bound, and the bucket size for different exponent values in the context of 32-bit numbers.

Table 7-3. *Windows for 32-Bit Floating-Point Numbers*

E	Lower	Upper	Bucket size
254	$2^{127} = 1.7 \cdot 10^{38}$	$2^{128} = 3.4 \cdot 10^{38}$	$2^{104} = 2.0 \cdot 10^{31}$
253	$2^{126} = 8.5 \cdot 10^{37}$	$2^{127} = 1.7 \cdot 10^{38}$	$2^{103} = 1.0 \cdot 10^{31}$
128	$2^{1} = 2$	$2^{2} = 4$	$2^{-22} = 2.4 \cdot 10^{-7}$
127	$2^{0} = 1$	$2^{1} = 2$	$2^{-23} = 1.2 \cdot 10^{-7}$
3	$2^{-124} = 4.7 \cdot 10^{-38}$	$2^{-123} = 9.4 \cdot 10^{-38}$	$2^{-147} = 5.6 \cdot 10^{-45}$
2	$2^{-125} = 2.4 \cdot 10^{-38}$	$2^{-124} = 4.7 \cdot 10^{-38}$	$2^{-148} = 2.8 \cdot 10^{-45}$
1	$2^{-126} = 1.2 \cdot 10^{-38}$	$2^{-125} = 2.4 \cdot 10^{-38}$	$2^{-149} = 1.4 \cdot 10^{-45}$
0	0	$2^{-126} = 1.2 \cdot 10^{-38}$	$2^{-149} = 1.4 \cdot 10^{-45}$

All the exponents follow the same rule except the last one ($E=0$). When the exponent equals to zero, we get an additional window that covers numbers from zero to 2^{-126}; the bucket size is 2^{-149} (we have the same value in the $E=1$ case). These numbers (except zero) are known as *denormalized numbers*. Typically, operations with denormalized numbers have serious performance issues. Let's learn how serious they can be by an example.

Source code

Consider the following BenchmarkDotNet-based benchmark:

```
public class Benchmarks
{
  [Params(100000, 1000000)]
  public int N;

  [Benchmark]
  public double PowerA()
  {
    double res = 1.0;
    for (int i = 0; i < N; i++)
      res = res * 0.96;
    return res;
  }
}
```

```
  private double resB;

  [Benchmark]
  public double PowerB()
  {
    resB = 1.0;
    for (int i = 0; i < N; i++)
      resB = resB * 0.96;
    return resB;
  }

  [Benchmark]
  public double PowerC()
  {
    double res = 1.0;
    for (int i = 0; i < N; i++)
      res = res * 0.96 + 0.1 - 0.1;
    return res;
  }
}
```

Here we calculate 0.96^N in three different ways. In PowerA, we just multiply a local variable by 0.96 N times. In PowerB, we use a field for the multiplication results instead of the local variable. In PowerC, we use a local variable, but we perform + 0.1 - 0.1 on it after each iteration.

Results

Here is an example of results (Windows 10.0.17763.195, Intel Core i7-6700HQ CPU 2.60GHz, .NET Framework 4.7.2, JIT 4.7.3260.0):

Method	Jit	Platform	N	Mean	StdDev
PowerA	LegacyJit	X86	100000	151.5 us	1.298 us
PowerB	LegacyJit	X86	100000	17,480.7 us	99.446 us
PowerC	LegacyJit	X86	100000	330.7 us	1.129 us
PowerA	RyuJit	X64	100000	3,547.9 us	11.868 us
PowerB	RyuJit	X64	100000	3,783.8 us	12.350 us

```
PowerC |    RyuJit |    X64 |  100000 |      366.6 us |     1.383 us |
PowerA | LegacyJit |    X86 | 1000000 |  150,718.6 us | 3,663.819 us |
PowerB | LegacyJit |    X86 | 1000000 |  219,923.4 us | 6,075.390 us |
PowerC | LegacyJit |    X86 | 1000000 |    3,521.8 us |    82.629 us |
PowerA |    RyuJit |    X64 | 1000000 |   43,119.9 us |   693.725 us |
PowerB |    RyuJit |    X64 | 1000000 |   45,739.5 us |   771.414 us |
PowerC |    RyuJit |    X64 | 1000000 |    3,755.5 us |    54.615 us |
```

And here are the mean values regrouped into a better summary table (without information about the standard deviation):

```
          JIT |        N |      PowerA |      PowerB |     PowerC |
-------------:| -------:| ------------:| ------------:| ----------:|
LegacyJIT-x86 |   100000 |    151.5 us | 17,480.7 us |   330.7 us |
 RyuJIT-x64   |   100000 |  3,547.9 us |  3,783.8 us |   366.6 us |
LegacyJIT-x86 |  1000000 | 150,718.6 us | 219,923.4 us | 3,521.8 us |
 RyuJIT-x64   |  1000000 |  43,119.9 us | 45,739.5 us | 3,755.5 us |
```

Some of these results may look surprising. Here we can ask the following questions about the summary table:

- Why does PowerC work so fast?

- Why are PowerA and PowerB so slow on LegacyJIT-x86 for $N = 10^6$?

- Why is PowerA much faster than PowerB and PowerC on LegacyJIT-x86 for $N = 10^5$?

Explanation

Let's try to answer these questions. First of all, let's compare PowerA and PowerC on RyuJIT. To understand why PowerC is faster, we should look at Table 7-4, in which the intermediate res values are presented in the real decimal form with internal hexadecimal representation.

Table 7-4. *RyuJIT-x64 Intermediate Results for Benchmark with Denormalized Numbers*

i	PowerA	PowerC
0	*1.0*	*1.0*
	3FF0000000000000	3FF0000000000000
1	*0.96*	*0.96000000000000008*
	3FEEB851EB851EB**8**	3FEEB851EB851EB**9**
885	*2.0419318345555615E-16*	*1.8041124150158794E-16*
	3CAD6D6617566397	**3CAA**000000000000
886	*1.9602545611733389E-16*	*1.6653345369377348E-16*
	3CAC4010166769D8	**3CA8**000000000000
887	*1.8818443787264053E-16*	*1.6653345369377348E-16*
	3CAB1EC7C3967A17	**3CA8**000000000000
18171	*6.42285339593621E-323*	*1.6653345369377348E-16*
	000000000000000**D**	3CA8000000000000
18172	*5.92878775009496E-323*	*1.6653345369377348E-16*
	000000000000000**C**	3CA8000000000000
18173	*5.92878775009496E-323*	*1.6653345369377348E-16*
	000000000000000**C**	3CA8000000000000

Let's learn what's going on here step by step:

- The initial value of res is 1.0, which is 3FF0000000000000 in the IEEE 754 format.

- After the first iteration (i=1), res becomes 0.96 (3FEEB851EB851EB8) in PowerA. In PowerC, res * 0.96 + 0.1 - 0.1 gives 0.96000000000000008 (3FEEB851EB851EB9). The difference between PowerA and PowerC is in a single bit.

- When i=886, we get 1.6653345369377348E-16 (3CA8000000000000) in PowerC. This magic number is an invariant for res * 0.96 + 0.1 - 0.1: this operation doesn't change this number. We can continue to perform iterations, but res will not be changed.

- When i=18172, we get 5.92878775009496E-323 (000000000000000C) in PowerA. This number is an invariant for res * 0.96: the res value will not be changed anymore in either method.

Now we can see that PowerA performs most of the operations with 5.92878775009496E-323, which is a denormalized number: that's why the performance is so bad. In PowerC, the + 0.1 - 0.1 trick helps to keep the intermediate results normalized. Since we don't have any operation with denormalized numbers in PowerC, this method works pretty fast.

Now let's look what's going on with LegacyJIT-x86. This JIT compiler uses x87 instruction. Here are disassembly listings for PowerA and PowerB:

```
; PowerA (N=10^5:    ~167us       N=10^6: ~152770us)
fld     qword ptr ds:[14D2E28h] ; 0.96
fmulp   st(1),st; In a register
; PowerB (N=10^5: ~19079us       N=10^6: ~226219us)
fld     qword ptr ds:[892E20h]  ; 0.96
fmul    qword ptr [ecx+4]
fstp    qword ptr [ecx+4]        ; In memory
```

As we can see, PowerA performs multiplication using a register; PowerB keeps the intermediate result in memory (because it should dump the value to a field). The next clue can be found in [Intel Manual]:

> §8.2 X87 FPU Data Types
>
> With the **exception of the 80-bit double extended-precision** format, all data types exist **in memory only.** When they are loaded into x87 FPU data registers, they are **converted into double extended-precision** format and operated on in that format.
>
> When a denormal number is used as a source operand, the x87 FPU **automatically normalizes** the number when it is converted to double extended-precision format.

Thus, `PowerA` actually uses 80-bit floating-point numbers for calculations. It doesn't hit the "denormalized zone" for $N = 10^5$, unlike `PowerB`, which uses 64-bit numbers. That's why `PowerA` is so fast for $N = 10^5$: it performs all calculations on normalized numbers using a register. For $N = 10^6$, we have a lot of denormalized operations even for 80-bit numbers (try to calculate the exact iteration when we get the first denormalized number and the iteration when we get the invariant value).

Discussion

As you can see, the denormalized number can be a cause of serious performance problems. Such numbers can also be used for timing side channel attacks (e.g., see [Andrysco 2015]). The performance effect of denormalized numbers significantly depends on the environment.

Case Study 2: Math.Abs

`Math.Abs` is a widely used static method that returns the absolute value of a specified number. Let's check its performance on different versions of .NET Core.

Source code

Consider the following BenchmarkDotNet-based benchmark:

```
public class Benchmarks
{
  private int positive = 1, negative = -1;

  [Benchmark]
  public int Positive()
  {
    return Math.Abs(positive);
  }

  [Benchmark]
  public int Negative()
  {
    return Math.Abs(negative);
  }
}
```

490

Here we have two benchmarks: Positive (measures Math.Abs for +1) and Negative (measures Math.Abs for -1).

Results

Here is an example of results (Windows 10.0.17763.195, Intel Core i7-6700HQ CPU 2.60GHz, .NET Core 2.0.9 and .NET Core 2.1.5):

```
 Method  |     Job     |   Mean    |  StdDev   |
 ------- |------------ |----------:|----------:|
 Positive | .NETCore20 | 0.2797 ns | 0.0182 ns |
 Negative | .NETCore20 | 0.9145 ns | 0.0239 ns |
 Positive | .NETCore21 | 0.2744 ns | 0.0077 ns |
 Negative | .NETCore21 | 0.2762 ns | 0.0126 ns |
```

As you can see, the Negative benchmark on .NET Core 2.0 works three times slower than other cases.

Explanation

Let's look at its implementation in .NET Core 2.0.0[40]:

```
public static int Abs(int value)
{
  if (value >= 0)
    return value;
  else
    return AbsHelper(value);
}

private static int AbsHelper(int value)
{
  Contract.Requires(value < 0,
    "AbsHelper should only be called for negative values!" +
    "(workaround for JIT inlining)");
  if (value == Int32.MinValue)
```

---

[40]https://github.com/dotnet/coreclr/blob/v2.0.0/src/mscorlib/src/System/Math. cs#L268

```
    throw new OverflowException(SR.Overflow_NegateTwosCompNum);
  Contract.EndContractBlock();
  return -value;
}
```

Here we can see that Math.Abs instantly returns value for positive input and calls additional method AbsHelper for the negative case. Thus, we always have an additional call for negative values. This call is not inlined, so we have a performance penalty for such cases. The performance was improved in .NET Core 2.1, and now the implementation looks as follows:

```
[MethodImpl(MethodImplOptions.AggressiveInlining)]
public static int Abs(int value)
{
  if (value < 0)
  {
    value = -value;
    if (value < 0)
    {
      ThrowAbsOverflow();
    }
  }
  return value;
}

[StackTraceHidden]
private static void ThrowAbsOverflow()
{
  throw new OverflowException(SR.Overflow_NegateTwosCompNum);
}
```

The updated implementation doesn't have an additional call for negative numbers. That's why the Positive and Negative benchmarks have the same duration on .NET Core 2.1.

Discussion

In the GitHub discussion, we can find a great explanation of this approach by Andy Ayers[41]:

> The general guidance is to separate out throws into helper methods that do the work of creating the exception object and any related data (eg formatted exception messages) and then unconditionally throw. The jit's inline performance heuristic will then block inlining of the helper. This has a number of performance benefits:
>
> - overall code size savings when are multiple callers or callers with multiple throw sites
>
> - call sites to helper are considered "rare" and so moved into the caller's cold code region
>
> - helper IL is only jitted if an exception about to be thrown, so caller jits faster
>
> - caller's prolog/epilog may be simplified with fewer register saves/ restores
>
> Native codegen for exception throws that use resource based strings is surprisingly large.
>
> There is no "correctness" reason preventing methods with throws from being inlined, and methods that conditionally throw (like the original AbsHelper in the preceding) may end up getting inlined, as they might contain a mixture of hot and cold code. Methods that unconditionally throw are much less likely to contain any hot code.

Many developers think that operations with numbers are so fundamental that they should have been written perfectly a long time ago and never changed since then. This is not true: most base operations that we use all the time get performance improvements all the time. For example, in [Icaza 2018], you can read a story about a 2× performance improvement of 32-bit floating-point calculations.

---

[41]https://github.com/dotnet/corefx/issues/26253#issuecomment-356736809

See also:

- corefx#26253[42] "Math.Abs is slow"

- coreclr#15823[43] "Improve performance for Math.Abs"

Case Study 3: double.ToString

A conversion from double to string is another popular operation used in most .NET applications. This conversion is pretty time-consuming. Let's measure its performance on .NET Core 2.0 and .NET Core 2.1

Source code

Consider the following BenchmarkDotNet-based benchmark:

```
public class Benchmarks
{
  private double value = -8.98846567431158E+307;

  [Benchmark]
  public string ConvertToString()
  {
    return value.ToString(CultureInfo.InvariantCulture);
  }
}
```

Here we have the only benchmark that measures ToString conversion for -8.98846567431158E+307.

Results

Here is an example of results (Windows 10.0.17763.195, Intel Core i7-6700HQ CPU 2.60GHz, .NET Core 2.0.9 and .NET Core 2.1.5):

---

[42]https://github.com/dotnet/corefx/issues/26253
[43]https://github.com/dotnet/coreclr/pull/15823

```
     Job |        Mean |      StdDev |
---------- |-----------:|------------:|
 .NETCore20 | 4,649.4 ns | 125.019 ns |
 .NETCore21 |   222.1 ns |   1.425 ns |
```

As you can see, double.ToString() works much faster for -8.98846567431158E+307 on .NET Core 2.1.

Explanation

In coreclr#14646,[44] the Grisu3 algorithm (read more about it in [Steele 1990] and [Andrysco 2016]) was added in double.ToString() implementation. This improvement was included in .NET Core 2.1 In the pull request comments, you can find benchmark results for different inputs (a fragment is presented in Table 7-5).

Table 7-5. *Grisu3 Performance Improvement for double.ToString*

Number	Arguments	Before	After
-1.79769313486232E+308	—	237.492	28.660
-8.98846567431158E+307	—	227.782	29.921
-1.79769313486232E+308	culture: "zh"	252.797	26.215
4.94065645841247E-324	format: "E"	222.350	40.334
-1.79769313486232E+308	format: "F50"	324.054	132.538
4.94065645841247E-324	format: "G"	213.085	39.974
-1.79769313486232E+308	format: "R"	443.718	45.578
4.94065645841247E-324	format: "R"	231.865	49.403

Discussion

The performance boost was noticed in some internal .NET Core benchmarks (see coreclr#16624[45] and coreclr#16625[46]).

---

[44]https://github.com/dotnet/coreclr/pull/14646
[45]https://github.com/dotnet/coreclr/issues/16624
[46]https://github.com/dotnet/coreclr/issues/16625

Note that the old and new implementations may return different values in some special cases. For example, consider the following lines:

```
var value = BitConverter.Int64BitsToDouble(-4585072949362425856);
Console.WriteLine(value);
```

It will print -122.194458007813 on .NET Core 2.0 and -122.194458007812 on .NET Core 2.1. You can find the corresponding discussion in coreclr#17805.[47]

Case Study 4: Integer Division

The integer division operation may be heavy when the divider is not a power of two. There is an old bit hack that allows replacing the division by a multiplication and a bit shift.[48] The following two methods produce the same result:

```
uint Div3Simple(uint n)   => n / 3;
uint Div3BitHacks(uint n) => (uint)((n * (ulong)0xAAAAAAAB) >> 33);
```

In theory, Div3BitHacks should work much faster because it doesn't perform the heavy division operation. Let's check how it works in practice.

Source code

Consider the following BenchmarkDotNet-based benchmark:

```
public class Benchmarks
{
  private uint x = 1, initialValue = uint.MaxValue;

  [Benchmark(OperationsPerInvoke = 16)]
  public void Simple()
  {
    x = initialValue;
    x = x / 3;
    x = x / 3;
```

---

[47]https://github.com/dotnet/coreclr/issues/17805

[48]You can find more details about it in [Lemire 2019] and [Tillaart 2007]. You can also find tons of interesting bit hacks in https://graphics.stanford.edu/~seander/bithacks.html

```
    x = x / 3;
    x = x / 3;
    x = x / 3;
    x = x / 3;
    x = x / 3;
    x = x / 3;
    x = x / 3;
    x = x / 3;
    x = x / 3;
    x = x / 3;
    x = x / 3;
    x = x / 3;
    x = x / 3;
    x = x / 3;
}

[Benchmark(OperationsPerInvoke = 16)]
public void BitHacks()
{
    x = initialValue;
    x = (uint) ((x * (ulong) 0xAAAAAAAB) >> 33);
    x = (uint) ((x * (ulong) 0xAAAAAAAB) >> 33);
    x = (uint) ((x * (ulong) 0xAAAAAAAB) >> 33);
    x = (uint) ((x * (ulong) 0xAAAAAAAB) >> 33);
    x = (uint) ((x * (ulong) 0xAAAAAAAB) >> 33);
    x = (uint) ((x * (ulong) 0xAAAAAAAB) >> 33);
    x = (uint) ((x * (ulong) 0xAAAAAAAB) >> 33);
    x = (uint) ((x * (ulong) 0xAAAAAAAB) >> 33);
    x = (uint) ((x * (ulong) 0xAAAAAAAB) >> 33);
    x = (uint) ((x * (ulong) 0xAAAAAAAB) >> 33);
    x = (uint) ((x * (ulong) 0xAAAAAAAB) >> 33);
    x = (uint) ((x * (ulong) 0xAAAAAAAB) >> 33);
    x = (uint) ((x * (ulong) 0xAAAAAAAB) >> 33);
    x = (uint) ((x * (ulong) 0xAAAAAAAB) >> 33);
```

```
    x = (uint) ((x * (ulong) 0xAAAAAAAB) >> 33);
    x = (uint) ((x * (ulong) 0xAAAAAAAB) >> 33);
  }
}
```

Here we have two benchmarks: Simple and BitHacks. Both of them divide x by 3 (16 times). In order to avoid ILP, all of the division operations use the same field x.

Results

Here is an example of results (Windows 10.0.17763.195, Intel Core i7-6700HQ CPU 2.60GHz, .NET Framework 4.7.2 with JIT 4.7.3260.0; Mono 5.18.0.225):

Method	JIT	Mean	StdDev
Simple	LegacyJIT-x86	5.6259 ns	0.0217 ns
BitHacks	LegacyJIT-x86	1.3119 ns	0.0123 ns
Simple	LegacyJIT-x64	1.2916 ns	0.0065 ns
BitHacks	LegacyJIT-x64	0.8484 ns	0.0039 ns
Simple	RyuJIT-x64	0.8491 ns	0.0099 ns
BitHacks	RyuJIT-x64	0.7035 ns	0.0081 ns
Simple	Mono-x86	3.5624 ns	0.0111 ns
BitHacks	Mono-x86	13.4624 ns	0.1121 ns
Simple	Mono-x64	1.1475 ns	0.0117 ns
BitHacks	Mono-x64	1.4359 ns	0.0074 ns

And here are the mean values regrouped into a better summary table (without information about the standard deviation):

JIT	Simple	BitHacks
LegacyJIT-x86	5.6259 ns	1.3119 ns
LegacyJIT-x64	1.2916 ns	0.8484 ns
RyuJIT-x64	0.8491 ns	0.7035 ns
Mono-x86	3.5624 ns	13.4624 ns
Mono-x64	1.1475 ns	1.4359 ns

We can make the following observations about the summary table:

- The `Simple` benchmark works much faster on `LegacyJIT-x64`, `RyuJIT-x64`, and `Mono-x64` than on `LegacyJIT-x86` and `Mono-x86`.

- The `BitHacks` benchmark works extremely slow on `Mono-x86`.

Explanation

To understand what's going on here, we should look at the generated native code for all JIT compilers. Let's start with `LegacyJIT-x86` because it produces the most straightforward native code:

```
; Simple/LegacyJIT-x86
mov   eax,dword ptr [esi+4]   ; eax = x
xor   edx,edx                 ; edx = 0
div   eax,ecx                 ; eax /= 3
mov   dword ptr [esi+4],eax   ; x = eax

; BitHacks/LegacyJIT-x86
mov   eax,dword ptr [ecx+4]   ; eax = x
mov   edx,0AAAAAAABh          ; edx = 0AAAAAAABh
mul   eax,edx                 ; eax * edx (result in edx)
mov   eax,edx                 ; eax = edx
shr   eax,1                   ; eax >>= 1
xor   edx,edx                 ; edx = 0
mov   dword ptr [ecx+4],eax   ; x = eax
```

No magic here: `LegacyJIT-x86` translated C# code to assembly in the most straightforward way. At the beginning of each division operation, we load the x value from the stack to a register, perform the division, and save the x value from the register to the stack. The `BitHacks` benchmark works faster than `Simple` because it uses multiplication instead of division.

Now let's look at the `LegacyJIT-x64` native code:

```
; Simple/LegacyJIT-x64
mov   ecx,dword ptr [r8+8]    ; ecx = x
mov   eax,0AAAAAAABh          ; eax = 0AAAAAAABh
mul   eax,ecx                 ; aex * ecx (result in edx)
```

```
shr   edx,1                     ; edx >>= 1
mov   dword ptr [r8+8],edx      ; x = edx
```

```
; BitHacks/LegacyJIT-x64
mov      eax,dword ptr [rcx+8]  ; eax = x
mov      edx,0AAAAAABh         ; edx = 0AAAAAABh
imul     rax,rdx                ; rax * rdx (result in rax)
shr      rax,21h                ; rax >>= 31
mov      dword ptr [rcx+8],eax  ; x = eax
```

LegacyJIT-x64 is smart enough to replace division by multiplication for the Simple benchmark! That's why the LegacyJIT-x64 version works faster than the LegacyJIT-x86 version.

Now let's look at the RyuJIT-x64 native code:

```
; Simple/RyuJIT-x64
mov      edx,0AAAAAABh         ; edx = 0AAAAAABh
mul      eax,edx                ; eax * edx (result in edx)
mov      eax,edx                ; eax = edx
shr      eax,1                  ; eax >>= 1
mov      dword ptr [rcx+8],eax  ; x = eax
```

```
; BitHacks/RyuJIT-x64
moveax,eax; eax = eax
imul     rax,rdx                ; rax * rdx (result in rax)
shr      rax,21h                ; rax >>= 31
mov      dword ptr [rcx+8],eax  ; x = eax
```

RyuJIT-x64 is also smart enough to replace division by multiplication. It works a little bit faster than LegacyJIT-x64 because it doesn't load the x value from the stack to the register at the beginning of the operation (the actual x value is already in the register after the previous operation).

Now let's look at the Mono-x86 native code:

```
; Simple/Mono-x86
movl    $0x0,-0xc(%rbp)        ; -0xc(%rbp) = 0
mov     -0x10(%rbp),%eax       ; eax = x
mov     %eax,0x8(%rdi)         ; 0x8(%rdi) = eax
```

```
mov    0x8(%rdi),%eax        ; eax = 0x8(%rdi)
mov    $0xaaaaaaab,%ecx      ; ecx = 0xaaaaaaab
mul    %ecx                  ; eax * ecx (result in edx)
mov    %edx,-0xc(%rbp)       ;  -0xc(%rbp) = edx
mov    %eax,-0x10(%rbp)      ; -0x10(%rbp) = eax
mov    -0xc(%rbp),%eax       ; eax = -0xc(%rbp) (mul result)
shr    %eax                  ; eax >>= 1
mov    %eax,-0x10(%rbp)      ; x = eax

; BitHacks/Mono-x86
mov    0x8(%rdi),%eax              ; %eax = x
movl   $0x0,0xc(%rsp)             ; 0xc(%rsp) = 0
movl   $0xaaaaaaab,0x8(%rsp)      ; 0x8(%rsp) = 0xaaaaaaab
movl   $0x0,0x4(%rsp)            ; 0x4(%rsp) = 0
mov    %eax,(%rsp)              ; (%rsp) = %eax
lea    0x0(%rbp),%ebp          ; %epb = 0x0(%rbp)
callq  fffffffffffffff4        ; Call external method
mov    %edx,-0xc(%rbp)         ; -0xc(%rbp) = %edx
mov    %eax,-0x10(%rbp)        ; -0x10(%rbp) = %eax
mov    -0xc(%rbp),%eax         ; %eax = -0xc(%rbp)
shr    %eax                    ; %eax >>= 1
mov    %eax,0x8(%rdi)          ; x = eax
```

Mono-x86 doesn't know how to handle our bit hacks with simple instructions: it generates a complicated code with an external call. That's why the BitHacks benchmark on Mono-x86 is so slow.

Now let's look at the Mono-x64 native code:

```
; Simple/Mono-x64
mov    0x10(%rsi),%eax  ; eax = x
mov    $0xaaaaaaab,%ecx ; ecx = 0xaaaaaaab
mov    %eax,%eax        ; eax = eax
imul   %rcx,%rax        ; rax * rcx (result in rax)
shr    $0x21,%rax       ; rax >>= 31
mov    %eax,0x10(%rsi)  ; x = eax
```

```
; BitHacks/Mono-x64
mov    0x10(%rsi),%eax  ; eax = x
mov    %eax,%eax        ; eax = eax
mov    $0xaaaaaaab,%ecx ; ecx = 0xaaaaaaab
imul   %rcx,%rax        ; rax * rcx (result in rax)
shr    $0x21,%rax       ; rax >>= 31
shr    $0x0,%eax        ; eax >>= 0
mov    %eax,0x10(%rsi)  ; x = eax
```

Mono-x64 is also smart enough to replace division by multiplication. Moreover, the optimized version of Simple is more efficient than BitHacks where we manually applied the optimization. Also, it can generate native code for BitHacks using only simple instructions (without external calls).

Discussion

As you can see, the division performance significantly depends on the environment. Some JIT compilers can apply the discussed optimization automatically. This automatic optimization may get a more efficient native code for the Simple benchmark than the native code for the BitHacks benchmark where we applied this optimization manually.

The preceding results are valid only for specified versions of runtimes; you never know what kind of optimization you will get on future versions of .NET.

- coreclr#8106[49] "Move magic division optimization from morph to lowering"

- [Akinshin 2016b]

- [Chen 2019]

Summing Up

In the IEEE 754 standard, each floating-point number is represented by a sign, an exponent, and a mantissa. Instead of the classic terms, we can use Sanglard's interpretation, which replaces the exponent with a window between two consecutive powers of two (e.g., [1; 2] or [8; 16]) and the mantissa by an offset within that window (each window is split by the fixed number of buckets). In .NET, float (32-bit) and double

---

[49]https://github.com/dotnet/coreclr/pull/8106

(64-bit) follow the IEEE 754 standard; decimal (128-bit) is a custom implemented floating-point struct useful for financial and monetary calculations (it has high precision but poor performance).

The same expression with floating-point numbers can return different results in different cases. For example, LegacyJIT-x86 can use 80-bit numbers for intermediate calculations even if you are using the float (32-bit) or double (64-bit) types in your code.

In the context of benchmarking, it's important to know about denormalized numbers. The denormalized numbers are IEEE 754 numbers with zero exponent. Usually, you don't have them in real code because they are very small (less than $1.2 \cdot 10^{-38}$ for float), but when you do, you can get a significant performance degradation (e.g., 100 times). Such a performance effect can be used for timing side channel attacks.

Almost all .NET applications use different operations with numbers. The performance of these operations depends on the number values, the compiler version, and the runtime version. It's not always easy to benchmark even a single arithmetic statement because there are too many different combinations of the input data and environments. Thus, we can't extrapolate results from a single environment to a general case.

Intrinsics

Intrinsic is a "smart" implementation of a specific method or a statement that the JIT compiler can use in specific situations. In this subsection, we are going to discuss several kinds of intrinsics that are available in different .NET JIT compilers.

Case Study 1: Math.Round

Let's discuss the Math.Round(double x) method: it rounds a value to the nearest integer.[50]

In .NET Core 2.1, it has the following implementation[51]:

---

[50]You can find more information about different overloads in the following documentation:
https://docs.microsoft.com/en-us/dotnet/api/system.math.round

[51]See https://github.com/dotnet/coreclr/blob/v2.1.7/src/mscorlib/shared/System/Math.cs#L647

```
[Intrinsic]
public static double Round(double a)
{
  // If the number has no fractional part do nothing
  // This shortcut is necessary to workaround precision loss
  // in borderline cases on some platforms
  if (a == (double)((long)a))
  {
    return a;
  }

  // We had a number that was equally close to 2 integers.
  // We need to return the even one.
  double flrTempVal = Floor(a + 0.5);
  if ((a == (Floor(a) + 0.5)) && (FMod(flrTempVal, 2.0) != 0))
  {
    flrTempVal -= 1.0;
  }

  return copysign(flrTempVal, a);
}
```

The [Intrinsic] attribute means that the JIT compiler can throw away this implementation and replace the method call by more efficient native instructions.

Source code

Consider the following BenchmarkDotNet-based benchmark:

```
public static class MyMath
{
  public static double Round(double a)
  {
    if (a == (double)((long)a))
    {
      return a;
    }
```

```
  double flrTempVal = Math.Floor(a + 0.5);
  if ((a == (Math.Floor(a) + 0.5)) && (flrTempVal % 2.0 != 0))
  {
    flrTempVal -= 1.0;
  }

  return copysign(flrTempVal, a);
}

private static double copysign(double x, double y)
{
  var xbits = BitConverter.DoubleToInt64Bits(x);
  var ybits = BitConverter.DoubleToInt64Bits(y);

  if (((xbits ^ ybits) >> 63) != 0)
  {
    return BitConverter.Int64BitsToDouble(xbits ^ long.MinValue);
  }

  return x;
  }
}

public class Benchmarks
{
  private double doubleValue = 1.3;

  [Benchmark]
  public double SystemRound()
  {
    return Math.Round(doubleValue);
  }

  [Benchmark]
  public double MyRound()
  {
    return MyMath.Round(doubleValue);
  }
}
```

Here we have the MyMath.Round method, which is a copy-pasted implementation of the system Math.Round method. We also have two benchmarks, SystemRound and MyRound, which call the corresponding Round implementations.

Results

Here is an example of results (Windows 10.0.17763.195, Intel Core i7-6700HQ CPU 2.60GHz, .NET Framework 4.7.2 with LegacyJIT 4.7.3260.0, .NET Core 2.1.5 with RyuJIT-x64):

```
      Method |          Job |     Mean |   StdDev |
------------ |------------- |--------- |---------:|
 SystemRound | LegacyJitX64 | 7.2785 ns | 0.2532 ns |
     MyRound | LegacyJitX64 | 7.1982 ns | 0.0876 ns |
 SystemRound |    RyuJitX64 | 0.4929 ns | 0.0184 ns |
     MyRound |    RyuJitX64 | 3.4426 ns | 0.0338 ns |
```

As you can see, SystemRound works much faster than MyRound on RyuJIT-x64. On LegacyJIT-x64, both methods have the same duration.

Explanation

The [Intrinsic] means that the JIT compiler has special knowledge about this method and can replace the preceding implementation by a more efficient native code. RyuJIT-x64 can generate a superefficient native code using the vroundsd AVX instruction:

```
; SystemRound/RyuJIT-x64
vzeroupper
vroundsd    xmm0,xmm0,mmword ptr [rcx+8],4
ret
```

That's why SystemRound works so fast on RyuJIT-x64 (it takes less than 1 nanosecond). The JIT compiler doesn't have special knowledge about the MyMath.Round method, so it generates a straightforward native code for the preceding implementation, which works slower.

On LegacyJIT-x64, we have the same duration for both benchmarks because this JIT compiler doesn't have a special intrinsic for the Math.Round method. Thus, it works with the same IL code in both cases.

Discussion

When we compare the performance of the same method on different JIT compilers, we should keep in mind that these JIT compilers may have different sets of intrinsics that can be applied to any system method.

See also:

- StackOverflow question 40460850[52] "Significant drop in performance of Math.Round on x64 platform"

- coreclr#8053[53] "A question about Math.Round intrinsic on x64"

Case Study 2: Rotate Bits

The JIT compiler can generate intrinsic not only for the known methods but also for statements of a specific form. Consider the following method, which implements the classic bit rotation for ulong value:

```
public static ulong RotateRight64(ulong value, int count)
{
  return (value >> count) | (value << (64 - count));
}
```

Such expression is widely used in different cryptographic algorithms. This method can be executed millions of times in a single method, so it would be nice to have a decent performance level here. Let's check the performance of this method on different JIT compilers.

Source code

Consider the following BenchmarkDotNet-based benchmark:

```
public class Benchmarks
{
  public static ulong RotateRight64(ulong value, int count)
  {
```

---

[52]https://stackoverflow.com/q/40460850
[53]https://github.com/dotnet/coreclr/issues/8053

507

```
    return (value >> count) | (value << (64 - count));
}

private ulong a = 100;
private int b = 2;

[Benchmark]
public ulong Foo()
{
    return RotateRight64(a, b);
}
}
```

Here we just apply the "Rotate Bit" operation for a private ulong field.

Results

Here is an example of results (Windows 10.0.17763.195, Intel Core i7-6700HQ CPU 2.60GHz, .NET Framework 4.7.2 with LegacyJIT-x86 4.7.3260.0, .NET Core 2.1.5 with RyuJIT-x64):

```
         Job |    Mean |    StdDev |
------------- |---------:|-----------:|
LegacyJitX86 | 4.676 ns | 0.1208 ns |
   RyuJitX64 | 1.217 ns | 0.0299 ns |
```

As you can see, this benchmark works much faster on .NET Core 2.1.5 with RyuJIT-x64 than on .NET Framework 4.7.2 with LegacyJIT-x86.

Explanation

RyuJIT is able to recognize the (value >> count) | (value << (64 - count)) pattern and generate fast implementation for it.

```
ror  rax,cl
```

LegacyJIT-x86 doesn't support this heuristic and generates a straightforward native code for the original expression. Of course, it works much slower than a single ror instruction.

Discussion

We already discussed a similar intrinsic in the "Integer Division" case study, in which some JIT compilers were able to replace a division operation by a multiplication operation. Each JIT compiler has its own set of "code patterns" that can be optimized. It's pretty hard to control this kind of intrinsics: any changes in the source code can prevent the JIT compiler from the optimization because it can recognize only some specific forms of these patterns.

See also:

- coreclr#1619[54] "RyuJIT: "Understand the idiomatic rotate bits"

- coreclr#1830[55] "Generate efficient code for rotation patterns"

Case Study 3: Vectorization

In the System.Numerics[56] namespace, there are a lot of useful structs including SIMD-enabled types: `Vector2`, `Vector3`, `Vector4`, `Matrix3x2`, `Matrix4x4`, `Plane`, and `Quaternion`. RyuJIT has hardware acceleration support for these types via SIMD intrinsics. The SIMD operations are another kind of parallelization on the hardware level: with the help of special instruction sets like SSE or AVX, we can explicitly perform an operation on multiple data at once. Other JIT compilers like LegacyJIT-x86 and LegacyJIT-x64 have no advanced support for these types: they are using a fallback option and perform the corresponding operations without smart intrinsics.

Source code

Consider the following BenchmarkDotNet-based benchmark:

```
public struct MyVector4
{
  public float X, Y, Z, W;

  public MyVector4(float x, float y, float z, float w)
```

---

[54]https://github.com/dotnet/coreclr/issues/1619

[55]https://github.com/dotnet/coreclr/pull/1830

[56]This has been available since .NET Framework 4.6 and .NET Core 1.0. See also: https://docs. microsoft.com/en-us/dotnet/api/system.numerics

```
  {
    X = x;
    Y = y;
    Z = z;
    W = w;
  }

  [MethodImpl(MethodImplOptions.AggressiveInlining)]
  public static MyVector4 operator *(MyVector4 left, MyVector4 right)
    => new MyVector4(
      left.X * right.X,
      left.Y * right.Y,
      left.Z * right.Z,
      left.W * right.W);
}

public class Benchmarks
{
  private Vector4 vectorA, vectorB, vectorC;
  private MyVector4 myVectorA, myVectorB, myVectorC;

  [Benchmark]
  public void MyMul() => myVectorC = myVectorA * myVectorB;

  [Benchmark]
  public void SystemMul() => vectorC = vectorA * vectorB;
}
```

Here we have two benchmarks: SystemMul and MyMy1. SystemMul multiplies two Vector4 instances. MyMul also multiplies two vectors, but it operates with MyVector instances. The MyVector type is a partial copy of the system Vector4 class.[57] The operator * method in the original method is marked with the [Intrinsic] attribute.

---

[57]You can find the .NET Core 2.2.1 version of this class here: https://github.com/dotnet/corefx/blob/v2.2.1/src/System.Numerics.Vectors/src/System/Numerics/Vector4_Intrinsics.cs#L252

Results

Here is an example of results (Windows 10.0.17763.195, Intel Core i7-6700HQ CPU 2.60GHz, .NET Framework 4.7.2, LegacyJIT-x64/RyuJIT-x64 v4.7.3260.0):

```
   Method |          Job |    Mean |   StdDev |
---------- |------------- |---------:|---------:|
    MyMul | LegacyJitX64 | 12.33 ns | 0.058 ns |
SystemMul | LegacyJitX64 | 12.37 ns | 0.109 ns |
    MyMul |    RyuJitX64 |  1.71 ns | 0.021 ns |
SystemMul |    RyuJitX64 |  0.00 ns | 0.009 ns |
```

As you can see, the SystemMul benchmark works instantly on RyuJIT-x64. The MyMul benchmark works pretty fast on RyuJIT-x64, but not as fast as SystemMul. On LegacyJIT-x64, both benchmarks take the same time, which is much bigger than the corresponding result on RyuJIT-x64.

Explanation

Let's look at the native code of both methods on LegacyJIT-x64:

```
; SystemMul/MyMul, LegacyJIT-x64
mov     eax,dword ptr [rcx+38h]
mov     dword ptr [rsp+20h],eax
mov     eax,dword ptr [rcx+3Ch]
mov     dword ptr [rsp+24h],eax
mov     eax,dword ptr [rcx+40h]
mov     dword ptr [rsp+28h],eax
mov     eax,dword ptr [rcx+44h]
mov     dword ptr [rsp+2Ch],eax
mov     eax,dword ptr [rcx+48h]
mov     dword ptr [rsp+10h],eax
mov     eax,dword ptr [rcx+4Ch]
mov     dword ptr [rsp+14h],eax
mov     eax,dword ptr [rcx+50h]
mov     dword ptr [rsp+18h],eax
mov     eax,dword ptr [rcx+54h]
mov     dword ptr [rsp+1Ch],eax
```

511

```
lea     rdx,[rsp+20h]
mov     rax,qword ptr [rdx]
mov     qword ptr [rsp+40h],rax
mov     rax,qword ptr [rdx+8]
mov     qword ptr [rsp+48h],rax
lea     rdx,[rsp+10h]
mov     rax,qword ptr [rdx]
mov     qword ptr [rsp+30h],rax
mov     rax,qword ptr [rdx+8]
mov     qword ptr [rsp+38h],rax
movss   xmm3,dword ptr [rsp+40h]
mulss   xmm3,dword ptr [rsp+30h]
movss   xmm2,dword ptr [rsp+44h]
mulss   xmm2,dword ptr [rsp+34h]
movss   xmm1,dword ptr [rsp+48h]
mulss   xmm1,dword ptr [rsp+38h]
movss   xmm0,dword ptr [rsp+4Ch]
mulss   xmm0,dword ptr [rsp+3Ch]
xor     eax,eax
mov     qword ptr [rsp],rax
mov     qword ptr [rsp+8],rax
lea     rax,[rsp]
movss   dword ptr [rax],xmm3
movss   dword ptr [rax+4],xmm2
movss   dword ptr [rax+8],xmm1
movss   dword ptr [rax+0Ch],xmm0
lea     rdx,[rsp]
mov     eax,dword ptr [rdx]
mov     dword ptr [rcx+58h],eax
mov     eax,dword ptr [rdx+4]
mov     dword ptr [rcx+5Ch],eax
mov     eax,dword ptr [rdx+8]
mov     dword ptr [rcx+60h],eax
mov     eax,dword ptr [rdx+0Ch]
mov     dword ptr [rcx+64h],eax
```

Both methods have the same implementation because they have the same IL representation. The native code uses SSE instruction to perform the multiplication.

Now let's look at the native code for MyMul on RyuJIT-x64:

```
; MyMul/RyuJIT-x64
lea     rax,[rcx+38h]
vmovss  xmm0,dword ptr [rax]
vmovss  xmm1,dword ptr [rax+4]
vmovss  xmm2,dword ptr [rax+8]
vmovss  xmm3,dword ptr [rax+0Ch]
lea     rax,[rcx+48h]
vmovss  xmm4,dword ptr [rax]
vmovss  xmm5,dword ptr [rax+4]
vmovss  xmm6,dword ptr [rax+8]
vmovss  xmm7,dword ptr [rax+0Ch]
vmulss  xmm0,xmm0,xmm4
vmulss  xmm1,xmm1,xmm5
vmulss  xmm2,xmm2,xmm6
vmulss  xmm3,xmm3,xmm7
lea     rax,[rcx+58h]
vmovss  dword ptr [rax],xmm0
vmovss  dword ptr [rax+4],xmm1
vmovss  dword ptr [rax+8],xmm2
vmovss  dword ptr [rax+0Ch],xmm3
vmovaps xmm6,xmmword ptr [rsp+10h]
```

This version is much shorter and much smarter: it uses AVX instructions, which are not available on LegacyJIT-x64.

Now let's look at the native code for SystemMul on RyuJIT-x64:

```
; SystemMul/RyuJIT-x64
vmovupd xmm0,xmmword ptr [rcx+8]
vmovupd xmm1,xmmword ptr [rcx+18h]
vmulps  xmm0,xmm0,xmm1
vmovupd xmmword ptr [rcx+28h],xmm0
```

The operator * method is marked with the [Intrinsic] attribute. RyuJIT-x64 has special knowledge about it: it's able to perform multiplication with a single AVX instructions vmulps. BenchmarkDotNet reports 0 ns for it because of the ILP effects.

Discussion

This example is pretty similar to the "Math.Round" case study. However, it deserves to be discussed independently because System.Numerics APIs were designed for using such a kind of intrinsics.

Sometimes, benchmarking of SSE/AVX instructions requires an advanced warm-up. Here is a quote from [Agner Microarch]:

> 11.9 Execution unit
>
> Warm-up period for YMM and ZMM vector instructions.
>
> The processor turns off the upper parts of the vector execution units when they are not used, in order to save power. Instructions with 256-bit vectors have a throughput that is approximately 4.5 times slower than normal during an initial warm-up period of approximately 56,000 clock cycles or 14 μs. A sequence of code containing 256-bit vector operations will run at full speed after this warm-up period. The processor returns to the mode of slow 256-bit execution 2.7 million clock cycles, or 675 μs, after the last 256-bit instruction (these times were measured on a 4 GHz processor). Similar times apply to 512-bit vectors.

Case Study 4: System.Runtime.Intrinsics

In the previous case studies, we discussed *implicit* intrinsics. This means that some JIT compilers *may* use advanced native instructions to generate efficient code. However, you can't control it: you should be ready to get "slow" native implementations in some cases.

Since .NET Core 3.0, we have System.Runtime.Intrinsics namespaces with various APIs, which provide direct access to different native instructions. Here we are talking about *explicit* intrinsics: we force the JIT compiler to use a specific instruction without any other options.

Let's say that we want to calculate the number of set bits in an uint value. In the SSE4, there is a native instruction for it called popcnt.[58] However, it may be unavailable on old hardware without SSE4 support. To handle this case correctly, we can write code like this:

```
public uint MyPopCount(uint x)
{
  if (Popcnt.IsSupported)
    return Popcnt.PopCount(x);
  else
  {
    // Manual implementation
  }
}
```

The Popcnt.PopCount(x) call always uses the popcnt instruction; the JIT compiler has no other options.

Source code

Consider the following BenchmarkDotNet-based benchmark:

```
public static unsafe class CompareHelper
{
  // Assuming x.Length == y.Length
  public static bool NotEqualManual(int[] x, int[] y)
  {
    for (int i = 0; i < x.Length; i++)
      if (x[i] == y[i])
        return false;
    return true;
  }

  // Assuming x.Length == y.Length; x.Length % 4 == 0
  public static bool NotEqualSse41(int[] x, int[] y)
  {
```

---

[58]https://www.felixcloutier.com/x86/popcnt

```
    fixed (int* xp = &x[0])
    fixed (int* yp = &y[0])
    {
      for (int i = 0; i < x.Length; i += 4)
      {
        Vector128<int> xVector = Sse2.LoadVector128(xp + i);
        Vector128<int> yVector = Sse2.LoadVector128(yp + i);
        Vector128<int> mask = Sse2.CompareEqual(xVector, yVector);
        if (!Sse41.TestAllZeros(mask, mask))
          return false;
      }
    }
    return true;
  }

  // Assuming x.Length == y.Length; x.Length % 8 == 0
  public static bool NotEqualAvx2(int[] x, int[] y)
  {
    fixed (int* xp = &x[0])
    fixed (int* yp = &y[0])
    {
      for (int i = 0; i < x.Length; i += 8)
      {
        Vector256<int> xVector = Avx.LoadVector256(xp + i);
        Vector256<int> yVector = Avx.LoadVector256(yp + i);
        Vector256<int> mask = Avx2.CompareEqual(xVector, yVector);
        if (!Avx.TestZ(mask, mask))
          return false;
      }
    }
    return true;
  }
}
```

```
public class Benchmarks
{
  private const int n = 100000;
  private int[] x = new int[n];
  private int[] y = new int[n];

  [GlobalSetup]
  public void Setup()
  {
    Array.Fill(x, 1);
    Array.Fill(y, 2);
  }

  [Benchmark(Baseline = true)]
  public bool Manual() => CompareHelper.NotEqualManual(x, y);

  [Benchmark]
  public bool Sse41() => CompareHelper.NotEqualSse41(x, y);

  [Benchmark]
  public bool Avx2() => CompareHelper.NotEqualAvx2(x, y);
}
```

Here we have three benchmarks: Manual, See41, and Avx2. All of them check that in the x and y arrays, there is no pair x[i]/y[i] where x[i] == y[i]. In the Manual benchmark, we have a simple loop that checks this condition for each pair of elements. In the Sse41 and Avx2 benchmarks, we do the same with the help of SSE4.1 and AVX2 instructions, which are called directly via System.Runtime.Intrinsics.

Results

Here is an example of results (Windows 10.0.17763.195, Intel Core i7-6700HQ CPU 2.60GHz, .NET Core 3.0.0-preview-27122-01):

```
Method  |     Mean |     StdDev | Ratio |
------- |---------:|-----------:|------:|
 Manual | 53.34 us |  0.5719 us |  1.00 |
  Sse41 | 40.45 us |  0.5451 us |  0.76 |
   Avx2 | 23.56 us |  0.1158 us |  0.44 |
```

As you can see, `Avx2` is the fastest benchmark, `Sse41` works slowly, and `Manual` is the slowest benchmark.

Explanation

With the help of `System.Runtime.Intrinsics` APIs, we can explicitly call SSE/AVX instructions that can process several array elements at once. That's why it allows getting better performance on hardware where these instructions are supported.

Discussion

Explicit intrinsics allows implementing different algorithms inside the same method based on the instruction availability. For example, if `Avx.IsSupported` is true, we can execute a fast AVX-based algorithm; if `Avx.IsSupported` is false, we can fall back to a slow algorithm without explicit intrinsics.

This is great for performance, but it's not so great for benchmarking: it makes harder to conduct "general" conclusions about method performance based on a single benchmark session. Of course, we have this problem without `System.Runtime.Intrinsics` usages: the JIT compiler is able to generate different native implementations on different hardware. However, now we have to check not only the JIT compiler "performance effects," but also hardware-specific user code in the benchmark execution paths.

See also:

- [Mijailovic 2018a], [Mijailovic 2018b], [Mijailovic 2018c], [Mijailovic 2018d]

- [Damageboy 2018a], [Damageboy 2018b], [Damageboy 2018c]

- [Lui 2018]

- https://github.com/EgorBo/IntrinsicsPlayground

- dotnet/designs: .NET Platform Dependent Intrinsics[59]

- dotnet/machinelearning#1292[60]: "Use FMA instruction in CpuMath for .NET Core 3"

Summing Up

In this section, we discussed several kinds of intrinsics:

- Some JIT compilers have special intrinsics for some standard methods. For example, in RyuJIT-x64, we have an intrinsic for Math. Round. Meanwhile, this method has an "honest" C# implementation, which is used by other JIT compilers.

- Some JIT compilers can recognize some patterns in the source code and generate a smart native code using special instructions. For example, RyuJIT-x64 can transform idiomatic bit rotation ((value >> count) | (value << (64 - count))) to a single ror instruction.

- In the System.Numerics namespace, we have SIMD-enabled types like Vector4 or Matrix4x4. These types were designed to be accelerated on the hardware level with the help of SIMD instructions. JIT compilers without knowledge of these types have a fallback option with slow implementation.

- Since .NET Core 3.0, we have had access to explicit intrinsics, which allows calling specific native instructions from different instruction sets. In the source code, we can also check which kinds of these sets are supported on the current CPU.

The variety of intrinsics in different JIT compilers makes benchmarks more hardware-specific. It's pretty hard to make general conclusions about method performance based on a single environment. If you change the runtime, the JIT version, or the hardware, it may dramatically distort your results. Fortunately, now you know one more thing that will help you to explain the difference in performance between different environments.

---

[59]https://github.com/dotnet/designs/blob/e55c517a1e7f8dc35b092397058029531209d610/accepted/platform-intrinsics.md

[60]https://github.com/dotnet/machinelearning/pull/1292

Summary

CPU-bound benchmarks are pretty popular, but it's not easy to design and analyze them because there are a lot of hardware and runtime features that may spoil our performance experiments. In this chapter, we discussed the following topics:

- **Registers and Stack**

  When the JIT compiler generates the native code for a method, it can put the local variable on the stack or in registers. Usually, operations with registers work much faster than operations with the stack. Unfortunately, you can't control the JIT compiler: even very small and harmless changes may affect its decisions.

- **Inlining**

  When the JIT compiler inlines a method, it replaces a method call by its body. Usually, this is a good optimization because it eliminates the call overhead and opens possibilities for other JIT compiler optimizations. However, it also can spoil performance because it may lead to worse register allocation or it can prevent further inlining that is more profitable. We can disable inlining for a specific method with the help of the [MethodImpl(MethodImplOptions.NoInlining)] attribute. There are a lot of other factors that may prevent inlining like method size, exception handling, virtual modifier, and recursion. Some of these factors are not obvious, and they may be valid only for specific JIT compilers (e.g., the starg IL instructions prevents method inlining on LegacyJIT-x86). We can tell the JIT compiler that we really want to inline a specific method with the help of the [MethodImpl(MethodImplOptions.AggressiveInlining)] attribute. However, we can't force it, because inlining is not always possible. AggressiveInlining may help to optimize some small hot methods, but it can also increase the duration of some methods.

- **ILP**

  ILP allows executing multiple instructions at the same time inside a single thread. As usual, this is good for performance, but not so good for benchmarking. For example, you can add some statements to the benchmark body without any performance changes because the new statements will be executed in parallel with previously existing code. The ILP capabilities depend on the dependency graph that you have in your C# code or on the native code level. When you have an extremely short loop, its performance may be significantly affected because of the native code alignment. In order to prevent such situations, it's recommended to unroll such loops manually.

- **Branch Prediction**

  When CPUs are able to predict taken branches correctly, it significantly improves conditions for ILP. The branch predictor uses the history of taken branches in your execution sessions. This means that performance can be affected by changes in the input data even if you execute the same number of native instructions.

- **Arithmetic**

  Performance of even the simplest arithmetic operations depends on the environment. The floating-point calculations are nondeterministic, so the program result may also be different with different runtimes and hardware. In the IEEE 754 standard, we have denormalized numbers which can be a cause of extremely slow calculations. Thus, the performance of `float` and `double` calculations also depends on the operand values.

- **Intrinsics**

  In C#, you have a lot of different implicit and explicit intrinsics, which allows getting an efficient native code for the current hardware. The implicit intrinsics are used by the JIT compiler to optimize specific statements or system methods using the best available hardware instructions. The explicit intrinsics are used by you to manually optimize your algorithms using any hardware instructions you want (if they are available).

All of these topics are important for benchmark design and analysis. The proper benchmark design requires careful work with all the components of the performance spaces. Changes in the *source code* can affect the native code generation for the local variables (they can be put on the stack or in registers), the JIT compiler inlining policy, and conditions for the ILP. Changes in the *environment* (e.g., runtime version or hardware) can affect generated native instructions and intrinsic availability. Changes in the *input data* can affect branch mispredict rate. When you analyze the *performance distributions* for a specific source code/environment/input data combination, you should keep in mind that you can get dramatic performance changes under other conditions. And now you know what can you check during performance investigations in the case of such changes in a CPU-bound benchmark.

References

[Agner Instructions] Fog, Agner. "Instruction Tables. Lists of Instruction Latencies, Throughputs and Micro-Operation Breakdowns for Intel, AMD and VIA CPUs." `www.agner.org/optimize/instruction_tables.pdf`.

[Agner Microarch] Fog, Agner. "The Microarchitecture of Intel, AMD and VIA CPUs. An Optimization Guide for Assembly Programmers and Compiler Makers." `www.agner.org/optimize/microarchitecture.pdf`.

[Akinshin 2015] Akinshin, Andrey. 2015. "A Story About JIT-X86 Inlining and Starg." February 26. `https://aakinshin.net/posts/inlining-and-starg/`.

[Akinshin 2016a] Akinshin, Andrey. 2016. "Performance Exercise: Minimum." December 20. `https://aakinshin.net/posts/perfex-min/`.

[Akinshin 2016b] Akinshin, Andrey. 2016. "Performance Exercise: Division." December 26. `https://aakinshin.net/posts/perfex-div/`.

[Amit 2018] Amit, Navad. 2018. "How New-Lines Affect the Linux Kernel Performance." `https://sites.google.com/site/nadavamit/blog/linux-inline`.

[Andrysco 2015] Andrysco, Marc, David Kohlbrenner, Keaton Mowery, Ranjit Jhala, Sorin Lerner, and Hovav Shacham. 2015. "On Subnormal Floating Point and Abnormal Timing." In *Security and Privacy (Sp), 2015 IEEE Symposium*, 623–39. IEEE.

[Andrysco 2016] Andrysco, Marc, Ranjit Jhala, and Sorin Lerner. 2016. "Printing Floating-Point Numbers: A Faster, Always Correct Method." In *ACM Sigplan Notices*, 51:555–67. 1. ACM.

[Ayers 2016] Ayers, Andy. 2016. "Some Notes on Using Machine Learning to Develop Inlining Heuristics." August. `https://github.com/AndyAyersMS/PerformanceExplorer/blob/master/notes/notes-aug-2016.md`.

[Chen 2019] Chen, Raymond. 2019. "The Intel 80386, Part 4: Arithmetic." January 24. https://blogs.msdn.microsoft.com/oldnewthing/20190124-00/?p=100775.

[Damageboy 2018a] Damageboy. 2018. "NET Core 3.0 Intrinsics in Real Life - 1/3." August 18. https://bits.houmus.org/2018-08-18/netcoreapp3.0-instrinsics-in-real-life-pt1.

[Damageboy 2018b] Damageboy. 2018. "NET Core 3.0 Intrinsics in Real Life - 2/3." August 19. https://bits.houmus.org/2018-08-19/netcoreapp3.0-instrinsics-in-real-life-pt2.

[Damageboy 2018c] Damageboy. 2018. "NET Core 3.0 Intrinsics in Real Life - 3/3." August 20. https://bits.houmus.org/2018-08-20/netcoreapp3.0-intrinsics-in-real-life-pt3.

[Edelkamp 2016] Edelkamp, Stefan, and Armin Weiß. 2016. "BlockQuicksort: How Branch Mispredictions Don't Affect QuickSort." *arXiv Preprint arXiv:1604.06697*, June. https://arxiv.org/abs/1604.06697v2.

[FPUx87] "Programming with the X87 Floating-Point Unit." http://home.agh.edu.pl/~amrozek/x87.pdf.

[Goldberg 1991] Goldberg, David. 1991. "What Every Computer Scientist Should Know About Floating-Point Arithmetic." *ACM Computing Surveys (CSUR)* 23 (1). ACM: 5–48.

[Hennessy 2011] Hennessy, John L., and David A. Patterson. 2011. *Computer Architecture: A Quantitative Approach*. 5th ed. Morgan Kaufmann.

[Icaza 2018] Icaza, Miguel de. 2018. "How We Doubled Mono's Float Speed." April 11. https://tirania.org/blog/archive/2018/Apr-11.html.

[Intel Manual] "Intel: Intel® 64 and IA-32 Architectures Software Developer's Manual (325462-061US)." 2016. www.intel.com/content/dam/www/public/us/en/documents/manuals/64-ia-32-architectures-software-developer-manual-325462.pdf.

[Lemire 2019] Lemire, Daniel, Owen Kaser, and Nathan Kurz. 2019. "Faster Remainder by Direct Computation: Applications to Compilers and Software Libraries." *arXiv Preprint arXiv:1902.01961*. https://arxiv.org/abs/1902.01961.

[Lui 2018] Lui, Brian. 2018. "Using .NET Hardware Intrinsics API to Accelerate Machine Learning Scenarios." October 10. https://blogs.msdn.microsoft.com/dotnet/2018/10/10/using-net-hardware-intrinsics-api-to-accelerate-machine-learning-scenarios/.

[Luu 2017] Luu, Dan. 2017. "Branch Prediction." August. `https://danluu.com/branch-prediction/`.

[Mijailovic 2018a] Mijailovic, Nemanja. 2018. "Exploring .NET Core Platform Intrinsics: Part 1 - Accelerating SHA-256 on ARMv8." June 6. `https://mijailovic.net/2018/06/06/sha256-armv8/`.

[Mijailovic 2018b] Mijailovic, Nemanja. 2018. "Exploring .NET Core Platform Intrinsics: Part 2 - Accelerating AES Encryption on ARMv8." June 18. `https://mijailovic.net/2018/06/18/aes-armv8/`.

[Mijailovic 2018c] Mijailovic, Nemanja. 2018. "Exploring .NET Core Platform Intrinsics: Part 3 - Viewing the Code Generated by the JIT." July 5. `https://mijailovic.net/2018/07/05/generated-code/`.

[Mijailovic 2018d] Mijailovic, Nemanja. 2018. "Exploring .NET Core Platform Intrinsics: Part 4 - Alignment and Pipelining." July 20. `https://mijailovic.net/2018/07/20/alignment-and-pipelining/`.

[Mittal 2018] Mittal, Sparsh. 2018. "A Survey of Techniques for Dynamic BranchPrediction." *arXiv Preprint arXiv:1804.00261*, April. `https://arxiv.org/pdf/1804.00261.pdf`.

[Morrison 2008] Morrison, Vance. 2008. "To Inline or Not to Inline: That Is the Question." August 19. `https://blogs.msdn.microsoft.com/vancem/2008/08/19/to-inline-or-not-to-inline-that-is-the-question/`.

[Notario 2004] Notario, David. 2004. "Jit Optimizations: Inlining (II)." November 1. `https://blogs.msdn.microsoft.com/davidnotario/2004/11/01/jit-optimizations-inlining-ii/`.

[Rohou 2015] Rohou, Erven, Bharath Narasimha Swamy, and André Seznec. 2015. "Branch Prediction and the Performance of Interpreters - Don't Trust Folklore." `https://hal.inria.fr/hal-01100647`.

[Sanglard 2017] Sanglard, Fabien. 2017. *Game Engine Black Book: Wolfenstein 3D*. CreateSpace Independent Publishing Platform.

[Skeet 2008] Skeet, Jon. 2008. *C# in Depth*. Manning.

[Steele 1990] Steele Jr., Guy L., and Jon L. White. 1990. "How to Print Floating-Point Numbers Accurately." In *ACM Sigplan Notices*, 25:112–126. 6. ACM.

[Tillaart 2007] Tillaart, Rob. 2007. "Optimizing Integer Divisions with Multiply Shift in C#." *CodeProject*. January 27. `www.codeproject.com/Articles/17480/Optimizing-integer-divisions-with-Multiply-Shift-i`.

CHAPTER 8

Memory-Bound Benchmarks

Blaming perf issues on Garbage Collection is like blaming your hangover on your liver...

Its the thing that's saving you from your code.

— Ben Adams

It's a common situation for memory to be a bottleneck in your code. In this case, it's very important to understand how memory works on different levels: from CPU to .NET runtime. This knowledge allows *designing* good benchmarks. On the other hand, if you don't know some memory "features,"[1] it's very easy for you to design a wrong benchmark: you can miss an important part of the performance space or measure the performance of some memory-specific things instead of the performance of your code.

The memory management in .NET is a huge topic: it deserves its own book. And this book has already been published: *Pro .NET Memory Management* ([Kokosa 2018a]). It contains more than 1000 pages with a detailed overview of the most important aspects of memory management.

If you want to know more low-level details about memory on the hardware level, it's recommended to read [Drepper 2007]. It's a pretty old paper, but it explains pretty fundamental concepts that are still valid for modern hardware.

When developers discuss program memory, they usually think about different kinds of memory on the OS level like virtual memory, management memory, private set,

---

[1]Some of these features are nonobvious if you don't know about them. Here is a pretty interesting example: [Majkowski 2018].

© Andrey Akinshin 2019
A. Akinshin, *Pro .NET Benchmarking*, https://doi.org/10.1007/978-1-4842-4941-3_8

shared memory, resident memory, working set, and so on. In this section, we are not going to talk about it.[2]

In this book, we don't cover theoretical topics around memory management. Instead, we are continuing to learn different case studies that demonstrate how different pitfalls may affect memory-bound benchmarks. We will use the same structure used in Chapter 7. Each case study contains four sections: *Source code*, *Results*, *Explanation*, and *Discussion*.

This chapter will help you to design better memory-bound benchmarks and avoid common mistakes. It's still good to have knowledge about low-level topics, but it's not mandatory for most simple benchmarks. As usual, it's enough just to understand general concepts (and how to use it during benchmark design and analysis).

CPU Cache

The *read* and *write* operations are very popular in any program. When we discuss the algorithmic complexity of different algorithms, we often use $O(1)$ as the complexity of a single I/O operation. This is correct, but it doesn't mean that all of the I/O operations have the same duration: the actual performance depends on the area of memory that we are working with.

For example, we can work with physical disks like HDD or SDD. The disks are great when we need persistent storage for our data. In terms of performance, this storage is not the best solution for algorithms that should process data because the disk access is pretty slow.

The main memory (RAM) works much faster than disks. In our benchmarks, we often operate with arrays and different data structures that exist in the RAM. The RAM access works faster than the disk access, but it's still not fast enough for many use cases.

That's why we have the CPU cache: it's pretty efficient storage for the hot data that is placed on the CPU. When you perform I/O operations on the same data several times, the CPU puts the corresponding memory chunks in the cache. It allows getting a very good performance boost.

---

[2]You can find some interesting information about different kinds of memory in [Goldshtein 2016] and [Gregg 2018]. In [Dawson 2018a] and [Dawson 2018b], you can also find relevant performance case studies.

We also have the CPU registers, which work even faster than the CPU cache, but we have only a few of them. It's enough to provide fast access to several variables, but it's not enough to handle a huge array.

While we can work directly with CPU registers or main memory on the native code level, we don't have direct access to the CPU cache. That's why the CPU cache topic is so important for benchmarking: it can significantly change the performance of our code without our direct involvement. Let's discuss a few case studies that show the corresponding performance effects.

Case Study 1: Memory Access Patterns

The understanding of the CPU cache effects is also important when you choose the memory access patterns in your benchmarks. Let's learn a case study that demonstrates why it's so important.

Source code

Consider the following BenchmarkDotNet-based benchmarks:

```
public class Benchmarks
{
  private int n = 512;
  private long[,] a;

  [GlobalSetup]
  public void Setup()
  {
    a = new long[n, n];
  }

  [Benchmark(Baseline = true)]
  public long SumIj()
  {
    long sum = 0;
    for (int i = 0; i < n; i++)
    for (int j = 0; j < n; j++)
      sum += a[i, j];
```

527

```
    return sum;
}

[Benchmark]
public long SumJi()
{
  long sum = 0;
  for (int i = 0; i < n; i++)
  for (int j = 0; j < n; j++)
    sum += a[j, i];
  return sum;
}
}
```

Here we have a square array a. In the SumIj benchmark, you can see the most classic way to calculate the sum of elements in this array. In the SumJi benchmark, you do the same, but we use a[j, i] elements instead of a[i, j] on each iteration.

Results

Here is an example of results (Windows 10.0.17763.195, Intel Core i7-6700HQ CPU 2.60GHz, .NET Core 2.1.5, RyuJIT-x64):

```
Method |     Mean |    StdDev | Ratio |
-------- |----------:|-----------:|------:|
  SumIj | 334.8 us |  6.466 us |  1.00 |
  SumJi | 692.0 us | 30.509 us |  2.13 |
```

As you can see, SumJi works much slower than SumIj.

Explanation

In the SumIj benchmark, we enumerate all elements line by line. If we don't have a[0, 0] in the cache, we have a situation called *cache miss*. It means that we have to load this value in the cache, which takes some time.

The atomic unit of the CPU cache is cache line. The typical cache line size is 64 bytes, which means that it can handle eight long values. When we load a[0, 0] in the cache, we actually load the whole cache line, which also contains a[0, 1], a[0, 2], a[0, 3], a[0, 4], a[0, 5], a[0, 6], and a[0, 7] (assuming that the array is aligned in the

528

memory). Once we loaded this cache line, the access for the following seven elements will be fast because these elements are already in the cache. On the a[0, 8], we will hit a cache miss again, and load the next 64 bytes in the cache. This means that the next seven read operations will be fast.

In the SumJi benchmark, we enumerate all elements column by column. When we read a value of a[0, 0], we also have a cache miss with a corresponding performance penalty. However, we don't need the a[0, 1]..a[0, 7] elements (which are loaded in the cache with a[0, 0]) right now. After the a[0, 0] element, we are reading the value of a[1, 0]. And we hit another cache miss! The elements we load in the cache with a[1, 0] (a[1, 1]..a[1, 7]) are not useful for us right now because the next used element is a[2, 0].

Both SumIj and SumJi benchmarks perform the same number of instructions. However, SumJi works much slower because it has more cache misses. The illustration of the memory layout for this case study is presented in Figure 8-1 (each cache line has its own color).

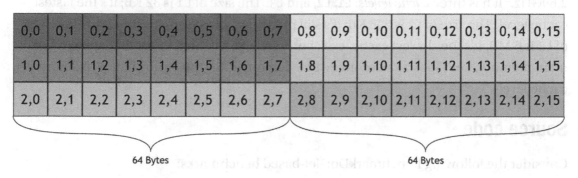

Figure 8-1. *Square array and CPU cache lines*

Discussion

In real life, you can't always control the memory access pattern, but you can control it in your benchmarks. If you want to get a proper overview of the performance space, it's recommended to check different access patterns (if it's possible): a sequential pattern (which should be the fastest one), a pattern when you never hit the same cache line twice (which should be the slowest one), a random pattern (which should be close to the slowest one), and some patterns that match real-life scenarios.

When you compare different algorithms, you can get the opposite results on different access patterns. In many cases, it's impossible to say which data structure is more efficient for your program, because one data structure may be faster in one kind of benchmark and slower in another kind. For example, the insert operation works much faster with a linked list than with a plain array, but the enumeration of the linked list may be much slower because of the high case miss rate.

If you want to use knowledge about CPU cache during optimization, you may be interested in the topic of cache-friendly algorithms and data structures (e.g., see [Hiroshi 2015] and [Kulukundis 2017]; "Data-Oriented Design" section in [Kokosa 2018a]). You can also find more interesting case studies about CPU caches in [Douillet 2018].

Case Study 2: Cache Levels

The core principles of the CPU cache are pretty similar on different hardware, but its physical layout depends on the CPU model. Let's consider the Intel Core i7-6700HQ CPU 2.60GHz.[3] It has three *cache levels*: L1, L2, and L3. The size of L1 is 32 KB; it's the fastest cache level. The size of L2 is 256 KB; it's still pretty fast, but it's not as fast as L1. The size of L3 is 6 MB; it's the slowest cache level, but it still works much faster than the physical main memory. Let's look at an example that demonstrates the performance of different cache levels.

Source code

Consider the following BenchmarkDotNet-based benchmarks:

```
[HardwareCounters(HardwareCounter.CacheMisses)]
public class Benchmarks
{
  private const int N = 16 * 1024 * 1024;
  private byte[] data;

  [Params(1, 2, 4, 8, 16, 32, 64, 128, 256,
          512, 1024, 2048, 4096, 8192, 16384, 32768)]
  public int SizeKb;
```

---

[3]https://ark.intel.com/products/88967/Intel-Core-i7-6700HQ-Processor-6M-Cache-up-to-3-50-GHz-

```
[GlobalSetup]
public void Setup()
{
  data = new byte[SizeKb * 1024];
}

[Benchmark]
public void Calc()
{
  int mask = data.Length - 1;
  for (int i = 0; i < N; i++)
    data[(i * 64) & mask]++;
}
}
```

Here we have a byte array data. We also have the SizeKb parameter, which defines the size of this array in kilobytes. In the only benchmark Calc, we increment elements of this array with the 64B delta. This is not a random number: it's the size of a single CPU *cache line*—the minimum chunk size processed by the cache. The CPU cache can't fetch a single variable from the main memory because it always works with cache lines. The number of increments in the benchmark is the same for all values of SizeKb. The [Har dwareCounters(HardwareCounter.CacheMisses)] attribute asks BenchmarkDotNet to measure the CPU cache misses via hardware counters.

Results

Here is an example of results (Windows 10.0.17763.195, Intel Core i7-6700HQ CPU 2.60GHz, .NET Core 2.1.5, RyuJIT-x64):

SizeKb	Mean	StdDev	CacheMisses/Op
1	18.75 ms	0.1259 ms	1,044
2	18.63 ms	0.1602 ms	1,058
4	18.62 ms	0.1656 ms	1,348
8	18.74 ms	0.1555 ms	1,065
16	18.75 ms	0.1675 ms	1,292
32	18.82 ms	0.1431 ms	1,841

```
   64 | 21.76 ms | 0.2145 ms |         2,743 |
  128 | 21.55 ms | 0.1594 ms |         3,702 |
  256 | 21.55 ms | 0.1367 ms |         3,076 |

  512 | 36.71 ms | 0.4937 ms |         2,791 |
 1024 | 36.31 ms | 0.2990 ms |         3,051 |
 2048 | 36.57 ms | 0.3610 ms |        49,448 |
 4096 | 40.92 ms | 0.4023 ms |       434,477 |

 8192 | 67.61 ms | 0.7010 ms |     3,162,028 |
16384 | 85.49 ms | 0.7213 ms |     5,493,341 |
32768 | 92.18 ms | 0.8848 ms |     6,240,472 |
```

As you can see, we have several groups of benchmark results. The SizeKb values from 1 to 32 give approximately the same result. The SizeKb values from 64 to 256 form another group of measurements that is two times slower than the first group. Next, we have a group of SizeKb values from 512 to 4096 that have bigger duration. After the SizeKb=8192, the duration becomes even bigger.

Explanation

When the work memory size is less than 32 KB, the CPU is able to keep the whole array in the L1 cache level. It's pretty efficient, and we have good performance results. Starting from 64 KB, the array can't be saved in L1 because it's too huge: the CPU has to use L2, which works slower. Starting from 512 KB, the CPU has to use L3 because L2 is not big enough: the performance becomes worse. Starting from 8192 KB, the array is too huge for all CPU cache levels: the read/write operations are starting to work directly with the main memory, which is even slower than L3.

The algorithmic complexity and the number of performed native instruction are the same for all SizeKb values. However, the benchmark with 32768 KB working memory works several times slower than the benchmark with 1 KB working memory.

Discussion

The knowledge about CPU cache is very important when you are starting to design small benchmarks based on real applications. In such applications, the working memory (memory that is actually used in the application lifecycle) may be pretty huge (dozens of megabytes or even gigabytes). Also, the CPU cache is typically cold: when we are working with the memory segment for the first time, the data is not loaded to the CPU cache yet. It means that memory access will be slow. In small artificial benchmarks, the CPU cache is typically warm (because we are performing several warm-up iterations to get the repeatable results), and the working memory is typically small (because we don't have gigabytes of memory, which are not necessary for this particular benchmark). Another common benchmarking pitfall is applying results of such benchmarks for optimizing real applications. Sometimes you can do it, but not always: the performance may be much worse in a real application because we don't have the benefits of the CPU cache that we have in a small benchmark. A general recommendation is simple: if you are working with arrays or other data structures, you should run your benchmarks on different sizes of the working memory.

The CPU cache performance also depends on the CPU microarchitecture. For example, there is a quote from [Intel OptManual], 2.1.3 "Cache and Memory Subsystem," about changes in Intel Skylake:

> *L3 write bandwidth increased from 4 cycles per line in previous generation to 2 per line.*

It's not easy to design small benchmarks that demonstrate such effects, but it may have a noticeable impact on application performance. It's also not easy to detect situations when we have performance changes between different CPUs because of the CPU cache efficiency, but it's one more factor that may affect the measurements.

Case Study 3: Cache Associativity

Another important "feature" of the CPU cache is the associativity. This is a special number used for matching main memory and cache lines. For example, in the Intel Core i7-6700HQ CPU 2.60GHz, the L1 cache level is 8-way associative, the L2 cache level is 4-way associative, and the L3 cache level is 12-way associative. Let's learn another example that will help us to understand how we should interpret these values during performance measurements.

Source code

Consider the following BenchmarkDotNet-based benchmarks:

```
public class Benchmarks
{
  private int[,] a;

  [Params(1023, 1024, 1025)]
  public int N;

  [GlobalSetup]
  public void Setup()
  {
    a = new int[N, N];
  }

  [Benchmark]
  public int Max()
  {
    int max = int.MinValue;
    for (int i = 0; i < N; i++)
      max = Math.Max(max, a[i, 0]);
    return max;
  }
}
```

Here we have a square array a. In the only benchmark, Max, we calculate the maximum element of the first column in this array. The array size is a benchmark parameter: we check 1023×1023, 1024×1024, and 1025×1025 arrays.

Results

Here is an example of results (Windows 10.0.17763.195, Intel Core i7-6700HQ CPU 2.60GHz, .NET Core 2.1.5, RyuJIT-x64):

N	Mean	StdDev
1023	2.026 us	0.0694 us
1024	4.452 us	0.2049 us
1025	2.012 us	0.0117 us

As we can see, the N=1023 and N=1025 cases have approximately the same duration. However, N=1024 case works much slower.

Explanation

Now it's time to discuss the meaning of the cache associativity. In Figure 8-2, you can see an illustration for a two-way associative cache.

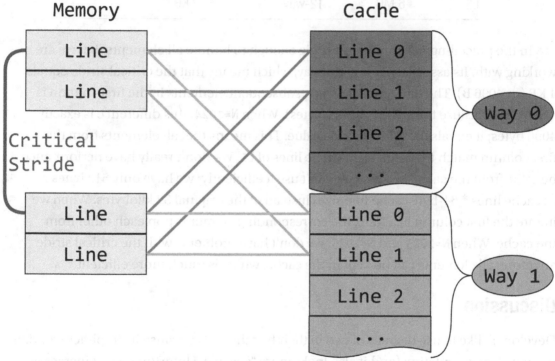

Figure 8-2. *Illustration of two-way associative cache*

As we mentioned before, the atomic unit of the CPU cache is the cache line (which is typically 64B). The "two-way" associativity means that for each 64B segment of the main memory, there are exactly two cache lines that can keep this segment. The total cache size is much lower than the main memory size, so it should reuse the same pair of cache lines for different 64B segments. The difference between 64B segments of the main memory that match the same set of cache lines is known as the *critical stride*. Its value can be easily calculated by dividing the cache size by the associativity value. In Table 8-1, you can see the critical stride values for different cache levels based on its associativity.

Table 8-1. *Critical Stride Values for Different CPU Caches*

Level	Size	Associativity	Critical stride
L1	32 KB	8-way	4 KB
L2	256 KB	4-way	64 KB
L2	256 KB	8-way	32 KB
L3	6 MB	12-way	512 KB

In the preceding benchmark, L1 is big enough to handle all elements that we are working with. Its associativity is eight-way, which means that the critical stride equals 4 KB (or 4096 B). The difference between subsequent elements in the first column is 4*N bytes (because the size of int is 4 bytes). When N=1024, this difference is exactly 4096 bytes; it equals the critical stride value. This means that all elements from the first column match the same eight cache lines of L1. We don't really have performance benefits from the cache because we can't use it efficiently: we have only 512 bytes (8 cache lines * 64-byte cache line size) instead of the original 32 kilobytes. When we iterate the first column in a loop, the corresponding elements pop each other from the cache. When N=1023 and N=1025, we don't have problems with the critical stride anymore: all elements can be kept in the cache, which is much more efficient.

Discussion

Developers like to use degrees of two in their benchmarks because it simplifies working memory size calculation (and it also looks more "geeky"). Unfortunately, it increases the probability of getting problems with the critical strides. You can easily get bad performance metrics because of that. The general recommendation is the same: you should check different sizes of the working memory in your performance experiments (including sizes that are not the power of two).

The critical stride effects also depend on the hardware. Here is another quote from [Intel OptManual], 2.1.3 "Cache and Memory Subsystem," about changes in Intel Skylake:

L2 associativity changed from 8 ways to 4 ways in Intel Skylake.

When you compare performance metrics in a memory-bound benchmark on two different CPUs, you can get a difference because of the different values of the cache associativity and the critical strides.

Case Study 4: False Sharing

False sharing is an effect that can spoil multithreading benchmarks. Let's look at an example that demonstrates it.

Source code

Consider the following BenchmarkDotNet-based benchmarks:

```
public class Benchmarks
{
  private static int[] x = new int[1024];

  private void Inc(int p)
  {
    for (int i = 0; i < 1000001; i++)
    {
      x[p]++; x[p]++; x[p]++; x[p]++;
      x[p]++; x[p]++; x[p]++; x[p]++;
      x[p]++; x[p]++; x[p]++; x[p]++;
      x[p]++; x[p]++; x[p]++; x[p]++;
    }
  }

  [Params(1, 256)]
  public int Step;

  [Benchmark]
  public void Run()
  {
    Task.WaitAll(
      Task.Factory.StartNew(() => Inc(0 * Step)),
      Task.Factory.StartNew(() => Inc(1 * Step)),
```

```
    Task.Factory.StartNew(() => Inc(2 * Step)),
    Task.Factory.StartNew(() => Inc(3 * Step)));
  }
}
```

Here we have the Inc method, which increments the same element of an array many times. It uses manual loop unrolling to avoid effects of the ILP that were discussed in Chapter 7. In the only Run benchmark, we start four tasks that are incrementing different array elements (each task has its own element index). The benchmark has the Step parameter, which defines the difference between indexes of the incremented elements. When Step=1, we are incrementing x[0], x[1], x[2], and x[3]. When Step=256, we are incrementing x[0], x[256], x[512], and x[768].

Results

Here is an example of results (Windows 10.0.17763.195, Intel Core i7-6700HQ CPU 2.60GHz, .NET Core 2.1.5, RyuJIT-x64):

```
Step |      Mean  |  StdDev |
----- |----------:|----------:|
    1 | 215.66 ms | 8.953 ms |
  256 |  61.54 ms | 4.002 ms |
```

As you can see, the case with Step=256 works much faster than the case with Step=1.

Explanation

Imagine a situation with two threads on two different CPU cores that perform read/write operations on the same variable. On Intel Core i7-6700HQ, each core has its own L1 and L2 caches. This means that CPU has to synchronize the variable value between the caches. Obviously, we will have a performance penalty because of this synchronization. This situation is known as *true sharing* (Figure 8-3, left side).

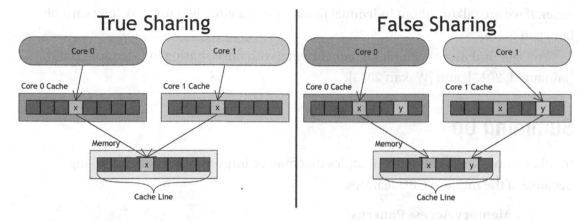

Figure 8-3. *True and false sharing*

Now imagine another situation: we still have two threads on two different CPU cores, but these threads perform read/write operations on *different* variables. We can assume that we will not have the synchronization performance penalty anymore because the threads don't share the same variable anymore. However, the CPU cache atomic unit for synchronization is not a single variable; it's a cache line! If these variables belong to the same cache line, the CPU cache still has to synchronize this cache line! It doesn't matter that we work with different variables. If we have read/write operations with the same cache line on two different cores, the CPU will synchronize it anyway (even if we don't actually share memory between threads). This situation is known as *false sharing* (Figure 8-3, right side). And it also has the performance penalty because of the synchronization.

Discussion

The discussed problem is valid only for multithreading benchmarks. Moreover, it's not a stable problem: you can observe the false sharing effect only if the target variables belong to the same cache line. Any changes in the source code or environment may move the variables into two different cache lines (the first variable will be at the end of one cache line; the second variable will be at the start of the next cache line). In this case, the false sharing effect will not affect the results anymore for these two variables.

The general recommendation: if you are writing a multithreading benchmark, make sure that the different variables which you use from different threads have a distance between them which is more than 64 bytes. In the preceding example, we did it with the help of Step=256: different tasks just use array elements that are pretty far from each other. If we are talking about individual fields, you can add eight unused `long` variables between them.

You can find more examples of benchmarks with false sharing in [Mendola 2008], [Jainam M. 2017], and [Wakart 2013].

Summing Up

In this section, we discussed four topics that may be important for benchmarking because of the modern CPU features:

- **Memory Access Patterns**

  The sequential access to the data is always faster than the random access because CPU cache operates with cache lines (the typical size is 64 B) instead of the variables. Once you load a variable in the cache, you also load the neighboring variables from the same cache line. After that, you can access these variables without additional cache miss penalty.

- **Cache Levels**

  Typically, the CPU cache has three levels: `L1`, `L2`, and `L3` (but you can also find other CPU cache configurations with two or four levels). The first level is the fastest one, but it's also the smallest one. The latest level is the biggest one, but it works much slower than other levels. Operations with any level of the CPU cache work faster than operations with data from the main memory, which is not presented in the cache.

- **Cache Associativity**

  Each byte of the main memory has a limited number of positions in the CPU cache that can handle its value. Typically, the associativity of the modern caches is between 4 and 24. The minimum positive difference between data segments that matches the same set of cache lines is known as the critical stride.

- **False Sharing**

    In multithreading benchmarks, you can get a situation when two
    different threads are performing read/write operations with two
    different variables on two different CPU cores. If these variables
    belong to the same cache line, we will get a situation called false
    sharing: the CPU has to synchronize this cache line between
    cores. As a result, we have a performance penalty for this kind of
    situation.

If you want to design a good CPU-bound benchmark, it's recommended to check the
different sizes of working memory. To reduce the number of these sizes, you can try the
sizes of L1, L2, L3, and the size that is much bigger than L3. In order to avoid problems
with critical strides, it makes sense also to check working sizes that are not powers
of two. It's also recommended to check different access patterns (if possible) like the
sequential access and random access. Such corner cases are useful to get an overview
of the performance space because they typically provide the best-case and worse-case
measurements. However, it's still important to check cases that are close to real-life
usage scenarios.

Memory Layout

In this section, we are going to discuss how performance depends on the actual
addresses of the variables that we are working with. In .NET, we can't always control the
alignment of our objects and structs, but there are still a lot of interesting performance
effects on the hardware level that may affect benchmark results.

In the previous section, we discussed typical problems with the CPU cache that affect
simple benchmarks pretty often. We will also continue to discuss the CPU cache effects
because this topic is closely related to the topic of the memory layout.

Case Study 1: Struct Alignment

In .NET, you can manually control the struct alignment via the [StructLayout] and
[FieldOffset] attributes (you can read more about it in [Kalapos 2018]). However, most
developers don't use these attributes and rely on default layout algorithms. Meanwhile,
different .NET runtimes have different layout policies that may produce a noticeable
impact on the application performance.

Source code

Consider the following BenchmarkDotNet-based benchmarks:

```
public struct Struct7
{
  public byte X0, X1, X2, X3, X4, X5, X6;
}

public struct Struct8
{
  public byte X0, X1, X2, X3, X4, X5, X6, X7;
}

[LegacyJitX86Job, MonoJob]
public class Benchmarks
{
  public const int Size = 256;

  private int[] sum = new int[Size];
  private Struct7[] struct7 = new Struct7[Size];
  private Struct8[] struct8 = new Struct8[Size];

  [Benchmark(OperationsPerInvoke = Size, Baseline = true)]
  public void Run7()
  {
    for (var i = 0; i < sum.Length; i++)
    {
      Struct7 s = struct7[i];
      sum[i] = s.X0 + s.X1;
    }
  }

  [Benchmark(OperationsPerInvoke = Size)]
  public void Run8()
  {
    for (var i = 0; i < sum.Length; i++)
    {
```

```
    Struct8 s = struct8[i];
    sum[i] = s.X0 + s.X1;
  }
 }
}
```

We have already discussed a similar benchmark in the "Struct Promotion" case study (Chapter 7). Here we have two structs: Struct7 with seven byte fields and Struct8 with eight byte fields. We also have two benchmarks: Run7 and Run8. In each benchmark, we calculate the sum of the first two struct fields in a loop. The only difference between Run7 and Run8 is the used struct.

Results

Here is an example of results (Windows 10.0.17763.195, Intel Core i7-6700HQ CPU 2.60GHz, .NET Framework 4.7.2, LegacyJIT-x86 v4.7.3260.0; Mono-x64 v5.18.0):

```
Method |           Job |     Mean |   StdDev | Ratio |
------- |-------------- |---------:|---------:|------:|
  Run7 | LegacyJitX86 | 7.331 ns | 0.0216 ns |  1.00 |
  Run8 | LegacyJitX86 | 2.409 ns | 0.0088 ns |  0.33 |
  Run7 |         Mono | 3.643 ns | 0.0177 ns |  1.00 |
  Run8 |         Mono | 3.716 ns | 0.0164 ns |  1.02 |
```

As you can see, Run8 works three times faster than Run7 on LegacyJIT-x86. On Mono-x64, Run8 works a little bit slower than Run7.

Explanation

When we have an array of structs, LegacyJIT-x86 tries to lay out its memory as compactly as possible. You can find the layout of the first eight elements of Struct7[] in the left side of Figure 8-4 (each struct instance has its own color). The elements are placed in memory one after another without padding. As you can see, most of the elements are unaligned. Access to the unaligned data usually works slower than access to the aligned data. That's why Run8 works much faster: all of its elements are naturally aligned because each element contains exactly eight bytes.

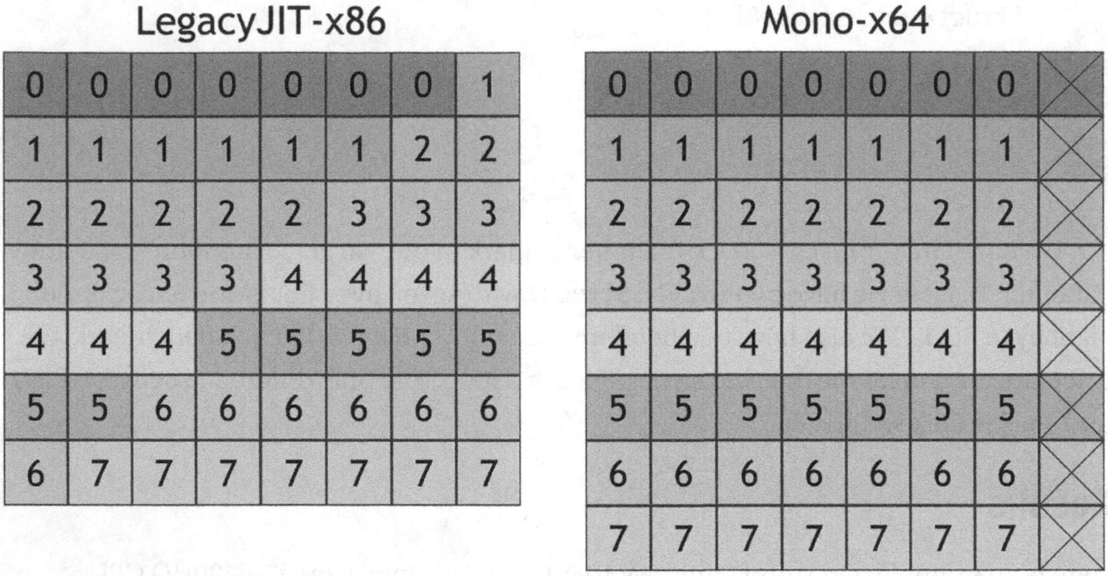

LegacyJIT-x86

0	0	0	0	0	0	0	1
1	1	1	1	1	1	2	2
2	2	2	2	2	3	3	3
3	3	3	3	4	4	4	4
4	4	4	5	5	5	5	5
5	5	6	6	6	6	6	6
6	7	7	7	7	7	7	7

Mono-x64

0	0	0	0	0	0	0	✕
1	1	1	1	1	1	1	✕
2	2	2	2	2	2	2	✕
3	3	3	3	3	3	3	✕
4	4	4	4	4	4	4	✕
5	5	5	5	5	5	5	✕
6	6	6	6	6	6	6	✕
7	7	7	7	7	7	7	✕

Figure 8-4. Struct7 layout in LegacyJIT-x86 and Mono-x64

In the right side of Figure 8-4, you can see the Struct7[] aligned on Mono: it uses one-byte padding after each element to make all Struct7 instances aligned. On the one hand, this is bad because such an alignment policy increases the total memory used for keeping the array. On the other hand, it's good because all the elements are properly aligned and access operation may be performed much faster than for the unaligned case.

Discussion

When you want to achieve the best possible performance for operation with struct arrays, it's a good idea to control the alignment for the struct instances manually. However, proper alignment may also increase the memory footprint because of the paddings. Also, note that unaligned access performance effects significantly depend on the used CPU model.

You can find more interesting information about memory alignment issues in [Sumedh 2013], [Sandler 2008], and [Lemirer 2012].

This case study is based on the StackOverflow question 38949304.[4]

---

[4]https://stackoverflow.com/q/38949304

Case Study 2: Cache Bank Conflicts

In the context of the CPU caches, a cache bank is a small segment inside a CPU cache line. When we match a byte from the main memory to the CPU cache line, we can also uniquely identify the number of a cache bank that contains this byte. In the next example, we will benchmark sequential operations with memory that works with the same cache bank from different cache lines.

Source code

Consider the following BenchmarkDotNet-based benchmark:

```
public unsafe class Benchmarks
{
  private readonly int[] data = new int[2 * 1024 * 1024];

  [Params(15, 16, 17)]
  public int Delta;

  [Benchmark]
  public bool Calc()
  {
    fixed (int* dataPtr = data)
    {
      int* ptr = dataPtr;
      int d = Delta;
      bool res = false;
      for (int i = 0; i < 1024 * 1024; i++)
      {
        res |= (ptr[0] < ptr[d]);
        ptr++;
      }
      return res;
    }
  }
}
```

Here we have a `data` array and a parameter called `Delta`. In the benchmark, we are enumerating the first `1024 * 1024` elements of this array. For each element `data[i]`, we compare it with `data[i + Delta]`. The algorithm is written with unsafe code to avoid bound checks during array element access. This code doesn't calculate anything useful; it's just another small example that demonstrates a pretty interesting CPU effect.

Results

Here is an example of results on Skylake (Windows 10.0.17763.195, Intel Core i7-6700HQ CPU 2.60GHz, .NET Framework 4.7.2, RyuJIT-x64 v4.7.3260):

Delta	Mean	StdDev
15	0.957 ms	0.0030 ms
16	0.955 ms	0.0045 ms
17	0.956 ms	0.0051 ms

And here is an example of results on Ivy Bridge (Windows 10.0.15063.1387, Intel Core i7-3615QM CPU 2.30GHz, .NET Framework 4.7.2, RyuJIT-x64 v4.7.3190):

Delta	Mean	StdDev
15	1.040 ms	0.0036 ms
16	1.243 ms	0.0063 ms
17	1.039 ms	0.0062 ms

As you can see, we have approximately the same duration of all runs on Skylake. However, on Ivy Bridge, the run with `Delta=16` works 20% slower.

Explanation

We can find an explanation for these results in [Intel OptManual], 3.6.1.3 "Handling L1D Cache Bank Conflict":

> *In Intel microarchitecture code name Sandy Bridge, the internal organization of the L1D cache may manifest a situation when two load micro-ops whose addresses have a bank conflict. When a bank conflict is present between two load operations, the more recent one will be delayed until the conflict is resolved. A bank conflict happens when two simultaneous load*

operations have the same bit 2–5 of their linear address but they are not from the same set in the cache (bits 6–12).

Bank conflicts should be handled only if the code is bound by load bandwidth. Some bank conflicts do not cause any performance degradation since they are hidden by other performance limiters. Eliminating such bank conflicts does not improve performance.

With the Haswell microarchitecture, the L1 DCache bank conflict issue does not apply.

Thus, each cache line can be split into 16 cache banks (this number also depends on the CPU model). Two load operations may collide on Ivy Bridge if they target values from different cache lines, but from cache banks with the same number.

Discussion

This problem is relevant only for old Intel processors (e.g., Ivy Bridge); you will not observe the described effect on processors since Haswell. Even on Sandy/Ivy Bridge processors, it's not so easy to hit the problem in real benchmarks. However, it's still good to know about such effects because they can unpredictably change the performance measurements. If you don't know about it, you may easily come up with the wrong conclusions.

Case Study 3: Cache Line Splits

Let's learn another case study about the CPU cache. This time, we will discuss it in the context of the data alignment.

Source code

Consider the following BenchmarkDotNet-based benchmarks:

```
[StructLayout(LayoutKind.Explicit, Pack = 8)]
public struct MyStruct
{
  [FieldOffset(0x04)] public ulong X0;
  [FieldOffset(0x0C)] public ulong X1;
  [FieldOffset(0x14)] public ulong X2;
  [FieldOffset(0x1C)] public ulong X3;
  [FieldOffset(0x24)] public ulong X4;
```

```
  [FieldOffset(0x2C)] public ulong X5;
  [FieldOffset(0x34)] public ulong X6;
  [FieldOffset(0x3C)] public ulong X7;
}

public unsafe class Benchmarks
{
  private int N = 1000;

  public void Run(int offset)
  {
    var myStruct = new MyStruct();
    if ((long) &myStruct.X0 % 64 == offset)
    {
      for (int i = 0; i < N; i++)
        myStruct.X0++;
    }
    else if ((long) &myStruct.X1 % 64 == offset)
    {
      for (int i = 0; i < N; i++)
        myStruct.X1++;
    }
    else if ((long) &myStruct.X2 % 64 == offset)
    {
      for (int i = 0; i < N; i++)
        myStruct.X2++;
    }
    else if ((long) &myStruct.X3 % 64 == offset)
    {
      for (int i = 0; i < N; i++)
        myStruct.X3++;
    }
    else if ((long) &myStruct.X4 % 64 == offset)
    {
      for (int i = 0; i < N; i++)
        myStruct.X4++;
    }
```

```
  else if ((long) &myStruct.X5 % 64 == offset)
  {
    for (int i = 0; i < N; i++)
      myStruct.X5++;
  }
  else if ((long) &myStruct.X6 % 64 == offset)
  {
    for (int i = 0; i < N; i++)
      myStruct.X6++;
  }
  else if ((long) &myStruct.X7 % 64 == offset)
  {
    for (int i = 0; i < N; i++)
      myStruct.X7++;
  }
}

[Benchmark(Baseline = true)]
public void InsideCacheLine() => Run(4);

[Benchmark]
public void CacheSplit() => Run(60);
}
```

Here we have the MyStruct value type with the explicit layout. It contains eight ulong fields with the following offsets: 0x04, 0x0C, 0x14, 0x1C, 0x24, 0x2C, 0x34, and 0x3C. In this case, .NET Framework will align this struct by eight bytes, which means that exactly one field will be placed on the boundary of two cache lines. The Run method takes offset and finds the field with an address that satisfies the following condition: "the remainder of dividing the address by 64 should be equal to offset." Next, it increments the corresponding field N times.

Also, we have two benchmarks: InsideCacheLine and CacheSplit. The InsideCacheLine benchmark invokes Run(4), which means that it will increment the field that is inside a cache line. The InsideCacheLine benchmark invokes Run(60), which means that it will increment the field on the boundary of two cache lines: the first four bytes of this field are located at the end of one cache line, and the last four are located at the start of another cache line.

Results

Here is an example of results on Skylake (Windows 10.0.17763.195, Intel Core i7-6700HQ CPU 2.60GHz, .NET Framework 4.7.2, RyuJIT-x64 v4.7.3260):

```
          Method |     Mean |    StdDev | Ratio |
---------------- |---------:|----------:|------:|
 InsideCacheLine | 1.630 us | 0.0063 us |  1.00 |
      CacheSplit | 3.041 us | 0.0089 us |  1.87 |
```

As you can see, the CacheSplit benchmark works significantly slower than the InsideCacheLine benchmark.

Explanation

We can find an explanation in [Intel OptManual], 3.6.4 "Alignment":

Misaligned data access can incur significant performance penalties. This is particularly true for cache line splits. The size of a cache line is 64 bytes in the Pentium 4 and other recent Intel processors, including processors based on Intel Core microarchitecture.

An access to data unaligned on 64-byte boundary leads to two memory accesses and requires several μops to be executed (instead of one). Accesses that span 64-byte boundaries are likely to incur a large performance penalty, the cost of each stall generally are greater on machines with longer pipelines.

Discussion

Cache line split is another effect that can unpredictably affect application performance. You will not get problems with it in most of the benchmarks because the data are usually properly aligned by the .NET runtime. However, you should be careful when you manually change the struct layout or when you are writing unsafe code.

You can find a lot of additional information about this topic in [Intel OptManual].

Case Study 4: 4K Aliasing

4K aliasing is a pretty exciting phenomenon that can also affect your measurements. It happens when we store a value to one memory location and load another value from a different memory location with a 4096-byte offset between these locations. Let's look at an example that demonstrates such a situation.

Source code

Consider the following BenchmarkDotNet-based benchmark:

```
public class Benchmarks
{
  private readonly byte[] data = new byte[32 * 1024 * 1024];
  private readonly int baseOffset;

  public Benchmarks()
  {
    GCHandle handle = GCHandle.Alloc(data, GCHandleType.Pinned);
    IntPtr addrOfPinnedObject = handle.AddrOfPinnedObject();
    long address = addrOfPinnedObject.ToInt64();
    const int align = 4 * 1024; // 4 KB
    baseOffset = (int) (align - address % align);
  }

  [Params(0, 1)]
  public int SrcOffset;

  [Params(
    -65, -64, -63, -34, -33, -32, -31, -3, -2, -1,
    0, 1, 2, 30, 31, 32, 33, 34, 63, 64, 65, 66)]
  public int StrideOffset;

  [Benchmark]
  public void ArrayCopy() => Array.Copy(
    sourceArray:      data,
    sourceIndex:      baseOffset + SrcOffset,
    destinationArray: data,
    destinationIndex: baseOffset + SrcOffset +
                      24 * 1024 +     // 24 KB
                      StrideOffset,
    length:           16 * 1024       // 16 KB
  );
}
```

Here we have the benchmark ArrayCopy, which copies 16 kilobytes from one array location to another. In the object constructor, we pin the array instance and prevent GC from moving the array. Also, we calculate the array address and find the baseOffset index, which is aligned by the 4 KB boundary. The SrcOffset parameter controls the alignment of the source data (sourceIndex equals to baseOffset + SrcOffset). The StrideOffset parameter controls the alignment of the destination address (destinationIndex equals to baseOffset + SrcOffset + 24 * 1024 + StrideOffset, which means that the difference between destinationIndex and sourceIndex equals to 24 * 1024 + StrideOffset).

Results

Here is an example of results on Haswell (Windows 10.0.17134.523, Intel Core i7-4702MQ CPU 2.20GHz, .NET Framework 4.7.2, RyuJIT-x64 v4.7.3260):

SrcOffset	StrideOffset	Mean	StdDev
0	-65	401.8 ns	4.727 ns
0	-64	335.2 ns	32.741 ns
0	-63	447.8 ns	29.978 ns
0	-34	502.1 ns	35.900 ns
0	-33	482.4 ns	30.916 ns
0	-32	369.1 ns	18.939 ns
0	-31	481.8 ns	27.200 ns
0	-3	487.4 ns	21.360 ns
0	-2	476.2 ns	25.476 ns
0	-1	496.1 ns	21.471 ns
0	0	364.3 ns	28.113 ns
0	1	1,184.3 ns	2.415 ns
0	2	1,224.3 ns	2.339 ns
0	30	2,079.1 ns	5.735 ns
0	31	1,197.0 ns	2.367 ns
0	32	315.5 ns	3.046 ns
0	33	1,117.5 ns	2.957 ns
0	34	1,150.7 ns	2.149 ns
0	63	1,106.0 ns	2.494 ns

0	64	317.4 ns	3.952 ns
0	65	881.8 ns	6.027 ns
0	66	856.9 ns	2.421 ns
1	-65	333.1 ns	3.071 ns
1	-64	434.8 ns	5.049 ns
1	-63	445.0 ns	3.903 ns
1	-34	436.0 ns	3.135 ns
1	-33	318.3 ns	2.898 ns
1	-32	444.9 ns	2.463 ns
1	-31	443.4 ns	6.471 ns
1	-3	417.3 ns	2.362 ns
1	-2	422.7 ns	2.393 ns
1	-1	357.7 ns	9.241 ns
1	0	430.4 ns	4.918 ns
1	1	1,020.1 ns	2.329 ns
1	2	1,015.7 ns	2.179 ns
1	30	1,021.5 ns	2.753 ns
1	31	412.8 ns	6.160 ns
1	32	834.7 ns	3.752 ns
1	33	709.2 ns	11.557 ns
1	34	708.8 ns	1.318 ns
1	63	608.8 ns	8.753 ns
1	64	663.9 ns	1.496 ns
1	65	625.9 ns	5.878 ns
1	66	648.8 ns	7.477 ns

This table is shown for all parameter values because it contains a lot of interesting alignment-related performance effects: we have dozens of different performance measurements for the same operations that just transfer 16 KB of memory. You can take this table (or build the same table on your own hardware) and try to explain the results. In the scope of this section, we will focus only on a small fragment of it:

SrcOffset	StrideOffset	Mean	StdDev
0	-1	496.1 ns	21.471 ns
0	0	364.3 ns	28.113 ns
0	1	1,184.3 ns	2.415 ns

```
0 |                  2 | 1,224.3 ns |   2.339 ns |
0 |                 30 | 2,079.1 ns |   5.735 ns |
0 |                 31 | 1,197.0 ns |   2.367 ns |
0 |                 32 |   315.5 ns |   3.046 ns |
```

As you can see, we have extremely high measurements for StrideOffset values from 1 to 31. In other fragments of the original table (e.g., for StrideOffset values from –31 to 1), the measurements are not so high, which means that it's not just unaligned memory access: we observe a more significant performance effect.

Explanation

When we perform read/write operations with memory, the CPU cache is used as an intermediate data storage. However, there is one more layer between the registers and the CPU, which is shown in Figure 8-5.

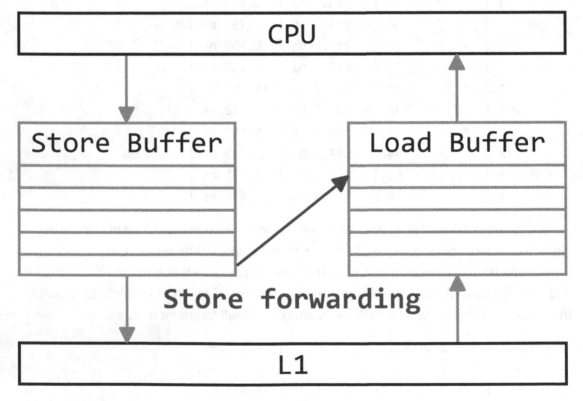

Figure 8-5. *Store buffer, load buffer, and store forwarding*

Imagine an instruction that moves data from the registers to the CPU cache. It performs an action that takes some time: CPU can't transfer data instantly. However, it doesn't make sense to wait until this transfer is finishing before CPU can start performing the next instruction. Instead of it, the register value is placed in the special *store buffer*. Next, it's possible to start the next instruction while the CPU moves values from the store buffer to the CPU cache.

The same approach is applied for getting data from the CPU cache: instead of waiting for transferring data from the CPU cache to the CPU registers, we fetch data in advance via the *load buffer*.

Now imagine the situation when we write a value to the memory and immediately read it again. In this case, the store and load buffers can introduce a significant delay because we should wait until the value is transferred from a register to the CPU cache via store buffer; next, we should wait until the value is transferred from the CPU cache to a register, and only after that can we use this value. Fortunately, this problem is already solved with the help of the *store forwarding*. This mechanism allows moving values from the store buffer to the load buffer bypassing the CPU cache!

To make the store forwarding efficient, the CPU has to understand very quickly that the required value is in the store buffer. Since it's not fast to enumerate the store buffer each time, the CPU uses a small hash table for the buffer values where the hash is the least significant 12 bits of the value address (it's valid for Intel CPUs). What do you think will happen in the case of a hash collision?

Now we are ready to read about 4K aliasing from [Intel OptManual], 11.8 "4K Aliasing":

> *4-KByte memory aliasing occurs when the code stores to one memory location and shortly after that it loads from a different memory location with a 4-KByte offset between them. For example, a load to linear address 0x400020 follows a store to linear address 0x401020.*

> *The load and store have the same value for bits 5–11 of their addresses and the accessed byte offsets should have partial or complete overlap.*

> *4K aliasing may have a five-cycle penalty on the load latency. This penalty may be significant when 4K aliasing happens repeatedly and the loads are on the critical path. If the load spans two cache lines it might be delayed until the conflicting store is committed to the cache. Therefore 4K aliasing that happens on repeated unaligned Intel AVX loads incurs a higher performance penalty.*

To detect 4K aliasing, use the LD_BLOCKS_PARTIAL.ADDRESS_ALIAS event that counts the number of times Intel AVX loads were blocked due to 4K aliasing.

To resolve 4K aliasing, try the following methods in the following order:

- *Align data to 32 Bytes.*

- *Change offsets between input and output buffers if possible.*

- *Use 16-Byte memory accesses on memory which is not 32-Byte aligned.*

The 4K aliasing explains the highlighted fragment of the summary table. The difference between the source and destination addresses is 24 * 1024 + StrideOffset. When the StrideOffset value belongs to the 1..31 interval, we have a situation that exactly matches to the preceding quote from the Intel manual.

Discussion

4K aliasing doesn't affect most benchmarks, but this effect may be very important when you copy chunks of bytes from one location to another.

You can find more interesting case studies about store forwarding and 4K aliasing in [Lemirer 2018], [Wong 2014], [Bakhvalov 2018], and JDK-8150730.[5]

Summing Up

In this section, we discussed several performance issues that are related to the data alignment:

- **Struct alignment**

  When we process an array of structs, performance *depends on the alignment and the size* of each struct instance. The layout strategy depends on the [StructLayout] and [FieldOffset] attributes and runtime version.

---

[5]https://bugs.openjdk.java.net/browse/JDK-8150730

- **Cache bank conflicts**

  A bank conflict happens when *two simultaneous load* operations
  have *the same bit 2–5* of their linear address but they are *not from
  the same set in the cache (bits 6–12)*. This problem is actual for
  Sandy Bridge and *Ivy Bridge*, but you shouldn't worry about it with
  Haswell and subsequent Intel CPU microarchitectures.

- **Cache line splits**

  A cache line split happens when you perform read/write
  operations on data that is unaligned on a 64-byte boundary.

- **4K aliasing**

  4K aliasing happens when the code stores to one memory location
  and shortly after that it loads from a different memory location
  with a 4-KByte offset between them.

You should remember about these effects when you work with structs, write unsafe code, or copy huge chunks for bytes.

Garbage Collector

Garbage collection is a huge and pretty interesting topic. If you want to learn it in detail, it's recommended to read [Jones 2016] and [Kokosa 2018a]. In this section, we are going to cover only *some aspects* that can be useful in terms of benchmarking and show corresponding effects with small case studies. You will also find a lot of useful links that help you to learn more information about GC in different runtimes.

Case Study 1: GC Modes

In .NET Framework and .NET Core, we have a few options to configure the GC behavior. One of the most important option is switching between Server and Workstation modes. Let's check how this setting can affect our measurements.

Source code

Consider the following BenchmarkDotNet-based benchmarks:

```
[Config(typeof(Config))]
[MemoryDiagnoser]
public class Benchmarks
{
  private class Config : ManualConfig
  {
    public Config()
    {
      Add(Job.Default.WithGcServer(true).WithId("Server"));
      Add(Job.Default.WithGcServer(false).WithId("Workstation"));
    }
  }

  [Benchmark]
  public byte[] Heap()
  {
    return new byte[10 * 1024];
  }

  [Benchmark]
  public unsafe void Stackalloc()
  {
    var array = stackalloc byte[10 * 1024];
    Consume(array);
  }

  [MethodImpl(MethodImplOptions.NoInlining)]
  private static unsafe void Consume(byte* input)
  {
  }
}
```

Here we have two benchmarks: Heap, which allocates 10 kilobytes in the managed heap, and Stackalloc, which allocates 10 kilobytes on the stack. The

Stackalloc benchmark uses empty Consume method (which is marked with the [MethodImpl(MethodImplOptions.NoInlining)] attribute) to prevent the DCE.

Also, we have two jobs, Server and Workstation, which are responsible for executing these benchmarks with corresponding GC modes.

Results

Here is an example of results (Windows 10.0.17763.195, Intel Core i7-6700HQ CPU 2.60GHz, .NET Framework 4.7.2, RyuJIT-x64 v4.7.3260):

```
     Method |         Job |       Mean |     StdDev |   Gen 0 |
----------- |------------ |-----------:|-----------:|-------:|
       Heap |      Server | 745.193 ns | 22.7130 ns |  0.1917 |
 Stackalloc |      Server |   4.531 ns |  0.0920 ns |       - |
       Heap | Workstation | 480.974 ns |  7.3521 ns |  3.2673 |
 Stackalloc | Workstation |   4.425 ns |  0.0537 ns |       - |
```

The Gen 0 column shows the number of GC Generation 0 collects per 1000 operations.

As you can see, the Heap benchmark works much slower in the Server GC mode than in the Workstation GC mode. However, this setting doesn't affect the Stackalloc benchmark.

Explanation

The Workstation GC mode is designed for interactive UI applications that should be responsive. In this mode, we have a lot of small GC sessions: the runtime tries to avoid long GC pauses that may lead to UI hangs.

The Server GC mode is designed for server applications that should have the maximum throughput. In this mode, we have a small number of huge GC sessions: the runtime doesn't care about long GC pauses.

In the Heap benchmark, we have many more garbage collections of the Generation 0 in the Workstation mode. The GC pauses are pretty small, and they don't hurt the "average" performance as much as in the Server mode.

It worth noting that it's not always easy to correctly measure the performance of methods that allocate a lot of objects. You may think of these allocations as getting a "performance loan": the allocation itself is processed pretty fast, but you have to "pay" for it in the future during garbage collection sessions. These "payments" significantly depend on the selected runtime and GC settings.

A common problem in handwriting benchmarks is excluding the GC time for the measurements. You can easily get such a situation if you stop the measurements before the GC is starting to collect objects that you allocated during the benchmark. You should not underestimate the duration of GC pauses. Some pauses can take 1 minute (see [Lemarchand 2018]) or even 15 minutes (see [Kokosa 2018b])! The general advice here is simple: if you have too many allocations in a benchmark, you should use more iterations! In this case, the performance metrics will include the "average" GC impact. Meanwhile, you can get better performance in real life because the garbage collection may happen outside the method scope. It doesn't mean that you shouldn't worry about it because it still affects performance. You still have to "repay the performance loan," but you can do it after the measured method is finished.

In the Heap benchmark, the actual duration of the object allocation is approximately the same for both GC modes. We can see the difference in measurements because of the garbage collections that occur during the benchmark. Meanwhile, the Stackalloc benchmark doesn't allocate anything in the managed heap (we have "-" in the Gen 0 column): that's why it's not affected by the GC mode.

Discussion

Here is a list of the most popular settings that you can change:

- **gcServer**: specifies whether CLR runs server GC or client GC. The default value is false for desktop applications and true for ASP.NET applications.

- **gcConcurrent**: specifies whether the CLR runs GC on a separate thread (or threads) concurrently with the application threads. The default value is true.

- **GCCpuGroup**: specifies whether garbage collection supports multiple CPU groups. When a computer has multiple CPU groups and server garbage collection is enabled, enabling this element extends garbage collection across all CPU groups and takes all cores into account when creating and balancing heaps. The default value is false.

- **gcAllowVeryLargeObjects**: on 64-bit platforms, enables arrays that are greater than 2 GB in total size. The default value is `false`.

- **GCHeapCount**: the desired number of server GC heaps. The default value is 0, which means "not specified."

In .NET Framework applications, you can control all these settings via `app.config`. A configuration example:

```
<configuration>
  <runtime>
    <gcServer enabled="true"/>
    <gcConcurrent enabled="true"/>
    <GCCpuGroup enabled="true"/>
    <gcAllowVeryLargeObjects enabled="true"/>
    <GCHeapCount enabled="6"/>
  </runtime>
</configuration>
```

In .NET Core, you can specify these values via `runtimeconfig.json`[6] file or via `COMPLUS_*` environment variables. Also, you can specify a lot of additional options like the smallest Generation 0 size (`GCgen0size`) or the heap segment size (`GCSegmentSize`).[7]

You can find a lot of useful information about GC in .NET Framework and .NET Core in [Kokosa 2018a] (see Chapter 11 therein) and [MSDOCS GC Fundamentals].

Case Study 2: Nursery Size in Mono

Mono has its own GC implementation. The first versions of Mono used the *Boehm* (Boehm–Demers–Weiser) GC. This is a classic conservative C/C++ GC. It wasn't efficient for .NET application, so it was decided to replace it with *SGen* (Generational GC), which was introduced in Mono 2.8. SGen has been the default GC since Mono 3.2; you can find a detailed description of it in [MONODOCS SGen].

The main thing that you should understand is that GC engines in .NET Framework/.NET Core and Mono are completely different. Thus, you can't apply observation from one GC to the .NET platform in general. For example, SGen uses two primary GC

---

[6]See `https://github.com/dotnet/cli/blob/v2.2.104/Documentation/specs/runtime-configuration-file.md`

[7]`https://github.com/dotnet/coreclr/blob/v2.2.2/src/gc/gcconfig.h`

generations (instead of three in .NET Framework/.NET Core): *Minor* (*Nursery*) and *Major*. It also has a lot of settings that you can configure. For example, you can tune the size of the nursery generation. Let's check how it can affect our measurements.

Source code

Consider the following BenchmarkDotNet-based benchmark:

```
[Config(typeof(Config))]
[MemoryDiagnoser]
public class Benchmarks
{
  private class Config : ManualConfig
  {
    public Config()
    {
      Add(Job.Mono
        .With(new[] {new EnvironmentVariable(
          "MONO_GC_PARAMS", "nursery-size=1m")})
        .WithId("Nursery=1MB"));
      Add(Job.Mono
        .With(new[] {new EnvironmentVariable(
          "MONO_GC_PARAMS", "nursery-size=4m")})
        .WithId("Nursery=4MB"));
    }
  }

  [Benchmark]
  public byte[] Heap()
  {
    return new byte[10 * 1024];
  }
}
```

Here we have only one benchmark which allocates 10 kilobytes in the managed heap. Also, we have two jobs that execute this benchmark with different nursery sizes: 1 megabyte and 4 megabytes.

Results

Here is an example of results (Windows 10.0.17763.195, Intel Core i7-6700HQ CPU 2.60GHz, Mono 5.18):

```
        Job |   Mean   |  StdDev   | Gen 0 |
----------- |---------:|----------:|------:|
Nursery=1MB |  6.058 us | 0.0321 us | 2.3193 |
Nursery=4MB |  7.669 us | 0.0473 us | 0.5951 |
```

The Gen 0 column shows the number of GC Generation 0 collects per 1000 operations.

As you can see, Nursery=1MB works faster than Nursery=4MB.

Explanation

If you change any of the GC settings, it is most likely that it affects measurements of a benchmark that allocates object *somehow*. However, you can't make any general conclusions about "better" GC setting values for all kinds of applications.

The default size of the nursery generation in Mono 5.18 is 4 megabytes. As we can see, 1 megabyte looks like a better value for our benchmark, which allocates just 10 kilobytes of memory. However, it doesn't mean that 1 megabyte is a better value for other applications. For example, in [Akinshin 2018], you can find a story about how I changed it from 4 MB to 64 MB and *increased* the Rider startup time twice on Linux and macOS.

Discussion

You can specify different parameters of SGen via MONO_GC_PARAMS environment variable (all parameters are joined in a single string by commas). Here is a list of some SGen parameters in Mono 5.18 (you can always get the actual list for your version of mono via man mono):

- max-heap-size=size: Sets the maximum size of the heap.

- nursery-size=size: Sets the size of the nursery generation.

- major=collector: Specifies which major collector to use. Available options: marksweep (Mark&Sweep collector), marksweep-conc (concurrent Mark&Sweep), and marksweep-conc-par (parallel and concurrent Mark&Sweep).

- `mode=balanced|throughput|pause[:max-pause]`: Specifies what should be the GC's target.

- `soft-heap-limit=size`: Once the heap size gets larger than this size, ignore what the default major collection trigger metric says and allow only four nursery sizes of major heap growth between major collections.

- `evacuation-threshold=threshold`: Sets the evacuation threshold as a percentage.

- `(no-)lazy-sweep`: Enables or disables lazy sweep for the Mark&Sweep collector.

- `(no-)concurrent-sweep`: Enables or disables concurrent sweep for the Mark&Sweep collector.

- `stack-mark=mark-mode`: Specifies how application threads should be scanned; options are `precise` and `conservative`.

- `save-target-ratio=ratio`: Specifies the target save ratio for the major collector.

- `default-allowance-ratio=ratio`: Specifies the default allocation allowance when the calculated size is too small.

- `minor=minor-collector`: Specifies which minor collector to use.

- `alloc-ratio=ratio`: Specifies the ratio of memory from the nursery to be used by the alloc space.

- `promotion-age=age`: Specifies the required age of an object must reach inside the nursery before been promoted to the old generation.

- `allow-synchronous-major`: Forbids the major collector from performing synchronous major collections.

The SGen implementation has a lot of pretty interesting features. For example, the nursery generation consists of slots of fixed size. Here is the definition of predefined sizes in Mono 5.18[8]:

---

[8]You can find the full source code here: `https://github.com/mono/mono/blob/mono-5.18.0.245/mono/sgen/sgen-internal.c#L38`

```
#if SIZEOF_VOID_P == 4
static const int allocator_sizes [] = {
     8,    16,    24,    32,    40,    48,    64,    80,
    96,   124,   160,   192,   224,   252,   292,   340,
   408,   452,   508,   584,   680,   816,  1020,
  1364,  2044,  2728,  4092,  5460,  8188 };
#else
static const int allocator_sizes [] = {
     8,    16,    24,    32,    40,    48,    64,    80,
    96,   128,   160,   192,   224,   248,   288,   336,
   368,   448,   504,   584,   680,   816,  1016,
  1360,  2040,  2728,  4088,  5456,  8184 };
#endif
```

Thus, if we create an object which needs 2729 bytes on x64, a 4088-byte slot will be used, because it's the smallest possible slot that can handle such an object. If you want to monitor and analyze memory traffic, you should know such details. Otherwise, you will not be able to interpret measurements right way.

If you want to get performance metrics for different GC modes, you can run `mono` with the `-stats` argument: it will print you a lot of useful GC statistics.

Case Study 3: Large Object Heaps

In .NET Framework and .NET Core, there are two kinds of heaps:

- Small Object Heap (SOH): objects that are smaller than 85,000 bytes.

- Large Object Heap (LOH)[9]: objects that are equal or larger than 85,000 bytes.

When we are talking about GC generations, we usually mean SOH. However, we shouldn't forget about LOH, which has its own rules of memory management. Let's look at another example that shows the performance impact of working with LOH objects.

---

[9]https://docs.microsoft.com/en-us/dotnet/standard/garbage-collection/
large-object-heap

Source code

Consider the following BenchmarkDotNet-based benchmarks:

```
[MemoryDiagnoser]
public class Benchmarks
{
  [Benchmark]
  public byte[] Allocate84900()
  {
    return new byte[84900];
  }

  [Benchmark]
  public byte[] Allocate85000()
  {
    return new byte[85000];
  }
}
```

Here we have two benchmarks: `Allocate84900`, which allocates 84900 bytes, and `Allocate85000`, which allocates 85000 bytes.

Results

Here is an example of results (Windows 10.0.17763.195, Intel Core i7-6700HQ CPU 2.60GHz, .NET Framework 4.7.2, RyuJIT-x64 v4.7.3260):

Method	Mean	StdDev	Gen 0	Gen 1	Gen 2
Allocate84900	3.017 us	0.0216 us	26.313	-	-
Allocate85000	4.511 us	0.0362 us	27.023	27.023	27.023

The Gen 0, Gen 1, and Gen 2 columns show the number of GC Generation 0/1/2 collects per 1000 operations. As you can see, `Allocate85000` works 1.5 times slower than `Allocate84900`. Also, `Allocate85000` has collects in Generation 1 and Generation 2, unlike `Allocate84900`.

Explanation

The concept of LOH was introduced because moving objects during compacting collection is a heavy operation. GC doesn't compact LOH by default, which means that it doesn't move objects.[10] This is a great decision for applications that operate with a high number of huge arrays because it reduces the overhead of garbage collection in complicated allocation scenarios. However, it also may spoil performance in some simple scenarios like the preceding benchmark because it triggers advanced GC techniques. `Allocate84900` works fast because GC is able to collect all the allocated objects in Generation 0. `Allocate85000` doesn't work so fast, because GC has to collect higher generations (all the allocated objects are placed to LOH instead of Generation 0).

Discussion

In general, it's not recommended to use knowledge of such heuristics in practice. However, the 85000 constant becomes so fundamental that it's used for different optimization heuristics in many applications. For example, you can find usages of this magic constant even in the implementation of standard classes.[11]

The LOH has one pretty interesting exception: `double` arrays on the 32-bit runtime. Here is a quote by Abhishek Mondal from [Bray 2011]:

> *In 32-bit architectures CLR's execution engine attempts to place these arrays > 1000 doubles on the LOH because of the performance benefit of accessing aligned doubles. However there are no benefits of applying the same heuristics on 64-bit architectures because doubles are already aligned on an 8-byte boundary. As such we have disabled this heuristics for 64-bit architectures in .NET 4.5.*

On Mono, we also have the concept of the LOH, which is known as the *large object space*. Its default threshold in Mono 5.18 is 8000 bytes.[12]

You can find more information about the LOH in [Kokosa 2018a] (see Chapter 5, section "Size Partitioning," therein), [Morter 2013], and [Goldshtein 2013].

---

[10]Since .NET Framework 4.5.1 and .NET Core 1.0, it's been possible to force GC to compact LOH via `GCSettings.LargeObjectHeapCompactionMode`. You can find more information about it in the official documentation: `https://docs.microsoft.com/en-us/dotnet/api/system.runtime.gcsettings.largeobjectheapcompactionmode`.

[11]For example, see `https://github.com/dotnet/corefx/blob/v2.2.1/src/Common/src/CoreLib/System/Text/StringBuilder.cs#L73`

[12]See `https://github.com/mono/mono/blob/mono-5.18.0.245/mono/sgen/sgen-conf.h#L161`

Case Study 4: Finalization

The last GC concept we are going to discuss is finalization. In .NET, each object can have a *finalizer*, which is executed by a dedicated finalization thread after GC collection stage. This technique may be useful when you have some unmanaged resources that you want to free with the help of GC. However, finalizers have a significant impact on the GC performance. Let's check how it may affect our measurements.

Source code

Consider the following BenchmarkDotNet-based benchmarks:

```
public class Benchmarks
{
  public class ClassWithoutFinalizer
  {
  }

  public class ClassWithFinalizer
  {
    ~ClassWithFinalizer()
    {
    }
  }

  [Benchmark(Baseline = true)]
  public object WithoutFinalizer()
  {
    return new ClassWithoutFinalizer();
  }

  [Benchmark]
  public object WithFinalizer()
  {
    return new ClassWithFinalizer();
  }
}
```

Here we have two classes: `ClassWithoutFinalizer` (an empty class) and `ClassWithFinalizer` (an empty class with an empty finalizer). In two declared benchmarks (`WithoutFinalizer` and `WithFinalizer`), we just allocate instances of the corresponding classes.

Results

Here is an example of results (Windows 10.0.17763.195, Intel Core i7-6700HQ CPU 2.60GHz, .NET Framework 4.7.2, RyuJIT-x64 v4.7.3260):

```
          Method |      Mean |   StdDev | Ratio |
----------------- |-----------:|----------:|------:|
WithoutFinalizer |   2.235 ns | 0.0422 ns |  1.00 |
   WithFinalizer | 153.198 ns | 1.7301 ns | 68.57 |
```

As you can see, `WithFinalizer` works ~70 times slower than `WithoutFinalizer`!

Explanation

This is another example of how GC may affect performance measurements. In the `WithFinalizer` benchmark, GC has much more work to do: it has to track all the finalizers and execute them. In the preceding example, the finalizer does nothing, but it doesn't mean the GC can skip it.

Discussion

It's pretty hard to perform accurate measurements while GC collects nonreachable objects and executes their finalizers. The GC in .NET is not deterministic. It means that you can't directly control when the finalizers should be executed. However, you can wait until all the finalizers are finished. Here is the most common pattern for the ultimate GC collect:

```
GC.Collect();
GC.WaitForPendingFinalizers();
GC.Collect();
```

Here we collect garbage, wait until all finalizers are executed, and collect garbage (that we have after the finalization) again. This pattern can be useful when you want to avoid the performance impact of collecting previously allocated objects during new measurements.

This case study is based on the "Finalization Overhead" example from [Kokosa 2018a] (see Listing 12-11 therein).

Summing Up

In this section, we discussed four case studies showing the impact of GC on application performance. We talked about different GC modes, about the size of the nursery generation in Mono, about the LOH in .NET Framework, and about the performance impact of GC finalization.

During benchmarking, you should keep in mind the following facts:

- If you allocate objects, the measurements will be affected by the GC.

- In the general case, you can't control GC and you can't exclude the GC overhead from your measurements. And this is OK: you shouldn't want to exclude the GC overhead, because it's one of the essential performance factors that affect all managed applications.

- If you have a huge standard deviation because of nondeterministic GC, the best thing that you can do is increase the number of iterations. This will help you to get "more stable" GC impact on the measurements.

- Benchmarks with huge memory traffic are very sensitive to the GC settings. Switching between different GC modes or tuning GC settings may completely change the benchmark results.

It's not always easy to write benchmarks with many object allocations because you can't control moments when the GC decides that you have to "repay your performance loans." Only knowledge of GC internals will help to correctly interpret the benchmark results. In most cases, it's enough to know the general concepts (GC impact on the measurements, GC generations, LOH, finalizers, GC settings). Some special cases may require deep knowledge of GC internals (here I want to recommend [Kokosa 2018a] one more time) and good tools that help you to investigate different memory issues (e.g., PerfView or dotMemory).

Summary

In this chapter, we covered three different topics that are related to the memory-bound benchmarks:

- **CPU Cache**

  When we perform read/write operations with the main memory, CPU can accelerate these operations with the help of CPU cache. It may significantly affect our performance measurements because of different memory access patterns, size and associativity of different CPU cache levels, and other cache-specific effects like false sharing.

- **Memory Layout**

  The alignment of the data (which we can't always control) also has a significant performance impact. Unaligned memory access, cache banks conflicts, cache line splits, and 4K aliasing can spoil your measurements when you don't expect that.

- **GC**

  GC also can unpredictably affect the performance measurements because it's nondeterministic and it can add overhead at random moments. This overhead depends on the GC settings (like Server/Workstation GC modes or mono nursery size) and internal GC features (like the LOH or finalization).

Knowledge about these hardware and runtime features will help you to design benchmarks and analyze their results better. The primary advice for this kind of benchmark is the advanced exploration of the performance space: you should check different sizes of the working memory, different access patterns, different memory layouts, and different GC settings. Based on these configurations, you can make conclusions that are valid not only for a specific benchmark, but for a variety of different cases. The proper description of the performance space helps to extrapolate these results and predict performance metrics in real applications based on individual benchmarks.

References

[Akinshin 2018] Akinshin, Andrey. 2018. "Analyzing Distribution of Mono GC Collections." February 20. https://aakinshin.net/posts/mono-gc-collects.

[Bakhvalov 2018] Bakhvalov, Denis. 2018. "Store Forwarding by Example." March 9. https://dendibakh.github.io/blog/2018/03/09/Store-forwarding.

[Bray 2011] Bray, Brandon. 2011. "Large Object Heap Improvements in .NET 4.5." October 3. https://blogs.msdn.microsoft.com/dotnet/2011/10/03/large-object-heap-improvements-in-net-4-5/.

[Dawson 2018a] Dawson, Bruce. 2018. "Zombie Processes Are Eating Your Memory." *Random ASCII*. https://randomascii.wordpress.com/2018/02/11/zombie-processes-are-eating-your-memory/.

[Dawson 2018b] Dawson, Bruce. 2018. "24-Core CPU and I Can't Type an Email (Part One)." *Random ASCII*. https://randomascii.wordpress.com/2018/08/16/24-core-cpu-and-i-cant-type-an-email-part-one/.

[Douillet 2018] Douillet, Nicolas. 2018. "Effects of CPU Caches." April 6. https://medium.com/@minimarcel/effect-of-cpu-caches-57db81490a7f.

[Drepper 2007] Drepper, Ulrich. 2007. "What Every Programmer Should Know About Memory." *Red Hat, Inc* 11 (July): 2007. https://people.freebsd.org/~lstewart/articles/cpumemory.pdf.

[Goldshtein 2013] Goldshtein, Sash. 2013. "On 'Stackalloc' Performance and the Large Object Heap." October 17. http://blogs.microsoft.co.il/sasha/2013/10/17/on-stackalloc-performance-and-the-large-object-heap/.

[Goldshtein 2016] Goldshtein, Sasha. 2016. "Windows Process Memory Usage Demystified." January 5. http://blogs.microsoft.co.il/sasha/2016/01/05/windows-process-memory-usage-demystified/.

[Gregg 2018] Gregg, Brendan. 2018. "How to Measure the Working Set Size on Linux." January 17. www.brendangregg.com/blog/2018-01-17/measure-working-set-size.html.

[Hiroshi 2015] Inoue, Hiroshi, and Kenjiro Taura. 2015. "SIMD-and Cache-Friendly Algorithm for Sorting an Array of Structures." *Proceedings of the VLDB Endowment* 8 (11). VLDB Endowment: 1274–85.

[Intel OptManual] "Intel® 64 and IA-32 Architectures Optimization Reference Manual (248966-033)." 2016. `www.intel.com/content/dam/www/public/us/en/documents/manuals/64-ia-32-architectures-optimization-manual.pdf`.

[Jainam M. 2017] M., Jainam. 2017. "Understanding False Sharing." March 17. `https://parallelcomputing2017.wordpress.com/2017/03/17/understanding-false-sharing/`.

[Jones 2016] Jones, Richard, Antony Hosking, and Eliot Moss. 2016. *The Garbage Collection Handbook: The Art of Automatic Memory Management*. Chapman; Hall/CRC.

[Kalapos 2018] Kalapos, Gergely. 2018. "Struct Layout in C# - .NET Concept of the Week - Episode 13." May 11. `https://kalapos.net/Blog/ShowPost/DotNetConceptOfTheWeek13_DotNetMemoryLayout`.

[Kokosa 2018a] Kokosa, Konrad. 2018. *Pro .NET Memory Management: For Better Code, Performance, and Scalability*. 1st ed. Apress. `https://prodotnetmemory.com/`.

[Kokosa 2018b] Kokosa, Konrad. 2018. "War Story – the Mystery of the Very Long GC Pauses in .NET Windows Service." December 13. `http://tooslowexception.com/scenario-mystery-of-the-very-long-gc-pauses-in-net-windows-service/`.

[Kulukundis 2017] Kulukundis, Matt. 2017. "Designing a Fast, Efficient, Cache-Friendly Hash Table, Step by Step." presented at the CppCon 2017, September 27. `www.youtube.com/watch?v=ncHmEUmJZf4`.

[Lemarchand 2018] Lemarchand, Remi. 2018. "The Mysterious Case of the 1 Minute Pauses." *Remi's World*. `https://theonlinedebugger.blogspot.com/2018/11/the-mysterious-case-of-1-minute-pauses.html`.

[Lemirer 2012] Lemire, Daniel. 2012. "Data Alignment for Speed: Myth or Reality?" May 31. `https://lemire.me/blog/2012/05/31/data-alignment-for-speed-myth-or-reality/`.

[Lemirer 2018] Lemire, Daniel. 2018. "Don't Make It Appear Like You Are Reading Your Own Recent Writes." January 4. `https://lemire.me/blog/2018/01/04/dont-make-it-appear-like-you-are-reading-your-own-recent-writes/`.

[Majkowski 2018] Majkowski, Marek. 2018. "Every 7.8us Your Computer's Memory Has a Hiccup." November 23. `https://blog.cloudflare.com/every-7-8us-your-computers-memory-has-a-hiccup/`.

[Mendola 2008] Mendola, Gaetano. 2008. May 31. `http://cpp-today.blogspot.com/2008/05/false-sharing-hits-again.html`.

[MONODOCS SGen] "Generational GC." Mono Docs. www.mono-project.com/docs/advanced/garbage-collector/sgen/.

[Morter 2013] Morter, Chris. 2013. "Large Object Heap Compaction: Should You Use It?" October 2. www.red-gate.com/simple-talk/dotnet/net-framework/large-object-heap-compaction-should-you-use-it/.

[MSDOCS GC Fundamentals] "Fundamentals of Garbage Collection." Microsoft Docs. https://docs.microsoft.com/en-us/dotnet/standard/garbage-collection/fundamentals.

[Sandler 2008] Sandler, Alexander. 2008. "Aligned Vs. Unaligned Memory Access." June 3. www.alexonlinux.com/aligned-vs-unaligned-memory-access.

[Sumedh 2013] Sumedh. 2013. "Coding for Performance: Data Alignment and Structures." September 26. https://software.intel.com/en-us/articles/coding-for-performance-data-alignment-and-structures.

[Wakart 2013] Wakart, Nitsan. 2013. "Using JMH to Benchmark Multi-Threaded Code." May 15. http://psy-lob-saw.blogspot.com/2013/05/using-jmh-to-benchmark-multi-threaded.html.

[Wong 2014] Wong, Henry. 2014. "Store-to-Load Forwarding and Memory Disambiguation in X86 Processors." January 9. http://blog.stuffedcow.net/2014/01/x86-memory-disambiguation/.

CHAPTER 9

Hardware and Software Timers

A man with a watch knows what time it is. A man with two watches is never sure.

—Segal's law

There are a lot of useful benchmarking tools that can simplify your benchmarking life, but they are usually optional. You can use them or not depending on your preferences. But there is one tool that is essential for benchmarking: *the timestamping API* (methods that help you to get the current time). You can't write a benchmark if you can't get a timestamp. It's critical to understand what kind of APIs you have on your system, how these APIs work internally, and what the main properties of these APIs are. Of course, you can write a benchmark without this knowledge. However, in-depth understanding of the hardware and software timers allows you to design better benchmarks, control the accuracy level, and avoid timestamping pitfalls. In this chapter, we are going to cover the following topics:

- **Terminology**

    We will learn the basic terms that are widely used in discussions about timers: time units, frequency units, tick generator, quantizing errors, resolution, granularity, latency, precision, accuracy, and so on.

© Andrey Akinshin 2019
A. Akinshin, *Pro .NET Benchmarking*, https://doi.org/10.1007/978-1-4842-4941-3_9

- **Hardware timers**

  We will cover the most used hardware components that provide timestamping capabilities: TSC, ACPI PM, and HPET. We will discuss the history and internals of these timers, the corresponding low-level API for getting timestamps, and how to switch between different time sources.

- **OS timestamping API**

  The operating systems have native timestamping API, which can be used in different programming platforms including .NET. We will learn what kind of API we have on Windows, Linux, and macOS.

- **.NET timestamping API**

  We will discuss three primary APIs that can be used in .NET Framework, .NET Core, and Mono: `DateTime.UtcNow`, `Environment.TickCount`, `Stopwatch.GetTimestamp`. We will learn how to use them, how they are implemented internally, and how to benchmark their resolution and latency.

- **Timestamping pitfalls**

  We will discuss the most common mistakes that developers usually make during timestamping with each kind of .NET timestamping API.

I want to be sure that we are speaking the same language, so let's discuss some essential terms first.

Terminology

In this book, we use a lot of specific terms and specific notation. Sometimes, these terms confuse people. In this section, we will briefly cover the basic concepts:

- **Time units:** d, h, m, s, ms, μs, ns, ps

- **Frequency units:** THz, GHz, MHz, kHz, Hz, mHz, μHz, nHz

- **Main components of a hardware timer:** tick generator, tick counter, and tick counter API

- **Ticks and quantizing errors:** how computers work with discrete time

- **Basic timer characteristics:** nominal frequency, actual frequency, nominal reciprocal frequency, nominal resolution, nominal granularity, actual reciprocal frequency, actual resolution, actual granularity, maximum frequency offset, timestamp latency, access time, timer overhead, precision, random errors, accuracy, systematic error.

It's very important to understand all the terms and symbols.

Time Units

You can't talk about time if you don't know basic time units, which help you to measure time intervals. I hope you understand what a *second* means; it's the base unit of time in the International System of Units (SI). The exact actual definition according to the National Institute of Standards and Technology is the following:

> *One second is the duration of 9 192 631 770 periods of the radiation corresponding to the transition between the two hyperfine levels of the ground state of the cesium 133 atom.*

Of course, you don't need to remember this definition for benchmarking; the usual domestic understanding used in civilian timekeeping will be enough. However, if you are curious why we have this definition (why 9,192,631,770 and why the cesium 133 atom), and if you are also interested in the history of timekeeping and the corresponding technical concepts, it's worth reading [Jones 2000].

In SI, there are some additional time units that are commonly used by software engineers. The most useful of them (with corresponding symbols and equivalents in seconds) are presented in Table 9-1.

Table 9-1. *Time Units*

Unit	Symbol	Duration in seconds
Day	d (day)	86400
Hour	h (hour)	3600
Minute	m (min)	60
Second	s (sec)	1
Millisecond	ms	10^{-3}
Microsecond	us (μs)	10^{-6}
Nanosecond	ns	10^{-9}
Picosecond	ps	10^{-12}

Someone may think that microsecond, nanosecond, and picosecond are very small time units and that we don't need them in real life. They are indeed very small. A picosecond relates to a second as a second relates to 31710 years! However, sometimes we should care about small time units like microseconds in real software (e.g., see [Cook 2017]). When we are writing benchmarks, we often need nanoseconds, a typical time unit for short code snippets. Many single CPU instructions take even less than 1 nanosecond, so picoseconds are also useful.

Common symbols for time and time intervals are t and T. Thus, if you see T=5s, it can mean "the time interval is equal to 5 seconds."

There are a couple of things that usually confuse people:

- Papers, articles, blog posts, and other texts about general topics usually use the day, hour, min/minutes, sec/second terms, which are widely used and understandable to everyone. In texts about time measurements and performance, we often use the d, h, m, and s symbols instead (to be short).

- The standard SI unit for microseconds is µs. Unfortunately, there is no µ[1] character on a typical keyboard. Also, you can have encoding troubles with this character in some text editors and terminals. Thus, developers often use the us symbol instead.

---

[1]Unicode Character 'GREEK SMALL LETTER MU' (U+03BC), ASCII code 230. You can type it via Alt+230 on Windows, Option+m on macOS, Ctrl+Shift+u00b5 on Linux.

There are also some informal time units that you may meet in different blog posts:

- *jiffy*: a short period of time with an unspecified length
- *flick*[2]: a time unit which was introduced by Oculus,
  1 flick = 1/705600000 second.

Now it's time to talk about frequency units, which can be easily expressed via time units.

Frequency Units

When we are talking about timer properties, there is another handy term: *frequency*. The frequency unit is 1 *Hertz* (Hz). If the frequency of some event is n Hz, it means that the event occurs n times per second. Thus, 1 Hz = 1/second = 1 second^{-1}. Each frequency value corresponds to a time period. For example, 20 Hz corresponds to 50 ms because

$$20\,\text{Hz} = \frac{20}{1\,\text{s}} = \frac{20}{1000\,\text{ms}} = \frac{1}{50\,\text{ms}}$$

Some additional useful frequency units (with corresponding time periods) are presented in Table 9-2.

Table 9-2. *Frequency Units*

Unit	Symbol	Value in Hz	Time period
Terahertz	THz	10^{12}	1ps
Gigahertz	GHz	10^{9}	1ns
Megahertz	MHz	10^{6}	1us
Kilohertz	kHz	10^{3}	1ms
Hertz	Hz	1	1s
Millihertz	mHz	10^{-3}	10^{3}s
Microhertz	uHz (μHz)	10^{-6}	10^{6}s
Nanohertz	nHz	10^{-9}	10^{9}s

---

[2]https://github.com/OculusVR/Flicks

The common symbol for frequency is f. If we want to calculate the frequency of an event, we should divide the number of events by a time interval that contains all these events. For example, if something happens 42 times per day, it means that the frequency of the e ollows:

$$f = \frac{42}{1d} = \frac{42}{86400s} \approx 0.000486s^{-1} = 486\mu\text{Hz}$$

The term "frequency" is widely used in many physics and engineering disciplines. Here are some famous examples:

- Humans can hear sounds with frequencies between 20 Hz and 20 kHz.

- Visible spectrum (the part of the electromagnetic spectrum that is visible to the human eye) is about 430..770 THz. The frequency range for the color yellow is about 508..526 THz.

- 440 Hz is the frequency of the musical note of A above middle C (A440, the pitch standard).

- Communication with submarines uses extremely low frequency: from 3 to 30 Hz.

- Shortwave radio uses frequencies in the range 1.6..30 MHz.

- The frequency of a typical microwave oven is about 2.45 GHz.

- The most popular WiFi frequencies are about 2.4 GHz (802.11b/g/n/ax) and 5 GHz (802.11a/h/j/n/ac/ax).

If we are talking about waves and we want to draw these waves on a plot, frequency can be easily compared at a glance. Look at Figure 9-1. Here we have three waves with different frequencies:

(a) Let's say that the first wave is a "reference" wave with frequency 1x

(b) The second wave frequency is twice (2x) that of the reference one

(c) The third wave has frequency = 8x (eight times more than the reference one; four times more than the second frequency)

As you can see, we can compare frequencies of different waves by a picture (even if we don't know the exact value of the reference frequency x).

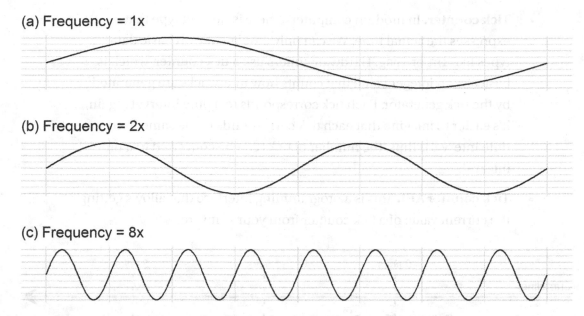

(a) Frequency = 1x

(b) Frequency = 2x

(c) Frequency = 8x

Figure 9-1. *Three waves with different frequencies*

The term "frequency" is also very useful for describing one of the most basic timer properties. Let's look at how we can use it for describing characteristics of hardware timers.

Main Components of a Hardware Timer

Real time is continuous. Unfortunately, it's impossible to work with continuous time and measure arbitrary time intervals. Any time measurements are based on hardware timers. You may think about a hardware timer as being composed of the following three parts (see Figure 9-2).

- **Tick generator.** This is a piece of hardware that generates a special kind of events (ticks) at a constant frequency. In practice, the generator frequency can be changeable, but in most cases, it's easier to imagine that the frequency is fixed. Typically, the generator is implemented with the help of a crystal oscillator (a small piece of quartz or other ceramic material).

- **Tick counter.** In modern computers, there is no data type that expresses the actual time. We can only emulate it with basic data types like int or long. Hardware timers use a tick counter, which is basically an integer value that counts how many ticks are generated by the tick generator. Each tick corresponds to a time interval (again, it's easier to imagine that each tick corresponds to the same fixed time interval). Thus, the number of ticks can be converted to a time interval.

- **Tick counter API.** This is a programming interface that allows getting the current value of a tick counter from your software.

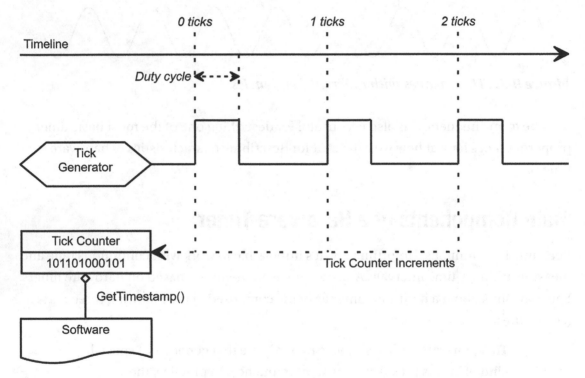

Figure 9-2. *Components of a hardware timer*

This construction allows measuring any time interval (with some limitations, which will be discussed soon). Usually, the tick duration is fixed and pretty small, and it's described in the timer documentation, or it can be obtained with the help of another API. Sometimes developers use the term "jiffy" for the duration of 1 tick.

An example. Let's say that we can get the tick counter value via the GetCurrentTicks() method and the frequency of our tick generator is 64 Hz. This means that one tick is $(1/64)$ s = 0.015625 s = 15.625 ms. Here is an example of measurements:

```
int startTicks = GetCurrentTicks();        // 100 ticks
SomeLogic();                               // Actual time: 0.5 s
int endTicks  = GetCurrentTicks();         // 132 ticks
int elapsedTicks = endTicks - startTicks;  // 32 ticks
double ticksInSec = 1.0 / 64.0;            // 1 tick = 0.015625 s
double elapsedTimeInSec =                  // Measure elapsed time
    elapsedTicks * ticksInSec;             // 32 * 0.015625 s = 0.5s
```

Here the SomeLogic() method takes 0.5 seconds, but we don't know this in advance; we want to get this value in the program. We get two timestamps (by calling GetCurrentTicks()): before and after the method invocation. Let's say the first value is 100 ticks, and the second one is 132 ticks. The difference between these timestamps is 32 ticks. We can easily convert ticks to seconds because we know the frequency (64 Hz):

$$\text{ElapsedTime} = \text{Ticks} \cdot \frac{1}{f} = 32 \cdot \frac{1}{64\text{Hz}} = 32 \cdot 15.625ms = 0.5s.$$

AN EXERCISE

Let's say frequency = 500 Hz, startTicks = 1280, endTicks = 1301. What is the value of the elapsed time in milliseconds?

I hope you solved this without any problems. It looks pretty easy, eh? However, it's not always as easy as in these examples. The tick-based approach has some problems, and one of the main problems is quantizing errors.

Ticks and Quantizing Errors

Thus, on the hardware level, we have discrete time (expressed in ticks) instead of continuous time. This time mapping (real time → number of ticks) is called *quantization*. The quantization process adds *quantizing errors* in our measurements. Let's figure out what that means with some examples.

Examples

Consider the three different measurements shown in Figure 9-3. In all these cases, we have two timestamps (A and B) and we are trying to measure the time between them. All timestamps are expressed in ticks, and we will use 1 `tick` as the time unit. For each timestamp, we will look at the actual and measured values. Here the measured value is always an integer (because the tick counter holds this value as an integer value); the actual time is expressed by a fractional number (it's a theoretical value that uniquely corresponds to a specific moment on the actual timeline).

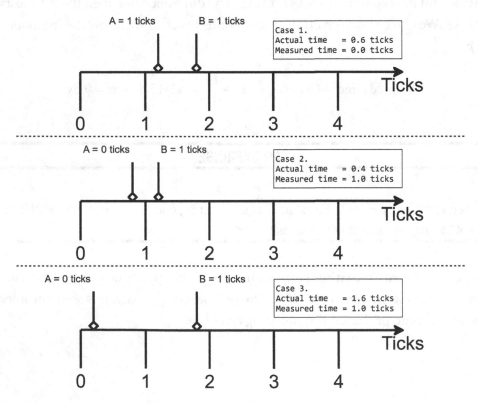

Figure 9-3. *Quantizing errors*

- **Case 1.** Actual(A) = 1.2 ticks, Actual(B) = 1.8 ticks. Because of the quantization, in both cases we have the same value of the tick counter: Measured(A) = Measured(B) = 1 tick. If we try to calculate the elapsed time based on these measurements, we get Measured(B) - Measured(A) = 0 ticks. The actual elapsed time is 0.6 ticks, but we just can't measure it because it's too small.

- **Case 2.** Actual(A) = 0.8 ticks, Actual(B) = 1.2 ticks, Measured(A) = 0 ticks, Measured(B) = 1 tick. The actual elapsed time is 0.4 ticks (smaller than in case 1), but the measured elapsed time is 1 tick (bigger than in case 1). Thus, we can't compare measured time intervals without knowledge about quantizing errors. If one measured interval is bigger than another, it doesn't mean that it's true for the actual time intervals!

- **Case 3.** Actual(A) = 0.2 ticks, Actual(B) = 1.8 ticks, Measured(A) = 0 ticks, Measured(B) = 1 tick. The actual elapsed time is 1.6 ticks (much bigger than in case 2), but the measured elapsed time is 1 tick (the same as in case 1). If two measured intervals are equal, the actual intervals may differ by up to 2 ticks.

Thus, the hardware time quantizing error is ±1 tick. Now we have to learn a few more terms in order to to describe errors.

Basic Timer Characteristics

There are many terms for describing basic timer characteristics. In this subsection, we are going to cover the following group of terms:

- Nominal and actual frequency, resolution, and granularity

- Frequency offset

- Timestamp latency, access time, and timer overhead

- Precision and accuracy

Nominal and actual frequency, resolution, and granularity

You may think that the minimum achievable positive difference between two timestamps is 1 tick. However, this is not always true. It's better to say that this difference is not less than 1 tick. A tick is the measurement unit of a timer, but it doesn't mean that you are always able to measure a 1 tick interval. For example, 1 tick for DateTime is 100 ns, but it's impossible to measure so small an interval with the help of DateTime (read more in the next section).

We can have some terminology troubles with the *frequency* term here. Sometimes "frequency" means how many ticks we have in 1 second. This is *the nominal frequency*. Sometimes "frequency" means how many counter increments we have per one second. This is *the actual frequency*.

If we have a value for frequency, we can calculate *reciprocal frequency*. The formula is simple: <reciprocal frequency> = 1 / <frequency>. Thus, if we are talking about the nominal frequency, *the nominal reciprocal frequency* is the duration of 1 tick. If we are talking about the actual frequency, *the actual reciprocal frequency* is the time interval between two sequential counter increments.

An example. The Stopwatch.Frequency value is the nominal stopwatch frequency because it can be used only for calculation of the 1 tick duration. There is nothing about it in the specification and the documentation, so it can return any value. And we can't make any conclusions about the actual Stopwatch frequency based on this value. For example, Stopwatch.Frequency in Mono is always 10000000.

"Reciprocal frequency" may sound clumsy, so we have another handy term: *resolution*. Unfortunately, here we also have some troubles with the definition. Sometimes people say "Resolution" and mean the duration of 1 tick. This is *the nominal resolution*. Sometimes people say "Resolution" and mean the minimum positive interval between two different measurements. This is *the actual resolution*.

There is another term for resolution: *granularity*. Usually, people use both words as synonyms (so, we can also talk about *the nominal granularity* and *the actual granularity*), but more often the granularity describes the actual reciprocal frequency (the actual resolution) instead of the 1 tick duration.

If we actually can measure the 1 tick interval, everything is OK. There is no difference between nominal and actual values: they are equal. Thus, people often say just "frequency" or "resolution" without any prefixes. However, if the actual resolution is more than 1 tick, there may be troubles with terminology. Be careful and always look at the context.

An example. The standard value of `DateTime.Ticks` is `100 ns`. On modern versions of Windows, the default timer frequency (which is responsible for `DateTime.Now`) is `64 Hz`. Thus, the actual resolution is the following:

$$ActualResolution = \frac{1}{ActualFrequency} = \frac{1}{64Hz} = 15.625ms = 15625000ns = 156250ticks.$$

Let's look once again on all these values:

```
NominalResolution = 100 ns
ActualResolution  = 15.625 ms
NominalFrequency  = 10 MHz
ActualFrequency   = 64 Hz
```

As you can see, it's important to distinguish between the nominal and actual values.

Frequency offset

As it was mentioned before, it's easy to think that the frequency is fixed. *Usually*, this assumption doesn't affect the calculations. However, it's good to know that the frequency may differ from the declared value. In this case, the actual frequency may differ from the declared value by the so-called *maximum frequency offset*, which is expressed in parts per million (ppm, 10^{-6}).

An example. The declared timer frequency is `2 GHz` with a maximum frequency offset of 70ppm. This means that the actual frequency should be in the range `1,999,930,000 Hz..2,000,070,000 Hz`. Let's say we measure a time interval, and the measured value is 1 second (or `2,000,000,000` ticks). If the actual frequency is `1,999,930,000 Hz`, the actual time interval is:

$$ElapsedTime = \frac{2\ 000\ 000\ 000\ ticks}{1\ 999\ 930\ 000\ ticks\,/\,sec} \approx 1.000035001225\,sec.$$

If the actual frequency is `2,000,070,000 Hz`, the actual time interval is:

$$ElapsedTime = \frac{2\ 000\ 000\ 000\ ticks}{2\ 000\ 070\ 000\ ticks\,/\,sec} \approx 0.999965001225\,sec.$$

Thus, the actual value of the measured interval (assuming there are no other errors) is in range `0.999965001225 sec..1.000035001225 sec`.

Once again: *usually* we shouldn't care about it because other errors have a greater impact on the final error.

Timestamp latency, access time, and timer overhead

When we discussed Figure 9-3, the timestamps were shown as instant events. In fact, a call of a timestamping API method also takes some time. Sometimes it interacts with the hardware, and such a call can be quite expensive. You may find different terms for this value: *timestamp latency*, *access time*, or *timer overhead*. All of these terms usually mean the same thing: a timer interval between two moments, calling a timestamping API and getting the value.

Precision and accuracy

There are two more important terms: *precision* and *accuracy*.

Precision (or *random error*) is the maximum difference between different measurements of the same time interval. Precision describes how repeatable measurements are. In other words, precision is defined by random errors of measured values around the actual value.

Accuracy (or *systematic error*) is the maximum difference between the measured value and the actual value.

In most cases, the timestamp latency is negligibly small compared to the actual resolution. However, sometimes the latency is huge, and it can affect total accuracy. We can say that the accuracy, in this case, is the sum of the latency and the resolution.

An example. On Windows 10 with enabled HPET (read more in further sections), the frequency of `Stopwatch` is `14.31818 MHz`, and the latency of `Stopwatch.GetTimestamp()` is about `700 ns`. It's easy to calculate the `Stopwatch` resolution: `(1/14318180)` second≈70 ns. Unfortunately, the latency is much bigger, so it's impossible to actually measure `70 ns` intervals:

$$\text{Accuracy} \approx \text{Latency} + \text{Resolution} \approx 700\text{ns} + 70\text{ns} \approx 770\text{ns}.$$

A typical measurement for such situation is presented in Figure 9-4.

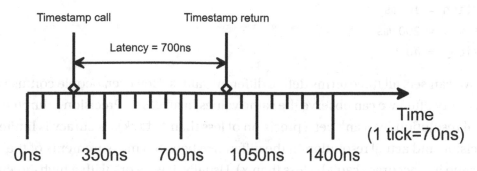

Figure 9-4. *Small resolution and big latency*

Thus, if you want to calculate the accuracy level, you should know both values: the actual resolution and the timestamp latency.

People often confuse resolution, precision, and accuracy. Let's look at the difference with a simple example.

An example. We have a timer with frequency = 100 Hz (this means that 1 sec = 100 ticks). We are trying to measure an exactly 1 second interval five times. Here are our results: 119 ticks, 121 ticks, 122 ticks, 120 ticks, 118 ticks. In this case:

- *Resolution* is the smallest difference between two measured values. We can't get a difference less than 1 tick (because we are working with an integer number of ticks), and we can get exactly 1 tick (the actual and nominal resolution are equal). Thus, the resolution is exactly 1 tick or 10 ms.

- *Accuracy* is the difference between actual and measured values. The actual value is 100 ticks, and the average of all measurements is 120 ticks. Thus, the accuracy is approximately equal to 20 ticks or 200 ms.

- *Precision* is the maximum difference between measurements that correspond to the same actual value. We measure exactly 1 second each time, but get different values (for example, because of the frequency offset): from 118 ticks to 122 ticks. Thus, precision is approximately equal to 4 ticks or 40 ms.

Thus, we get

```
Resolution = 10 ms
Accuracy   = 200 ms
Precision  = 40 ms
```

As we can see, all three terms define different values. However, people confuse them because very often we can observe the same values in all cases. Precision is limited by nominal resolution (we can't get a precision of less than 1 `tick`). Accuracy is limited by precision and actual resolution (if the difference between measurements of the same value if x, accuracy can't be less than x). Usually, if we work with a high-precision timer and a low access time, precision, resolution, and accuracy have the same order (sometimes these values can be equal). So, if everyone knows the context (exact values of all timer properties), the terms can replace each other (e.g., we can say "precision level" instead of "accuracy level" because they are the same). Formally, this is wrong. Despite this, people do it anyway. If you read a description of some measurements, always look at the context and be ready for incorrect statements.

Summing Up

In this section, we learned the following terms:

- *Time unit*: a unit for time measurement. The basic time unit is 1 second, but benchmarks often operate with very small units like 1 microsecond (10^{-6} *seconds*, notation: μs or us) or 1 nanosecond (10^{-9}*seconds*, notation: ns). Commonly used time units: d, h, m, s, ms, μs, ns, ps. Common symbols for time and time intervals are t and T. There are some informal time units like "jiffy," which means a short period of time with unspecified length, but developers often use it to denote the duration of 1 tick.

- *Frequency unit*: a unit for frequency measurements, reciprocal of time unit: 1 Hz = 1 second^{-1} Commonly used frequency units: nHz, μHz, mHz, Hz, kHz, MHz, GHz, THz. The common symbol for frequency is f.

- *Tick generator*: a piece of hardware that generates a special kind of event (*ticks*) at a constant frequency.

- *Tick counter*: an integer counter that holds the number of elapsed ticks.

- *Tick counter API*: a programming interface that allows getting the current value of a tick counter from your software.

- *Hardware timer*: a combination of a tick generator, a tick counter, and tick counter API.

- *Quantization*: a mapping from real continuous time to discrete time (number of ticks).

- *Quantizing errors*: errors that are introduced by quantization (we can't express real time by an integer value).

- *Nominal frequency*: how many ticks we have in 1 second.

- *Actual frequency*: how many counter increments we have in 1 second.

- *Nominal reciprocal frequency, nominal resolution, nominal granularity*: duration of 1 `tick`.

- *Actual reciprocal frequency, actual resolution, actual granularity*: the minimum positive interval between two different measurements.

- *Maximum frequency offset*: a difference between actual and declared frequency.

- *Timestamp latency, access time, timer overhead*: duration of a tick counter API call that returns the current value of a tick counter.

- *Precision, random errors*: the maximum difference between different measurements of the same time interval.

- *Accuracy, systematic error*: the maximum difference between the measured and actual value.

Now we know basic terminology. In the next section, we will use these terms to discuss the origin of the tick generators: hardware timers.

Hardware Timers

All of the timestamp methods use hardware in one way or another. So, first of all, we have to learn which hardware timers we have and how they can be used. In this section, we will cover the following timers:

- TSC (Time Stamp Counter)

- HPET (High Precision Event Timer)

- ACPI PM (Power Management Timer)

We will also talk about

- A brief history of the different kinds of these timers

- Basic timer properties (like actual frequency and timestamp latency) on different hardware

- How to work with TSC directly from C#

- How to switch between TSC, HPET, and ACPI PM on Windows and Linux

- What problems we might have with each timer

TSC

TSC is a common abbreviation for **Time Stamp Counter**. It is an internal 64-bit register that has been presented on all x86 processors since the Pentium. The TSC is an independent counter and can't be affected by changes in the current system time. It keeps monotonically increasing values of ticks; the tick duration depends on the CPU model. The TSC frequency is usually close to the nominal CPU frequency.

The value of the TSC can be read into EDX:EAX registers using the RDTSC instruction. The opcode for this instruction is 0F 31 ([Intel Manual], Vol. 2B 4-545). C# and other .NET languages are high level, so we are not typically working directly with assembly opcodes (because we have the powerful BCL, which contains managed wrappers for all useful functions). However, if you really want to do it, there are some special tricks. For a better understanding of internals, we will learn how to get the value of the TSC without standard .NET classes. On Windows, it can be read directly from C# code with the help of the following assembly injection:

```csharp
const uint PAGE_EXECUTE_READWRITE = 0x40;
const uint MEM_COMMIT = 0x1000;

[DllImport("kernel32.dll", SetLastError = true)]
static extern IntPtr VirtualAlloc(IntPtr lpAddress,
                                  uint dwSize,
                                  uint flAllocationType,
                                  uint flProtect);

static IntPtr Alloc(byte[] asm)
{
  var ptr = VirtualAlloc(IntPtr.Zero,
                         (uint)asm.Length,
                         MEM_COMMIT,
                         PAGE_EXECUTE_READWRITE);
  Marshal.Copy(asm, 0, ptr, asm.Length);
  return ptr;
}

delegate long RdtscDelegate();

static readonly byte[] rdtscAsm =
{
  0x0F, 0x31, // RDTSC
  0xC3        // RET
};

static void Main()
{
  var rdtsc = Marshal
    .GetDelegateForFunctionPointer<RdtscDelegate>(Alloc(rdtscAsm));
  Console.WriteLine(rdtsc());
}
```

Let's discuss this code in detail.

- For an assembly injection, we need the `VirtualAlloc` function from `kernel32.dll`. This function will help us to manually allocate memory in the virtual address space of the current process.

- The `Alloc` function takes a `byte` array with assembly instruction opcodes, allocates memory with the help of `VirtualAlloc`, copies the opcodes there, and returns a pointer to the address of the allocated and filled memory chunk. The penultimate argument of `VirtualAlloc` (flAllocationType) is responsible for what we are going to do with this memory: `MEM_COMMIT` means that we are going to commit memory changes. The last argument of `VirtualAlloc` (flProtect) is responsible for the memory protection mode: `PAGE_ EXECUTE_READWRITE` means that we can execute code directly from the allocated pages.

- We define a signature for the new managed `rdtsc` function via `RdtscDelegate` (it doesn't have any arguments and returns a `long` value).

- The `rdtscAsm` array contains all the target assembly opcodes: `0F 31` for RDTSC and `C3` for RET.

- The `Main` method uses `Marshal.GetDelegateForFunctionPointer` for converting an unmanaged function pointer to a delegate. The generic overload is supported only in the .NET Framework 4.5.1 and later versions. The argument of this method is `Alloc(rdtscAsm)`: here we take the byte array with the assembly opcodes and transform it into an `IntPtr`, which points to a piece of memory with these opcodes.

This approach allows calling RDTSC from the managed code. Usually, it's not a good idea to do so because there are a lot of troubles with the TSC that can spoil your measurements (many of them will be covered soon). Operating systems have special APIs that allow getting high-precision timestamps without assembly injection and direct knowledge about TSC. These APIs protect you from problems that you can get with the direct RDTSC call. However, sometimes the described assembly injection can be useful for research and diagnostics.

If you want to read the TSC value directly via the RDTSC instruction, you should know that the processor can reorder your instructions and spoil your measurements. From [Intel Manual], Vol. 3B 17-41, section 17.15:

> *The RDTSC instruction is not serializing or ordered with other instructions. It does not necessarily wait until all previous instructions have been executed before reading the counter. Similarly, subsequent instructions may begin execution before the RDTSC instruction operation is performed.*

We can find a classic way to solve this problem in [Agner Optimizing Assembly] (section 18.1):

> *On all processors with out-of-order execution, you have to insert XOR EAX, EAX/CPUID before and after each read of the counter to prevent it from executing in parallel with anything else. CPUID is a serializing instruction, which means that it flushes the pipeline and waits for all pending operations to finish before proceeding. This is very useful for testing purposes.*

In [Agner Optimizing Cpp] (section 16, "Testing Speed"), you can find a C++ example of direct RDTSC call with a memory barrier via CPUID.

There is another timestamping native instruction which prevents instruction reordering: RDTSCP. It also reads the TSC value, but it waits until all previous instructions have been executed before reading the counter. From [Intel Manual], Vol. 2B 4-545:

> *If software requires RDTSC to be executed only after all previous instructions have completed locally, it can either use RDTSCP (if the processor supports that instruction) or execute the sequence LFENCE;RDTSC.*

You can use RDTSCP instead of RDTSC and not be afraid of out-of-order execution. In addition to TSC reading, RDTSCP also reads the processor ID, but you don't need it for time measurements.

Now let's talk about the RDTSCP access time. In Table 9-3, you can see the list of reciprocal RDTSC throughputs (CPU clock cycles) for different processors (the data is taken from [Agner Instructions]).

Table 9-3. *Reciprocal Throughput of RDTSC on Different Processors*

Processor Name	Reciprocal throughput
AMD K7	11
AMD K8	7
AMD K10	67
AMD Bulldozer	42
AMD Piledriver	42
AMD Steamroller	78
AMD Bobcat	87
AMD Jaguar	41
Intel Pentium M, Core Solo, Core Duo	42
Intel Pentium 4	80
Intel Pentium 4 w. EM64T (Prescott)	100
Intel Core 2 (Merom)	64
Intel Core 2 (Wolfdale)	32
Intel Nehalem	24
Intel Sandy Bridge	28
Intel Ivy Bridge	27
Intel Haswell	24
Intel Broadwell	24
Intel Skylake	25
Intel SkylakeX	25

How can we interpret these numbers? Let's say that we have Intel Haswell (our reciprocal throughput is 24) with fixed CPU frequency = 2.2G Hz. So, 1 CPU clock cycle is about 0.45 ns (this is our resolution). We can say that a RDTSC invocation takes approximately 24 × 0.45ns ≈ 10.8ns (for RDTSC, we can assume that latency is approximately equal to reciprocal throughput).

You can also evaluate the throughput of RDTSC on your machine. Download `testp.`
`zip`[3] from the Agner Fog site, build it, and run `misc_int.sh1`. Here are typical results for
Intel Haswell:

```
rdtsc Throughput
```

```
Processor 0
```

Clock	Core cyc	Instruct	Uops	uop p0	uop p1	uop p2
1686	2384	100	1500	255	399	0
1686	2384	100	1500	255	399	0
1686	2384	100	1500	255	399	0
1686	2384	100	1500	254	399	0
1686	2384	100	1500	255	399	0
1686	2384	100	1500	255	399	0
1686	2384	100	1500	255	399	0
1686	2384	100	1500	254	399	0
1686	2384	100	1500	255	399	0
1686	2384	100	1500	255	399	0

Here we have 2384 CPU cycles per 100 RDTSC instructions, which means
approximately 24 CPI.

On modern hardware and modern operating systems, TSC works very well, but it has
a long history,[4] and people often consider TSC as an unreliable source of timestamps.
Let's discuss different generations of TSC and problems that we can get with it (you can
find more information about it in [Intel Manual], Vol. 3B 17-40, section 17.16).

Generation 1: Variant TSC

The first version of TSC (see the list of the processor's families in [Intel Manual], Vol. 3B
17-40, section 17.16) was very simple: it just counted internal processor clock cycles.
This is not a good way to measure time on modern hardware because the processor
can dynamically change its own frequency (e.g., the SpeedStep and Turbo Boost
technologies by Intel).

There is another problem: each processor core has its own TSC, and these TSCs are
not synchronized. If a thread starts a measurement on one core and ends on another

---

[3]http://www.agner.org/optimize/testp.zip
[4]https://stackoverflow.com/a/19942784

core, the obtained result can't be reliable. For example, there is a nice bug report on support.microsoft.com (see [MSSupport 895980]); the author had the following output for the ping command:

```
C:\>ping x.x.x.x

Pinging x.x.x.x with 32 bytes of data:

Reply from x.x.x.x: bytes=32 time=-59ms TTL=128
Reply from x.x.x.x: bytes=32 time=-59ms TTL=128
Reply from x.x.x.x: bytes=32 time=-59ms TTL=128
Reply from x.x.x.x: bytes=32 time=-59ms TTL=128
```

The cause:

This problem occurs when the computer has the AMD Cool'n'Quiet technology (AMD dual cores) enabled in the BIOS or some Intel multicore processors. Multicore or multiprocessor systems may encounter TSC drift when the times between different cores are not synchronized. Operating systems that use TSC as a timekeeping resource may experience this issue.

If you want to use TSC on old hardware/software, it's a good idea to set the processor affinity of your thread or process. If you are working with native code, you can do it via SetThreadAffinityMask on Windows or sched_setaffinity on Linux. In managed C# code, you can use the ProcessorAffinity property of the process like this:

```
IntPtr affinityMask = (IntPtr) 0x0002; // Second core only
Process.GetCurrentProcess().ProcessorAffinity = affinityMask;
```

Fortunately, we don't have these problems on modern hardware because the TSC internals were significantly improved.

Generation 2: Constant TSC

Constant TSC is the next generation of TSC; it solves the dynamic frequency problem by incrementing at a constant rate. This is a good step forward, but Constant TSC still has some issues (e.g., it could be stopped when CPU runs into deep C-state; read more in [Kidd 2014]). These problems were solved in the next incarnation of TSC.

Generation 3: Invariant TSC

Invariant TSC, the latest version of the counter, works well. A quote from [Intel Manual]:

> *The invariant TSC will run at a constant rate in all ACPI P-, C-. and T-states. This is the architectural behavior moving forward. On processors with invariant TSC support, the OS may use the TSC for wall clock timer services (instead of ACPI or HPET timers).*

You can check which kind of TSC you have with the help of the CPUID opcode. Fortunately, you don't need to write another assembly injection for that because there are existing tools that can detect the TSC kind. On Windows, you can check it via the Coreinfo[5] utility (a part of the Sysinternals Suite):

Here is a partial output example with TSC-specific lines:

```
Coreinfo v3.31 - Dump information on system CPU and memory topology
Copyright (C) 2008-2014 Mark Russinovich
Sysinternals - www.sysinternals.com
Intel(R) Core(TM) i7-6700HQ CPU @ 2.60GHz
Intel64 Family 6 Model 94 Stepping 3, GenuineIntel
RDTSCP          *          Supports RDTSCP instruction
TSC             *          Supports RDTSC instruction
TSC-INVARIANT   *          TSC runs at constant rate
```

This tells us that both RDTSC and RDTSCP are supported and the invariant TSC is available. You can do the same thing on Linux with the following command:

```
$ cat /proc/cpuinfo | tr ' ' '\n' | sort -u | grep -i "tsc"
```

If RDTSC, RDTSCP, and the invariant TSC are available, you should have the following lines in the output:

```
constant_tsc
nonstop_tsc
rdtscp
tsc
```

---

[5]https://docs.microsoft.com/en-us/sysinternals/downloads/coreinfo

The invariant TSC is indicated by a combination of `constant_tsc` (synchronization between cores) and `nonstop_tsc` (power management independence) flags.

In most cases, you can trust `Invariant TSC` and use it as a wall-clock timer for high-precision measurements. In rare cases, you can still have some problems (like synchronization problems on large *multiprocessor* systems), but you typically shouldn't worry about it. Nowadays, `Invariant TSC` is a very popular kind of TSC; you can find it in most modern Intel processors.

Now we know some basic information about different generations of TSC, assembly instructions for getting counter values, how to call it from the managed C# code, and what kinds of problems we may have with the TSC. But there are also other hardware timers.

HPET and ACPI PM

Along with TSC, many processors have two additional timers: *HPET* and *ACPI PM*. These are also independent counters that can't be affected by changes in the current system time.

HPET is the *High-Precision Event Timer*. HPET was designed by Microsoft and AMD to replace old timers like TSC and be the main timer for high-precision measurements. However, HPET didn't become the main timer, mainly because of the huge access time. On modern hardware and operating systems, HPET is usually disabled (the invariant TSC is used as the primary timestamp source), but it's usually possible to enable it (if you want it for some reason).

According to [HPET Specifications], section 2.2, the minimum HPET clock frequency is 10 MHz, but the actual HPET frequency is always 14.31818 MHz (the origin of this number is explained in the "History of Magic Numbers" section).

ACPI PM is a timer in the power management system. The most common abbreviations are *ACPI PM* and *ACPI PMT*. ACPI means *Advanced Configuration and Power Interface*, and PMT means *Power Management Timer*. However, it's common to call it *ACPI PM*, *PMC*, or just *Power Management Timer*.

According to [ACPI Specifications] (section 4.8.2.1), the frequency of this timer is always 3.579545 MHz. Both HPET and ACPI PM use the same master oscillator crystal (14.31818 MHz is 4·3.579545 MHz). Consequently, ACPI PM also has a huge access time.

The operating system has the "primary" hardware timer, which is used by default for timestamping. Typically, the default is TSC, but you can change this value manually.

On Windows, you can enable or disable HPET with the help of the `bcdedit`[6] utility. For enabling, you should run it with `/set useplatformclock true` arguments and reboot your computer.

```
:: Enable HPET (reboot is required):
bcdedit /set useplatformclock true
```

This sets the `useplatformclock` value in Boot Manager, which requires HPET instead of TSC. If you don't want to use it anymore, you should delete this value by `/deletevalue` and reboot:

```
:: Disable HPET (reboot is required):
bcdedit /deletevalue useplatformclock
```

If you want to check whether HPET is enabled or not, you should look for `useplatformclock` in the output of the following command:

```
bcdedit /enum
```

On Linux, all the time source–related files are typically placed in `/sys/devices/system/clocksource/clocksource0/`. You can look at the full list of available clock sources in `available_clocksource`. For example, I have TSC, HPET, and ACPI PM on my Linux laptop:

```
# Get available clocksource:
$ cat /sys/devices/system/clocksource/clocksource0/available_clocksource
tsc hpet acpi_pm
```

The current clock source can be find in `current_clocksource`:

```
# Get current clocksource:
$ cat /sys/devices/system/clocksource/clocksource0/current_clocksource
tsc
```

---

[6]A command-line tool for managing Boot Configuration Data (BCD). You can find more information about in https://docs.microsoft.com/en-us/windows-hardware/manufacture/desktop/bcdedit-command-line-options and https://msdn.microsoft.com/en-us/library/windows/hardware/ff542202.aspx

This value can be easily changed. For example, for enabling HPET, you should run the following:

```
# Set current clocksource:
$ sudo /bin/sh -c \
  'echo hpet > /sys/devices/system/clocksource/clocksource0/current_clocksource'
```

Usually, HPET is disabled, but you shouldn't assume that TSC is always the default. For example, you can meet enabled HPET on many legacy servers (which didn't have OS reinstallation for several years). It can be also enabled manually for some specific scenarios or because of the bugs.[7]

History of Magic Numbers

We already know that the HPET frequency is 14.31818 MHz and that the ACPI PM frequency is 3.579545 MHz. Why are these numbers used for hardware timers? If we want to understand this, we have to take an intriguing history lesson (you can skip it if you don't like history).

In 1950, the National Television System Committee (NTSC) started to construct a new standard for color television. This standard was approved in 1953. It was a complicated technical task because the new standard had to be backward compatible with old black-and-white television (B&W TV). The new standard uses the luminance-chrominance encoding system: a color image is represented as a sum of luminance and chrominance signals. The luminance signal corresponds to the monochrome signal in B&W TV, so that B&W TV could accept the new standard. The chrominance signal contains only information about color (two additional signals with different phases). Now let's solve a simple task: we should choose the chrominance signal frequency f_c (also known as color subcarrier frequency) which doesn't affect B&W TV. Consider several basic conditions that we should satisfy.

Condition 1 "Bandwidth for the chrominance signal"

The frequency of chrominance signal f_c should be as high as possible: it allows getting small noise structure. By the American standard, the maximum video frequency is f_{max}=4.18 MHz. After a series of experiments, it turned out that the difference $f_{max} - f_c$

---

[7]For example, there was a firmware bug in CentOS 7: "available_clocksource" contained only "hpet acpi_pm" without "tsc". The discussion is here: https://stackoverflow.com/q/45803565

can't be less than 0.6 MHz (otherwise, we will get image distortions). Thus, we have the following requirement:

$$f_{max} - f_c \geq 0.6 \text{ MHz}$$

Now we have the upper limit for f_c:

$$f_c \leq 3.58 \text{ MHz}$$

Condition 2 "Line frequency"

To minimize the visibility of the color subcarrier on B&W screens, its frequency should be chosen as an odd half-integer multiple of the **h**orizontal line rate f_h:

$$f_c = (2n+1)\frac{f_h}{2}$$

Thanks to this, the chrominance signal peaks would fit neatly between the luminance signal peaks, which minimizes the interference. In case of an even multiplier 2n, we get a strong noise pattern (a set of vertical lines).

Condition 3 "Audio signal"

We also have to minimize the interference between the audio signal (sound carrier) and the chrominance signal (chrominance carrier). So, we have to introduce an additional requirement (by analogy with Condition 2) for the distance between the sound carrier spacing $f_{\Delta s}$ and the frequency of chrominance carrier f_c:

$$f_{\Delta s} - f_c = (2m+1)\frac{f_h}{2}$$

Substituting $(2n+1) \cdot f_h/2$ for f_c, we get

$$f_{\Delta s} = (2m+1)\frac{f_h}{2} + (2n+1)\frac{f_h}{2}$$

It follows that

$$\frac{f_{\Delta s}}{f_h} = m + n + 1 = k$$

where k is an integer number.

The original standard had a frame rate of 30 Hz with 525 lines per frame (15750 lines per second). This number was chosen because of the vacuum-tube-based technology limitations of the day. Thus, the original horizontal line rate was f_h=15750 Hz. By the American standard for B&W TV, the sound carrier spacing $f_{\Delta s}$ between the audio and video frequency is exactly 4.5 MHz. Thereby, we have

$$\frac{f_{\Delta s}}{f_h} = \frac{4.5 \text{ MHz}}{15750 \text{ Hz}} \approx 285.714285714.$$

To minimize interference between audio and color video signals, $f_{\Delta s}/f_h$ should be an integer number. It was decided to make $f_{\Delta s}$ 286th harmonic of f_h (286 is the closest integer number to 285.714285714). However, we can't change the audio carrier frequency (the legacy TV receivers will not decode it), but we can change the horizontal line frequency! It's easy to calculate the new horizontal line rate:

$$f_h = \frac{f_s}{286} = 15734.26573 \text{ Hz}.$$

The frequency reduction coefficient is 15750 Hz/15734.26573 Hz≈ 1.001. An interesting implication from this is that now we have 29.97 Hz as the frame rate instead of 30 Hz and 59.94 Hz as the field frequency instead of the common 60 Hz.[8]

Condition 4 "Simple construction"

We also want to have an oscillator that is easy to implement. It is easier to create frequency divider chains when (2n+1) is a product of small prime numbers. We know that

$$f_c = (2n+1)\frac{f_h}{2}.$$

From $f_c \leq 3.58$ MHz and $f_h = 15734.26573$ Hz, we have

$$2n+1 = \frac{2f_h}{f_h} \leq \frac{2.3580000 \text{ Hz}}{15734.26573 \text{ Hz}} \approx 455.0578$$

---

[8]It's a special kind of fun to convert "24 frames per second" films to the 59.94 Hz NTSC video standard. Long story short, it requires slowing the film motion by 1/1000 to 23.976 frames per second, which increases a 1.5-hour film by 5.4 seconds. Google for "Three-two pull down."

We know that the chrominance signal frequency f_c should be as high as possible. The maximum possible value for $(2n+1)$ (which should be an odd integer number) is 455. This is a great number because it has small frequency divisors, namely, 5, 7, and 13:

$$(2n+1) = 5 \cdot 7 \cdot 13 = 455.$$

Solution

Hooray, now we can calculate f_c, which became the default NTSC color burst frequency:

$$f_c = (2n+1)\frac{f_h}{2} = 455 \cdot \frac{15734.26573 \text{ Hz}}{2} \approx 3.579545 \text{ MHz}.$$

If you like the history of television, you can also find a lot of interesting technical details in [Schlyter] and [Stephens 1999]. The 3.579545 MHz value had a significant impact on modern hardware timers. But how? Well, it's time to learn more about one of the first clock oscillators: **the Intel 8284 clock oscillator**.

Let's remember some old-fashioned processor models and clock oscillators. Intel 8284 is a clock oscillator for Intel 8086/8088 microprocessors. By specification, the maximum frequency for 8088 is 5 MHz. The signal should have 33.3% duty clock cycle (1/3 of the time high; 2/3 of the time low), so the original signal should be around 15 MHz (we can get 5 MHz by dividing the original frequency by 3).

At that time, it was a common practice to use TVs instead of monitors. Thus, the Color Graphics Adapter (CGA) required the 3.579545 MHz signal for creating the NTSC color subcarrier.

Also, it was expensive to have several crystal oscillators on the same chip. It was decided to use the same crystal for both CGA and CPU. Thereby, the master oscillator has the 14.31818 MHz frequency (4× NTSC). It allows getting 3.579545 MHz for CGA video controller (dividing the master frequency by 4) and 4.77272666 MHz for CPU (dividing it by 3). Yes, it was less than the 5 MHz limit (4.6% performance drop), but it's a good trade-off that allowed producing cheap CPU chips. You can find this story in a blog post by Tim Paterson (the original author of MS-DOS) (see [Paterson 2009]). Also, it is worth it to read the same story by Calvin Hsia (see [Hsia 2004]). Some additional technical information about Intel 8284 can be found in [Karna 2017] and [Govindarajalu 2002].

Now we can understand the origin of ACPI PM and HPET frequencies. The ACPI PM reuses the 3.579545 MHz NTSC frequency because we already have hardware support for this. HPET has a the minimum frequency requirement: 10 MHz. Since it was expensive to introduce an additional oscillator for HPET, it was decided to reuse the 14.31818 MHz frequency, which is also already implemented at the hardware level. Another hardware timer affected by these magic numbers is the PIT (Programmable Interval Timer) (also known as Intel 8253/8254 chip). The frequency of this timer is 1.193182 MHz. It uses the same 14.31818 MHz master frequency, which is divided by 12, so it's compatible with CGA (CGA Frequency = 3 * PIT Frequency) and CPU (CPU Frequency = 4 * PIT Frequency).

Summing Up

At the present time, the most popular and reliable hardware timer is TSC. You can read the value of the TSC via the RDTSC instruction, which has a high resolution and a low latency. However, you don't want to use it directly in general because there are a lot of problems with TSC. Here is a summary:

- Some old processors don't have TSC registers.

- The processor can change the frequency and affect the old version of TSC.

- There are synchronization problems on multicore systems.

- Even if we have Invariant TSC, there are still synchronization problems on large multiprocessor systems.

- Some processors can execute RDTSC out of order.

Thus, a direct RDTSC call is not a good choice for time measurements in general, because you can't be sure in advance that it produces reliable measurements. Fortunately, modern operating systems provide nice APIs that allow getting the most reliable timestamps for your current hardware.

TSC is not the only tick generator; there are also ACPI PM, and HPET. You can meet ACPI PM (frequency = 3.579545 MHz) or HPET (frequency = 14.31818 MHz) even on modern versions of Windows or Linux, but they are not popular because of the high latency.

Now we know the basic hardware sources of ticks. In the next section, we are going to learn different ways to get tick values from the software.

OS Timestamping API

We already know about hardware timers and how to use them. However, it's not a good idea to interact with them directly: it requires knowledge of these timers on different hardware and deep understanding of what can go wrong for all target environments. Fortunately, operating systems introduce a higher level of abstraction by providing special APIs.

There are three main groups of timestamping APIs on Windows:

- **System timer**

  - GetSystemTime: Retrieves the current *system* date and time in coordinated universal time (UTC) format as SYSTEMTIME.

  - GetLocalTime: Retrieves the current *local* date and time as SYSTEMTIME.

  - GetSystemTimeAsFileTime: Retrieves the current system date and time in UTC format as FILETIME.

- **System ticks**

  - GetTickCount: Retrieves the number of milliseconds that have elapsed since the system was started. The first version returns a 32-bit number up to 49.7 days.

  - GetTickCount64: 64-bit version of GetTickCount

- **High-resolution timer**

  - QueryPerformanceCounter and QueryPerformanceFrequency: Retrieves the current value and the frequency of the performance counter, which is a high-resolution timestamp that can be used for time interval measurements.

  - KeQueryPerformanceCounter: An analogue of QueryPerformanceCounter that can be used in device drivers (kernel-mode API).

  - GetSystemTimePreciseAsFileTime: Retrieves the current system date and time with the highest possible level of precision.

The second group (System ticks) is not very interesting,[9] so we are going to focus on the first and third groups (system timer and high-resolution timer), which will be covered in the next two subsections.

We will also discuss some Unix timestamping APIs like clock_gettime, clock_settime, clock_getres, mach_absolute_time, mach_timebase_info, gethrtime, read_real_time, gettimeofday, and settimeofday.

Timestamping API on Windows: System Timer

On Windows, there are several types of time representations. Here are two of the most popular options:

- SYSTEMTIME: Specifies a date and time, using individual members for the month, day, year, weekday, hour, minute, second, and millisecond. The time is either in UTC or local time, depending on the function that is being called.

- FILETIME: Contains a 64-bit value representing the number of 100-nanosecond intervals since January 1, 1601 (UTC).

If we want to know what time is it now (and don't need high-resolution measurements), Windows provides another useful mechanism called *system timer*. The primary API is the GetSystemTimeAsFileTime function. It returns FILETIME, which represents the current system date and time in the UTC format. If we want to get this value as SYSTEMTIME, we can also use GetSystemTime: it works slowly, but it returns the current date and time in a well-suited format. You can convert FILETIME to SYSTEMTIME manually with the help of FileTimeToSystemTime. If we want to get the local date and time (instead of UTC), we can use the GetLocalTime function.

All of the preceding APIs use the Windows system timer internally. It's important to understand the resolution of this timer, how the resolution can be changed, and how this can affect your application.

---

[9]It's useful only for some specific situations, and there is no really interesting information about it. We will discuss it in the next section because it's the underlying API for Environment.TickCount on Windows.

System timer and its resolution

The actual resolution of the system timer may take different values. You can easily get the configuration of your OS with the help of the ClockRes[10] utility (a part of the Sysinternals Suite). Here is a typical output on modern versions of Windows:

```
> Clockres.exe
Clockres v2.1 - Clock resolution display utility
Copyright (C) 2016 Mark Russinovich
Sysinternals

Maximum timer interval: 15.625 ms
Minimum timer interval: 0.500 ms
Current timer interval: 1.000 ms
```

First of all, look at the maximum timer interval: it equals to 15.625 ms (this corresponds to a frequency of 64 Hz). This is the default DateTime resolution when we don't have any nonsystem running applications. This value can be changed programmatically by *any application*. In the preceding example, the current timer interval is 1 ms (frequency = 1000 Hz). However, there are limits for this value: the minimum timer interval equals 0.5 ms (frequency = 2000 Hz) and the maximum is 15.625 ms. The current timer interval may take its value only from the specified range.

This is a typical configuration for the modern version of Windows. However, you can observe other resolution values on the older version of Windows. Here are two examples:

- Windows 95/98/Me: 55 ms (We already discussed this value in the "Hardware Timers" section; we have it thanks to the NTSC)

- Windows NT/2000/XP: 10 ms or 15 ms

You can also find a lot of useful information about different configurations in [The Windows Timestamp Project].

---

[10]https://docs.microsoft.com/en-us/sysinternals/downloads/clockres

System timer resolution API

So, how can the timer resolution be changed? There are some Windows APIs that can be used:

- timeBeginPeriod, timeEndPeriod from winmm.dll

- NtQueryTimerResolution, NtSetTimerResolution from ntdll.dll

You can use it directly from C#; here is a helper class for you:

```
public struct ResolutionInfo
{
  public uint Min;
  public uint Max;
  public uint Current;
}

public static class WinApi
{
  [DllImport("winmm.dll",
             EntryPoint = "timeBeginPeriod",
             SetLastError = true)]
  public static extern uint TimeBeginPeriod(uint uMilliseconds);

  [DllImport("winmm.dll",
             EntryPoint = "timeEndPeriod",
             SetLastError = true)]
  public static extern uint TimeEndPeriod(uint uMilliseconds);

  [DllImport("ntdll.dll", SetLastError = true)]
  private static extern uint NtQueryTimerResolution
        (out uint min,
          out uint max,
          out uint current);

  [DllImport("ntdll.dll", SetLastError = true)]
  private static extern uint NtSetTimerResolution
        (uint desiredResolution,
```

```
            bool setResolution,
            ref uint currentResolution);

  public static ResolutionInfo QueryTimerResolution()
  {
    var info = new ResolutionInfo();
    NtQueryTimerResolution(out info.Min,
                           out info.Max,
                           out info.Current);
    return info;
  }

  public static ulong SetTimerResolution(uint ticks)
  {
    uint currentRes = 0;
    NtSetTimerResolution(ticks, true, ref currentRes);
    return currentRes;
  }
}
}
```

The ResolutionInfo data structure represents the minimum, maximum, and current resolution of the system timer. In the WinApi static class, we import four target functions from winmm.dll and ntdll.dll. The custom methods QueryTimerResolution and SetTimerResolution are just wrappers for the imported NtQueryTimerResolution and NtSetTimerResolution.

Now let's play a little bit with this class. First of all, we can write our own ClockRes based on the described API:

```
var resolutionInfo = WinApi.QueryTimerResolution();
Console.WriteLine($"Min     = {resolutionInfo.Min}");
Console.WriteLine($"Max     = {resolutionInfo.Max}");
Console.WriteLine($"Current = {resolutionInfo.Current}");
```

Output (without any running apps):

```
Min     = 156250
Max     = 5000
Current = 156250
```

The only difference between ClockRes and our program is that ClockRes prints time in milliseconds, while we print time in 100 ns units. Max = 5000 means MaxResolution = 5000 * 100 ns = 0.5 ms.

Now, let's manually check that resolutionInfo.Current is the actual resolution of DateTime. Here is a very simple code that shows observed DateTime behavior:

```
// DateTimeResolutionObserver
for (int i = 0; i < 5; i++)
{
  DateTime current = DateTime.UtcNow;
  DateTime last = current;
  while (last == current)
    current = DateTime.UtcNow;
  TimeSpan diff = current - last;
  Console.WriteLine(diff.Ticks);
}
```

Here we save the current value of DateTime.UtcNow in current, and then we wait for another DateTime.UtcNow value in the while loop (by updating the last variable). This is not the most beautiful and correct way to get the DateTime resolution, but it's a simple program that should be affected by the actual DateTime resolution.

Typical output (without any running apps):

```
155934
156101
156237
156256
156237
```

Here is the output for case resolutionInfo.Current = 5000:

```
5574
4634
5353
5014
4271
```

As you can see, the received numbers are not exactly equal to 156250 or 5000. So, the difference between two sequential different DateTime values is approximately equal to the current timer interval.

PLAY WITH WINAPI CLASS

- Run ClockRes on your system. Next, get the minimum, maximum, and current resolution of the system timer from C# code.

- Try to increase or decrease the current resolution via SetTimerResolution. Check the new resolution value via API and via DateTimeResolutionObserver.

- Try to change the current resolution via TimeBeginPeriod/TimeEndPeriod functions.

- Try to set the current resolution to an invalid value (less than minimum or bigger than maximum).

It will probably be hard to change this value because other applications already requested high timer frequency. So, it's a good idea to terminate them before the experiments. But how do we know which applications changed the resolution? The powercfg utility will help us!

System timer analysis: powercfg

Let's say your current timer interval is not the maximum timer interval. How do you know what's to blame? Which program increased the system timer frequency? You can check it with the help of powercfg. This is a command-line utility that helps to control power system settings. Typically, you can find it in C:\Windows\System32\powercfg.exe.

Let's check how it works. Run the following command as administrator:

```
> powercfg -energy duration 10
```

This command will monitor your system for 10 seconds and generate an HTML report (energy-report.html in the current directory) with a lot of useful information including information about the platform timer resolution. Here is an example of output:

```
Platform Timer Resolution:Platform Timer Resolution
The default platform timer resolution is 15.6ms (15625000ns)
```

and should be used whenever the system is idle. If the timer
resolution is increased, processor power management technologies
may not be effective. The timer resolution may be increased due
to multimedia playback or graphical animations.

  Current Timer Resolution (100ns units) 5003
  Maximum Timer Period (100ns units) 156250

Platform Timer Resolution: Outstanding Timer Request
A program or service has requested a timer resolution smaller
than the platform maximum timer resolution.
  Requested Period 5000
  Requesting Process ID 6676
  Requesting Process Path
    \Device\HarddiskVolume4\Users\akinshin\ConsoleApplication1.exe

Platform Timer Resolution: Outstanding Timer Request
A program or service has requested a timer resolution smaller
than the platform maximum timer resolution.
  Requested Period 10000
  Requesting Process ID 10860
  Requesting Process Path
    \Device\HarddiskVolume4\Program Files (x86)\Mozilla Firefox\firefox.exe

   As you can see, the default interval is 15.6 ms, Firefox requires a 1.0 ms interval,
and ConsoleApplication1.exe in the home directory (which just calls WinApi.
SetTimerResolution(5000)) requires a 0.5 ms interval. ConsoleApplication1.exe
won; now we have the maximum possible platform timer frequency.

AN EXERCISE

Run all your favorite applications and monitor your system for 10 seconds via powercfg. Look
at the report and find all applications which have requested small timer resolution.

   And we have one more topic that is related to the system timer: Thread.Sleep.

System timer and `Thread.Sleep`

All this sounds very interesting, but where is the practical value? Why should we care about the system timer resolution? Here I want to ask you a question: what does the following call do?

```
Thread.Sleep(1);
```

Somebody might probably answer: it suspends the current thread for 1 ms. Unfortunately, that is not the correct answer. The documentation states the following:

> *The actual timeout might not be exactly the specified timeout, because the specified timeout will be adjusted to coincide with clock ticks.*

In fact, the elapsed time depends on system timer resolution. Let's write another naive benchmark (we don't need any accuracy here; we just want to show the Sleep behavior in a simple way, so we don't need usual benchmarking routines here like a warm-up, statistics, and so on):

```
for (int i = 0; i < 5; i++)
{
  var stopwatch = Stopwatch.StartNew();
  Thread.Sleep(1);
  stopwatch.Stop();
  var time = stopwatch.ElapsedTicks * 1000.0 / Stopwatch.Frequency;
  Console.WriteLine(time + " ms");
}
```

This code just tries to measure the duration of `Thread.Sleep(1)` with the help of Stopwatch five times. Typical output for current timer interval = `15.625` ms:

```
14.8772437280584 ms
15.5369201880125 ms
18.6300283418281 ms
15.5728431635545 ms
15.6129649284456 ms
```

As you can see, the elapsed intervals are much more than 1 ms. Now, let's run Firefox (which sets the interval to 1 ms) and repeat this stupid benchmark:

```
1.72057056881932 ms
1.48123957592228 ms
1.47983997947259 ms
1.47237546507424 ms
1.49756820116866 ms
```

Firefox affected the Sleep call and reduced the elapsed interval by ~10 times. You can find a good explanation of the Sleep behavior in [The Windows Timestamp Project]:

> *Say the ActualResolution is set to 156250, the interrupt heartbeat of the system will run at 15.625 ms periods or 64 Hz, and a call to Sleep is made with the desired delay of 1 ms. Two scenarios are to be looked at:*
>
> - *The call was made < 1ms (ΔT) ahead of the next interrupt. The next interrupt will not confirm that the desired period of time has expired. Only the following interrupt will cause the call to return. The resulting sleep delay will be ΔT + 15.625ms.*
>
> - *The call was made $\geq$ 1ms (ΔT) ahead of the next interrupt. The next interrupt will force the call to return. The resulting sleep delay will be ΔT.*

There are many other Sleep "features," but they are beyond the scope of this book. Of course, there is another Windows API that depends on the system timer resolution (e.g., WaitableTimer). We will not discuss this class in detail; I just want to recommend once again that you read it in [The Windows Timestamp Project].

Timestamping API on Windows: QPC

The primary APIs for high-resolution timestamping on Windows are QueryPerformanceCounter (QPC) and QueryPerformanceFrequency (QPF). QPC is completely independent of the system time and UTC (it is not affected by daylight savings time, leap seconds, or time zones). If you need high-resolution time-of-day measurements, use GetSystemTimePreciseAsFileTime (available since Windows 8 / Windows Server 2012). Thus, it is the best option if you want to measure the duration of an operation.

Here are some important facts about QPC and different versions of Windows:

- QPC is available on *Windows XP and Windows 2000* and works well on most systems. However, some hardware systems' BIOS did not indicate the hardware CPU characteristics correctly (a noninvariant TSC), and some multicore or multiprocessor systems used processors with TSCs that could not be synchronized across cores. Systems with flawed firmware that run these versions of Windows might not provide the same QPC reading on different cores if they used the TSC as the basis for QPC.

- All computers that shipped with *Windows Vista* and *Windows Server 2008* used the HPET or the ACPI PM as the basis for QPC.

- The majority of *Windows 7* and *Windows Server 2008 R2* computers have processors with constant-rate TSCs and use these counters as the basis for QPC.

- *Windows 8, Windows 8.1, Windows Server 2012*, and *Windows Server 2012 R2* use TSCs as the basis for the performance counter.

There are two main functions for high-resolution timestamps in `kernel32.dll` that can be imported to C# program with the following lines:

```
[DllImport("kernel32.dll")]
static extern bool QueryPerformanceCounter(out long value);
```

```
[DllImport("kernel32.dll")]
static extern bool QueryPerformanceFrequency(out long value);
```

As you can guess from the title, `QueryPerformanceCounter` allows getting counter value (via `out long value`), and `QueryPerformanceFrequency` allows getting the tick generator frequency. But how does it work? Let's find out!

Consider a simple program:

```
static void Main()
{
  long ticks;
  QueryPerformanceCounter(out ticks);
}

[DllImport("kernel32.dll")]
static extern bool QueryPerformanceCounter(out long value);
```

Build this in Release-x64 and open the executable in WinDbg. There is a difference between x86 and x64 asm code, but x64 asm code will be enough to understand what's going on. Let's set a breakpoint on KERNEL32!QueryPerformanceCounter (bp command) and go to it (g command). For simplification, address prefixes like 00007ff are removed from the listings:

> bp KERNEL32!QueryPerformanceCounter

> g

```
KERNEL32!QueryPerformanceCounter:
e6ccbb720  jmp  qword ptr [KERNEL32!QuirkIsEnabled2Worker+0x9ec8 (e6cd16378)]
  ds:00007ffe6cd16378={ntdll!RtlQueryPerformanceCounter (e6d83a7b0)}
```

If you are not able to set a breakpoint to KERNEL32!QueryPerformanceCounter, you can try to use KERNEL32!QueryPerformanceCounterStub (different versions of Windows have different naming styles):

> bp KERNEL32!QueryPerformanceCounterStub

> g

```
KERNEL32!QueryPerformanceCounterStub:/
f431f5750  jmp  qword ptr [KERNEL32!_imp_QueryPerformanceCounter (f43255290)]
  ds:00007fff43255290={ntdll!RtlQueryPerformanceCounter (f45300ff0)}
```

KERNEL32!QueryPerformanceCounter (or KERNEL32!QueryPerformanceCounterStub) just redirects us to ntdll!RtlQueryPerformanceCounter. Let's look at the disassembly of this method (uf command):

> uf ntdll!RtlQueryPerformanceCounter

```
ntdll!RtlQueryPerformanceCounter:
e6d83a7b0 push     rbx
e6d83a7b2 sub      rsp,20h
; Checking special flag
e6d83a7b6 mov      al,byte ptr [SharedUserData+0x3c6 (e03c6)]
e6d83a7bd mov      rbx,rcx
e6d83a7c0 cmp      al,1
e6d83a7c2 jne      ntdll!RtlQueryPerformanceCounter+0x44 (e6d83a7f4)

; The fast rdtsc version
ntdll!RtlQueryPerformanceCounter+0x14:
e6d83a7c4 mov      rcx,qword ptr [SharedUserData+0x3b8 (e03b8)]
e6d83a7cc rdtsc
e6d83a7ce shl      rdx,20h
e6d83a7d2 or       rax,rdx
e6d83a7d5 mov      qword ptr [rbx],rax
e6d83a7d8 lea      rdx,[rax+rcx]
e6d83a7dc mov      cl,byte ptr [SharedUserData+0x3c7 (e03c7)]
e6d83a7e3 shr      rdx,cl
e6d83a7e6 mov      qword ptr [rbx],rdx

ntdll!RtlQueryPerformanceCounter+0x39:
e6d83a7e9 mov      eax,1
e6d83a7ee add      rsp,20h
e6d83a7f2 pop      rbx
e6d83a7f3 ret

; The slow syscall version
ntdll!RtlQueryPerformanceCounter+0x44:
e6d83a7f4 lea      rdx,[rsp+40h]
e6d83a7f9 lea      rcx,[rsp+38h]
e6d83a7fe call     ntdll!NtQueryPerformanceCounter (e6d8956f0)
e6d83a803 mov      rax,qword ptr [rsp+38h]
e6d83a808 mov      qword ptr [rbx],rax
e6d83a80b jmp      ntdll!RtlQueryPerformanceCounter+0x39 (e6d83a7e9)
```

There is a special flag in [SharedUserData+0x3c6 (e03c6)] that determines which QPC algorithm will be used. If everything is fine (we are working on modern hardware with invariant TSC, and we can directly use it), we are going to the fast algorithm (ntdll!RtlQueryPerformanceCounter+0x14). Otherwise, we are going to call ntdll!NtQueryPerformanceCounter, which produces a syscall:

```
> uf ntdll!NtQueryPerformanceCounter
```

```
ntdll!NtQueryPerformanceCounter:
e6d8956f0  mov     r10,rcx
e6d8956f3  mov     eax,31h
e6d8956f8  test    byte ptr [SharedUserData+0x308 (e0308)],1
e6d895700  jne     ntdll!NtQueryPerformanceCounter+0x15 (e6d895705)

ntdll!NtQueryPerformanceCounter+0x12:
e6d895702  syscall
e6d895704  ret

ntdll!NtQueryPerformanceCounter+0x15:
e6d895705  int     2Eh
e6d895707  ret
```

Here is an important fact about the fast algorithm (ntdll!RtlQueryPerformance Counter+0x14): it directly calls RDTSC without any syscalls. It allows achieving low latency for simple situations (when we really can use TSC without any troubles).

Another interesting fact: QPC uses a shifted value of RDTSC: it puts the full value of the counter in rdx, and then it performs shr rdx,cl (where cl typically equals to 0xA). Thus, one QPC tick equals to 1024 rdtsc ticks. We can say the same thing about QPF: nominal Windows frequency for high-precision measurements is 1024 times less than the RDTSC frequency.

A remark: in the modern world, versions of Windows are changing very quickly, so you can get different asm on different versions of Windows and hardware.

AN EXERCISE

Try to repeat this experiment on your machine and explain the assembly code that you get.

Timestamping API on Unix

On Unix, there are many different time functions:

- Linux: `clock_gettime`, `clock_settime`, `clock_getres`[11]

- macOS: `mach_absolute_time`, `mach_timebase_info`[12]

- Oracle Solaris: `gethrtime`[13]

- PowerPC: `read_real_time`[14]

- All Unix systems: `gettimeofday`, `settimeofday`[15]

Let's briefly talk about some of these functions.

clock_getttime, clock_settime, clock_getres

On Linux, there are the following useful functions for timestamping:

```
int clock_getres(clockid_t clock_id, struct timespec *res);
int clock_gettime(clockid_t clock_id, struct timespec *tp);
int clock_settime(clockid_t clock_id, const struct timespec *tp);
```

Here is some useful information from the documentation:

> *The function* `clock_getres()` *finds the resolution (precision) of the specified* `clock_id`, *and, if* `res` *is non-NULL, stores it in the struct* `timespec` *pointed to by* `res`. *The resolution of clocks depends on the implementation and cannot be configured by a particular process. If the time value pointed to by the argument tp of* `clock_settime()` *is not a multiple of res, then it is truncated to a multiple of res. The functions* `clock_gettime()` *and* `clock_settime()` *retrieve and set the time of the specified clock clk_id.*

---

[11]http://man7.org/linux/man-pages/man2/clock_gettime.2.html

[12]https://developer.apple.com/library/mac/#qa/qa1398/_index.html

[13]https://docs.oracle.com/cd/E23824_01/html/821-1465/gethrtime-3c.html

[14]http://ps-2.kev009.com/tl/techlib/manuals/adoclib/aixprggd/genprogc/highrest.htm

[15]http://linux.die.net/man/2/gettimeofday

clock_getttime allows getting a timespec value:

```
struct timespec {
    time_t tv_sec; /* seconds */
    long tv_nsec;  /* nanoseconds */
};
```

The timespec structure has two fields: tv_sec for seconds and tv_nsec for nanoseconds. Thus, the minimal possible resolution of functions that returns timespec is 1 ns.

The clock_id argument is the ID of the target clocks. Some typical values:

- CLOCK_REALTIME: System-wide real-time clock. Setting this clock requires appropriate privileges.

- CLOCK_REALTIME_COARSE: A faster but less precise version of CLOCK_REALTIME. Use when you need very fast, but not fine-grained timestamps. Available since Linux 2.6.32.

- CLOCK_MONOTONIC: Clock that cannot be set and represents monotonic time from some unspecified starting point.

- CLOCK_MONOTONIC_COARSE: A faster but less precise version of CLOCK_MONOTONIC. Use when you need very fast, but not fine-grained timestamps. Available since Linux 2.6.32.

- CLOCK_MONOTONIC_RAW: Similar to CLOCK_MONOTONIC, but provides access to a raw hardware-based time that is not subject to NTP adjustments or the incremental adjustments performed by adjtime(3). Available since Linux 2.6.28.

- CLOCK_BOOTTIME: Identical to CLOCK_MONOTONIC, except it also includes any time that the system is suspended. Available since Linux 2.6.39.

- CLOCK_PROCESS_CPUTIME_ID: High-resolution per-process timer from the CPU.

- CLOCK_THREAD_CPUTIME_ID: Thread-specific CPU-time clock.

For high-precision timestamping, you should use CLOCK_MONOTONIC (if this option is available on current hardware) but there are other clock options (like CLOCK_REALTIME for the real-time clock or CLOCK_THREAD_CPUTIME_ID for thread-specific CPU-time clock).

A usage example:

```
struct timespec ts;
uint64_t timestamp;
clock_gettime(CLOCK_MONOTONIC, &ts);
timestamp = (static_cast<uint64_t>(ts.tv_sec) * 1000000000) +
            static_cast<uint64_t>(ts.tv_nsec);
```

Internally, clock_gettime(CLOCK_MONOTONIC, ...) is based on the current high-precision hardware timer (usually TSC, but it can also be HPET or ACPI_PM).

To reduce clock_gettime latency, Linux kernel uses the vsyscalls (virtual system calls) and VDSOs (Virtual Dynamically Linked Shared Objects) instead of a direct syscall.

If Invariant TSC is available, clock_gettime(CLOCK_MONOTONIC, ...) will use it directly via the rdtsc instruction. Of course, it adds some overhead, but in general, you should use clock_gettime instead of rdtsc because it solves a lot of portability problems.[16]

clock_gettime has been available on macOS since macOS 10.12 Sierra.

mach_absolute_time

If you want to write a portable code that supports old versions of macOS (before 10.12), the mach_absolute_time() is the primary timestamping API. This function returns ticks as unsigned 64-bit integers. For the conversation from these ticks to real time, we need the following struct:

```
struct mach_timebase_info {
    uint32_t  numer;
    uint32_t  denom;
};
```

You can get mach_timebase_info for your system with the help of the mach_timebase_info function. If you multiply ticks by numer and then divide into denom, you will get the time in nanoseconds.

---

[16]There is a nice commit in the Linux repository: "x86: tsc prevent time going backward" https://github.com/torvalds/linux/commit/d8bb6f4c1670c8324e4135c61ef07486f7f17379

A usage example:

```
mach_timebase_info_data_t timebase;
mach_timebase_info(&timebase);
uint64_t timestamp = mach_absolute_time();
uint64_t timestampInNanoseconds = timestamp * timebase.numer / timebase.
denom;
```

gettimeofday

The gettimeofday function is available almost everywhere and allows you to get the current date and time as well as a time zone. We also can set the current date and time with the help of the settimeofday functions. Here are the signatures of these functions:

```
int gettimeofday(struct timeval *tv, struct timezone *tz);
int settimeofday(const struct timeval *tv, const struct timezone *tz);
```

The functions work with the timeval structure, which is similar to timespec:

```
struct timeval {
    time_t       tv_sec;    /* seconds */
    suseconds_t tv_usec;    /* microseconds */
};
```

Be careful: the first field in both types are seconds, but the second field is nanoseconds for timespec and microseconds for timeval. The minimal possible resolution of gettimeofday is 1 us.

A usage example:

```
struct timeval tv;
if (gettimeofday(&tv, NULL) == 0)
{
  return tv.tv_sec * 1000000000 +
         tv.tv_usec * 1000; // Nanoseconds
}
```

Summing Up

In this section, we learned a lot of useful information about software timers. Let's briefly recall it.

On Windows, we have three groups of Timestamping API: system timer, system ticks, and high-resolution timer.

The system timer is used for WinAPI functions like GetSystemTime, GetLocalTime, and GetSystemTimeAsFileTime. This timer has poor accuracy. Typically, its resolution is between 0.5 ms and 15.625 ms; this value can be changed manually via timeBegin Period/timeEndPeriod or NtQueryTimerResolution/NtSetTimerResolution. You can get the current values with the help of ClockRes; powercfg will help you to get the list of applications that try to change this value. Thread.Sleep also uses the system timer under the hood, so Thread.Sleep(1) can easily take 15 ms.

System ticks can be obtained via GetTickCount and GetTickCount64 WinAPI functions.

If you want to perform high-precision measurements, you can use QueryPerformanceCounter and QueryPerformanceFrequency (in kernel-mode API, you should use KeQueryPerformanceCounter). If you want to get the current system date and time with the highest possible level of precision, you should use GetSystemTimePreciseAsFileTime.

On Unix there are also a lot of timestamping APIs: clock_gettime, clock_settime, clock_getres, mach_absolute_time, mach_timebase_info, gethrtime, read_real_time, gettimeofday, and settimeofday. Some of them are available only on specific Unix distributions. clock_getttime is the best option on Linux (available if HAVE_CLOCK_MONOTONIC is defined). mach_absolute_time is the best option on macOS (available if HAVE_MACH_ABSOLUTE_TIME is defined; clock_getttime has been available on macOS since 10.12). gettimeofday is available almost everywhere, so it's a good fallback option (but this API has worse accuracy than clock_getttime and mach_absolute_time).

Now we know what kind of timestamping APIs we have on different operating systems. But what's about the managed APIs? Let's time to check what do we have on the .NET platform!

.NET Timestamping API

In this section, we are going to cover three primary .NET timestamping APIs:

- `DateTime.UtcNow`

- `Environment.TickCount`

- `Stopwatch.GetTimestamp`

For each API, we will briefly discuss how to use it and how it's implemented internally. You can find the detailed source code overview for .NET Framework, .NET Core, and Mono in the attachment to this book. We will also benchmark each API and calculate the latency and the resolution. The source code of benchmarks also can be found in the attachment to this book. The following configuration was used for the presented values:

Benchmark setup Hardware (the same for all benchmarks): Mac mini, Intel Core i7-3615QM CPU 2.30GHz (Ivy Bridge). Operating systems: Windows 10.0.15063.1155, macOS High Sierra 10.13.4, Ubuntu 16.04. Runtimes: .NET Framework 4.6 (CLR 4.0.30319.42000), Mono 5.12.0, .NET Core 1.1.8, .NET Core 2.1.0. Hardware timers: TSC, HPET, ACPI_PM. Windows Current Timer Interval (CTI): 5000, 156250. BenchmarkDotNet v0.10.14 is used for benchmarking. Source code of all benchmarks and the detailed results can be found in the attachment to this book.

For each benchmark, it's recommended to try it in your own environment and then explain the results.

This section will help you to understand the API internals and their basic characteristics that can affect measurements.

DateTime.UtcNow

`System.DateTime` is a widely used .NET type. A lot of developers use it all the time, but not all of them really know how it works. The `DateTime` structure represents an instant in time, typically expressed as a date and time of day. Here are some important `DateTime` properties:

- `int Year, int Month, int Day, int Hour, int Minute, int Second, int Millisecond`: Gets the corresponding components of the date represented by this instance. All of the values are non-negative.

- `long Ticks`: Gets the number of ticks that represent the date and time of this instance (expressed as a value between `DateTime.MinValue.Ticks` and `DateTime.MaxValue.Ticks`). A single tick equals to `100 ns`. The number of ticks represents the number of `100 ns` time units elapsed since 12:00:00 midnight, January 1, 0001 (0:00:00 UTC on January 1, 0001, in the Gregorian calendar).

- `DateTimeKind Kind`: Gets a value that indicates whether the time represented by this instance is based on local time (`DateTimeKind.Local`), UTC (`DateTimeKind.Utc`), or neither (`DateTimeKind.Unspecified`).

`DateTime` provides two important properties: `UtcNow` (the current *UTC* date and time on a local computer) and `Now` (the current *local* date and time on a local computer). `DateTime.Now` is based on `DateTime.UtcNow`, so we will focus only on `DateTime.UtcNow`.

We can evaluate the difference between two DateTimes with the help of the `TimeSpan` class:

```
DateTime a = DateTime.UtcNow;
// <Measured logic>
DateTime b = DateTime.UtcNow;
TimeSpan span = b - a;
```

Here are some important `TimeSpan` properties:

- `int Days, int Hours, int Minutes, int Seconds, int Milliseconds`: these properties correspond to the same properties of `DateTime`. Be careful: these values represent *the corresponding time component*. Thus, the value range of Seconds is `-59..59`, and the value range of Milliseconds is `-999..999`.

- `double TotalDays, double TotalHours, double TotalMinutes, double TotalSeconds, double Milliseconds, long Ticks`: these properties express total elapsed time in the specified time unit.

An example of measurements with `DateTime`:

```
DateTime start = DateTime.UtcNow;
// Logic
DateTime end = DateTime.UtcNow;
TimeSpan elapsed = end - start;
Console.WriteLine(elapsed.TotalMilliseconds);
```

Internally, it uses different native APIs depending on environment:

- Windows, .NET Framework/.NET Core 1.x/Mono: `GetSystemTimeAsFileTime`

- Windows, .NET Core 2.x: `GetSystemTimePreciseAsFileTime` (if available) or `GetSystemTimeAsFileTime` (as a fallback)

- Unix, .NET Core 1.x/Mono: `gettimeofday`

- Unix, .NET Core 2.x: `clock_gettime` (if available) or `gettimeofday` (as a fallback)

Since .NET Core 2.0, it was decided to use `GetSystemTimePreciseAsFileTime` instead of `GetSystemTimeAsFileTime` to get a better accuracy (see coreclr#5061[17] and coreclr#9736[18]). However, another problem was introduced: on misconfigured systems, the `GetSystemTimePreciseAsFileTime` drifts and returns incorrect results (see coreclr#14187[19]) So, it was decided to introduce a workaround (see coreclr#14283[20]): now .NET Core checks whether `GetSystemTimePreciseAsFileTime` is trustable or not. If `GetSystemTimePreciseAsFileTime` has a drift, the runtime uses `GetSystemTimeAsFileTime` as a fallback option.

Now let's benchmark the `DateTime.UtcNow` resolution and latency.

```
[Benchmark]
public long DateTimeNowLatency() => DateTime.Now.Ticks;
```

---

[17]https://github.com/dotnet/coreclr/issues/5061
[18]https://github.com/dotnet/coreclr/pull/9736
[19]https://github.com/dotnet/coreclr/issues/14187
[20]https://github.com/dotnet/coreclr/pull/14283

```
[Benchmark]
public long DateTimeNowResolution()
{
    long lastTicks = DateTime.Now.Ticks;
    while (DateTime.Now.Ticks == lastTicks)
    {
    }
    return lastTicks;
}

[Benchmark]
public long DateTimeUtcNowLatency() => DateTime.UtcNow.Ticks;

[Benchmark]
public long DateTimeUtcNowResolution()
{
    long lastTicks = DateTime.UtcNow.Ticks;
    while (DateTime.UtcNow.Ticks == lastTicks)
    {
    }
    return lastTicks;
}
```

The results of these benchmarks are presented in Table 9-4 ("*" means "Any runtime"; CTI means "Current Timer Interval" of the system timer). Remember that it's only an example of possible measurements in some specific configurations; you can get other results on your machine.

Table 9-4. *DateTime.UtcNow Resolution and Latency*

OS	Runtime	Env	Resolution	Latency
Windows	.NET Framework	TSC, CTI=5000	500 us	6–7 ns
Windows	.NET Framework	TSC, CTI=156250	15625 us	6–7 ns
Windows	Mono	TSC, CTI=5000	500 us	19–20 ns
Windows	Mono	TSC, CTI=156250	15625 us	19–20 ns
Windows	.NET Core 1.x	TSC, CTI=5000	500 us	6–7 ns
Windows	.NET Core 1.x	TSC, CTI=156250	15625 us	6–7 ns
Windows	.NET Core 2.x	TSC	0.4–0.5 us	18–19 ns
macOS	*	TSC	1 us	36–40 ns
Linux	Mono	TSC	1 us	26–30 ns
Linux	.NET Core 1.x	TSC	1 us	26–30 ns
Linux	.NET Core 2.x	TSC	0.1 us	26–30 ns
Linux	*	HPET/ACPI_PM	1.8–1.9 us	900–950 ns

These numbers and the knowledge of `DateTime.UtcNow` internals allow making some important conclusions:

- On Windows, the resolution equals to the Windows CTI (except .NET Core 2.0). Usually, it's about `0.5 ms..15.625 ms`. This value can be changed programmatically by any application.

- On Linux, the resolution equals to `1 us` (except .NET Core 2.0). As mentioned before, on Linux, `DateTime.UtcNow` uses the `gettimeofday` function. `gettimeofday` allows you to get the time in microseconds. Thus, `1 us` is the minimal possible resolution.

- In .NET Core 2.0, the implementation of `DateTime.UtcNow` was changed: now it uses `GetSystemTimePreciseAsFileTime` on Windows and `clock_gettime(CLOCK_REALTIME)` on Unix. Thus, resolution was reduced to `0.4-0.5 us` on Windows and `0.1 us` on Linux.

As you may notice, only results for `DateTime.UtcNow` are shown. Try to repeat these benchmarks for `DateTime.Now` in your environment and explain the results.

Typically, `DateTime` is a good choice when you want to know the actual current time (e.g., for logging) and you don't need high precision. You should understand that the measurements can be spoiled if the current time is changing during measurements (more about that in the next section). If you need to measure some time interval (not just put an approximate timestamp into a log file), you probably need a better API. OK, let's check what other kinds of timestamping APIs we have. The next one is `Environment.TickCount`.

Environment.TickCount

`System.Environment.TickCount` returns the number of milliseconds elapsed since the system started. You can measure elapsed milliseconds of some logic with the following code:

```
int start = Environment.TickCount;
// <Measured logic>
int end = Environment.TickCount;
int elapsedMilliseconds = end - start;
```

The internal implementation depends on the OS and the runtime:

- On Windows, `TickCount` just calls the `GetTickCount64` WinAPI function.

- On Unix+.NET Core, it uses the `clock_gettime()`, `mach_absolute_time()`, `gethrtime()`, `read_real_time()`, `gettimeofday()` functions.

- On Unix+Mono, it uses `mono_100ns_datetime()` - `get_boot_time()`.

The nominal resolution is always 1 ms and the nominal frequency is always 1 kHz.

Now, let's benchmark the `Environment.TickCount` resolution and latency:

```
[Benchmark]
public long TickCountLatency() => Environment.TickCount;

[Benchmark]
public long TickCountResolution()
{
  long lastTimestamp = Environment.TickCount;
  while (Environment.TickCount == lastTimestamp)
  {
  }
  return lastTimestamp;
}
```

The results of these benchmarks are presented in Table 9-5. Remember that it's only an example of possible measurements in some specific configurations; you can get other results on your machine.

Table 9-5. *Environment.TickCount Resolution and Latency*

OS	Runtime	Resolution	Latency
Windows	.NET Framework	15.625 ms	2–3 ns
Windows	.NET Core	15.625 ms	2–3 ns
Windows	Mono	15.625 ms	11–12 ns
macOS	Mono	1 ms	30–40 ns
macOS	.NET Core 1.x	1 ms	30–40 ns
macOS	.NET Core 2.x	1 ms	70–80 ns
Linux	Mono	3.9–4.0 ms	12–20 ns
Linux	.NET Core	3.9–4.0 ms	8–10 ns

These numbers and the knowledge of `Environment.TickCount` internals allow making some important conclusions:

- The resolution on Windows is always `15.625` `ms` for all runtimes. You may notice that this is not an integer number. The actual difference between two consecutive calls of `TickCount` is always an integer number (typically, it's 0, 15, or 16). Technically, you can't measure a `15.625` `ms` time interval by values of two timestamps. However, it's the exact value between two counter increments.

- The resolution on macOS is 1 `ms` for all runtimes.

- The resolution on Linux is `3.9-4.0` `ms` for all runtimes.

- The latency is pretty small. It equals to `2-3` `ns` on Windows for .NET Core and .NET Framework. However, it can take up to 80 `ns` in some environments (e.g., macOS + .NET Core 2.x).

Well, `Environment.TickCount` is also not the best timestamping API for benchmarking. Now it's time to learn the most powerful API: Stopwatch!

Stopwatch.GetTimestamp

The `Stopwatch` class is the best tool for high-precision time measurements on .NET. We have already used it a lot of times, so just recall the main use cases. The method pair `StartNew()`/`Stop()` allows measuring the time of any operation:

```
// Simple time measurement
Stopwatch stopwatch = Stopwatch.StartNew();
// <Measured logic>
stopwatch.Stop();
```

Next, we can get the elapsed time with the help of `Elapsed`, `ElapsedMilliseconds`, or `ElapsedTicks`:

```
// Elapsed time in different measurement units
TimeSpan elapsed = stopwatch.Elapsed;
long elapsedMilliseconds = stopwatch.ElapsedMilliseconds;
long elapsedTicks = stopwatch.ElapsedTicks;
double elapsedNanoseconds = stopwatch.ElapsedTicks * 1_000_000_000.0 /
                            Stopwatch.Frequency;
```

After that, we can restart the Stopwatch instance and use it again without additional allocations:

```
// Reusing existed stopwatch
stopwatch.Restart();
// <Measured logic>
stopwatch.Stop();
```

Internally, it calls `Stopwatch.GetTimestamp()`, which can be used directly. Thus, we can compare several timestamps without `Stopwatch` instances:

```
// Measurements without an instance of Stopwatch
long timestamp1 = Stopwatch.GetTimestamp();
// <Measured logic>
long timestamp2 = Stopwatch.GetTimestamp();
double elapsedSeconds = (timestamp2 - timestamp1) * 1.0 /
                        Stopwatch.Frequency;
```

The implementation depends on the operating system and the runtime:

- *Windows (.NET Framework, .NET Core, Mono)*: the QueryPerformanceFrequency and QueryPerformanceCounter WinAPI functions

- *Linux (.NET Core, Mono)*: uses clock_gettime as a primary way (with fallbacks gettimeofday)

- *macOS (.NET Core 2.0.x, .NET Core 2.1.0-2.1.2)*: uses clock_gettime as a primary way (with fallbacks to mach_absolute_time and gettimeofday)

- *macOS (.NET Core 1.x, .NET Core 2.1.3+, Mono)*: uses mach_absolute_time as a primary way (with fallbacks to gettimeofday)

An interesting problem was introduced in .NET Core 2.0 (see corefx#30391[21]). In .NET Core 1.0, we had the following implementation of `Stopwatch.GetTimestamp()`: we tried to call clock_gettime, next we tried to call mach_absolute_time (if clock_gettime is not available), and then we called gettimeofday (if mach_absolute_time is not available). clock_gettime is available on macOS since macOS 10.12. .NET Core 1.0

---

[21]https://github.com/dotnet/corefx/issues/30391

supports macOS 10.11,[22] so it was compiled against macOS 10.11 SDK, which doesn't support clock_gettime. As a result, .NET Core 1.0 uses mach_absolute_time as a time source for Stopwatch.GetTimestamp(). In .NET Core 2.0, it was decided to drop macOS 10.11 support: only macOS 10.12+ is supported.[23] .NET Core 2.0 was compiled against macOS 10.12 SDK, which has the clock_gettime support. Thus, without any changes in the source code, clock_gettime becomes the primary time source for Stopwatch. GetTimestamp(). Unfortunately, it had worse accuracy than mach_absolute_time on macOS: the default resolution of clock_gettime is 1000ns. The problem was fixed in .NET Core 3.0 (see coreclr#18505[24] and corefx#30457[25]); the fix was back-ported to .NET 2.1.3 (but it's not available in .NET Core 2.0.x).

The Stopwatch.Frequency value also depends on the environment:

- *Windows (.NET Framework, .NET Core) with enabled HPET*: TSC frequency divided by 1024 (usually, it's about $2 \cdot 10^6..4 \cdot 10^6$)

- *Windows (.NET Framework, .NET Core) with disabled HPET*: 14,318,180

- *Windows/Linux/macOS (Mono)*: 10^7

- *Linux/macOS (.NET Core)*: 10^9

Now, let's benchmark the Stopwatch resolution and latency:

```
[Benchmark]
public long StopwatchLatency() => Stopwatch.GetTimestamp();

[Benchmark]
public long StopwatchResolution()
{
  long lastTimestamp = Stopwatch.GetTimestamp();
  while (Stopwatch.GetTimestamp() == lastTimestamp)
  {
  }
  return lastTimestamp;
}
```

[22]See https://github.com/dotnet/core/blob/master/release-notes/1.0/1.0-supported-os.md
[23]See https://github.com/dotnet/core/blob/master/release-notes/2.0/2.0-supported-os.md
[24]https://github.com/dotnet/coreclr/pull/18505
[25]https://github.com/dotnet/corefx/pull/30457

Results of these benchmarks are presented in Table 9-6 ("*" means "Any runtime"). Remember that it's only an example of possible measurements in some specific configurations; you can get other results on your machine.

Table 9-6. *Stopwatch Resolution and Latency*

OS	Runtime	Timer	Resolution	Latency
Windows	*	TSC	400–500 ns	15–25 ns
Windows	*	HPET	1800–1900 ns	900–950 ns
macOS	Mono	TSC	100 ns	30–40 ns
macOS	.NET Core 1.x	TSC	70–80 ns	30–40 ns
macOS	.NET Core 2.0.x	TSC	1000 ns	90–100 ns
macOS	.NET Core 2.1.3+	TSC	70–80 ns	30–40 ns
Linux	Mono	TSC	100 ns	25–30 ns
Linux	.NET Core	TSC	70–80 ns	30–40 ns
Linux	*	HPET/ACPI_PM	1800–1900 ns	900–950 ns

These numbers and the knowledge of Stopwatch internals allow making some important conclusions:

- Windows+TSC: In this case we get Resolution≈ (1 second / Stopwatch.Frequency) ≈ (1 second / (rdstc Frequency / 1024)).

- HPET/ACPI_PM: benchmarks show that Resolution≈2 x Latency because we call Stopwatch.GetTimestamp at least twice per the Resolution method invocation. It's hard to say something about real resolution because the value of HPET/ACPI_PM ticks is much smaller than the latency. For practical use, you can assume that the resolution has the same order as latency.

- macOS/Linux+TSC: In Mono, we have Resolution = 100 ns because it is the value of 1 tick (and it can be achieved). In .NET Core, 1 ticks is 1 ns, and it uses rdtsc, which works on frequency (2.30 GHz for the preceding example). Thus, we have a situation which is similar to the HPET/ACPI_PM case: latency is much bigger than resolution. So, it's hard to evaluate it via a microbenchmark.

Stopwatch is the best available .NET API for high-precision measurements, but this doesn't mean that all Stopwatch-based measurements are correct. With this knowledge of internals, oyou can not only get raw numbers, but also interpret it in the right way and make good error estimations.

Summing Up

On .NET, we have several ways to get timestamps:

- Stopwatch is the best solution when you need high-precision timestamping. When HPET is disabled, the typical resolution is about 300–500 ns on Windows and 70–100 ns on Linux/macOS. When HPET is enabled, the situation is worse because the actual resolution rises up to ~2000 ns.

- Environment.TickCount is the best solution on Windows when you don't care about precision (±1 sec is enough) and you need extremely low latency (2–3 ns).

- DateTime.Now/DateTime.UtcNow is the best solution when you don't care about precision and you want to connect timestamps and real-time (e.g., for logging).

Thus, if you want to write a proper benchmark, Stopwatch is your friend. However, correct benchmarks still require a lot of benchmark routine in order to get proper results.

Timestamping Pitfalls

The timestamping APIs look simple, but it's not always easy to use them correctly. In this section, we are going to cover the most common mistakes that developers usually make with usages of DateTime, Environment.TickCount, and Stopwatch.

Small Resolution

The timestamping resolution depends on different factors including runtime and OS. In general, you can expect the following values:

- **DateTime.UtcNow:** 0.1 us .. 15625 us

- **Environment.TickCount:** 1000 us .. 15625 us

- **Stopwatch.GetTimestamp:** 0.07 us .. 2 us

If the timestamping resolution is q, the final random measurement error is about $\pm 2q$ (because we have two timestamps: "before" and "after"). Thus, if the measured operation takes several minutes, we shouldn't worry about the timer resolution. However, if it takes several nanoseconds, the error is too high. Even 1000 repetitions of the operation will not save us: the worst-case Stopwatch resolution is 2 us, which means that we will get ±4 ns error.

Counter Overflow

All timestamping API counters are represented by integer types and can handle a limited number of values. Of course, we can get a counter overflow at any moment. Let's check whether should we worry about it or not.

- **DateTime**

  The DateTime.Tick property contains the number of ticks since January 1, 0001; one tick is 100 ns. The type of this property is long; the maximum long value equals to $\approx 9.22 \cdot 10^{18}$. However, the actual maximum value for DateTime.Ticks is $\approx 3.16 \cdot 10^{18}$ (three times less). It corresponds to 11:59:59 PM, December 31, 9999. Thus, we shouldn't worry about overflow problems for the next eight thousand years.

- **Environment.TickCount**

  TickCount returns an int value that can hold timestamps up to $(2^{31} - 1)$ ms or 49 days, 17 hours, 2 minutes, 47 seconds, and 295 milliseconds. If you are writing a system with uptime that takes months, Environment.TickCount isn't a good tool for time measurements. Some developers think that TickCount equals to

0 on system startup. But this isn't always true, and the software shouldn't use this fact. In order to catch wrong TickCount usages, Windows debug builds use "one hour before 32-bit timer tick rollover" as the initial value (see [Chen 2014] for details).

- **Stopwatch**

    In theory, the duration of a single Stopwatch tick can be arbitrary. In practice, the smallest used value is 1 ns (.NET Core + Unix). Stopwatch.GetTimestamp() returns a long value, which means that it can handle $\approx 9.22 \cdot 10^{18}$ nanoseconds or approximately 292 years. Thus, we will not have any overflow problems with Stopwatch.

The only timestamping API that has a potential counter overflow problem is Environment.TickCount. It can handle intervals up to approximately 50 days. You can use it for short time measurements, but it's not recommended to use it in services that can be active for months.

Time Components and Total Properties

When we are working with TimeSpan, we have the time-component properties (Days, Hours, ...) and the total properties (TotalDays, TotalHours, ...). There is a huge difference between them. Let's look at a small example that demonstrates it:

```
TimeSpan span = new TimeSpan(
  days: 8,
  hours: 19,
  minutes: 46,
  seconds: 57,
  milliseconds: 876
);
WriteLine("TimeSpan = {0}", span);

WriteLine("Days:        {0,3} TotalDays:        {1}",
          span.Days,        span.TotalDays);
WriteLine("Hours:       {0,3} TotalHours:       {1}",
          span.Hours,       span.TotalHours);
```

```
WriteLine("Minutes:      {0,3} TotalMinutes:       {1}",
          span.Minutes,           span.TotalMinutes);
WriteLine("Seconds:       {0,3} TotalSeconds:        {1}",
          span.Seconds,          span.TotalSeconds);
WriteLine("Milliseconds: {0,3} TotalMilliseconds: {1}",
          span.Milliseconds,  span.TotalMilliseconds);
WriteLine("               Ticks:            {0}",
                       span.Ticks);
```

Here is the output:

```
TimeSpan = 8.19:46:57.8760000
Days:          8 TotalDays:           8.82428097222222
Hours:        19 TotalHours:          211.782743333333
Minutes:      46 TotalMinutes:        12706.9646
Seconds:      57 TotalSeconds:        762417.876
Milliseconds: 876 TotalMilliseconds: 762417876
                Ticks:                7624178760000
```

The difference is huge! For example, Hours = 19 (an integer time-component that is less than 24) and TotalHours (a double total property that can be much bigger than 24). Thus, it's easy to mix up these values and write something like that:

```
var start = DateTime.UtcNow;
Thread.Sleep(2500);
var end = DateTime.UtcNow;
WriteLine((end - start).Milliseconds); // prints 500 instead of 2500
```

This is a very popular bug that is easy to write and hard to detect.

Changes in Current Time

If you are using DateTime.UtcNow or DateTime.Now, the measurements can be spoiled if the current time is changing during the benchmark. Let's discuss a few possible reasons for that.

Time synchronization

If you have enabled time synchronization, the current time can be changed at any moment. Moreover, some servers have several time synchronization services. There are many stories about Linux servers with enabled ntp and systemd-timesyncd at the same time.[26] Such services can have desynchronized time sources with several seconds delta. In this case, these services can constantly change time backward or forward. It leads to flaky bugs with incorrect time measurements.

Daylight saving time

The DateTime.Now returns the local user's date and time. This value uses the current time zones, which are full of surprises. For example, the practice of daylight saving time in some countries can accidentally affect your benchmark: you will get a 1 hour error if you run a benchmark at an unfortunate moment in time.

Changes in time zones

The time zone of a region can be changed. For example, here are some historical data for the Netherlands time zone:

```
1909–1937:   GMT+00:19:32.13
1937–1940:   GMT+00:20
1940–1942:   UTC+02:00
```

Another recent example: the time zone of Samoa was changed in 2011 from UTC-10 to UTC+14. Because of that, December 30 was cancelled. Just imagine that somebody ran a DateTime-based benchmark in Samoa on this day: such measurements had a 1-day error!

For time measurements, it's almost always better to use UTC time (DateTime.UtcNow).

Time can be manually changed

Finally, a user is always able to change the system time at any moment. If this happens during time measurements, the measurements will be spoiled. Probably, you will not manually change the time yourself, but you can have some time measurements inside a real application; for instance, a user might run this application in the background and decide to change the time.

---

[26]For example, see https://bugs.launchpad.net/ubuntu/+source/ntp/+bug/1597909

Sequential Reads

Let's say that we do two sequential reads of `Stopwatch.GetTimestamp()`:

```
var a = Stopwatch.GetTimestamp();
var b = Stopwatch.GetTimestamp();
var delta = b - a;
```

Can you name the possible values of `delta`? Let's check it out with the help of the following program, which builds the delta histogram:

```
// (1)
const int N = 100000000;
var values = new long[N];
for (int i = 0; i < N; i++)
  values[i] = Stopwatch.GetTimestamp();
// (2)
var deltas = new long[N - 1];
for (int i = 0; i < N - 1; i++)
  deltas[i] = values[i + 1] - values[i];
// (3)
var table =
  from d in deltas
  group d by d into g
  orderby g.Key
  select new
  {
    Ticks = g.Key,
    Microseconds = g.Key * 1000000.0 / Stopwatch.Frequency,
    Count = g.Count()
  };
// (4)
WriteLine("Ticks      | Time(us) | Count    ");
WriteLine("-----------|----------|---------");
foreach (var line in table)
{
  var ticks = line.Ticks.ToString().PadRight(8);
  var us = line.Microseconds.ToString("0.0").PadRight(8);
```

```
    var count = line.Count.ToString();
    WriteLine($"{ticks}    | {us} | {count}");
}
```

Let's discuss what's going on here:

1. We do N measurements (in this case N=100000000, but you are free to choose any positive value). The measurement here is just a call of `Stopwatch.GetTimestamp()`. We save N sequential measurements in the `value` array. There is a small overhead of the `for` loop but it doesn't matter in this case (fortunately we know the latency of `GetTimestamp()`; it's huge in comparison with the `for` overhead of a single iteration).

2. We calculate differences between each pair of sequential measurements and save it in the `deltas` array.

3. Next, we group `deltas` and calculate the number of `delta` values in each group (LINQ allows doing it in a simple way).

4. We print the results with nice formatting. This means a table with three columns: `Ticks` (the raw difference between sequential measurements in ticks), `Time(us)` (it's not convenient to work with ticks, so we convert them to microseconds), and `Count` (how many times we observed such differences in our small experiment).

Here is an example of output on macOS 10.13 + .NET Core 2.1.0 (the middle part was removed):

Ticks	Time(us)	Count
0	0.0	91961519
1000	1.0	7820660
2000	2.0	129139
3000	3.0	55617
4000	4.0	4378
5000	5.0	2619
6000	6.0	1484
7000	7.0	1272
...	...	...

```
822000      | 822.0     | 1
875000      | 875.0     | 1
1083000     | 1083.0    | 1
1177000     | 1177.0    | 1
1479000     | 1479.0    | 1
1991000     | 1991.0    | 1
2751000     | 2751.0    | 1
8317000     | 8317.0    | 1
12341000    | 12341.0   | 1
```

In this pseudohistogram, there are three very important lines:

- **The first line (zero time value).** And we get a zero difference between sequential measurements 91961519 times!

- **The second line (minimum positive time value).** In the "Terminology" section, we already discussed that the nominal and actual resolutions are not always equal. The nominal resolution of Stopwatch (1 tick) is defined by Stopwatch.Frequency. However, in some cases, we can't measure exactly one tick: the actual resolution (the minimum possible interval that can be measured) contains more than one tick. The second line of the histogram shows this value (sometimes, it's only an approximation). In the current example, Stopwatch.Frequency is 10^9. This means that 1 tick = 1 ns.

- **The last line (maximum time value).** As you can see, once I had a delta between two sequential GetTimestamp calls, which equals to 12341000 ticks or 12.3 ms! Note that we even don't have any target method here; we are trying to measure nothing! Of course, this is a rare situation. Usually, you get plausible measurements. But you can never be sure! This approach is methodologically wrong; such benchmarks cannot be trusted. A good microbenchmark always performs many method invocations. It allows getting better accuracy because the error is divided by the number of invocations.

The positive difference between sequential timestamping calls can cause tricky bugs. Can you say where there is a problem in the following expression?

```
var stopwatch = Stopwatch.StartNew();
// ... some logic
var value = stopwatch.ElapsedMilliseconds > timeout
  ? 0
  : timeout - (int)stopwatch.ElapsedMilliseconds;
```

The answer: we can't be sure that two invocations of stopwatch. ElapsedMilliseconds will return the same value. For example, let's say that timeout equals to 100. We are trying to evaluate stopwatch.ElapsedMilliseconds > timeout; stopwatch.ElapsedMilliseconds returns 99, and the expression value is false. Next, we are going to evaluate timeout - (int)stopwatch.ElapsedMilliseconds. But we have another stopwatch.ElapsedMilliseconds here! Let's say it returns 101. Then, the resulting value will be equal to –1! Probably, the author of this code did not expect negative values here.

This is an example of a real bug from the AsyncIO library. The bug is already fixed,[27] but it was a cause of a very tricky bug in Rider. We spent several days on an investigation because such kinds of bugs are *really* hard to reproduce.

AN EXERCISE

Build this histogram in different environments and compare the results. Write the same logic for DateTime.Now, DateTime.UtcNow, and Environment.TickCount, compare histograms for different timestamping APIs.

---

[27]https://github.com/somdoron/AsyncIO/commit/5c838f3d30d483dcadb4181233a4437fb5 e7f327

Summing Up

In this section, we discussed five timestamping pitfalls:

- **Small Resolution**

  The timer resolution is typically not enough to measure a method that takes several nanoseconds. In such cases, you have to invoke the method many times inside each iteration to achieve good accuracy.

- **Counter Overflow**

  `Environment.TickCount` overflows every ≈50 days. You shouldn't use this API in services that can be active for months.

- **Time Components and Total Properties**

  Another common mistake is using properties like `TimeSpan.Milliseconds` instead of `TimeSpan.TotalMilliseconds`. `Milliseconds` always returns values from –999 to 999. If you want to report the *total* number of elapsed milliseconds, you need `TotalMilliseconds`.

- **Changes in Current Time**

  `DateTime.Now` and `DateTime.UtcNow` can be useful for logging, but it's not recommended to use these properties for time measurements. They use the actual time, which can be changed because of different reasons like a time synchronization service.

- **Sequential Reads**

  The difference between two sequential calls of a timestamping API can be any non-negative number. Even if you are using `Stopwatch` with 1 us resolution, this difference can be several milliseconds.

Even if you are using `Stopwatch`, you can get huge measurement errors if the number of method invocations inside an iteration is not big enough. `Stopwatch.Elapsed` returns a `TimeSpan` that can be misused.

Summary

In this chapter, we learned a lot about timers. We covered the following topics:

- **Terminology**

  We discussed the basic timer and frequency units, including the common notation (symbols like µs, ps, THz), the main components of a hardware timer (tick generator, tick counter, tick counter API), quantizing errors, and basic timer characteristics (now we know the difference between accuracy and precision or between the nominal and the actual resolution).

- **Hardware timers**

  On the hardware level, there are several time sources like TSC, ACPI PM, and HPET. TSC is the most reliable way to get timestamps in most configurations. The TSC frequency is usually close to the nominal CPU frequency. ACPI PM (frequency = 3.579545 MHz) and HPET (frequency = 14.31818 MHz) are usually disabled by default on modern versions of operating systems because of the high latency. However, you still should be ready to meet ACPI PM or HPET. The frequency values of these two timers have a long history, which was started when NTSC started to construct a new standard for color television.

- **OS timestamping API**

  Operating systems provide you many APIs that internally interact with hardware timers. On Windows, the best high-resolution timestamping APIs are QueryPerformanceCounter (QPC) and QueryPerformanceFrequency (QPF). The value doesn't relate to the current local time. If you want to know the current time, you can use GetSystemTime, GetLocalTime, and GetSystemTimeAsFileTime. These APIs use the Windows system timer with resolution between 0.5 ms and 15.625 ms. If you want to know the current time with better accuracy, you should use GetSystemTimePreciseAsFileTime. On Unix, you can use clock_gettime/mach_absolute_time (if available) for high-precision timestamping and gettimeofday for regular timestamping.

647

- **.NET timestamping API**

  The best high-resolution timestamping API in .NET is `Stopwatch`; internally it uses the best API, which is provided by the OS. `Environment.TickCount` can be used on Windows if you don't need good accuracy, but you do need extremely low latency. `DateTime.Now` and `DateTime.UtcNow` can be useful for logging.

- **Timestamping pitfalls**

  Even if you are using `Stopwatch`, you can still get huge errors for short operations because of the small resolution or a huge delta between sequential reads. The `Stopwatch.Elapsed` is a `TimeSpan` that can be misused (taking `Milliseconds` instead of `TotalMilliseconds`). The `Environment.TickCount` counter overflows after ≈50 days. Measurements based on `DateTime.Now` or `DateTime.UtcNow` can be spoiled by a time synchronization service or other changes in the current time.

Now we have learned the internals of the hardware and the software timers. This knowledge will help us choose a proper timer in each situation, design better benchmarks, and avoid common mistakes.

References

[ACPI Specifications] "Advanced Configuration and Power Interface Specification (Version 6.0)." 2015. `www.uefi.org/sites/default/files/resources/ACPI_6.0.pdf`.

[Agner Instructions] Fog, Agner. "Instruction Tables. Lists of Instruction Latencies, Throughputs and Micro-Operation Breakdowns for Intel, AMD and VIA CPUs." `www.agner.org/optimize/instruction_tables.pdf`.

[Agner Optimizing Assembly] Fog, Agner. "Optimizing Subroutines in Assembly Language. An Optimization Guide for X86 Platforms." `www.agner.org/optimize/optimizing_assembly.pdf`.

[Agner Optimizing Cpp] Fog, Agner. "Optimizing Software in C++. An Optimization Guide for Windows, Linux and Mac Platforms." `www.agner.org/optimize/optimizing_cpp.pdf`.

[Chen 2014] Chen, Raymond. 2014. "When Does GetTickCount Consider the System to Have Started?" November 13. https://blogs.msdn.microsoft.com/oldnewthing/20141113-00/?p=43623.

[Cook 2017] Cook, Carl. 2017. "When a Microsecond Is an Eternity: High Performance Trading Systems in C++." Presented at the CppCon 2017. www.youtube.com/watch?v=NH1Tta7purM.

[Govindarajalu 2002] Govindarajalu, B. 2002. *IBM PC AND CLONES: Hardware, Troubleshooting and Maintenance*. Tata McGraw-Hill Education.

[HPET Specifications] "IA-PC HPET (High Precision Event Timers) Specification (Version 1.0a)." 2004. www.intel.com/content/dam/www/public/us/en/documents/technical-specifications/software-developers-hpet-spec-1-0a.pdf.

[Hsia 2004] Hsia, Calvin. 2004. "Why Was the Original IBM PC 4.77 Megahertz?" August. https://blogs.msdn.microsoft.com/calvin_hsia/2004/08/12/why-was-the-original-ibm-pc-4-77-megahertz/.

[Intel Manual] "Intel: Intel® 64 and IA-32 Architectures Software Developer's Manual (325462-061US)." 2016. www.intel.com/content/dam/www/public/us/en/documents/manuals/64-ia-32-architectures-software-developer-manual-325462.pdf.

[Jones 2000] Jones, Anthony. 2000. *Splitting the Second: The Story of Atomic Time*. CRC Press.

[Karna 2017] Karna, Satish K. 2017. *Microprocessors—GATE, PSUS AND ES Examination*. Vikas Publishing House.

[Kidd 2014] Taylor, Randy. 2014. "Power Management States: P-States, C-States, and Package C-States." April. https://software.intel.com/en-us/articles/power-management-states-p-states-c-states-and-package-c-states.

[MSSupport 895980] "Programs That Use the QueryPerformanceCounter Function May Perform Poorly in Windows Server 2000, in Windows Server 2003, and in Windows XP." Microsoft Support. https://support.microsoft.com/en-us/kb/895980.

[Paterson 2009] Paterson, Tim. 2009. "IBM PC Design Antics." May. http://dosmandrivel.blogspot.ru/2009/03/ibm-pc-design-antics.html.

[Schlyter] Schlyter, Paul. "Analog TV Broadcast Systems." http://stjarnhimlen.se/tv/tv.html.

[Solntsev 2017] Solntsev, Andrey. 2017. "Flaky Tests (in Russian)." presented at the Heisenbug Moscow, December 9. www.youtube.com/watch?v=jLG3RXECQU8.

[Stephens 1999] Stephens, Randy. 1999. "Measuring Differential Gain and Phase." *Application Report SLOA040*. www.ti.com/lit/an/sloa040/sloa040.pdf.

[The Windows Timestamp Project] Lentfer, Arno. "Microsecond Resolution Time Services for Windows." www.windowstimestamp.com/description.

Index

A

Absolute threshold, 344–347

Adaptive threshold, 344, 348, 349

Add method, 60

Address space layout randomization (ASLR), 42

Ahead-Of-Time (AOT) compilation, 93
- advantage, 133, 134
- CoreRT, 137
- CrossGen, 135
- disadvantage, 134, 135
- Mono, 136
- .NET Native, 136
- NGen, 135
- RuntimeHelpers, 137

AMD64, 159

Arithmetic
- characteristics, 481–484
- denormalized numbers, 484, 486, 487, 489
- double to string, 494, 495
- integer division, 496, 498–500, 502, 503
- Math.Abs, 490–493
- operations, 480
- Sanglard interpretation, 480

ASM decompiler, 366

Asserts and alarms, performance
- absolute threshold, 345–347
- adaptive threshold, 348, 349
- manual threshold, 349, 350
- relative thresholds, 347, 348

Asymptotic analysis, 227

Asymptotic complexity, 340

Asymptotic tests, 282, 283

Asynchronous methods, 129

B

Bad benchmark (N mistakes), 32

Bar method, 416, 434

Base Class Libraries (BCL), 103

BenchmarkDotNet, 366, 408

Benchmarking
- data dredging, 254
- goals, 10, 244, 245
  - marketing tools, 12–14
  - performance analysis, 11, 12
  - puzzles, 14
  - scientific interest, 14
- Holm–Bonferroni correction, 254, 255
- multiple comparison problem, 255
- percentages, 247, 248
- ratios, 248–250
- small samples, 245, 246
- statistics knowledge, 245

Bessel's correction, 202

Bimodal distribution, 199, 316

BitHacks method, 475

Printed in the United States
By Bookmasters